CIPM® PROGRAM LEVEL I VOLUME 1

CFA Institute

2024

ISBN 978-1-953337-86-3

September 2023

CONTENTS

◘ indicates an optional segment

◘ indicates an optional segment

How to Use the CIPM Program Curriculum

Congratulations on your decision to enter the Certificate in Investment Performance Measurement (CIPM®) Program. This exciting and rewarding program of study reflects your desire to become a serious portfolio evaluation professional. You are embarking on a program noted for its high ethical standards and the depth of knowledge, skills, and abilities it develops. Your commitment to the CIPM Program should be educationally and professionally rewarding. CIPM certificants are dedicated to life-long learning and maintaining currency with the ever-changing dynamics of a challenging profession. The CIPM Program represents the first step towards a career-long commitment to professional education.

To begin your study:

1 Schedule your examination.

2 Access the CIPM Learning Ecosystem and access your study materials.

EXAM SCHEDULING

Examinations are provided online by our testing partner, Pearson VUE. We suggest you schedule your exam appointment with them as soon as possible, because appointments are first-come, first-served. With 24 hours notice, Pearson VUE allows you to reschedule your exam to another available time and place within the same exam window. Rescheduling your exam appointment must be completed within the exam scheduling window. When you schedule or reschedule your exam appointment with Pearson VUE, you will receive an e-mail confirmation. Contact Pearson VUE www.pearsonvue.com/contact/ if you do not receive a confirmation of your appointment.

CIPM LEARNING ECOSYSTEM

The Learning Ecosystem is a customized learning program that makes studying for the CIPM Exam enjoyable, efficient, and effective. The Learning Ecosystem is an online portal that adapts to your needs, strengths, and weaknesses, serving you the right material at the right time and focusing on the areas you need to focus on the most. It helps you stay focused, engaged, and on track while you study.

TIP

Everything you need is in one place. We provide an eBook version of the curriculum for your convenience should that be your preferred method of study. The Learning Ecosystem contains the exact same content. There is no need to do both. If you elect to use the eBook, you may still log into the Learning Ecosystem to take advantage of study tools, such as flashcards, practice tests, and the mock exam.

FEATURES OVERVIEW

The Learning Ecosystem is web-based and accessible through all common browsers.

- The Learning Ecosystem is designed to work well on whatever device is convenient at the moment, whether your desktop, tablet, or smartphone.
- Your progress through the course is automatically recorded so you can seamlessly switch between devices.

TIP

If you are accessing the Learning Ecosystem on a mobile device, it is possible to preload some content for times when you will not have continuous internet access. While you still have Internet access, log in to the Learning Ecosystem and launch your next study activity. This content will remain available when internet access is cut off, for example if you are on mass transit.

Home: Dashboard

Here you will find a summary of your progress through the material and a summary of your strengths and weaknesses with the content.

Study Plans

There are two kinds of study plans from which to choose: structured and adaptive.

- The structured plan will help you keep track of the time remaining before your exam and will suggest the number of activities to complete each day to stay on track. The structured plan will take you through the content in the same order as it appears in the eBook.
- The adaptive plan will begin with a short pre-test to establish a baseline for your existing knowledge. From that point forward, the system will track and adapt to your strengths and weaknesses with the content each time you interact with it. For example, it may adjust your pace through the material to spend less time on content where you are strong and more time on content where you comparatively weaker.

TIP

You are not stuck with your choice of study plan. You can switch back and forth between the structured and adaptive plans. When you switch from one study plan to the other your progress is not lost, and you do not need to start again at the beginning.

TIP

Whichever study plan you choose, studying consistently is the key to success.

Study Tasks

Whichever study plan you are using, the Learning Ecosystem will always let you know which study task is next. Study tasks can include reading a lesson, completing practice questions, completing chapter review questions, reviewing flashcards, or taking a mock exam.

- Lessons are composed of the same content found in the eBook.
- Practiced questions help you review and make sure you understood what you have learned.
- Flashcards test your understanding and recall of important terms and definitions.
- The mock exam is of similar length and weight as the live examination and can help gauge your overall readiness for the live exam.

TIP

As you work through lessons, practice problems, and flashcards, the Learning Ecosystem will frequently ask you to assess your confidence in knowing the material being covered. This information is tracked and presented to you in your Learning History. In the case of the adaptive plan, this information may supplement the system's understanding of your relative strengths and weaknesses.

TIP

If you are studying primarily from the eBook, you can still access the study tools in the Learning Ecosystem without working through a study plan. All of the study tools are accessible directly through the tabs within the menu bar on the left side of the Learning Ecosystem screen.

Other Study Resources

The Learning Ecosystem provides resources that supplement your study tasks.

- The Game Center makes reviewing your flashcards more enjoyable by presenting them within the context of a game in which you may compete with fellow candidates.
- Discussion boards are a place where you can confer with fellow candidates when you need a little extra help or a motivational nudge.

TIP

Discussion boards are **not** actively monitored or moderated by CFA Institute; please use them with that caution in mind. Our vendor monitors the boards for vulgarity and inflammatory language; to speak with a CFA Institute representative please contact us at info@cfainstitute.org.

TIP

For technical support assistance or to give us feedback on the Learning Ecosystem or course of study, you may also use the messaging feature.

- The Learning History tab reports trends in your performance over time with tracking on how you have done on practice tests and the mock exam. Additionally, the learning history summarizes your confidence in the topics within the program.

CURRICULUM DEVELOPMENT

The CIPM Program curriculum is grounded in the practice of the portfolio evaluation profession. CFA Institute performs a continuous practice analysis with investment professionals around the world to determine the knowledge, skills, and abilities that are relevant to the profession. Regional expert panels and targeted surveys are conducted to verify and reinforce the insights from practice analysis. The practice analysis process ultimately defines the CIPM Candidate Body of Knowledge (CBOK™).

The examinations are written by practicing certificants and are designed to allow you to demonstrate your mastery of the CBOK as set forth in the CIPM Program curriculum. As you structure your personal study program, you should emphasize mastery of the CBOK and the practical application of that knowledge. For more information on the practice analysis, CBOK, and development of the CIPM Program curriculum, please visit https://www.cfainstitute.org/programs/cipm/curriculum.

ORGANIZATION OF THE CURRICULUM

The reading assignments are the basis for all examination questions, and are selected or developed specifically to teach the CBOK. These readings are drawn from CIPM Program-commissioned content, textbook chapters, and professional journal articles. Learning outcome statements are listed with each lesson. These LOS indicate what you should be able to accomplish after studying the lesson. We encourage you to review how to properly use LOS, and the descriptions of commonly used LOS "command words," at www.cfainstitute.org/programs/cipm/curriculum/overview. The command words signal the depth of learning you are expected to achieve from the reading. You should use the LOS to guide and focus your study, as each examination question is based on an assigned lesson and one or more LOS. However, the lessons provide context for the LOS and enable you to apply a principle or concept in a variety of scenarios. *Candidates are responsible for the entirety of all required material in the curriculum.*

CANDIDATE RESOURCES

CFA Institute provides a web page that contains numerous resources to help in your successful completion of the CIPM Program. On this page you will find links to testing policies (calculator policy, ID policy, and others); exam details and logistics; testing

Ethical and Professional Standards

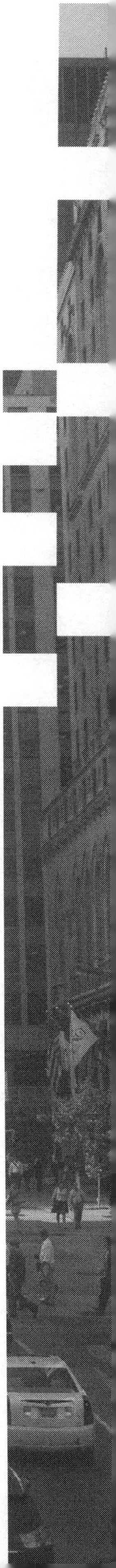

Study Session 1 Ethical and Professional Standards

TOPIC LEVEL LEARNING OUTCOME

The candidate should be able to summarize the importance of ethical standards to the investment profession, demonstrate ethically sound reasoning, and identify and explain the responsibilities required by the CFA Institute Code of Ethics and Standards of Professional Conduct.

accommodations; curriculum errata; and a detailed glossary of terms. You should visit this site often to obtain current information: www.cfainstitute.org/programs/cipm/candidate.

FEEDBACK

At CFA Institute, we are committed to delivering a comprehensive and rigorous curriculum for the development of competent, ethically grounded investment professionals. We rely on candidate and member feedback as we work to incorporate content, design, and packaging improvements. You can be assured that we will continue to listen to your suggestions. Please send any comments or feedback—or perceived errors—to info@cfainstitute.org. Ongoing improvements in the curriculum will help you prepare for success on the upcoming examinations, and for a lifetime of learning as a serious investment professional.

ETHICAL AND PROFESSIONAL STANDARDS

STUDY SESSION 1

Ethical and Professional Standards

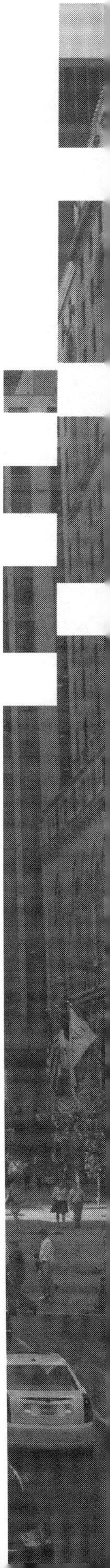

The readings in this study session set forth the provisions of the CFA Institute Code of Ethics (the Code) and Standards of Professional Conduct (the Standards) and illustrate the practical application of the Code and Standards in investment practice.

CIPM candidates and members of the CIPM Association and CFA Institute are subject to the Code and Standards.[1] The Code articulates the ethical principles governing the investment profession. The Standards set forth the responsibilities of covered persons in the areas of professionalism; integrity of capital markets; duties to clients; duties to employers; investment analysis, recommendations, and action; conflicts of interest; and responsibilities as a CIPM Association or CFA Institute member or CIPM candidate.

Note: This study session makes use of the 11th edition of the CFA Institute *Standards of Practice Handbook* (SOPH) to focus on applications of the Code and Standards and recommended procedures for complying with them. The guidance, recommendations, and applications provided in the SOPH supplement the Code and Standards. Recognizing that the following list is not exhaustive, the following exchanges may help CIPM candidates with understanding the reading:

SOPH Terminology		
CFA Institute	→	CIPM Association
CFA	→	CIPM
Members and Membership	→	Pertains to the CIPM Association and CFA Institute

(continued)

1 Until October 1, 2019, existing CIPM Certificants may be members of either the CIPM Association or CFA Institute. While the Code and Standards for each organization are substantially similar, each certificant will be held to the Code and Standards of the organization of which they are a member. New CIPM certificants will join CFA Institute, thus this material is focused on the CFA Institute Code of Ethics and Standards of Professional Conduct.

SOPH Terminology		
Program, Candidates and Candidacy	→	Pertains to the CIPM Program and the CFA Program
Designation	→	Pertains to the Certificate in Investment Performance Measurement (CIPM) designation and the CFA designation
Exams	→	CIPM and CFA exams
CFA marks	→	CIPM marks (“Certificate in Investment Performance Measurement” or “CIPM”)
Charter/Charterholders	→	Certificate/Certificants or Certificate Holders

READING ASSIGNMENTS

1 CFA Institute Code of Ethics and Standards of Professional Conduct

2 *Standards of Practice Handbook*, Eleventh Edition

READING

1

CFA Institute Code of Ethics and Standards of Professional Conduct

LEARNING OUTCOMES

Mastery	*The candidate should be able to:*
☐	**a.** explain the relationship between ethics and laws and regulations;
☐	**b.** state and explain the provisions of the CFA Institute Code of Ethics and Standards of Professional Conduct;
☐	**c.** determine potential violations of the CFA Institute Code of Ethics and Standards of Professional Conduct and select appropriate preventive or corrective actions.

PREAMBLE

The CFA Institute Code of Ethics and Standards of Professional Conduct are fundamental to the values of CFA Institute and essential to achieving its mission to lead the investment profession globally by promoting the highest standards of ethics, education, and professional excellence for the ultimate benefit of society. High ethical standards are critical to maintaining the public's trust in financial markets and in the investment profession. Since their creation in the 1960s, the Code and Standards have promoted the integrity of CFA Institute members and served as a model for measuring the ethics of investment professionals globally, regardless of job function, cultural differences, or local laws and regulations. All CFA Institute members (including holders of the Chartered Financial Analyst [CFA] and Certificate in Investment Performance Measurement [CIPM] designations) and CFA and CIPM Program candidates have the personal responsibility to embrace and uphold the provisions of the Code and Standards and are encouraged to notify their employer of this responsibility. Violations may result in disciplinary sanctions by CFA Institute. Sanctions can include revocation of membership, revocation of candidacy in the CFA or CIPM Program, and revocation of the right to use the CFA or CIPM designation.

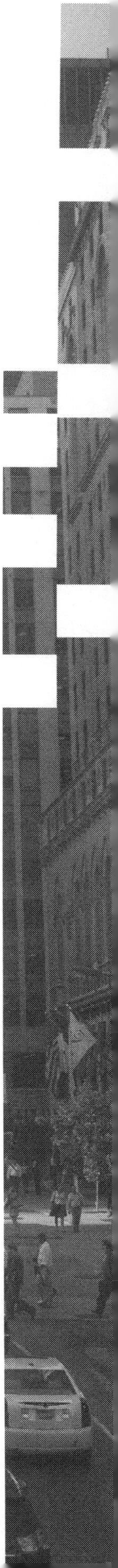

THE CODE OF ETHICS

Members of CFA Institute (including CFA charterholders and CIPM certificants) and candidates for the CFA and CIPM designations ("Members and Candidates") must:

- Act with integrity, competence, diligence, and respect and in an ethical manner with the public, clients, prospective clients, employers, employees, colleagues in the investment profession, and other participants in the global capital markets.
- Place the integrity of the investment profession and the interests of clients above their own personal interests.
- Use reasonable care and exercise independent professional judgment when conducting investment analysis, making investment recommendations, taking investment actions, and engaging in other professional activities.
- Practice and encourage others to practice in a professional and ethical manner that will reflect credit on themselves and the profession.
- Promote the integrity and viability of the global capital markets for the ultimate benefit of society.
- Maintain and improve their professional competence and strive to maintain and improve the competence of other investment professionals.

STANDARDS OF PROFESSIONAL CONDUCT

I. PROFESSIONALISM

A Knowledge of the Law

Members and Candidates must understand and comply with all applicable laws, rules, and regulations (including the CFA Institute Code of Ethics and Standards of Professional Conduct) of any government, regulatory organization, licensing agency, or professional association governing their professional activities. In the event of conflict, Members and Candidates must comply with the more strict law, rule, or regulation. Members and Candidates must not knowingly participate or assist in and must dissociate from any violation of such laws, rules, or regulations.

B Independence and Objectivity

Members and Candidates must use reasonable care and judgment to achieve and maintain independence and objectivity in their professional activities. Members and Candidates must not offer, solicit, or accept any gift, benefit, compensation, or consideration that reasonably could be expected to compromise their own or another's independence and objectivity.

C Misrepresentation

Members and Candidates must not knowingly make any misrepresentations relating to investment analysis, recommendations, actions, or other professional activities.

D Misconduct

Members and Candidates must not engage in any professional conduct involving dishonesty, fraud, or deceit or commit any act that reflects adversely on their professional reputation, integrity, or competence.

II. INTEGRITY OF CAPITAL MARKETS

A Material Nonpublic Information

Members and Candidates who possess material nonpublic information that could affect the value of an investment must not act or cause others to act on the information.

B Market Manipulation

Members and Candidates must not engage in practices that distort prices or artificially inflate trading volume with the intent to mislead market participants.

III. DUTIES TO CLIENTS

A Loyalty, Prudence, and Care

Members and Candidates have a duty of loyalty to their clients and must act with reasonable care and exercise prudent judgment. Members and Candidates must act for the benefit of their clients and place their clients' interests before their employer's or their own interests.

B Fair Dealing

Members and Candidates must deal fairly and objectively with all clients when providing investment analysis, making investment recommendations, taking investment action, or engaging in other professional activities.

C Suitability

1 When Members and Candidates are in an advisory relationship with a client, they must:

a Make a reasonable inquiry into a client's or prospective client's investment experience, risk and return objectives, and financial constraints prior to making any investment recommendation or taking investment action and must reassess and update this information regularly.

b Determine that an investment is suitable to the client's financial situation and consistent with the client's written objectives, mandates, and constraints before making an investment recommendation or taking investment action.

c Judge the suitability of investments in the context of the client's total portfolio.

2 When Members and Candidates are responsible for managing a portfolio to a specific mandate, strategy, or style, they must make only investment recommendations or take only investment actions that are consistent with the stated objectives and constraints of the portfolio.

D Performance Presentation

When communicating investment performance information, Members and Candidates must make reasonable efforts to ensure that it is fair, accurate, and complete.

E Preservation of Confidentiality

Members and Candidates must keep information about current, former, and prospective clients confidential unless:

1 The information concerns illegal activities on the part of the client or prospective client,

2 Disclosure is required by law, or

3 The client or prospective client permits disclosure of the information.

IV. DUTIES TO EMPLOYERS

A Loyalty

In matters related to their employment, Members and Candidates must act for the benefit of their employer and not deprive their employer of the advantage of their skills and abilities, divulge confidential information, or otherwise cause harm to their employer.

B Additional Compensation Arrangements

Members and Candidates must not accept gifts, benefits, compensation, or consideration that competes with or might reasonably be expected to create a conflict of interest with their employer's interest unless they obtain written consent from all parties involved.

C Responsibilities of Supervisors

Members and Candidates must make reasonable efforts to ensure that anyone subject to their supervision or authority complies with applicable laws, rules, regulations, and the Code and Standards.

V. INVESTMENT ANALYSIS, RECOMMENDATIONS, AND ACTIONS

A Diligence and Reasonable Basis

Members and Candidates must:

1 Exercise diligence, independence, and thoroughness in analyzing investments, making investment recommendations, and taking investment actions.

2 Have a reasonable and adequate basis, supported by appropriate research and investigation, for any investment analysis, recommendation, or action.

B Communication with Clients and Prospective Clients

Members and Candidates must:

1 Disclose to clients and prospective clients the basic format and general principles of the investment processes they use to analyze investments, select securities, and construct portfolios and must promptly disclose any changes that might materially affect those processes.

2 Disclose to clients and prospective clients significant limitations and risks associated with the investment process.

3 Use reasonable judgment in identifying which factors are important to their investment analyses, recommendations, or actions and include those factors in communications with clients and prospective clients.

4 Distinguish between fact and opinion in the presentation of investment analysis and recommendations.

C Record Retention

Members and Candidates must develop and maintain appropriate records to support their investment analyses, recommendations, actions, and other investment-related communications with clients and prospective clients.

VI. CONFLICTS OF INTEREST

A Disclosure of Conflicts

Members and Candidates must make full and fair disclosure of all matters that could reasonably be expected to impair their independence and objectivity or interfere with respective duties to their clients, prospective clients, and employer. Members and Candidates must ensure that such disclosures are prominent, are delivered in plain language, and communicate the relevant information effectively.

B Priority of Transactions

Investment transactions for clients and employers must have priority over investment transactions in which a Member or Candidate is the beneficial owner.

C Referral Fees

Members and Candidates must disclose to their employer, clients, and prospective clients, as appropriate, any compensation, consideration, or benefit received from or paid to others for the recommendation of products or services.

VII. RESPONSIBILITIES AS A CFA INSTITUTE MEMBER OR CFA CANDIDATE

A Conduct as Participants in CFA Institute Programs

Members and Candidates must not engage in any conduct that compromises the reputation or integrity of CFA Institute or the CFA designation or the integrity, validity, or security of CFA Institute programs.

B Reference to CFA Institute, the CFA Designation, and the CFA Program

When referring to CFA Institute, CFA Institute membership, the CFA designation, or candidacy in the CFA Program, Members and Candidates must not misrepresent or exaggerate the meaning or implications of membership in CFA Institute, holding the CFA designation, or candidacy in the CFA Program.

READING

2

Standards of Practice Handbook, Eleventh Edition

STANDARD I: PROFESSIONALISM

Standard I(A) Knowledge of the Law

Members and Candidates must understand and comply with all applicable laws, rules, and regulations (including the CFA Institute Code of Ethics and Standards of Professional Conduct) of any government, regulatory organization, licensing agency, or professional association governing their professional activities. In the event of conflict, Members and Candidates must comply with the more strict law, rule, or regulation. Members and Candidates must not knowingly participate or assist in and must dissociate from any violation of such laws, rules, or regulations.

Guidance

Highlights:

- *Relationship between the Code and Standards and Applicable Law*
- *Participation in or Association with Violations by Others*
- *Investment Products and Applicable Laws*

Members and candidates must understand the applicable laws and regulations of the countries and jurisdictions where they engage in professional activities. These activities may include, but are not limited to, trading of securities or other financial instruments, providing investment advice, conducting research, or performing other investment services. On the basis of their reasonable and good faith understanding, members and candidates must comply with the laws and regulations that directly govern their professional activities and resulting outcomes and that protect the interests of the clients.

When questions arise, members and candidates should know their firm's policies and procedures for accessing compliance guidance. This standard does not require members and candidates to become experts, however, in compliance. Additionally, members and candidates are not required to have detailed knowledge of or be experts on all the laws that could potentially govern their activities.

During times of changing regulations, members and candidates must remain vigilant in maintaining their knowledge of the requirements for their professional activities. New financial products and processes, along with uncovered ethical missteps, create an environment for recurring and potentially wide-ranging regulatory changes. Members and candidates are also continually provided improved and enhanced methods of communicating with both clients and potential clients, such as mobile applications and web-based social networking platforms. As new local, regional, and global requirements are updated to address these and other changes, members, candidates, and their firms must adjust their procedures and practices to remain in compliance.

Relationship between the Code and Standards and Applicable Law

Some members or candidates may live, work, or provide investment services to clients living in a country that has no law or regulation governing a particular action or that has laws or regulations that differ from the requirements of the Code and Standards. When applicable law and the Code and Standards require different conduct, members and candidates must follow the more strict of the applicable law or the Code and Standards.

"Applicable law" is the law that governs the member's or candidate's conduct. Which law applies will depend on the particular facts and circumstances of each case. The "more strict" law or regulation is the law or regulation that imposes greater restrictions on the action of the member or candidate or calls for the member or candidate to exert a greater degree of action that protects the interests of investors. For example, applicable law or regulation may not require members and candidates to disclose referral fees received from or paid to others for the recommendation of investment products or services. Because the Code and Standards impose this obligation, however, members and candidates must disclose the existence of such fees.

Members and candidates must adhere to the following principles:

- Members and candidates must comply with applicable laws or regulations related to their professional activities.
- Members and candidates must not engage in conduct that constitutes a violation of the Code and Standards, even though it may otherwise be legal.
- In the absence of any applicable law or regulation or when the Code and Standards impose a higher degree of responsibility than applicable laws and regulations, members and candidates must adhere to the Code and Standards. Applications of these principles are outlined in Exhibit 1.

The applicable laws governing the responsibilities of a member or candidate should be viewed as the minimal threshold of acceptable actions. When members and candidates take actions that exceed the minimal requirements, they further support the conduct required of Standard I(A).

CFA Institute members are obligated to abide by the CFA Institute Articles of Incorporation, Bylaws, Code of Ethics, Standards of Professional Conduct, Rules of Procedure, Membership Agreement, and other applicable rules promulgated by CFA Institute, all as amended periodically. CFA candidates who are not members must also abide by these documents (except for the Membership Agreement) as well as rules and regulations related to the administration of the CFA examination, the Candidate Responsibility Statement, and the Candidate Pledge.

Participation in or Association with Violations by Others

Members and candidates are responsible for violations in which they *knowingly* participate or assist. Although members and candidates are presumed to have knowledge of all applicable laws, rules, and regulations, CFA Institute acknowledges that members may not recognize violations if they are not aware of all the facts giving rise to the violations. Standard I(A) applies when members and candidates know or should know that their conduct may contribute to a violation of applicable laws, rules, or regulations or the Code and Standards.

If a member or candidate has reasonable grounds to believe that imminent or ongoing client or employer activities are illegal or unethical, the member or candidate must dissociate, or separate, from the activity. In extreme cases, dissociation may require a member or candidate to leave his or her employment. Members and candidates may take the following intermediate steps to dissociate from ethical violations of others when direct discussions with the person or persons committing the violation are unsuccessful. The first step should be to attempt to stop the behavior by bringing it to the attention of the employer through a supervisor or the firm's compliance department. If this attempt is unsuccessful, then members and candidates have a responsibility to step away and dissociate from the activity. Dissociation practices will differ on the basis of the member's or candidate's role in the investment industry. It may include removing one's name from written reports or recommendations, asking for a different assignment, or refusing to accept a new client or continue to advise a current client. Inaction combined with continuing association with those involved in illegal or unethical conduct may be construed as participation or assistance in the illegal or unethical conduct.

CFA Institute strongly encourages members and candidates to report potential violations of the Code and Standards committed by fellow members and candidates. Although a failure to report is less likely to be construed as a violation than a failure to dissociate from unethical conduct, the impact of inactivity on the integrity of capital markets can be significant. Although the Code and Standards do not compel members and candidates to report violations to their governmental or regulatory organizations unless such disclosure is mandatory under applicable law (voluntary reporting is often referred to as whistleblowing), such disclosure may be prudent under certain circumstances. Members and candidates should consult their legal and compliance advisers for guidance.

Additionally, CFA Institute encourages members, nonmembers, clients, and the investing public to report violations of the Code and Standards by CFA Institute members or CFA candidates by submitting a complaint in writing to the CFA Institute Professional Conduct Program via e-mail (pcprogram@cfainstitute.org) or the CFA Institute website (www.cfainstitute.org).

Investment Products and Applicable Laws

Members and candidates involved in creating or maintaining investment services or investment products or packages of securities and/or derivatives should be mindful of where these products or packages will be sold as well as their places of origination. The applicable laws and regulations of the countries or regions of origination and expected sale should be understood by those responsible for the supervision of the services or creation and maintenance of the products or packages. Members or candidates should make reasonable efforts to review whether associated firms that are distributing products or services developed by their employing firm also abide by the laws and regulations of the countries and regions of distribution. Members and candidates should undertake the necessary due diligence when transacting cross-border business to understand the multiple applicable laws and regulations in order to protect the reputation of their firm and themselves.

Given the complexity that can arise with business transactions in today's market, there may be some uncertainty surrounding which laws or regulations are considered applicable when activities are being conducted in multiple jurisdictions. Members and candidates should seek the appropriate guidance, potentially including the firm's compliance or legal departments and legal counsel outside the organization, to gain a reasonable understanding of their responsibilities and how to implement them appropriately.

Exhibit 1 Global Application of the Code and Standards

Members and candidates who practice in multiple jurisdictions may be subject to varied securities laws and regulations. If applicable law is stricter than the requirements of the Code and Standards, members and candidates must adhere to applicable law; otherwise, they must adhere to the Code and Standards. The following chart provides illustrations involving a member who may be subject to the securities laws and regulations of three different types of countries:

NS: country with no securities laws or regulations

LS: country with ***less*** strict securities laws and regulations than the Code and Standards

MS: country with ***more*** strict securities laws and regulations than the Code and Standards

Applicable Law	Duties	Explanation
Member resides in NS country, does business in LS country; LS law applies.	Member must adhere to the Code and Standards.	Because applicable law is less strict than the Code and Standards, the member must adhere to the Code and Standards.
Member resides in NS country, does business in MS country; MS law applies.	Member must adhere to the law of MS country.	Because applicable law is stricter than the Code and Standards, member must adhere to the more strict applicable law.
Member resides in LS country, does business in NS country; LS law applies.	Member must adhere to the Code and Standards.	Because applicable law is less strict than the Code and Standards, member must adhere to the Code and Standards.
Member resides in LS country, does business in MS country; MS law applies.	Member must adhere to the law of MS country.	Because applicable law is stricter than the Code and Standards, member must adhere to the more strict applicable law.
Member resides in LS country, does business in NS country; LS law applies, but it states that law of locality where business is conducted governs.	Member must adhere to the Code and Standards.	Because applicable law states that the law of the locality where the business is conducted governs and there is no local law, the member must adhere to the Code and Standards.

Exhibit 1 (Continued)

Applicable Law	Duties	Explanation
Member resides in LS country, does business in MS country; LS law applies, but it states that law of locality where business is conducted governs.	Member must adhere to the law of MS country.	Because applicable law of the locality where the business is conducted governs and local law is stricter than the Code and Standards, member must adhere to the more strict applicable law.
Member resides in MS country, does business in LS country; MS law applies.	Member must adhere to the law of MS country.	Because applicable law is stricter than the Code and Standards, member must adhere to the more strict applicable law.
Member resides in MS country, does business in LS country; MS law applies, but it states that law of locality where business is conducted governs.	Member must adhere to the Code and Standards.	Because applicable law states that the law of the locality where the business is conducted governs and local law is less strict than the Code and Standards, member must adhere to the Code and Standards.
Member resides in MS country, does business in LS country with a client who is a citizen of LS country; MS law applies, but it states that the law of the client's home country governs.	Member must adhere to the Code and Standards.	Because applicable law states that the law of the client's home country governs (which is less strict than the Code and Standards), member must adhere to the Code and Standards.
Member resides in MS country, does business in LS country with a client who is a citizen of MS country; MS law applies, but it states that the law of the client's home country governs.	Member must adhere to the law of MS country.	Because applicable law states that the law of the client's home country governs and the law of the client's home country is stricter than the Code and Standards, the member must adhere to the more strict applicable law.

Recommended Procedures for Compliance

Members and Candidates

Suggested methods by which members and candidates can acquire and maintain understanding of applicable laws, rules, and regulations include the following:

- *Stay informed*: Members and candidates should establish or encourage their employers to establish a procedure by which employees are regularly informed about changes in applicable laws, rules, regulations, and case law. In many instances, the employer's compliance department or legal counsel can provide such information in the form of memorandums distributed to employees in the organization. Also, participation in an internal or external continuing education program is a practical method of staying current.

- *Review procedures*: Members and candidates should review, or encourage their employers to review, the firm's written compliance procedures on a regular basis to ensure that the procedures reflect current law and provide adequate guidance to employees about what is permissible conduct under the law and/or the Code and Standards. Recommended compliance procedures for specific items of the Code and Standards are discussed in this *Handbook* in the "Guidance" sections associated with each standard.
- *Maintain current files*: Members and candidates should maintain or encourage their employers to maintain readily accessible current reference copies of applicable statutes, rules, regulations, and important cases.

Distribution Area Laws

Members and candidates should make reasonable efforts to understand the applicable laws—both country and regional—for the countries and regions where their investment products are developed and are most likely to be distributed to clients.

Legal Counsel

When in doubt about the appropriate action to undertake, it is recommended that a member or candidate seek the advice of compliance personnel or legal counsel concerning legal requirements. If a potential violation is being committed by a fellow employee, it may also be prudent for the member or candidate to seek the advice of the firm's compliance department or legal counsel.

Dissociation

When dissociating from an activity that violates the Code and Standards, members and candidates should document the violation and urge their firms to attempt to persuade the perpetrator(s) to cease such conduct. To dissociate from the conduct, a member or candidate may have to resign his or her employment.

Firms

The formality and complexity of compliance procedures for firms depend on the nature and size of the organization and the nature of its investment operations. Members and candidates should encourage their firms to consider the following policies and procedures to support the principles of Standard I(A):

- *Develop and/or adopt a code of ethics*: The ethical culture of an organization starts at the top. Members and candidates should encourage their supervisors or managers to adopt a code of ethics. Adhering to a code of ethics facilitates solutions when people face ethical dilemmas and can prevent the need for employees to resort to a "whistleblowing" solution publicly alleging concealed misconduct. CFA Institute has published the *Asset Manager Code of Professional Conduct*, which firms may adopt or use as the basis for their codes (visit www.cfainstitute.org).
- *Provide information on applicable laws*: Pertinent information that highlights applicable laws and regulations might be distributed to employees or made available in a central location. Information sources might include primary information developed by the relevant government, governmental agencies, regulatory organizations, licensing agencies, and professional associations (e.g., from their websites); law firm memorandums or newsletters; and association memorandums or publications (e.g., *CFA Institute Magazine*).
- *Establish procedures for reporting violations*: Firms might provide written protocols for reporting suspected violations of laws, regulations, or company policies.

Application of the Standard

Example 1 (Notification of Known Violations):

Michael Allen works for a brokerage firm and is responsible for an underwriting of securities. A company official gives Allen information indicating that the financial statements Allen filed with the regulator overstate the issuer's earnings. Allen seeks the advice of the brokerage firm's general counsel, who states that it would be difficult for the regulator to prove that Allen has been involved in any wrongdoing.

> *Comment*: Although it is recommended that members and candidates seek the advice of legal counsel, the reliance on such advice does not absolve a member or candidate from the requirement to comply with the law or regulation. Allen should report this situation to his supervisor, seek an independent legal opinion, and determine whether the regulator should be notified of the error.

Example 2 (Dissociating from a Violation):

Lawrence Brown's employer, an investment banking firm, is the principal underwriter for an issue of convertible debentures by the Courtney Company. Brown discovers that the Courtney Company has concealed severe third-quarter losses in its foreign operations. The preliminary prospectus has already been distributed.

> *Comment*: Knowing that the preliminary prospectus is misleading, Brown should report his findings to the appropriate supervisory persons in his firm. If the matter is not remedied and Brown's employer does not dissociate from the underwriting, Brown should sever all his connections with the underwriting. Brown should also seek legal advice to determine whether additional reporting or other action should be taken.

Example 3 (Dissociating from a Violation):

Kamisha Washington's firm advertises its past performance record by showing the 10-year return of a composite of its client accounts. Washington discovers, however, that the composite omits the performance of accounts that have left the firm during the 10-year period, whereas the description of the composite indicates the inclusion of all firm accounts. This omission has led to an inflated performance figure. Washington is asked to use promotional material that includes the erroneous performance number when soliciting business for the firm.

> *Comment*: Misrepresenting performance is a violation of the Code and Standards. Although she did not calculate the performance herself, Washington would be assisting in violating Standard I(A) if she were to use the inflated performance number when soliciting clients. She must dissociate herself from the activity. If discussing the misleading number with the person responsible is not an option for correcting the problem, she can bring the situation to the attention of her supervisor or the compliance department at her firm. If her firm is unwilling to recalculate performance, she must refrain from using the misleading promotional material and should notify the firm of her reasons. If the firm insists that she use the material, she should consider whether her obligation to dissociate from the activity requires her to seek other employment.

Example 4 (Following the Highest Requirements):

James Collins is an investment analyst for a major Wall Street brokerage firm. He works in a developing country with a rapidly modernizing economy and a growing capital market. Local securities laws are minimal—in form and content—and include no punitive prohibitions against insider trading.

> *Comment*: Collins must abide by the requirements of the Code and Standards, which might be more strict than the rules of the developing country. He should be aware of the risks that a small market and the absence of a fairly regulated flow of information to the market represent to his ability to obtain information and make timely judgments. He should include this factor in formulating his advice to clients. In handling material nonpublic information that accidentally comes into his possession, he must follow Standard II(A)–Material Nonpublic Information.

Example 5 (Following the Highest Requirements):

Laura Jameson works for a multinational investment adviser based in the United States. Jameson lives and works as a registered investment adviser in the tiny, but wealthy, island nation of Karramba. Karramba's securities laws state that no investment adviser registered and working in that country can participate in initial public offerings (IPOs) for the adviser's personal account. Jameson, believing that, as a US citizen working for a US-based company, she should comply only with US law, has ignored this Karrambian law. In addition, Jameson believes that as a charterholder, as long as she adheres to the Code and Standards requirement that she disclose her participation in any IPO to her employer and clients when such ownership creates a conflict of interest, she is meeting the highest ethical requirements.

> *Comment*: Jameson is in violation of Standard I(A). As a registered investment adviser in Karramba, Jameson is prevented by Karrambian securities law from participating in IPOs regardless of the law of her home country. In addition, because the law of the country where she is working is stricter than the Code and Standards, she must follow the stricter requirements of the local law rather than the requirements of the Code and Standards.

Example 6 (Laws and Regulations Based on Religious Tenets):

Amanda Janney is employed as a fixed-income portfolio manager for a large international firm. She is on a team within her firm that is responsible for creating and managing a fixed-income hedge fund to be sold throughout the firm's distribution centers to high-net-worth clients. Her firm receives expressions of interest from potential clients from the Middle East who are seeking investments that comply with Islamic law. The marketing and promotional materials for the fixed-income hedge fund do not specify whether or not the fund is a suitable investment for an investor seeking compliance with Islamic law. Because the fund is being distributed globally, Janney is concerned about the reputation of the fund and the firm and believes disclosure of whether or not the fund complies with Islamic law could help minimize potential mistakes with placing this investment.

> *Comment*: As the financial market continues to become globalized, members and candidates will need to be aware of the differences between cultural and religious laws and requirements as well as the different governmental laws and regulations. Janney and the firm could be proactive in their efforts to acknowledge areas where the new fund may not be suitable for clients.

Example 7 (Reporting Potential Unethical Actions):

Krista Blume is a junior portfolio manager for high-net-worth portfolios at a large global investment manager. She observes a number of new portfolios and relationships coming from a country in Europe where the firm did not have previous business and is told that a broker in that country is responsible for this new business. At a meeting on allocation of research resources to third-party research firms, Blume notes that this broker has been added to the list and is allocated payments for research. However, she knows the portfolios do not invest in securities in the broker's country, and she has not seen any research come from this broker. Blume asks her supervisor about the name being on the list and is told that someone in marketing is receiving the research and that the name being on the list is OK. She believes that what may be going on is that the broker is being paid for new business through the inappropriate research payments, and she wishes to dissociate from the misconduct.

> *Comment*: Blume should follow the firm's policies and procedures for reporting potential unethical activity, which may include discussions with her supervisor or someone in a designated compliance department. She should communicate her concerns appropriately while advocating for disclosure between the new broker relationship and the research payments.

Example 8 (Failure to Maintain Knowledge of the Law):

Colleen White is excited to use new technology to communicate with clients and potential clients. She recently began posting investment information, including performance reports and investment opinions and recommendations, to her Facebook page. In addition, she sends out brief announcements, opinions, and thoughts via her Twitter account (for example, "Prospects for future growth of XYZ company look good! #makingmoney4U"). Prior to White's use of these social media platforms, the local regulator had issued new requirements and guidance governing online electronic communication. White's communications appear to conflict with the recent regulatory announcements.

> *Comment*: White is in violation of Standard I(A) because her communications do not comply with the existing guidance and regulation governing use of social media. White must be aware of the evolving legal requirements pertaining to new and dynamic areas of the financial services industry that are applicable to her. She should seek guidance from appropriate, knowledgeable, and reliable sources, such as her firm's compliance department, external service providers, or outside counsel, unless she diligently follows legal and regulatory trends affecting her professional responsibilities.

Standard I(B) Independence and Objectivity

> Members and Candidates must use reasonable care and judgment to achieve and maintain independence and objectivity in their professional activities. Members and Candidates must not offer, solicit, or accept any gift, benefit, compensation, or consideration that reasonably could be expected to compromise their own or another's independence and objectivity.

Guidance

Highlights:

- *Buy-Side Clients*
- *Fund Manager and Custodial Relationships*
- *Investment Banking Relationships*
- *Performance Measurement and Attribution*
- *Public Companies*
- *Credit Rating Agency Opinions*
- *Influence during the Manager Selection/Procurement Process*
- *Issuer-Paid Research*
- *Travel Funding*

Standard I(B) states the responsibility of CFA Institute members and candidates in the CFA Program to maintain independence and objectivity so that their clients will have the benefit of their work and opinions unaffected by any potential conflict of interest or other circumstance adversely affecting their judgment. Every member and candidate should endeavor to avoid situations that could cause or be perceived to cause a loss of independence or objectivity in recommending investments or taking investment action.

External sources may try to influence the investment process by offering analysts and portfolio managers a variety of benefits. Corporations may seek expanded research coverage, issuers and underwriters may wish to promote new securities offerings, brokers may want to increase commission business, and independent rating agencies may be influenced by the company requesting the rating. Benefits may include gifts, invitations to lavish functions, tickets, favors, or job referrals. One type of benefit is the allocation of shares in oversubscribed IPOs to investment managers for their personal accounts. This practice affords managers the opportunity to make quick profits that may not be available to their clients. Such a practice is prohibited under Standard I(B). Modest gifts and entertainment are acceptable, but special care must be taken by members and candidates to resist subtle and not-so-subtle pressures to act in conflict with the interests of their clients. Best practice dictates that members and candidates reject any offer of gift or entertainment that could be expected to threaten their independence and objectivity.

Receiving a gift, benefit, or consideration from a *client* can be distinguished from gifts given by entities seeking to influence a member or candidate to the detriment of other clients. In a client relationship, the client has already entered some type of compensation arrangement with the member, candidate, or his or her firm. A gift from a client could be considered supplementary compensation. The potential for obtaining influence to the detriment of other clients, although present, is not as great as in situations where no compensation arrangement exists. When possible, prior to accepting "bonuses" or gifts from clients, members and candidates should disclose to their employers such benefits offered by clients. If notification is not possible prior to acceptance, members and candidates must disclose to their employer benefits previously accepted from clients. Disclosure allows the employer of a member or candidate to make an independent determination about the extent to which the gift may affect the member's or candidate's independence and objectivity.

Members and candidates may also come under pressure from their own firms to, for example, issue favorable research reports or recommendations for certain companies with potential or continuing business relationships with the firm. The situation may be aggravated if an executive of the company sits on the bank or investment firm's board and attempts to interfere in investment decision making. Members and candidates acting in a sales or marketing capacity must be especially mindful of their objectivity in promoting appropriate investments for their clients.

Left unmanaged, pressures that threaten independence place research analysts in a difficult position and may jeopardize their ability to act independently and objectively. One of the ways that research analysts have coped with these pressures in the past is to use subtle and ambiguous language in their recommendations or to temper the tone of their research reports. Such subtleties are lost on some investors, however, who reasonably expect research reports and recommendations to be straightforward and transparent and to communicate clearly an analyst's views based on unbiased analysis and independent judgment.

Members and candidates are personally responsible for maintaining independence and objectivity when preparing research reports, making investment recommendations, and taking investment action on behalf of clients. Recommendations must convey the member's or candidate's true opinions, free of bias from internal or external pressures, and be stated in clear and unambiguous language.

Members and candidates also should be aware that some of their professional or social activities within CFA Institute or its member societies may subtly threaten their independence or objectivity. When seeking corporate financial support for conventions, seminars, or even weekly society luncheons, the members or candidates responsible for the activities should evaluate both the actual effect of such solicitations on their independence and whether their objectivity might be perceived to be compromised in the eyes of their clients.

Buy-Side Clients

One source of pressure on sell-side analysts is buy-side clients. Institutional clients are traditionally the primary users of sell-side research, either directly or with soft dollar brokerage. Portfolio managers may have significant positions in the security of a company under review. A rating downgrade may adversely affect the portfolio's performance, particularly in the short term, because the sensitivity of stock prices to ratings changes has increased in recent years. A downgrade may also affect the manager's compensation, which is usually tied to portfolio performance. Moreover, portfolio performance is subject to media and public scrutiny, which may affect the manager's professional reputation. Consequently, some portfolio managers implicitly or explicitly support sell-side ratings inflation.

Portfolio managers have a responsibility to respect and foster the intellectual honesty of sell-side research. Therefore, it is improper for portfolio managers to threaten or engage in retaliatory practices, such as reporting sell-side analysts to the covered company in order to instigate negative corporate reactions. Although most portfolio managers do not engage in such practices, the perception by the research analyst that a reprisal is possible may cause concern and make it difficult for the analyst to maintain independence and objectivity.

Fund Manager and Custodial Relationships

Research analysts are not the only people who must be concerned with maintaining their independence. Members and candidates who are responsible for hiring and retaining outside managers and third-party custodians should not accepts gifts, entertainment, or travel funding that may be perceived as impairing their decisions. The use of secondary fund managers has evolved into a common practice to manage specific asset allocations. The use of third-party custodians is common practice for independent investment advisory firms and helps them with trading capabilities and reporting requirements. Primary and secondary fund managers, as well as third-party custodians, often arrange educational and marketing events to inform others about their business strategies, investment process, or custodial services. Members and candidates must review the merits of each offer individually in determining whether they may attend yet maintain their independence.

Investment Banking Relationships

Some sell-side firms may exert pressure on their analysts to issue favorable research reports on current or prospective investment banking clients. For many of these firms, income from investment banking has become increasingly important to overall firm profitability because brokerage income has declined as a result of price competition. Consequently, firms offering investment banking services work hard to develop and maintain relationships with investment banking clients and prospects. These companies are often covered by the firm's research analysts because companies often select their investment banks on the basis of the reputation of their research analysts, the quality of their work, and their standing in the industry.

In some countries, research analysts frequently work closely with their investment banking colleagues to help evaluate prospective investment banking clients. In other countries, because of past abuses in managing the obvious conflicts of interest, regulators have established clear rules prohibiting the interaction of these groups. Although collaboration between research analysts and investment banking colleagues may benefit the firm and enhance market efficiency (e.g., by allowing firms to assess risks more accurately and make better pricing assumptions), it requires firms to carefully balance the conflicts of interest inherent in the collaboration. Having analysts work with investment bankers is appropriate only when the conflicts are adequately and effectively managed and disclosed. Firm managers have a responsibility to provide an environment in which analysts are neither coerced nor enticed into issuing research that does not reflect their true opinions. Firms should require public disclosure of actual conflicts of interest to investors.

Members, candidates, and their firms must adopt and follow perceived best practices in maintaining independence and objectivity in the corporate culture and protecting analysts from undue pressure by their investment banking colleagues. The "firewalls" traditionally built between these two functions must be managed to minimize conflicts of interest; indeed, enhanced firewall policies may go as far as prohibiting all communications between these groups. A key element of an enhanced firewall is separate reporting structures for personnel on the research side and personnel on the investment banking side. For example, investment banking personnel should not have any authority to approve, disapprove, or make changes to research reports or recommendations. Another element should be a compensation arrangement that minimizes the pressures on research analysts and rewards objectivity and accuracy. Compensation arrangements should not link analyst remuneration directly to investment banking assignments in which the analyst may participate as a team member. Firms should also regularly review their policies and procedures to determine whether analysts are adequately safeguarded and to improve the transparency of disclosures relating to conflicts of interest. The highest level of transparency is achieved when disclosures are prominent and specific rather than marginalized and generic.

Performance Measurement and Attribution

Members and candidates working within a firm's investment performance measurement department may also be presented with situations that challenge their independence and objectivity. As performance analysts, their analyses may reveal instances where managers may appear to have strayed from their mandate. Additionally, the performance analyst may receive requests to alter the construction of composite indexes owing to negative results for a selected account or fund. The member or candidate must not allow internal or external influences to affect their independence and objectivity as they faithfully complete their performance calculation and analysis-related responsibilities.

Public Companies

Analysts may be pressured to issue favorable reports and recommendations by the companies they follow. Not every stock is a "buy," and not every research report is favorable—for many reasons, including the cyclical nature of many business activities and market fluctuations. For instance, a "good company" does not always translate into a "good stock" rating if the current stock price is fully valued. In making an investment recommendation, the analyst is responsible for anticipating, interpreting, and assessing a company's prospects and stock price performance in a factual manner. Many company managers, however, believe that their company's stock is undervalued, and these managers may find it difficult to accept critical research reports or ratings downgrades. Company managers' compensation may also be dependent on stock performance.

Due diligence in financial research and analysis involves gathering information from a wide variety of sources, including public disclosure documents (such as proxy statements, annual reports, and other regulatory filings) and also company management and investor-relations personnel, suppliers, customers, competitors, and other relevant sources. Research analysts may justifiably fear that companies will limit their ability to conduct thorough research by denying analysts who have "negative" views direct access to company managers and/or barring them from conference calls and other communication venues. Retaliatory practices include companies bringing legal action against analysts personally and/or their firms to seek monetary damages for the economic effects of negative reports and recommendations. Although few companies engage in such behavior, the perception that a reprisal is possible is a reasonable concern for analysts. This concern may make it difficult for them to conduct the comprehensive research needed to make objective recommendations. For further information and guidance, members and candidates should refer to the CFA Institute publication *Best Practice Guidelines Governing Analyst/Corporate Issuer Relations* (www.cfainstitute.org).

Credit Rating Agency Opinions

Credit rating agencies provide a service by grading the fixed-income products offered by companies. Analysts face challenges related to incentives and compensation schemes that may be tied to the final rating and successful placement of the product. Members and candidates employed at rating agencies should ensure that procedures and processes at the agencies prevent undue influences from a sponsoring company during the analysis. Members and candidates should abide by their agencies' and the industry's standards of conduct regarding the analytical process and the distribution of their reports.

The work of credit rating agencies also raises concerns similar to those inherent in investment banking relationships. Analysts may face pressure to issue ratings at a specific level because of other services the agency offers companies—namely, advising on the development of structured products. The rating agencies need to develop the necessary firewalls and protections to allow the independent operations of their different business lines.

When using information provided by credit rating agencies, members and candidates should be mindful of the potential conflicts of interest. And because of the potential conflicts, members and candidates may need to independently validate the rating granted.

Influence during the Manager Selection/Procurement Process

Members and candidates may find themselves on either side of the manager selection process. An individual may be on the hiring side as a representative of a pension organization or an investment committee member of an endowment or a charitable organization. Additionally, other members may be representing their organizations in attempts to earn new investment allocation mandates. The responsibility of members and candidates to maintain their independence and objectivity extends to the hiring or firing of those who provide business services beyond investment management.

When serving in a hiring capacity, members and candidates should not solicit gifts, contributions, or other compensation that may affect their independence and objectivity. Solicitations do not have to benefit members and candidates personally to conflict with Standard I(B). Requesting contributions to a favorite charity or political organization may also be perceived as an attempt to influence the decision-making process. Additionally, members and candidates serving in a hiring capacity should refuse gifts, donations, and other offered compensation that may be perceived to influence their decision-making process.

When working to earn a new investment allocation, members and candidates should not offer gifts, contributions, or other compensation to influence the decision of the hiring representative. The offering of these items with the intent to impair the independence and objectivity of another person would not comply with Standard I(B). Such prohibited actions may include offering donations to a charitable organization or political candidate referred by the hiring representative.

A clear example of improperly influencing hiring representatives was displayed in the "pay-to-play" scandal involving government-sponsored pension funds in the United States. Managers looking to gain lucrative allocations from the large funds made requested donations to the political campaigns of individuals directly responsible for the hiring decisions. This scandal and other similar events have led to new laws requiring additional reporting concerning political contributions and bans on hiring—or hiring delays for—managers that made campaign contributions to representatives associated with the decision-making process.

Issuer-Paid Research

In light of the recent reduction of sell-side research coverage, many companies, seeking to increase visibility both in the financial markets and with potential investors, have hired analysts to produce research reports analyzing their companies. These reports bridge the gap created by the lack of coverage and can be an effective method of communicating with investors.

Issuer-paid research conducted by independent analysts, however, is fraught with potential conflicts. Depending on how the research is written and distributed, investors may be misled into believing that the research is from an independent source when, in reality, it has been paid for by the subject company.

Members and candidates must adhere to strict standards of conduct that govern how the research is to be conducted and what disclosures must be made in the report. Analysts must engage in thorough, independent, and unbiased analysis and must fully disclose potential conflicts of interest, including the nature of their compensation. Otherwise, analysts risk misleading investors.

Investors need clear, credible, and thorough information about companies, and they need research based on independent thought. At a minimum, issuer-paid research should include a thorough analysis of the company's financial statements based on publicly disclosed information, benchmarking within a peer group, and industry analysis. Analysts must exercise diligence, independence, and thoroughness in conducting their research in an objective manner. Analysts must distinguish between fact and opinion in their reports. Conclusions must have a reasonable and adequate basis and must be supported by appropriate research.

Independent analysts must also strictly limit the type of compensation that they accept for conducting issuer-paid research. Otherwise, the content and conclusions of the reports could reasonably be expected to be determined or affected by compensation from the sponsoring companies. Compensation that might influence the research report could be direct, such as payment based on the conclusions of the report, or indirect, such as stock warrants or other equity instruments that could increase in value on the basis of positive coverage in the report. In such instances, the independent analyst has an incentive to avoid including negative information or making negative conclusions. Best practice is for independent analysts, prior to writing their reports, to negotiate only a flat fee for their work that is not linked to their conclusions or recommendations.

Travel Funding

The benefits related to accepting paid travel extend beyond the cost savings to the member or candidate and his firm, such as the chance to talk exclusively with the executives of a company or learning more about the investment options provided by an investment organization. Acceptance also comes with potential concerns; for example, members and candidates may be influenced by these discussions when flying on a corporate or chartered jet or attending sponsored conferences where many expenses, including airfare and lodging, are covered. To avoid the appearance of compromising their independence and objectivity, best practice dictates that members and candidates always use commercial transportation at their expense or at the expense of their firm rather than accept paid travel arrangements from an outside company. Should commercial transportation be unavailable, members and candidates may accept modestly arranged travel to participate in appropriate information-gathering events, such as a property tour.

Recommended Procedures for Compliance

Members and candidates should adhere to the following practices and should encourage their firms to establish procedures to avoid violations of Standard I(B):

- *Protect the integrity of opinions*: Members, candidates, and their firms should establish policies stating that every research report concerning the securities of a corporate client should reflect the unbiased opinion of the analyst. Firms should also design compensation systems that protect the integrity of the investment decision process by maintaining the independence and objectivity of analysts.
- *Create a restricted list*: If the firm is unwilling to permit dissemination of adverse opinions about a corporate client, members and candidates should encourage the firm to remove the controversial company from the research universe and put it on a restricted list so that the firm disseminates only factual information about the company.
- *Restrict special cost arrangements*: When attending meetings at an issuer's headquarters, members and candidates should pay for commercial transportation and hotel charges. No corporate issuer should reimburse members or candidates for air transportation. Members and candidates should encourage issuers to limit the use of corporate aircraft to situations in which commercial transportation is not available or in which efficient movement could not otherwise be arranged. Members and candidates should take particular care that when frequent meetings are held between an individual issuer and an individual member or candidate, the issuer should not always host the member or candidate.

- *Limit gifts*: Members and candidates must limit the acceptance of gratuities and/or gifts to token items. Standard I(B) does not preclude customary, ordinary business-related entertainment as long as its purpose is not to influence or reward members or candidates. Firms should consider a strict value limit for acceptable gifts that is based on the local or regional customs and should address whether the limit is per gift or an aggregate annual value.
- *Restrict investments*: Members and candidates should encourage their investment firms to develop formal policies related to employee purchases of equity or equity-related IPOs. Firms should require prior approval for employee participation in IPOs, with prompt disclosure of investment actions taken following the offering. Strict limits should be imposed on investment personnel acquiring securities in private placements.
- *Review procedures*: Members and candidates should encourage their firms to implement effective supervisory and review procedures to ensure that analysts and portfolio managers comply with policies relating to their personal investment activities.
- *Independence policy*: Members, candidates, and their firms should establish a formal written policy on the independence and objectivity of research and implement reporting structures and review procedures to ensure that research analysts do not report to and are not supervised or controlled by any department of the firm that could compromise the independence of the analyst. More detailed recommendations related to a firm's policies regarding research objectivity are set forth in the CFA Institute statement *Research Objectivity Standards* (www.cfainstitute.org).
- *Appointed officer*: Firms should appoint a senior officer with oversight responsibilities for compliance with the firm's code of ethics and all regulations concerning its business. Firms should provide every employee with the procedures and policies for reporting potentially unethical behavior, violations of regulations, or other activities that may harm the firm's reputation.

Application of the Standard

Example 1 (Travel Expenses):

Steven Taylor, a mining analyst with Bronson Brokers, is invited by Precision Metals to join a group of his peers in a tour of mining facilities in several western US states. The company arranges for chartered group flights from site to site and for accommodations in Spartan Motels, the only chain with accommodations near the mines, for three nights. Taylor allows Precision Metals to pick up his tab, as do the other analysts, with one exception—John Adams, an employee of a large trust company who insists on following his company's policy and paying for his hotel room himself.

> *Comment*: The policy of the company where Adams works complies closely with Standard I(B) by avoiding even the appearance of a conflict of interest, but Taylor and the other analysts were not necessarily violating Standard I(B). In general, when allowing companies to pay for travel and/or accommodations in these circumstances, members and candidates must use their judgment. They must be on guard that such arrangements not impinge on a member's or candidate's independence and objectivity. In this example, the trip was strictly for business and Taylor was not accepting irrelevant or lavish hospitality. The itinerary required chartered flights, for which analysts were not expected to pay. The accommodations were modest. These arrangements are not unusual and did not violate Standard I(B) as long as Taylor's independence and objectivity were not compromised. In

the final analysis, members and candidates should consider both whether they can remain objective and whether their integrity might be perceived by their clients to have been compromised.

Example 2 (Research Independence):

Susan Dillon, an analyst in the corporate finance department of an investment services firm, is making a presentation to a potential new business client that includes the promise that her firm will provide full research coverage of the potential client.

Comment: Dillon may agree to provide research coverage, but she must not commit her firm's research department to providing a favorable recommendation. The firm's recommendation (favorable, neutral, or unfavorable) must be based on an independent and objective investigation and analysis of the company and its securities.

Example 3 (Research Independence and Intrafirm Pressure):

Walter Fritz is an equity analyst with Hilton Brokerage who covers the mining industry. He has concluded that the stock of Metals & Mining is overpriced at its current level, but he is concerned that a negative research report will hurt the good relationship between Metals & Mining and the investment banking division of his firm. In fact, a senior manager of Hilton Brokerage has just sent him a copy of a proposal his firm has made to Metals & Mining to underwrite a debt offering. Fritz needs to produce a report right away and is concerned about issuing a less-than-favorable rating.

Comment: Fritz's analysis of Metals & Mining must be objective and based solely on consideration of company fundamentals. Any pressure from other divisions of his firm is inappropriate. This conflict could have been eliminated if, in anticipation of the offering, Hilton Brokerage had placed Metals & Mining on a restricted list for its sales force.

Example 4 (Research Independence and Issuer Relationship Pressure):

As in Example 3, Walter Fritz has concluded that Metals & Mining stock is overvalued at its current level, but he is concerned that a negative research report might jeopardize a close rapport that he has nurtured over the years with Metals & Mining's CEO, chief finance officer, and investment relations officer. Fritz is concerned that a negative report might result also in management retaliation—for instance, cutting him off from participating in conference calls when a quarterly earnings release is made, denying him the ability to ask questions on such calls, and/or denying him access to top management for arranging group meetings between Hilton Brokerage clients and top Metals & Mining managers.

Comment: As in Example 3, Fritz's analysis must be objective and based solely on consideration of company fundamentals. Any pressure from Metals & Mining is inappropriate. Fritz should reinforce the integrity of his conclusions by stressing that his investment recommendation is based on relative valuation, which may include qualitative issues with respect to Metals & Mining's management.

Example 5 (Research Independence and Sales Pressure):

As support for the sales effort of her corporate bond department, Lindsey Warner offers credit guidance to purchasers of fixed-income securities. Her compensation is closely linked to the performance of the corporate bond department. Near the quarter's end, Warner's firm has a large inventory position in the bonds of Milton, Ltd., and has been unable to sell the bonds because of Milton's recent announcement of an operating problem. Salespeople have asked her to contact large clients to push the bonds.

> *Comment*: Unethical sales practices create significant potential violations of the Code and Standards. Warner's opinion of the Milton bonds must not be affected by internal pressure or compensation. In this case, Warner must refuse to push the Milton bonds unless she is able to justify that the market price has already adjusted for the operating problem.

Example 6 (Research Independence and Prior Coverage):

Jill Jorund is a securities analyst following airline stocks and a rising star at her firm. Her boss has been carrying a "buy" recommendation on International Airlines and asks Jorund to take over coverage of that airline. He tells Jorund that under no circumstances should the prevailing buy recommendation be changed.

> *Comment*: Jorund must be independent and objective in her analysis of International Airlines. If she believes that her boss's instructions have compromised her, she has two options: She can tell her boss that she cannot cover the company under these constraints, or she can take over coverage of the company, reach her own independent conclusions, and if they conflict with her boss's opinion, share the conclusions with her boss or other supervisors in the firm so that they can make appropriate recommendations. Jorund must issue only recommendations that reflect her independent and objective opinion.

Example 7 (Gifts and Entertainment from Related Party):

Edward Grant directs a large amount of his commission business to a New York–based brokerage house. In appreciation for all the business, the brokerage house gives Grant two tickets to the World Cup in South Africa, two nights at a nearby resort, several meals, and transportation via limousine to the game. Grant fails to disclose receiving this package to his supervisor.

> *Comment*: Grant has violated Standard I(B) because accepting these substantial gifts may impede his independence and objectivity. Every member and candidate should endeavor to avoid situations that might cause or be perceived to cause a loss of independence or objectivity in recommending investments or taking investment action. By accepting the trip, Grant has opened himself up to the accusation that he may give the broker favored treatment in return.

Example 8 (Gifts and Entertainment from Client):

Theresa Green manages the portfolio of Ian Knowlden, a client of Tisbury Investments. Green achieves an annual return for Knowlden that is consistently better than that of the benchmark she and the client previously agreed to. As a reward, Knowlden offers Green two tickets to Wimbledon and the use of Knowlden's flat in London for a week. Green discloses this gift to her supervisor at Tisbury.

> *Comment*: Green is in compliance with Standard I(B) because she disclosed the gift from one of her clients in accordance with the firm's policies. Members and candidates may accept bonuses or gifts from clients as long as they disclose them to their employer because gifts in a client relationship are deemed less likely to affect a member's or candidate's objectivity and independence than gifts in other situations. Disclosure is required, however, so that supervisors can monitor such situations to guard against

employees favoring a gift-giving client to the detriment of other fee-paying clients (such as by allocating a greater proportion of IPO stock to the gift-giving client's portfolio).

Best practices for monitoring include comparing the transaction costs of the Knowlden account with the costs of other accounts managed by Green and other similar accounts within Tisbury. The supervisor could also compare the performance returns with the returns of other clients with the same mandate. This comparison will assist in determining whether a pattern of favoritism by Green is disadvantaging other Tisbury clients or the possibility that this favoritism could affect her future behavior.

Example 9 (Travel Expenses from External Manager):

Tom Wayne is the investment manager of the Franklin City Employees Pension Plan. He recently completed a successful search for a firm to manage the foreign equity allocation of the plan's diversified portfolio. He followed the plan's standard procedure of seeking presentations from a number of qualified firms and recommended that his board select Penguin Advisors because of its experience, well-defined investment strategy, and performance record. The firm claims compliance with the Global Investment Performance Standards (GIPS) and has been verified. Following the selection of Penguin, a reporter from the *Franklin City Record* calls to ask if there was any connection between this action and the fact that Penguin was one of the sponsors of an "investment fact-finding trip to Asia" that Wayne made earlier in the year. The trip was one of several conducted by the Pension Investment Academy, which had arranged the itinerary of meetings with economic, government, and corporate officials in major cities in several Asian countries. The Pension Investment Academy obtains support for the cost of these trips from a number of investment managers, including Penguin Advisors; the Academy then pays the travel expenses of the various pension plan managers on the trip and provides all meals and accommodations. The president of Penguin Advisors was also one of the travelers on the trip.

Comment: Although Wayne can probably put to good use the knowledge he gained from the trip in selecting portfolio managers and in other areas of managing the pension plan, his recommendation of Penguin Advisors may be tainted by the possible conflict incurred when he participated in a trip partly paid for by Penguin Advisors and when he was in the daily company of the president of Penguin Advisors. To avoid violating Standard I(B), Wayne's basic expenses for travel and accommodations should have been paid by his employer or the pension plan; contact with the president of Penguin Advisors should have been limited to informational or educational events only; and the trip, the organizer, and the sponsor should have been made a matter of public record. Even if his actions were not in violation of Standard I(B), Wayne should have been sensitive to the public perception of the trip when reported in the newspaper and the extent to which the subjective elements of his decision might have been affected by the familiarity that the daily contact of such a trip would encourage. This advantage would probably not be shared by firms competing with Penguin Advisors.

Example 10 (Research Independence and Compensation Arrangements):

Javier Herrero recently left his job as a research analyst for a large investment adviser. While looking for a new position, he was hired by an investor-relations firm to write a research report on one of its clients, a small educational software company. The investor-relations firm hopes to generate investor interest in the technology company. The firm will pay Herrero a flat fee plus a bonus if any new investors buy stock in the company as a result of Herrero's report.

Comment: If Herrero accepts this payment arrangement, he will be in violation of Standard I(B) because the compensation arrangement can reasonably be expected to compromise his independence and objectivity. Herrero will receive a bonus for attracting investors, which provides an incentive to draft a positive report regardless of the facts and to ignore or play down any negative information about the company. Herrero should accept only a flat fee that is not tied to the conclusions or recommendations of the report. Issuer-paid research that is objective and unbiased can be done under the right circumstances as long as the analyst takes steps to maintain his or her objectivity and includes in the report proper disclosures regarding potential conflicts of interest.

Example 11 (Recommendation Objectivity and Service Fees):

Two years ago, Bob Wade, trust manager for Central Midas Bank, was approached by Western Funds about promoting its family of funds, with special interest in the service-fee class of funds. To entice Central to promote this class, Western Funds offered to pay the bank a service fee of 0.25%. Without disclosing the fee being offered to the bank, Wade asked one of the investment managers to review Western's funds to determine whether they were suitable for clients of Central Midas Bank. The manager completed the normal due diligence review and determined that the new funds were fairly valued in the market with fee structures on a par with competitors. Wade decided to accept Western's offer and instructed the team of portfolio managers to exclusively promote these funds and the service-fee class to clients seeking to invest new funds or transfer from their current investments.

Now, two years later, the funds managed by Western begin to underperform their peers. Wade is counting on the fees to reach his profitability targets and continues to push these funds as acceptable investments for Central's clients.

Comment: Wade is violating Standard I(B) because the fee arrangement has affected the objectivity of his recommendations. Wade is relying on the fee as a component of the department's profitability and is unwilling to offer other products that may affect the fees received.

See also Standard VI(A)–Disclosure of Conflicts.

Example 12 (Recommendation Objectivity):

Bob Thompson has been doing research for the portfolio manager of the fixed-income department. His assignment is to do sensitivity analysis on securitized subprime mortgages. He has discussed with the manager possible scenarios to use to calculate expected returns. A key assumption in such calculations is housing price appreciation (HPA) because it drives "prepays" (prepayments of mortgages) and losses. Thompson is concerned with the significant appreciation experienced over the previous five years as a result of the increased availability of funds from subprime mortgages. Thompson insists that the analysis should include a scenario run with −10% for Year 1, −5% for Year 2, and then (to project a worst-case scenario) 0% for Years 3 through 5. The manager replies that these assumptions are too dire because there has never been a time in their available database when HPA was negative.

Thompson conducts his research to better understand the risks inherent in these securities and evaluates these securities in the worst-case scenario, an unlikely but possible environment. Based on the results of the enhanced scenarios, Thompson does not recommend the purchase of the securitization. Against the general market trends, the manager follows Thompson's recommendation and does not invest. The following year, the housing market collapses. In avoiding the subprime investments, the manager's portfolio outperforms its peer group that year.

Comment: Thompson's actions in running the worst-case scenario against the protests of the portfolio manager are in alignment with the principles of Standard I(B). Thompson did not allow his research to be pressured by the general trends of the market or the manager's desire to limit the research to historical norms.

See also Standard V(A)–Diligence and Reasonable Basis.

Example 13 (Influencing Manager Selection Decisions):

Adrian Mandel, CFA, is a senior portfolio manager for ZZYY Capital Management who oversees a team of investment professionals who manage labor union pension funds. A few years ago, ZZYY sought to win a competitive asset manager search to manage a significant allocation of the pension fund of the United Doughnut and Pretzel Bakers Union (UDPBU). UDPBU's investment board is chaired by a recognized key decision maker and long-time leader of the union, Ernesto Gomez. To improve ZZYY's chances of winning the competition, Mandel made significant monetary contributions to Gomez's union reelection campaign fund. Even after ZZYY was hired as a primary manager of the pension, Mandel believed that his firm's position was not secure. Mandel continued to contribute to Gomez's reelection campaign chest as well as to entertain lavishly the union leader and his family at top restaurants on a regular basis. All of Mandel's outlays were routinely handled as marketing expenses reimbursed by ZZYY's expense accounts and were disclosed to his senior management as being instrumental in maintaining a strong close relationship with an important client.

Comment: Mandel not only offered but actually gave monetary gifts, benefits, and other considerations that reasonably could be expected to compromise Gomez's objectivity. Therefore, Mandel was in violation of Standard I(B).

Example 14 (Influencing Manager Selection Decisions):

Adrian Mandel, CFA, had heard about the manager search competition for the UDPBU Pension Fund through a broker/dealer contact. The contact told him that a well-known retired professional golfer, Bobby "The Bear" Finlay, who had become a licensed broker/dealer serving as a pension consultant, was orchestrating the UDPBU manager search. Finlay had gained celebrity status with several labor union pension fund boards by entertaining their respective board members and regaling them with colorful stories of fellow pro golfers' antics in clubhouses around the world. Mandel decided to improve ZZYY's chances of being invited to participate in the search competition by befriending Finlay to curry his favor. Knowing Finlay's love of entertainment, Mandel wined and dined Finlay at high-profile bistros where Finlay could glow in the fan recognition lavished on him by all the other patrons. Mandel's endeavors paid off handsomely when Finlay recommended to the UDPBU board that ZZYY be entered as one of three finalist asset management firms in its search.

Comment: Similar to Example 13, Mandel lavished gifts, benefits, and other considerations in the form of expensive entertainment that could reasonably be expected to influence the consultant to recommend the hiring of his firm. Therefore, Mandel was in violation of Standard I(B).

Example 15 (Fund Manager Relationships):

Amie Scott is a performance analyst within her firm with responsibilities for analyzing the performance of external managers. While completing her quarterly analysis, Scott notices a change in one manager's reported composite construction. The change concealed the bad performance of a particularly large account by placing that account into a new residual composite. This change allowed the manager to remain at the top of the list of manager performance. Scott knows her firm has a large allocation to this manager, and the fund's manager is a close personal friend of the CEO. She needs to deliver her final report but is concerned with pointing out the composite change.

> *Comment*: Scott would be in violation of Standard I(B) if she did not disclose the change in her final report. The analysis of managers' performance should not be influenced by personal relationships or the size of the allocation to the outside managers. By not including the change, Scott would not be providing an independent analysis of the performance metrics for her firm.

Example 16 (Intrafirm Pressure):

Jill Stein is head of performance measurement for her firm. During the last quarter, many members of the organization's research department were removed because of the poor quality of their recommendations. The subpar research caused one larger account holder to experience significant underperformance, which resulted in the client withdrawing his money after the end of the quarter. The head of sales requests that Stein remove this account from the firm's performance composite because the performance decline can be attributed to the departed research team and not the client's adviser.

> *Comment*: Pressure from other internal departments can create situations that cause a member or candidate to violate the Code and Standards. Stein must maintain her independence and objectivity and refuse to exclude specific accounts from the firm's performance composites to which they belong. As long as the client invested under a strategy similar to that of the defined composite, it cannot be excluded because of the poor stock selections that led to the underperformance and asset withdrawal.

Standard I(C) Misrepresentation

> Members and Candidates must not knowingly make any misrepresentations relating to investment analysis, recommendations, actions, or other professional activities.

Guidance

Highlights:

- *Impact on Investment Practice*
- *Performance Reporting*
- *Social Media*
- *Omissions*
- *Plagiarism*
- *Work Completed for Employer*

Trust is the foundation of the investment profession. Investors must be able to rely on the statements and information provided to them by those with whom the investors have trusted their financial well-being. Investment professionals who make false or misleading statements not only harm investors but also reduce the level of investor confidence in the investment profession and threaten the integrity of capital markets as a whole.

A misrepresentation is any untrue statement or omission of a fact or any statement that is otherwise false or misleading. A member or candidate must not knowingly omit or misrepresent information or give a false impression of a firm, organization, or security in the member's or candidate's oral representations, advertising (whether in the press or through brochures), electronic communications, or written materials (whether publicly disseminated or not). In this context, "knowingly" means that the member or candidate either knows or should have known that the misrepresentation was being made or that omitted information could alter the investment decision-making process.

Written materials include, but are not limited to, research reports, underwriting documents, company financial reports, market letters, newspaper columns, and books. Electronic communications include, but are not limited to, internet communications, webpages, mobile applications, and e-mails. Members and candidates who use webpages should regularly monitor materials posted on these sites to ensure that they contain current information. Members and candidates should also ensure that all reasonable precautions have been taken to protect the site's integrity and security and that the site does not misrepresent any information and does provide full disclosure.

Standard I(C) prohibits members and candidates from guaranteeing clients any specific return on volatile investments. Most investments contain some element of risk that makes their return inherently unpredictable. For such investments, guaranteeing either a particular rate of return or a guaranteed preservation of investment capital (e.g., "I can guarantee that you will earn 8% on equities this year" or "I can guarantee that you will not lose money on this investment") is misleading to investors. Standard I(C) does not prohibit members and candidates from providing clients with information on investment products that have guarantees built into the structure of the products themselves or for which an institution has agreed to cover any losses.

Impact on Investment Practice

Members and candidates must not misrepresent any aspect of their practice, including (but not limited to) their qualifications or credentials, the qualifications or services provided by their firm, their performance record and the record of their firm, and the characteristics of an investment. Any misrepresentation made by a member or candidate relating to the member's or candidate's professional activities is a breach of this standard.

Members and candidates should exercise care and diligence when incorporating third-party information. Misrepresentations resulting from the use of the credit ratings, research, testimonials, or marketing materials of outside parties become the responsibility of the investment professional when it affects that professional's business practices.

Investing through outside managers continues to expand as an acceptable method of investing in areas outside a firm's core competencies. Members and candidates must disclose their intended use of external managers and must not represent those managers' investment practices as their own. Although the level of involvement of outside managers may change over time, appropriate disclosures by members and candidates are important in avoiding misrepresentations, especially if the primary activity is to invest directly with a single external manager. Standard V(B)–Communication with Clients and Prospective Clients discusses in further detail communicating the firm's investment practices.

Performance Reporting

The performance benchmark selection process is another area where misrepresentations may occur. Members and candidates may misrepresent the success of their performance record through presenting benchmarks that are not comparable to their strategies. Further, clients can be misled if the benchmark's results are not reported on a basis comparable to that of the fund's or client's results. Best practice is selecting the most appropriate available benchmark from a universe of available options. The transparent presentation of appropriate performance benchmarks is an important aspect in providing clients with information that is useful in making investment decisions.

However, Standard I(C) does not require that a benchmark always be provided in order to comply. Some investment strategies may not lend themselves to displaying an appropriate benchmark because of the complexity or diversity of the investments included. Furthermore, some investment strategies may use reference indexes that do not reflect the opportunity set of the invested assets—for example, a hedge fund comparing its performance with a "cash plus" basis. When such a benchmark is used, members and candidates should make reasonable efforts to ensure that they disclose the reasons behind the use of this reference index to avoid misrepresentations of their performance. Members and candidates should discuss with clients on a continuous basis the appropriate benchmark to be used for performance evaluations and related fee calculations.

Reporting misrepresentations may also occur when valuations for illiquid or non-traded securities are available from more than one source. When different options are available, members and candidates may be tempted to switch providers to obtain higher security valuations. The process of shopping for values may misrepresent a security's worth, lead to misinformed decisions to sell or hold an investment, and result in overcharging clients advisory fees.

Members and candidates should take reasonable steps to provide accurate and reliable security pricing information to clients on a consistent basis. Changing pricing providers should not be based solely on the justification that the new provider reports a higher current value of a security. Consistency in the reported information will improve the perception of the valuation process for illiquid securities. Clients will likely have additional confidence that they were able to make an informed decision about continuing to hold these securities in their portfolios.

Social Media

The advancement of online discussion forums and communication platforms, commonly referred to as "social media," is placing additional responsibilities on members and candidates. When communicating through social media channels, members and candidates should provide only the same information they are allowed to distribute to clients and potential clients through other traditional forms of communication. The online or interactive aspects of social media do not remove the need to be open and honest about the information being distributed.

Along with understanding and following existing and newly developing rules and regulations regarding the allowed use of social media, members and candidates should also ensure that all communications in this format adhere to the requirements of the Code and Standards. The perceived anonymity granted through these platforms may entice individuals to misrepresent their qualifications or abilities or those of their employer. Actions undertaken through social media that knowingly misrepresent investment recommendations or professional activities are considered a violation of Standard I(C).

Omissions

The omission of a fact or outcome can be misleading, especially given the growing use of models and technical analysis processes. Many members and candidates rely on such models and processes to scan for new investment opportunities, to develop investment vehicles, and to produce investment recommendations and ratings. When inputs are knowingly omitted, the resulting outcomes may provide misleading information to those who rely on it for making investment decisions. Additionally, the outcomes from models shall not be presented as fact because they represent the expected results based on the inputs and analysis process incorporated.

Omissions in the performance measurement and attribution process can also misrepresent a manager's performance and skill. Members and candidates should encourage their firms to develop strict policies for composite development to prevent cherry picking—situations in which selected accounts are presented as representative of the firm's abilities. The omission of any accounts appropriate for the defined composite may misrepresent to clients the success of the manager's implementation of its strategy.

Plagiarism

Standard I(C) also prohibits plagiarism in the preparation of material for distribution to employers, associates, clients, prospects, or the general public. Plagiarism is defined as copying or using in substantially the same form materials prepared by others without acknowledging the source of the material or identifying the author and publisher of such material. Members and candidates must not copy (or represent as their own) original ideas or material without permission and must acknowledge and identify the source of ideas or material that is not their own.

The investment profession uses a myriad of financial, economic, and statistical data in the investment decision-making process. Through various publications and presentations, the investment professional is constantly exposed to the work of others and to the temptation to use that work without proper acknowledgment.

Misrepresentation through plagiarism in investment management can take various forms. The simplest and most flagrant example is to take a research report or study done by another firm or person, change the names, and release the material as one's own original analysis. This action is a clear violation of Standard I(C). Other practices include (1) using excerpts from articles or reports prepared by others either verbatim or with only slight changes in wording without acknowledgment, (2) citing specific quotations as attributable to "leading analysts" and "investment experts" without naming the specific references, (3) presenting statistical estimates of forecasts prepared by others and identifying the sources but without including the qualifying statements or caveats that may have been used, (4) using charts and graphs without stating their sources, and (5) copying proprietary computerized spreadsheets or algorithms without seeking the cooperation or authorization of their creators.

In the case of distributing third-party, outsourced research, members and candidates may use and distribute such reports as long as they do not represent themselves as the report's authors. Indeed, the member or candidate may add value for the client by sifting through research and repackaging it for clients. In such cases, clients should be fully informed that they are paying for the ability of the member or candidate to find the best research from a wide variety of sources. Members and candidates must not misrepresent their abilities, the extent of their expertise, or the extent of their work in a way that would mislead their clients or prospective clients. Members and candidates should disclose whether the research being presented to clients comes from another source—from either within or outside the member's or candidate's firm. This allows clients to understand who has the expertise behind the report or whether the work is being done by the analyst, other members of the firm, or an outside party.

Standard I(C) also applies to plagiarism in oral communications, such as through group meetings; visits with associates, clients, and customers; use of audio/video media (which is rapidly increasing); and telecommunications, including electronic data transfer and the outright copying of electronic media.

One of the most egregious practices in violation of this standard is the preparation of research reports based on multiple sources of information without acknowledging the sources. Examples of information from such sources include ideas, statistical compilations, and forecasts combined to give the appearance of original work. Although there is no monopoly on ideas, members and candidates must give credit where it is clearly due. Analysts should not use undocumented forecasts, earnings projections, asset values, and so on. Sources must be revealed to bring the responsibility directly back to the author of the report or the firm involved.

Work Completed for Employer

The preceding paragraphs address actions that would constitute a violation of Standard I(C). In some situations, however, members or candidates may use research conducted or models developed by others within the same firm without committing a violation. The most common example relates to the situation in which one (or more) of the original analysts is no longer with the firm. Research and models developed while employed by a firm are the property of the firm. The firm retains the right to continue using the work completed after a member or candidate has left the organization. The firm may issue future reports without providing attribution to the prior analysts. A member or candidate cannot, however, reissue a previously released report solely under his or her name.

Recommended Procedures for Compliance

Factual Presentations

Members and candidates can prevent unintentional misrepresentations of their qualifications or the services they or their firms provide if each member and candidate understands the limit of the firm's or individual's capabilities and the need to be accurate and complete in presentations. Firms can provide guidance for employees who make written or oral presentations to clients or potential clients by providing a written list of the firm's available services and a description of the firm's qualifications. This list should suggest ways of describing the firm's services, qualifications, and compensation that are both accurate and suitable for client or customer presentations. Firms can also help prevent misrepresentation by specifically designating which employees are authorized to speak on behalf of the firm. Regardless of whether the firm provides guidance, members and candidates should make certain that they understand the services the firm can perform and its qualifications.

Qualification Summary

In addition, to ensure accurate presentations to clients, each member and candidate should prepare a summary of his or her own qualifications and experience and a list of the services the member or candidate is capable of performing. Firms can assist member and candidate compliance by periodically reviewing employee correspondence and documents that contain representations of individual or firm qualifications.

Verify Outside Information

When providing information to clients from a third party, members and candidates share a responsibility for the accuracy of the marketing and distribution materials that pertain to the third party's capabilities, services, and products. Misrepresentation by third parties can damage the member's or candidate's reputation, the reputation of the firm, and the integrity of the capital markets. Members and candidates should encourage their employers to develop procedures for verifying information of third-party firms.

Maintain Webpages

Members and candidates who publish a webpage should regularly monitor materials posted on the site to ensure that the site contains current information. Members and candidates should also ensure that all reasonable precautions have been taken to protect the site's integrity, confidentiality, and security and that the site does not misrepresent any information and provides full disclosure.

Plagiarism Policy

To avoid plagiarism in preparing research reports or conclusions of analysis, members and candidates should take the following steps:

- *Maintain copies*: Keep copies of all research reports, articles containing research ideas, material with new statistical methodologies, and other materials that were relied on in preparing the research report.
- *Attribute quotations*: Attribute to their sources any direct quotations, including projections, tables, statistics, model/product ideas, and new methodologies prepared by persons other than recognized financial and statistical reporting services or similar sources.
- *Attribute summaries*: Attribute to their sources any paraphrases or summaries of material prepared by others. For example, to support his analysis of Brown Company's competitive position, the author of a research report on Brown might summarize another analyst's report on Brown's chief competitor, but the author of the Brown report must acknowledge in his own report the reliance on the other analyst's report.

Application of the Standard

Example 1 (Disclosure of Issuer-Paid Research):

Anthony McGuire is an issuer-paid analyst hired by publicly traded companies to electronically promote their stocks. McGuire creates a website that promotes his research efforts as a seemingly independent analyst. McGuire posts a profile and a strong buy recommendation for each company on the website indicating that the stock is expected to increase in value. He does not disclose the contractual relationships with the companies he covers on his website, in the research reports he issues, or in the statements he makes about the companies in internet chat rooms.

> *Comment*: McGuire has violated Standard I(C) because the website is misleading to potential investors. Even if the recommendations are valid and supported with thorough research, his omissions regarding the true relationship between himself and the companies he covers constitute a misrepresentation. McGuire has also violated Standard VI(A)–Disclosure of Conflicts by not disclosing the existence of an arrangement with the companies through which he receives compensation in exchange for his services.

Example 2 (Correction of Unintentional Errors):

Hijan Yao is responsible for the creation and distribution of the marketing materials for his firm, which claims compliance with the GIPS standards. Yao creates and distributes a presentation of performance by the firm's Asian equity composite that states the composite has ¥350 billion in assets. In fact, the composite has only ¥35 billion in assets, and the higher figure on the presentation is a result of a typographical error. Nevertheless, the erroneous material is distributed to a number of clients before Yao catches the mistake.

> *Comment*: Once the error is discovered, Yao must take steps to cease distribution of the incorrect material and correct the error by informing those who have received the erroneous information. Because Yao did not knowingly make the misrepresentation, however, he did not violate Standard I(C). Because his firm claims compliance with the GIPS standards, it must also comply with the GIPS Guidance Statement on Error Correction in relation to the error.

Example 3 (Noncorrection of Known Errors):

Syed Muhammad is the president of an investment management firm. The promotional material for the firm, created by the firm's marketing department, incorrectly claims that Muhammad has an advanced degree in finance from a prestigious business school in addition to the CFA designation. Although Muhammad attended the school for a short period of time, he did not receive a degree. Over the years, Muhammad and others in the firm have distributed this material to numerous prospective clients and consultants.

> *Comment*: Even though Muhammad may not have been directly responsible for the misrepresentation of his credentials in the firm's promotional material, he used this material numerous times over an extended period and should have known of the misrepresentation. Thus, Muhammad has violated Standard I(C).

Example 4 (Plagiarism):

Cindy Grant, a research analyst for a Canadian brokerage firm, has specialized in the Canadian mining industry for the past 10 years. She recently read an extensive research report on Jefferson Mining, Ltd., by Jeremy Barton, another analyst. Barton provided extensive statistics on the mineral reserves, production capacity, selling rates, and marketing factors affecting Jefferson's operations. He also noted that initial drilling results on a new ore body, which had not been made public, might show the existence of mineral zones that could increase the life of Jefferson's main mines, but Barton cited no specific data as to the initial drilling results. Grant called an officer of Jefferson, who gave her the initial drilling results over the telephone. The data indicated that the expected life of the main mines would be tripled. Grant added these statistics to Barton's report and circulated it within her firm as her own report.

> *Comment*: Grant plagiarized Barton's report by reproducing large parts of it in her own report without acknowledgment.

Example 5 (Misrepresentation of Information):

When Ricki Marks sells mortgage-backed derivatives called "interest-only strips" (IOs) to public pension plan clients, she describes them as "guaranteed by the US government." Purchasers of the IOs are entitled only to the interest stream generated by the mortgages, however, not the notional principal itself. One particular municipality's investment policies and local law require that securities purchased by its public pension plans be guaranteed by the US government. Although the underlying mortgages are guaranteed, neither the investor's investment nor the interest stream on the IOs is guaranteed. When interest rates decline, causing an increase in prepayment of mortgages, interest payments to the IOs' investors decline, and these investors lose a portion of their investment.

> *Comment*: Marks violated Standard I(C) by misrepresenting the terms and character of the investment.

Example 6 (Potential Information Misrepresentation):

Khalouck Abdrabbo manages the investments of several high-net-worth individuals in the United States who are approaching retirement. Abdrabbo advises these individuals that a portion of their investments be moved from equity to bank-sponsored certificates of deposit and money market accounts so that the principal will be "guaranteed" up to a certain amount. The interest is not guaranteed.

> *Comment*: Although there is risk that the institution offering the certificates of deposits and money market accounts could go bankrupt, in the United States, these accounts are insured by the US government through the Federal Deposit Insurance Corporation. Therefore, using the term "guaranteed" in this context is not inappropriate as long as the amount is within the government-insured limit. Abdrabbo should explain these facts to the clients.

Example 7 (Plagiarism):

Steve Swanson is a senior analyst in the investment research department of Ballard and Company. Apex Corporation has asked Ballard to assist in acquiring the majority ownership of stock in the Campbell Company, a financial consulting firm, and to prepare a report recommending that stockholders of Campbell agree to the acquisition. Another investment firm, Davis and Company, had already prepared a report for Apex analyzing both Apex and Campbell and recommending an exchange ratio. Apex has given the Davis report to Ballard officers, who have passed it on to Swanson. Swanson reviews the Davis report and other available material on Apex and Campbell. From his analysis, he concludes that the common stocks of Campbell and Apex represent good value at their current prices; he believes, however, that the Davis report does not consider all the factors a Campbell stockholder would need to know to make a decision. Swanson reports his conclusions to the partner in charge, who tells him to "use the Davis report, change a few words, sign your name, and get it out."

> *Comment*: If Swanson does as requested, he will violate Standard I(C). He could refer to those portions of the Davis report that he agrees with if he identifies Davis as the source; he could then add his own analysis and conclusions to the report before signing and distributing it.

Example 8 (Plagiarism):

Claude Browning, a quantitative analyst for Double Alpha, Inc., returns from a seminar in great excitement. At that seminar, Jack Jorrely, a well-known quantitative analyst at a national brokerage firm, discussed one of his new models in great detail, and Browning is intrigued by the new concepts. He proceeds to test the model, making some minor mechanical changes but retaining the concepts, until he produces some very positive results. Browning quickly announces to his supervisors at Double Alpha that he has discovered a new model and that clients and prospective clients should be informed of this positive finding as ongoing proof of Double Alpha's continuing innovation and ability to add value.

Comment: Although Browning tested Jorrely's model on his own and even slightly modified it, he must still acknowledge the original source of the idea. Browning can certainly take credit for the final, practical results; he can also support his conclusions with his own test. The credit for the innovative thinking, however, must be awarded to Jorrely.

Example 9 (Plagiarism):

Fernando Zubia would like to include in his firm's marketing materials some "plain-language" descriptions of various concepts, such as the price-to-earnings (P/E) multiple and why standard deviation is used as a measure of risk. The descriptions come from other sources, but Zubia wishes to use them without reference to the original authors. Would this use of material be a violation of Standard I(C)?

Comment: Copying verbatim any material without acknowledgement, including plain-language descriptions of the P/E multiple and standard deviation, violates Standard I(C). Even though these concepts are general, best practice would be for Zubia to describe them in his own words or cite the sources from which the descriptions are quoted. Members and candidates would be violating Standard I(C) if they either were responsible for creating marketing materials without attribution or knowingly use plagiarized materials.

Example 10 (Plagiarism):

Through a mainstream media outlet, Erika Schneider learns about a study that she would like to cite in her research. Should she cite both the mainstream intermediary source as well as the author of the study itself when using that information?

Comment: In all instances, a member or candidate must cite the actual source of the information. Best practice for Schneider would be to obtain the information directly from the author and review it before citing it in a report. In that case, Schneider would not need to report how she found out about the information. For example, suppose Schneider read in the *Financial Times* about a study issued by CFA Institute; best practice for Schneider would be to obtain a copy of the study from CFA Institute, review it, and then cite it in her report. If she does not use any interpretation of the report from the *Financial Times* and the newspaper does not add value to the report itself, the newspaper is merely a conduit of the original information and does not need to be cited. If she does not obtain the report and review the information, Schneider runs the risk of relying on second-hand information that may misstate facts. If, for example, the *Financial Times* erroneously reported some information from the original CFA Institute study and Schneider copied that erroneous information without acknowledging CFA Institute, she could be the object of complaints. Best practice would be either to obtain the complete study from its original author and cite only that author or to use the information provided by the intermediary and cite both sources.

Example 11 (Misrepresentation of Information):

Paul Ostrowski runs a two-person investment management firm. Ostrowski's firm subscribes to a service from a large investment research firm that provides research reports that can be repackaged by smaller firms for those firms' clients. Ostrowski's firm distributes these reports to clients as its own work.

Comment: Ostrowski can rely on third-party research that has a reasonable and adequate basis, but he cannot imply that he is the author of such research. If he does, Ostrowski is misrepresenting the extent of his work in a way that misleads the firm's clients or prospective clients.

Example 12 (Misrepresentation of Information):

Tom Stafford is part of a team within Appleton Investment Management responsible for managing a pool of assets for Open Air Bank, which distributes structured securities to offshore clients. He becomes aware that Open Air is promoting the structured securities as a much less risky investment than the investment management policy followed by him and the team to manage the original pool of assets. Also, Open Air has procured an independent rating for the pool that significantly overstates the quality of the investments. Stafford communicates his concerns to his supervisor, who responds that Open Air owns the product and is responsible for all marketing and distribution. Stafford's supervisor goes on to say that the product is outside of the US regulatory regime that Appleton follows and that all risks of the product are disclosed at the bottom of page 184 of the prospectus.

Comment: As a member of the investment team, Stafford is qualified to recognize the degree of accuracy of the materials that characterize the portfolio, and he is correct to be worried about Appleton's responsibility for a misrepresentation of the risks. Thus, he should continue to pursue the issue of Open Air's inaccurate promotion of the portfolio according to the firm's policies and procedures.

The Code and Standards stress protecting the reputation of the firm and the sustainability and integrity of the capital markets. Misrepresenting the quality and risks associated with the investment pool may lead to negative consequences for others well beyond the direct investors.

Example 13 (Avoiding a Misrepresentation):

Trina Smith is a fixed-income portfolio manager at a pension fund. She has observed that the market for highly structured mortgages is the focus of salespeople she meets and that these products represent a significant number of trading opportunities. In discussions about this topic with her team, Smith learns that calculating yields on changing cash flows within the deal structure requires very specialized vendor software. After more research, they find out that each deal is unique and that deals can have more than a dozen layers and changing cash flow priorities. Smith comes to the conclusion that, because of the complexity of these securities, the team cannot effectively distinguish between potentially good and bad investment options. To avoid misrepresenting their understanding, the team decides that the highly structured mortgage segment of the securitized market should not become part of the core of the fund's portfolio; they will allow some of the less complex securities to be part of the core.

Comment: Smith is in compliance with Standard I(C) by not investing in securities that she and her team cannot effectively understand. Because she is not able to describe the risk and return profile of the securities to the pension fund beneficiaries and trustees, she appropriately limits the fund's exposure to this sector.

Example 14 (Misrepresenting Composite Construction):

Robert Palmer is head of performance for a fund manager. When asked to provide performance numbers to fund rating agencies, he avoids mentioning that the fund manager is quite liberal in composite construction. The reason accounts are included/

excluded is not fully explained. The performance values reported to the rating agencies for the composites, although accurate for the accounts shown each period, may not present a true representation of the fund manager's ability.

Comment: "Cherry picking" accounts to include in either published reports or information provided to rating agencies conflicts with Standard I(C). Moving accounts into or out of a composite to influence the overall performance results materially misrepresents the reported values over time. Palmer should work with his firm to strengthen its reporting practices concerning composite construction to avoid misrepresenting the firm's track record or the quality of the information being provided.

Example 15 (Presenting Out-of-Date Information):

David Finch is a sales director at a commercial bank, where he directs the bank's client advisers in the sale of third-party mutual funds. Each quarter, he holds a division-wide training session where he provides fact sheets on investment funds the bank is allowed to offer to clients. These fact sheets, which can be redistributed to potential clients, are created by the fund firms and contain information about the funds, including investment strategy and target distribution rates.

Finch knows that some of the fact sheets are out of date; for example, one long-only fund approved the use of significant leverage last quarter as a method to enhance returns. He continues to provide the sheets to the sales team without updates because the bank has no control over the marketing material released by the mutual fund firms.

Comment: Finch is violating Standard I(C) by providing information that misrepresents aspects of the funds. By not providing the sales team and, ultimately, the clients with the updated information, he is misrepresenting the potential risks associated with the funds with outdated fact sheets. Finch can instruct the sales team to clarify the deficiencies in the fact sheets with clients and ensure they have the most recent fund prospectus document before accepting orders for investing in any fund.

Example 16 (Overemphasis of Firm Results):

Bob Anderson is chief compliance officer for Optima Asset Management Company, a firm currently offering eight funds to clients. Seven of the eight had 10-year returns below the median for their respective sectors. Anderson approves a recent advertisement, which includes this statement: "Optima Asset Management is achieving excellent returns for its investors. The Optima Emerging Markets Equity fund, for example, has 10-year returns that exceed the sector median by more than 10%."

Comment: From the information provided it is difficult to determine whether a violation has occurred as long as the sector outperformance is correct. Anderson may be attempting to mislead potential clients by citing the performance of the sole fund that achieved such results. Past performance is often used to demonstrate a firm's skill and abilities in comparison to funds in the same sectors.

However, if all the funds outperformed their respective benchmarks, then Anderson's assertion that the company "is achieving excellent returns" may be factual. Funds may exhibit positive returns for investors, exceed benchmarks, and yet have returns below the median in their sectors.

Members and candidates need to ensure that their marketing efforts do not include statements that misrepresent their skills and abilities to remain compliant with Standard I(C). Unless the returns of a single fund reflect the performance of a firm as a whole, the use of a singular fund for performance comparisons should be avoided.

Standard I(D) Misconduct

> Members and Candidates must not engage in any professional conduct involving dishonesty, fraud, or deceit or commit any act that reflects adversely on their professional reputation, integrity, or competence.

Guidance

Whereas Standard I(A) addresses the obligation of members and candidates to comply with applicable law that governs their professional activities, Standard I(D) addresses *all* conduct that reflects poorly on the professional integrity, good reputation, or competence of members and candidates. Any act that involves lying, cheating, stealing, or other dishonest conduct is a violation of this standard if the offense reflects adversely on a member's or candidate's professional activities. Although CFA Institute discourages any sort of unethical behavior by members and candidates, the Code and Standards are primarily aimed at conduct and actions related to a member's or candidate's professional life.

Conduct that damages trustworthiness or competence may include behavior that, although not illegal, nevertheless negatively affects a member's or candidate's ability to perform his or her responsibilities. For example, abusing alcohol during business hours might constitute a violation of this standard because it could have a detrimental effect on the member's or candidate's ability to fulfill his or her professional responsibilities. Personal bankruptcy may not reflect on the integrity or trustworthiness of the person declaring bankruptcy, but if the circumstances of the bankruptcy involve fraudulent or deceitful business conduct, the bankruptcy may be a violation of this standard.

In some cases, the absence of appropriate conduct or the lack of sufficient effort may be a violation of Standard I(D). The integrity of the investment profession is built on trust. A member or candidate—whether an investment banker, rating or research analyst, or portfolio manager—is expected to conduct the necessary due diligence to properly understand the nature and risks of an investment before making an investment recommendation. By not taking these steps and, instead, relying on someone else in the process to perform them, members or candidates may violate the trust their clients have placed in them. This loss of trust may have a significant impact on the reputation of the member or candidate and the operations of the financial market as a whole.

Individuals may attempt to abuse the CFA Institute Professional Conduct Program by actively seeking CFA Institute enforcement of the Code and Standards, and Standard I(D) in particular, as a method of settling personal, political, or other disputes unrelated to professional ethics. CFA Institute is aware of this issue, and appropriate disciplinary policies, procedures, and enforcement mechanisms are in place to address misuse of the Code and Standards and the Professional Conduct Program in this way.

Recommended Procedures for Compliance

In addition to ensuring that their own behavior is consistent with Standard I(D), to prevent general misconduct, members and candidates should encourage their firms to adopt the following policies and procedures to support the principles of Standard I(D):

- *Code of ethics*: Develop and/or adopt a code of ethics to which every employee must subscribe, and make clear that any personal behavior that reflects poorly on the individual involved, the institution as a whole, or the investment industry will not be tolerated.

- *List of violations*: Disseminate to all employees a list of potential violations and associated disciplinary sanctions, up to and including dismissal from the firm.
- *Employee references*: Check references of potential employees to ensure that they are of good character and not ineligible to work in the investment industry because of past infractions of the law.

Application of the Standard

Example 1 (Professionalism and Competence):

Simon Sasserman is a trust investment officer at a bank in a small affluent town. He enjoys lunching every day with friends at the country club, where his clients have observed him having numerous drinks. Back at work after lunch, he clearly is intoxicated while making investment decisions. His colleagues make a point of handling any business with Sasserman in the morning because they distrust his judgment after lunch.

> *Comment*: Sasserman's excessive drinking at lunch and subsequent intoxication at work constitute a violation of Standard I(D) because this conduct has raised questions about his professionalism and competence. His behavior reflects poorly on him, his employer, and the investment industry.

Example 2 (Fraud and Deceit):

Howard Hoffman, a security analyst at ATZ Brothers, Inc., a large brokerage house, submits reimbursement forms over a two-year period to ATZ's self-funded health insurance program for more than two dozen bills, most of which have been altered to increase the amount due. An investigation by the firm's director of employee benefits uncovers the inappropriate conduct. ATZ subsequently terminates Hoffman's employment and notifies CFA Institute.

> *Comment*: Hoffman violated Standard I(D) because he engaged in intentional conduct involving fraud and deceit in the workplace that adversely reflected on his integrity.

Example 3 (Fraud and Deceit):

Jody Brink, an analyst covering the automotive industry, volunteers much of her spare time to local charities. The board of one of the charitable institutions decides to buy five new vans to deliver hot lunches to low-income elderly people. Brink offers to donate her time to handle purchasing agreements. To pay a long-standing debt to a friend who operates an automobile dealership—and to compensate herself for her trouble—she agrees to a price 20% higher than normal and splits the surcharge with her friend. The director of the charity ultimately discovers the scheme and tells Brink that her services, donated or otherwise, are no longer required.

> *Comment*: Brink engaged in conduct involving dishonesty, fraud, and misrepresentation and has violated Standard I(D).

Example 4 (Personal Actions and Integrity):

Carmen Garcia manages a mutual fund dedicated to socially responsible investing. She is also an environmental activist. As the result of her participation in nonviolent protests, Garcia has been arrested on numerous occasions for trespassing on the property of a large petrochemical plant that is accused of damaging the environment.

Comment: Generally, Standard I(D) is not meant to cover legal transgressions resulting from acts of civil disobedience in support of personal beliefs because such conduct does not reflect poorly on the member's or candidate's professional reputation, integrity, or competence.

Example 5 (Professional Misconduct):

Meredith Rasmussen works on a buy-side trading desk of an investment management firm and concentrates on in-house trades for a hedge fund subsidiary managed by a team at the investment management firm. The hedge fund has been very successful and is marketed globally by the firm. From her experience as the trader for much of the activity of the fund, Rasmussen has become quite knowledgeable about the hedge fund's strategy, tactics, and performance. When a distinct break in the market occurs and many of the securities involved in the hedge fund's strategy decline markedly in value, Rasmussen observes that the reported performance of the hedge fund does not reflect this decline. In her experience, the lack of effect is a very unlikely occurrence. She approaches the head of trading about her concern and is told that she should not ask any questions and that the fund is big and successful and is not her concern. She is fairly sure something is not right, so she contacts the compliance officer, who also tells her to stay away from the issue of the hedge fund's reporting.

Comment: Rasmussen has clearly come across an error in policies, procedures, and compliance practices within the firm's operations. According to the firm's procedures for reporting potentially unethical activity, she should pursue the issue by gathering some proof of her reason for doubt. Should all internal communications within the firm not satisfy her concerns, Rasmussen should consider reporting the potential unethical activity to the appropriate regulator.

See also Standard IV(A) for guidance on whistleblowing and Standard IV(C) for the duties of a supervisor.

STANDARD II: INTEGRITY OF CAPITAL MARKETS

Standard II(A) Material Nonpublic Information

Members and Candidates who possess material nonpublic information that could affect the value of an investment must not act or cause others to act on the information.

Guidance

Highlights:

- *What Is "Material" Information?*
- *What Constitutes "Nonpublic" Information?*
- *Mosaic Theory*
- *Social Media*

- *Using Industry Experts*
- *Investment Research Reports*

Trading or inducing others to trade on material nonpublic information erodes confidence in capital markets, institutions, and investment professionals by supporting the idea that those with inside information and special access can take unfair advantage of the general investing public. Although trading on inside information may lead to short-term profits, in the long run, individuals and the profession as a whole suffer from such trading. These actions have caused and will continue to cause investors to avoid capital markets because the markets are perceived to be "rigged" in favor of the knowledgeable insider. When the investing public avoids capital markets, the markets and capital allocation become less efficient and less supportive of strong and vibrant economies. Standard II(A) promotes and maintains a high level of confidence in market integrity, which is one of the foundations of the investment profession.

The prohibition on using this information goes beyond the direct buying and selling of individual securities or bonds. Members and candidates must not use material nonpublic information to influence their investment actions related to derivatives (e.g., swaps or option contracts), mutual funds, or other alternative investments. *Any* trading based on material nonpublic information constitutes a violation of Standard II(A). The expansion of financial products and the increasing interconnectivity of financial markets globally have resulted in new potential opportunities for trading on material nonpublic information.

What Is "Material" Information?

Information is "material" if its disclosure would probably have an impact on the price of a security or if reasonable investors would want to know the information before making an investment decision. In other words, information is material if it would significantly alter the total mix of information currently available about a security in such a way that the price of the security would be affected.

The specificity of the information, the extent of its difference from public information, its nature, and its reliability are key factors in determining whether a particular piece of information fits the definition of material. For example, material information may include, but is not limited to, information on the following:

- earnings;
- mergers, acquisitions, tender offers, or joint ventures;
- changes in assets or asset quality;
- innovative products, processes, or discoveries (e.g., new product trials or research efforts);
- new licenses, patents, registered trademarks, or regulatory approval/rejection of a product;
- developments regarding customers or suppliers (e.g., the acquisition or loss of a contract);
- changes in management;
- change in auditor notification or the fact that the issuer may no longer rely on an auditor's report or qualified opinion;
- events regarding the issuer's securities (e.g., defaults on senior securities, calls of securities for redemption, repurchase plans, stock splits, changes in dividends, changes to the rights of security holders, and public or private sales of additional securities);
- bankruptcies;
- significant legal disputes;

- government reports of economic trends (employment, housing starts, currency information, etc.);
- orders for large trades before they are executed; and
- new or changing equity or debt ratings issued by a third party (e.g., sell-side recommendations and credit ratings).

In addition to the substance and specificity of the information, the source or relative reliability of the information also determines materiality. The less reliable a source, the less likely the information provided would be considered material. For example, factual information from a corporate insider regarding a significant new contract for a company is likely to be material, whereas an assumption based on speculation by a competitor about the same contract is likely to be less reliable and, therefore, not material. Additionally, information about trials of a new drug, product, or service under development from qualified personnel involved in the trials is likely to be material, whereas educated conjecture by subject experts not connected to the trials is unlikely to be material.

Also, the more ambiguous the effect of the information on price, the less material that information is considered. If it is unclear whether and to what extent the information will affect the price of a security, the information may not be considered material. The passage of time may also render information that was once important immaterial.

What Constitutes "Nonpublic" Information?

Information is "nonpublic" until it has been disseminated or is available to the marketplace in general (as opposed to a select group of investors). "Disseminated" can be defined as "made known." For example, a company report of profits that is posted on the internet and distributed widely through a press release or accompanied by a filing has been effectively disseminated to the marketplace. Members and candidates must have a reasonable expectation that people have received the information before it can be considered public. It is not necessary, however, to wait for the slowest method of delivery. Once the information is disseminated to the market, it is public information that is no longer covered by this standard.

Members and candidates must be particularly aware of information that is selectively disclosed by corporations to a small group of investors, analysts, or other market participants. Information that is made available to analysts remains nonpublic until it is made available to investors in general. Corporations that disclose information on a limited basis create the potential for insider-trading violations.

Issues of selective disclosure often arise when a corporate insider provides material information to analysts in a briefing or conference call before that information is released to the public. Analysts must be aware that a disclosure made to a room full of analysts does not necessarily make the disclosed information "public." Analysts should also be alert to the possibility that they are selectively receiving material nonpublic information when a company provides them with guidance or interpretation of such publicly available information as financial statements or regulatory filings.

A member or candidate may use insider information provided legitimately by the source company for the specific purpose of conducting due diligence according to the business agreement between the parties for such activities as mergers, loan underwriting, credit ratings, and offering engagements. In such instances, the investment professional would not be considered in violation of Standard II(A) by using the material information. However, the use of insider information provided by the source company for other purposes, especially to trade or entice others to trade the securities of the firm, conflicts with this standard.

Mosaic Theory

A financial analyst gathers and interprets large quantities of information from many sources. The analyst may use significant conclusions derived from the analysis of public and nonmaterial nonpublic information as the basis for investment recommendations and decisions even if those conclusions would have been material inside information had they been communicated directly to the analyst by a company. Under the "mosaic theory," financial analysts are free to act on this collection, or mosaic, of information without risking violation.

The practice of financial analysis depends on the free flow of information. For the fair and efficient operation of the capital markets, analysts and investors must have the greatest amount of information possible to facilitate making well-informed investment decisions about how and where to invest capital. Accurate, timely, and intelligible communication is essential if analysts and investors are to obtain the data needed to make informed decisions about how and where to invest capital. These disclosures must go beyond the information mandated by the reporting requirements of the securities laws and should include specific business information about items used to guide a company's future growth, such as new products, capital projects, and the competitive environment. Analysts seek and use such information to compare and contrast investment alternatives.

Much of the information used by analysts comes directly from companies. Analysts often receive such information through contacts with corporate insiders, especially investor-relations staff and financial officers. Information may be disseminated in the form of press releases, through oral presentations by company executives in analysts' meetings or conference calls, or during analysts' visits to company premises. In seeking to develop the most accurate and complete picture of a company, analysts should also reach beyond contacts with companies themselves and collect information from other sources, such as customers, contractors, suppliers, and the companies' competitors.

Analysts are in the business of formulating opinions and insights that are not obvious to the general investing public about the attractiveness of particular securities. In the course of their work, analysts actively seek out corporate information not generally known to the market for the express purpose of analyzing that information, forming an opinion on its significance, and informing their clients, who can be expected to trade on the basis of the recommendation. Analysts' initiatives to discover and analyze information and communicate their findings to their clients significantly enhance market efficiency, thus benefiting all investors (see *Dirks v. Securities and Exchange Commission*). Accordingly, violations of Standard II(A) will *not* result when a perceptive analyst reaches a conclusion about a corporate action or event through an analysis of public information and items of nonmaterial nonpublic information.

Investment professionals should note, however, that although analysts are free to use mosaic information in their research reports, they should save and document all their research [see Standard V(C)–Record Retention]. Evidence of the analyst's knowledge of public and nonmaterial nonpublic information about a corporation strengthens the assertion that the analyst reached his or her conclusions solely through appropriate methods rather than through the use of material nonpublic information.

Social Media

The continuing advancement in technology allows members, candidates, and the industry at large to exchange information at rates not previously available. It is important for investment professionals to understand the implications of using information from the internet and social media platforms because all such information may not actually be considered public.

Some social media platforms require membership in specific groups in order to access the published content. Members and candidates participating in groups with membership limitations should verify that material information obtained from these sources can also be accessed from a source that would be considered available to the public (e.g., company filings, webpages, and press releases).

Members and candidates may use social media platforms to communicate with clients or investors without conflicting with this standard. As long as the information reaches all clients or is open to the investing public, the use of these platforms would be comparable with other traditional forms of communications, such as e-mails and press releases. Members and candidates, as required by Standard I(A), should also complete all appropriate regulatory filings related to information distributed through social media platforms.

Using Industry Experts

The increased demand for insights for understanding the complexities of some industries has led to an expansion of engagement with outside experts. As the level of engagement increased, new businesses formed to connect analysts and investors with individuals who have specialized knowledge of their industry (e.g., technology or pharmaceuticals). These networks offer investors the opportunity to reach beyond their usual business circles to speak with experts regarding economic conditions, industry trends, and technical issues relating to specific products and services.

Members and candidates may provide compensation to individuals for their insights without violating this standard. However, members and candidates are ultimately responsible for ensuring that they are not requesting or acting on confidential information received from external experts, which is in violation of security regulations and laws or duties to others. As the recent string of insider-trading cases displayed, some experts are willing to provide confidential and protected information for the right incentive.

Firms connecting experts with members or candidates often require both parties to sign agreements concerning the disclosure of material nonpublic information. Even with the protections from such compliance practices, if an expert provides material nonpublic information, members and candidates would be prohibited from taking investment actions on the associated firm until the information became publicly known to the market.

Investment Research Reports

When a particularly well-known or respected analyst issues a report or makes changes to his or her recommendation, that information alone may have an effect on the market and thus may be considered material. Theoretically, under Standard II(A), such a report would have to be made public at the time it was distributed to clients. The analyst is not a company insider, however, and does not have access to inside information. Presumably, the analyst created the report from information available to the public (mosaic theory) and by using his or her expertise to interpret the information. The analyst's hard work, paid for by the client, generated the conclusions.

Simply because the public in general would find the conclusions material does not require that the analyst make his or her work public. Investors who are not clients of the analyst can either do the work themselves or become clients of the analyst to gain access to the analyst's expertise.

Recommended Procedures for Compliance

Achieve Public Dissemination

If a member or candidate determines that information is material, the member or candidate should make reasonable efforts to achieve public dissemination of the information. These efforts usually entail encouraging the issuing company to make the information public. If public dissemination is not possible, the member or candidate must communicate the information only to the designated supervisory and compliance personnel within the member's or candidate's firm and must not take investment action or alter current investment recommendations on the basis of the information. Moreover, members and candidates must not knowingly engage in any conduct that may induce company insiders to privately disclose material nonpublic information.

Adopt Compliance Procedures

Members and candidates should encourage their firms to adopt compliance procedures to prevent the misuse of material nonpublic information. Particularly important is improving compliance in such areas as the review of employee and proprietary trading, the review of investment recommendations, documentation of firm procedures, and the supervision of interdepartmental communications in multiservice firms. Compliance procedures should suit the particular characteristics of a firm, including its size and the nature of its business.

Members and candidates are encouraged to inform their supervisor and compliance personnel of suspected inappropriate use of material nonpublic information as the basis for security trading activities or recommendations being made within their firm.

Adopt Disclosure Procedures

Members and candidates should encourage their firms to develop and follow disclosure policies designed to ensure that information is disseminated to the marketplace in an equitable manner. For example, analysts from small firms should receive the same information and attention from a company as analysts from large firms receive. Similarly, companies should not provide certain information to buy-side analysts but not to sell-side analysts, or vice versa. Furthermore, a company should not discriminate among analysts in the provision of information or "blackball" particular analysts who have given negative reports on the company in the past.

Within investment and research firms, members and candidates should encourage the development of and compliance with procedures for distributing new and updated investment opinions to clients. Recommendations of this nature may represent material market-moving information that needs to be communicated to all clients fairly.

Issue Press Releases

Companies should consider issuing press releases prior to analyst meetings and conference calls and scripting those meetings and calls to decrease the chance that further information will be disclosed. If material nonpublic information is disclosed for the first time in an analyst meeting or call, the company should promptly issue a press release or otherwise make the information publicly available.

Firewall Elements

An information barrier commonly referred to as a "firewall" is the most widely used approach for preventing the communication of material nonpublic information within firms. It restricts the flow of confidential information to those who need to know the information to perform their jobs effectively. The minimum elements of such a system include, but are not limited to, the following:

- substantial control of relevant interdepartmental communications, preferably through a clearance area within the firm in either the compliance or legal department;
- review of employee trading through the maintenance of "watch," "restricted," and "rumor" lists;
- documentation of the procedures designed to limit the flow of information between departments and of the actions taken to enforce those procedures; and
- heightened review or restriction of proprietary trading while a firm is in possession of material nonpublic information.

Appropriate Interdepartmental Communications

Although documentation requirements must, for practical reasons, take into account the differences between the activities of small firms and those of large, multiservice firms, firms of all sizes and types benefit by improving the documentation of their internal enforcement of firewall procedures. Therefore, even at small firms, procedures concerning interdepartmental communication, the review of trading activity, and the investigation of possible violations should be compiled and formalized.

Physical Separation of Departments

As a practical matter, to the greatest extent possible, firms should consider the physical separation of departments and files to prevent the communication of sensitive information that should not be shared. For example, the investment banking and corporate finance areas of a brokerage firm should be separated from the sales and research departments, and a bank's commercial lending department should be segregated from its trust and research departments.

Prevention of Personnel Overlap

There should be no overlap of personnel between the investment banking and corporate finance areas of a brokerage firm and the sales and research departments or between a bank's commercial lending department and its trust and research departments. For a firewall to be effective in a multiservice firm, an employee should be on only one side of the firewall at any time. Inside knowledge may not be limited to information about a specific offering or the current financial condition of a company. Analysts may be exposed to much information about the company, including new product developments or future budget projections that clearly constitute inside knowledge and thus preclude the analyst from returning to his or her research function. For example, an analyst who follows a particular company may provide limited assistance to the investment bankers under carefully controlled circumstances when the firm's investment banking department is involved in a deal with the company. That analyst must then be treated as though he or she were an investment banker; the analyst must remain on the investment banking side of the wall until any information he or she learns is publicly disclosed. In short, the analyst cannot use any information learned in the course of the project for research purposes and cannot share that information with colleagues in the research department.

A Reporting System

A primary objective of an effective firewall procedure is to establish a reporting system in which authorized people review and approve communications between departments. If an employee behind a firewall believes that he or she needs to share confidential information with someone on the other side of the wall, the employee should consult a designated compliance officer to determine whether sharing the information is necessary and how much information should be shared. If the sharing is necessary, the compliance officer should coordinate the process of "looking over the wall" so that the necessary information will be shared and the integrity of the procedure will be maintained.

A single supervisor or compliance officer should have the specific authority and responsibility of deciding whether information is material and whether it is sufficiently public to be used as the basis for investment decisions. Ideally, the supervisor or compliance officer responsible for communicating information to a firm's research or brokerage area would not be a member of that area.

Personal Trading Limitations

Firms should consider restrictions or prohibitions on personal trading by employees and should carefully monitor both proprietary trading and personal trading by employees. Firms should require employees to make periodic reports (to the extent that such reporting is not already required by securities laws) of their own transactions and transactions made for the benefit of family members. Securities should be placed on a restricted list when a firm has or may have material nonpublic information. The broad distribution of a restricted list often triggers the sort of trading the list was developed to avoid. Therefore, a watch list shown to only the few people responsible for compliance should be used to monitor transactions in specified securities. The use of a watch list in combination with a restricted list is an increasingly common means of ensuring effective control of personal trading.

Record Maintenance

Multiservice firms should maintain written records of the communications between various departments. Firms should place a high priority on training and should consider instituting comprehensive training programs, particularly for employees in sensitive areas.

Proprietary Trading Procedures

Procedures concerning the restriction or review of a firm's proprietary trading while the firm possesses material nonpublic information will necessarily depend on the types of proprietary trading in which the firm may engage. A prohibition on all types of proprietary activity when a firm comes into possession of material nonpublic information is *not* appropriate. For example, when a firm acts as a market maker, a prohibition on proprietary trading may be counterproductive to the goals of maintaining the confidentiality of information and market liquidity. This concern is particularly important in the relationships between small, regional broker/dealers and small issuers. In many situations, a firm will take a small issuer public with the understanding that the firm will continue to be a market maker in the stock. In such instances, a withdrawal by the firm from market-making activities would be a clear tip to outsiders. Firms that continue market-making activity while in the possession of material nonpublic information should, however, instruct their market makers to remain passive with respect to the market—that is, to take only the contra side of unsolicited customer trades.

In risk-arbitrage trading, the case for a trading prohibition is more compelling than it is in the case of market making. The impetus for arbitrage trading is neither passive nor reactive, and the potential for illegal profits is greater than in market making. The most prudent course for firms is to suspend arbitrage activity when a security is placed on the watch list. Those firms that continue arbitrage activity face a high hurdle in proving the adequacy of their internal procedures for preventing trading on material nonpublic information and must demonstrate a stringent review and documentation of firm trades.

Communication to All Employees

Members and candidates should encourage their employers to circulate written compliance policies and guidelines to all employees. Policies and guidelines should be used in conjunction with training programs aimed at enabling employees to recognize material nonpublic information. Such information is not always clearly identifiable.

Employees must be given sufficient training to either make an informed decision or to realize they need to consult a supervisor or compliance officer before engaging in questionable transactions. Appropriate policies reinforce that using material nonpublic information is illegal in many countries. Such trading activities based on material nonpublic information undermine the integrity of the individual, the firm, and the capital markets.

Application of the Standard

Example 1 (Acting on Nonpublic Information):

Frank Barnes, the president and controlling shareholder of the SmartTown clothing chain, decides to accept a tender offer and sell the family business at a price almost double the market price of its shares. He describes this decision to his sister (SmartTown's treasurer), who conveys it to her daughter (who owns no stock in the family company at present), who tells her husband, Staple. Staple, however, tells his stockbroker, Alex Halsey, who immediately buys SmartTown stock for himself.

> *Comment*: The information regarding the pending sale is both material and nonpublic. Staple has violated Standard II(A) by communicating the inside information to his broker. Halsey also has violated the standard by buying the shares on the basis of material nonpublic information.

Example 2 (Controlling Nonpublic Information):

Samuel Peter, an analyst with Scotland and Pierce Incorporated, is assisting his firm with a secondary offering for Bright Ideas Lamp Company. Peter participates, via telephone conference call, in a meeting with Scotland and Pierce investment banking employees and Bright Ideas' CEO. Peter is advised that the company's earnings projections for the next year have significantly dropped. Throughout the telephone conference call, several Scotland and Pierce salespeople and portfolio managers walk in and out of Peter's office, where the telephone call is taking place. As a result, they are aware of the drop in projected earnings for Bright Ideas. Before the conference call is concluded, the salespeople trade the stock of the company on behalf of the firm's clients and other firm personnel trade the stock in a firm proprietary account and in employees' personal accounts.

> *Comment*: Peter has violated Standard II(A) because he failed to prevent the transfer and misuse of material nonpublic information to others in his firm. Peter's firm should have adopted information barriers to prevent the communication of nonpublic information between departments of the firm. The salespeople and portfolio managers who traded on the information have also violated Standard II(A) by trading on inside information.

Example 3 (Selective Disclosure of Material Information):

Elizabeth Levenson is based in Taipei and covers the Taiwanese market for her firm, which is based in Singapore. She is invited, together with the other 10 largest shareholders of a manufacturing company, to meet the finance director of that company. During the meeting, the finance director states that the company expects its workforce to strike next Friday, which will cripple productivity and distribution. Can Levenson use this information as a basis to change her rating on the company from “buy” to “sell”?

> *Comment*: Levenson must first determine whether the material information is public. According to Standard II(A), if the company has not made this information public (a small group forum does not qualify as a method of public dissemination), she cannot use the information.

Example 4 (Determining Materiality):

Leah Fechtman is trying to decide whether to hold or sell shares of an oil-and-gas exploration company that she owns in several of the funds she manages. Although the company has underperformed the index for some time already, the trends in the industry sector signal that companies of this type might become takeover targets. While she is considering her decision, her doctor, who casually follows the markets, mentions that she thinks that the company in question will soon be bought out by a large multinational conglomerate and that it would be a good idea to buy the stock right now. After talking to various investment professionals and checking their opinions on the company as well as checking industry trends, Fechtman decides the next day to accumulate more stock in the oil-and-gas exploration company.

> *Comment*: Although information on an expected takeover bid may be of the type that is generally material and nonpublic, in this case, the source of information is unreliable, so the information cannot be considered material. Therefore, Fechtman is not prohibited from trading the stock on the basis of this information.

Example 5 (Applying the Mosaic Theory):

Jagdish Teja is a buy-side analyst covering the furniture industry. Looking for an attractive company to recommend as a buy, he analyzes several furniture makers by studying their financial reports and visiting their operations. He also talks to some designers and retailers to find out which furniture styles are trendy and popular. Although none of the companies that he analyzes are a clear buy, he discovers that one of them, Swan Furniture Company (SFC), may be in financial trouble. SFC’s extravagant new designs have been introduced at substantial cost. Even though these designs initially attracted attention, the public is now buying more conservative furniture from other makers. Based on this information and on a profit-and-loss analysis, Teja believes that SFC’s next quarter earnings will drop substantially. He issues a sell recommendation for SFC. Immediately after receiving that recommendation, investment managers start reducing the SFC stock in their portfolios.

> *Comment*: Information on quarterly earnings data is material and nonpublic. Teja arrived at his conclusion about the earnings drop on the basis of public information and on pieces of nonmaterial nonpublic information (such as opinions of designers and retailers). Therefore, trading based on Teja’s correct conclusion is not prohibited by Standard II(A).

Example 6 (Applying the Mosaic Theory):

Roger Clement is a senior financial analyst who specializes in the European automobile sector at Rivoli Capital. Because he has been repeatedly nominated by many leading industry magazines and newsletters as a "best analyst" for the automobile industry, he is widely regarded as an authority on the sector. After speaking with representatives of Turgot Chariots—a European auto manufacturer with sales primarily in South Korea—and after conducting interviews with salespeople, labor leaders, his firm's Korean currency analysts, and banking officials, Clement analyzed Turgot Chariots and concluded that (1) its newly introduced model will probably not meet sales expectations, (2) its corporate restructuring strategy may well face serious opposition from unions, (3) the depreciation of the Korean won should lead to pressure on margins for the industry in general and Turgot's market segment in particular, and (4) banks could take a tougher-than-expected stance in the upcoming round of credit renegotiations with the company. For these reasons, he changes his conclusion about the company from "market outperform" to "market underperform." Clement retains the support material used to reach his conclusion in case questions later arise.

> *Comment*: To reach a conclusion about the value of the company, Clement has pieced together a number of nonmaterial or public bits of information that affect Turgot Chariots. Therefore, under the mosaic theory, Clement has not violated Standard II(A) in drafting the report.

Example 7 (Analyst Recommendations as Material Nonpublic Information):

The next day, Clement is preparing to be interviewed on a global financial news television program where he will discuss his changed recommendation on Turgot Chariots for the first time in public. While preparing for the program, he mentions to the show's producers and Mary Zito, the journalist who will be interviewing him, the information he will be discussing. Just prior to going on the air, Zito sells her holdings in Turgot Chariots. She also phones her father with the information because she knows that he and other family members have investments in Turgot Chariots.

> *Comment*: When Zito receives advance notice of Clement's change of opinion, she knows it will have a material impact on the stock price, even if she is not totally aware of Clement's underlying reasoning. She is not a client of Clement but obtains early access to the material nonpublic information prior to publication. Her trades are thus based on material nonpublic information and violate Standard II(A).
>
> Zito further violates the Standard by relaying the information to her father. It would not matter if he or any other family member traded; the act of providing the information violates Standard II(A). The fact that the information is provided to a family member does not absolve someone of the prohibition of using or communicating material nonpublic information.

Example 8 (Acting on Nonpublic Information):

Ashton Kellogg is a retired investment professional who manages his own portfolio. He owns shares in National Savings, a large local bank. A close friend and golfing buddy, John Mayfield, is a senior executive at National. National has seen its stock price drop considerably, and the news and outlook are not good. In a conversation about the economy and the banking industry on the golf course, Mayfield relays the information that National will surprise the investment community in a few days when it announces excellent earnings for the quarter. Kellogg is pleasantly surprised by this information, and thinking that Mayfield, as a senior executive, knows the law and would not disclose inside information, he doubles his position in the bank. Subsequently,

National announces that it had good operating earnings but had to set aside reserves for anticipated significant losses on its loan portfolio. The combined news causes the stock to go down 60%.

> *Comment*: Even though Kellogg believes that Mayfield would not break the law by disclosing inside information and money was lost on the purchase, Kellogg should not have purchased additional shares of National. It is the member's or candidate's responsibility to make sure, before executing investment actions, that comments about earnings are not material nonpublic information. Kellogg has violated Standard II(A).

Example 9 (Mosaic Theory):

John Doll is a research analyst for a hedge fund that also sells its research to a select group of paying client investment firms. Doll's focus is medical technology companies and products, and he has been in the business long enough and has been successful enough to build up a very credible network of friends and experts in the business. Doll has been working on a major research report recommending Boyce Health, a medical device manufacturer. He recently ran into an old acquaintance at a wedding who is a senior executive at Boyce, and Doll asked about the business. Doll was drawn to a statement that the executive, who has responsibilities in the new products area, made about a product: "I would not get too excited about the medium-term prospects; we have a lot of work to do first." Doll incorporated this and other information about the new Boyce product in his long-term recommendation of Boyce.

> *Comment*: Doll's conversation with the senior executive is part of the mosaic of information used in recommending Boyce. When holding discussions with a firm executive, Doll would need to guard against soliciting or obtaining material nonpublic information. Before issuing the report, the executive's statement about the continuing development of the product would need to be weighed against the other known public facts to determine whether it would be considered material.

Example 10 (Materiality Determination):

Larry Nadler, a trader for a mutual fund, gets a text message from another firm's trader, whom he has known for years. The message indicates a software company is going to report strong earnings when the firm publicly announces in two days. Nadler has a buy order from a portfolio manager within his firm to purchase several hundred thousand shares of the stock. Nadler is aggressive in placing the portfolio manager's order and completes the purchases by the following morning, a day ahead of the firm's planned earnings announcement.

> *Comment*: There are often rumors and whisper numbers before a release of any kind. The text message from the other trader would most likely be considered market noise. Unless Nadler knew that the trader had an ongoing business relationship with the public firm, he had no reason to suspect he was receiving material nonpublic information that would prevent him from completing the trading request of the portfolio manager.

Example 11 (Using an Expert Network):

Mary McCoy is the senior drug analyst at a mutual fund. Her firm hires a service that connects her to experts in the treatment of cancer. Through various phone conversations, McCoy enhances her understanding of the latest therapies for successful treatment. This information is critical to Mary making informed recommendations of the companies producing these drugs.

Comment: McCoy is appropriately using the expert networks to enhance her evaluation process. She has neither asked for nor received information that may be considered material and nonpublic, such as preliminary trial results. McCoy is allowed to seek advice from professionals within the industry that she follows.

Example 12 (Using an Expert Network):

Tom Watson is a research analyst working for a hedge fund. To stay informed, Watson relies on outside experts for information on such industries as technology and pharmaceuticals, where new advancements occur frequently. The meetings with the industry experts often are arranged through networks or placement agents that have specific policies and procedures in place to deter the exchange of material non-public information.

Watson arranges a call to discuss future prospects for one of the fund's existing technology company holdings, a company that was testing a new semiconductor product. The scientist leading the tests indicates his disappointment with the performance of the new semiconductor. Following the call, Watson relays the insights he received to others at the fund. The fund sells its current position in the company and buys many put options because the market is anticipating the success of the new semiconductor and the share price reflects the market's optimism.

Comment: Watson has violated Standard II(A) by passing along material nonpublic information concerning the ongoing product tests, which the fund used to trade in the securities and options of the related company. Watson cannot simply rely on the agreements signed by individuals who participate in expert networks that state that he has not received information that would prohibit his trading activity. He must make his own determination whether information he received through these arrangements reaches a materiality threshold that would affect his trading abilities.

Standard II(B) Market Manipulation

Members and Candidates must not engage in practices that distort prices or artificially inflate trading volume with the intent to mislead market participants.

Guidance

Highlights:

- *Information-Based Manipulation*
- *Transaction-Based Manipulation*

Standard II(B) requires that members and candidates uphold market integrity by prohibiting market manipulation. Market manipulation includes practices that distort security prices or trading volume with the intent to deceive people or entities that rely on information in the market. Market manipulation damages the interests of all investors by disrupting the smooth functioning of financial markets and lowering investor confidence.

Market manipulation may lead to a lack of trust in the fairness of the capital markets, resulting in higher risk premiums and reduced investor participation. A reduction in the efficiency of a local capital market may negatively affect the growth and economic health of the country and may also influence the operations of the globally interconnected capital markets. Although market manipulation may be less likely to occur in mature financial markets than in emerging markets, cross-border investing increasingly exposes all global investors to the potential for such practices.

Market manipulation includes (1) the dissemination of false or misleading information and (2) transactions that deceive or would be likely to mislead market participants by distorting the price-setting mechanism of financial instruments. The development of new products and technologies increases the incentives, means, and opportunities for market manipulation. Additionally, the increasing complexity and sophistication of the technologies used for communicating with market participants have created new avenues for manipulation.

Information-Based Manipulation

Information-based manipulation includes, but is not limited to, spreading false rumors to induce trading by others. For example, members and candidates must refrain from "pumping up" the price of an investment by issuing misleading positive information or overly optimistic projections of a security's worth only to later "dump" the investment (i.e., sell it) once the price, fueled by the misleading information's effect on other market participants, reaches an artificially high level.

Transaction-Based Manipulation

Transaction-based manipulation involves instances where a member or candidate knew or should have known that his or her actions could affect the pricing of a security. This type of manipulation includes, but is not limited to, the following:

- transactions that artificially affect prices or volume to give the impression of activity or price movement in a financial instrument, which represent a diversion from the expectations of a fair and efficient market, and
- securing a controlling, dominant position in a financial instrument to exploit and manipulate the price of a related derivative and/or the underlying asset.

Standard II(B) is not intended to preclude transactions undertaken on legitimate trading strategies based on perceived market inefficiencies. The intent of the action is critical to determining whether it is a violation of this standard.

Application of the Standard

Example 1 (Independent Analysis and Company Promotion):

The principal owner of Financial Information Services (FIS) entered into an agreement with two microcap companies to promote the companies' stock in exchange for stock and cash compensation. The principal owner caused FIS to disseminate e-mails, design and maintain several websites, and distribute an online investment newsletter—all of which recommended investment in the two companies. The systematic publication of purportedly independent analyses and recommendations containing inaccurate and highly promotional and speculative statements increased public investment in the companies and led to dramatically higher stock prices.

> *Comment*: The principal owner of FIS violated Standard II(B) by using inaccurate reporting and misleading information under the guise of independent analysis to artificially increase the stock price of the companies. Furthermore, the principal owner violated Standard V(A)–Diligence and Reasonable Basis by not having a reasonable and adequate basis for recommending the two

companies and violated Standard VI(A)–Disclosure of Conflicts by not disclosing to investors the compensation agreements (which constituted a conflict of interest).

Example 2 (Personal Trading Practices and Price):

John Gray is a private investor in Belgium who bought a large position several years ago in Fame Pharmaceuticals, a German small-cap security with limited average trading volume. He has now decided to significantly reduce his holdings owing to the poor price performance. Gray is worried that the low trading volume for the stock may cause the price to decline further as he attempts to sell his large position.

Gray devises a plan to divide his holdings into multiple accounts in different brokerage firms and private banks in the names of family members, friends, and even a private religious institution. He then creates a rumor campaign on various blogs and social media outlets promoting the company.

Gray begins to buy and sell the stock using the accounts in hopes of raising the trading volume and the price. He conducts the trades through multiple brokers, selling slightly larger positions than he bought on a tactical schedule, and over time, he is able to reduce his holding as desired without negatively affecting the sale price.

Comment: John violated Standard II(B) by fraudulently creating the appearance that there was a greater investor interest in the stock through the online rumors. Additionally, through his trading strategy, he created the appearance that there was greater liquidity in the stock than actually existed. He was able to manipulate the price through both misinformation and trading practices.

Example 3 (Creating Artificial Price Volatility):

Matthew Murphy is an analyst at Divisadero Securities & Co., which has a significant number of hedge funds among its most important brokerage clients. Some of the hedge funds hold short positions on Wirewolf Semiconductor. Two trading days before the publication of a quarter-end report, Murphy alerts his sales force that he is about to issue a research report on Wirewolf that will include the following opinions:

- quarterly revenues are likely to fall short of management's guidance,
- earnings will be as much as 5 cents per share (or more than 10%) below consensus, and
- Wirewolf's highly respected chief financial officer may be about to join another company.

Knowing that Wirewolf has already entered its declared quarter-end "quiet period" before reporting earnings (and thus would be reluctant to respond to rumors), Murphy times the release of his research report specifically to sensationalize the negative aspects of the message in order to create significant downward pressure on Wirewolf's stock—to the distinct advantage of Divisadero's hedge fund clients. The report's conclusions are based on speculation, not on fact. The next day, the research report is broadcast to all of Divisadero's clients and to the usual newswire services.

Before Wirewolf's investor-relations department can assess the damage on the final trading day of the quarter and refute Murphy's report, its stock opens trading sharply lower, allowing Divisadero's clients to cover their short positions at substantial gains.

Comment: Murphy violated Standard II(B) by aiming to create artificial price volatility designed to have a material impact on the price of an issuer's stock. Moreover, by lacking an adequate basis for the recommendation, Murphy also violated Standard V(A)–Diligence and Reasonable Basis.

Example 4 (Personal Trading and Volume):

Rajesh Sekar manages two funds—an equity fund and a balanced fund—whose equity components are supposed to be managed in accordance with the same model. According to that model, the funds' holdings in stock of Digital Design Inc. (DD) are excessive. Reduction of the DD holdings would not be easy, however, because the stock has low liquidity in the stock market. Sekar decides to start trading larger portions of DD stock back and forth between his two funds to slowly increase the price; he believes market participants will see growing volume and increasing price and become interested in the stock. If other investors are willing to buy the DD stock because of such interest, then Sekar will be able to get rid of at least some of his overweight position without inducing price decreases. In this way, the whole transaction will be for the benefit of fund participants, even if additional brokers' commissions are incurred.

> *Comment*: Sekar's plan would be beneficial for his funds' participants but is based on artificial distortion of both trading volume and the price of the DD stock and thus constitutes a violation of Standard II(B).

Example 5 ("Pump-Priming" Strategy):

ACME Futures Exchange is launching a new bond futures contract. To convince investors, traders, arbitrageurs, hedgers, and so on, to use its contract, the exchange attempts to demonstrate that it has the best liquidity. To do so, it enters into agreements with members in which they commit to a substantial minimum trading volume on the new contract over a specific period in exchange for substantial reductions of their regular commissions.

> *Comment*: The formal liquidity of a market is determined by the obligations set on market makers, but the actual liquidity of a market is better estimated by the actual trading volume and bid–ask spreads. Attempts to mislead participants about the actual liquidity of the market constitute a violation of Standard II(B). In this example, investors have been intentionally misled to believe they chose the most liquid instrument for some specific purpose, but they could eventually see the actual liquidity of the contract significantly reduced after the term of the agreement expires. If the ACME Futures Exchange fully discloses its agreement with members to boost transactions over some initial launch period, it will not violate Standard II(B). ACME's intent is not to harm investors but, on the contrary, to give them a better service. For that purpose, it may engage in a liquidity-pumping strategy, but the strategy must be disclosed.

Example 6 (Creating Artificial Price Volatility):

Emily Gordon, an analyst of household products companies, is employed by a research boutique, Picador & Co. Based on information that she has gathered during a trip through Latin America, she believes that Hygene, Inc., a major marketer of personal care products, has generated better-than-expected sales from its new product initiatives in South America. After modestly boosting her projections for revenue and for gross profit margin in her worksheet models for Hygene, Gordon estimates that her earnings projection of US$2.00 per diluted share for the current year may be as much as 5% too low. She contacts the chief financial officer (CFO) of Hygene to try to gain confirmation of her findings from her trip and to get some feedback regarding her revised models. The CFO declines to comment and reiterates management's most recent guidance of US$1.95–US$2.05 for the year.

Gordon decides to try to force a comment from the company by telling Picador & Co. clients who follow a momentum investment style that consensus earnings projections for Hygene are much too low; she explains that she is considering raising her published estimate by an ambitious US$0.15 to US$2.15 per share. She believes that when word of an unrealistically high earnings projection filters back to Hygene's investor-relations department, the company will feel compelled to update its earnings guidance. Meanwhile, Gordon hopes that she is at least correct with respect to the earnings direction and that she will help clients who act on her insights to profit from a quick gain by trading on her advice.

> *Comment*: By exaggerating her earnings projections in order to try to fuel a quick gain in Hygene's stock price, Gordon is in violation of Standard II(B). Furthermore, by virtue of previewing her intentions of revising upward her earnings projections to only a select group of clients, she is in violation of Standard III(B)–Fair Dealing. However, it would have been acceptable for Gordon to write a report that
>
> - framed her earnings projection in a range of possible outcomes,
> - outlined clearly the assumptions used in her Hygene models that took into consideration the findings from her trip through Latin America, and
> - was distributed to all Picador & Co. clients in an equitable manner.

Example 7 (Pump and Dump Strategy):

In an effort to pump up the price of his holdings in Moosehead & Belfast Railroad Company, Steve Weinberg logs on to several investor chat rooms on the internet to start rumors that the company is about to expand its rail network in anticipation of receiving a large contract for shipping lumber.

> *Comment*: Weinberg has violated Standard II(B) by disseminating false information about Moosehead & Belfast with the intent to mislead market participants.

Example 8 (Manipulating Model Inputs):

Bill Mandeville supervises a structured financing team for Superior Investment Bank. His responsibilities include packaging new structured investment products and managing Superior's relationship with relevant rating agencies. To achieve the best rating possible, Mandeville uses mostly positive scenarios as model inputs—scenarios that reflect minimal downside risk in the assets underlying the structured products. The resulting output statistics in the rating request and underwriting prospectus support the idea that the new structured products have minimal potential downside risk. Additionally, Mandeville's compensation from Superior is partially based on both the level of the rating assigned and the successful sale of new structured investment products but does not have a link to the long-term performance of the instruments.

Mandeville is extremely successful and leads Superior as the top originator of structured investment products for the next two years. In the third year, the economy experiences difficulties and the values of the assets underlying structured products significantly decline. The subsequent defaults lead to major turmoil in the capital markets, the demise of Superior Investment Bank, and the loss of Mandeville's employment.

> *Comment*: Mandeville manipulates the inputs of a model to minimize associated risk to achieve higher ratings. His understanding of structured products allows him to skillfully decide which inputs to include in support of the desired rating and price. This information manipulation for short-term gain, which is in violation of Standard II(B), ultimately causes significant damage to many parties and the capital markets as a whole. Mandeville should have realized that promoting a rating and price with inaccurate

information could cause not only a loss of price confidence in the particular structured product but also a loss of investor trust in the system. Such loss of confidence affects the ability of the capital markets to operate efficiently.

Example 9 (Information Manipulation):

Allen King is a performance analyst for Torrey Investment Funds. King believes that the portfolio manager for the firm's small- and microcap equity fund dislikes him because the manager never offers him tickets to the local baseball team's games but does offer tickets to other employees. To incite a potential regulatory review of the manager, King creates user profiles on several online forums under the portfolio manager's name and starts rumors about potential mergers for several of the smaller companies in the portfolio. As the prices of these companies' stocks increase, the portfolio manager sells the position, which leads to an investigation by the regulator as King desired.

Comment: King has violated Standard II(B) even though he did not personally profit from the market's reaction to the rumor. In posting the false information, King misleads others into believing the companies were likely to be acquired. Although his intent was to create trouble for the portfolio manager, his actions clearly manipulated the factual information that was available to the market.

STANDARD III: DUTIES TO CLIENTS

Standard III(A) Loyalty, Prudence, and Care

Members and Candidates have a duty of loyalty to their clients and must act with reasonable care and exercise prudent judgment. Members and Candidates must act for the benefit of their clients and place their clients' interests before their employer's or their own interests.

Guidance

Highlights:

- *Understanding the Application of Loyalty, Prudence, and Care*
- *Identifying the Actual Investment Client*
- *Developing the Client's Portfolio*
- *Soft Commission Policies*
- *Proxy Voting Policies*

Standard III(A) clarifies that client interests are paramount. A member's or candidate's responsibility to a client includes a duty of loyalty and a duty to exercise reasonable care. Investment actions must be carried out for the sole benefit of the client and in a manner the member or candidate believes, given the known facts and circumstances, to be in the best interest of the client. Members and candidates must exercise the same level of prudence, judgment, and care that they would apply in the management and disposition of their own interests in similar circumstances.

Prudence requires caution and discretion. The exercise of prudence by investment professionals requires that they act with the care, skill, and diligence that a reasonable person acting in a like capacity and familiar with such matters would use. In the context of managing a client's portfolio, prudence requires following the investment parameters set forth by the client and balancing risk and return. Acting with care requires members and candidates to act in a prudent and judicious manner in avoiding harm to clients.

Standard III(A) sets minimum expectations for members and candidates when fulfilling their responsibilities to their clients. Regulatory and legal requirements for such duties can vary across the investment industry depending on a variety of factors, including job function of the investment professional, the existence of an adviser/client relationship, and the nature of the recommendations being offered. From the perspective of the end user of financial services, these different standards can be arcane and confusing, leaving investors unsure of what level of service to expect from investment professionals they employ. The single standard of conduct described in Standard III(A) benefits investors by establishing a benchmark for the duties of loyalty, prudence, and care and clarifies that all CFA Institute members and candidates, regardless of job title, local laws, or cultural differences, are required to comply with these fundamental responsibilities. Investors hiring members or candidates who must adhere to the duty of loyalty, prudence, and care set forth in this standard can be confident that these responsibilities are a requirement regardless of any legally imposed fiduciary duties.

Standard III(A), however, is not a substitute for a member's or candidate's legal or regulatory obligations. As stated in Standard I(A), members and candidates must abide by the most strict requirements imposed on them by regulators or the Code and Standards, including any legally imposed fiduciary duty. Members and candidates must also be aware of whether they have "custody" or effective control of client assets. If so, a heightened level of responsibility arises. Members and candidates are considered to have custody if they have any direct or indirect access to client funds. Members and candidates must manage any pool of assets in their control in accordance with the terms of the governing documents (such as trust documents and investment management agreements), which are the primary determinant of the manager's powers and duties. Whenever their actions are contrary to provisions of those instruments or applicable law, members and candidates are at risk of violating Standard III(A).

Understanding the Application of Loyalty, Prudence, and Care

Standard III(A) establishes a minimum benchmark for the duties of loyalty, prudence, and care that are required of all members and candidates regardless of whether a legal fiduciary duty applies. Although fiduciary duty often encompasses the principles of loyalty, prudence, and care, Standard III(A) does not render all members and candidates fiduciaries. The responsibilities of members and candidates for fulfilling their obligations under this standard depend greatly on the nature of their professional responsibilities and the relationships they have with clients. The conduct of members and candidates may or may not rise to the level of being a fiduciary, depending on the type of client, whether the member or candidate is giving investment advice, and the many facts and circumstances surrounding a particular transaction or client relationship.

Fiduciary duties are often imposed by law or regulation when an individual or institution is charged with the duty of acting for the benefit of another party, such as managing investment assets. The duty required in fiduciary relationships exceeds what is acceptable in many other business relationships because a fiduciary is in an enhanced position of trust. Although members and candidates must comply with any legally imposed fiduciary duty, the Code and Standards neither impose such a legal responsibility nor require all members or candidates to act as fiduciaries. However, Standard III(A) requires members and candidates to work in the client's best interest no matter what the job function.

A member or candidate who does not provide advisory services to a client but who acts only as a trade execution professional must prudently work in the client's interest when completing requested trades. Acting in the client's best interest requires these professionals to use their skills and diligence to execute trades in the most favorable terms that can be achieved. Members and candidates operating in such positions must use care to operate within the parameters set by the client's trading instructions.

Members and candidates may also operate in a blended environment where they execute client trades and offer advice on a limited set of investment options. The extent of the advisory arrangement and limitations should be outlined in the agreement with the client at the outset of the relationship. For instance, members and candidates should inform clients that the advice provided will be limited to the propriety products of the firm and not include other products available on the market. Clients who want access to a wider range of investment products would have the information necessary to decide not to engage with members or candidates working under these restrictions.

Members and candidates operating in this blended context would comply with their obligations by recommending the allowable products that are consistent with the client's objectives and risk tolerance. They would exercise care through diligently aligning the client's needs with the attributes of the products being recommended. Members and candidates should place the client's interests first by disregarding any firm or personal interest in motivating a recommended transaction.

There is a large variety of professional relationships that members and candidates have with their clients. Standard III(A) requires them to fulfill the obligations outlined explicitly or implicitly in the client agreements to the best of their abilities and with loyalty, prudence, and care. Whether a member or candidate is structuring a new securitization transaction, completing a credit rating analysis, or leading a public company, he or she must work with prudence and care in delivering the agreed-on services.

Identifying the Actual Investment Client

The first step for members and candidates in fulfilling their duty of loyalty to clients is to determine the identity of the "client" to whom the duty of loyalty is owed. In the context of an investment manager managing the personal assets of an individual, the client is easily identified. When the manager is responsible for the portfolios of pension plans or trusts, however, the client is not the person or entity who hires the manager but, rather, the beneficiaries of the plan or trust. The duty of loyalty is owed to the ultimate beneficiaries.

In some situations, an actual client or group of beneficiaries may not exist. Members and candidates managing a fund to an index or an expected mandate owe the duty of loyalty, prudence, and care to invest in a manner consistent with the stated mandate. The decisions of a fund's manager, although benefiting all fund investors, do not have to be based on an individual investor's requirements and risk profile. Client loyalty and care for those investing in the fund are the responsibility of members and candidates who have an advisory relationship with those individuals.

Situations involving potential conflicts of interest with respect to responsibilities to clients may be extremely complex because they may involve a number of competing interests. The duty of loyalty, prudence, and care applies to a large number of persons in varying capacities, but the exact duties may differ in many respects in accord with the relationship with each client or each type of account in which the assets are managed. Members and candidates must not only put their obligations to clients first in all dealings but also endeavor to avoid all real or potential conflicts of interest.

Members and candidates with positions whose responsibilities do not include direct investment management also have "clients" that must be considered. Just as there are various types of advisory relationships, members and candidates must look at their roles and responsibilities when making a determination of who their clients are. Sometimes the client is easily identifiable; such is the case in the relationship between a company executive and the firm's public shareholders. At other times, the client may be the investing public as a whole, in which case the goals of independence and objectivity of research surpass the goal of loyalty to a single organization.

Developing the Client's Portfolio

The duty of loyalty, prudence, and care owed to the individual client is especially important because the professional investment manager typically possesses greater knowledge in the investment arena than the client does. This disparity places the individual client in a vulnerable position; the client must trust the manager. The manager in these situations should ensure that the client's objectives and expectations for the performance of the account are realistic and suitable to the client's circumstances and that the risks involved are appropriate. In most circumstances, recommended investment strategies should relate to the long-term objectives and circumstances of the client.

Particular care must be taken to detect whether the goals of the investment manager or the firm in conducting business, selling products, and executing security transactions potentially conflict with the best interests and objectives of the client. When members and candidates cannot avoid potential conflicts between their firm and clients' interests, they must provide clear and factual disclosures of the circumstances to the clients.

Members and candidates must follow any guidelines set by their clients for the management of their assets. Some clients, such as charitable organizations and pension plans, have strict investment policies that limit investment options to certain types or classes of investment or prohibit investment in certain securities. Other organizations have aggressive policies that do not prohibit investments by type but, instead, set criteria on the basis of the portfolio's total risk and return.

Investment decisions must be judged in the context of the total portfolio rather than by individual investment within the portfolio. The member's or candidate's duty is satisfied with respect to a particular investment if the individual has thoroughly considered the investment's place in the overall portfolio, the risk of loss and opportunity for gains, tax implications, and the diversification, liquidity, cash flow, and overall return requirements of the assets or the portion of the assets for which the manager is responsible.

Soft Commission Policies

An investment manager often has discretion over the selection of brokers executing transactions. Conflicts may arise when an investment manager uses client brokerage to purchase research services, a practice commonly called "soft dollars" or "soft commissions." A member or candidate who pays a higher brokerage commission than he or she would normally pay to allow for the purchase of goods or services, without corresponding benefit to the client, violates the duty of loyalty to the client.

From time to time, a client will direct a manager to use the client's brokerage to purchase goods or services for the client, a practice that is commonly called "directed brokerage." Because brokerage commission is an asset of the client and is used to benefit that client, not the manager, such a practice does not violate any duty of loyalty. However, a member or candidate is obligated to seek "best price" and "best execution" and be assured by the client that the goods or services purchased from the brokerage will benefit the account beneficiaries. "Best execution" refers to a trading process that seeks to maximize the value of the client's portfolio within the client's stated investment objectives and constraints. In addition, the member or candidate should disclose to the client that the client may not be getting best execution from the directed brokerage.

Proxy Voting Policies

The duty of loyalty, prudence, and care may apply in a number of situations facing the investment professional besides those related directly to investing assets.

Part of a member's or candidate's duty of loyalty includes voting proxies in an informed and responsible manner. Proxies have economic value to a client, and members and candidates must ensure that they properly safeguard and maximize this value. An investment manager who fails to vote, casts a vote without considering the impact of the question, or votes blindly with management on nonroutine governance issues (e.g., a change in company capitalization) may violate this standard. Voting of proxies is an integral part of the management of investments.

A cost–benefit analysis may show that voting all proxies may not benefit the client, so voting proxies may not be necessary in all instances. Members and candidates should disclose to clients their proxy voting policies.

Recommended Procedures for Compliance

Regular Account Information

Members and candidates with control of client assets (1) should submit to each client, at least quarterly, an itemized statement showing the funds and securities in the custody or possession of the member or candidate plus all debits, credits, and transactions that occurred during the period, (2) should disclose to the client where the assets are to be maintained, as well as where or when they are moved, and (3) should separate the client's assets from any other party's assets, including the member's or candidate's own assets.

Client Approval

If a member or candidate is uncertain about the appropriate course of action with respect to a client, the member or candidate should consider what he or she would expect or demand if the member or candidate were the client. If in doubt, a member or candidate should disclose the questionable matter in writing to the client and obtain client approval.

Firm Policies

Members and candidates should address and encourage their firms to address the following topics when drafting the statements or manuals containing their policies and procedures regarding responsibilities to clients:

- *Follow all applicable rules and laws*: Members and candidates must follow all legal requirements and applicable provisions of the Code and Standards.
- *Establish the investment objectives of the client*: Make a reasonable inquiry into a client's investment experience, risk and return objectives, and financial constraints prior to making investment recommendations or taking investment actions.
- *Consider all the information when taking actions*: When taking investment actions, members and candidates must consider the appropriateness and suitability of the investment relative to (1) the client's needs and circumstances, (2) the investment's basic characteristics, and (3) the basic characteristics of the total portfolio.

- *Diversify*: Members and candidates should diversify investments to reduce the risk of loss, unless diversification is not consistent with plan guidelines or is contrary to the account objectives.
- *Carry out regular reviews*: Members and candidates should establish regular review schedules to ensure that the investments held in the account adhere to the terms of the governing documents.
- *Deal fairly with all clients with respect to investment actions*: Members and candidates must not favor some clients over others and should establish policies for allocating trades and disseminating investment recommendations.
- *Disclose conflicts of interest*: Members and candidates must disclose all actual and potential conflicts of interest so that clients can evaluate those conflicts.
- *Disclose compensation arrangements*: Members and candidates should make their clients aware of all forms of manager compensation.
- *Vote proxies*: In most cases, members and candidates should determine who is authorized to vote shares and vote proxies in the best interests of the clients and ultimate beneficiaries.
- *Maintain confidentiality*: Members and candidates must preserve the confidentiality of client information.
- *Seek best execution*: Unless directed by the client as ultimate beneficiary, members and candidates must seek best execution for their clients. (Best execution is defined in the preceding text.)
- *Place client interests first*: Members and candidates must serve the best interests of clients.

Application of the Standard

Example 1 (Identifying the Client—Plan Participants):

First Country Bank serves as trustee for the Miller Company's pension plan. Miller is the target of a hostile takeover attempt by Newton, Inc. In attempting to ward off Newton, Miller's managers persuade Julian Wiley, an investment manager at First Country Bank, to purchase Miller common stock in the open market for the employee pension plan. Miller's officials indicate that such action would be favorably received and would probably result in other accounts being placed with the bank. Although Wiley believes the stock is overvalued and would not ordinarily buy it, he purchases the stock to support Miller's managers, to maintain Miller's good favor toward the bank, and to realize additional new business. The heavy stock purchases cause Miller's market price to rise to such a level that Newton retracts its takeover bid.

> *Comment*: Standard III(A) requires that a member or candidate, in evaluating a takeover bid, act prudently and solely in the interests of plan participants and beneficiaries. To meet this requirement, a member or candidate must carefully evaluate the long-term prospects of the company against the short-term prospects presented by the takeover offer and by the ability to invest elsewhere. In this instance, Wiley, acting on behalf of his employer, which was the trustee for a pension plan, clearly violated Standard III(A). He used the pension plan to perpetuate existing management, perhaps to the detriment of plan participants and the company's shareholders, and to benefit himself. Wiley's responsibilities to the plan participants and beneficiaries should have taken precedence over any ties of his bank to corporate managers and over his self-interest. Wiley had a duty to examine the takeover offer on its own merits and to make an independent decision.

The guiding principle is the appropriateness of the investment decision to the pension plan, not whether the decision benefited Wiley or the company that hired him.

Example 2 (Client Commission Practices):

JNI, a successful investment counseling firm, serves as investment manager for the pension plans of several large regionally based companies. Its trading activities generate a significant amount of commission-related business. JNI uses the brokerage and research services of many firms, but most of its trading activity is handled through a large brokerage company, Thompson, Inc., because the executives of the two firms have a close friendship. Thompson's commission structure is high in comparison with charges for similar brokerage services from other firms. JNI considers Thompson's research services and execution capabilities average. In exchange for JNI directing its brokerage to Thompson, Thompson absorbs a number of JNI overhead expenses, including those for rent.

Comment: JNI executives are breaching their responsibilities by using client brokerage for services that do not benefit JNI clients and by not obtaining best price and best execution for their clients. Because JNI executives are not upholding their duty of loyalty, they are violating Standard III(A).

Example 3 (Brokerage Arrangements):

Charlotte Everett, a struggling independent investment adviser, serves as investment manager for the pension plans of several companies. One of her brokers, Scott Company, is close to consummating management agreements with prospective new clients whereby Everett would manage the new client accounts and trade the accounts exclusively through Scott. One of Everett's existing clients, Crayton Corporation, has directed Everett to place securities transactions for Crayton's account exclusively through Scott. But to induce Scott to exert efforts to send more new accounts to her, Everett also directs transactions to Scott from other clients without their knowledge.

Comment: Everett has an obligation at all times to seek best price and best execution on all trades. Everett may direct new client trades exclusively through Scott Company as long as Everett receives best price and execution on the trades or receives a written statement from new clients that she is *not* to seek best price and execution and that they are aware of the consequence for their accounts. Everett may trade other accounts through Scott as a reward for directing clients to Everett only if the accounts receive best price and execution and the practice is disclosed to the accounts. Because Everett does not disclose the directed trading, Everett has violated Standard III(A).

Example 4 (Brokerage Arrangements):

Emilie Rome is a trust officer for Paget Trust Company. Rome's supervisor is responsible for reviewing Rome's trust account transactions and her monthly reports of personal stock transactions. Rome has been using Nathan Gray, a broker, almost exclusively for trust account brokerage transactions. When Gray makes a market in stocks, he has been giving Rome a lower price for personal purchases and a higher price for sales than he gives to Rome's trust accounts and other investors.

Comment: Rome is violating her duty of loyalty to the bank's trust accounts by using Gray for brokerage transactions simply because Gray trades Rome's personal account on favorable terms. Rome is placing her own interests before those of her clients.

Example 5 (Client Commission Practices):

Lauren Parker, an analyst with Provo Advisors, covers South American equities for her firm. She likes to travel to the markets for which she is responsible and decides to go on a trip to Chile, Argentina, and Brazil. The trip is sponsored by SouthAM, Inc., a research firm with a small broker/dealer affiliate that uses the clearing facilities of a larger New York brokerage house. SouthAM specializes in arranging South American trips for analysts during which they can meet with central bank officials, government ministers, local economists, and senior executives of corporations. SouthAM accepts commission dollars at a ratio of 2 to 1 against the hard-dollar costs of the research fee for the trip. Parker is not sure that SouthAM's execution is competitive, but without informing her supervisor, she directs the trading desk at Provo to start giving commission business to SouthAM so she can take the trip. SouthAM has conveniently timed the briefing trip to coincide with the beginning of Carnival season, so Parker also decides to spend five days of vacation in Rio de Janeiro at the end of the trip. Parker uses commission dollars to pay for the five days of hotel expenses.

> *Comment*: Parker is violating Standard III(A) by not exercising her duty of loyalty to her clients. She should have determined whether the commissions charged by SouthAM are reasonable in relation to the benefit of the research provided by the trip. She also should have determined whether best execution and prices could be received from SouthAM. In addition, the five extra days are not part of the research effort because they do not assist in the investment decision making. Thus, the hotel expenses for the five days should not be paid for with client assets.

Example 6 (Excessive Trading):

Vida Knauss manages the portfolios of a number of high-net-worth individuals. A major part of her investment management fee is based on trading commissions. Knauss engages in extensive trading for each of her clients to ensure that she attains the minimum commission level set by her firm. Although the securities purchased and sold for the clients are appropriate and fall within the acceptable asset classes for the clients, the amount of trading for each account exceeds what is necessary to accomplish the client's investment objectives.

> *Comment*: Knauss has violated Standard III(A) because she is using the assets of her clients to benefit her firm and herself.

Example 7 (Managing Family Accounts):

Adam Dill recently joined New Investments Asset Managers. To assist Dill in building a book of clients, both his father and brother opened new fee-paying accounts. Dill followed all the firm's procedures in noting his relationships with these clients and in developing their investment policy statements.

After several years, the number of Dill's clients has grown, but he still manages the original accounts of his family members. An IPO is coming to market that is a suitable investment for many of his clients, including his brother. Dill does not receive the amount of stock he requested, so to avoid any appearance of a conflict of interest, he does not allocate any shares to his brother's account.

> *Comment*: Dill has violated Standard III(A) because he is not acting for the benefit of his brother's account as well as his other accounts. The brother's account is a regular fee-paying account comparable to the accounts of his other clients. By not allocating the shares proportionately across *all* accounts for which he thought the IPO was suitable, Dill is disadvantaging specific clients.

Dill would have been correct in not allocating shares to his brother's account if that account was being managed outside the normal fee structure of the firm.

Example 8 (Identifying the Client):

Donna Hensley has been hired by a law firm to testify as an expert witness. Although the testimony is intended to represent impartial advice, she is concerned that her work may have negative consequences for the law firm. If the law firm is Hensley's client, how does she ensure that her testimony will not violate the required duty of loyalty, prudence, and care to one's client?

Comment: In this situation, the law firm represents Hensley's employer and the aspect of "who is the client" is not well defined. When acting as an expert witness, Hensley is bound by the standard of independence and objectivity in the same manner as an independent research analyst would be bound. Hensley must not let the law firm influence the testimony she provides in the legal proceedings.

Example 9 (Identifying the Client):

Jon Miller is a mutual fund portfolio manager. The fund is focused on the global financial services sector. Wanda Spears is a private wealth manager in the same city as Miller and is a friend of Miller. At a local CFA Institute society meeting, Spears mentions to Miller that her new client is an investor in Miller's fund. She states that the two of them now share a responsibility to this client.

Comment: Spears' statement is not totally correct. Because she provides the advisory services to her new client, she alone is bound by the duty of loyalty to this client. Miller's responsibility is to manage the fund according to the investment policy statement of the fund. His actions should not be influenced by the needs of any particular fund investor.

Example 10 (Client Loyalty):

After providing client account investment performance to the external-facing departments but prior to it being finalized for release to clients, Teresa Nguyen, an investment performance analyst, notices the reporting system missed a trade. Correcting the omission resulted in a large loss for a client that had previously placed the firm on "watch" for potential termination owing to underperformance in prior periods. Nguyen knows this news is unpleasant but informs the appropriate individuals that the report needs to be updated before releasing it to the client.

Comment: Nguyen's actions align with the requirements of Standard III(A). Even though the correction may lead to the firm's termination by the client, withholding information on errors would not be in the best interest of the client.

Example 11 (Execution-Only Responsibilities):

Baftija Sulejman recently became a candidate in the CFA Program. He is a broker who executes client-directed trades for several high-net-worth individuals. Sulejman does not provide any investment advice and only executes the trading decisions made by clients. He is concerned that the Code and Standards impose a fiduciary duty on him in his dealing with clients and sends an e-mail to the CFA Ethics Helpdesk (ethics@cfainstitute.org) to seek guidance on this issue.

Comment: In this instance, Sulejman serves in an execution-only capacity and his duty of loyalty, prudence, and care is centered on the skill and diligence used when executing trades—namely, by seeking best execution and making trades within the parameters set by the clients (instructions on quantity, price, timing, etc.). Acting in the best interests of the client dictates that trades are executed on the most favorable terms that can be achieved for the client. Given this job function, the requirements of the Code and Standards for loyalty, prudence, and care clearly do not impose a fiduciary duty.

Standard III(B) Fair Dealing

> Members and Candidates must deal fairly and objectively with all clients when providing investment analysis, making investment recommendations, taking investment action, or engaging in other professional activities.

Guidance

Highlights:

- *Investment Recommendations*
- *Investment Action*

Standard III(B) requires members and candidates to treat all clients fairly when disseminating investment recommendations or making material changes to prior investment recommendations or when taking investment action with regard to general purchases, new issues, or secondary offerings. Only through the fair treatment of all parties can the investment management profession maintain the confidence of the investing public.

When an investment adviser has multiple clients, the potential exists for the adviser to favor one client over another. This favoritism may take various forms—from the quality and timing of services provided to the allocation of investment opportunities.

The term "fairly" implies that the member or candidate must take care not to discriminate against any clients when disseminating investment recommendations or taking investment action. Standard III(B) does not state "equally" because members and candidates could not possibly reach all clients at exactly the same time—whether by printed mail, telephone (including text messaging), computer (including internet updates and e-mail distribution), facsimile (fax), or wire. Each client has unique needs, investment criteria, and investment objectives, so not all investment opportunities are suitable for all clients. In addition, members and candidates may provide more personal, specialized, or in-depth service to clients who are willing to pay for premium services through higher management fees or higher levels of brokerage. Members and candidates may differentiate their services to clients, but different levels of service must not disadvantage or negatively affect clients. In addition, the different service levels should be disclosed to clients and prospective clients and should be available to everyone (i.e., different service levels should not be offered selectively).

Standard III(B) covers conduct in two broadly defined categories—investment recommendations and investment action.

Investment Recommendations

The first category of conduct involves members and candidates whose primary function is the preparation of investment recommendations to be disseminated either to the public or within a firm for the use of others in making investment decisions. This group includes members and candidates employed by investment counseling, advisory, or consulting firms as well as banks, brokerage firms, and insurance companies. The criterion is that the member's or candidate's primary responsibility is the preparation of recommendations to be acted on by others, including those in the member's or candidate's organization.

An investment recommendation is any opinion expressed by a member or candidate in regard to purchasing, selling, or holding a given security or other investment. The opinion may be disseminated to customers or clients through an initial detailed research report, through a brief update report, by addition to or deletion from a list of recommended securities, or simply by oral communication. A recommendation that is distributed to anyone outside the organization is considered a communication for general distribution under Standard III(B).

Standard III(B) addresses the manner in which investment recommendations or changes in prior recommendations are disseminated to clients. Each member or candidate is obligated to ensure that information is disseminated in such a manner that all clients have a fair opportunity to act on every recommendation. Communicating with all clients on a uniform basis presents practical problems for members and candidates because of differences in timing and methods of communication with various types of customers and clients. Members and candidates should encourage their firms to design an equitable system to prevent selective or discriminatory disclosure and should inform clients about what kind of communications they will receive.

The duty to clients imposed by Standard III(B) may be more critical when members or candidates change their recommendations than when they make initial recommendations. Material changes in a member's or candidate's prior investment recommendations because of subsequent research should be communicated to all current clients; particular care should be taken that the information reaches those clients who the member or candidate knows have acted on or been affected by the earlier advice. Clients who do not know that the member or candidate has changed a recommendation and who, therefore, place orders contrary to a current recommendation should be advised of the changed recommendation before the order is accepted.

Investment Action

The second category of conduct includes those members and candidates whose primary function is taking investment action (portfolio management) on the basis of recommendations prepared internally or received from external sources. Investment action, like investment recommendations, can affect market value. Consequently, Standard III(B) requires that members or candidates treat all clients fairly in light of their investment objectives and circumstances. For example, when making investments in new offerings or in secondary financings, members and candidates should distribute the issues to all customers for whom the investments are appropriate in a manner consistent with the policies of the firm for allocating blocks of stock. If the issue is oversubscribed, then the issue should be prorated to all subscribers. This action should be taken on a round-lot basis to avoid odd-lot distributions. In addition, if the issue is oversubscribed, members and candidates should forgo any sales to themselves or their immediate families in order to free up additional shares for clients. If the investment professional's family-member accounts are managed similarly to the accounts of other clients of the firm, however, the family-member accounts should not be excluded from buying such shares.

Members and candidates must make every effort to treat all individual and institutional clients in a fair and impartial manner. A member or candidate may have multiple relationships with an institution; for example, the member or candidate may be a corporate trustee, pension fund manager, manager of funds for individuals employed by the customer, loan originator, or creditor. A member or candidate must exercise care to treat all clients fairly.

Members and candidates should disclose to clients and prospective clients the documented allocation procedures they or their firms have in place and how the procedures would affect the client or prospect. The disclosure should be clear and complete so that the client can make an informed investment decision. Even when complete disclosure is made, however, members and candidates must put client interests ahead of their own. A member's or candidate's duty of fairness and loyalty to clients can never be overridden by client consent to patently unfair allocation procedures.

Treating clients fairly also means that members and candidates should not take advantage of their position in the industry to the detriment of clients. For instance, in the context of IPOs, members and candidates must make bona fide public distributions of "hot issue" securities (defined as securities of a public offering that are trading at a premium in the secondary market whenever such trading commences because of the great demand for the securities). Members and candidates are prohibited from withholding such securities for their own benefit and must not use such securities as a reward or incentive to gain benefit.

Recommended Procedures for Compliance

Develop Firm Policies

Although Standard III(B) refers to a member's or candidate's responsibility to deal fairly and objectively with clients, members and candidates should also encourage their firms to establish compliance procedures requiring all employees who disseminate investment recommendations or take investment actions to treat customers and clients fairly. At the very least, a member or candidate should recommend appropriate procedures to management if none are in place. And the member or candidate should make management aware of possible violations of fair-dealing practices within the firm when they come to the attention of the member or candidate.

The extent of the formality and complexity of such compliance procedures depends on the nature and size of the organization and the type of securities involved. An investment adviser who is a sole proprietor and handles only discretionary accounts might not disseminate recommendations to the public, but that adviser should have formal written procedures to ensure that all clients receive fair investment action.

Good business practice dictates that initial recommendations be made available to all customers who indicate an interest. Although a member or candidate need not communicate a recommendation to all customers, the selection process by which customers receive information should be based on suitability and known interest, not on any preferred or favored status. A common practice to assure fair dealing is to communicate recommendations simultaneously within the firm and to customers.

Members and candidates should consider the following points when establishing fair-dealing compliance procedures:

- *Limit the number of people involved*: Members and candidates should make reasonable efforts to limit the number of people who are privy to the fact that a recommendation is going to be disseminated.
- *Shorten the time frame between decision and dissemination*: Members and candidates should make reasonable efforts to limit the amount of time that elapses between the decision to make an investment recommendation and the time the actual recommendation is disseminated. If a detailed institutional

recommendation that might take two or three weeks to publish is in preparation, a short summary report including the conclusion might be published in advance. In an organization where both a research committee and an investment policy committee must approve a recommendation, the meetings should be held on the same day if possible. The process of reviewing reports and printing and mailing them, faxing them, or distributing them by e-mail necessarily involves the passage of time, sometimes long periods of time. In large firms with extensive review processes, the time factor is usually not within the control of the analyst who prepares the report. Thus, many firms and their analysts communicate to customers and firm personnel the new or changed recommendations by an update or "flash" report. The communication technique might be fax, e-mail, wire, or short written report.

- *Publish guidelines for pre-dissemination behavior*: Members and candidates should encourage firms to develop guidelines that prohibit personnel who have prior knowledge of an investment recommendation from discussing or taking any action on the pending recommendation.
- *Simultaneous dissemination*: Members and candidates should establish procedures for the timing of dissemination of investment recommendations so that all clients are treated fairly—that is, are informed at approximately the same time. For example, if a firm is going to announce a new recommendation, supervisory personnel should time the announcement to avoid placing any client or group of clients at an unfair advantage relative to other clients. A communication to all branch offices should be sent at the time of the general announcement. (When appropriate, the firm should accompany the announcement of a new recommendation with a statement that trading restrictions for the firm's employees are now in effect. The trading restrictions should stay in effect until the recommendation is widely distributed to all relevant clients.) Once this distribution has occurred, the member or candidate may follow up separately with individual clients, but members and candidates should not give favored clients advance information when such advance notification may disadvantage other clients.
- *Maintain a list of clients and their holdings*: Members and candidates should maintain a list of all clients and the securities or other investments each client holds in order to facilitate notification of customers or clients of a change in an investment recommendation. If a particular security or other investment is to be sold, such a list can be used to ensure that all holders are treated fairly in the liquidation of that particular investment.
- *Develop and document trade allocation procedures*: When formulating procedures for allocating trades, members and candidates should develop a set of guiding principles that ensure
  - fairness to advisory clients, both in priority of execution of orders and in the allocation of the price obtained in execution of block orders or trades,
  - timeliness and efficiency in the execution of orders, and
  - accuracy of the member's or candidate's records as to trade orders and client account positions.

With these principles in mind, members and candidates should develop or encourage their firm to develop written allocation procedures, with particular attention to procedures for block trades and new issues. Procedures to consider are as follows:

- requiring orders and modifications or cancellations of orders to be documented and time stamped;

- processing and executing orders on a first-in, first-out basis with consideration of bundling orders for efficiency as appropriate for the asset class or the security;
- developing a policy to address such issues as calculating execution prices and "partial fills" when trades are grouped, or in a block, for efficiency;
- giving all client accounts participating in a block trade the same execution price and charging the same commission;
- when the full amount of the block order is not executed, allocating partially executed orders among the participating client accounts pro rata on the basis of order size while not going below an established minimum lot size for some securities (e.g., bonds); and
- when allocating trades for new issues, obtaining advance indications of interest, allocating securities by client (rather than portfolio manager), and providing a method for calculating allocations.

Disclose Trade Allocation Procedures

Members and candidates should disclose to clients and prospective clients how they select accounts to participate in an order and how they determine the amount of securities each account will buy or sell. Trade allocation procedures must be fair and equitable, and disclosure of inequitable allocation methods does not relieve the member or candidate of this obligation.

Establish Systematic Account Review

Member and candidate supervisors should review each account on a regular basis to ensure that no client or customer is being given preferential treatment and that the investment actions taken for each account are suitable for each account's objectives. Because investments should be based on individual needs and circumstances, an investment manager may have good reasons for placing a given security or other investment in one account while selling it from another account and should fully document the reasons behind both sides of the transaction. Members and candidates should encourage firms to establish review procedures, however, to detect whether trading in one account is being used to benefit a favored client.

Disclose Levels of Service

Members and candidates should disclose to all clients whether the organization offers different levels of service to clients for the same fee or different fees. Different levels of service should not be offered to clients selectively.

Application of the Standard

Example 1 (Selective Disclosure):

Bradley Ames, a well-known and respected analyst, follows the computer industry. In the course of his research, he finds that a small, relatively unknown company whose shares are traded over the counter has just signed significant contracts with some of the companies he follows. After a considerable amount of investigation, Ames decides to write a research report on the small company and recommend purchase of its shares. While the report is being reviewed by the company for factual accuracy, Ames schedules a luncheon with several of his best clients to discuss the company. At the luncheon, he mentions the purchase recommendation scheduled to be sent early the following week to all the firm's clients.

Comment: Ames has violated Standard III(B) by disseminating the purchase recommendation to the clients with whom he has lunch a week before the recommendation is sent to all clients.

Example 2 (Fair Dealing between Funds):

Spencer Rivers, president of XYZ Corporation, moves his company's growth-oriented pension fund to a particular bank primarily because of the excellent investment performance achieved by the bank's commingled fund for the prior five-year period. Later, Rivers compares the results of his pension fund with those of the bank's commingled fund. He is startled to learn that, even though the two accounts have the same investment objectives and similar portfolios, his company's pension fund has significantly underperformed the bank's commingled fund. Questioning this result at his next meeting with the pension fund's manager, Rivers is told that, as a matter of policy, when a new security is placed on the recommended list, Morgan Jackson, the pension fund manager, first purchases the security for the commingled account and then purchases it on a pro rata basis for all other pension fund accounts. Similarly, when a sale is recommended, the security is sold first from the commingled account and then sold on a pro rata basis from all other accounts. Rivers also learns that if the bank cannot get enough shares (especially of hot issues) to be meaningful to all the accounts, its policy is to place the new issues only in the commingled account.

Seeing that Rivers is neither satisfied nor pleased by the explanation, Jackson quickly adds that nondiscretionary pension accounts and personal trust accounts have a lower priority on purchase and sale recommendations than discretionary pension fund accounts. Furthermore, Jackson states, the company's pension fund had the opportunity to invest up to 5% in the commingled fund.

Comment: The bank's policy does not treat all customers fairly, and Jackson has violated her duty to her clients by giving priority to the growth-oriented commingled fund over all other funds and to discretionary accounts over nondiscretionary accounts. Jackson must execute orders on a systematic basis that is fair to all clients. In addition, trade allocation procedures should be disclosed to all clients when they become clients. Of course, in this case, disclosure of the bank's policy would not change the fact that the policy is unfair.

Example 3 (Fair Dealing and IPO Distribution):

Dominic Morris works for a small regional securities firm. His work consists of corporate finance activities and investing for institutional clients. Arena, Ltd., is planning to go public. The partners have secured rights to buy an arena football league franchise and are planning to use the funds from the issue to complete the purchase. Because arena football is the current rage, Morris believes he has a hot issue on his hands. He has quietly negotiated some options for himself for helping convince Arena to do the financing through his securities firm. When he seeks expressions of interest, the institutional buyers oversubscribe the issue. Morris, assuming that the institutions have the financial clout to drive the stock up, then fills all orders (including his own) and decreases the institutional blocks.

Comment: Morris has violated Standard III(B) by not treating all customers fairly. He should not have taken any shares himself and should have prorated the shares offered among all clients. In addition, he should have disclosed to his firm and to his clients that he received options as part of the deal [see Standard VI(A)–Disclosure of Conflicts].

Example 4 (Fair Dealing and Transaction Allocation):

Eleanor Preston, the chief investment officer of Porter Williams Investments (PWI), a medium-size money management firm, has been trying to retain a client, Colby Company. Management at Colby, which accounts for almost half of PWI's revenues, recently told Preston that if the performance of its account did not improve, it would find a new money manager. Shortly after this threat, Preston purchases mortgage-backed securities (MBSs) for several accounts, including Colby's. Preston is busy with a number of transactions that day, so she fails to allocate the trades immediately or write up the trade tickets. A few days later, when Preston is allocating trades, she notes that some of the MBSs have significantly increased in price and some have dropped. Preston decides to allocate the profitable trades to Colby and spread the losing trades among several other PWI accounts.

> *Comment*: Preston has violated Standard III(B) by failing to deal fairly with her clients in taking these investment actions. Preston should have allocated the trades prior to executing the orders, or she should have had a systematic approach to allocating the trades, such as pro rata, as soon as practical after they were executed. Among other things, Preston must disclose to the client that the adviser may act as broker for, receive commissions from, and have a potential conflict of interest regarding both parties in agency cross-transactions. After the disclosure, she should obtain from the client consent authorizing such transactions in advance.

Example 5 (Selective Disclosure):

Saunders Industrial Waste Management (SIWM) publicly indicates to analysts that it is comfortable with the somewhat disappointing earnings-per-share projection of US$1.16 for the quarter. Bernard Roberts, an analyst at Coffey Investments, is confident that SIWM management has understated the forecasted earnings so that the real announcement will cause an "upside surprise" and boost the price of SIWM stock. The "whisper number" (rumored) estimate based on extensive research and discussed among knowledgeable analysts is higher than US$1.16. Roberts repeats the US$1.16 figure in his research report to all Coffey clients but informally tells his large clients that he expects the earnings per share to be higher, making SIWM a good buy.

> *Comment*: By not sharing his opinion regarding the potential for a significant upside earnings surprise with all clients, Roberts is not treating all clients fairly and has violated Standard III(B).

Example 6 (Additional Services for Select Clients):

Jenpin Weng uses e-mail to issue a new recommendation to all his clients. He then calls his three largest institutional clients to discuss the recommendation in detail.

> *Comment*: Weng has not violated Standard III(B) because he widely disseminated the recommendation and provided the information to all his clients prior to discussing it with a select few. Weng's largest clients received additional personal service because they presumably pay higher fees or because they have a large amount of assets under Weng's management. If Weng had discussed the report with a select group of clients prior to distributing it to all his clients, he would have violated Standard III(B).

Example 7 (Minimum Lot Allocations):

Lynn Hampton is a well-respected private wealth manager in her community with a diversified client base. She determines that a new 10-year bond being offered by Healthy Pharmaceuticals is appropriate for five of her clients. Three clients request to purchase US$10,000 each, and the other two request US$50,000 each. The minimum lot size is established at US$5,000, and the issue is oversubscribed at the time of placement. Her firm's policy is that odd-lot allocations, especially those below the minimum, should be avoided because they may affect the liquidity of the security at the time of sale.

Hampton is informed she will receive only US$55,000 of the offering for all accounts. Hampton distributes the bond investments as follows: The three accounts that requested US$10,000 are allocated US$5,000 each, and the two accounts that requested US$50,000 are allocated US$20,000 each.

> *Comment*: Hampton has not violated Standard III(B), even though the distribution is not on a completely pro rata basis because of the required minimum lot size. With the total allocation being significantly below the amount requested, Hampton ensured that each client received at least the minimum lot size of the issue. This approach allowed the clients to efficiently sell the bond later if necessary.

Example 8 (Excessive Trading):

Ling Chan manages the accounts for many pension plans, including the plan of his father's employer. Chan developed similar but not identical investment policies for each client, so the investment portfolios are rarely the same. To minimize the cost to his father's pension plan, he intentionally trades more frequently in the accounts of other clients to ensure the required brokerage is incurred to continue receiving free research for use by all the pensions.

> *Comment*: Chan is violating Standard III(B) because his trading actions are disadvantaging his clients to enhance a relationship with a preferred client. All clients are benefiting from the research being provided and should incur their fair portion of the costs. This does not mean that additional trading should occur if a client has not paid an equal portion of the commission; trading should occur only as required by the strategy.

Example 9 (Limited Social Media Disclosures):

Mary Burdette was recently hired by Fundamental Investment Management (FIM) as a junior auto industry analyst. Burdette is expected to expand the social media presence of the firm because she is active with various networks, including Facebook, LinkedIn, and Twitter. Although Burdette's supervisor, Joe Graf, has never used social media, he encourages Burdette to explore opportunities to increase FIM's online presence and ability to share content, communicate, and broadcast information to clients. In response to Graf's encouragement, Burdette is working on a proposal detailing the advantages of getting FIM onto Twitter in addition to launching a company Facebook page.

As part of her auto industry research for FIM, Burdette is completing a report on the financial impact of Sun Drive Auto Ltd.'s new solar technology for compact automobiles. This research report will be her first for FIM, and she believes Sun Drive's technology could revolutionize the auto industry. In her excitement, Burdette sends a quick tweet to FIM Twitter followers summarizing her "buy" recommendation for Sun Drive Auto stock.

> *Comment*: Burdette has violated Standard III(B) by sending an investment recommendation to a select group of contacts prior to distributing it to all clients. Burdette must make sure she has received the appropriate training about FIM's policies and procedures, including the appropriate business use of personal social media networks before engaging in such activities.
>
> See Standard IV(C) for guidance related to the duties of the supervisor.

Example 10 (Fair Dealing between Clients):

Paul Rove, performance analyst for Alpha-Beta Investment Management, is describing to the firm's chief investment officer (CIO) two new reports he would like to develop to assist the firm in meeting its obligations to treat clients fairly. Because many of the firm's clients have similar investment objectives and portfolios, Rove suggests a report detailing securities owned across several clients and the percentage of the portfolio the security represents. The second report would compare the monthly performance of portfolios with similar strategies. The outliers within each report would be submitted to the CIO for review.

> *Comment*: As a performance analyst, Rove likely has little direct contact with clients and thus has limited opportunity to treat clients differently. The recommended reports comply with Standard III(B) while helping the firm conduct after-the-fact reviews of how effectively the firm's advisers are dealing with their clients' portfolios. Reports that monitor the fair treatment of clients are an important oversight tool to ensure that clients are treated fairly.

Standard III(C) Suitability

1 When Members and Candidates are in an advisory relationship with a client, they must:

- **a** Make a reasonable inquiry into a client's or prospective client's investment experience, risk and return objectives, and financial constraints prior to making any investment recommendation or taking investment action and must reassess and update this information regularly.
- **b** Determine that an investment is suitable to the client's financial situation and consistent with the client's written objectives, mandates, and constraints before making an investment recommendation or taking investment action.
- **c** Judge the suitability of investments in the context of the client's total portfolio.

2 When Members and Candidates are responsible for managing a portfolio to a specific mandate, strategy, or style, they must make only investment recommendations or take only investment actions that are consistent with the stated objectives and constraints of the portfolio.

Guidance

Highlights:

- *Developing an Investment Policy*
- *Understanding the Client's Risk Profile*
- *Updating an Investment Policy*
- *The Need for Diversification*
- *Addressing Unsolicited Trading Requests*
- *Managing to an Index or Mandate*

Standard III(C) requires that members and candidates who are in an investment advisory relationship with clients consider carefully the needs, circumstances, and objectives of the clients when determining the appropriateness and suitability of a given investment or course of investment action. An appropriate suitability determination will not, however, prevent some investments or investment actions from losing value.

In judging the suitability of a potential investment, the member or candidate should review many aspects of the client's knowledge, experience related to investing, and financial situation. These aspects include, but are not limited to, the risk profile of the investment as compared with the constraints of the client, the impact of the investment on the diversity of the portfolio, and whether the client has the means or net worth to assume the associated risk. The investment professional's determination of suitability should reflect only the investment recommendations or actions that a prudent person would be willing to undertake. Not every investment opportunity will be suitable for every portfolio, regardless of the potential return being offered.

The responsibilities of members and candidates to gather information and make a suitability analysis prior to making a recommendation or taking investment action fall on those members and candidates who provide investment advice in the course of an advisory relationship with a client. Other members and candidates may be simply executing specific instructions for retail clients when buying or selling securities, such as shares in mutual funds. These members and candidates and some others, such as sell-side analysts, may not have the opportunity to judge the suitability of a particular investment for the ultimate client.

Developing an Investment Policy

When an advisory relationship exists, members and candidates must gather client information at the inception of the relationship. Such information includes the client's financial circumstances, personal data (such as age and occupation) that are relevant to investment decisions, attitudes toward risk, and objectives in investing. This information should be incorporated into a written investment policy statement (IPS) that addresses the client's risk tolerance, return requirements, and all investment constraints (including time horizon, liquidity needs, tax concerns, legal and regulatory factors, and unique circumstances). Without identifying such client factors, members and candidates cannot judge whether a particular investment or strategy is suitable for a particular client. The IPS also should identify and describe the roles and responsibilities of the parties to the advisory relationship and investment process, as well as schedules for review and evaluation of the IPS. After formulating long-term capital market expectations, members and candidates can assist in developing an appropriate strategic asset allocation and investment program for the client, whether these are presented in separate documents or incorporated in the IPS or in appendices to the IPS.

Understanding the Client's Risk Profile

One of the most important factors to be considered in matching appropriateness and suitability of an investment with a client's needs and circumstances is measuring that client's tolerance for risk. The investment professional must consider the possibilities of rapidly changing investment environments and their likely impact on a client's holdings, both individual securities and the collective portfolio. The risk of many investment strategies can and should be analyzed and quantified in advance.

The use of synthetic investment vehicles and derivative investment products has introduced particular issues of risk. Members and candidates should pay careful attention to the leverage inherent in many of these vehicles or products when considering them for use in a client's investment program. Such leverage and limited liquidity, depending on the degree to which they are hedged, bear directly on the issue of suitability for the client.

Updating an Investment Policy

Updating the IPS should be repeated at least annually and also prior to material changes to any specific investment recommendations or decisions on behalf of the client. The effort to determine the needs and circumstances of each client is not a one-time occurrence. Investment recommendations or decisions are usually part of an ongoing process that takes into account the diversity and changing nature of portfolio and client characteristics. The passage of time is bound to produce changes that are important with respect to investment objectives.

For an individual client, important changes might include the number of dependents, personal tax status, health, liquidity needs, risk tolerance, amount of wealth beyond that represented in the portfolio, and extent to which compensation and other income provide for current income needs. With respect to an institutional client, such changes might relate to the magnitude of unfunded liabilities in a pension fund, the withdrawal privileges in an employee savings plan, or the distribution requirements of a charitable foundation. Without efforts to update information concerning client factors, one or more factors could change without the investment manager's knowledge.

Suitability review can be done most effectively when the client fully discloses his or her complete financial portfolio, including those portions not managed by the member or candidate. If clients withhold information about their financial portfolios, the suitability analysis conducted by members and candidates cannot be expected to be complete; it must be based on the information provided.

The Need for Diversification

The investment profession has long recognized that combining several different investments is likely to provide a more acceptable level of risk exposure than having all assets in a single investment. The unique characteristics (or risks) of an individual investment may become partially or entirely neutralized when it is combined with other individual investments within a portfolio. Some reasonable amount of diversification is thus the norm for many portfolios, especially those managed by individuals or institutions that have some degree of legal fiduciary responsibility.

An investment with high relative risk on its own may be a suitable investment in the context of the entire portfolio or when the client's stated objectives contemplate speculative or risky investments. The manager may be responsible for only a portion of the client's total portfolio, or the client may not have provided a full financial picture. Members and candidates can be responsible for assessing the suitability of an investment only on the basis of the information and criteria actually provided by the client.

Addressing Unsolicited Trading Requests

Members and candidates may receive requests from a client for trades that do not properly align with the risk and return objectives outlined in the client's investment policy statement. These transaction requests may be based on the client's individual biases or professional experience. Members and candidates will need to make reasonable efforts to balance their clients' trading requests with their responsibilities to follow the agreed-on investment policy statement.

In cases of unsolicited trade requests that a member or candidate knows are unsuitable for a client, the member or candidate should refrain from making the trade until he or she discusses the concerns with the client. The discussions and resulting actions may encompass a variety of scenarios depending on how the requested unsuitable investment relates to the client's full portfolio.

Many times, an unsolicited request may be expected to have only a minimum impact on the entire portfolio because the size of the requested trade is small or the trade would result in a limited change to the portfolio's risk profile. In discussing the trade, the member or candidate should focus on educating the investor on how the request deviates from the current policy statement. Following the discussion, the member or candidate may follow his or her firm's policies regarding the necessary client approval for executing unsuitable trades. At a minimum, the client should acknowledge the discussion and accept the conditions that make the recommendation unsuitable.

Should the unsolicited request be expected to have a material impact on the portfolio, the member or candidate should use this opportunity to update the investment policy statement. Doing so would allow the client to fully understand the potential effect of the requested trade on his or her current goals or risk levels.

Members and candidates may have some clients who decline to modify their policy statements while insisting an unsolicited trade be made. In such instances, members or candidates will need to evaluate the effectiveness of their services to the client. The options available to the members or candidates will depend on the services provided by their employer. Some firms may allow for the trade to be executed in a new unmanaged account. If alternative options are not available, members and candidates ultimately will need to determine whether they should continue the advisory arrangement with the client.

Managing to an Index or Mandate

Some members and candidates do not manage money for individuals but are responsible for managing a fund to an index or an expected mandate. The responsibility of these members and candidates is to invest in a manner consistent with the stated mandate. For example, a member or candidate who serves as the fund manager for a large-cap income fund would not be following the fund mandate by investing heavily in small-cap or start-up companies whose stock is speculative in nature. Members and candidates who manage pooled assets to a specific mandate are not responsible for determining the suitability of the *fund* as an investment for investors who may be purchasing shares in the fund. The responsibility for determining the suitability of an investment for clients can be conferred only on members and candidates who have an advisory relationship with clients.

Recommended Procedures for Compliance

Investment Policy Statement

To fulfill the basic provisions of Standard III(C), a member or candidate should put the needs and circumstances of each client and the client's investment objectives into a written investment policy statement. In formulating an investment policy for the client, the member or candidate should take the following into consideration:

- client identification—(1) type and nature of client, (2) the existence of separate beneficiaries, and (3) approximate portion of total client assets that the member or candidate is managing;
- investor objectives—(1) return objectives (income, growth in principal, maintenance of purchasing power) and (2) risk tolerance (suitability, stability of values);
- investor constraints—(1) liquidity needs, (2) expected cash flows (patterns of additions and/or withdrawals), (3) investable funds (assets and liabilities or other commitments), (4) time horizon, (5) tax considerations, (6) regulatory and legal circumstances, (7) investor preferences, prohibitions, circumstances, and unique needs, and (8) proxy voting responsibilities and guidance; and
- performance measurement benchmarks.

Regular Updates

The investor's objectives and constraints should be maintained and reviewed periodically to reflect any changes in the client's circumstances. Members and candidates should regularly compare client constraints with capital market expectations to arrive at an appropriate asset allocation. Changes in either factor may result in a fundamental change in asset allocation. Annual review is reasonable unless business or other reasons, such as a major change in market conditions, dictate more frequent review. Members and candidates should document attempts to carry out such a review if circumstances prevent it.

Suitability Test Policies

With the increase in regulatory required suitability tests, members and candidates should encourage their firms to develop related policies and procedures. The procedures will differ according to the size of the firm and the scope of the services offered to its clients.

The test procedures should require the investment professional to look beyond the potential return of the investment and include the following:

- an analysis of the impact on the portfolio's diversification,
- a comparison of the investment risks with the client's assessed risk tolerance, and
- the fit of the investment with the required investment strategy.

Application of the Standard

Example 1 (Investment Suitability—Risk Profile):

Caleb Smith, an investment adviser, has two clients: Larry Robertson, 60 years old, and Gabriel Lanai, 40 years old. Both clients earn roughly the same salary, but Robertson has a much higher risk tolerance because he has a large asset base. Robertson is willing to invest part of his assets very aggressively; Lanai wants only to achieve a steady rate of return with low volatility to pay for his children's education. Smith recommends investing 20% of both portfolios in zero-yield, small-cap, high-technology equity issues.

> *Comment*: In Robertson's case, the investment may be appropriate because of his financial circumstances and aggressive investment position, but this investment is not suitable for Lanai. Smith is violating Standard III(C) by applying Robertson's investment strategy to Lanai because the two clients' financial circumstances and objectives differ.

Example 2 (Investment Suitability—Entire Portfolio):

Jessica McDowell, an investment adviser, suggests to Brian Crosby, a risk-averse client, that covered call options be used in his equity portfolio. The purpose would be to enhance Crosby's income and partially offset any untimely depreciation in the portfolio's value should the stock market or other circumstances affect his holdings unfavorably. McDowell educates Crosby about all possible outcomes, including the risk of incurring an added tax liability if a stock rises in price and is called away and, conversely, the risk of his holdings losing protection on the downside if prices drop sharply.

> *Comment*: When determining suitability of an investment, the primary focus should be the characteristics of the client's entire portfolio, not the characteristics of single securities on an issue-by-issue basis. The basic characteristics of the entire portfolio will largely determine whether investment recommendations are taking client factors into account. Therefore,

the most important aspects of a particular investment are those that will affect the characteristics of the total portfolio. In this case, McDowell properly considers the investment in the context of the entire portfolio and thoroughly explains the investment to the client.

Example 3 (IPS Updating):

In a regular meeting with client Seth Jones, the portfolio managers at Blue Chip Investment Advisors are careful to allow some time to review his current needs and circumstances. In doing so, they learn that some significant changes have recently taken place in his life. A wealthy uncle left Jones an inheritance that increased his net worth fourfold, to US$1 million.

> *Comment*: The inheritance has significantly increased Jones's ability (and possibly his willingness) to assume risk and has diminished the average yield required to meet his current income needs. Jones's financial circumstances have definitely changed, so Blue Chip managers must update Jones's investment policy statement to reflect how his investment objectives have changed. Accordingly, the Blue Chip portfolio managers should consider a somewhat higher equity ratio for his portfolio than was called for by the previous circumstances, and the managers' specific common stock recommendations might be heavily tilted toward low-yield, growth-oriented issues.

Example 4 (Following an Investment Mandate):

Louis Perkowski manages a high-income mutual fund. He purchases zero-dividend stock in a financial services company because he believes the stock is undervalued and is in a potential growth industry, which makes it an attractive investment.

> *Comment*: A zero-dividend stock does not seem to fit the mandate of the fund that Perkowski is managing. Unless Perkowski's investment fits within the mandate or is within the realm of allowable investments the fund has made clear in its disclosures, Perkowski has violated Standard III(C).

Example 5 (IPS Requirements and Limitations):

Max Gubler, chief investment officer of a property/casualty insurance subsidiary of a large financial conglomerate, wants to improve the diversification of the subsidiary's investment portfolio and increase its returns. The subsidiary's investment policy statement provides for highly liquid investments, such as large-cap equities and government, supranational, and corporate bonds with a minimum credit rating of AA and maturity of no more than five years. In a recent presentation, a venture capital group offered very attractive prospective returns on some of its private equity funds that provide seed capital to ventures. An exit strategy was already contemplated, but investors would have to observe a minimum three-year lockup period and a subsequent laddered exit option for a maximum of one-third of their shares per year. Gubler does not want to miss this opportunity. After extensive analysis, with the intent to optimize the return on the equity assets within the subsidiary's current portfolio, he invests 4% in this seed fund, leaving the portfolio's total equity exposure still well below its upper limit.

> *Comment*: Gubler is violating Standard III(A)–Loyalty, Prudence, and Care as well as Standard III(C). His new investment locks up part of the subsidiary's assets for at least three years and up to as many as five years and possibly beyond. The IPS requires investments in highly liquid investments and describes accepted asset classes; private equity investments with a lockup period certainly do not qualify. Even without a lockup period, an asset class with only an occasional, and thus implicitly illiquid, market

may not be suitable for the portfolio. Although an IPS typically describes objectives and constraints in great detail, the manager must also make every effort to understand the client's business and circumstances. Doing so should enable the manager to recognize, understand, and discuss with the client other factors that may be or may become material in the investment management process.

Example 6 (Submanager and IPS Reviews):

Paul Ostrowski's investment management business has grown significantly over the past couple of years, and some clients want to diversify internationally. Ostrowski decides to find a submanager to handle the expected international investments. Because this will be his first subadviser, Ostrowski uses the CFA Institute model "request for proposal" to design a questionnaire for his search. By his deadline, he receives seven completed questionnaires from a variety of domestic and international firms trying to gain his business. Ostrowski reviews all the applications in detail and decides to select the firm that charges the lowest fees because doing so will have the least impact on his firm's bottom line.

Comment: When selecting an external manager or subadviser, Ostrowski needs to ensure that the new manager's services are appropriate for his clients. This due diligence includes comparing the risk profile of the clients with the investment strategy of the manager. In basing the decision on the fee structure alone, Ostrowski may be violating Standard III(C).

When clients ask to diversify into international products, it is an appropriate time to review and update the clients' IPSs. Ostrowski's review may determine that the risk of international investments modifies the risk profiles of the clients or does not represent an appropriate investment.

See also Standard V(A)–Diligence and Reasonable Basis for further discussion of the review process needed in selecting appropriate submanagers.

Example 7 (Investment Suitability—Risk Profile):

Samantha Snead, a portfolio manager for Thomas Investment Counsel, Inc., specializes in managing public retirement funds and defined benefit pension plan accounts, all of which have long-term investment objectives. A year ago, Snead's employer, in an attempt to motivate and retain key investment professionals, introduced a bonus compensation system that rewards portfolio managers on the basis of quarterly performance relative to their peers and to certain benchmark indexes. In an attempt to improve the short-term performance of her accounts, Snead changes her investment strategy and purchases several high-beta stocks for client portfolios. These purchases are seemingly contrary to the clients' investment policy statements. Following their purchase, an officer of Griffin Corporation, one of Snead's pension fund clients, asks why Griffin Corporation's portfolio seems to be dominated by high-beta stocks of companies that often appear among the most actively traded issues. No change in objective or strategy has been recommended by Snead during the year.

Comment: Snead violated Standard III(C) by investing the clients' assets in high-beta stocks. These high-risk investments are contrary to the long-term risk profile established in the clients' IPSs. Snead has changed the investment strategy of the clients in an attempt to reap short-term rewards offered by her firm's new compensation arrangement, not in response to changes in clients' investment policy statements.

See also Standard VI(A)–Disclosure of Conflicts.

Example 8 (Investment Suitability):

Andre Shrub owns and operates Conduit, an investment advisory firm. Prior to opening Conduit, Shrub was an account manager with Elite Investment, a hedge fund managed by his good friend Adam Reed. To attract clients to a new Conduit fund, Shrub offers lower-than-normal management fees. He can do so because the fund consists of two top-performing funds managed by Reed. Given his personal friendship with Reed and the prior performance record of these two funds, Shrub believes this new fund is a winning combination for all parties. Clients quickly invest with Conduit to gain access to the Elite funds. No one is turned away because Conduit is seeking to expand its assets under management.

> *Comment*: Shrub has violated Standard III(C) because the risk profile of the new fund may not be suitable for every client. As an investment adviser, Shrub needs to establish an investment policy statement for each client and recommend only investments that match each client's risk and return profile in the IPS. Shrub is required to act as more than a simple sales agent for Elite.
>
> Although Shrub cannot disobey the direct request of a client to purchase a specific security, he should fully discuss the risks of a planned purchase and provide reasons why it might not be suitable for a client. This requirement may lead members and candidates to decline new customers if those customers' requested investment decisions are significantly out of line with their stated requirements.
>
> See also Standard V(A)–Diligence and Reasonable Basis.

Standard III(D) Performance Presentation

When communicating investment performance information, Members and Candidates must make reasonable efforts to ensure that it is fair, accurate, and complete.

Guidance

Standard III(D) requires members and candidates to provide credible performance information to clients and prospective clients and to avoid misstating performance or misleading clients and prospective clients about the investment performance of members or candidates or their firms. This standard encourages full disclosure of investment performance data to clients and prospective clients.

Standard III(D) covers any practice that would lead to misrepresentation of a member's or candidate's performance record, whether the practice involves performance presentation or performance measurement. This standard prohibits misrepresentations of past performance or reasonably expected performance. A member or candidate must give a fair and complete presentation of performance information whenever communicating data with respect to the performance history of individual accounts, composites or groups of accounts, or composites of an analyst's or firm's performance results. Furthermore, members and candidates should not state or imply that clients will obtain or benefit from a rate of return that was generated in the past.

The requirements of this standard are not limited to members and candidates managing separate accounts. Whenever a member or candidate provides performance information for which the manager is claiming responsibility, such as for pooled funds, the history must be accurate. Research analysts promoting the success or accuracy of their recommendations must ensure that their claims are fair, accurate, and complete.

If the presentation is brief, the member or candidate must make available to clients and prospects, on request, the detailed information supporting that communication. Best practice dictates that brief presentations include a reference to the limited nature of the information provided.

Recommended Procedures for Compliance

Apply the GIPS Standards

For members and candidates who are showing the performance history of the assets they manage, compliance with the GIPS standards is the best method to meet their obligations under Standard III(D). Members and candidates should encourage their firms to comply with the GIPS standards.

Compliance without Applying GIPS Standards

Members and candidates can also meet their obligations under Standard III(D) by

- considering the knowledge and sophistication of the audience to whom a performance presentation is addressed,
- presenting the performance of the weighted composite of similar portfolios rather than using a single representative account,
- including terminated accounts as part of performance history with a clear indication of when the accounts were terminated,
- including disclosures that fully explain the performance results being reported (for example, stating, when appropriate, that results are simulated when model results are used, clearly indicating when the performance record is that of a prior entity, or disclosing whether the performance is gross of fees, net of fees, or after tax), and
- maintaining the data and records used to calculate the performance being presented.

Application of the Standard

Example 1 (Performance Calculation and Length of Time):

Kyle Taylor of Taylor Trust Company, noting the performance of Taylor's common trust fund for the past two years, states in a brochure sent to his potential clients, "You can expect steady 25% annual compound growth of the value of your investments over the year." Taylor Trust's common trust fund did increase at the rate of 25% per year for the past year, which mirrored the increase of the entire market. The fund has never averaged that growth for more than one year, however, and the average rate of growth of all of its trust accounts for five years is 5% per year.

> *Comment*: Taylor's brochure is in violation of Standard III(D). Taylor should have disclosed that the 25% growth occurred only in one year. Additionally, Taylor did not include client accounts other than those in the firm's common trust fund. A general claim of firm performance should take into account the performance of all categories of accounts. Finally, by

stating that clients can expect a steady 25% annual compound growth rate, Taylor is also violating Standard I(C)–Misrepresentation, which prohibits assurances or guarantees regarding an investment.

Example 2 (Performance Calculation and Asset Weighting):

Anna Judd, a senior partner of Alexander Capital Management, circulates a performance report for the capital appreciation accounts for the years 1988 through 2004. The firm claims compliance with the GIPS standards. Returns are not calculated in accordance with the requirements of the GIPS standards, however, because the composites are not asset weighted.

> *Comment*: Judd is in violation of Standard III(D). When claiming compliance with the GIPS standards, firms must meet *all* of the requirements, make mandatory disclosures, and meet any other requirements that apply to that firm's specific situation. Judd's violation is not from any misuse of the data but from a false claim of GIPS compliance.

Example 3 (Performance Presentation and Prior Fund/Employer):

Aaron McCoy is vice president and managing partner of the equity investment group of Mastermind Financial Advisors, a new business. Mastermind recruited McCoy because he had a proven six-year track record with G&P Financial. In developing Mastermind's advertising and marketing campaign, McCoy prepares an advertisement that includes the equity investment performance he achieved at G&P Financial. The advertisement for Mastermind does not identify the equity performance as being earned while at G&P. The advertisement is distributed to existing clients and prospective clients of Mastermind.

> *Comment*: McCoy has violated Standard III(D) by distributing an advertisement that contains material misrepresentations about the historical performance of Mastermind. Standard III(D) requires that members and candidates make every reasonable effort to ensure that performance information is a fair, accurate, and complete representation of an individual's or firm's performance. As a general matter, this standard does not prohibit showing past performance of funds managed at a prior firm as part of a performance track record as long as showing that record is accompanied by appropriate disclosures about where the performance took place and the person's specific role in achieving that performance. If McCoy chooses to use his past performance from G&P in Mastermind's advertising, he should make full disclosure of the source of the historical performance.

Example 4 (Performance Presentation and Simulated Results):

Jed Davis has developed a mutual fund selection product based on historical information from the 1990–95 period. Davis tested his methodology by applying it retroactively to data from the 1996–2003 period, thus producing simulated performance results for those years. In January 2004, Davis's employer decided to offer the product and Davis began promoting it through trade journal advertisements and direct dissemination to clients. The advertisements included the performance results for the 1996–2003 period but did not indicate that the results were simulated.

> *Comment*: Davis violated Standard III(D) by failing to clearly identify simulated performance results. Standard III(D) prohibits members and candidates from making any statements that misrepresent the performance achieved by them or their firms and requires members and candidates to make every reasonable effort to ensure that performance information

presented to clients is fair, accurate, and complete. Use of simulated results should be accompanied by full disclosure as to the source of the performance data, including the fact that the results from 1995 through 2003 were the result of applying the model retroactively to that time period.

Example 5 (Performance Calculation and Selected Accounts Only):

In a presentation prepared for prospective clients, William Kilmer shows the rates of return realized over a five-year period by a "composite" of his firm's discretionary accounts that have a "balanced" objective. This composite, however, consisted of only a few of the accounts that met the balanced criterion set by the firm, excluded accounts under a certain asset level without disclosing the fact of their exclusion, and included accounts that did not have the balanced mandate because those accounts would boost the investment results. In addition, to achieve better results, Kilmer manipulated the narrow range of accounts included in the composite by changing the accounts that made up the composite over time.

Comment: Kilmer violated Standard III(D) by misrepresenting the facts in the promotional material sent to prospective clients, distorting his firm's performance record, and failing to include disclosures that would have clarified the presentation.

Example 6 (Performance Attribution Changes):

Art Purell is reviewing the quarterly performance attribution reports for distribution to clients. Purell works for an investment management firm with a bottom-up, fundamentals-driven investment process that seeks to add value through stock selection. The attribution methodology currently compares each stock with its sector. The attribution report indicates that the value added this quarter came from asset allocation and that stock selection contributed negatively to the calculated return.

Through running several different scenarios, Purell discovers that calculating attribution by comparing each stock with its industry and then rolling the effect to the sector level improves the appearance of the manager's stock selection activities. Because the firm defines the attribution terms and the results better reflect the stated strategy, Purell recommends that the client reports should use the revised methodology.

Comment: Modifying the attribution methodology without proper notifications to clients would fail to meet the requirements of Standard III(D). Purrell's recommendation is being done solely for the interest of the firm to improve its perceived ability to meet the stated investment strategy. Such changes are unfair to clients and obscure the facts regarding the firm's abilities.

Had Purell believed the new methodology offered improvements to the original model, then he would have needed to report the results of both calculations to the client. The report should also include the reasons why the new methodology is preferred, which would allow the client to make a meaningful comparison to prior results and provide a basis for comparing future attributions.

Example 7 (Performance Calculation Methodology Disclosure):

While developing a new reporting package for existing clients, Alisha Singh, a performance analyst, discovers that her company's new system automatically calculates both time-weighted and money-weighted returns. She asks the head of client services and retention which value would be preferred given that the firm has various investment strategies that include bonds, equities, securities without leverage, and alternatives. Singh is told not to label the return value so that the firm may show whichever value is greatest for the period.

> *Comment*: Following these instructions would lead to Singh violating Standard III(D). In reporting inconsistent return values, Singh would not be providing complete information to the firm's clients. Full information is provided when clients have sufficient information to judge the performance generated by the firm.

Example 8 (Performance Calculation Methodology Disclosure):

Richmond Equity Investors manages a long–short equity fund in which clients can trade once a week (on Fridays). For transparency reasons, a daily net asset value of the fund is calculated by Richmond. The monthly fact sheets of the fund report month-to-date and year-to-date performance. Richmond publishes the performance based on the higher of the last trading day of the month (typically, not the last business day) or the last business day of the month as determined by Richmond. The fact sheet mentions only that the data are as of the end of the month, without giving the exact date. Maggie Clark, the investment performance analyst in charge of the calculations, is concerned about the frequent changes and asks her supervisor whether they are appropriate.

> *Comment*: Clark's actions in questioning the changing performance metric comply with Standard III(D). She has shown concern that these changes are not presenting an accurate and complete picture of the performance generated.

Standard III(E) Preservation of Confidentiality

Members and Candidates must keep information about current, former, and prospective clients confidential unless:

1 The information concerns illegal activities on the part of the client;

2 Disclosure is required by law; or

3 The client or prospective client permits disclosure of the information.

Guidance

Highlights:

- *Status of Client*
- *Compliance with Laws*
- *Electronic Information and Security*
- *Professional Conduct Investigations by CFA Institute*

Standard III(E) requires that members and candidates preserve the confidentiality of information communicated to them by their clients, prospective clients, and former clients. This standard is applicable when (1) the member or candidate receives information because of his or her special ability to conduct a portion of the client's business or personal affairs and (2) the member or candidate receives information that arises from or is relevant to that portion of the client's business that is the subject of the special or confidential relationship. If disclosure of the information is required by law or the information concerns illegal activities by the client, however, the member or candidate may have an obligation to report the activities to the appropriate authorities.

Status of Client

This standard protects the confidentiality of client information even if the person or entity is no longer a client of the member or candidate. Therefore, members and candidates must continue to maintain the confidentiality of client records even after the client relationship has ended. If a client or former client expressly authorizes the member or candidate to disclose information, however, the member or candidate may follow the terms of the authorization and provide the information.

Compliance with Laws

As a general matter, members and candidates must comply with applicable law. If applicable law requires disclosure of client information in certain circumstances, members and candidates must comply with the law. Similarly, if applicable law requires members and candidates to maintain confidentiality, even if the information concerns illegal activities on the part of the client, members and candidates should not disclose such information. Additionally, applicable laws, such as inter-departmental communication restrictions within financial institutions, can impose limitations on information flow about a client within an entity that may lead to a violation of confidentiality. When in doubt, members and candidates should consult with their employer's compliance personnel or legal counsel before disclosing confidential information about clients.

Electronic Information and Security

Because of the ever-increasing volume of electronically stored information, members and candidates need to be particularly aware of possible accidental disclosures. Many employers have strict policies about how to electronically communicate sensitive client information and store client information on personal laptops, mobile devices, or portable disk/flash drives. In recent years, regulatory authorities have imposed stricter data security laws applying to the use of mobile remote digital communication, including the use of social media, that must be considered. Standard III(E) does not require members or candidates to become experts in information security technology, but they should have a thorough understanding of the policies of their employer. The size and operations of the firm will lead to differing policies for ensuring the security of confidential information maintained within the firm. Members and candidates should encourage their firm to conduct regular periodic training on confidentiality procedures for all firm personnel, including portfolio associates, receptionists, and other non-investment staff who have routine direct contact with clients and their records.

Professional Conduct Investigations by CFA Institute

The requirements of Standard III(E) are not intended to prevent members and candidates from cooperating with an investigation by the CFA Institute Professional Conduct Program (PCP). When permissible under applicable law, members and candidates shall consider the PCP an extension of themselves when requested to provide information about a client in support of a PCP investigation into their own conduct. Members and candidates are encouraged to cooperate with investigations into the conduct of others. Any information turned over to the PCP is kept in the strictest confidence. Members and candidates will not be considered in violation of this standard by forwarding confidential information to the PCP.

Recommended Procedures for Compliance

The simplest, most conservative, and most effective way to comply with Standard III(E) is to avoid disclosing any information received from a client except to authorized fellow employees who are also working for the client. In some instances, however, a member or candidate may want to disclose information received from clients that is outside the scope of the confidential relationship and does not involve illegal activities. Before making such a disclosure, a member or candidate should ask the following:

- In what context was the information disclosed? If disclosed in a discussion of work being performed for the client, is the information relevant to the work?
- Is the information background material that, if disclosed, will enable the member or candidate to improve service to the client?

Members and candidates need to understand and follow their firm's electronic information communication and storage procedures. If the firm does not have procedures in place, members and candidates should encourage the development of procedures that appropriately reflect the firm's size and business operations.

Communicating with Clients

Technological changes are constantly enhancing the methods that are used to communicate with clients and prospective clients. Members and candidates should make reasonable efforts to ensure that firm-supported communication methods and compliance procedures follow practices designed for preventing accidental distribution of confidential information. Given the rate at which technology changes, a regular review of privacy protection measures is encouraged.

Members and candidates should be diligent in discussing with clients the appropriate methods for providing confidential information. It is important to convey to clients that not all firm-sponsored resources may be appropriate for such communications.

Application of the Standard

Example 1 (Possessing Confidential Information):

Sarah Connor, a financial analyst employed by Johnson Investment Counselors, Inc., provides investment advice to the trustees of City Medical Center. The trustees have given her a number of internal reports concerning City Medical's needs for physical plant renovation and expansion. They have asked Connor to recommend investments that would generate capital appreciation in endowment funds to meet projected capital expenditures. Connor is approached by a local businessman, Thomas Kasey, who is considering a substantial contribution either to City Medical Center or to another local hospital. Kasey wants to find out the building plans of both institutions before making a decision, but he does not want to speak to the trustees.

> *Comment*: The trustees gave Connor the internal reports so she could advise them on how to manage their endowment funds. Because the information in the reports is clearly both confidential and within the scope of the confidential relationship, Standard III(E) requires that Connor refuse to divulge information to Kasey.

Example 2 (Disclosing Confidential Information):

Lynn Moody is an investment officer at the Lester Trust Company. She has an advisory customer who has talked to her about giving approximately US$50,000 to charity to reduce her income taxes. Moody is also treasurer of the Home for Indigent Widows (HIW), which is planning its annual giving campaign. HIW hopes to expand its list of prospects, particularly those capable of substantial gifts. Moody recommends that HIW's vice president for corporate gifts call on her customer and ask for a donation in the US$50,000 range.

> *Comment*: Even though the attempt to help the Home for Indigent Widows was well intended, Moody violated Standard III(E) by revealing confidential information about her client.

Example 3 (Disclosing Possible Illegal Activity):

Government officials approach Casey Samuel, the portfolio manager for Garcia Company's pension plan, to examine pension fund records. They tell her that Garcia's corporate tax returns are being audited and the pension fund is being reviewed. Two days earlier, Samuel had learned in a regular investment review with Garcia officers that potentially excessive and improper charges were being made to the pension plan by Garcia. Samuel consults her employer's general counsel and is advised that Garcia has probably violated tax and fiduciary regulations and laws.

> *Comment*: Samuel should inform her supervisor of these activities, and her employer should take steps, with Garcia, to remedy the violations. If that approach is not successful, Samuel and her employer should seek advice of legal counsel to determine the appropriate steps to be taken. Samuel may well have a duty to disclose the evidence she has of the continuing legal violations and to resign as asset manager for Garcia.

Example 4 (Disclosing Possible Illegal Activity):

David Bradford manages money for a family-owned real estate development corporation. He also manages the individual portfolios of several of the family members and officers of the corporation, including the chief financial officer (CFO). Based on the financial records of the corporation and some questionable practices of the CFO that Bradford has observed, Bradford believes that the CFO is embezzling money from the corporation and putting it into his personal investment account.

> *Comment*: Bradford should check with his firm's compliance department or appropriate legal counsel to determine whether applicable securities regulations require reporting the CFO's financial records.

Example 5 (Accidental Disclosure of Confidential Information):

Lynn Moody is an investment officer at the Lester Trust Company (LTC). She has stewardship of a significant number of individually managed taxable accounts. In addition to receiving quarterly written reports, about a dozen high-net-worth individuals have indicated to Moody a willingness to receive communications about overall economic and financial market outlooks directly from her by way of a social media platform. Under the direction of her firm's technology and compliance departments, she established a new group page on an existing social media platform specifically for her clients. In the instructions provided to clients, Moody asked them to "join" the group so they may be granted access to the posted content. The instructions also advised clients that all comments posted would be available to the public and thus the platform was not an appropriate method for communicating personal or confidential information.

Six months later, in early January, Moody posted LTC's year-end "Market Outlook." The report outlined a new asset allocation strategy that the firm is adding to its recommendations in the new year. Moody introduced the publication with a note informing her clients that she would be discussing the changes with them individually in their upcoming meetings.

One of Moody's clients responded directly on the group page that his family recently experienced a major change in their financial profile. The client described highly personal and confidential details of the event. Unfortunately, all clients that were part of the group were also able to read the detailed posting until Moody was able to have the comment removed.

> *Comment*: Moody has taken reasonable steps for protecting the confidentiality of client information while using the social media platform. She provided instructions clarifying that all information posted to the site would be publically viewable to all group members and warned against using this method for communicating confidential information. The accidental disclosure of confidential information by a client is not under Moody's control. Her actions to remove the information promptly once she became aware further align with Standard III(E).
>
> In understanding the potential sensitivity clients express surrounding the confidentiality of personal information, this event highlights a need for further training. Moody might advocate for additional warnings or controls for clients when they consider using social media platforms for two-way communications.

STANDARD IV: DUTIES TO EMPLOYERS

Standard IV(A) Loyalty

> In matters related to their employment, Members and Candidates must act for the benefit of their employer and not deprive their employer of the advantage of their skills and abilities, divulge confidential information, or otherwise cause harm to their employer.

Guidance

Highlights:

- *Employer Responsibilities*
- *Independent Practice*
- *Leaving an Employer*
- *Use of Social Media*
- *Whistleblowing*
- *Nature of Employment*

Standard IV(A) requires members and candidates to protect the interests of their firm by refraining from any conduct that would injure the firm, deprive it of profit, or deprive it of the member's or candidate's skills and ability. Members and candidates must always place the interests of clients above the interests of their employer but should also consider the effects of their conduct on the sustainability and integrity of the employer firm. In matters related to their employment, members and candidates must not engage in conduct that harms the interests of their employer. Implicit in this standard is the obligation of members and candidates to comply with the policies and procedures established by their employers that govern the employer–employee relationship—to the extent that such policies and procedures do not conflict with applicable laws, rules, or regulations or the Code and Standards.

This standard is not meant to be a blanket requirement to place employer interests ahead of personal interests in all matters. The standard does not require members and candidates to subordinate important personal and family obligations to their work. Members and candidates should enter into a dialogue with their employer about balancing personal and employment obligations when personal matters may interfere with their work on a regular or significant basis.

Employer Responsibilities

The employer–employee relationship imposes duties and responsibilities on both parties. Employers must recognize the duties and responsibilities that they owe to their employees if they expect to have content and productive employees.

Members and candidates are encouraged to provide their employer with a copy of the Code and Standards. These materials will inform the employer of the responsibilities of a CFA Institute member or a candidate in the CFA Program. The Code and Standards also serve as a basis for questioning employer policies and practices that conflict with these responsibilities.

Employers are not obligated to adhere to the Code and Standards. In expecting to retain competent employees who are members and candidates, however, they should not develop conflicting policies and procedures. The employer is responsible for a positive working environment, which includes an ethical workplace. Senior management has the additional responsibility to devise compensation structures and incentive arrangements that do not encourage unethical behavior.

Independent Practice

Included in Standard IV(A) is the requirement that members and candidates abstain from independent competitive activity that could conflict with the interests of their employer. Although Standard IV(A) does not preclude members or candidates from entering into an independent business while still employed, members and candidates who plan to engage in independent practice for compensation must notify their employer and describe the types of services they will render to prospective independent clients, the expected duration of the services, and the compensation for the services. Members and candidates should not render services until they receive consent from their employer to all of the terms of the arrangement. "Practice" means any service that the employer currently makes available for remuneration. "Undertaking independent practice" means engaging in competitive business, as opposed to making preparations to begin such practice.

Leaving an Employer

When members and candidates are planning to leave their current employer, they must continue to act in the employer's best interest. They must not engage in any activities that would conflict with this duty until their resignation becomes effective. It is difficult to define specific guidelines for those members and candidates who are planning to compete with their employer as part of a new venture. The circumstances of each situation must be reviewed to distinguish permissible preparations from violations of duty. Activities that might constitute a violation, especially in combination, include the following:

- misappropriation of trade secrets,
- misuse of confidential information,
- solicitation of the employer's clients prior to cessation of employment,

- self-dealing (appropriating for one's own property a business opportunity or information belonging to one's employer), and
- misappropriation of clients or client lists.

A departing employee is generally free to make arrangements or preparations to go into a competitive business before terminating the relationship with his or her employer as long as such preparations do not breach the employee's duty of loyalty. A member or candidate who is contemplating seeking other employment must not contact existing clients or potential clients prior to leaving his or her employer for purposes of soliciting their business for the new employer. Once notice is provided to the employer of the intent to resign, the member or candidate must follow the employer's policies and procedures related to notifying clients of his or her planned departure. In addition, the member or candidate must not take records or files to a new employer without the written permission of the previous employer.

Once an employee has left the firm, the skills and experience that an employee obtained while employed are not "confidential" or "privileged" information. Similarly, simple knowledge of the names and existence of former clients is generally not confidential information unless deemed such by an agreement or by law. Standard IV(A) does not prohibit experience or knowledge gained at one employer from being used at another employer. Firm records or work performed on behalf of the firm that is stored in paper copy or electronically for the member's or candidate's convenience while employed, however, should be erased or returned to the employer unless the firm gives permission to keep those records after employment ends.

The standard does not prohibit former employees from contacting clients of their previous firm as long as the contact information does not come from the records of the former employer or violate an applicable "noncompete agreement." Members and candidates are free to use public information after departing to contact former clients without violating Standard IV(A) as long as there is no specific agreement not to do so.

Employers often require employees to sign noncompete agreements that preclude a departing employee from engaging in certain conduct. Members and candidates should take care to review the terms of any such agreement when leaving their employer to determine what, if any, conduct those agreements may prohibit.

In some markets, there are agreements between employers within an industry that outline information that departing employees are permitted to take upon resignation, such as the "Protocol for Broker Recruiting" in the United States. These agreements ease individuals' transition between firms that have agreed to follow the outlined procedures. Members and candidates who move between firms that sign such agreements may rely on the protections provided as long as they faithfully adhere to all the procedures outlined.

For example, under the agreement between many US brokers, individuals are allowed to take some general client contact information when departing. To be protected, a copy of the information the individual is taking must be provided to the local management team for review. Additionally, the specific client information may only be used by the departing employee and not others employed by the new firm.

Use of Social Media

The growth in various online networking platforms, such as LinkedIn, Twitter, and Facebook (commonly referred to as social media platforms), is providing new opportunities and challenges for businesses. Members and candidates should understand and abide by all applicable firm policies and regulations as to the acceptable use of social media platforms to interact with clients and prospective clients. This is especially important when a member or candidate is planning to leave an employer.

Social media use makes determining how and when departure notification is delivered to clients more complex. Members and candidates may have developed profiles on these platforms that include connections with individuals who are clients of the firm, as well as individuals unrelated to their employer. Communications through social media platforms that potentially reach current clients should adhere to the employer's policies and procedures regarding notification of departing employees.

Social media connections with clients are also raising questions concerning the differences between public information and firm property. Specific accounts and user profiles of members and candidates may be created for solely professional reasons, including firm-approved accounts for client engagements. Such firm-approved business-related accounts would be considered part of the firm's assets, thus requiring members and candidates to transfer or delete the accounts as directed by their firm's policies and procedures. Best practice for members and candidates is to maintain separate accounts for their personal and professional social media activities. Members and candidates should discuss with their employers how profiles should be treated when a single account includes personal connections and also is used to conduct aspects of their professional activities.

Whistleblowing

A member's or candidate's personal interests, as well as the interests of his or her employer, are secondary to protecting the integrity of capital markets and the interests of clients. Therefore, circumstances may arise (e.g., when an employer is engaged in illegal or unethical activity) in which members and candidates must act contrary to their employer's interests in order to comply with their duties to the market and clients. In such instances, activities that would normally violate a member's or candidate's duty to his or her employer (such as contradicting employer instructions, violating certain policies and procedures, or preserving a record by copying employer records) may be justified. Such action would be permitted only if the intent is clearly aimed at protecting clients or the integrity of the market, not for personal gain.

Nature of Employment

A wide variety of business relationships exists within the investment industry. For instance, a member or candidate may be an employee or an independent contractor. Members and candidates must determine whether they are employees or independent contractors in order to determine the applicability of Standard IV(A). This issue will be decided largely by the degree of control exercised by the employing entity over the member or candidate. Factors determining control include whether the member's or candidate's hours, work location, and other parameters of the job are set; whether facilities are provided to the member or candidate; whether the member's or candidate's expenses are reimbursed; whether the member or candidate seeks work from other employers; and the number of clients or employers the member or candidate works for.

A member's or candidate's duties within an independent contractor relationship are governed by the oral or written agreement between the member and the client. Members and candidates should take care to define clearly the scope of their responsibilities and the expectations of each client within the context of each relationship. Once a member or candidate establishes a relationship with a client, the member or candidate has a duty to abide by the terms of the agreement.

Recommended Procedures for Compliance

Employers may establish codes of conduct and operating procedures for their employees to follow. Members and candidates should fully understand the policies to ensure that they are not in conflict with the Code and Standards. The following topics identify policies that members and candidates should encourage their firms to adopt if the policies are not currently in place.

Competition Policy

A member or candidate must understand any restrictions placed by the employer on offering similar services outside the firm while employed by the firm. The policy may outline the procedures for requesting approval to undertake the outside service or may be a strict prohibition of such service. If a member's or candidate's employer elects to have its employees sign a noncompete agreement as part of the employment agreement, the member or candidate should ensure that the details are clear and fully explained prior to signing the agreement.

Termination Policy

Members and candidates should clearly understand the termination policies of their employer. Termination policies should establish clear procedures regarding the resignation process, including addressing how the termination will be disclosed to clients and staff and whether updates posted through social media platforms will be allowed. The firm's policy may also outline the procedures for transferring ongoing research and account management responsibilities. Finally, the procedures should address agreements that allow departing employees to remove specific client-related information upon resignation.

Incident-Reporting Procedures

Members and candidates should be aware of their firm's policies related to whistleblowing and encourage their firm to adopt industry best practices in this area. Many firms are required by regulatory mandates to establish confidential and anonymous reporting procedures that allow employees to report potentially unethical and illegal activities in the firm.

Employee Classification

Members and candidates should understand their status within their employer firm. Firms are encouraged to adopt a standardized classification structure (e.g., part time, full time, outside contractor) for their employees and indicate how each of the firm's policies applies to each employee class.

Application of the Standard

Example 1 (Soliciting Former Clients):

Samuel Magee manages pension accounts for Trust Assets, Inc., but has become frustrated with the working environment and has been offered a position with Fiduciary Management. Before resigning from Trust Assets, Magee asks four big accounts to leave that firm and open accounts with Fiduciary. Magee also persuades several prospective clients to sign agreements with Fiduciary Management. Magee had previously made presentations to these prospects on behalf of Trust Assets.

> *Comment*: Magee violated the employee–employer principle requiring him to act solely for his employer's benefit. Magee's duty is to Trust Assets as long as he is employed there. The solicitation of Trust Assets' current clients and prospective clients is unethical and violates Standard IV(A).

Example 2 (Former Employer's Documents and Files):

James Hightower has been employed by Jason Investment Management Corporation for 15 years. He began as an analyst but assumed increasing responsibilities and is now a senior portfolio manager and a member of the firm's investment policy committee. Hightower has decided to leave Jason Investment and start his own investment management business. He has been careful not to tell any of Jason's clients that he is leaving; he does not want to be accused of breaching his duty to Jason by soliciting Jason's clients before his departure. Hightower is planning to copy and take with him the following documents and information he developed or worked on while at Jason: (1) the client list, with addresses, telephone numbers, and other pertinent client information; (2) client account statements; (3) sample marketing presentations to prospective clients containing Jason's performance record; (4) Jason's recommended list of securities; (5) computer models to determine asset allocations for accounts with various objectives; (6) computer models for stock selection; and (7) personal computer spreadsheets for Hightower's major corporate recommendations, which he developed when he was an analyst.

> *Comment*: Except with the consent of their employer, departing members and candidates may not take employer property, which includes books, records, reports, and other materials, because taking such materials may interfere with their employer's business opportunities. Taking any employer records, even those the member or candidate prepared, violates Standard IV(A). Employer records include items stored in hard copy or any other medium (e.g., home computers, portable storage devices, cell phones).

Example 3 (Addressing Rumors):

Reuben Winston manages all-equity portfolios at Target Asset Management (TAM), a large, established investment counselor. Ten years previously, Philpott & Company, which manages a family of global bond mutual funds, acquired TAM in a diversification move. After the merger, the combined operations prospered in the fixed-income business but the equity management business at TAM languished. Lately, a few of the equity pension accounts that had been with TAM before the merger have terminated their relationships with TAM. One day, Winston finds on his voice mail the following message from a concerned client: "Hey! I just heard that Philpott is close to announcing the sale of your firm's equity management business to Rugged Life. What is going on?" Not being aware of any such deal, Winston and his associates are stunned. Their internal inquiries are met with denials from Philpott management, but the rumors persist. Feeling left in the dark, Winston contemplates leading an employee buyout of TAM's equity management business.

> *Comment*: An employee-led buyout of TAM's equity asset management business would be consistent with Standard IV(A) because it would rest on the permission of the employer and, ultimately, the clients. In this case, however, in which employees suspect the senior managers or principals are not truthful or forthcoming, Winston should consult legal counsel to determine appropriate action.

Example 4 (Ownership of Completed Prior Work):

Laura Clay, who is unemployed, wants part-time consulting work while seeking a full-time analyst position. During an interview at Bradley Associates, a large institutional asset manager, Clay is told that the firm has no immediate research openings but would be willing to pay her a flat fee to complete a study of the wireless communications industry within a given period of time. Clay would be allowed unlimited access to Bradley's research files and would be welcome to come to the offices and use whatever support facilities are available during normal working hours. Bradley's research director does not seek any exclusivity for Clay's output, and the two agree to the arrangement on a handshake. As Clay nears completion of the study, she is offered an analyst job in the research department of Winston & Company, a brokerage firm, and she is pondering submitting the draft of her wireless study for publication by Winston.

Comment: Although she is under no written contractual obligation to Bradley, Clay has an obligation to let Bradley act on the output of her study before Winston & Company or Clay uses the information to their advantage. That is, unless Bradley gives permission to Clay and waives its rights to her wireless report, Clay would be in violation of Standard IV(A) if she were to immediately recommend to Winston the same transactions recommended in the report to Bradley. Furthermore, Clay must not take from Bradley any research file material or other property that she may have used.

Example 5 (Ownership of Completed Prior Work):

Emma Madeline, a recent college graduate and a candidate in the CFA Program, spends her summer as an unpaid intern at Murdoch and Lowell. The senior managers at Murdoch are attempting to bring the firm into compliance with the GIPS standards, and Madeline is assigned to assist in its efforts. Two months into her internship, Madeline applies for a job at McMillan & Company, which has plans to become GIPS compliant. Madeline accepts the job with McMillan. Before leaving Murdoch, she copies the firm's software that she helped develop because she believes this software will assist her in her new position.

Comment: Even though Madeline does not receive monetary compensation for her services at Murdoch, she has used firm resources in creating the software and is considered an employee because she receives compensation and benefits in the form of work experience and knowledge. By copying the software, Madeline violated Standard IV(A) because she misappropriated Murdoch's property without permission.

Example 6 (Soliciting Former Clients):

Dennis Elliot has hired Sam Chisolm, who previously worked for a competing firm. Chisolm left his former firm after 18 years of employment. When Chisolm begins working for Elliot, he wants to contact his former clients because he knows them well and is certain that many will follow him to his new employer. Is Chisolm in violation of Standard IV(A) if he contacts his former clients?

Comment: Because client records are the property of the firm, contacting former clients for any reason through the use of client lists or other information taken from a former employer without permission would be a violation of Standard IV(A). In addition, the nature and extent of the contact with former clients may be governed by the terms of any noncompete agreement signed by the employee and the former employer that covers contact with former clients after employment.

Simple knowledge of the names and existence of former clients is not confidential information, just as skills or experience that an employee obtains while employed are not "confidential" or "privileged" information. The Code and Standards do not impose a prohibition on the use of experience or knowledge gained at one employer from being used at another employer. The Code and Standards also do not prohibit former employees from contacting clients of their previous firm, in the absence of a noncompete agreement. Members and candidates are free to use public information about their former firm after departing to contact former clients without violating Standard IV(A).

In the absence of a noncompete agreement, as long as Chisolm maintains his duty of loyalty to his employer before joining Elliot's firm, does not take steps to solicit clients until he has left his former firm, and does not use material from his former employer without its permission after he has left, he is not in violation of the Code and Standards.

Example 7 (Starting a New Firm):

Geraldine Allen currently works at a registered investment company as an equity analyst. Without notice to her employer, she registers with government authorities to start an investment company that will compete with her employer, but she does not actively seek clients. Does registration of this competing company with the appropriate regulatory authorities constitute a violation of Standard IV(A)?

Comment: Allen's preparation for the new business by registering with the regulatory authorities does not conflict with the work for her employer if the preparations have been done on Allen's own time outside the office and if Allen will not be soliciting clients for the business or otherwise operating the new company until she has left her current employer.

Example 8 (Competing with Current Employer):

Several employees are planning to depart their current employer within a few weeks and have been careful to not engage in any activities that would conflict with their duty to their current employer. They have just learned that one of their employer's clients has undertaken a request for proposal (RFP) to review and possibly hire a new investment consultant. The RFP has been sent to the employer and all of its competitors. The group believes that the new entity to be formed would be qualified to respond to the RFP and be eligible for the business. The RFP submission period is likely to conclude before the employees' resignations are effective. Is it permissible for the group of departing employees to respond to the RFP for their anticipated new firm?

Comment: A group of employees responding to an RFP that their employer is also responding to would lead to direct competition between the employees and the employer. Such conduct violates Standard IV(A) unless the group of employees receives permission from their employer as well as the entity sending out the RFP.

Example 9 (Externally Compensated Assignments):

Alfonso Mota is a research analyst with Tyson Investments. He works part time as a mayor for his hometown, a position for which he receives compensation. Must Mota seek permission from Tyson to serve as mayor?

Comment: If Mota's mayoral duties are so extensive and time-consuming that they might detract from his ability to fulfill his responsibilities at Tyson, he should discuss his outside activities with his employer and come to a mutual agreement regarding how to manage his personal commitments with his responsibilities to his employer.

Example 10 (Soliciting Former Clients):

After leaving her employer, Shawna McQuillen establishes her own money management business. While with her former employer, she did not sign a noncompete agreement that would have prevented her from soliciting former clients. Upon her departure, she does not take any of her client lists or contact information and she clears her personal computer of any employer records, including client contact information. She obtains the phone numbers of her former clients through public records and contacts them to solicit their business.

> *Comment*: McQuillen is not in violation of Standard IV(A) because she has not used information or records from her former employer and is not prevented by an agreement with her former employer from soliciting her former clients.

Example 11 (Whistleblowing Actions):

Meredith Rasmussen works on a buy-side trading desk and concentrates on in-house trades for a hedge fund subsidiary managed by a team at the investment management firm. The hedge fund has been very successful and is marketed globally by the firm. From her experience as the trader for much of the activity of the fund, Rasmussen has become quite knowledgeable about the hedge fund's strategy, tactics, and performance. When a distinct break in the market occurs, however, and many of the securities involved in the hedge fund's strategy decline markedly in value, Rasmussen observes that the reported performance of the hedge fund does not reflect this decline. In her experience, the lack of any effect is a very unlikely occurrence. She approaches the head of trading about her concern and is told that she should not ask any questions and that the fund is big and successful and is not her concern. She is fairly sure something is not right, so she contacts the compliance officer, who also tells her to stay away from the issue of this hedge fund's reporting.

> *Comment*: Rasmussen has clearly come upon an error in policies, procedures, and compliance practices in the firm's operations. Having been unsuccessful in finding a resolution with her supervisor and the compliance officer, Rasmussen should consult the firm's whistleblowing policy to determine the appropriate next step toward informing management of her concerns. The potentially unethical actions of the investment management division are appropriate grounds for further disclosure, so Rasmussen's whistleblowing would not represent a violation of Standard IV(A).
>
> See also Standard I(D)–Misconduct and Standard IV(C)–Responsibilities of Supervisors.

Example 12 (Soliciting Former Clients):

Angel Crome has been a private banker for YBSafe Bank for the past eight years. She has been very successful and built a considerable client portfolio during that time but is extremely frustrated by the recent loss of reputation by her current employer and subsequent client insecurity. A locally renowned headhunter contacted Crome a few days ago and offered her an interesting job with a competing private bank. This bank offers a substantial signing bonus for advisers with their own client portfolios. Crome figures that she can solicit at least 70% of her clients to follow her and gladly enters into the new employment contract.

> *Comment*: Crome may contact former clients upon termination of her employment with YBSafe Bank, but she is prohibited from using client records built by and kept with her in her capacity as an employee of YBSafe Bank. Client lists are proprietary information of her former employer and must not be used for her or her new employer's benefit. The use of written, electronic, or any other form of records other than publicly available information to contact her former clients at YBSafe Bank will be a violation of Standard IV(A).

Example 13 (Notification of Code and Standards):

Krista Smith is a relatively new assistant trader for the fixed-income desk of a major investment bank. She is on a team responsible for structuring collateralized debt obligations (CDOs) made up of securities in the inventory of the trading desk. At a meeting of the team, senior executives explain the opportunity to eventually separate the CDO into various risk-rated tranches to be sold to the clients of the firm. After the senior executives leave the meeting, the head trader announces various responsibilities of each member of the team and then says, "This is a good time to unload some of the junk we have been stuck with for a while and disguise it with ratings and a thick, unreadable prospectus, so don't be shy in putting this CDO together. Just kidding." Smith is worried by this remark and asks some of her colleagues what the head trader meant. They all respond that he was just kidding but that there is some truth in the remark because the CDO is seen by management as an opportunity to improve the quality of the securities in the firm's inventory.

Concerned about the ethical environment of the workplace, Smith decides to talk to her supervisor about her concerns and provides the head trader with a copy of the Code and Standards. Smith discusses the principle of placing the client above the interest of the firm and the possibility that the development of the new CDO will not adhere to this responsibility. The head trader assures Smith that the appropriate analysis will be conducted when determining the appropriate securities for collateral. Furthermore, the ratings are assigned by an independent firm and the prospectus will include full and factual disclosures. Smith is reassured by the meeting, but she also reviews the company's procedures and requirements for reporting potential violations of company policy and securities laws.

> *Comment*: Smith's review of the company policies and procedures for reporting violations allows her to be prepared to report through the appropriate whistleblower process if she decides that the CDO development process involves unethical actions by others. Smith's actions comply with the Code and Standards principles of placing the client's interests first and being loyal to her employer. In providing her supervisor with a copy of the Code and Standards, Smith is highlighting the high level of ethical conduct she is required to adhere to in her professional activities.

Example 14 (Leaving an Employer):

Laura Webb just left her position as portfolio analyst at Research Systems, Inc. (RSI). Her employment contract included a non-solicitation agreement that requires her to wait two years before soliciting RSI clients for any investment-related services. Upon leaving, Webb was informed that RSI would contact clients immediately about her departure and introduce her replacement.

While working at RSI, Webb connected with clients, other industry associates, and friends through her LinkedIn network. Her business and personal relationships were intermingled because she considered many of her clients to be personal friends. Realizing that her LinkedIn network would be a valuable resource for new employment opportunities, she updated her profile several days following her departure from RSI. LinkedIn automatically sent a notification to Webb's entire network that her employment status had been changed in her profile.

> *Comment*: Prior to her departure, Webb should have discussed any client information contained in her social media networks. By updating her LinkedIn profile after RSI notified clients and after her employment ended, she has appropriately placed her employer's interests ahead of her own personal interests. In addition, she has not violated the non-solicitation agreement with RSI, unless it prohibited any contact with clients during the two-year period.

Example 15 (Confidential Firm Information):

Sanjay Gupta is a research analyst at Naram Investment Management (NIM). NIM uses a team-based research process to develop recommendations on investment opportunities covered by the team members. Gupta, like others, provides commentary for NIM's clients through the company blog, which is posted weekly on the NIM password-protected website. According to NIM's policy, every contribution to the website must be approved by the company's compliance department before posting. Any opinions expressed on the website are disclosed as representing the perspective of NIM.

Gupta also writes a personal blog to share his experiences with friends and family. As with most blogs, Gupta's personal blog is widely available to interested readers through various internet search engines. Occasionally, when he disagrees with the team-based research opinions of NIM, Gupta uses his personal blog to express his own opinions as a counterpoint to the commentary posted on the NIM website. Gupta believes this provides his readers with a more complete perspective on these investment opportunities.

> *Comment*: Gupta is in violation of Standard IV(A) for disclosing confidential firm information through his personal blog. The recommendations on the firm's blog to clients are not freely available across the internet, but his personal blog post indirectly provides the firm's recommendations.
>
> Additionally, by posting research commentary on his personal blog, Gupta is using firm resources for his personal advantage. To comply with Standard IV(A), members and candidates must receive consent from their employer prior to using company resources.

Standard IV(B) Additional Compensation Arrangements

> Members and Candidates must not accept gifts, benefits, compensation, or consideration that competes with or might reasonably be expected to create a conflict of interest with their employer's interest unless they obtain written consent from all parties involved.

Guidance

Standard IV(B) requires members and candidates to obtain permission from their employer before accepting compensation or other benefits from third parties for the services rendered to the employer or for any services that might create a conflict with their employer's interest. Compensation and benefits include direct compensation by the client and any indirect compensation or other benefits received from third parties. "Written consent" includes any form of communication that can be documented (for example, communication via e-mail that can be retrieved and documented).

Members and candidates must obtain permission for additional compensation/benefits because such arrangements may affect loyalties and objectivity and create potential conflicts of interest. Disclosure allows an employer to consider the outside arrangements when evaluating the actions and motivations of members and candidates. Moreover, the employer is entitled to have full knowledge of all compensation/benefit arrangements so as to be able to assess the true cost of the services members or candidates are providing.

There may be instances in which a member or candidate is hired by an employer on a "part-time" basis. "Part-time" status applies to employees who do not commit the full number of hours required for a normal work week. Members and candidates should discuss possible limitations to their abilities to provide services that may be competitive with their employer during the negotiation and hiring process. The requirements of Standard IV(B) would be applicable to limitations identified at that time.

Recommended Procedures for Compliance

Members and candidates should make an immediate written report to their supervisor and compliance officer specifying any compensation they propose to receive for services in addition to the compensation or benefits received from their employer. The details of the report should be confirmed by the party offering the additional compensation, including performance incentives offered by clients. This written report should state the terms of any agreement under which a member or candidate will receive additional compensation; "terms" include the nature of the compensation, the approximate amount of compensation, and the duration of the agreement.

Application of the Standard

Example 1 (Notification of Client Bonus Compensation):

Geoff Whitman, a portfolio analyst for Adams Trust Company, manages the account of Carol Cochran, a client. Whitman is paid a salary by his employer, and Cochran pays the trust company a standard fee based on the market value of assets in her portfolio. Cochran proposes to Whitman that "any year that my portfolio achieves at least a 15% return before taxes, you and your wife can fly to Monaco at my expense and use my condominium during the third week of January." Whitman does not inform his employer of the arrangement and vacations in Monaco the following January as Cochran's guest.

> *Comment*: Whitman violated Standard IV(B) by failing to inform his employer in writing of this supplemental, contingent compensation arrangement. The nature of the arrangement could have resulted in partiality to Cochran's account, which could have detracted from Whitman's performance with respect to other accounts he handles for Adams Trust. Whitman must obtain the consent of his employer to accept such a supplemental benefit.

Example 2 (Notification of Outside Compensation):

Terry Jones sits on the board of directors of Exercise Unlimited, Inc. In return for his services on the board, Jones receives unlimited membership privileges for his family at all Exercise Unlimited facilities. Jones purchases Exercise Unlimited stock for the client accounts for which it is appropriate. Jones does not disclose this arrangement to his employer because he does not receive monetary compensation for his services to the board.

> *Comment*: Jones has violated Standard IV(B) by failing to disclose to his employer benefits received in exchange for his services on the board of directors. The nonmonetary compensation may create a conflict of interest in the same manner as being paid to serve as a director.

Example 3 (Prior Approval for Outside Compensation):

Jonathan Hollis is an analyst of oil-and-gas companies for Specialty Investment Management. He is currently recommending the purchase of ABC Oil Company shares and has published a long, well-thought-out research report to substantiate his recommendation. Several weeks after publishing the report, Hollis receives a call from the investor-relations office of ABC Oil saying that Thomas Andrews, CEO of the company, saw the report and really liked the analyst's grasp of the business and his company. The investor-relations officer invites Hollis to visit ABC Oil to discuss the industry further. ABC Oil offers to send a company plane to pick Hollis up and arrange for his accommodations while visiting. Hollis, after gaining the appropriate approvals, accepts the meeting with the CEO but declines the offered travel arrangements.

Several weeks later, Andrews and Hollis meet to discuss the oil business and Hollis's report. Following the meeting, Hollis joins Andrews and the investment relations officer for dinner at an upscale restaurant near ABC Oil's headquarters.

Upon returning to Specialty Investment Management, Hollis provides a full review of the meeting to the director of research, including a disclosure of the dinner attended.

> *Comment*: Hollis's actions did not violate Standard IV(B). Through gaining approval before accepting the meeting and declining the offered travel arrangements, Hollis sought to avoid any potential conflicts of interest between his company and ABC Oil. Because the location of the dinner was not available prior to arrival and Hollis notified his company of the dinner upon his return, accepting the dinner should not impair his objectivity. By disclosing the dinner, Hollis has enabled Specialty Investment Management to assess whether it has any impact on future reports and recommendations by Hollis related to ABC Oil.

Standard IV(C) Responsibilities of Supervisors

> Members and Candidates must make reasonable efforts to ensure that anyone subject to their supervision or authority complies with applicable laws, rules, regulations, and the Code and Standards.

Guidance

Highlights:

- *System for Supervision*
- *Supervision Includes Detection*

Standard IV(C) states that members and candidates must promote actions by all employees under their supervision and authority to comply with applicable laws, rules, regulations, and firm policies and the Code and Standards.

Any investment professional who has employees subject to her or his control or influence—whether or not the employees are CFA Institute members, CFA charterholders, or candidates in the CFA Program—exercises supervisory responsibility. Members and candidates acting as supervisors must also have in-depth knowledge of the Code and Standards so that they can apply this knowledge in discharging their supervisory responsibilities.

The conduct that constitutes reasonable supervision in a particular case depends on the number of employees supervised and the work performed by those employees. Members and candidates with oversight responsibilities for large numbers of employees may not be able to personally evaluate the conduct of these employees on a continuing basis. These members and candidates may delegate supervisory duties to subordinates who directly oversee the other employees. A member's or candidate's responsibilities under Standard IV(C) include instructing those subordinates to whom supervision is delegated about methods to promote compliance, including preventing and detecting violations of laws, rules, regulations, firm policies, and the Code and Standards.

At a minimum, Standard IV(C) requires that members and candidates with supervisory responsibility make reasonable efforts to prevent and detect violations by ensuring the establishment of effective compliance systems. However, an effective compliance system goes beyond enacting a code of ethics, establishing policies and procedures to achieve compliance with the code and applicable law, and reviewing employee actions to determine whether they are following the rules.

To be effective supervisors, members and candidates should implement education and training programs on a recurring or regular basis for employees under their supervision. Such programs will assist the employees with meeting their professional obligations to practice in an ethical manner within the applicable legal system. Further, establishing incentives—monetary or otherwise—for employees not only to meet business goals but also to reward ethical behavior offers supervisors another way to assist employees in complying with their legal and ethical obligations.

Often, especially in large organizations, members and candidates may have supervisory responsibility but not the authority to establish or modify firm-wide compliance policies and procedures or incentive structures. Such limitations should not prevent a member or candidate from working with his or her own superiors and within the firm structure to develop and implement effective compliance tools, including but not limited to:

- a code of ethics,
- compliance policies and procedures,
- education and training programs,
- an incentive structure that rewards ethical conduct, and
- adoption of firm-wide best practice standards (e.g., the GIPS standards, the CFA Institute Asset Manager Code of Professional Conduct).

A member or candidate with supervisory responsibility should bring an inadequate compliance system to the attention of the firm's senior managers and recommend corrective action. If the member or candidate clearly cannot discharge supervisory responsibilities because of the absence of a compliance system or because of an inadequate compliance system, the member or candidate should decline in writing to accept supervisory responsibility until the firm adopts reasonable procedures to allow adequate exercise of supervisory responsibility.

System for Supervision

Members and candidates with supervisory responsibility must understand what constitutes an adequate compliance system for their firms and make reasonable efforts to see that appropriate compliance procedures are established, documented, communicated to covered personnel, and followed. "Adequate" procedures are those designed to meet industry standards, regulatory requirements, the requirements of the Code and Standards, and the circumstances of the firm. Once compliance procedures are established, the supervisor must also make reasonable efforts to ensure that the procedures are monitored and enforced.

To be effective, compliance procedures must be in place prior to the occurrence of a violation of the law or the Code and Standards. Although compliance procedures cannot be designed to anticipate every potential violation, they should be designed to anticipate the activities most likely to result in misconduct. Compliance programs must be appropriate for the size and nature of the organization. The member or candidate should review model compliance procedures or other industry programs to ensure that the firm's procedures meet the minimum industry standards.

Once a supervisor learns that an employee has violated or may have violated the law or the Code and Standards, the supervisor must promptly initiate an assessment to determine the extent of the wrongdoing. Relying on an employee's statements about the extent of the violation or assurances that the wrongdoing will not reoccur is not enough. Reporting the misconduct up the chain of command and warning the employee to cease the activity are also not enough. Pending the outcome of the investigation, a supervisor should take steps to ensure that the violation will not be repeated, such as placing limits on the employee's activities or increasing the monitoring of the employee's activities.

Supervision Includes Detection

Members and candidates with supervisory responsibility must also make reasonable efforts to detect violations of laws, rules, regulations, firm policies, and the Code and Standards. The supervisors exercise reasonable supervision by establishing and implementing written compliance procedures and ensuring that those procedures are followed through periodic review. If a member or candidate has adopted reasonable procedures and taken steps to institute an effective compliance program, then the member or candidate may not be in violation of Standard IV(C) if he or she does not detect violations that occur despite these efforts. The fact that violations do occur may indicate, however, that the compliance procedures are inadequate. In addition, in some cases, merely enacting such procedures may not be sufficient to fulfill the duty required by Standard IV(C). A member or candidate may be in violation of Standard IV(C) if he or she knows or should know that the procedures designed to promote compliance, including detecting and preventing violations, are not being followed.

Recommended Procedures for Compliance

Codes of Ethics or Compliance Procedures

Members and candidates are encouraged to recommend that their employers adopt a code of ethics. Adoption of a code of ethics is critical to establishing a strong ethical foundation for investment advisory firms and their employees. Codes of ethics formally emphasize and reinforce the client loyalty responsibilities of investment firm personnel, protect investing clients by deterring misconduct, and protect the firm's reputation for integrity.

There is a distinction, however, between codes of ethics and the specific policies and procedures needed to ensure compliance with the codes and with securities laws and regulations. Although both are important, codes of ethics should consist of fundamental, principle-based ethical and fiduciary concepts that are applicable to all of the firm's employees. In this way, firms can best convey to employees and clients the ethical ideals that investment advisers strive to achieve. These concepts need to be implemented, however, by detailed, firm-wide compliance policies and procedures. Compliance procedures assist the firm's personnel in fulfilling the responsibilities enumerated in the code of ethics and make probable that the ideals expressed in the code of ethics will be adhered to in the day-to-day operation of the firm.

Stand-alone codes of ethics should be written in plain language and should address general fiduciary concepts. They should be unencumbered by numerous detailed procedures. Codes presented in this way are the most effective in stressing to employees that they are in positions of trust and must act with integrity at all times. Mingling compliance procedures in the firm's code of ethics goes against the goal of reinforcing the ethical obligations of employees.

Separating the code of ethics from compliance procedures will also reduce, if not eliminate, the legal terminology and "boilerplate" language that can make the underlying ethical principles incomprehensible to the average person. Above all, to ensure the creation of a culture of ethics and integrity rather than one that merely focuses on following the rules, the principles in the code of ethics must be stated in a way that is accessible and understandable to everyone in the firm.

Members and candidates should encourage their employers to provide their codes of ethics to clients. In this case also, a simple, straightforward code of ethics will be best understood by clients. Unencumbered by the compliance procedures, the code of ethics will be effective in conveying that the firm is committed to conducting business in an ethical manner and in the best interests of the clients.

Adequate Compliance Procedures

A supervisor complies with Standard IV(C) by identifying situations in which legal violations or violations of the Code and Standards are likely to occur and by establishing and enforcing compliance procedures to prevent such violations. Adequate compliance procedures should

- be contained in a clearly written and accessible manual that is tailored to the firm's operations,
- be drafted so that the procedures are easy to understand,
- designate a compliance officer whose authority and responsibility are clearly defined and who has the necessary resources and authority to implement the firm's compliance procedures,
- describe the hierarchy of supervision and assign duties among supervisors,
- implement a system of checks and balances,
- outline the scope of the procedures,
- outline procedures to document the monitoring and testing of compliance procedures,
- outline permissible conduct, and
- delineate procedures for reporting violations and sanctions.

Once a compliance program is in place, a supervisor should

- disseminate the contents of the program to appropriate personnel,
- periodically update procedures to ensure that the measures are adequate under the law,
- continually educate personnel regarding the compliance procedures,
- issue periodic reminders of the procedures to appropriate personnel,
- incorporate a professional conduct evaluation as part of an employee's performance review,
- review the actions of employees to ensure compliance and identify violators, and
- take the necessary steps to enforce the procedures once a violation has occurred.

Once a violation is discovered, a supervisor should

- respond promptly,

- conduct a thorough investigation of the activities to determine the scope of the wrongdoing,
- increase supervision or place appropriate limitations on the wrongdoer pending the outcome of the investigation, and
- review procedures for potential changes necessary to prevent future violations from occurring.

Implementation of Compliance Education and Training

No amount of ethics education and awareness will deter someone determined to commit fraud for personal enrichment. But the vast majority of investment professionals strive to achieve personal success with dedicated service to their clients and employers.

Regular ethics and compliance training, in conjunction with adoption of a code of ethics, is critical to investment firms seeking to establish a strong culture of integrity and to provide an environment in which employees routinely engage in ethical conduct in compliance with the law. Training and education assist individuals in both recognizing areas that are prone to ethical and legal pitfalls and identifying those circumstances and influences that can impair ethical judgment.

By implementing educational programs, supervisors can train their subordinates to put into practice what the firm's code of ethics requires. Education helps employees make the link between legal and ethical conduct and the long-term success of the business; a strong culture of compliance signals to clients and potential clients that the firm has truly embraced ethical conduct as fundamental to the firm's mission to serve its clients.

Establish an Appropriate Incentive Structure

Even if individuals want to make the right choices and follow an ethical course of conduct and are aware of the obstacles that may trip them up, they can still be influenced to act improperly by a corporate culture that embraces a "succeed at all costs" mentality, stresses results regardless of the methods used to achieve those results, and does not reward ethical behavior. Supervisors can reinforce an individual's natural desire to "do the right thing" by building a culture of integrity in the workplace.

Supervisors and firms must look closely at their incentive structure to determine whether the structure encourages profits and returns at the expense of ethically appropriate conduct. Reward structures may turn a blind eye to how desired outcomes are achieved and encourage dysfunctional or counterproductive behavior. Only when compensation and incentives are firmly tied to client interests and *how* outcomes are achieved, rather than *how much* is generated for the firm, will employees work to achieve a culture of integrity.

Application of the Standard

Example 1 (Supervising Research Activities):

Jane Mattock, senior vice president and head of the research department of H&V, Inc., a regional brokerage firm, has decided to change her recommendation for Timber Products from buy to sell. In line with H&V's procedures, she orally advises certain other H&V executives of her proposed actions before the report is prepared for publication. As a result of Mattock's conversation with Dieter Frampton, one of the H&V executives accountable to Mattock, Frampton immediately sells Timber's stock from his own account and from certain discretionary client accounts. In addition, other personnel inform certain institutional customers of the changed recommendation before it is printed and disseminated to all H&V customers who have received previous Timber reports.

Comment: Mattock has violated Standard IV(C) by failing to reasonably and adequately supervise the actions of those accountable to her. She did not prevent or establish reasonable procedures designed to prevent dissemination of or trading on the information by those who knew of her changed recommendation. She must ensure that her firm has procedures for reviewing or recording any trading in the stock of a corporation that has been the subject of an unpublished change in recommendation. Adequate procedures would have informed the subordinates of their duties and detected sales by Frampton and selected customers.

Example 2 (Supervising Research Activities):

Deion Miller is the research director for Jamestown Investment Programs. The portfolio managers have become critical of Miller and his staff because the Jamestown portfolios do not include any stock that has been the subject of a merger or tender offer. Georgia Ginn, a member of Miller's staff, tells Miller that she has been studying a local company, Excelsior, Inc., and recommends its purchase. Ginn adds that the company has been widely rumored to be the subject of a merger study by a well-known conglomerate and discussions between them are under way. At Miller's request, Ginn prepares a memo recommending the stock. Miller passes along Ginn's memo to the portfolio managers prior to leaving for vacation, and he notes that he has not reviewed the memo. As a result of the memo, the portfolio managers buy Excelsior stock immediately. The day Miller returns to the office, he learns that Ginn's only sources for the report were her brother, who is an acquisitions analyst with Acme Industries, the "well-known conglomerate," and that the merger discussions were planned but not held.

Comment: Miller violated Standard IV(C) by not exercising reasonable supervision when he disseminated the memo without checking to ensure that Ginn had a reasonable and adequate basis for her recommendations and that Ginn was not relying on material nonpublic information.

Example 3 (Supervising Trading Activities):

David Edwards, a trainee trader at Wheeler & Company, a major national brokerage firm, assists a customer in paying for the securities of Highland, Inc., by using anticipated profits from the immediate sale of the same securities. Despite the fact that Highland is not on Wheeler's recommended list, a large volume of its stock is traded through Wheeler in this manner. Roberta Ann Mason is a Wheeler vice president responsible for supervising compliance with the securities laws in the trading department. Part of her compensation from Wheeler is based on commission revenues from the trading department. Although she notices the increased trading activity, she does nothing to investigate or halt it.

Comment: Mason's failure to adequately review and investigate purchase orders in Highland stock executed by Edwards and her failure to supervise the trainee's activities violate Standard IV(C). Supervisors should be especially sensitive to actual or potential conflicts between their own self-interests and their supervisory responsibilities.

Example 4 (Supervising Trading Activities and Record Keeping):

Samantha Tabbing is senior vice president and portfolio manager for Crozet, Inc., a registered investment advisory and registered broker/dealer firm. She reports to Charles Henry, the president of Crozet. Crozet serves as the investment adviser and principal underwriter for ABC and XYZ public mutual funds. The two funds' prospectuses allow Crozet to trade financial futures for the funds for the limited purpose of hedging against market risks. Henry, extremely impressed by Tabbing's performance in the past two years, directs Tabbing to act as portfolio manager for the funds. For the benefit of its employees, Crozet has also organized the Crozet Employee Profit-Sharing Plan (CEPSP), a defined contribution retirement plan. Henry assigns Tabbing to manage 20% of the assets of CEPSP. Tabbing's investment objective for her portion of CEPSP's assets is aggressive growth. Unbeknownst to Henry, Tabbing frequently places S&P 500 Index purchase and sale orders for the funds and the CEPSP without providing the futures commission merchants (FCMs) who take the orders with any prior or simultaneous designation of the account for which the trade has been placed. Frequently, neither Tabbing nor anyone else at Crozet completes an internal trade ticket to record the time an order was placed or the specific account for which the order was intended. FCMs often designate a specific account only after the trade, when Tabbing provides such designation. Crozet has no written operating procedures or compliance manual concerning its futures trading, and its compliance department does not review such trading. After observing the market's movement, Tabbing assigns to CEPSP the S&P 500 positions with more favorable execution prices and assigns positions with less favorable execution prices to the funds.

Comment: Henry violated Standard IV(C) by failing to adequately supervise Tabbing with respect to her S&P 500 trading. Henry further violated Standard IV(C) by failing to establish record-keeping and reporting procedures to prevent or detect Tabbing's violations. Henry must make a reasonable effort to determine that adequate compliance procedures covering all employee trading activity are established, documented, communicated, and followed.

Example 5 (Accepting Responsibility):

Meredith Rasmussen works on a buy-side trading desk and concentrates on in-house trades for a hedge fund subsidiary managed by a team at the investment management firm. The hedge fund has been very successful and is marketed globally by the firm. From her experience as the trader for much of the activity of the fund, Rasmussen has become quite knowledgeable about the hedge fund's strategy, tactics, and performance. When a distinct break in the market occurs and many of the securities involved in the hedge fund's strategy decline markedly in value, however, Rasmussen observes that the reported performance of the hedge fund does not at all reflect this decline. From her experience, this lack of an effect is a very unlikely occurrence. She approaches the head of trading about her concern and is told that she should not ask any questions and that the fund is too big and successful and is not her concern. She is fairly sure something is not right, so she contacts the compliance officer and is again told to stay away from the hedge fund reporting issue.

Comment: Rasmussen has clearly come upon an error in policies, procedures, and compliance practices within the firm's operations. According to Standard IV(C), the supervisor and the compliance officer have the responsibility to review the concerns brought forth by Rasmussen. Supervisors have the responsibility of establishing and encouraging an ethical culture in the firm. The dismissal of Rasmussen's question violates Standard IV(C) and undermines the firm's ethical operations.

See also Standard I(D)–Misconduct and, for guidance on whistleblowing, Standard IV(A)–Loyalty.

Example 6 (Inadequate Procedures):

Brendan Witt, a former junior sell-side technology analyst, decided to return to school to earn an MBA. To keep his research skills and industry knowledge sharp, Witt accepted a position with On-line and Informed, an independent internet-based research company. The position requires the publication of a recommendation and report on a different company every month. Initially, Witt is a regular contributor of new research and a participant in the associated discussion boards that generally have positive comments on the technology sector. Over time, his ability to manage his educational requirements and his work requirements begin to conflict with one another. Knowing a recommendation is due the next day for On-line, Witt creates a report based on a few news articles and what the conventional wisdom of the markets has deemed the "hot" security of the day.

Comment: Allowing the report submitted by Witt to be posted highlights a lack of compliance procedures by the research firm. Witt's supervisor needs to work with the management of On-line to develop an appropriate review process to ensure that all contracted analysts comply with the requirements.

See also Standard V(A)–Diligence and Reasonable Basis because it relates to Witt's responsibility for substantiating a recommendation.

Example 7 (Inadequate Supervision):

Michael Papis is the chief investment officer of his state's retirement fund. The fund has always used outside advisers for the real estate allocation, and this information is clearly presented in all fund communications. Thomas Nagle, a recognized sell-side research analyst and Papis's business school classmate, recently left the investment bank he worked for to start his own asset management firm, Accessible Real Estate. Nagle is trying to build his assets under management and contacts Papis about gaining some of the retirement fund's allocation. In the previous few years, the performance of the retirement fund's real estate investments was in line with the fund's benchmark but was not extraordinary. Papis decides to help out his old friend and also to seek better returns by moving the real estate allocation to Accessible. The only notice of the change in adviser appears in the next annual report in the listing of associated advisers.

Comment: Papis's actions highlight the need for supervision and review at all levels in an organization. His responsibilities may include the selection of external advisers, but the decision to change advisers appears arbitrary. Members and candidates should ensure that their firm has appropriate policies and procedures in place to detect inappropriate actions, such as the action taken by Papis.

See also Standard V(A)–Diligence and Reasonable Basis, Standard V(B)–Communication with Clients and Prospective Clients, and Standard VI(A)–Disclosure of Conflicts.

Example 8 (Supervising Research Activities):

Mary Burdette was recently hired by Fundamental Investment Management (FIM) as a junior auto industry analyst. Burdette is expected to expand the social media presence of the firm because she is active with various networks, including Facebook, LinkedIn, and Twitter. Although Burdette's supervisor, Joe Graf, has never used social media, he encourages Burdette to explore opportunities to increase FIM's online presence and ability to share content, communicate, and broadcast information to clients. In response to Graf's encouragement, Burdette is working on a proposal detailing the advantages of getting FIM onto Twitter in addition to launching a company Facebook page.

As part of her auto industry research for FIM, Burdette is completing a report on the financial impact of Sun Drive Auto Ltd.'s new solar technology for compact automobiles. This research report will be her first for FIM, and she believes Sun Drive's technology could revolutionize the auto industry. In her excitement, Burdette sends a quick tweet to FIM Twitter followers summarizing her "buy" recommendation for Sun Drive Auto stock.

> *Comment*: Graf has violated Standard IV(C) by failing to reasonably supervise Burdette with respect to the contents of her tweet. He did not establish reasonable procedures to prevent the unauthorized dissemination of company research through social media networks. Graf must make sure all employees receive regular training about FIM's policies and procedures, including the appropriate business use of personal social media networks.
>
> See Standard III(B) for additional guidance.

Example 9 (Supervising Research Activities):

Chen Wang leads the research department at YYRA Retirement Planning Specialists. Chen supervises a team of 10 analysts in a fast-paced and understaffed organization. He is responsible for coordinating the firm's approved process to review all reports before they are provided to the portfolio management team for use in rebalancing client portfolios.

One of Chen's direct reports, Huang Mei, covers the banking industry. Chen must submit the latest updates to the portfolio management team tomorrow morning. Huang has yet to submit her research report on ZYX Bank because she is uncomfortable providing a "buy" or "sell" opinion of ZYX on the basis of the completed analysis. Pressed for time and concerned that Chen will reject a "hold" recommendation, she researches various websites and blogs on the banking sector for whatever she can find on ZYX. One independent blogger provides a new interpretation of the recently reported data Huang has analyzed and concludes with a strong "sell" recommendation for ZYX. She is impressed by the originality and resourcefulness of this blogger's report.

Very late in the evening, Huang submits her report and "sell" recommendation to Chen without any reference to the independent blogger's report. Given the late time of the submission and the competence of Huang's prior work, Chen compiles this report with the recommendations from each of the other analysts and meets with the portfolio managers to discuss implementation.

> *Comment*: Chen has violated Standard IV(C) by neglecting to reasonably and adequately follow the firm's approved review process for Huang's research report. The delayed submission and the quality of prior work do not remove Chen's requirement to uphold the designated review process. A member or candidate with supervisory responsibility must make reasonable efforts to see that appropriate procedures are established, documented, communicated to covered personnel, and followed.

STANDARD V: INVESTMENT ANALYSIS, RECOMMENDATIONS, AND ACTIONS

Standard V(A) Diligence and Reasonable Basis

Members and Candidates must:

1 Exercise diligence, independence, and thoroughness in analyzing investments, making investment recommendations, and taking investment actions.

2 Have a reasonable and adequate basis, supported by appropriate research and investigation, for any investment analysis, recommendation, or action.

Guidance

Highlights:

- *Defining Diligence and Reasonable Basis*
- *Using Secondary or Third-Party Research*
- *Using Quantitatively Oriented Research*
- *Developing Quantitatively Oriented Techniques*
- *Selecting External Advisers and Subadvisers*
- *Group Research and Decision Making*

The application of Standard V(A) depends on the investment philosophy the member, candidate, or firm is following, the role of the member or candidate in the investment decision-making process, and the support and resources provided by the member's or candidate's employer. These factors will dictate the nature of the diligence and thoroughness of the research and the level of investigation required by Standard V(A).

The requirements for issuing conclusions based on research will vary in relation to the member's or candidate's role in the investment decision-making process, but the member or candidate must make reasonable efforts to cover all pertinent issues when arriving at a recommendation. Members and candidates enhance transparency by providing or offering to provide supporting information to clients when recommending a purchase or sale or when changing a recommendation.

Defining Diligence and Reasonable Basis

Every investment decision is based on a set of facts known and understood at the time. Clients turn to members and candidates for advice and expect these advisers to have more information and knowledge than they do. This information and knowledge is the basis from which members and candidates apply their professional judgment in taking investment actions and making recommendations.

At a basic level, clients want assurance that members and candidates are putting forth the necessary effort to support the recommendations they are making. Communicating the level and thoroughness of the information reviewed before the member or candidate makes a judgment allows clients to understand the reasonableness of the recommended investment actions.

As with determining the suitability of an investment for the client, the necessary level of research and analysis will differ with the product, security, or service being offered. In providing an investment service, members and candidates typically use a variety of resources, including company reports, third-party research, and results from quantitative models. A reasonable basis is formed through a balance of these resources appropriate for the security or decision being analyzed.

The following list provides some, but definitely not all, examples of attributes to consider while forming the basis for a recommendation:

- global, regional, and country macroeconomic conditions,
- a company's operating and financial history,
- the industry's and sector's current conditions and the stage of the business cycle,
- a mutual fund's fee structure and management history,
- the output and potential limitations of quantitative models,
- the quality of the assets included in a securitization, and
- the appropriateness of selected peer-group comparisons.

Even though an investment recommendation may be well informed, downside risk remains for any investment. Members and candidates can base their decisions only on the information available at the time decisions are made. The steps taken in developing a diligent and reasonable recommendation should minimize unexpected downside events.

Using Secondary or Third-Party Research

If members and candidates rely on secondary or third-party research, they must make reasonable and diligent efforts to determine whether such research is sound. Secondary research is defined as research conducted by someone else in the member's or candidate's firm. Third-party research is research conducted by entities outside the member's or candidate's firm, such as a brokerage firm, bank, or research firm. If a member or candidate has reason to suspect that either secondary or third-party research or information comes from a source that lacks a sound basis, the member or candidate must not rely on that information.

Members and candidates should make reasonable enquiries into the source and accuracy of all data used in completing their investment analysis and recommendations. The sources of the information and data will influence the level of the review a member or candidate must undertake. Information and data taken from internet sources, such as personal blogs, independent research aggregation websites, or social media websites, likely require a greater level of review than information from more established research organizations.

Criteria that a member or candidate can use in forming an opinion on whether research is sound include the following:

- assumptions used,
- rigor of the analysis performed,
- date/timeliness of the research, and
- evaluation of the objectivity and independence of the recommendations.

A member or candidate may rely on others in his or her firm to determine whether secondary or third-party research is sound and use the information in good faith unless the member or candidate has reason to question its validity or the processes and procedures used by those responsible for the research. For example, a portfolio manager may not have a choice of a data source because the firm's senior managers conducted due diligence to determine which vendor would provide services; the member or candidate can use the information in good faith assuming the due diligence process was deemed adequate.

A member or candidate should verify that the firm has a policy about the timely and consistent review of approved research providers to ensure that the quality of the research continues to meet the necessary standards. If such a policy is not in place at the firm, the member or candidate should encourage the development and adoption of a formal review practice.

Using Quantitatively Oriented Research

Standard V(A) applies to the rapidly expanding use of quantitatively oriented research models and processes, such as computer-generated modeling, screening, and ranking of investment securities; the creation or valuation of derivative instruments; and quantitative portfolio construction techniques. These models and processes are being used for much more than the back testing of investment strategies, especially with continually advancing technology and techniques. The continued broad development of quantitative methods and models is an important part of capital market developments.

Members and candidates need to have an understanding of the parameters used in models and quantitative research that are incorporated into their investment recommendations. Although they are not required to become experts in every technical aspect of the models, they must understand the assumptions and limitations inherent in any model and how the results were used in the decision-making process.

The reliance on and potential limitations of financial models became clear through the investment crisis that unfolded in 2007 and 2008. In some cases, the financial models used to value specific securities and related derivative products did not adequately demonstrate the level of associated risks. Members and candidates should make reasonable efforts to test the output of investment models and other pre-programed analytical tools they use. Such validation should occur before incorporating the process into their methods, models, or analyses.

Although not every model can test for every factor or outcome, members and candidates should ensure that their analyses incorporate a broad range of assumptions sufficient to capture the underlying characteristics of investments. The omission from the analysis of potentially negative outcomes or of levels of risk outside the norm may misrepresent the true economic value of an investment. The possible scenarios for analysis should include factors that are likely to have a substantial influence on the investment value and may include extremely positive and negative scenarios.

Developing Quantitatively Oriented Techniques

Individuals who create new quantitative models and services must exhibit a higher level of diligence in reviewing new products than the individuals who ultimately use the analytical output. Members and candidates involved in the development and oversight of quantitatively oriented models, methods, and algorithms must understand the technical aspects of the products they provide to clients. A thorough testing of the model and resulting analysis should be completed prior to product distribution.

Members and candidates need to consider the source and time horizon of the data used as inputs in financial models. The information from many commercially available databases may not effectively incorporate both positive and negative market cycles. In the development of a recommendation, the member or candidate may need to test the models by using volatility and performance expectations that represent scenarios outside the observable databases. In reviewing the computer models or the resulting output, members and candidates need to pay particular attention to the assumptions used in the analysis and the rigor of the analysis to ensure that the model incorporates a wide range of possible input expectations, including negative market events.

Selecting External Advisers and Subadvisers

Financial instruments and asset allocation techniques continue to develop and evolve. This progression has led to the use of specialized managers to invest in specific asset classes or diversification strategies that complement a firm's in-house expertise. Standard V(A) applies to the level of review necessary in selecting an external adviser or subadviser to manage a specifically mandated allocation. Members and candidates must review managers as diligently as they review individual funds and securities.

Members and candidates who are directly involved with the use of external advisers need to ensure that their firms have standardized criteria for reviewing these selected external advisers and managers. Such criteria would include, but would not be limited to, the following:

- reviewing the adviser's established code of ethics,
- understanding the adviser's compliance and internal control procedures,
- assessing the quality of the published return information, and
- reviewing the adviser's investment process and adherence to its stated strategy.

Codes, standards, and guides to best practice published by CFA Institute provide members and candidates with examples of acceptable practices for external advisers and advice in selecting a new adviser. The following guides are available at the CFA Institute website (www.cfainstitute.org): Asset Manager Code of Professional Conduct, Global Investment Performance Standards, and Model Request for Proposal (for equity, credit, or real estate managers).

Group Research and Decision Making

Commonly, members and candidates are part of a group or team that is collectively responsible for producing investment analysis or research. The conclusions or recommendations of the group report represent the consensus of the group and are not necessarily the views of the member or candidate, even though the name of the member or candidate is included on the report. In some instances, a member or candidate will not agree with the view of the group. If, however, the member or candidate believes that the consensus opinion has a reasonable and adequate basis and is independent and objective, the member or candidate need not decline to be identified with the report. If the member or candidate is confident in the process, the member or candidate does not need to dissociate from the report even if it does not reflect his or her opinion.

Recommended Procedures for Compliance

Members and candidates should encourage their firms to consider the following policies and procedures to support the principles of Standard V(A):

- Establish a policy requiring that research reports, credit ratings, and investment recommendations have a basis that can be substantiated as reasonable and adequate. An individual employee (a supervisory analyst) or a group of employees (a review committee) should be appointed to review and approve such items prior to external circulation to determine whether the criteria established in the policy have been met.
- Develop detailed, written guidance for analysts (research, investment, or credit), supervisory analysts, and review committees that establishes the due diligence procedures for judging whether a particular recommendation has a reasonable and adequate basis.

- Develop measurable criteria for assessing the quality of research, the reasonableness and adequacy of the basis for any recommendation or rating, and the accuracy of recommendations over time. In some cases, firms may consider implementing compensation arrangements that depend on these measurable criteria and that are applied consistently to all related analysts.
- Develop detailed, written guidance that establishes minimum levels of scenario testing of all computer-based models used in developing, rating, and evaluating financial instruments. The policy should contain criteria related to the breadth of the scenarios tested, the accuracy of the output over time, and the analysis of cash flow sensitivity to inputs.
- Develop measurable criteria for assessing outside providers, including the quality of information being provided, the reasonableness and adequacy of the provider's collection practices, and the accuracy of the information over time. The established policy should outline how often the provider's products are reviewed.
- Adopt a standardized set of criteria for evaluating the adequacy of external advisers. The policy should include how often and on what basis the allocation of funds to the adviser will be reviewed.

Application of the Standard

Example 1 (Sufficient Due Diligence):

Helen Hawke manages the corporate finance department of Sarkozi Securities, Ltd. The firm is anticipating that the government will soon close a tax loophole that currently allows oil-and-gas exploration companies to pass on drilling expenses to holders of a certain class of shares. Because market demand for this tax-advantaged class of stock is currently high, Sarkozi convinces several companies to undertake new equity financings at once, before the loophole closes. Time is of the essence, but Sarkozi lacks sufficient resources to conduct adequate research on all the prospective issuing companies. Hawke decides to estimate the IPO prices on the basis of the relative size of each company and to justify the pricing later when her staff has time.

> *Comment*: Sarkozi should have taken on only the work that it could adequately handle. By categorizing the issuers by general size, Hawke has bypassed researching all the other relevant aspects that should be considered when pricing new issues and thus has not performed sufficient due diligence. Such an omission can result in investors purchasing shares at prices that have no actual basis. Hawke has violated Standard V(A).

Example 2 (Sufficient Scenario Testing):

Babu Dhaliwal works for Heinrich Brokerage in the corporate finance group. He has just persuaded Feggans Resources, Ltd., to allow his firm to do a secondary equity financing at Feggans Resources' current stock price. Because the stock has been trading at higher multiples than similar companies with equivalent production, Dhaliwal presses the Feggans Resources managers to project what would be the maximum production they could achieve in an optimal scenario. Based on these numbers, he is able to justify the price his firm will be asking for the secondary issue. During a sales pitch to the brokers, Dhaliwal then uses these numbers as the base-case production levels that Feggans Resources will achieve.

> *Comment*: When presenting information to the brokers, Dhaliwal should have given a range of production scenarios and the probability of Feggans Resources achieving each level. By giving the maximum production level

as the likely level of production, he has misrepresented the chances of achieving that production level and seriously misled the brokers. Dhaliwal has violated Standard V(A).

Example 3 (Developing a Reasonable Basis):

Brendan Witt, a former junior sell-side technology analyst, decided to return to school to earn an MBA. To keep his research skills and industry knowledge sharp, Witt accepted a position with On-line and Informed, an independent internet-based research company. The position requires the publication of a recommendation and report on a different company every month. Initially, Witt is a regular contributor of new research and a participant in the associated discussion boards that generally have positive comments on the technology sector. Over time, his ability to manage his educational requirements and his work requirements begin to conflict with one another. Knowing a recommendation is due the next day for On-line, Witt creates a report based on a few news articles and what the conventional wisdom of the markets has deemed the "hot" security of the day.

Comment: Witt's knowledge of and exuberance for technology stocks, a few news articles, and the conventional wisdom of the markets do not constitute, without more information, a reasonable and adequate basis for a stock recommendation that is supported by appropriate research and investigation. Therefore, Witt has violated Standard V(A).

See also Standard IV(C)–Responsibilities of Supervisors because it relates to the firm's inadequate procedures.

Example 4 (Timely Client Updates):

Kristen Chandler is an investment consultant in the London office of Dalton Securities, a major global investment consultant firm. One of her UK pension funds has decided to appoint a specialist US equity manager. Dalton's global manager of research relies on local consultants to cover managers within their regions and, after conducting thorough due diligence, puts their views and ratings in Dalton's manager database. Chandler accesses Dalton's global manager research database and conducts a screen of all US equity managers on the basis of a match with the client's desired philosophy/style, performance, and tracking-error targets. She selects the five managers that meet these criteria and puts them in a briefing report that is delivered to the client 10 days later. Between the time of Chandler's database search and the delivery of the report to the client, Chandler is told that Dalton has updated the database with the information that one of the firms that Chandler has recommended for consideration lost its chief investment officer, the head of its US equity research, and the majority of its portfolio managers on the US equity product—all of whom have left to establish their own firm. Chandler does not revise her report with this updated information.

Comment: Chandler has failed to satisfy the requirement of Standard V(A). Although Dalton updated the manager ratings to reflect the personnel turnover at one of the firms, Chandler did not update her report to reflect the new information.

Example 5 (Group Research Opinions):

Evelyn Mastakis is a junior analyst who has been asked by her firm to write a research report predicting the expected interest rate for residential mortgages over the next six months. Mastakis submits her report to the fixed-income investment committee of her firm for review, as required by firm procedures. Although some committee members support Mastakis's conclusion, the majority of the committee disagrees with her conclusion, and the report is significantly changed to indicate that interest rates are likely to increase more than originally predicted by Mastakis. Should Mastakis ask that her name be taken off the report when it is disseminated?

> *Comment*: The results of research are not always clear, and different people may have different opinions based on the same factual evidence. In this case, the committee may have valid reasons for issuing a report that differs from the analyst's original research. The firm can issue a report that is different from the original report of an analyst as long as there is a reasonable and adequate basis for its conclusions.
>
> Generally, analysts must write research reports that reflect their own opinion and can ask the firm not to put their name on reports that ultimately differ from that opinion. When the work is a group effort, however, not all members of the team may agree with all aspects of the report. Ultimately, members and candidates can ask to have their names removed from the report, but if they are satisfied that the process has produced results or conclusions that have a reasonable and adequate basis, members and candidates do not have to dissociate from the report even when they do not agree with its contents. If Mastakis is confident in the process, she does not need to dissociate from the report even if it does not reflect her opinion.

Example 6 (Reliance on Third-Party Research):

Gary McDermott runs a two-person investment management firm. McDermott's firm subscribes to a service from a large investment research firm that provides research reports. McDermott's firm makes investment recommendations on the basis of these reports.

> *Comment*: Members and candidates can rely on third-party research but must make reasonable and diligent efforts to determine that such research is sound. If McDermott undertakes due diligence efforts on a regular basis to ensure that the research produced by the large firm is objective and reasonably based, McDermott can rely on that research when making investment recommendations to clients.

Example 7 (Due Diligence in Submanager Selection):

Paul Ostrowski's business has grown significantly over the past couple of years, and some clients want to diversify internationally. Ostrowski decides to find a submanager to handle the expected international investments. Because this will be his first subadviser, Ostrowski uses the CFA Institute model "request for proposal" to design a questionnaire for his search. By his deadline, he receives seven completed questionnaires from a variety of domestic and international firms trying to gain his business. Ostrowski reviews all the applications in detail and decides to select the firm that charges the lowest fees because doing so will have the least impact on his firm's bottom line.

> *Comment*: The selection of an external adviser or subadviser should be based on a full and complete review of the adviser's services, performance history, and cost structure. In basing the decision on the fee structure alone, Ostrowski may be violating Standard V(A).
>
> See also Standard III(C)–Suitability because it relates to the ability of the selected adviser to meet the needs of the clients.

Example 8 (Sufficient Due Diligence):

Michael Papis is the chief investment officer of his state's retirement fund. The fund has always used outside advisers for the real estate allocation, and this information is clearly presented in all fund communications. Thomas Nagle, a recognized sell-side research analyst and Papis's business school classmate, recently left the investment bank he worked for to start his own asset management firm, Accessible Real Estate. Nagle is trying to build his assets under management and contacts Papis about gaining some of the retirement fund's allocation. In the previous few years, the performance of the retirement fund's real estate investments was in line with the fund's benchmark but was not extraordinary. Papis decides to help out his old friend and also to seek better returns by moving the real estate allocation to Accessible. The only notice of the change in adviser appears in the next annual report in the listing of associated advisers.

> *Comment*: Papis violated Standard V(A). His responsibilities may include the selection of the external advisers, but the decision to change advisers appears to have been arbitrary. If Papis was dissatisfied with the current real estate adviser, he should have conducted a proper solicitation to select the most appropriate adviser.
>
> See also Standard IV(C)–Responsibilities of Supervisors, Standard V(B)–Communication with Clients and Prospective Clients, and Standard VI(A)–Disclosure of Conflicts.

Example 9 (Sufficient Due Diligence):

Andre Shrub owns and operates Conduit, an investment advisory firm. Prior to opening Conduit, Shrub was an account manager with Elite Investment, a hedge fund managed by his good friend Adam Reed. To attract clients to a new Conduit fund, Shrub offers lower-than-normal management fees. He can do so because the fund consists of two top-performing funds managed by Reed. Given his personal friendship with Reed and the prior performance record of these two funds, Shrub believes this new fund is a winning combination for all parties. Clients quickly invest with Conduit to gain access to the Elite funds. No one is turned away because Conduit is seeking to expand its assets under management.

> *Comment*: Shrub violated Standard V(A) by not conducting a thorough analysis of the funds managed by Reed before developing the new Conduit fund. Shrub's reliance on his personal relationship with Reed and his prior knowledge of Elite are insufficient justification for the investments. The funds may be appropriately considered, but a full review of their operating procedures, reporting practices, and transparency are some elements of the necessary due diligence.
>
> See also Standard III(C)–Suitability.

Example 10 (Sufficient Due Diligence):

Bob Thompson has been doing research for the portfolio manager of the fixed-income department. His assignment is to do sensitivity analysis on securitized subprime mortgages. He has discussed with the manager possible scenarios to use to calculate expected returns. A key assumption in such calculations is housing price appreciation (HPA) because it drives "prepays" (prepayments of mortgages) and losses. Thompson is concerned with the significant appreciation experienced over the previous five years as a result of the increased availability of funds from subprime mortgages. Thompson insists that the analysis should include a scenario run with –10% for Year 1, –5% for Year 2, and then (to project a worst-case scenario) 0% for Years 3 through 5. The manager replies that these assumptions are too dire because there has never been a time in their available database when HPA was negative.

Thompson conducts his research to better understand the risks inherent in these securities and evaluates these securities in the worst-case scenario, a less likely but possible environment. Based on the results of the enhanced scenarios, Thompson does not recommend the purchase of the securitization. Against the general market trends, the manager follows Thompson's recommendation and does not invest. The following year, the housing market collapses. In avoiding the subprime investments, the manager's portfolio outperforms its peer group that year.

> *Comment*: Thompson's actions in running the scenario test with inputs beyond the historical trends available in the firm's databases adhere to the principles of Standard V(A). His concerns over recent trends provide a sound basis for further analysis. Thompson understands the limitations of his model, when combined with the limited available historical information, to accurately predict the performance of the funds if market conditions change negatively.
>
> See also Standard I(B)–Independence and Objectivity.

Example 11 (Use of Quantitatively Oriented Models):

Espacia Liakos works in sales for Hellenica Securities, a firm specializing in developing intricate derivative strategies to profit from particular views on market expectations. One of her clients is Eugenie Carapalis, who has become convinced that commodity prices will become more volatile over the coming months. Carapalis asks Liakos to quickly engineer a strategy that will benefit from this expectation. Liakos turns to Hellenica's modeling group to fulfill this request. Because of the tight deadline, the modeling group outsources parts of the work to several trusted third parties. Liakos implements the disparate components of the strategy as the firms complete them.

Within a month, Carapalis is proven correct: Volatility across a range of commodities increases sharply. But her derivatives position with Hellenica returns huge losses, and the losses increase daily. Liakos investigates and realizes that although each of the various components of the strategy had been validated, they had never been evaluated as an integrated whole. In extreme conditions, portions of the model worked at cross-purposes with other portions, causing the overall strategy to fail dramatically.

> *Comment*: Liakos violated Standard V(A). Members and candidates must understand the statistical significance of the results of the models they recommend and must be able to explain them to clients. Liakos did not take adequate care to ensure a thorough review of the whole model; its components were evaluated only individually. Because Carapalis clearly intended to implement the strategy as a whole rather than as separate parts, Liakos should have tested how the components of the strategy interacted as well as how they performed individually.

Example 12 (Successful Due Diligence/Failed Investment):

Alton Newbury is an investment adviser to high-net-worth clients. A client with an aggressive risk profile in his investment policy statement asks about investing in the Top Shelf hedge fund. This fund, based in Calgary, Alberta, Canada, has reported 20% returns for the first three years. The fund prospectus states that its strategy involves long and short positions in the energy sector and extensive leverage. Based on his analysis of the fund's track record, the principals involved in managing the fund, the fees charged, and the fund's risk profile, Newbury recommends the fund to the client and secures a position in it. The next week, the fund announces that it has suffered a loss of 60% of its value and is suspending operations and redemptions until after a regulatory review. Newbury's client calls him in a panic and asks for an explanation.

> *Comment*: Newbury's actions were consistent with Standard V(A). Analysis of an investment that results in a reasonable basis for recommendation does not guarantee that the investment has no downside risk. Newbury should discuss the analysis process with the client while reminding him or her that past performance does not lead to guaranteed future gains and that losses in an aggressive investment portfolio should be expected.

Example 13 (Quantitative Model Diligence):

Barry Cannon is the lead quantitative analyst at CityCenter Hedge Fund. He is responsible for the development, maintenance, and enhancement of the proprietary models the fund uses to manage its investors' assets. Cannon reads several high-level mathematical publications and blogs to stay informed of current developments. One blog, run by Expert CFA, presents some intriguing research that may benefit one of CityCenter's current models. Cannon is under pressure from firm executives to improve the model's predictive abilities, and he incorporates the factors discussed in the online research. The updated output recommends several new investments to the fund's portfolio managers.

> *Comment*: Cannon has violated Standard V(A) by failing to have a reasonable basis for the new recommendations made to the portfolio managers. He needed to diligently research the effect of incorporating the new factors before offering the output recommendations. Cannon may use the blog for ideas, but it is his responsibility to determine the effect on the firm's proprietary models.
>
> See Standard VII(B) regarding the violation by "Expert CFA" in the use of the CFA designation.

Example 14 (Selecting a Service Provider):

Ellen Smith is a performance analyst at Artic Global Advisors, a firm that manages global equity mandates for institutional clients. She was asked by her supervisor to review five new performance attribution systems and recommend one that would more appropriately explain the firm's investment strategy to clients. On the list was a system she recalled learning about when visiting an exhibitor booth at a recent conference. The system is highly quantitative and something of a "black box" in how it calculates the attribution values. Smith recommended this option without researching the others because the sheer complexity of the process was sure to impress the clients.

> *Comment*: Smith's actions do not demonstrate a sufficient level of diligence in reviewing this product to make a recommendation for selecting the service. Besides not reviewing or considering the other four potential systems, she did not determine whether the "black box" attribution process aligns with the investment practices of the firm, including its investments in different countries and currencies. Smith must review and understand the process of any software or system before recommending its use as the firm's attribution system.

Example 15 (Subadviser Selection):

Craig Jackson is working for Adams Partners, Inc., and has been assigned to select a hedge fund subadviser to improve the diversification of the firm's large fund-of-funds product. The allocation must be in place before the start of the next quarter. Jackson uses a consultant database to find a list of suitable firms that claim compliance with the GIPS standards. He calls more than 20 firms on the list to confirm their potential interest and to determine their most recent quarterly and annual total return values. Because of the short turnaround, Jackson recommends the firm with the greatest total return values for selection.

> *Comment*: By considering only performance and GIPS compliance, Jackson has not conducted sufficient review of potential firms to satisfy the requirements of Standard V(A). A thorough investigation of the firms and their operations should be conducted to ensure that their addition would increase the diversity of clients' portfolios and that they are suitable for the fund-of-funds product.

Example 16 (Manager Selection):

Timothy Green works for Peach Asset Management, where he creates proprietary models that analyze data from the firm request for proposal questionnaires to identify managers for possible inclusion in the firm's fund-of-funds investment platform. Various criteria must be met to be accepted to the platform. Because of the number of respondents to the questionnaires, Green uses only the data submitted to make a recommendation for adding a new manager.

> *Comment*: By failing to conduct any additional outside review of the information to verify what was submitted through the request for proposal, Green has likely not satisfied the requirements of Standard V(A). The amount of information requested from outside managers varies among firms. Although the requested information may be comprehensive, Green should ensure sufficient effort is undertaken to verify the submitted information before recommending a firm for inclusion. This requires that he go beyond the information provided by the manager on the request for proposal questionnaire and may include interviews with interested managers, reviews of regulatory filings, and discussions with the managers' custodian or auditor.

Example 17 (Technical Model Requirements):

Jérôme Dupont works for the credit research group of XYZ Asset Management, where he is in charge of developing and updating credit risk models. In order to perform accurately, his models need to be regularly updated with the latest market data.

Dupont does not interact with or manage money for any of the firm's clients. He is in contact with the firm's US corporate bond fund manager, John Smith, who has only very superficial knowledge of the model and who from time to time asks very basic questions regarding the output recommendations. Smith does not consult Dupont with respect to finalizing his clients' investment strategies.

Dupont's recently assigned objective is to develop a new emerging market corporate credit risk model. The firm is planning to expand into emerging credit, and the development of such a model is a critical step in this process. Because Smith seems to follow the model's recommendations without much concern for its quality as he develops his clients' investment strategies, Dupont decides to focus his time on the development of the new emerging market model and neglects to update the US model.

After several months without regular updates, Dupont's diagnostic statistics start to show alarming signs with respect to the quality of the US credit model. Instead of conducting the long and complicated data update, Dupont introduces new codes into his model with some limited new data as a quick "fix." He thinks this change will address the issue without needing to complete the full data update, so he continues working on the new emerging market model.

Several months following the quick "fix," another set of diagnostic statistics reveals nonsensical results and Dupont realizes that his earlier change contained an error. He quickly corrects the error and alerts Smith. Smith realizes that some of the prior trades he performed were due to erroneous model results. Smith rebalances the portfolio to remove the securities purchased on the basis of the questionable results without reporting the issue to anyone else.

Comment: Smith violated standard V(A) because exercising "diligence, independence, and thoroughness in analyzing investments, making investment recommendations, and taking investment actions" means that members and candidates must understand the technical aspects of the products they provide to clients. Smith does not understand the model he is relying on to manage money. Members and candidates should also make reasonable enquiries into the source and accuracy of all data used in completing their investment analysis and recommendations.

Dupont violated V(A) even if he does not trade securities or make investment decisions. Dupont's models give investment recommendations, and Dupont is accountable for the quality of those recommendations. Members and candidates should make reasonable efforts to test the output of preprogramed analytical tools they use. Such validation should occur before incorporating the tools into their decision-making process.

See also Standard V(B)–Communication with Clients and Prospective Clients.

Standard V(B) Communication with Clients and Prospective Clients

Members and Candidates must:

1 Disclose to clients and prospective clients the basic format and general principles of the investment processes they use to analyze investments, select securities, and construct portfolios and must promptly disclose any changes that might materially affect those processes.

2 Disclose to clients and prospective clients significant limitations and risks associated with the investment process.

3 Use reasonable judgment in identifying which factors are important to their investment analyses, recommendations, or actions and include those factors in communications with clients and prospective clients.

4 Distinguish between fact and opinion in the presentation of investment analyses and recommendations.

Guidance

Highlights:

- *Informing Clients of the Investment Process*
- *Different Forms of Communication*
- *Identifying Risk and Limitations*
- *Report Presentation*
- *Distinction between Facts and Opinions in Reports*

Standard V(B) addresses member and candidate conduct with respect to communicating with clients. Developing and maintaining clear, frequent, and thorough communication practices is critical to providing high-quality financial services to clients. When clients understand the information communicated to them, they also can understand exactly how members and candidates are acting on their behalf, which gives clients the opportunity to make well-informed decisions about their investments. Such understanding can be accomplished only through clear communication.

Standard V(B) states that members and candidates should communicate in a recommendation the factors that were instrumental in making the investment recommendation. A critical part of this requirement is to distinguish clearly between opinions and facts. In preparing a research report, the member or candidate must present the basic characteristics of the security(ies) being analyzed, which will allow the reader to evaluate the report and incorporate information the reader deems relevant to his or her investment decision-making process.

Similarly, in preparing a recommendation about, for example, an asset allocation strategy, alternative investment vehicle, or structured investment product, the member or candidate should include factors that are relevant to the asset classes that are being discussed. Follow-up communication of significant changes in the risk characteristics of a security or asset strategy is required. Providing regular updates to any changes in the risk characteristics is recommended.

Informing Clients of the Investment Process

Members and candidates must adequately describe to clients and prospective clients the manner in which they conduct the investment decision-making process. Such disclosure should address factors that have positive and negative influences on the recommendations, including significant risks and limitations of the investment process used. The member or candidate must keep clients and other interested parties informed on an ongoing basis about changes to the investment process, especially newly identified significant risks and limitations. Only by thoroughly understanding the nature of the investment product or service can a client determine whether changes to that product or service could materially affect his or her investment objectives.

Understanding the basic characteristics of an investment is of great importance in judging the suitability of that investment on a standalone basis, but it is especially important in determining the impact each investment will have on the characteristics of a portfolio. Although the risk and return characteristics of a common stock might seem to be essentially the same for any investor when the stock is viewed in isolation, the effects of those characteristics greatly depend on the other investments held. For instance, if the particular stock will represent 90% of an individual's investments, the stock's importance in the portfolio is vastly different from what it would be to an investor with a highly diversified portfolio for whom the stock will represent only 2% of the holdings.

A firm's investment policy may include the use of outside advisers to manage various portions of clients' assets under management. Members and candidates should inform the clients about the specialization or diversification expertise provided by the external adviser(s). This information allows clients to understand the full mix of products and strategies being applied that may affect their investment objectives.

Different Forms of Communication

For purposes of Standard V(B), communication is not confined to a written report of the type traditionally generated by an analyst researching a security, company, or industry. A presentation of information can be made via any means of communication, including in-person recommendation or description, telephone conversation, media broadcast, or transmission by computer (e.g., on the internet).

Computer and mobile device communications have rapidly evolved over the past few years. Members and candidates using any social media service to communicate business information must be diligent in their efforts to avoid unintended problems because these services may not be available to all clients. When providing information to clients through new technologies, members and candidates should take reasonable steps to ensure that such delivery would treat all clients fairly and, if necessary, be considered publicly disseminated.

The nature of client communications is highly diverse—from one word ("buy" or "sell") to in-depth reports of more than 100 pages. A communication may contain a general recommendation about the market, asset allocations, or classes of investments (e.g., stocks, bonds, real estate) or may relate to a specific security. If recommendations are contained in capsule form (such as a recommended stock list), members and candidates should notify clients that additional information and analyses are available from the producer of the report.

Identifying Risks and Limitations

Members and candidates must outline to clients and prospective clients significant risks and limitations of the analysis contained in their investment products or recommendations. The type and nature of significant risks will depend on the investment process that members and candidates are following and on the personal circumstances of the client. In general, the use of leverage constitutes a significant risk and should be disclosed.

Members and candidates must adequately disclose the general market-related risks and the risks associated with the use of complex financial instruments that are deemed significant. Other types of risks that members and candidates may consider disclosing include, but are not limited to, counterparty risk, country risk, sector or industry risk, security-specific risk, and credit risk.

Investment securities and vehicles may have limiting factors that influence a client's or potential client's investment decision. Members and candidates must report to clients and prospective clients the existence of limitations significant to the decision-making process. Examples of such factors and attributes include, but are not limited to, investment liquidity and capacity. Liquidity is the ability to liquidate an investment on a timely basis at a reasonable cost. Capacity is the investment amount beyond which returns will be negatively affected by new investments.

The appropriateness of risk disclosure should be assessed on the basis of what was known at the time the investment action was taken (often called an *ex ante* basis). Members and candidates must disclose significant risks known to them at the time of the disclosure. Members and candidates cannot be expected to disclose risks they are unaware of at the time recommendations or investment actions are made. In assessing compliance with Standard V(B), it is important to establish knowledge of a purported significant risk or limitation. A one-time investment loss that occurs after the disclosure does not constitute a pertinent factor in assessing whether significant risks and limitations were properly disclosed. Having no knowledge of a risk or limitation that subsequently triggers a loss may reveal a deficiency in the diligence and reasonable basis of the research of the member or candidate but may not reveal a breach of Standard V(B).

Report Presentation

Once the analytical process has been completed, the member or candidate who prepares the report must include those elements that are important to the analysis and conclusions of the report so that the reader can follow and challenge the report's reasoning. A report writer who has done adequate investigation may emphasize certain areas, touch briefly on others, and omit certain aspects deemed unimportant. For instance, a report may dwell on a quarterly earnings release or new-product introduction and omit other matters as long as the analyst clearly stipulates the limits to the scope of the report.

Investment advice based on quantitative research and analysis must be supported by readily available reference material and should be applied in a manner consistent with previously applied methodology. If changes in methodology are made, they should be highlighted.

Distinction between Facts and Opinions in Reports

Standard V(B) requires that opinion be separated from fact. Violations often occur when reports fail to separate the past from the future by not indicating that earnings estimates, changes in the outlook for dividends, or future market price information are *opinions* subject to future circumstances.

In the case of complex quantitative analyses, members and candidates must clearly separate fact from statistical conjecture and should identify the known limitations of an analysis. Members and candidates may violate Standard V(B) by failing to identify the limits of statistically developed projections because such omission leaves readers unaware of the limits of the published projections.

Members and candidates should explicitly discuss with clients and prospective clients the assumptions used in the investment models and processes to generate the analysis. Caution should be used in promoting the perceived accuracy of any model or process to clients because the ultimate output is merely an estimate of future results and not a certainty.

Recommended Procedures for Compliance

Because the selection of relevant factors is an analytical skill, determination of whether a member or candidate has used reasonable judgment in excluding and including information in research reports depends heavily on case-by-case review rather than a specific checklist.

Members and candidates should encourage their firms to have a rigorous methodology for reviewing research that is created for publication and dissemination to clients.

To assist in the after-the-fact review of a report, the member or candidate must maintain records indicating the nature of the research and should, if asked, be able to supply additional information to the client (or any user of the report) covering factors not included in the report.

Application of the Standard

Example 1 (Sufficient Disclosure of Investment System):

Sarah Williamson, director of marketing for Country Technicians, Inc., is convinced that she has found the perfect formula for increasing Country Technicians' income and diversifying its product base. Williamson plans to build on Country Technicians' reputation as a leading money manager by marketing an exclusive and expensive investment advice letter to high-net-worth individuals. One hitch in the plan is the complexity of Country Technicians' investment system—a combination of technical trading rules (based on historical price and volume fluctuations) and portfolio construction rules designed to minimize risk. To simplify the newsletter, she decides to include only each week's top five "buy" and "sell" recommendations and to leave out details of the valuation models and the portfolio structuring scheme.

> *Comment*: Williamson's plans for the newsletter violate Standard V(B). Williamson need not describe the investment system in detail in order to implement the advice effectively, but she must inform clients of Country

Technicians' basic process and logic. Without understanding the basis for a recommendation, clients cannot possibly understand its limitations or its inherent risks.

Example 2 (Providing Opinions as Facts):

Richard Dox is a mining analyst for East Bank Securities. He has just finished his report on Boisy Bay Minerals. Included in his report is his own assessment of the geological extent of mineral reserves likely to be found on the company's land. Dox completed this calculation on the basis of the core samples from the company's latest drilling. According to Dox's calculations, the company has more than 500,000 ounces of gold on the property. Dox concludes his research report as follows: "Based on the fact that the company has 500,000 ounces of gold to be mined, I recommend a strong BUY."

> *Comment*: If Dox issues the report as written, he will violate Standard V(B). His calculation of the total gold reserves for the property based on the company's recent sample drilling is a quantitative opinion, not a fact. Opinion must be distinguished from fact in research reports.

Example 3 (Proper Description of a Security):

Olivia Thomas, an analyst at Government Brokers, Inc., which is a brokerage firm specializing in government bond trading, has produced a report that describes an investment strategy designed to benefit from an expected decline in US interest rates. The firm's derivative products group has designed a structured product that will allow the firm's clients to benefit from this strategy. Thomas's report describing the strategy indicates that high returns are possible if various scenarios for declining interest rates are assumed. Citing the proprietary nature of the structured product underlying the strategy, the report does not describe in detail how the firm is able to offer such returns or the related risks in the scenarios, nor does the report address the likely returns of the strategy if, contrary to expectations, interest rates rise.

> *Comment*: Thomas has violated Standard V(B) because her report fails to describe properly the basic characteristics of the actual and implied risks of the investment strategy, including how the structure was created and the degree to which leverage was embedded in the structure. The report should include a balanced discussion of how the strategy would perform in the case of rising as well as falling interest rates, preferably illustrating how the strategies might be expected to perform in the event of a reasonable variety of interest rate and credit risk–spread scenarios. If liquidity issues are relevant with regard to the valuation of either the derivatives or the underlying securities, provisions the firm has made to address those risks should also be disclosed.

Example 4 (Notification of Fund Mandate Change):

May & Associates is an aggressive growth manager that has represented itself since its inception as a specialist at investing in small-cap US stocks. One of May's selection criteria is a maximum capitalization of US$250 million for any given company. After a string of successful years of superior performance relative to its peers, May has expanded its client base significantly, to the point at which assets under management now exceed US$3 billion. For liquidity purposes, May's chief investment officer (CIO) decides to lift the maximum permissible market-cap ceiling to US$500 million and change the firm's sales and marketing literature accordingly to inform prospective clients and third-party consultants.

Comment: Although May's CIO is correct about informing potentially interested parties as to the change in investment process, he must also notify May's existing clients. Among the latter group might be a number of clients who not only retained May as a small-cap manager but also retained mid-cap and large-cap specialists in a multiple-manager approach. Such clients could regard May's change of criteria as a style change that distorts their overall asset allocations.

Example 5 (Notification of Fund Mandate Change):

Rather than lifting the ceiling for its universe from US$250 million to US$500 million, May & Associates extends its small-cap universe to include a number of non-US companies.

Comment: Standard V(B) requires that May's CIO advise May's clients of this change because the firm may have been retained by some clients specifically for its prowess at investing in US small-cap stocks. Other changes that require client notification are introducing derivatives to emulate a certain market sector or relaxing various other constraints, such as portfolio beta. In all such cases, members and candidates must disclose changes to all interested parties.

Example 6 (Notification of Changes to the Investment Process):

RJZ Capital Management is an active value-style equity manager that selects stocks by using a combination of four multifactor models. The firm has found favorable results when back testing the most recent 10 years of available market data in a new dividend discount model (DDM) designed by the firm. This model is based on projected inflation rates, earnings growth rates, and interest rates. The president of RJZ decides to replace its simple model that uses price to trailing 12-month earnings with the new DDM.

Comment: Because the introduction of a new and different valuation model represents a material change in the investment process, RJZ's president must communicate the change to the firm's clients. RJZ is moving away from a model based on hard data toward a new model that is at least partly dependent on the firm's forecasting skills. Clients would likely view such a model as a significant change rather than a mere refinement of RJZ's process.

Example 7 (Notification of Changes to the Investment Process):

RJZ Capital Management loses the chief architect of its multifactor valuation system. Without informing its clients, the president of RJZ decides to redirect the firm's talents and resources toward developing a product for passive equity management—a product that will emulate the performance of a major market index.

Comment: By failing to disclose to clients a substantial change to its investment process, the president of RJZ has violated Standard V(B).

Example 8 (Notification of Changes to the Investment Process):

At Fundamental Asset Management, Inc., the responsibility for selecting stocks for addition to the firm's "approved" list has just shifted from individual security analysts to a committee consisting of the research director and three senior portfolio managers. Eleanor Morales, a portfolio manager with Fundamental Asset Management, thinks this change is not important enough to communicate to her clients.

Comment: Morales must disclose the process change to all her clients. Some of Fundamental's clients might be concerned about the morale and motivation among the firm's best research analysts after such a change. Moreover, clients might challenge the stock-picking track record of the portfolio managers and might even want to monitor the situation closely.

Example 9 (Sufficient Disclosure of Investment System):

Amanda Chinn is the investment director for Diversified Asset Management, which manages the endowment of a charitable organization. Because of recent staff departures, Diversified has decided to limit its direct investment focus to large-cap securities and supplement the needs for small-cap and mid-cap management by hiring outside fund managers. In describing the planned strategy change to the charity, Chinn's update letter states, "As investment director, I will directly oversee the investment team managing the endowment's large-capitalization allocation. I will coordinate the selection and ongoing review of external managers responsible for allocations to other classes." The letter also describes the reasons for the change and the characteristics external managers must have to be considered.

Comment: Standard V(B) requires the disclosure of the investment process used to construct the portfolio of the fund. Changing the investment process from managing all classes of investments within the firm to the use of external managers is one example of information that needs to be communicated to clients. Chinn and her firm have embraced the principles of Standard V(B) by providing their client with relevant information. The charity can now make a reasonable decision about whether Diversified Asset Management remains the appropriate manager for its fund.

Example 10 (Notification of Changes to the Investment Process):

Michael Papis is the chief investment officer of his state's retirement fund. The fund has always used outside advisers for the real estate allocation, and this information is clearly presented in all fund communications. Thomas Nagle, a recognized sell-side research analyst and Papis's business school classmate, recently left the investment bank he worked for to start his own asset management firm, Accessible Real Estate. Nagle is trying to build his assets under management and contacts Papis about gaining some of the retirement fund's allocation. In the previous few years, the performance of the retirement fund's real estate investments was in line with the fund's benchmark but was not extraordinary. Papis decides to help out his old friend and also to seek better returns by moving the real estate allocation to Accessible. The only notice of the change in adviser appears in the next annual report in the listing of associated advisers.

Comment: Papis has violated Standard V(B). He attempted to hide the nature of his decision to change external managers by making only a limited disclosure. The plan recipients and the fund's trustees need to be aware when changes are made to ensure that operational procedures are being followed.

See also Standard IV(C)–Responsibilities of Supervisors, Standard V(A)–Diligence and Reasonable Basis, and Standard VI(A)–Disclosure of Conflicts.

Example 11 (Notification of Errors):

Jérôme Dupont works for the credit research group of XYZ Asset Management, where he is in charge of developing and updating credit risk models. In order to perform accurately, his models need to be regularly updated with the latest market data.

Dupont does not interact with or manage money for any of the firm's clients. He is in contact with the firm's US corporate bond fund manager, John Smith, who has only very superficial knowledge of the model and who from time to time asks very basic questions regarding the output recommendations. Smith does not consult Dupont with respect to finalizing his clients' investment strategies.

Dupont's recently assigned objective is to develop a new emerging market corporate credit risk model. The firm is planning to expand into emerging credit, and the development of such a model is a critical step in this process. Because Smith seems to follow the model's recommendations without much concern for its quality as he develops his clients' investment strategies, Dupont decides to focus his time on the development of the new emerging market model and neglects to update the US model.

After several months without regular updates, Dupont's diagnostic statistics start to show alarming signs with respect to the quality of the US credit model. Instead of conducting the long and complicated data update, Dupont introduces new codes into his model with some limited new data as a quick "fix." He thinks this change will address the issue without needing to complete the full data update, so he continues working on the new emerging market model.

Several months following the quick "fix," another set of diagnostic statistics reveals nonsensical results and Dupont realizes that his earlier change contained an error. He quickly corrects the error and alerts Smith. Smith realizes that some of the prior trades he performed were due to erroneous model results. Smith rebalances the portfolio to remove the securities purchased on the basis of the questionable results without reporting the issue to anyone else.

> *Comment*: Smith violated V(B) by not disclosing a material error in the investment process. Clients should have been informed about the error and the corrective actions the firm was undertaking on their behalf.
>
> See also Standard V(A)–Diligence and Reasonable Basis.

Example 12 (Notification of Risks and Limitations):

Quantitative analyst Yuri Yakovlev has developed an investment strategy that selects small-cap stocks on the basis of quantitative signals. Yakovlev's strategy typically identifies only a small number of stocks (10–20) that tend to be illiquid, but according to his backtests, the strategy generates significant risk-adjusted returns. The partners at Yakovlev's firm, QSC Capital, are impressed by these results. After a thorough examination of the strategy's risks, stress testing, historical back testing, and scenario analysis, QSC decides to seed the strategy with US$10 million of internal capital in order for Yakovlev to create a track record for the strategy.

After two years, the strategy has generated performance returns greater than the appropriate benchmark and the Sharpe ratio of the fund is close to 1.0. On the basis of these results, QSC decides to actively market the fund to large institutional investors. While creating the offering materials, Yakovlev informs the marketing team that the capacity of the strategy is limited. The extent of the limitation is difficult to ascertain with precision; it depends on market liquidity and other factors in his model that can evolve over time. Yakovlev indicates that given the current market conditions, investments in the fund beyond US$100 million of capital could become more difficult and negatively affect expected fund returns.

Alan Wellard, the manager of the marketing team, is a partner with 30 years of marketing experience and explains to Yakovlev that these are complex technical issues that will muddy the marketing message. According to Wellard, the offering material should focus solely on the great track record of the fund. Yakovlev does not object because the fund has only US$12 million of capital, very far from the US$100 million threshold.

Comment: Yakovlev and Wellard have not appropriately disclosed a significant limitation associated with the investment product. Yakovlev believes this limitation, once reached, will materially affect the returns of the fund. Although the fund is currently far from the US$100 million mark, current and prospective investors must be made aware of this capacity issue. If significant limitations are complicated to grasp and clients do not have the technical background required to understand them, Yakovlev and Wellard should either educate the clients or ascertain whether the fund is suitable for each client.

Example 13 (Notification of Risks and Limitations):

Brickell Advisers offers investment advisory services mainly to South American clients. Julietta Ramon, a risk analyst at Brickell, describes to clients how the firm uses value at risk (VaR) analysis to track the risk of its strategies. Ramon assures clients that calculating a VaR at a 99% confidence level, using a 20-day holding period, and applying a methodology based on an *ex ante* Monte Carlo simulation is extremely effective. The firm has never had losses greater than those predicted by this VaR analysis.

Comment: Ramon has not sufficiently communicated the risks associated with the investment process to satisfy the requirements of Standard V(B). The losses predicted by a VaR analysis depend greatly on the inputs used in the model. The size and probability of losses can differ significantly from what an individual model predicts. Ramon must disclose how the inputs were selected and the potential limitations and risks associated with the investment strategy.

Example 14 (Notification of Risks and Limitations):

Lily Smith attended an industry conference and noticed that John Baker, an investment manager with Baker Associates, attracted a great deal of attention from the conference participants. On the basis of her knowledge of Baker's reputation and the interest he received at the conference, Smith recommends adding Baker Associates to the approved manager platform. Her recommendation to the approval committee included the statement "John Baker is well respected in the industry, and his insights are consistently sought after by investors. Our clients are sure to benefit from investing with Baker Associates."

Comment: Smith is not appropriately separating facts from opinions in her recommendation to include the manager within the platform. Her actions conflict with the requirements of Standard V(B). Smith is relying on her opinions about Baker's reputation and the fact that many attendees were talking with him at the conference. Smith should also review the requirements of Standard V(A) regarding reasonable basis to determine the level of review necessary to recommend Baker Associates.

Standard V(C) Record Retention

Members and Candidates must develop and maintain appropriate records to support their investment analyses, recommendations, actions, and other investment-related communications with clients and prospective clients.

Guidance

Highlights:

- *New Media Records*
- *Records Are Property of the Firm*
- *Local Requirements*

Members and candidates must retain records that substantiate the scope of their research and reasons for their actions or conclusions. The retention requirement applies to decisions to buy or sell a security as well as reviews undertaken that do not lead to a change in position. Which records are required to support recommendations or investment actions depends on the role of the member or candidate in the investment decision-making process. Records may be maintained either in hard copy or electronic form.

Some examples of supporting documentation that assists the member or candidate in meeting the requirements for retention are as follows:

- personal notes from meetings with the covered company,
- press releases or presentations issued by the covered company,
- computer-based model outputs and analyses,
- computer-based model input parameters,
- risk analyses of securities' impacts on a portfolio,
- selection criteria for external advisers,
- notes from clients from meetings to review investment policy statements, and
- outside research reports.

New Media Records

The increased use of new and evolving technological formats (e.g., social media) for gathering and sharing information creates new challenges in maintaining the appropriate records and files. The nature or format of the information does not remove a member's or candidate's responsibility to maintain a record of information used in his or her analysis or communicated to clients.

Members and candidates should understand that although employers and local regulators are developing digital media retention policies, these policies may lag behind the advent of new communication channels. Such lag places greater responsibility on the individual for ensuring that all relevant information is retained. Examples of non-print media formats that should be retained include, but are not limited to,

- e-mails,
- text messages,
- blog posts, and
- Twitter posts.

Records Are Property of the Firm

As a general matter, records created as part of a member's or candidate's professional activity on behalf of his or her employer are the property of the firm. When a member or candidate leaves a firm to seek other employment, the member or candidate cannot take the property of the firm, including original forms or copies of supporting records of the member's or candidate's work, to the new employer without the express consent of the previous employer. The member or candidate cannot use historical recommendations or research reports created at the previous firm because the supporting documentation is unavailable. For future use, the member or candidate must re-create the supporting records at the new firm with information gathered through public sources or directly from the covered company and not from memory or sources obtained at the previous employer.

Local Requirements

Local regulators often impose requirements on members, candidates, and their firms related to record retention that must be followed. Firms may also implement policies detailing the applicable time frame for retaining research and client communication records. Fulfilling such regulatory and firm requirements satisfies the requirements of Standard V(C). In the absence of regulatory guidance or firm policies, CFA Institute recommends maintaining records for at least seven years.

Recommended Procedures for Compliance

The responsibility to maintain records that support investment action generally falls with the firm rather than individuals. Members and candidates must, however, archive research notes and other documents, either electronically or in hard copy, that support their current investment-related communications. Doing so will assist their firms in complying with requirements for preservation of internal or external records.

Application of the Standard

Example 1 (Record Retention and IPS Objectives and Recommendations):

One of Nikolas Lindstrom's clients is upset by the negative investment returns of his equity portfolio. The investment policy statement for the client requires that the portfolio manager follow a benchmark-oriented approach. The benchmark for the client includes a 35% investment allocation in the technology sector. The client acknowledges that this allocation was appropriate, but over the past three years, technology stocks have suffered severe losses. The client complains to the investment manager for allocating so much money to this sector.

> *Comment*: For Lindstrom, having appropriate records is important to show that over the past three years, the portion of technology stocks in the benchmark index was 35%, as called for in the IPS. Lindstrom should also have the client's IPS stating that the benchmark was appropriate for the client's investment objectives. He should also have records indicating that the investment has been explained appropriately to the client and that the IPS was updated on a regular basis. Taking these actions, Lindstrom would be in compliance with Standard V(C).

Example 2 (Record Retention and Research Process):

Malcolm Young is a research analyst who writes numerous reports rating companies in the luxury retail industry. His reports are based on a variety of sources, including interviews with company managers, manufacturers, and economists; on-site company visits; customer surveys; and secondary research from analysts covering related industries.

> *Comment*: Young must carefully document and keep copies of all the information that goes into his reports, including the secondary or third-party research of other analysts. Failure to maintain such files would violate Standard V(C).

Example 3 (Records as Firm, Not Employee, Property):

Martin Blank develops an analytical model while he is employed by Green Partners Investment Management, LLP (GPIM). While at the firm, he systematically documents the assumptions that make up the model as well as his reasoning behind the assumptions. As a result of the success of his model, Blank is hired to be the head of the research department of one of GPIM's competitors. Blank takes copies of the records supporting his model to his new firm.

> *Comment*: The records created by Blank supporting the research model he developed at GPIM are the records of GPIM. Taking the documents with him to his new employer without GPIM's permission violates Standard V(C). To use the model in the future, Blank must re-create the records supporting his model at the new firm.

STANDARD VI: CONFLICTS OF INTEREST

Standard VI(A) Disclosure of Conflicts

> Members and Candidates must make full and fair disclosure of all matters that could reasonably be expected to impair their independence and objectivity or interfere with respective duties to their clients, prospective clients, and employer. Members and Candidates must ensure that such disclosures are prominent, are delivered in plain language, and communicate the relevant information effectively.

Guidance

Highlights:

- *Disclosure of Conflicts to Employers*
- *Disclosure to Clients*
- *Cross-Departmental Conflicts*
- *Conflicts with Stock Ownership*
- *Conflicts as a Director*

Best practice is to avoid actual conflicts or the appearance of conflicts of interest when possible. Conflicts of interest often arise in the investment profession. Conflicts can occur between the interests of clients, the interests of employers, and the member's or candidate's own personal interests. Common sources for conflict are compensation structures, especially incentive and bonus structures that provide immediate returns for members and candidates with little or no consideration of long-term value creation.

Identifying and managing these conflicts is a critical part of working in the investment industry and can take many forms. When conflicts cannot be reasonably avoided, clear and complete disclosure of their existence is necessary.

Standard VI(A) protects investors and employers by requiring members and candidates to fully disclose to clients, potential clients, and employers all actual and potential conflicts of interest. Once a member or candidate has made full disclosure, the member's or candidate's employer, clients, and prospective clients will have the information needed to evaluate the objectivity of the investment advice or action taken on their behalf.

To be effective, disclosures must be prominent and must be made in plain language and in a manner designed to effectively communicate the information. Members and candidates have the responsibility of determining how often, in what manner, and in what particular circumstances the disclosure of conflicts must be made. Best practices dictate updating disclosures when the nature of a conflict of interest changes materially—for example, if the nature of a conflict of interest worsens through the introduction of bonuses based on each quarter's profits as to opposed annual profits. In making and updating disclosures of conflicts of interest, members and candidates should err on the side of caution to ensure that conflicts are effectively communicated.

Disclosure of Conflicts to Employers

Disclosure of conflicts to employers may be appropriate in many instances. When reporting conflicts of interest to employers, members and candidates must give their employers enough information to assess the impact of the conflict. By complying with employer guidelines, members and candidates allow their employers to avoid potentially embarrassing and costly ethical or regulatory violations.

Reportable situations include conflicts that would interfere with rendering unbiased investment advice and conflicts that would cause a member or candidate to act not in the employer's best interest. The same circumstances that generate conflicts to be reported to clients and prospective clients also would dictate reporting to employers. Ownership of stocks analyzed or recommended, participation on outside boards, and financial or other pressures that could influence a decision are to be promptly reported to the employer so that their impact can be assessed and a decision on how to resolve the conflict can be made.

The mere appearance of a conflict of interest may create problems for members, candidates, and their employers. Therefore, many of the conflicts previously mentioned could be explicitly prohibited by an employer. For example, many employers restrict personal trading, outside board membership, and related activities to prevent situations that might not normally be considered problematic from a conflict-of-interest point of view but that could give the appearance of a conflict of interest. Members and candidates must comply with these restrictions. Members and candidates must take reasonable steps to avoid conflicts and, if they occur inadvertently, must report them promptly so that the employer and the member or candidate can resolve them as quickly and effectively as possible.

Standard VI(A) also deals with a member's or candidate's conflicts of interest that might be detrimental to the employer's business. Any potential conflict situation that could prevent clear judgment about or full commitment to the execution of a member's or candidate's duties to the employer should be reported to the member's or candidate's employer and promptly resolved.

Disclosure to Clients

Members and candidates must maintain their objectivity when rendering investment advice or taking investment action. Investment advice or actions may be perceived to be tainted in numerous situations. Can a member or candidate remain objective if, on behalf of the firm, the member or candidate obtains or assists in obtaining fees for services? Can a member or candidate give objective advice if he or she owns stock in the company that is the subject of an investment recommendation or if the member or candidate has a close personal relationship with the company managers? Requiring members and candidates to disclose all matters that reasonably could be expected to impair the member's or candidate's objectivity allows clients and prospective clients to judge motives and possible biases for themselves.

Often in the investment industry, a conflict, or the perception of a conflict, cannot be avoided. The most obvious conflicts of interest, which should always be disclosed, are relationships between an issuer and the member, the candidate, or his or her firm (such as a directorship or consultancy by a member; investment banking, underwriting, and financial relationships; broker/dealer market-making activities; and material beneficial ownership of stock). For the purposes of Standard VI(A), members and candidates beneficially own securities or other investments if they have a direct or indirect pecuniary interest in the securities, have the power to vote or direct the voting of the shares of the securities or investments, or have the power to dispose or direct the disposition of the security or investment.

A member or candidate must take reasonable steps to determine whether a conflict of interest exists and disclose to clients any known conflicts of the member's or candidate's firm. Disclosure of broker/dealer market-making activities alerts clients that a purchase or sale might be made from or to the firm's principal account and that the firm has a special interest in the price of the stock.

Additionally, disclosures should be made to clients regarding fee arrangements, subadvisory agreements, or other situations involving nonstandard fee structures. Equally important is the disclosure of arrangements in which the firm benefits directly from investment recommendations. An obvious conflict of interest is the rebate of a portion of the service fee some classes of mutual funds charge to investors. Members and candidates should ensure that their firms disclose such relationships so clients can fully understand the costs of their investments and the benefits received by their investment manager's employer.

Cross-Departmental Conflicts

Other circumstances can give rise to actual or potential conflicts of interest. For instance, a sell-side analyst working for a broker/dealer may be encouraged, not only by members of her or his own firm but by corporate issuers themselves, to write research reports about particular companies. The buy-side analyst is likely to be faced with similar conflicts as banks exercise their underwriting and security-dealing powers. The marketing division may ask an analyst to recommend the stock of a certain company in order to obtain business from that company.

The potential for conflicts of interest also exists with broker-sponsored limited partnerships formed to invest venture capital. Increasingly, members and candidates are expected not only to follow issues from these partnerships once they are offered to the public but also to promote the issues in the secondary market after public offerings. Members, candidates, and their firms should attempt to resolve situations presenting potential conflicts of interest or disclose them in accordance with the principles set forth in Standard VI(A).

Conflicts with Stock Ownership

The most prevalent conflict requiring disclosure under Standard VI(A) is a member's or candidate's ownership of stock in companies that he or she recommends to clients or that clients hold. Clearly, the easiest method for preventing a conflict is to prohibit members and candidates from owning any such securities, but this approach is overly burdensome and discriminates against members and candidates.

Therefore, sell-side members and candidates should disclose any materially beneficial ownership interest in a security or other investment that the member or candidate is recommending. Buy-side members and candidates should disclose their procedures for reporting requirements for personal transactions. Conflicts arising from personal investing are discussed more fully in the guidance for Standard VI(B).

Conflicts as a Director

Service as a director poses three basic conflicts of interest. First, a conflict may exist between the duties owed to clients and the duties owed to shareholders of the company. Second, investment personnel who serve as directors may receive the securities or options to purchase securities of the company as compensation for serving on the board, which could raise questions about trading actions that might increase the value of those securities. Third, board service creates the opportunity to receive material nonpublic information involving the company. Even though the information is confidential, the perception could be that information not available to the public is being communicated to a director's firm—whether a broker, investment adviser, or other type of organization. When members or candidates providing investment services also serve as directors, they should be isolated from those making investment decisions by the use of firewalls or similar restrictions.

Recommended Procedures for Compliance

Members or candidates should disclose special compensation arrangements with the employer that might conflict with client interests, such as bonuses based on short-term performance criteria, commissions, incentive fees, performance fees, and referral fees. If the member's or candidate's firm does not permit such disclosure, the member or candidate should document the request and may consider dissociating from the activity.

Members' and candidates' firms are encouraged to include information on compensation packages in firms' promotional literature. If a member or candidate manages a portfolio for which the fee is based on capital gains or capital appreciation (a performance fee), this information should be disclosed to clients. If a member, a candidate, or a member's or candidate's firm has outstanding agent options to buy stock as part of the compensation package for corporate financing activities, the amount and expiration date of these options should be disclosed as a footnote to any research report published by the member's or candidate's firm.

Application of the Standard

Example 1 (Conflict of Interest and Business Relationships):

Hunter Weiss is a research analyst with Farmington Company, a broker and investment banking firm. Farmington's merger and acquisition department has represented Vimco, a conglomerate, in all of Vimco's acquisitions for 20 years. From time to time, Farmington officers sit on the boards of directors of various Vimco subsidiaries. Weiss is writing a research report on Vimco.

> *Comment*: Weiss must disclose in his research report Farmington's special relationship with Vimco. Broker/dealer management of and participation in public offerings must be disclosed in research reports. Because the position of underwriter to a company entails a special past and potential future relationship with a company that is the subject of investment advice, it threatens the independence and objectivity of the report writer and must be disclosed.

Example 2 (Conflict of Interest and Business Stock Ownership):

The investment management firm of Dover & Roe sells a 25% interest in its partnership to a multinational bank holding company, First of New York. Immediately after the sale, Margaret Hobbs, president of Dover & Roe, changes her recommendation for First of New York's common stock from "sell" to "buy" and adds First of New York's commercial paper to Dover & Roe's approved list for purchase.

Comment: Hobbs must disclose the new relationship with First of New York to all Dover & Roe clients. This relationship must also be disclosed to clients by the firm's portfolio managers when they make specific investment recommendations or take investment actions with respect to First of New York's securities.

Example 3 (Conflict of Interest and Personal Stock Ownership):

Carl Fargmon, a research analyst who follows firms producing office equipment, has been recommending purchase of Kincaid Printing because of its innovative new line of copiers. After his initial report on the company, Fargmon's wife inherits from a distant relative US$3 million of Kincaid stock. He has been asked to write a follow-up report on Kincaid.

Comment: Fargmon must disclose his wife's ownership of the Kincaid stock to his employer and in his follow-up report. Best practice would be to avoid the conflict by asking his employer to assign another analyst to draft the follow-up report.

Example 4 (Conflict of Interest and Personal Stock Ownership):

Betty Roberts is speculating in penny stocks for her own account and purchases 100,000 shares of Drew Mining, Inc., for US$0.30 a share. She intends to sell these shares at the sign of any substantial upward price movement of the stock. A week later, her employer asks her to write a report on penny stocks in the mining industry to be published in two weeks. Even without owning the Drew stock, Roberts would recommend it in her report as a "buy." A surge in the price of the stock to the US$2 range is likely to result once the report is issued.

Comment: Although this holding may not be material, Roberts must disclose it in the report and to her employer before writing the report because the gain for her will be substantial if the market responds strongly to her recommendation. The fact that she has only recently purchased the stock adds to the appearance that she is not entirely objective.

Example 5 (Conflict of Interest and Compensation Arrangements):

Samantha Snead, a portfolio manager for Thomas Investment Counsel, Inc., specializes in managing public retirement funds and defined benefit pension plan accounts, all of which have long-term investment objectives. A year ago, Snead's employer, in an attempt to motivate and retain key investment professionals, introduced a bonus compensation system that rewards portfolio managers on the basis of quarterly performance relative to their peers and to certain benchmark indexes. In an attempt to improve the short-term performance of her accounts, Snead changes her investment strategy and purchases several high-beta stocks for client portfolios. These purchases are seemingly contrary to the clients' investment policy statements. Following their purchase, an officer of Griffin Corporation, one of Snead's pension fund clients, asks why Griffin Corporation's portfolio seems to be dominated by high-beta stocks of companies that often appear among the most actively traded issues. No change in objective or strategy has been recommended by Snead during the year.

Comment: Snead has violated Standard VI(A) by failing to inform her clients of the changes in her compensation arrangement with her employer, which created a conflict of interest between her compensation and her clients' IPSs. Firms may pay employees on the basis of performance, but pressure by Thomas Investment Counsel to achieve short-term performance goals is in basic conflict with the objectives of Snead's accounts.

See also Standard III(C)–Suitability.

Example 6 (Conflict of Interest, Options, and Compensation Arrangements):

Wayland Securities works with small companies doing IPOs or secondary offerings. Typically, these deals are in the US$10 million to US$50 million range, and as a result, the corporate finance fees are quite small. To compensate for the small fees, Wayland Securities usually takes "agent options"—that is, rights (exercisable within a two-year time frame) to acquire up to an additional 10% of the current offering. Following an IPO performed by Wayland for Falk Resources, Ltd., Darcy Hunter, the head of corporate finance at Wayland, is concerned about receiving value for her Falk Resources options. The options are due to expire in one month, and the stock is not doing well. She contacts John Fitzpatrick in the research department of Wayland Securities, reminds him that he is eligible for 30% of these options, and indicates that now would be a good time to give some additional coverage to Falk Resources. Fitzpatrick agrees and immediately issues a favorable report.

> *Comment*: For Fitzpatrick to avoid being in violation of Standard VI(A), he must indicate in the report the volume and expiration date of agent options outstanding. Furthermore, because he is personally eligible for some of the options, Fitzpatrick must disclose the extent of this compensation. He also must be careful to not violate his duty of independence and objectivity under Standard I(B).

Example 7 (Conflict of Interest and Compensation Arrangements):

Gary Carter is a representative with Bengal International, a registered broker/dealer. Carter is approached by a stock promoter for Badger Company, who offers to pay Carter additional compensation for sales of Badger Company's stock to Carter's clients. Carter accepts the stock promoter's offer but does not disclose the arrangements to his clients or to his employer. Carter sells shares of the stock to his clients.

> *Comment*: Carter has violated Standard VI(A) by failing to disclose to clients that he is receiving additional compensation for recommending and selling Badger stock. Because he did not disclose the arrangement with Badger to his clients, the clients were unable to evaluate whether Carter's recommendations to buy Badger were affected by this arrangement. Carter's conduct also violated Standard VI(A) by failing to disclose to his employer monetary compensation received in addition to the compensation and benefits conferred by his employer. Carter was required by Standard VI(A) to disclose the arrangement with Badger to his employer so that his employer could evaluate whether the arrangement affected Carter's objectivity and loyalty.

Example 8 (Conflict of Interest and Directorship):

Carol Corky, a senior portfolio manager for Universal Management, recently became involved as a trustee with the Chelsea Foundation, a large not-for-profit foundation in her hometown. Universal is a small money manager (with assets under management of approximately US$100 million) that caters to individual investors. Chelsea has assets in excess of US$2 billion. Corky does not believe informing Universal of her involvement with Chelsea is necessary.

> *Comment*: By failing to inform Universal of her involvement with Chelsea, Corky violated Standard VI(A). Given the large size of the endowment at Chelsea, Corky's new role as a trustee can reasonably be expected to be time consuming, to the possible detriment of Corky's portfolio responsibilities with Universal. Also, as a trustee, Corky may become involved in

the investment decisions at Chelsea. Therefore, Standard VI(A) obligates Corky to discuss becoming a trustee at Chelsea with her compliance officer or supervisor at Universal before accepting the position, and she should have disclosed the degree to which she would be involved in investment decisions at Chelsea.

Example 9 (Conflict of Interest and Personal Trading):

Bruce Smith covers eastern European equities for Marlborough Investments, an investment management firm with a strong presence in emerging markets. While on a business trip to Russia, Smith learns that investing in Russian equities directly is difficult but that equity-linked notes that replicate the performance of underlying Russian equities can be purchased from a New York–based investment bank. Believing that his firm would not be interested in such a security, Smith purchases a note linked to a Russian telecommunications company for his own account without informing Marlborough. A month later, Smith decides that the firm should consider investing in Russian equities by way of the equity-linked notes. He prepares a write-up on the market that concludes with a recommendation to purchase several of the notes. One note he recommends is linked to the same Russian telecom company that Smith holds in his personal account.

> *Comment*: Smith has violated Standard VI(A) by failing to disclose his purchase and ownership of the note linked to the Russian telecom company. Smith is required by the standard to disclose the investment opportunity to his employer and look to his company's policies on personal trading to determine whether it was proper for him to purchase the note for his own account. By purchasing the note, Smith may or may not have impaired his ability to make an unbiased and objective assessment of the appropriateness of the derivative instrument for his firm, but Smith's failure to disclose the purchase to his employer impaired his employer's ability to decide whether his ownership of the security is a conflict of interest that might affect Smith's future recommendations. Then, when he recommended the particular telecom notes to his firm, Smith compounded his problems by not disclosing that he owned the notes in his personal account—a clear conflict of interest.

Example 10 (Conflict of Interest and Requested Favors):

Michael Papis is the chief investment officer of his state's retirement fund. The fund has always used outside advisers for the real estate allocation, and this information is clearly presented in all fund communications. Thomas Nagle, a recognized sell-side research analyst and Papis's business school classmate, recently left the investment bank he worked for to start his own asset management firm, Accessible Real Estate. Nagle is trying to build his assets under management and contacts Papis about gaining some of the retirement fund's allocation. In the previous few years, the performance of the retirement fund's real estate investments was in line with the fund's benchmark but was not extraordinary. Papis decides to help out his old friend and also to seek better returns by moving the real estate allocation to Accessible. The only notice of the change in adviser appears in the next annual report in the listing of associated advisers.

> *Comment*: Papis has violated Standard VI(A) by not disclosing to his employer his personal relationship with Nagle. Disclosure of his past history with Nagle would allow his firm to determine whether the conflict may have impaired Papis's independence in deciding to change managers.

See also Standard IV(C)–Responsibilities of Supervisors, Standard V(A)–Diligence and Reasonable Basis, and Standard V(B)–Communication with Clients and Prospective Clients.

Example 11 (Conflict of Interest and Business Relationships):

Bob Wade, trust manager for Central Midas Bank, was approached by Western Funds about promoting its family of funds, with special interest in the service-fee class. To entice Central to promote this class, Western Funds offered to pay the bank a service fee of 0.25%. Without disclosing the fee being offered to the bank, Wade asked one of the investment managers to review the Western Funds family of funds to determine whether they were suitable for clients of Central. The manager completed the normal due diligence review and determined that the funds were fairly valued in the market with fee structures on a par with their competitors. Wade decided to accept Western's offer and instructed the team of portfolio managers to exclusively promote these funds and the service-fee class to clients seeking to invest new funds or transfer from their current investments. So as to not influence the investment managers, Wade did not disclose the fee offer and allowed that income to flow directly to the bank.

Comment: Wade is violating Standard VI(A) by not disclosing the portion of the service fee being paid to Central. Although the investment managers may not be influenced by the fee, neither they nor the client have the proper information about Wade's decision to exclusively market this fund family and class of investments. Central may come to rely on the new fee as a component of the firm's profitability and may be unwilling to offer other products in the future that could affect the fees received.

See also Standard I(B)–Independence and Objectivity.

Example 12 (Disclosure of Conflicts to Employers):

Yehudit Dagan is a portfolio manager for Risk Management Bank (RMB), whose clients include retirement plans and corporations. RMB provides a defined contribution retirement plan for its employees that offers 20 large diversified mutual fund investment options, including a mutual fund managed by Dagan's RMB colleagues. After being employed for six months, Dagan became eligible to participate in the retirement plan, and she intends to allocate her retirement plan assets in six of the investment options, including the fund managed by her RMB colleagues. Dagan is concerned that joining the plan will lead to a potentially significant amount of paperwork for her (e.g., disclosure of her retirement account holdings and needing preclearance for her transactions), especially with her investing in the in-house fund.

Comment: Standard VI(A) would not require Dagan to disclosure her personal or retirement investments in large diversified mutual funds, unless specifically required by her employer. For practical reasons, the standard does not require Dagan to gain preclearance for ongoing payroll deduction contributions to retirement plan account investment options.

Dagan should ensure that her firm does not have a specific policy regarding investment—whether personal or in the retirement account—for funds managed by the company's employees. These mutual funds may be subject to the company's disclosure, preclearance, and trading restriction procedures to identify possible conflicts prior to the execution of trades.

Standard VI(B) Priority of Transactions

> Investment transactions for clients and employers must have priority over investment transactions in which a Member or Candidate is the beneficial owner.

Guidance

Highlights:

- *Avoiding Potential Conflicts*
- *Personal Trading Secondary to Trading for Clients*
- *Standards for Nonpublic Information*
- *Impact on All Accounts with Beneficial Ownership*

Standard VI(B) reinforces the responsibility of members and candidates to give the interests of their clients and employers priority over their personal financial interests. This standard is designed to prevent any potential conflict of interest or the appearance of a conflict of interest with respect to personal transactions. Client interests have priority. Client transactions must take precedence over transactions made on behalf of the member's or candidate's firm or personal transactions.

Avoiding Potential Conflicts

Conflicts between the client's interest and an investment professional's personal interest may occur. Although conflicts of interest exist, nothing is inherently unethical about individual managers, advisers, or mutual fund employees making money from personal investments as long as (1) the client is not disadvantaged by the trade, (2) the investment professional does not benefit personally from trades undertaken for clients, and (3) the investment professional complies with applicable regulatory requirements.

Some situations occur where a member or candidate may need to enter a personal transaction that runs counter to current recommendations or what the portfolio manager is doing for client portfolios. For example, a member or candidate may be required at some point to sell an asset to make a college tuition payment or a down payment on a home, to meet a margin call, or so on. The sale may be contrary to the long-term advice the member or candidate is currently providing to clients. In these situations, the same three criteria given in the preceding paragraph should be applied in the transaction so as to not violate Standard VI(B).

Personal Trading Secondary to Trading for Clients

Standard VI(B) states that transactions for clients and employers must have priority over transactions in securities or other investments for which a member or candidate is the beneficial owner. The objective of the standard is to prevent personal transactions from adversely affecting the interests of clients or employers. A member or candidate having the same investment positions or being co-invested with clients does not always create a conflict. Some clients in certain investment situations require members or candidates to have aligned interests. Personal investment positions or transactions of members or candidates or their firm should never, however, adversely affect client investments.

Standards for Nonpublic Information

Standard VI(B) covers the activities of members and candidates who have knowledge of pending transactions that may be made on behalf of their clients or employers, who have access to nonpublic information during the normal preparation of research recommendations, or who take investment actions. Members and candidates are prohibited from conveying nonpublic information to any person whose relationship to the member or candidate makes the member or candidate a beneficial owner of the person's securities. Members and candidates must not convey this information to any other person if the nonpublic information can be deemed material.

Impact on All Accounts with Beneficial Ownership

Members or candidates may undertake transactions in accounts for which they are a beneficial owner only after their clients and employers have had adequate opportunity to act on a recommendation. Personal transactions include those made for the member's or candidate's own account, for family (including spouse, children, and other immediate family members) accounts, and for accounts in which the member or candidate has a direct or indirect pecuniary interest, such as a trust or retirement account. Family accounts that are client accounts should be treated like any other firm account and should neither be given special treatment nor be disadvantaged because of the family relationship. If a member or candidate has a beneficial ownership in the account, however, the member or candidate may be subject to preclearance or reporting requirements of the employer or applicable law.

Recommended Procedures for Compliance

Policies and procedures designed to prevent potential conflicts of interest, and even the appearance of a conflict of interest, with respect to personal transactions are critical to establishing investor confidence in the securities industry. Therefore, members and candidates should urge their firms to establish such policies and procedures. Because investment firms vary greatly in assets under management, types of clients, number of employees, and so on, each firm should have policies regarding personal investing that are best suited to the firm. Members and candidates should then prominently disclose these policies to clients and prospective clients.

The specific provisions of each firm's standards will vary, but all firms should adopt certain basic procedures to address the conflict areas created by personal investing. These procedures include the following:

- *Limited participation in equity IPOs*: Some eagerly awaited IPOs rise significantly in value shortly after the issue is brought to market. Because the new issue may be highly attractive and sought after, the opportunity to participate in the IPO may be limited. Therefore, purchases of IPOs by investment personnel create conflicts of interest in two principal ways. First, participation in an IPO may have the appearance of taking away an attractive investment opportunity from clients for personal gain—a clear breach of the duty of loyalty to clients. Second, personal purchases in IPOs may have the appearance that the investment opportunity is being bestowed as an incentive to make future investment decisions for the benefit of the party providing the opportunity. Members and candidates can avoid these conflicts or appearances of conflicts of interest by not participating in IPOs.

  Reliable and systematic review procedures should be established to ensure that conflicts relating to IPOs are identified and appropriately dealt with by supervisors. Members and candidates should preclear their participation in IPOs, even in situations without any conflict of interest between a member's or candidate's participation in an IPO and the client's interests. Members and candidates should not benefit from the position that their clients occupy in the marketplace—through preferred trading, the allocation of limited offerings, or oversubscription.

- *Restrictions on private placements*: Strict limits should be placed on investment personnel acquiring securities in private placements, and appropriate supervisory and review procedures should be established to prevent noncompliance.

  Firms do not routinely use private placements for clients (e.g., venture capital deals) because of the high risk associated with them. Conflicts related to private placements are more significant to members and candidates who manage large pools of assets or act as plan sponsors because these managers may be offered special opportunities, such as private placements, as a reward or an enticement for continuing to do business with a particular broker.

  Participation in private placements raises conflict-of-interest issues that are similar to issues surrounding IPOs. Investment personnel should not be involved in transactions, including (but not limited to) private placements, that could be perceived as favors or gifts that seem designed to influence future judgment or to reward past business deals.

  Whether the venture eventually proves to be good or bad, managers have an immediate conflict concerning private placement opportunities. If and when the investments go public, participants in private placements have an incentive to recommend the investments to clients regardless of the suitability of the investments for their clients. Doing so increases the value of the participants' personal portfolios.

- *Establish blackout/restricted periods*: Investment personnel involved in the investment decision-making process should establish blackout periods prior to trades for clients so that managers cannot take advantage of their knowledge of client activity by "front-running" client trades (trading for one's personal account before trading for client accounts).

  Individual firms must decide who within the firm should be required to comply with the trading restrictions. At a minimum, all individuals who are involved in the investment decision-making process should be subject to the same restricted period. Each firm must determine specific requirements related to blackout and restricted periods that are most relevant to the firm while ensuring that the procedures are governed by the guiding principles set forth in the Code and Standards. Size of firm and type of securities purchased are relevant factors. For example, in a large firm, a blackout requirement is, in effect, a total trading ban because the firm is continually trading in most securities. In a small firm, the blackout period is more likely to prevent the investment manager from front-running.

- *Reporting requirements*: Supervisors should establish reporting procedures for investment personnel, including disclosure of personal holdings/beneficial ownerships, confirmations of trades to the firm and the employee, and preclearance procedures. Once trading restrictions are in place, they must be enforced. The best method for monitoring and enforcing procedures to eliminate conflicts of interest in personal trading is through reporting requirements, including the following:

  - **Disclosure of holdings in which the employee has a beneficial interest**. Disclosure by investment personnel to the firm should be made upon commencement of the employment relationship and at least annually thereafter. To address privacy considerations, disclosure of personal holdings should be handled in a confidential manner by the firm.

- **Providing duplicate confirmations of transactions**. Investment personnel should be required to direct their brokers to supply to firms duplicate copies or confirmations of all their personal securities transactions and copies of periodic statements for all securities accounts. The duplicate confirmation requirement has two purposes: (1) The requirement sends a message that there is independent verification, which reduces the likelihood of unethical behavior, and (2) it enables verification of the accounting of the flow of personal investments that cannot be determined from merely looking at holdings.
- **Preclearance procedures**. Investment personnel should examine all planned personal trades to identify possible conflicts prior to the execution of the trades. Preclearance procedures are designed to identify possible conflicts before a problem arises.

■ *Disclosure of policies*: Members and candidates should fully disclose to investors their firm's policies regarding personal investing. The information about employees' personal investment activities and policies will foster an atmosphere of full and complete disclosure and calm the public's legitimate concerns about the conflicts of interest posed by investment personnel's personal trading. The disclosure must provide helpful information to investors; it should not be simply boilerplate language, such as "investment personnel are subject to policies and procedures regarding their personal trading."

Application of the Standard

Example 1 (Personal Trading):

Research analyst Marlon Long does not recommend purchase of a common stock for his employer's account because he wants to purchase the stock personally and does not want to wait until the recommendation is approved and the stock is purchased by his employer.

> *Comment*: Long has violated Standard VI(B) by taking advantage of his knowledge of the stock's value before allowing his employer to benefit from that information.

Example 2 (Trading for Family Member Account):

Carol Baker, the portfolio manager of an aggressive growth mutual fund, maintains an account in her husband's name at several brokerage firms with which the fund and a number of Baker's other individual clients do a substantial amount of business. Whenever a hot issue becomes available, she instructs the brokers to buy it for her husband's account. Because such issues normally are scarce, Baker often acquires shares in hot issues but her clients are not able to participate in them.

> *Comment*: To avoid violating Standard VI(B), Baker must acquire shares for her mutual fund first and acquire them for her husband's account only after doing so, even though she might miss out on participating in new issues via her husband's account. She also must disclose the trading for her husband's account to her employer because this activity creates a conflict between her personal interests and her employer's interests.

Example 3 (Family Accounts as Equals):

Erin Toffler, a portfolio manager at Esposito Investments, manages the retirement account established with the firm by her parents. Whenever IPOs become available, she first allocates shares to all her other clients for whom the investment is appropriate;

only then does she place any remaining portion in her parents' account, if the issue is appropriate for them. She has adopted this procedure so that no one can accuse her of favoring her parents.

Comment: Toffler has violated Standard VI(B) by breaching her duty to her parents by treating them differently from her other accounts simply because of the family relationship. As fee-paying clients of Esposito Investments, Toffler's parents are entitled to the same treatment as any other client of the firm. If Toffler has beneficial ownership in the account, however, and Esposito Investments has preclearance and reporting requirements for personal transactions, she may have to preclear the trades and report the transactions to Esposito.

Example 4 (Personal Trading and Disclosure):

Gary Michaels is an entry-level employee who holds a low-paying job serving both the research department and the investment management department of an active investment management firm. He purchases a sports car and begins to wear expensive clothes after only a year of employment with the firm. The director of the investment management department, who has responsibility for monitoring the personal stock transactions of all employees, investigates and discovers that Michaels has made substantial investment gains by purchasing stocks just before they were put on the firm's recommended "buy" list. Michaels was regularly given the firm's quarterly personal transaction form but declined to complete it.

Comment: Michaels violated Standard VI(B) by placing personal transactions ahead of client transactions. In addition, his supervisor violated Standard IV(C)–Responsibilities of Supervisors by permitting Michaels to continue to perform his assigned tasks without having signed the quarterly personal transaction form. Note also that if Michaels had communicated information about the firm's recommendations to a person who traded the security, that action would be a misappropriation of the information and a violation of Standard II(A)–Material Nonpublic Information.

Example 5 (Trading Prior to Report Dissemination):

A brokerage's insurance analyst, Denise Wilson, makes a closed-circuit TV report to her firm's branches around the country. During the broadcast, she includes negative comments about a major company in the insurance industry. The following day, Wilson's report is printed and distributed to the sales force and public customers. The report recommends that both short-term traders and intermediate investors take profits by selling that insurance company's stock. Seven minutes after the broadcast, however, Ellen Riley, head of the firm's trading department, had closed out a long "call" position in the stock. Shortly thereafter, Riley established a sizable "put" position in the stock. When asked about her activities, Riley claimed she took the actions to facilitate anticipated sales by institutional clients.

Comment: Riley did not give customers an opportunity to buy or sell in the options market before the firm itself did. By taking action before the report was disseminated, Riley's firm may have depressed the price of the calls and increased the price of the puts. The firm could have avoided a conflict of interest if it had waited to trade for its own account until its clients had an opportunity to receive and assimilate Wilson's recommendations. As it is, Riley's actions violated Standard VI(B).

Standard VI(C) Referral Fees

> Members and Candidates must disclose to their employer, clients, and prospective clients, as appropriate, any compensation, consideration, or benefit received from or paid to others for the recommendation of products or services.

Guidance

Standard VI(C) states the responsibility of members and candidates to inform their employer, clients, and prospective clients of any benefit received for referrals of customers and clients. Such disclosures allow clients or employers to evaluate (1) any partiality shown in any recommendation of services and (2) the full cost of the services. Members and candidates must disclose when they pay a fee or provide compensation to others who have referred prospective clients to the member or candidate.

Appropriate disclosure means that members and candidates must advise the client or prospective client, before entry into any formal agreement for services, of any benefit given or received for the recommendation of any services provided by the member or candidate. In addition, the member or candidate must disclose the nature of the consideration or benefit—for example, flat fee or percentage basis, one-time or continuing benefit, based on performance, benefit in the form of provision of research or other noncash benefit—together with the estimated dollar value. Consideration includes all fees, whether paid in cash, in soft dollars, or in kind.

Recommended Procedures for Compliance

Members and candidates should encourage their employers to develop procedures related to referral fees. The firm may completely restrict such fees. If the firm does not adopt a strict prohibition of such fees, the procedures should indicate the appropriate steps for requesting approval.

Employers should have investment professionals provide to the clients notification of approved referral fee programs and provide the employer regular (at least quarterly) updates on the amount and nature of compensation received.

Application of the Standard

Example 1 (Disclosure of Referral Arrangements and Outside Parties):

Brady Securities, Inc., a broker/dealer, has established a referral arrangement with Lewis Brothers, Ltd., an investment counseling firm. In this arrangement, Brady Securities refers all prospective tax-exempt accounts, including pension, profit-sharing, and endowment accounts, to Lewis Brothers. In return, Lewis Brothers makes available to Brady Securities on a regular basis the security recommendations and reports of its research staff, which registered representatives of Brady Securities use in serving customers. In addition, Lewis Brothers conducts monthly economic and market reviews for Brady Securities personnel and directs all stock commission business generated by referral accounts to Brady Securities.

Willard White, a partner in Lewis Brothers, calculates that the incremental costs involved in functioning as the research department of Brady Securities are US$20,000 annually.

Referrals from Brady Securities last year resulted in fee income of US$200,000 for Lewis Brothers, and directing all stock trades through Brady Securities resulted in additional costs to Lewis Brothers' clients of US$10,000.

Diane Branch, the chief financial officer of Maxwell Inc., contacts White and says that she is seeking an investment manager for Maxwell's profit-sharing plan. She adds, "My friend Harold Hill at Brady Securities recommended your firm without qualification, and that's good enough for me. Do we have a deal?" White accepts the new account but does not disclose his firm's referral arrangement with Brady Securities.

> *Comment*: White has violated Standard VI(C) by failing to inform the prospective customer of the referral fee payable in services and commissions for an indefinite period to Brady Securities. Such disclosure could have caused Branch to reassess Hill's recommendation and make a more critical evaluation of Lewis Brothers' services.

Example 2 (Disclosure of Interdepartmental Referral Arrangements):

James Handley works for the trust department of Central Trust Bank. He receives compensation for each referral he makes to Central Trust's brokerage department and personal financial management department that results in a sale. He refers several of his clients to the personal financial management department but does not disclose the arrangement within Central Trust to his clients.

> *Comment*: Handley has violated Standard VI(C) by not disclosing the referral arrangement at Central Trust Bank to his clients. Standard VI(C) does not distinguish between referral payments paid by a third party for referring clients to the third party and internal payments paid within the firm to attract new business to a subsidiary. Members and candidates must disclose all such referral fees. Therefore, Handley is required to disclose, at the time of referral, any referral fee agreement in place among Central Trust Bank's departments. The disclosure should include the nature and the value of the benefit and should be made in writing.

Example 3 (Disclosure of Referral Arrangements and Informing Firm):

Katherine Roberts is a portfolio manager at Katama Investments, an advisory firm specializing in managing assets for high-net-worth individuals. Katama's trading desk uses a variety of brokerage houses to execute trades on behalf of its clients. Roberts asks the trading desk to direct a large portion of its commissions to Naushon, Inc., a small broker/dealer run by one of Roberts' business school classmates. Katama's traders have found that Naushon is not very competitive on pricing, and although Naushon generates some research for its trading clients, Katama's other analysts have found most of Naushon's research to be not especially useful. Nevertheless, the traders do as Roberts asks, and in return for receiving a large portion of Katama's business, Naushon recommends the investment services of Roberts and Katama to its wealthiest clients. This arrangement is not disclosed to either Katama or the clients referred by Naushon.

> *Comment*: Roberts is violating Standard VI(C) by failing to inform her employer of the referral arrangement.

Example 4 (Disclosure of Referral Arrangements and Outside Organizations):

Alex Burl is a portfolio manager at Helpful Investments, a local investment advisory firm. Burl is on the advisory board of his child's school, which is looking for ways to raise money to purchase new playground equipment for the school. Burl discusses a plan with his supervisor in which he will donate to the school a portion of his service fee from new clients referred by the parents of students at the school. Upon getting the approval from Helpful, Burl presents the idea to the school's advisory board and directors. The school agrees to announce the program at the next parent event and asks Burl to provide the appropriate written materials to be distributed. A week following the distribution of the flyers, Burl receives the first school-related referral. In establishing the client's investment policy statement, Burl clearly discusses the school's referral and outlines the plans for distributing the donation back to the school.

> *Comment*: Burl has not violated Standard VI(C) because he secured the permission of his employer, Helpful Investments, and the school prior to beginning the program and because he discussed the arrangement with the client at the time the investment policy statement was designed.

Example 5 (Disclosure of Referral Arrangements and Outside Parties):

The sponsor of a state employee pension is seeking to hire a firm to manage the pension plan's emerging market allocation. To assist in the review process, the sponsor has hired Thomas Arrow as a consultant to solicit proposals from various advisers. Arrow is contracted by the sponsor to represent its best interest in selecting the most appropriate new manager. The process runs smoothly, and Overseas Investments is selected as the new manager.

The following year, news breaks that Arrow is under investigation by the local regulator for accepting kickbacks from investment managers after they are awarded new pension allocations. Overseas Investments is included in the list of firms allegedly making these payments. Although the sponsor is happy with the performance of Overseas since it has been managing the pension plan's emerging market funds, the sponsor still decides to have an independent review of the proposals and the selection process to ensure that Overseas was the appropriate firm for its needs. This review confirms that, even though Arrow was being paid by both parties, the recommendation of Overseas appeared to be objective and appropriate.

> *Comment*: Arrow has violated Standard VI(C) because he did not disclose the fee being paid by Overseas. Withholding this information raises the question of a potential lack of objectivity in the recommendation of Overseas by Arrow; this aspect is in addition to questions about the legality of having firms pay to be considered for an allocation.
>
> Regulators and governmental agencies may adopt requirements concerning allowable consultant activities. Local regulations sometimes include having a consultant register with the regulatory agency's ethics board. Regulator policies may include a prohibition on acceptance of payments from investment managers receiving allocations and require regular reporting of contributions made to political organizations and candidates. Arrow would have to adhere to these requirements as well as the Code and Standards.

STANDARD VII: RESPONSIBILITIES AS A CFA INSTITUTE MEMBER OR CFA CANDIDATE

Standard VII(A) Conduct as Participants in CFA Institute Programs

Members and Candidates must not engage in any conduct that compromises the reputation or integrity of CFA Institute or the CFA designation or the integrity, validity, or security of CFA Institute programs.

Guidance

Highlights:

- *Confidential Program Information*
- *Additional CFA Program Restrictions*
- *Expressing an Opinion*

Standard VII(A) covers the conduct of CFA Institute members and candidates involved with the CFA Program and prohibits any conduct that undermines the public's confidence that the CFA charter represents a level of achievement based on merit and ethical conduct. There is an array of CFA Institute programs beyond the CFA Program that provide additional educational and credentialing opportunities, including the Certificate in Investment Performance Measurement (CIPM) Program and the CFA Institute Investment Foundations™ Program. The standard's function is to hold members and candidates to a high ethical criterion while they are participating in or involved with any CFA Institute program. Conduct covered includes but is not limited to

- giving or receiving assistance (cheating) on any CFA Institute examinations;
- violating the rules, regulations, and testing policies of CFA Institute programs;
- providing confidential program or exam information to candidates or the public;
- disregarding or attempting to circumvent security measures established for any CFA Institute examinations;
- improperly using an association with CFA Institute to further personal or professional goals; and
- misrepresenting information on the Professional Conduct Statement or in the CFA Institute Continuing Education Program.

Confidential Program Information

CFA Institute is vigilant about protecting the integrity of CFA Institute programs' content and examination processes. CFA Institute program rules, regulations, and policies prohibit candidates from disclosing confidential material gained during the exam process.

Examples of information that cannot be disclosed by candidates sitting for an exam include but are not limited to

- specific details of questions appearing on the exam and
- broad topical areas and formulas tested or not tested on the exam.

All aspects of the exam, including questions, broad topical areas, and formulas, tested or not tested, are considered confidential until such time as CFA Institute elects to release them publicly. This confidentiality requirement allows CFA Institute to maintain the integrity and rigor of exams for future candidates. Standard VII(A) does not prohibit candidates from discussing nonconfidential information or curriculum material with others or in study groups in preparation for the exam.

Candidates increasingly use online forums and new technology as part of their exam preparations. CFA Institute actively polices blogs, forums, and related social networking groups for information considered confidential. The organization works with both individual candidates and the sponsors of online or offline services to promptly remove any and all violations. As noted in the discussion of Standard I(A)–Knowledge of the Law, candidates, members, and the public are encouraged to report suspected violations to CFA Institute.

Additional CFA Program Restrictions

The CFA Program rules, regulations, and policies define additional allowed and disallowed actions concerning the exams. Violating any of the testing policies, such as the calculator policy, personal belongings policy, or the Candidate Pledge, constitutes a violation of Standard VII(A). Candidates will find all of these policies on the CFA Program portion of the CFA Institute website (www.cfainstitute.org). Exhibit 2 provides the Candidate Pledge, which highlights the respect candidates must have for the integrity, validity, and security of the CFA exam.

Members may participate as volunteers in various aspects of the CFA Program. Standard VII(A) prohibits members from disclosing and/or soliciting confidential material gained prior to or during the exam and grading processes with those outside the CFA exam development process.

Examples of information that cannot be shared by members involved in developing, administering, or grading the exams include but are not limited to

- questions appearing on the exam or under consideration,
- deliberation related to the exam process, and
- information related to the scoring of questions.

Members may also be asked to offer assistance with other CFA Institute programs, including but not limited to the CIPM and Investment Foundations programs. Members participating in any CFA Institute program should do so with the same level of integrity and confidentiality as is required of participation in the CFA Program.

Expressing an Opinion

Standard VII(A) does *not* cover expressing opinions regarding CFA Institute, the CFA Program, or other CFA Institute programs. Members and candidates are free to disagree and express their disagreement with CFA Institute on its policies, its procedures, or any advocacy positions taken by the organization. When expressing a personal opinion, a candidate is prohibited from disclosing content-specific information, including any actual exam question and the information as to subject matter covered or not covered in the exam.

Exhibit 2 Sample of CFA Program Testing Policies

Candidate Pledge	As a candidate in the CFA Program, I am obligated to follow Standard VII(A) of the CFA Institute Standards of Professional Conduct, which states that members and candidates must not engage in any conduct that compromises the reputation or integrity of CFA Institute or the CFA designation or the integrity, validity, or security of the CFA exam. ■ Prior to this exam, I have not given or received information regarding the content of this exam. During this exam, I will not give or receive any information regarding the content of this exam. ■ After this exam, I will not disclose **ANY** portion of this exam and I will not remove **ANY** exam materials from the testing room in original or copied form. I understand that all exam materials, including my answers, are the property of CFA Institute and will not be returned to me in any form. ■ I will follow **ALL** rules of the CFA Program as stated on the CFA Institute website and the back cover of the exam book. My violation of any rules of the CFA Program will result in CFA Institute voiding my exam results and may lead to suspension or termination of my candidacy in the CFA Program.

Application of the Standard

Example 1 (Sharing Exam Questions):

Travis Nero serves as a proctor for the administration of the CFA examination in his city. In the course of his service, he reviews a copy of the Level II exam on the evening prior to the exam's administration and provides information concerning the exam questions to two candidates who use it to prepare for the exam.

> *Comment*: Nero and the two candidates have violated Standard VII(A). By giving information about the exam questions to two candidates, Nero provided an unfair advantage to the two candidates and undermined the integrity and validity of the Level II exam as an accurate measure of the knowledge, skills, and abilities necessary to earn the right to use the CFA designation. By accepting the information, the candidates also compromised the integrity and validity of the Level II exam and undermined the ethical framework that is a key part of the designation.

Example 2 (Bringing Written Material into Exam Room):

Loren Sullivan is enrolled to take the Level II CFA examination. He has been having difficulty remembering a particular formula, so prior to entering the exam room, he writes the formula on the palm of his hand. During the afternoon section of the exam, a proctor notices Sullivan looking at the palm of his hand. She asks to see his hand and finds the formula.

> *Comment*: Because Sullivan wrote down information from the Candidate Body of Knowledge (CBOK) and took that written information into the exam room, his conduct compromised the validity of his exam performance and violated Standard VII(A). Sullivan's conduct was also in direct contradiction with the rules and regulations of the CFA Program, the Candidate Pledge, and the CFA Institute Code and Standards.

Example 3 (Writing after Exam Period End):

At the conclusion of the morning section of the Level I CFA examination, the proctors announce, "Stop writing now." John Davis has not completed the exam, so he continues to randomly fill in ovals on his answer sheet. A proctor approaches Davis's desk and reminds him that he should stop writing immediately. Davis, however, continues to complete the answer sheet. After the proctor asks him to stop writing two additional times, Davis finally puts down his pencil.

> *Comment*: By continuing to complete his exam after time was called, Davis has violated Standard VII(A). By continuing to write, Davis took an unfair advantage over other candidates, and his conduct compromised the validity of his exam performance. Additionally, by not heeding the proctor's repeated instructions, Davis violated the rules and regulations of the CFA Program.

Example 4 (Sharing Exam Content):

After completing Level II of the CFA exam, Annabelle Rossi posts on her blog about her experience. She posts the following: "Level II is complete! I think I did fairly well on the exam. It was really difficult, but fair. I think I did especially well on the derivatives questions. And there were tons of them! I think I counted 18! The ethics questions were really hard. I'm glad I spent so much time on the Code and Standards. I was surprised to see there were no questions at all about IPO allocations. I expected there to be a couple. Well, off to celebrate getting through it. See you tonight?"

> *Comment*: Rossi did not violate Standard VII(A) when she wrote about how difficult she found the exam or how well she thinks she may have done. By revealing portions of the CBOK covered on the exam and areas not covered, however, she did violate Standard VII(A) and the Candidate Pledge. Depending on the time frame in which the comments were posted, Rossi not only may have assisted future candidates but also may have provided an unfair advantage to candidates yet to sit for the same exam, thereby undermining the integrity and validity of the Level II exam.

Example 5 (Sharing Exam Content):

Level I candidate Etienne Gagne has been a frequent visitor to an internet forum designed specifically for CFA Program candidates. The week after completing the Level I examination, Gagne and several others begin a discussion thread on the forum about the most challenging questions and attempt to determine the correct answers.

> *Comment*: Gagne has violated Standard VII(A) by providing and soliciting confidential exam information, which compromises the integrity of the exam process and violates the Candidate Pledge. In trying to determine correct answers to specific questions, the group's discussion included question-specific details considered to be confidential to the CFA Program.

Example 6 (Sharing Exam Content):

CFA4Sure is a company that produces test-preparation materials for CFA Program candidates. Many candidates register for and use the company's products. The day after the CFA examination, CFA4Sure sends an e-mail to all its customers asking them to share with the company the hardest questions from the exam so that CFA4Sure can better prepare its customers for the next exam administration. Marisol Pena e-mails a summary of the questions she found most difficult on the exam.

Comment: Pena has violated Standard VII(A) by disclosing a portion of the exam questions. The information provided is considered confidential until publicly released by CFA Institute. CFA4Sure is likely to use such feedback to refine its review materials for future candidates. Pena's sharing of the specific questions undermines the integrity of the exam while potentially making the exam easier for future candidates.

If the CFA4Sure employees who participated in the solicitation of confidential CFA Program information are CFA Institute members or candidates, they also have violated Standard VII(A).

Example 7 (Discussion of Exam Grading Guidelines and Results):

Prior to participating in grading CFA examinations, Wesley Whitcomb is required to sign a CFA Institute Grader Agreement. As part of the Grader Agreement, Whitcomb agrees not to reveal or discuss the exam materials with anyone except CFA Institute staff or other graders. Several weeks after the conclusion of the CFA exam grading, Whitcomb tells several colleagues who are candidates in the CFA Program which question he graded. He also discusses the guideline answer and adds that few candidates scored well on the question.

Comment: Whitcomb violated Standard VII(A) by breaking the Grader Agreement and disclosing information related to a specific question on the exam, which compromised the integrity of the exam process.

Example 8 (Compromising CFA Institute Integrity as a Volunteer):

Jose Ramirez is an investor-relations consultant for several small companies that are seeking greater exposure to investors. He is also the program chair for the CFA Institute society in the city where he works. Ramirez schedules only companies that are his clients to make presentations to the society and excludes other companies.

Comment: Ramirez, by using his volunteer position at CFA Institute to benefit himself and his clients, compromises the reputation and integrity of CFA Institute and thus violates Standard VII(A).

Example 9 (Compromising CFA Institute Integrity as a Volunteer):

Marguerite Warrenski is a member of the CFA Institute GIPS Executive Committee, which oversees the creation, implementation, and revision of the GIPS standards. As a member of the Executive Committee, she has advance knowledge of confidential information regarding the GIPS standards, including any new or revised standards the committee is considering. She tells her clients that her Executive Committee membership will allow her to better assist her clients in keeping up with changes to the Standards and facilitating their compliance with the changes.

Comment: Warrenski is using her association with the GIPS Executive Committee to promote her firm's services to clients and potential clients. In defining her volunteer position at CFA Institute as a strategic business advantage over competing firms and implying to clients that she would use confidential information to further their interests, Warrenski is compromising the reputation and integrity of CFA Institute and thus violating Standard VII(A). She may factually state her involvement with the Executive Committee but cannot infer any special advantage to her clients from such participation.

Standard VII(B) Reference to CFA Institute, the CFA Designation, and the CFA Program

When referring to CFA Institute, CFA Institute membership, the CFA designation, or candidacy in the CFA Program, Members and Candidates must not misrepresent or exaggerate the meaning or implications of membership in CFA Institute, holding the CFA designation, or candidacy in the CFA Program.

Guidance

Highlights:

- *CFA Institute Membership*
- *Using the CFA Designation*
- *Referring to Candidacy in the CFA Program*

Standard VII(B) is intended to prevent promotional efforts that make promises or guarantees that are tied to the CFA designation. Individuals must not exaggerate the meaning or implications of membership in CFA Institute, holding the CFA designation, or candidacy in the CFA Program.

Standard VII(B) is not intended to prohibit factual statements related to the positive benefit of earning the CFA designation. However, statements referring to CFA Institute, the CFA designation, or the CFA Program that overstate the competency of an individual or imply, either directly or indirectly, that superior performance can be expected from someone with the CFA designation are not allowed under the standard.

Statements that highlight or emphasize the commitment of CFA Institute members, CFA charterholders, and CFA candidates to ethical and professional conduct or mention the thoroughness and rigor of the CFA Program are appropriate. Members and candidates may make claims about the relative merits of CFA Institute, the CFA Program, or the Code and Standards as long as those statements are implicitly or explicitly stated as the opinion of the speaker. Statements that do not express opinions have to be supported by facts.

Standard VII(B) applies to any form of communication, including but not limited to communications made in electronic or written form (such as on firm letterhead, business cards, professional biographies, directory listings, printed advertising, firm brochures, or personal resumes) and oral statements made to the public, clients, or prospects.

CFA Institute Membership

The term "CFA Institute member" refers to "regular" and "affiliate" members of CFA Institute who have met the membership requirements as defined in the CFA Institute Bylaws. Once accepted as a CFA Institute member, the member must satisfy the following requirements to maintain his or her status:

- remit annually to CFA Institute a completed Professional Conduct Statement, which renews the commitment to abide by the requirements of the Code and Standards and the CFA Institute Professional Conduct Program, and
- pay applicable CFA Institute membership dues on an annual basis.

If a CFA Institute member fails to meet any of these requirements, the individual is no longer considered an active member. Until membership is reactivated, individuals must not present themselves to others as active members. They may state, however, that they were CFA Institute members in the past or refer to the years when their membership was active.

Using the CFA Designation

Those who have earned the right to use the Chartered Financial Analyst designation are encouraged to do so but only in a manner that does not misrepresent or exaggerate the meaning or implications of the designation. The use of the designation may be accompanied by an accurate explanation of the requirements that have been met to earn the right to use the designation.

"CFA charterholders" are those individuals who have earned the right to use the CFA designation granted by CFA Institute. These people have satisfied certain requirements, including completion of the CFA Program and required years of acceptable work experience. Once granted the right to use the designation, individuals must also satisfy the CFA Institute membership requirements (see above) to maintain their right to use the designation.

If a CFA charterholder fails to meet any of the membership requirements, he or she forfeits the right to use the CFA designation. Until membership is reactivated, individuals must not present themselves to others as CFA charterholders. They may state, however, that they were charterholders in the past.

Given the growing popularity of social media, where individuals may anonymously express their opinions, pseudonyms or online profile names created to hide a member's identity should not be tagged with the CFA designation.

Use of the CFA designation by a CFA charterholder is governed by the terms and conditions of the annual Professional Conduct Statement Agreement, entered into between CFA Institute and its membership prior to commencement of use of the CFA designation and reaffirmed annually.

Referring to Candidacy in the CFA Program

Candidates in the CFA Program may refer to their participation in the CFA Program, but such references must clearly state that an individual is a *candidate* in the CFA Program and must not imply that the candidate has achieved any type of partial designation. A person is a candidate in the CFA Program if

- the person's application for registration in the CFA Program has been accepted by CFA Institute, as evidenced by issuance of a notice of acceptance, and the person is enrolled to sit for a specified examination or
- the registered person has sat for a specified examination but exam results have not yet been received.

If an individual is registered for the CFA Program but declines to sit for an exam or otherwise does not meet the definition of a candidate as described in the CFA Institute Bylaws, then that individual is no longer considered an active candidate. Once the person is enrolled to sit for a future examination, his or her CFA Program candidacy resumes.

CFA Program candidates must never state or imply that they have a partial designation as a result of passing one or more levels or cite an expected completion date of any level of the CFA Program. Final award of the charter is subject to meeting the CFA Program requirements and approval by the CFA Institute Board of Governors.

If a candidate passes each level of the exam in consecutive years and wants to state that he or she did so, that is not a violation of Standard VII(B) because it is a statement of fact. If the candidate then goes on to claim or imply superior ability by obtaining the designation in only three years, however, he or she is in violation of Standard VII(B).

Exhibit 3 provides examples of proper and improper references to the CFA designation.

Exhibit 3 Proper and Improper References to the CFA Designation

Proper References	Improper References
"Completion of the CFA Program has enhanced my portfolio management skills."	"CFA charterholders achieve better performance results."
"John Smith passed all three CFA Program examinations in three consecutive years."	"John Smith is among the elite, having passed all three CFA examinations in three consecutive attempts."
"The CFA designation is globally recognized and attests to a charterholder's success in a rigorous and comprehensive study program in the field of investment management and research analysis."	"As a CFA charterholder, I am the most qualified to manage client investments."
"The credibility that the CFA designation affords and the skills the CFA Program cultivates are key assets for my future career development."	"As a CFA charterholder, Jane White provides the best value in trade execution."
"I enrolled in the CFA Program to obtain the highest set of credentials in the global investment management industry."	"Enrolling as a candidate in the CFA Program ensures one of becoming better at valuing debt securities."
"I passed Level I of the CFA Program."	"CFA, Level II"
"I am a 2010 Level III candidate in the CFA Program."	"CFA, Expected 2011"
"I passed all three levels of the CFA Program and may be eligible for the CFA charter upon completion of the required work experience."	"CFA, Expected 2011" "John Smith, Charter Pending"

Recommended Procedures for Compliance

Misuse of a member's CFA designation or CFA candidacy or improper reference to it is common by those in a member's or candidate's firm who do not possess knowledge of the requirements of Standard VII(B). As an appropriate step to reduce this risk, members and candidates should disseminate written information about Standard VII(B) and the accompanying guidance to their firm's legal, compliance, public relations, and marketing departments (see www.cfainstitute.org).

For materials that refer to employees' affiliation with CFA Institute, members and candidates should encourage their firms to create templates that are approved by a central authority (such as the compliance department) as being consistent with Standard VII(B). This practice promotes consistency and accuracy in the firm of references to CFA Institute membership, the CFA designation, and CFA candidacy.

Application of the Standard

Example 1 (Passing Exams in Consecutive Years):

An advertisement for AZ Investment Advisors states that all the firm's principals are CFA charterholders and all passed the three examinations on their first attempt. The advertisement prominently links this fact to the notion that AZ's mutual funds have achieved superior performance.

> *Comment*: AZ may state that all principals passed the three examinations on the first try as long as this statement is true, but it must not be linked to performance or imply superior ability. Implying that (1) CFA charterholders achieve better investment results and (2) those who pass the exams on the first try may be more successful than those who do not violates Standard VII(B).

Example 2 (Right to Use CFA Designation):

Five years after receiving his CFA charter, Louis Vasseur resigns his position as an investment analyst and spends the next two years traveling abroad. Because he is not actively engaged in the investment profession, he does not file a completed Professional Conduct Statement with CFA Institute and does not pay his CFA Institute membership dues. At the conclusion of his travels, Vasseur becomes a self-employed analyst accepting assignments as an independent contractor. Without reinstating his CFA Institute membership by filing his Professional Conduct Statement and paying his dues, he prints business cards that display "CFA" after his name.

> *Comment*: Vasseur has violated Standard VII(B) because his right to use the CFA designation was suspended when he failed to file his Professional Conduct Statement and stopped paying dues. Therefore, he no longer is able to state or imply that he is an active CFA charterholder. When Vasseur files his Professional Conduct Statement, resumes paying CFA Institute dues to activate his membership, and completes the CFA Institute reinstatement procedures, he will be eligible to use the CFA designation.

Example 3 ("Retired" CFA Institute Membership Status):

After a 25-year career, James Simpson retires from his firm. Because he is not actively engaged in the investment profession, he does not file a completed Professional Conduct Statement with CFA Institute and does not pay his CFA Institute membership dues. Simpson designs a plain business card (without a corporate logo) to hand out to friends with his new contact details, and he continues to put "CFA" after his name.

> *Comment*: Simpson has violated Standard VII(B). Because he failed to file his Professional Conduct Statement and ceased paying dues, his membership has been suspended and he has given up the right to use the CFA designation. CFA Institute has procedures, however, for reclassifying a member and charterholder as "retired" and reducing the annual dues. If he wants to obtain retired status, he needs to file the appropriate paperwork with CFA Institute. When Simpson receives his notification from CFA Institute that his membership has been reclassified as retired and he resumes paying reduced dues, his membership will be reactivated and his right to use the CFA designation will be reinstated.

Example 4 (Stating Facts about CFA Designation and Program):

Rhonda Reese has been a CFA charterholder since 2000. In a conversation with a friend who is considering enrolling in the CFA Program, she states that she has learned a great deal from the CFA Program and that many firms require their employees to be CFA charterholders. She would recommend the CFA Program to anyone pursuing a career in investment management.

> *Comment*: Reese's comments comply with Standard VII(B). Her statements refer to facts: The CFA Program enhanced her knowledge, and many firms require the CFA designation for their investment professionals.

Example 5 (Order of Professional and Academic Designations):

Tatiana Prittima has earned both her CFA designation and a PhD in finance. She would like to cite both her accomplishments on her business card but is unsure of the proper method for doing so.

> *Comment*: The order of designations cited on such items as resumes and business cards is a matter of personal preference. Prittima is free to cite the CFA designation either before or after citing her PhD. Multiple designations must be separated by a comma.

Example 6 (Use of Fictitious Name):

Barry Glass is the lead quantitative analyst at CityCenter Hedge Fund. Glass is responsible for the development, maintenance, and enhancement of the proprietary models the fund uses to manage its investors' assets. Glass reads several high-level mathematical publications and blogs to stay informed on current developments. One blog, run by Expert CFA, presents some intriguing research that may benefit one of CityCenter's current models. Glass is under pressure from firm executives to improve the model's predictive abilities, and he incorporates the factors discussed in the online research. The updated output recommends several new investments to the fund's portfolio managers.

> *Comment*: "Expert CFA" has violated Standard VII(B) by using the CFA designation inappropriately. As with any research report, authorship of online comments must include the charterholder's full name along with any reference to the CFA designation.
>
> See also Standard V(A), which Glass has violated for guidance on diligence and reasonable basis.

PRACTICE PROBLEMS

Unless otherwise stated in the question, all individuals in the following questions are CFA Institute members or candidates in the CFA Program and, therefore, are subject to the CFA Institute Code of Ethics and Standards of Professional Conduct.

1 Smith, a research analyst with a brokerage firm, decides to change his recommendation for the common stock of Green Company, Inc., from a "buy" to a "sell." He mails this change in investment advice to all the firm's clients on Wednesday. The day after the mailing, a client calls with a buy order for 500 shares of Green Company. In this circumstance, Smith should:

A Accept the order.

B Advise the customer of the change in recommendation before accepting the order.

C Not accept the order because it is contrary to the firm's recommendation.

2 Which statement about a manager's use of client brokerage commissions violates the Code and Standards?

A A client may direct a manager to use that client's brokerage commissions to purchase goods and services for that client.

B Client brokerage commissions should be used to benefit the client and should be commensurate with the value of the brokerage and research services received.

C Client brokerage commissions may be directed to pay for the investment manager's operating expenses.

3 Jamison is a junior research analyst with Howard & Howard, a brokerage and investment banking firm. Howard & Howard's mergers and acquisitions department has represented the Britland Company in all of its acquisitions for the past 20 years. Two of Howard & Howard's senior officers are directors of various Britland subsidiaries. Jamison has been asked to write a research report on Britland. What is the best course of action for her to follow?

A Jamison may write the report but must refrain from expressing any opinions because of the special relationships between the two companies.

B Jamison should not write the report because the two Howard & Howard officers serve as directors for subsidiaries of Britland.

C Jamison may write the report if she discloses the special relationships with the company in the report.

4 Which of the following statements clearly *conflicts* with the recommended procedures for compliance presented in the CFA Institute *Standards of Practice Handbook*?

A Firms should disclose to clients the personal investing policies and procedures established for their employees.

B Prior approval must be obtained for the personal investment transactions of all employees.

C For confidentiality reasons, personal transactions and holdings should not be reported to employers unless mandated by regulatory organizations.

5 Bronson provides investment advice to the board of trustees of a private university endowment fund. The trustees have provided Bronson with the fund's financial information, including planned expenditures. Bronson receives a phone call on Friday afternoon from Murdock, a prominent alumnus, requesting that Bronson fax him comprehensive financial information about the fund. According to Murdock, he has a potential contributor but needs the information that day to close the deal and cannot contact any of the trustees. Based on the CFA Institute Standards, Bronson should:

A Send Murdock the information because disclosure would benefit the client.

B Not send Murdock the information to preserve confidentiality.

C Send Murdock the information, provided Bronson promptly notifies the trustees.

6 Miller heads the research department of a large brokerage firm. The firm has many analysts, some of whom are subject to the Code and Standards. If Miller delegates some supervisory duties, which statement best describes her responsibilities under the Code and Standards?

A Miller's supervisory responsibilities do not apply to those subordinates who are not subject to the Code and Standards.

B Miller no longer has supervisory responsibility for those duties delegated to her subordinates.

C Miller retains supervisory responsibility for all subordinates despite her delegation of some duties.

7 Willier is the research analyst responsible for following Company X. All the information he has accumulated and documented suggests that the outlook for the company's new products is poor, so the stock should be rated a weak "hold." During lunch, however, Willier overhears a financial analyst from another firm whom he respects offer opinions that conflict with Willier's forecasts and expectations. Upon returning to his office, Willier releases a strong "buy" recommendation to the public. Willier:

A Violated the Standards by failing to distinguish between facts and opinions in his recommendation.

B Violated the Standards because he did not have a reasonable and adequate basis for his recommendation.

C Was in full compliance with the Standards.

8 An investment management firm has been hired by ETV Corporation to work on an additional public offering for the company. The firm's brokerage unit now has a "sell" recommendation on ETV, but the head of the investment banking department has asked the head of the brokerage unit to change the recommendation from "sell" to "buy." According to the Standards, the head of the brokerage unit would be permitted to:

A Increase the recommendation by no more than one increment (in this case, to a "hold" recommendation).

B Place the company on a restricted list and give only factual information about the company.

C Assign a new analyst to decide if the stock deserves a higher rating.

9 Albert and Tye, who recently started their own investment advisory business, have registered to take the Level III CFA examination. Albert's business card reads, "Judy Albert, CFA Level II." Tye has not put anything about the CFA designation on his business card, but promotional material that he designed for the business describes the CFA requirements and indicates that Tye participates in the CFA Program and has completed Levels I and II. According to the Standards:

A Albert has violated the Standards, but Tye has not.

B Tye has violated the Standards, but Albert has not.

C Both Albert and Tye have violated the Standards.

10 Scott works for a regional brokerage firm. He estimates that Walkton Industries will increase its dividend by US$1.50 a share during the next year. He realizes that this increase is contingent on pending legislation that would, if enacted, give Walkton a substantial tax break. The US representative for Walkton's home district has told Scott that, although she is lobbying hard for the bill and prospects for its passage are favorable, concern of the US Congress over the federal deficit could cause the tax bill to be voted down. Walkton Industries has not made any statements about a change in dividend policy. Scott writes in his research report, "We expect Walkton's stock price to rise by at least US$8.00 a share by the end of the year because the dividend will increase by US$1.50 a share. Investors buying the stock at the current time should expect to realize a total return of at least 15% on the stock." According to the Standards:

A Scott violated the Standards because he used material inside information.

B Scott violated the Standards because he failed to separate opinion from fact.

C Scott violated the Standards by basing his research on uncertain predictions of future government action.

11 Which one of the following actions will help to ensure the fair treatment of brokerage firm clients when a new investment recommendation is made?

A Informing all people in the firm in advance that a recommendation is to be disseminated.

B Distributing recommendations to institutional clients prior to individual accounts.

C Minimizing the time between the decision and the dissemination of a recommendation.

12 The mosaic theory holds that an analyst:

A Violates the Code and Standards if the analyst fails to have knowledge of and comply with applicable laws.

B Can use material public information and nonmaterial nonpublic information in the analyst's analysis.

C Should use all available and relevant information in support of an investment recommendation.

13 Jurgen is a portfolio manager. One of her firm's clients has told Jurgen that he will compensate her beyond the compensation provided by her firm on the basis of the capital appreciation of his portfolio each year. Jurgen should:

A Turn down the additional compensation because it will result in conflicts with the interests of other clients' accounts.

B Turn down the additional compensation because it will create undue pressure on her to achieve strong short-term performance.

C Obtain permission from her employer prior to accepting the compensation arrangement.

14 One of the discretionary accounts managed by Farnsworth is the Jones Corporation employee profit-sharing plan. Jones, the company president, recently asked Farnsworth to vote the shares in the profit-sharing plan in favor of the slate of directors nominated by Jones Corporation and against the directors sponsored by a dissident stockholder group. Farnsworth does not want to lose this account because he directs all the account's trades to a brokerage firm that provides Farnsworth with useful information about tax-free investments. Although this information is not of value in managing the Jones Corporation account, it does help in managing several other accounts. The brokerage firm providing this information also offers the lowest commissions for trades and

provides best execution. Farnsworth investigates the director issue, concludes that the management-nominated slate is better for the long-run performance of the company than the dissident group's slate, and votes accordingly. Farnsworth:

A Violated the Standards in voting the shares in the manner requested by Jones but not in directing trades to the brokerage firm.

B Did not violate the Standards in voting the shares in the manner requested by Jones or in directing trades to the brokerage firm.

C Violated the Standards in directing trades to the brokerage firm but not in voting the shares as requested by Jones.

15 Brown works for an investment counseling firm. Green, a new client of the firm, is meeting with Brown for the first time. Green used another counseling firm for financial advice for years, but she has switched her account to Brown's firm. After spending a few minutes getting acquainted, Brown explains to Green that she has discovered a highly undervalued stock that offers large potential gains. She recommends that Green purchase the stock. Brown has committed a violation of the Standards. What should she have done differently?

A Brown should have determined Green's needs, objectives, and tolerance for risk before making a recommendation of any type of security.

B Brown should have thoroughly explained the characteristics of the company to Green, including the characteristics of the industry in which the company operates.

C Brown should have explained her qualifications, including her education, training, and experience and the meaning of the CFA designation.

16 Grey recommends the purchase of a mutual fund that invests solely in long-term US Treasury bonds. He makes the following statements to his clients:

I. "The payment of the bonds is guaranteed by the US government; therefore, the default risk of the bonds is virtually zero."

II. "If you invest in the mutual fund, you will earn a 10% rate of return each year for the next several years based on historical performance of the market."

Did Grey's statements violate the CFA Institute Code and Standards?

A Neither statement violated the Code and Standards.

B Only statement I violated the Code and Standards.

C Only statement II violated the Code and Standards.

17 Anderb, a portfolio manager for XYZ Investment Management Company—a registered investment organization that advises investment firms and private accounts—was promoted to that position three years ago. Bates, her supervisor, is responsible for reviewing Anderb's portfolio account transactions and her required monthly reports of personal stock transactions. Anderb has been using Jonelli, a broker, almost exclusively for brokerage transactions for the portfolio account. For securities in which Jonelli's firm makes a market, Jonelli has been giving Anderb lower prices for personal purchases and higher prices for personal sales than Jonelli gives to Anderb's portfolio accounts and other investors. Anderb has been filing monthly reports with Bates only for those months in which she has no personal transactions, which is about every fourth month. Which of the following is *most likely* to be a violation of the Code and Standards?

A Anderb failed to disclose to her employer her personal transactions.

B Anderb owned the same securities as those of her clients.

C Bates allowed Anderb to use Jonelli as her broker for personal trades.

18 Which of the following is a correct statement of a member's or candidate's duty under the Code and Standards?

A In the absence of specific applicable law or other regulatory requirements, the Code and Standards govern the member's or candidate's actions.

B A member or candidate is required to comply only with applicable local laws, rules, regulations, or customs, even though the Code and Standards may impose a higher degree of responsibility or a higher duty on the member or candidate.

C A member or candidate who trades securities in a securities market where no applicable local laws or stock exchange rules regulate the use of material nonpublic information may take investment action based on material nonpublic information.

19 Ward is scheduled to visit the corporate headquarters of Evans Industries. Ward expects to use the information he obtains there to complete his research report on Evans stock. Ward learns that Evans plans to pay all of Ward's expenses for the trip, including costs of meals, hotel room, and air transportation. Which of the following actions would be the *best* course for Ward to take under the Code and Standards?

A Accept the expense-paid trip and write an objective report.

B Pay for all travel expenses, including costs of meals and incidental items.

C Accept the expense-paid trip but disclose the value of the services accepted in the report.

20 Which of the following statements is *correct* under the Code and Standards?

A CFA Institute members and candidates are prohibited from undertaking independent practice in competition with their employer.

B Written consent from the employer is necessary to permit independent practice that could result in compensation or other benefits in competition with a member's or candidate's employer.

C Members and candidates are prohibited from making arrangements or preparations to go into a competitive business before terminating their relationship with their employer.

21 Smith is a financial analyst with XYZ Brokerage Firm. She is preparing a purchase recommendation on JNI Corporation. Which of the following situations is *most likely* to represent a conflict of interest for Smith that would have to be disclosed?

A Smith frequently purchases items produced by JNI.

B XYZ holds for its own account a substantial common stock position in JNI.

C Smith's brother-in-law is a supplier to JNI.

22 Michelieu tells a prospective client, "I may not have a long-term track record yet, but I'm sure that you'll be very pleased with my recommendations and service. In the three years that I've been in the business, my equity-oriented clients have averaged a total return of more than 26% a year." The statement is true, but Michelieu only has a few clients, and one of his clients took a large position in a penny stock (against Michelieu's advice) and realized a huge gain. This large return caused the average of all of Michelieu's clients to exceed 26% a year. Without this one investment, the average gain would have been 8% a year. Has Michelieu violated the Standards?

A No, because Michelieu is not promising that he can earn a 26% return in the future.

B No, because the statement is a true and accurate description of Michelieu's track record.

C Yes, because the statement misrepresents Michelieu's track record.

23 An investment banking department of a brokerage firm often receives material nonpublic information that could have considerable value if used in advising the firm's brokerage clients. In order to conform to the Code and Standards, which one of the following is the best policy for the brokerage firm?

A Permanently prohibit both "buy" and "sell" recommendations of the stocks of clients of the investment banking department.

B Establish physical and informational barriers within the firm to prevent the exchange of information between the investment banking and brokerage operations.

C Monitor the exchange of information between the investment banking department and the brokerage operation.

24 Stewart has been hired by Goodner Industries, Inc., to manage its pension fund. Stewart's duty of loyalty, prudence, and care is owed to:

A The management of Goodner.

B The participants and beneficiaries of Goodner's pension plan.

C The shareholders of Goodner.

25 Which of the following statements is a stated purpose of disclosure in Standard VI(C)–Referral Fees?

A Disclosure will allow the client to request discounted service fees.

B Disclosure will help the client evaluate any possible partiality shown in the recommendation of services.

C Disclosure means advising a prospective client about the referral arrangement once a formal client relationship has been established.

26 Rose, a portfolio manager for a local investment advisory firm, is planning to sell a portion of his personal investment portfolio to cover the costs of his child's academic tuition. Rose wants to sell a portion of his holdings in Household Products, but his firm recently upgraded the stock to "strong buy." Which of the following describes Rose's options under the Code and Standards?

A Based on his firm's "buy" recommendation, Rose cannot sell the shares because he would be improperly prospering from the inflated recommendation.

B Rose is free to sell his personal holdings once his firm is properly informed of his intentions.

C Rose can sell his personal holdings but only when a client of the firm places an order to buy shares of Household.

27 A former hedge fund manager, Jackman, has decided to launch a new private wealth management firm. From his prior experiences, he believes the new firm needs to achieve US$1 million in assets under management in the first year. Jackman offers a $10,000 incentive to any adviser who joins his firm with the minimum of $200,000 in committed investments. Jackman places notice of the opening on several industry web portals and career search sites. Which of the following is *correct* according to the Code and Standards?

A A member or candidate is eligible for the new position and incentive if he or she can arrange for enough current clients to switch to the new firm and if the member or candidate discloses the incentive fee.

B A member or candidate may not accept employment with the new firm because Jackman's incentive offer violates the Code and Standards.

C A member or candidate is not eligible for the new position unless he or she is currently unemployed because soliciting the clients of the member's or candidate's current employer is prohibited.

28 Carter works for Invest Today, a local asset management firm. A broker that provides Carter with proprietary research through client brokerage arrangements is offering a new trading service. The broker is offering low-fee, execution-only trades to complement its traditional full-service, execution-and-research trades. To entice Carter and other asset managers to send additional business its way, the broker will apply the commissions paid on the new service toward satisfying the brokerage commitment of the prior full-service arrangements. Carter has always been satisfied with the execution provided on the full-service trades, and the new low-fee trades are comparable to the fees of other brokers currently used for the accounts that prohibit soft dollar arrangements.

A Carter can trade for his accounts that prohibit soft dollar arrangements under the new low-fee trading scheme.

B Carter cannot use the new trading scheme because the commissions are prohibited by the soft dollar restrictions of the accounts.

C Carter should trade only through the new low-fee scheme and should increase his trading volume to meet his required commission commitment.

29 Rule has worked as a portfolio manager for a large investment management firm for the past 10 years. Rule earned his CFA charter last year and has decided to open his own investment management firm. After leaving his current employer, Rule creates some marketing material for his new firm. He states in the material, "In earning the CFA charter, a highly regarded credential in the investment management industry, I further enhanced the portfolio management skills learned during my professional career. While completing the examination process in three consecutive years, I consistently received the highest possible scores on the topics of Ethics, Alternative Investments, and Portfolio Management." Has Rule violated Standard VII(B)–Reference to CFA Institute, the CFA Designation, and the CFA Program in his marketing material?

A Rule violated Standard VII(B) in stating that he completed the exams in three consecutive years.

B Rule violated Standard VII(B) in stating that he received the highest scores in the topics of Ethics, Alternative Investments, and Portfolio Management.

C Rule did not violate Standard VII(B).

30 Stafford is a portfolio manager for a specialized real estate mutual fund. Her firm clearly describes in the fund's prospectus its soft dollar policies. Stafford decides that entering the CFA Program will enhance her investment decision-making skill and decides to use the fund's soft dollar account to pay the registration and exam fees for the CFA Program. Which of the following statements is *most likely* correct?

A Stafford did not violate the Code and Standards because the prospectus informed investors of the fund's soft dollar policies.

B Stafford violated the Code and Standards because improving her investment skills is not a reasonable use of the soft dollar account.

C Stafford violated the Code and Standards because the CFA Program does not meet the definition of research allowed to be purchased with brokerage commissions.

31 Long has been asked to be the keynote speaker at an upcoming investment conference. The event is being hosted by one of the third-party investment managers currently used by his pension fund. The manager offers to cover all conference and travel costs for Long and make the conference registrations free for three additional members of his investment management team. To ensure that the conference obtains the best speakers, the host firm has arranged for an exclusive golf outing for the day following the conference on a local championship-caliber course. Which of the following is *least likely* to violate Standard I(B)?

A Long may accept only the offer to have his conference-related expenses paid by the host firm.

B Long may accept the offer to have his conference-related expenses paid and may attend the exclusive golf outing at the expense of the hosting firm.

C Long may accept the entire package of incentives offered to speak at this conference.

32 Andrews, a private wealth manager, is conducting interviews for a new research analyst for his firm. One of the candidates is Wright, an analyst with a local investment bank. During the interview, while Wright is describing his analytical skills, he mentions a current merger in which his firm is acting as the adviser. Andrews has heard rumors of a possible merger between the two companies, but no releases have been made by the companies concerned. Which of the following actions by Andrews is *least likely* a violation of the Code and Standards?

A Waiting until the next day before trading on the information to allow time for it to become public.

B Notifying all investment managers in his firm of the new information so none of their clients are disadvantaged.

C Placing the securities mentioned as part of the merger on the firm's restricted trading list.

33 Pietro, president of Local Bank, has hired the bank's market maker, Vogt, to seek a merger partner. Local is currently not listed on a stock exchange and has not reported that it is seeking strategic alternatives. Vogt has discussed the possibility of a merger with several firms, but they have all decided to wait until after the next period's financial data are available. The potential buyers believe the results will be worse than the results of prior periods and will allow them to pay less for Local Bank.

Pietro wants to increase the likelihood of structuring a merger deal quickly. Which of the following actions would *most likely* be a violation of the Code and Standards?

A Pietro could instruct Local Bank to issue a press release announcing that it has retained Vogt to find a merger partner.

B Pietro could place a buy order for 2,000 shares (or four times the average weekly volume) through Vogt for his personal account.

C After confirming with Local's chief financial officer, Pietro could instruct Local to issue a press release reaffirming the firm's prior announced earnings guidance for the full fiscal year.

34 ABC Investment Management acquires a new, very large account with two concentrated positions. The firm's current policy is to add new accounts for the purpose of performance calculation after the first full month of management. Cupp is responsible for calculating the firm's performance returns. Before the end of the initial month, Cupp notices that one of the significant holdings of the new accounts is acquired by another company, causing the value of the investment to double. Because of this holding, Cupp decides to account for the new portfolio as of the date of transfer, thereby allowing ABC Investment to reap the positive impact of that month's portfolio return.

A Cupp did not violate the Code and Standards because the GIPS standards allow composites to be updated on the date of large external cash flows.

B Cupp did not violate the Code and Standards because companies are allowed to determine when to incorporate new accounts into their composite calculation.

C Cupp violated the Code and Standards because the inclusion of the new account produces an inaccurate calculation of the monthly results according to the firm's stated policies.

35 Cannan has been working from home on weekends and occasionally saves correspondence with clients and completed work on her home computer. Because of worsening market conditions, Cannan is one of several employees released by her firm. While Cannan is looking for a new job, she uses the files she saved at home to request letters of recommendation from former clients. She also provides to prospective clients some of the reports as examples of her abilities.

A Cannan violated the Code and Standards because she did not receive permission from her former employer to keep or use the files after her employment ended.

B Cannan did not violate the Code and Standards because the files were created and saved on her own time and computer.

C Cannan violated the Code and Standards because she is prohibited from saving files on her home computer.

36 Quinn sat for the Level III CFA exam this past weekend. He updates his resume with the following statement: "In finishing the CFA Program, I improved my skills related to researching investments and managing portfolios. I will be eligible for the CFA charter upon completion of the required work experience."

A Quinn violated the Code and Standards by claiming he improved his skills through the CFA Program.

B Quinn violated the Code and Standards by incorrectly stating that he is eligible for the CFA charter.

C Quinn did not violate the Code and Standards with his resume update.

37 During a round of golf, Rodriguez, chief financial officer of Mega Retail, mentions to Hart, a local investment adviser and long-time personal friend, that Mega is having an exceptional sales quarter. Rodriguez expects the results to be almost 10% above the current estimates. The next day, Hart initiates the purchase of a large stake in the local exchange-traded retail fund for her personal account.

A Hart violated the Code and Standards by investing in the exchange-traded fund that included Mega Retail.

B Hart did not violate the Code and Standards because she did not invest directly in securities of Mega Retail.

C Rodriguez did not violate the Code and Standards because the comments made to Hart were not intended to solicit an investment in Mega Retail.

38 Park is very frustrated after taking her Level II exam. While she was studying for the exam, to supplement the curriculum provided, she ordered and used study material from a third-party provider. Park believes the additional material focused her attention on specific topic areas that were not tested while ignoring other areas. She posts the following statement on the provider's discussion board: "I am very dissatisfied with your firm's CFA Program Level II material. I found the exam extremely difficult and myself unprepared for specific questions after using your product. How could your service provide such limited

instructional resources on the analysis of inventories and taxes when the exam had multiple questions about them? I will not recommend your products to other candidates."

- **A** Park violated the Code and Standards by purchasing third-party review material.
- **B** Park violated the Code and Standards by providing her opinion on the difficulty of the exam.
- **C** Park violated the Code and Standards by providing specific information on topics tested on the exam.

39 Paper was recently terminated as one of a team of five managers of an equity fund. The fund had two value-focused managers and terminated one of them to reduce costs. In a letter sent to prospective employers, Paper presents, with written permission of the firm, the performance history of the fund to demonstrate his past success.

- **A** Paper did not violate the Code and Standards.
- **B** Paper violated the Code and Standards by claiming the performance of the entire fund as his own.
- **C** Paper violated the Code and Standards by including the historical results of his prior employer.

40 Townsend was recently appointed to the board of directors of a youth golf program that is the local chapter of a national not-for-profit organization. The program is beginning a new fund-raising campaign to expand the number of annual scholarships it provides. Townsend believes many of her clients make annual donations to charity. The next week in her regular newsletter to all clients, she includes a small section discussing the fund-raising campaign and her position on the organization's board.

- **A** Townsend did not violate the Code and Standards.
- **B** Townsend violated the Code and Standards by soliciting donations from her clients through the newsletter.
- **C** Townsend violated the Code and Standards by not getting approval of the organization before soliciting her clients.

41 Danvers is the head of investment operations at an asset management firm in Country A. The chief investment officer (CIO) of the firm requested that Danvers provide him with a performance report that complies with Country A's performance reporting standards. The CIO used this same performance report to market to prospective clients in Country B. Danvers was not responsible for monitoring the CIO's activities and did not know that the CIO used the report for marketing purposes. Compared to Country A, Country B's local laws require a stricter methodology for performance reporting. Has Danvers violated the Standards?

- **A** Yes.
- **B** No, because the performance was calculated in Country A.
- **C** No, because Danvers was unaware of the CIO's use of the performance data.

42 An investment management firm has been selected as one of three finalists to manage a large investment allocation for a local government pension fund. The CEO of the firm knows that one of the fund's board members is very involved with a local children's charity. The CEO historically has supported this charity by making anonymous cash donations every December. Which of the following actions by the firm's CEO would *most likely* be prohibited under Standard I(B)–Independence and Objectivity?

- **A** Continuing to send anonymous cash donations every year

B Publicly endorsing the charity during a luncheon that the board member will be attending prior to the selection of the investment management firm

C Waiting until after the board decides on who receives the investment allocation to encourage family members to anonymously volunteer their time at this charity by not disclosing their family connection

43 Drake is a portfolio manager at a large investment firm and is managing some seed capital for a concentrated microcap stock portfolio. Drake believes that the price will decline as he is liquidating his firm's position in one of the holdings that is thinly traded and negatively impact the performance of the portfolio. Drake has also been managing a concentrated microcap portfolio within a personal account that holds the same stocks as the first portfolio. Drake trades using his personal account to raise the trading volume and create the appearance of higher volume. Drake *most likely* violated:

A Standard IV(A)–Loyalty.

B Standard I(C)–Misrepresentation.

C Standard II(B)–Market Manipulation.

44 Dent provides investment advice to the board of trustees of a local private university endowment fund. He calculates investment performance and attribution for the fund on a monthly basis. Dent receives an email on the second day of the month from Wayne, a large donor, requesting that Dent send him the past month's preliminary fund performance data. According to Wayne, he has been thinking about making a substantial donation but wants to make sure that the endowment is performing well. Based on the Standards of Professional Conduct, Dent should:

A not send Wayne the information to preserve confidentiality.

B send Wayne the performance data because disclosing it would benefit the client.

C send Wayne the performance data, provided Wayne promptly notifies the trustees.

45 Howard has just left his prior firm to open his own investment consulting business. While at his prior firm, Howard developed a complicated investment model that is still being used by the firm. Since departing his prior firm, he has been able to re-create the model using his own research. He now wants to solicit business for his new firm by reaching out to previous clients from a list that he found in his briefcase after leaving his old firm. The clients already knew about his departure as it was company policy for him to notify all fee-paying clients of his leaving. They were not made aware of his future plans at that time. Howard has violated the Standards of Professional Conduct by:

A using the list of clients.

B re-creating the investment model.

C notifying all of his fee-paying clients of his departure.

46 According to Standard V(B)–Communication with Clients and Prospective Clients, which of the following statements is *correct*?

A Members and candidates must not insert their opinions when presenting investment analyses and recommendations to clients.

B Disclosure of all limitations and risks associated with the investment process must be made to prospective clients.

C Reasonable judgment must be used in identifying factors that are important to the investment analyses, and those factors must be included in communication with clients.

47 Lindsay works for an investment consultant and oversees the verification of Company A's compliance with the GIPS standards. As part of the verification, Lindsay is asked by Company A to help review the company's marketing materials and provide advice on any missing GIPS-required disclosures. Upon reviewing a specific presentation, Lindsay learns that Company A will be presenting its performance data to a state retirement fund for which Lindsay is on the board of directors. Lindsay also learns from the biography section of the marketing materials that one of Company A's portfolio managers is a member of a local society that Lindsay recently joined. Under Standard VI(A)–Disclosure of Conflicts, Lindsay will *most likely* be required to disclose to his employer his:

A membership in the local society.

B review of Company A's marketing materials.

C involvement on the state retirement fund's board of directors.

48 Harley sat for the Level II exam of the CIPM Program this past week. While she waits for the release of the exam results, she updates her LinkedIn account with the following statement: "In finishing the CIPM Program, I improved my skills related to the calculation and analysis of attribution models. I will be a CIPM certificate holder upon completion of the required work experience." Did Harley violate the Code and Standards?

A No.

B Yes, because Harley stated that she will become a CIPM certificate holder.

C Yes, because Harley claimed that she improved her skills through the CIPM Program.

49 Gilmore is a performance analyst and is reviewing the performance of a micro-cap equity fund. Performance in the fund has been very strong over the past three years. Gilmore notes that the fund manager engaged in frequent trading of some fund holdings that are also in the manager's own personal account. After the stock price of these holdings rose, the manager would sell the positions at higher prices. Did the fund manager *most likely* violate Standard II(B)–Market Manipulation?

A No.

B Yes, through transaction-based manipulation.

C Yes, through information-based manipulation.

50 Standard IV(A)–Loyalty allows for whistleblowing to protect the:

A employer from a lawsuit.

B interests of a firm's clients.

C employee from losing his or her job.

51 Taylor sits on the board of directors for a state retirement plan that recently released a request for proposal to hire a firm to take over management of the plan's large-cap equity assets. Unknown to the other members of the board, Taylor's sister is the lead portfolio manager for one of the four finalists, and her firm currently manages his personal retirement account. The sister's investment firm has hinted to Taylor that the fees on his personal account may be reduced if the firm acquires this new business. Taylor has violated the Code and Standards by failing to disclose:

A only that his sister is a portfolio manager for the finalist firm.

B only that his sister's firm manages his retirement account.

C both that his sister is a portfolio manager for the finalist firm and that his sister manages his retirement account.

52 Firm A provides investment services to clients and operates in a country with no laws addressing the acceptance of gifts. To abide by the Code and Standards, members and candidates employed by Firm A:

A can accept all gifts.

B must reject all gifts.

C must reject gifts that could compromise their independence and objectivity.

53 Which of the following is a suggested method for members and candidates to maintain understanding of applicable laws, rules, and regulations?

A Participate in external continuing education programs.

B Review their firm's compliance procedures when hired.

C Update reference copies of applicable statutes, rules, regulations, and important cases every three years.

54 A performance analyst is instructed by her boss to change the benchmark of her firm's high-yield bond composite to an index with higher-quality bonds. The performance analyst concludes that this change would mislead the firm's clients and prospects. The performance analyst should:

A update the composite to the new benchmark.

B share her conclusions with her boss or other supervisors.

C compare performance evaluations using the new and the old indexes.

55 Matthew Hill, a performance analyst, maintains his firm's Large-Cap Composite. A client of the Large-Cap Strategy requires a significant portion of his account to remain invested in small-cap stocks inherited from his grandfather. Hill and the strategy's portfolio manager agreed to exclude the account from the composite. During the latest quarter, the small-cap stocks outperformed the Large-Cap Strategy's benchmark. Later, Hill was directed by the portfolio manager to include the client's account in the Large-Cap Composite for the quarter. Hill should:

A include the account in the composite.

B exclude the account from the composite because the small-cap stocks outperformed.

C exclude the account from the composite because it was not reflective of the Large-Cap Strategy.

56 Anna Schmidt is reviewing the performance and valuations for her firm's municipal bond strategy. The firm is provided valuations by two bond pricing services. After researching the portfolios and the benchmark, Schmidt noted the following facts:

Fact 1: The strategy is benchmarked against a municipal bond index following a similar strategy but containing different constituents.

Fact 2: The firm selects valuations from the two pricing services on an ad hoc basis.

Which of the two facts *most likely* indicates misrepresentation?

A Only Fact 1

B Only Fact 2

C Both Fact 1 and Fact 2

57 Jackson Foreman is a performance analyst developing marketing materials for his firm's all-cap equity strategy. The strategy underperformed because of several accounts where the portfolio manager decided to overweight, with the clients' approval, some stocks that ended up performing poorly. The accounts were still reflective of the strategy and met the composite's definition. Foreman decides to remove those portfolios from the composite performance calculations because of their underperformance. Foreman's decision is:

A appropriate.

B inappropriate because excluding these accounts misrepresents the portfolio manager's decision making.

C inappropriate because he should exclude only the poorly performing stocks from the accounts' performance calculations.

58 Lance Elliot works at an investment management firm claiming Global Investment Performance Standards (GIPS) compliance. Elliot calculated the performance of the firm's Mid-Cap Composite for the most recent year. In preparing the performance report, Elliot asset weighted the composite accounts that were open for the entire time period, excluding accounts that were closed during the year or accounts that were below a specific asset size. None of these decisions were disclosed in the composite's performance report. Elliot's failure to disclose was *most* appropriate for which of his decisions?

A Asset weighting the composite's accounts

B Excluding only accounts below a specific asset size

C Excluding only accounts that were closed during the year

59 Firm ABC has been managing client accounts for three years through 2017. In order to present a 10-year track record in the firm's pitch book, ABC includes simulated results for the years 2008–2014 in a section labeled "Supplemental Information" and discloses the simulated periods. In constructing the strategy's GIPS-compliant composite, ABC includes an account with significant trading restrictions. The account's returns improve the composite's results. Which of ABC's actions was *most likely* a violation of the Code and Standards?

A Only the composite construction

B Only the presentation of simulated results

C Both the composite construction and the presentation of simulated results

60 Mindy Lane has been hired recently to lead the performance department of a large fixed-income money manager. While preparing the first quarter-end performance, she noted that the pricing team had the ability to choose between bid and ask prices. The team was expected to use the price that reported the most favorable performance. Additionally, the performance shown for one of their flagship products included results for a period when the portfolio manager was at a prior firm. The above information was appropriately disclosed in marketing materials. Which of the situations noted above *most likely* violates the Code and Standards?

A Only the pricing policy

B Only the use of prior firm performance

C Both the pricing policy and the use of prior firm performance

61 According to Standard III(E): Preservation of Confidentiality, is it permissible for a member or candidate to disclose information received from a client that is outside the scope of the confidential relationship?

A Only if the information is relevant to work being performed for the client

B Only if the information will improve services available to prospective clients

C If the information is relevant to work being performed for the client and the information will improve services available to prospective clients

62 James Lee oversees the performance department of an investment management firm. In reviewing the firm's newest strategy, Lee noted that the firm's largest client has outperformed the benchmark over the past four quarters whereas the rest of the accounts underperformed the benchmark. Lee traced the client's outperformance to a few illiquid securities due to the use of inaccurate market data. Lee discussed his concerns about the outperformance with his supervisor. His supervisor claimed the results were due to superior stock selection and told Lee to stop conducting this review. Lee then decided to submit his concerns to the compliance department. Was Lee correct in his actions?

A Yes

B No, because his supervisor told Lee to stop conducting this review

C No, because his supervisor has determined the reason for the outperformance

63 Michael Reed has decided to start an investment management firm. Reed developed the quantitative model used by his current firm, TMA Management. Reed takes copies of the records necessary to support the past performance of the model to his new firm, along with the documentation needed to run the model. Because he developed the model, Reed does not request permission from TMA to use the performance records and documentation. Which of Reed's actions is *most likely* an acceptable practice according to the Code and Standards?

A Managing the same strategy at a new firm

B Taking the records to support performance

C Taking documents to recreate the methodology used to run the model

SOLUTIONS

1 The correct answer is B. This question involves Standard III(B)–Fair Dealing. Smith disseminated a change in the stock recommendation to his clients but then received a request contrary to that recommendation from a client who probably had not yet received the recommendation. Prior to executing the order, Smith should take additional steps to ensure that the customer has received the change of recommendation. Answer A is incorrect because the client placed the order prior to receiving the recommendation and, therefore, does not have the benefit of Smith's most recent recommendation. Answer C is also incorrect; simply because the client request is contrary to the firm's recommendation does not mean a member can override a direct request by a client. After Smith contacts the client to ensure that the client has received the changed recommendation, if the client still wants to place a buy order for the shares, Smith is obligated to comply with the client's directive.

2 The correct answer is C. This question involves Standard III(A)–Loyalty, Prudence, and Care and the specific topic of soft dollars or soft commissions. Answer C is the correct choice because client brokerage commissions may not be directed to pay for the investment manager's operating expenses. Answer B describes how members and candidates should determine how to use brokerage commissions—that is, if the use is in the best interests of clients and is commensurate with the value of the services provided. Answer A describes a practice that is commonly referred to as "directed brokerage." Because brokerage is an asset of the client and is used to benefit the client, not the manager, such practice does not violate a duty of loyalty to the client. Members and candidates are obligated in all situations to disclose to clients their practices in the use of client brokerage commissions.

3 The correct answer is C. This question involves Standard VI(A)–Disclosure of Conflicts. The question establishes a conflict of interest in which an analyst, Jamison, is asked to write a research report on a company that is a client of the analyst's employer. In addition, two directors of the company are senior officers of Jamison's employer. Both facts establish that there are conflicts of interest that must be disclosed by Jamison in her research report. Answer B is incorrect because an analyst is not prevented from writing a report simply because of the special relationship the analyst's employer has with the company as long as that relationship is disclosed. Answer A is incorrect because whether or not Jamison expresses any opinions in the report is irrelevant to her duty to disclose a conflict of interest. Not expressing opinions does not relieve the analyst of the responsibility to disclose the special relationships between the two companies.

4 The correct answer is C. This question asks about compliance procedures relating to personal investments of members and candidates. The statement in answer C clearly conflicts with the recommended procedures in the *Standards of Practice Handbook*. Employers should compare personal transactions of employees with those of clients on a regular basis regardless of the existence of a requirement by any regulatory organization. Such comparisons ensure that employees' personal trades do not conflict with their duty to their clients, and the comparisons can be conducted in a confidential manner. The statement in answer A does not conflict with the procedures in the *Handbook*. Disclosure of such policies will give full information to clients regarding potential conflicts of interest on the part of those entrusted to manage their money. Answer B is incorrect because firms are encouraged to establish policies whereby employees clear their personal holdings and transactions with their employers.

5 The correct answer is B. This question relates to Standard III(A)–Loyalty, Prudence, and Care and Standard III(E)–Preservation of Confidentiality. In this case, the member manages funds of a private endowment. Clients, who are, in this case, the trustees of the fund, must place some trust in members and candidates. Bronson cannot disclose confidential financial information to anyone without the permission of the fund, regardless of whether the disclosure may benefit the fund. Therefore, answer A is incorrect. Answer C is incorrect because Bronson must notify the fund and obtain the fund's permission before publicizing the information.

6 The correct answer is C. Under Standard IV(C)–Responsibilities of Supervisors, members and candidates may delegate supervisory duties to subordinates but such delegation does not relieve members or candidates of their supervisory responsibilities. As a result, answer B is incorrect. Moreover, whether or not Miller's subordinates are subject to the Code and Standards is irrelevant to her supervisory responsibilities. Therefore, answer A is incorrect.

7 The correct answer is B. This question relates to Standard V(A)–Diligence and Reasonable Basis. The opinion of another financial analyst is not an adequate basis for Willier's action in changing the recommendation. Answer C is thus incorrect. So is answer A because, although it is true that members and candidates must distinguish between facts and opinions in recommendations, the question does not illustrate a violation of that nature. If the opinion overheard by Willier had sparked him to conduct additional research and investigation that justified a change of opinion, then a changed recommendation would be appropriate.

8 The correct answer is B. This question relates to Standard I(B)–Independence and Objectivity. When asked to change a recommendation on a company stock to gain business for the firm, the head of the brokerage unit must refuse in order to maintain his independence and objectivity in making recommendations. He must not yield to pressure by the firm's investment banking department. To avoid the appearance of a conflict of interest, the firm should discontinue issuing recommendations about the company. Answer A is incorrect; changing the recommendation in any manner that is contrary to the analyst's opinion violates the duty to maintain independence and objectivity. Answer C is incorrect because merely assigning a new analyst to decide whether the stock deserves a higher rating will not address the conflict of interest.

9 The correct answer is A. Standard VII(B)–Reference to CFA Institute, the CFA Designation, and the CFA Program is the subject of this question. The reference on Albert's business card implies that there is a "CFA Level II" designation; Tye merely indicates in promotional material that he is participating in the CFA Program and has completed Levels I and II. Candidates may not imply that there is some sort of partial designation earned after passing a level of the CFA exam. Therefore, Albert has violated Standard VII(B). Candidates may communicate that they are participating in the CFA Program, however, and may state the levels that they have completed. Therefore, Tye has not violated Standard VII(B).

10 The correct answer is B. This question relates to Standard V(B)–Communication with Clients and Prospective Clients. Scott has issued a research report stating that he expects the price of Walkton Industries stock to rise by US$8 a share "because the dividend will increase" by US$1.50 per share. He has made this statement knowing that the dividend will increase only if Congress enacts certain legislation, an uncertain prospect. By stating that the dividend will increase, Scott failed to separate fact from opinion.

The information regarding passage of legislation is not material nonpublic information because it is conjecture, and the question does not state whether the US representative gave Scott her opinion on the passage of the legislation in confidence. She could have been offering this opinion to anyone who asked. Therefore, statement A is incorrect. It may be acceptable to base a recommendation, in part, on an expectation of future events, even though they may be uncertain. Therefore, answer C is incorrect.

11 The correct answer is C. This question, which relates to Standard III(B)–Fair Dealing, tests the knowledge of the procedures that will assist members and candidates in treating clients fairly when making investment recommendations. The step listed in C will help ensure the fair treatment of clients. Answer A may have negative effects on the fair treatment of clients. The more people who know about a pending change, the greater the chance that someone will inform some clients before the information's release. The firm should establish policies that limit the number of people who are aware in advance that a recommendation is to be disseminated. Answer B, distributing recommendations to institutional clients before distributing them to individual accounts, discriminates among clients on the basis of size and class of assets and is a violation of Standard III(B).

12 The correct answer is B. This question deals with Standard II(A)–Material Nonpublic Information. The mosaic theory states that an analyst may use material public information and nonmaterial nonpublic information in creating a larger picture than shown by any individual piece of information and the conclusions the analyst reaches become material only after the pieces are assembled. Answers A and C are accurate statements relating to the Code and Standards but do not describe the mosaic theory.

13 The correct answer is C. This question involves Standard IV(B)–Additional Compensation Arrangements. The arrangement described in the question—whereby Jurgen would be compensated beyond the compensation provided by her firm, on the basis of an account's performance—is not a violation of the Standards as long as Jurgen discloses the arrangement in writing to her employer and obtains permission from her employer prior to entering into the arrangement. Answers A and B are incorrect; although the private compensation arrangement could conflict with the interests of other clients and lead to short-term performance pressures, members and candidates may enter into such agreements as long as they have disclosed the arrangements to their employer and obtained permission for the arrangement from their employer.

14 The correct answer is B. This question relates to Standard III(A)–Loyalty, Prudence, and Care—specifically, a member's or candidate's responsibility for voting proxies and the use of client brokerage. According to the facts stated in the question, Farnsworth did not violate Standard III(A). Although the company president asked Farnsworth to vote the shares of the Jones Corporation profit-sharing plan a certain way, Farnsworth investigated the issue and concluded, independently, the best way to vote. Therefore, even though his decision coincided with the wishes of the company president, Farnsworth is not in violation of his responsibility to be loyal and to provide care to his clients. In this case, the participants and the beneficiaries of the profit-sharing plan are the clients, not the company's management. Had Farnsworth not investigated the issue or had he yielded to the president's wishes and voted for a slate of directors that he had determined was not in the best interest of the company, Farnsworth would have violated his responsibilities to the beneficiaries of the plan. In addition, because the brokerage firm provides the lowest commissions and best execution for securities transactions, Farnsworth has met his obligations to the client in using this brokerage firm. It does not matter that the brokerage firm also

provides research information that is not useful for the account generating the commission because Farnsworth is not paying extra money of the client's for that information.

15 The correct answer is A. In this question, Brown is providing investment recommendations before making inquiries about the client's financial situation, investment experience, or investment objectives. Brown is thus violating Standard III(C)–Suitability. Answers B and C provide examples of information members and candidates should discuss with their clients at the outset of the relationship, but these answers do not constitute a complete list of those factors. Answer A is the best answer.

16 The correct answer is C. This question involves Standard I(C)–Misrepresentation. Statement I is a factual statement that discloses to clients and prospects accurate information about the terms of the investment instrument. Statement II, which guarantees a specific rate of return for a mutual fund, is an opinion stated as a fact and, therefore, violates Standard I(C). If statement II were rephrased to include a qualifying statement, such as "in my opinion, investors may earn . . . ," it would not be in violation of the Standards.

17 The correct answer is A. This question involves three of the Standards. Anderb, the portfolio manager, has been obtaining more favorable prices for her personal securities transactions than she gets for her clients, which is a breach of Standard III(A)–Loyalty, Prudence, and Care. In addition, she violated Standard I(D)–Misconduct by failing to adhere to company policy and by hiding her personal transactions from her firm. Anderb's supervisor, Bates, violated Standard IV(C)–Responsibilities of Supervisors; although the company had requirements for reporting personal trading, Bates failed to adequately enforce those requirements. Answer B does not represent a violation because Standard VI(B)–Priority of Transactions requires that personal trading in a security be conducted after the trading in that security of clients and the employer. The Code and Standards do not prohibit owning such investments, although firms may establish policies that limit the investment opportunities of members and candidates. Answer C does not represent a violation because the Code and Standards do not contain a prohibition against employees using the same broker for their personal accounts that they use for their client accounts. This arrangement should be disclosed to the employer so that the employer may determine whether a conflict of interest exists.

18 The correct answer is A because this question relates to Standard I(A)–Knowledge of the Law—specifically, global application of the Code and Standards. Members and candidates who practice in multiple jurisdictions may be subject to various securities laws and regulations. If applicable law is more strict than the requirements of the Code and Standards, members and candidates must adhere to applicable law; otherwise, members and candidates must adhere to the Code and Standards. Therefore, answer A is correct. Answer B is incorrect because members and candidates must adhere to the higher standard set by the Code and Standards if local applicable law is less strict. Answer C is incorrect because when no applicable law exists, members and candidates are required to adhere to the Code and Standards, and the Code and Standards prohibit the use of material nonpublic information.

19 The correct answer is B. The best course of action under Standard I(B)–Independence and Objectivity is to avoid a conflict of interest whenever possible. Therefore, for Ward to pay for all his expenses is the correct answer. Answer C details a course of action in which the conflict would be disclosed, but the solution is not as appropriate as avoiding the conflict of interest.

Answer A would not be the best course because it would not remove the appearance of a conflict of interest; even though the report would not be affected by the reimbursement of expenses, it could appear to be.

20 The correct answer is B. Under Standard IV(A)–Loyalty, members and candidates may undertake independent practice that may result in compensation or other benefit in competition with their employer as long as they obtain consent from their employer. Answer C is not consistent with the Standards because the Standards allow members and candidates to make arrangements or preparations to go into competitive business as long as those arrangements do not interfere with their duty to their current employer. Answer A is not consistent with the Standards because the Standards do not include a complete prohibition against undertaking independent practice.

21 The correct answer is B. This question involves Standard VI(A)–Disclosure of Conflicts—specifically, the holdings of an analyst's employer in company stock. Answers A and C do not describe conflicts of interest that Smith would have to disclose. Answer A describes the use of a firm's products, which would not be a required disclosure. In answer C, the relationship between the analyst and the company through a relative is so tangential that it does not create a conflict of interest necessitating disclosure.

22 The correct answer is C. This question relates to Standard I(C)–Misrepresentation. Although Michelieu's statement about the total return of his clients' accounts on average may be technically true, it is misleading because the majority of the gain resulted from one client's large position taken against Michelieu's advice. Therefore, this statement misrepresents the investment performance the member is responsible for. He has not taken steps to present a fair, accurate, and complete presentation of performance. Answer B is thus incorrect. Answer A is incorrect because although Michelieu is not guaranteeing future results, his words are still a misrepresentation of his performance history.

23 The correct answer is B. The best policy to prevent violation of Standard II(A)–Material Nonpublic Information is the establishment of firewalls in a firm to prevent exchange of insider information. The physical and informational barrier of a firewall between the investment banking department and the brokerage operation prevents the investment banking department from providing information to analysts on the brokerage side who may be writing recommendations on a company stock. Prohibiting recommendations of the stock of companies that are clients of the investment banking department is an alternative, but answer A states that this prohibition would be permanent, which is not the best answer. Once an offering is complete and the material nonpublic information obtained by the investment banking department becomes public, resuming publishing recommendations on the stock is not a violation of the Code and Standards because the information of the investment banking department no longer gives the brokerage operation an advantage in writing the report. Answer C is incorrect because no exchange of information should be occurring between the investment banking department and the brokerage operation, so monitoring of such exchanges is not an effective compliance procedure for preventing the use of material nonpublic information.

24 The correct answer is B. Under Standard III(A)–Loyalty, Prudence, and Care, members and candidates who manage a company's pension fund owe these duties to the participants and beneficiaries of the pension plan, not the management of the company or the company's shareholders.

25 The correct answer is B. Answer B gives one of the two primary reasons listed in the *Handbook* for disclosing referral fees to clients under Standard VI(C)–Referral Fees. (The other is to allow clients and employers to evaluate the full cost of the services.) Answer A is incorrect because Standard VI(C) does not require members or candidates to discount their fees when they receive referral fees. Answer C is inconsistent with Standard VI(C) because disclosure of referral fees, to be effective, should be made to prospective clients before entering into a formal client relationship with them.

26 The correct answer is B. Standard VI(B)–Priority of Transactions does not limit transactions of company employees that differ from current recommendations as long as the sale does not disadvantage current clients. Thus, answer A is incorrect. Answer C is incorrect because the Standard does not require the matching of personal and client trades.

27 Answer C is correct. Standard IV(A)–Loyalty discusses activities permissible to members and candidates when they are leaving their current employer; soliciting clients is strictly prohibited. Thus, answer A is inconsistent with the Code and Standards even with the required disclosure. Answer B is incorrect because the offer does not directly violate the Code and Standards. There may be out-of-work members and candidates who can arrange the necessary commitments without violating the Code and Standards.

28 Answer A is correct. The question relates to Standard III(A)–Loyalty, Prudence, and Care. Carter believes the broker offers effective execution at a fee that is comparable with those of other brokers, so he is free to use the broker for all accounts. Answer B is incorrect because the accounts that prohibit soft dollar arrangements do not want to fund the purchase of research by Carter. The new trading scheme does not incur additional commissions from clients, so it would not go against the prohibitions. Answer C is incorrect because Carter should not incur unnecessary or excessive "churning" of the portfolios (excessive trading) for the purpose of meeting the brokerage commitments of soft dollar arrangements.

29 Answer B is correct according to Standard VII(B)–Reference to CFA Institute, the CFA Designation, and the CFA Program. CFA Program candidates do not receive their actual scores on the exam. Topic and subtopic results are grouped into three broad categories, and the exam is graded only as "pass" or "fail." Although a candidate may have achieved a topical score of "above 70%," she or he cannot factually state that she or he received the highest possible score because that information is not reported. Thus, answer C is incorrect. Answer A is incorrect as long as the member or candidate actually completed the exams consecutively. Standard VII(B) does not prohibit the communication of factual information about completing the CFA Program in three consecutive years.

30 Answer C is correct. According to Standard III(A)–Loyalty, Prudence, and Care, the CFA Program would be considered a personal or firm expense and should not be paid for with the fund's brokerage commissions. Soft dollar accounts should be used only to purchase research services that directly assist the investment manager in the investment decision-making process, not to assist the management of the firm or to further education. Thus, answer A is incorrect. Answer B is incorrect because the reasonableness of how the money is used is not an issue; the issue is that educational expense is not research.

31 Answer A is correct. Standard I(B)–Independence and Objectivity emphasizes the need for members and candidates to maintain their independence and objectivity. Best practices dictate that firms adopt a strict policy not to accept compensation for travel arrangements. At times, however, accepting paid travel would not compromise one's independence and objectivity. Answers B

and C are incorrect because the added benefits—free conference admission for additional staff members and an exclusive golf retreat for the speaker—could be viewed as inducements related to the firm's working arrangements and not solely related to the speaking engagement. Should Long wish to bring other team members or participate in the golf outing, he or his firm should be responsible for the associated fees.

32 Answer C is correct. The guidance to Standard II(A)–Material Nonpublic Information recommends adding securities to the firm's restricted list when the firm has or may have material nonpublic information. By adding these securities to this list, Andrews would uphold this standard. Because waiting until the next day will not ensure that news of the merger is made public, answer A is incorrect. Negotiations may take much longer between the two companies, and the merger may never happen. Andrews must wait until the information is disseminated to the market before he trades on that information. Answer B is incorrect because Andrews should not disclose the information to other managers; no trading is allowed on material nonpublic information.

33 Answer B is correct. Through placing a personal purchase order that is significantly greater than the average volume, Pietro is violating Standard IIB–Market Manipulation. He is attempting to manipulate an increase in the share price and thus bring a buyer to the negotiating table. The news of a possible merger and confirmation of the firm's earnings guidance may also have positive effects on the price of Local Bank, but Pietro's actions in instructing the release of the information does not represent a violation through market manipulation. Announcements of this nature are common and practical to keep investors informed. Thus, answers A and C are incorrect.

34 Answer C is correct. Cupp violated Standard III(D)–Performance Presentations when he deviated from the firm's stated policies solely to capture the gain from the holding being acquired. Answer A is incorrect because the firm does not claim GIPS compliance and the GIPS standards require external cash flows to be treated in a consistent manner with the firm's documented policies. Answer B is incorrect because the firm does not state that it is updating its composite policies. If such a change were to occur, all cash flows for the month would have to be reviewed to ensure their consistent treatment under the new policy.

35 Answer A is correct. According to Standard V(C)–Record Retention, Cannan needed the permission of her employer to maintain the files at home after her employment ended. Without that permission, she should have deleted the files. All files created as part of a member's or candidate's professional activity are the property of the firm, even those created outside normal work hours. Thus, answer B is incorrect. Answer C is incorrect because the Code and Standards do not prohibit using one's personal computer to complete work for one's employer.

36 Answer B is correct. According to Standard VII(B)–Reference to CFA Institute, the CFA Designation, and the CFA Program, Quinn cannot claim to have finished the CFA Program or be eligible for the CFA charter until he officially learns that he has passed the Level III exam. Until the results for the most recent exam are released, those who sat for the exam should continue to refer to themselves as "candidates." Thus, answer C is incorrect. Answer A is incorrect because members and candidates may discuss areas of practice in which they believe the CFA Program improved their personal skills.

37 Answer A is correct. Hart's decision to invest in the retail fund appears directly correlated with Rodriguez's statement about the successful quarter of Mega Retail and thus violates Standard II(A)–Material Nonpublic Information. Rodriguez's information would be considered material because it would influence the share price of Mega Retail and probably influence the price of the entire exchange-traded retail fund. Thus, answer B is incorrect. Answer C is also incorrect because Rodriguez shared information that was both material and nonpublic. Company officers regularly have such knowledge about their firms, which is not a violation. The sharing of such information, however, even in a conversation between friends, does violate Standard II(A).

38 Answer C is correct. Standard VII(A)–Conduct as Members and Candidates in the CFA Program prohibits providing information to candidates or the public that is considered confidential to the CFA Program. In revealing that questions related to the analysis of inventories and analysis of taxes were on the exam, Park has violated this standard. Answer B is incorrect because the guidance for the standard explicitly acknowledges that members and candidates are allowed to offer their opinions about the CFA Program. Answer A is incorrect because candidates are not prohibited from using outside resources.

39 Answer B is correct. Paper has violated Standard III(D)–Performance Presentation by not disclosing that he was part of a team of managers that achieved the results shown. If he had also included the return of the portion he directly managed, he would not have violated the standard. Thus, answer A is incorrect. Answer C is incorrect because Paper received written permission from his prior employer to include the results.

40 Answer A is correct. Townsend has not provided any information about her clients to the leaders or managers of the golf program; thus, she has not violated Standard III(E)–Preservation of Confidentiality. Providing contact information about her clients for a direct-mail solicitation would have been a violation. Answer B is incorrect because the notice in the newsletter does not violate Standard III(E). Answer C is incorrect because the golf program's fund-raising campaign had already begun, so discussing the opportunity to donate was appropriate.

41 C is correct. This question relates to Standard I(A)–Knowledge of the Law. A member or candidate must not knowingly participate or assist in any violation of laws, rules, or regulations. Danvers was not aware—or reasonably expected to be aware—that the CIO was distributing this information in Country B.

42 B is correct. This question relates to Standard I(B)–Independence and Objectivity. Publicly endorsing a charity during a luncheon that the board member is known to be attending could be perceived as an attempt by the CEO to impair the objectivity of the board member.

43 C is correct. This question relates to Standard II(B)–Market Manipulation. By trading the stock within his own personal account, he has created the appearance that the stock had greater liquidity than it actually did. Standard II(B) states that members and candidates must not engage in practices that distort prices or artificially inflate trading volume with the intent to mislead market participants.

44 A is correct. This question relates to Standard III(A)–Loyalty, Prudence, and Care and Standard III(E)–Preservation of Confidentiality. Dent cannot disclose confidential information to anyone without the permission of the fund, regardless of whether the disclosure may benefit the fund.

45 A is correct. This question relates to Standard IV(A)–Loyalty. Howard has violated the Standards by using the list of clients without permission from his prior firm. The Standards state that firm records that are stored in paper copy should be returned to the employer unless the firm gives the employee permission to keep those records after employment has ended. Howard would not have violated this standard if he had re-created the list from memory.

46 C is correct. This question relates to Standard V(B)–Communication with Clients and Prospective Clients. The Standards state that members and candidates must use reasonable judgment in identifying which factors are important to their investment analyses, recommendations, or actions and include those factors in communication with clients and prospective clients.

47 C is correct. This question relates to Standard VI(A)–Disclosure of Conflicts. According to this standard, members and candidates must make full and fair disclosure of all matters that could reasonably be expected to impair their independence and objectivity or interfere with respective duties to their clients, prospective clients, and employer. Participation on outside boards would most likely be considered a conflict that members should disclose to their employers. The potential conflict that arises is that serving on the board of the state retirement fund allows Lindsay to have a say over which firm is chosen for the investment allocation, and he would likely have an interest in ensuring that his client receives the mandate.

48 B is correct. According to Standard VII(B)–References to the CIPM Association, the CIPM Designation, and the CIPM Program, Harley cannot claim that she will become a CIPM certificate holder until she officially learns that she has completed the requirements of the program. Until the results for the most recent exam are released, those who sat for the exam can refer to themselves only as "candidates."

49 B is correct. According to Standard II(B)–Market Manipulation, transaction-based manipulation involves instances where a member or candidate knew or should have known that his or her actions could affect the pricing of a security. The portfolio manager's actions were clearly intended to manipulate the price of the client's holdings.

50 B is correct. According to Standard IV(A)–Loyalty, whistleblowing is intended to protect the integrity of the capital markets and the interests of clients.

51 C is correct. This question relates to Standard VI(A)–Disclosure of Conflicts. Taylor's personal relationship with a key member of the finalist firm may be perceived as a conflict of interest for the retirement plan and needs to be disclosed to the other members of the board. Additionally, the fact that the firm manages Taylor's retirement account and will lower his fees if the business is won constitutes a conflict of interest.

52 C is correct. Standard I(A): Knowledge of the Law states, "In the event of conflict, Members and Candidates must comply with the more strict law, rule, or regulation." In this situation, the absence of any local laws would require members to follow the Code and Standards. Standard I(B): Independence and Objectivity states that "Members and Candidates must not offer, solicit, or accept any gift, benefit, compensation, or consideration that could be expected to compromise their own or another's independence and objectivity."

A is incorrect because the Code and Standards require members and candidates to reject gifts that could be expected to compromise their own or another's independence and objectivity.

B is incorrect because Standard I(B) does not preclude customary, ordinary business-related entertainment as long as its purpose is not to influence or reward members or candidates. However, members and candidates must limit the acceptance of gratuities or gifts to token items. A gift from a client can be distinguished from gifts given by entities seeking to influence a member or candidate to the detriment of other clients.

53 A is correct. Participation in an external continuing education program is a suggested method for members and candidates to acquire and maintain understanding of applicable laws, rules, and regulations. Under Standard I(A): Knowledge of the Law, members and candidates must understand and comply with all applicable laws, rules, and regulations. Procedures should be established to keep employees regularly informed of changes.

B is incorrect because under Standard I(A): Knowledge of the Law, members and candidates should review or encourage their employers to review their firm's written compliance procedures on a *regular* basis.

C is incorrect because under Standard I(A): Knowledge of the Law, members and candidates should maintain or encourage their employers to maintain readily accessible *current* reference copies of applicable statutes, rules, regulations, and important cases.

54 B is correct. Under Standard I(B): Independence and Objectivity, a performance analyst must not allow internal or external influences to affect her independence and objectivity as she faithfully completes her performance calculation and analysis-related responsibilities. The performance analyst should share her conclusions with her boss or other supervisors, potentially a senior officer appointed to have oversight responsibilities for compliance.

A is incorrect because the analyst concludes that using the new index would be misleading and she must not allow internal or external influences to affect her independence and objectivity.

C is incorrect because the analyst concludes that using the new index would be misleading. Comparing performance evaluations with the two indexes would not resolve the issue, even if there were no material difference in a particular time frame.

55 C is correct. According to Standard I(B), Hill must maintain his independence and objectivity and refuse to include specific accounts in the firm's performance composite in which they should not belong. As long as the client requires a portion of his account remain invested in inherited small-cap stocks, it cannot be included in the Large-Cap Composite because the holdings are not reflective of the strategy. Their inclusion in the composite would violate Standard I(C): Misrepresentation regarding performance reporting.

A is incorrect because the account does not reflect the Large-Cap Strategy and, therefore, should not be included in the composite. By including the account that includes small-cap stocks, Hill would be violating Standard I(B): Independence and Objectivity, because their inclusion would violate Standard I(C): Misrepresentation regarding performance reporting.

B is incorrect because the relative performance of small-cap stocks is not a reason to exclude the account from the composite. According to Standard I(B), Hill must maintain his independence and objectivity and refuse to include specific accounts in the firm's performance composite in which they should not belong. As long as the client requires a portion of his account remain invested in inherited small-cap stocks, it cannot be included in the Large-Cap Composite because the holdings are not reflective of the strategy. Their inclusion in the composite would violate Standard I(C): Misrepresentation regarding performance reporting.

56 B is correct. Under Standard I(C): Misrepresentation, members and candidates should take reasonable steps to provide accurate and reliable security pricing information to clients on a consistent basis. By selecting valuations on an ad hoc basis in a manner that is not clear or consistent, the firm will misrepresent performance for some time frames.

A is incorrect because a benchmark for a municipal bond strategy is not expected to have the same constituents as the strategy. Therefore, Fact 1 is not an indication of misrepresentation.

C is incorrect because a benchmark for a municipal bond strategy is not expected to have the same constituents as the strategy. Therefore, Fact 1 is not an indication of misrepresentation.

57 B is correct. Moving accounts into or out of a composite to influence the overall performance results materially misrepresents the reported values over time and conflicts with Standard I(C): Misrepresentation. Foreman should work with his firm to strengthen its reporting practices concerning composite construction to avoid misrepresenting the composite's track record.

A is incorrect because the removal of these accounts represents cherry picking. The composite performance should be a representation of all accounts managed to the indicated strategy and reflect the portfolio manager's investment decisions. The portfolio manager made the decision to overweight the securities, and the results of this decision need to be reflected in the composite performance.

C is incorrect because by excluding the poorly performing stocks from the accounts' performance calculations, the composite's performance results will not reflect the impact of the portfolio manager's decision to overweight some stocks.

58 A is correct. The firm claims compliance with the GIPS standards, which means that the firm must meet all the requirements of the Standards, including making mandatory disclosures that apply to the firm's specific situation. Elliot's asset weighting of the composite's accounts is not a violation of the GIPS standards and, therefore, meets members' and candidates' obligations under Standard III(D).

B is incorrect because Elliot's failure to disclose that only accounts above a specific asset size were included in the composite is a violation of the GIPS standards and, therefore, does not meet members' and candidates' obligations under Standard III(D).

C is incorrect because Elliot's decision to exclude accounts not open for the entire time period is in violation of the GIPS standards and, therefore, does not meet members' and candidates' obligations under Standard III(D).

59 A is correct because the firm is violating Standard III(D) by distorting the performance record by including a portfolio that is not reflective of the strategy.

B and C are incorrect because simulated results are allowed to be presented, assuming appropriate disclosures are included.

60 A is correct. In reporting inconsistent valuations, Lane is failing the fairness test for claims made in communications to the firm's clients and is violating Standard III(D).

B and C are incorrect because the Code and Standards do not prohibit showing past performance of accounts managed at a prior firm as part of a performance track record as long as that record is accompanied by appropriate disclosures about where the performance took place and the person's specific role in achieving that performance.

61 A is correct. Before making a decision to disclose non-confidential information received from a client, members and candidates should ask the following: If disclosed in a discussion of work being performed for the client, is the information relevant to the work? Is the information background material that, if disclosed, will enable the member or candidate to improve service to the client? Affirmative responses to these questions would likely indicate that it is permissible to disclose the client's non-confidential information.

B and C are incorrect because members should ask themselves, If the information is disclosed, will it enable the member or candidate to improve service to the client? The decision of whether to disclose such information should include consideration of the potential impact on the firm's existing, not prospective, clients.

62 A is correct. Lee has come across an error in policies, procedures, and compliance practices within the firm's operations. Lee was correct in submitting his concerns to the compliance department when his supervisor appeared unwilling to address his concerns.

B is incorrect because supervisors have the responsibility of establishing and encouraging an ethical culture in the firm. The dismissal of Lee's concerns violates Standard IV(C) and undermines the firm's ethical operations.

C is incorrect because according to Standard IV(C), the supervisor has the responsibility to review the concerns brought forth by Lee.

63 A is correct. There is nothing in the Code and Standards that restricts a member or candidate from continuing to run a similar strategy at a new firm, assuming that he either recreates the model at the new firm or is given permission to take the documentation by his prior firm.

B is incorrect because under Standard V(C): Record Retention, records are the property of firm, not the individual. To use this model and prior performance, Reed would first need to obtain the express consent from the previous employer to take the records or recreate the records at the new firm.

C is incorrect because under Standard V(C): Record Retention, records created as part of a member's or candidate's professional activity on behalf of his or her employer are the property of the firm, not the individual. To use this model and prior performance, Reed would first need to obtain the express consent from the previous employer to take the documents to recreate the methodologies uses to run the model. Read can use the model at the new firm if he recreates the methodology from memory.

Performance Evaluation:

Measurement, Attribution, and Appraisal

Study Session 2	Overview and Return Measurement
Study Session 3	Return Attribution and Benchmark Analysis
Study Session 4	Risk Measurement, Risk Attribution, and Security Characteristics
Study Session 5	Performance Appraisal

TOPIC LEVEL LEARNING OUTCOME

The candidate should be able to calculate rates of return; explain and apply analytical techniques to determine the sources of returns relative to appropriate benchmarks; and calculate and interpret basic risk measures.

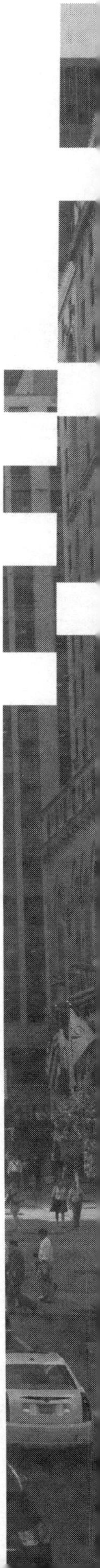

PERFORMANCE EVALUATION:
STUDY SESSION

2

Overview and Return Measurement

Fund sponsors use the techniques of performance evaluation to assess investment results relative to investment objectives, to determine the sources of returns, and to evaluate investment managers. Investment managers apply the techniques of performance evaluation to assess the effectiveness of various elements of their research and decision-making processes. For both fund sponsors and investment managers, performance evaluation is a productive feedback and control mechanism.

The first reading provides an overview of performance evaluation. The second reading examines return measurement as the foundation of all subsequent performance analysis.

READING ASSIGNMENTS

3 Performance Evaluation: An Introduction
by Stefan J. Illmer, PhD, and Dmitri A. Senik, FCCA, CFA

4 Performance Evaluation: Rate-of-Return Measurement
by Carl R. Bacon, CIPM, David R. Cariño, PhD, and Arin Stancil, CFA, CIPM

5 Data Integrity
by Marcus Boudville and Adam Taylor

READING

3

Performance Evaluation: An Introduction

by Stefan J. Illmer, PhD, and Dmitri A. Senik, FCCA, CFA

Stefan J. Illmer, PhD, is at Illmer Investment Performance Consulting AG (Switzerland). Dmitri A. Senik, FCCA, CFA (Switzerland).

LEARNING OUTCOMES

Mastery	*The candidate should be able to:*
☐	**a.** describe the feedback role of performance evaluation in the overall investment management process;
☐	**b.** describe how information provided by performance evaluation is useful to a variety of stakeholders;
☐	**c.** describe the major components of investment performance evaluation, including the questions they address;
☐	**d.** describe the factors that determine the specific characteristics of performance evaluation output;
☐	**e.** describe the scope of the performance evaluation process and its major activities, including how these activities are interrelated;
☐	**f.** explain ethical concerns related to investment performance presentations.

INTRODUCTION

1

Investors and investment managers need timely and accurate information on the performance of their investment portfolios. Performance evaluation provides such information. Without it, investors and investment managers would find it increasingly difficult to meet stakeholders' current and future needs in a very competitive investment management industry.

In the investment management industry, performance evaluation broadly refers to the measurement, analysis, interpretation, assessment, and presentation of investment results. In particular, performance evaluation provides information about the return and risk of investment portfolios over specified periods. Selection of investment managers is a closely related topic.

Performance evaluation, because of its function in monitoring portfolios, is an integral part of investment management. Among the questions addressed by performance evaluation are the following:

- What were the consequences of investment decisions?

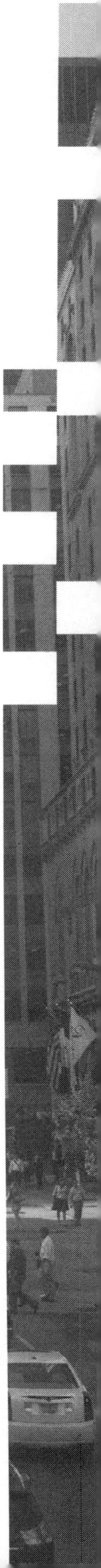

- Are portfolios being managed within their mandates and to investors' expectations?
- What progress has been made toward achieving clients' investment goals?
- How skillful is a portfolio manager?

Professionals involved in performance evaluation have such titles as investment officer, investment controller, investment consultant, financial adviser, equity analyst, fixed-income analyst, compliance officer, risk manager, performance analyst, and performance presentation specialist, depending on their responsibilities and focus.

This reading introduces performance evaluation and is organized as follows. Section 2 explains how performance evaluation fits into the investment management process, highlights the importance of performance evaluation, and describes its major activities and the factors that define the specific characteristics of its output. Section 3 describes the scope of the major activities of performance evaluation in more detail. Section 4 provides a summary.[1]

2 OVERVIEW OF PERFORMANCE EVALUATION

This section explains why performance evaluation is an integral part of the overall investment management process and how it plays a feedback role in investment management. The process of performance evaluation is also outlined.

2.1 Integration into the Investment Management Process

Performance evaluation covers many distinct but interrelated activities, beginning with return calculation. These activities provide information on both final investment results and the investment decisions producing those results.

Performance evaluation's place in portfolio management is shown in Exhibit 1, which illustrates a model of the investment management process as an integrated set of activities aimed at attaining investor objectives.[2]

1 In this reading, the terms "asset owners" and "clients"—that is, the clients of investment managers—are used interchangeably. "Investment portfolio" is used broadly to refer to investment accounts or mandates managed by investment managers. A portfolio might be one investment account, multiple distinct investment accounts managed by different portfolio managers, or all investment portfolios of a certain investment product or of an investment manager. Furthermore, in this reading, "asset" and "investment" manager are used in a very broad sense to refer not only to asset management companies but also to all organizations that manage assets—including family offices, pension plans, and endowment funds. As used here, an "investment manager" may employ one or more portfolio managers.

2 For a detailed discussion of the investment management process, see John L. Maginn, Donald L. Tuttle, Jerald E. Pinto, and Dennis W. McLeavey, eds., *Managing Investment Portfolios: A Dynamic Process*, 3rd ed. (Hoboken, NJ: Wiley, 2007).

Exhibit 1 The Portfolio Construction, Monitoring, and Revision Process

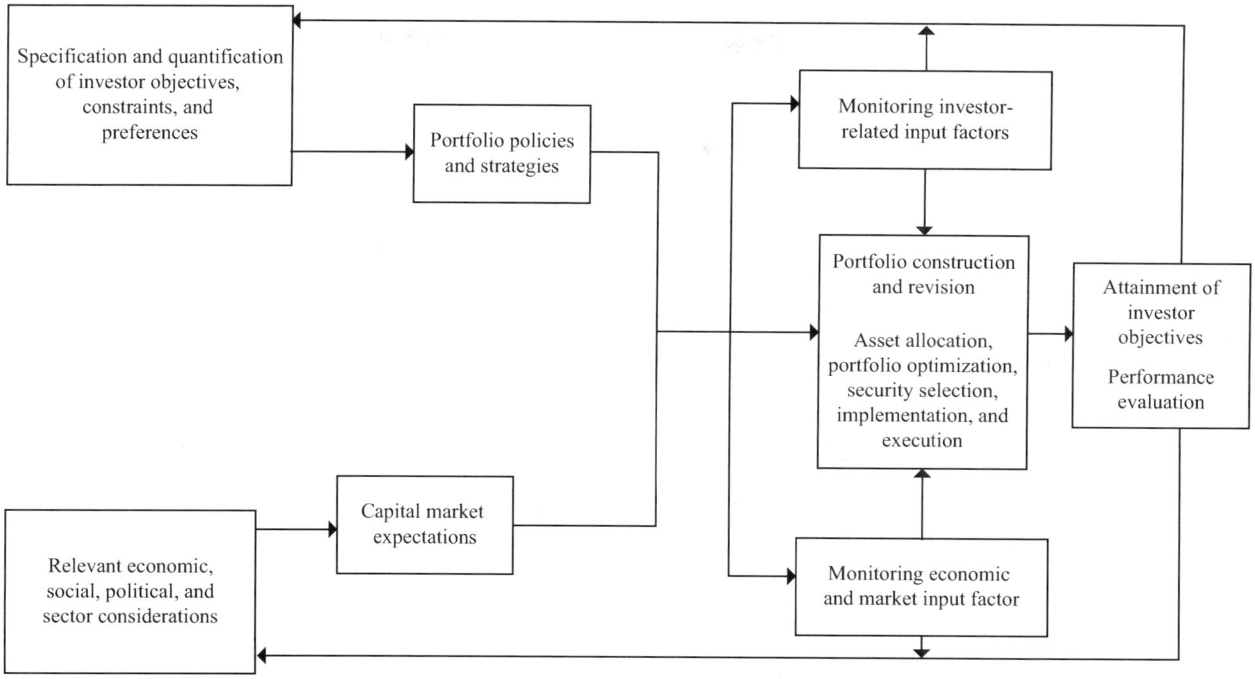

Source: John L. Maginn, Donald L. Tuttle, Jerald E. Pinto, and Dennis W. McLeavey, eds., "The Portfolio Management Process and the Investment Policy Statement," Chapter 1 in *Managing Investment Portfolios: A Dynamic Approach*, 3rd ed. (Hoboken, NJ: Wiley, 2007), p. 6.

Exhibit 1 shows a sequence of activities that begins with understanding investor objectives, constraints, and preferences. These investor-related input factors determine the range of portfolio policies and strategies that may be pursued. Such factors, in conjunction with capital market considerations, form the basis for asset allocation and the selection of individual investments. Portfolio managers or their traders then execute those decisions. The portfolio is reviewed on a regular basis to determine whether a revision of the current asset allocation or portfolio composition is required or advisable. Performance evaluation, as the final step, describes performance and analyzes why progress toward investor objectives turned out as it did. Such information may also be useful in judging whether an investment manager is likely to help an investor reach her investment goals in the future, which is why performance evaluation supports manager selection. Performance evaluation is a feedback mechanism that helps align portfolio characteristics with investor objectives.

This information provided by performance evaluation is of great interest to all stakeholders in the investment management process because of its value in evaluating the overall quality of the investment management process as well as individual investment decisions. One very important stakeholder is the investor/client/asset owner whose financial well-being is affected by how effectively his portfolio is managed. Other individuals and entities, however, also have an interest in the information provided by performance evaluation. Exhibit 2 illustrates major stakeholders classified as internal or external to the investment manager.[3]

3 Performance analysis may be conducted internally and externally to the investment manager (e.g., by custodians, investment consultants, independent performance measurement firms, and the asset owners themselves).

Exhibit 2 Major Stakeholders in Performance Evaluation

Among external stakeholders, regulators are concerned that investment results are reported fairly and accurately and that prospective clients are aware of potential risks to their investment; investment consultants are stakeholders because they may be hired for advice on the selection of investment managers. Internally, portfolio managers and risk controllers (or risk managers) need performance information to control investment processes and manage risk; a firm's marketing and sales departments needs such information to answer prospective client' questions. Senior management needs to oversee individual portfolio managers as well as the entire investment process, and the operations function can use performance analysis to identify pricing and transaction errors and improve the overall quality of information provided.

2.2 Why Performance Evaluation Is Important

This section summarizes and extends the discussion of why performance evaluation is important and its benefits to various stakeholders.

By providing accurate data and analysis on investment decisions and their consequences, performance evaluation allows investment managers (and the portfolio managers they employ) to take corrective measures to improve investment decision-making and management processes. Performance evaluation information helps in understanding and controlling investment risk and should, therefore, lead to improved risk management.

For asset owners and prospective clients, performance evaluation communicates portfolio managers' results. Broadly, it permits asset owners and prospective clients to make better decisions (including selection, continuance, and dismissal) about investment managers by providing relevant information on performance and its drivers. Accurate performance presentations are especially important for asset owners and prospective clients in facilitating accurate analysis.

Performance evaluation in its feedback role may have a large impact on investment managers, asset owners, and other stakeholders. An effective performance evaluation process facilitates the following outcomes:

For investment managers:

- Prompt attention to potential performance issues and unintended business or investment risks
- Effective monitoring of risk and return in relation to the investor's objectives and the designated benchmark

- An effective internal management information system
- Effective internal monitoring and oversight management/mechanisms

For both investment managers and asset owners:

- Clear understanding of the different activities and decisions within the investment management process, as well as their performance contributions
- Reduction in non-fact-based discussions by using more objective and less subjective investment performance information during the performance assessment process
- Dialogue among stakeholders that may lead to innovation, change in practices, strengthened brand and reputation, and new attractive investment products for investors

For asset owners:

- Finding evidence of skill (or lack thereof)

Because of different perspectives held by participants in the investment management process, performance evaluation sometimes involves emotional discussions among the concerned stakeholders. Such discussions often hinder achieving appropriate solutions and may lead to unintended consequences. To minimize the chance of such discussions, performance evaluation should follow appropriate guiding principles. Such principles include the following:

- The intended user and the expected use of the performance information are taken into account in deciding what types of performance evaluation analysis to conduct and what methodologies to use.
- The performance evaluation considers and provides information on changes in investment strategy, investment style, or investment restrictions.
- The performance evaluation is an accurate and unbiased representation of the investments made, results achieved, risks taken, and taxes and fees incurred.
- The performance evaluation is relevant and appropriate for the presented asset classes, investment strategies, investment styles, and investment products.
- The performance evaluation takes into account both risk and return.
- The performance evaluation provides information on past (*ex post*) and expected (*ex ante*) investment risks and compares *ex post* realized risk with the *ex ante* forecast of risk (risk efficiency).
- The performance evaluation analyzes taxes and their effect on investment portfolio performance, where such analysis is feasible and relevant.
- The performance evaluation analyzes fees and associated remuneration (e.g., commissions and referral fees) received for management or administration of the investment portfolio, as well as transaction costs and trading expenses incurred in the portfolio.
- The performance evaluation provides comparatives, such as an appropriate benchmark, to enable assessment of the investment portfolio's relative performance.

Besides attention to these principles, other factors promoting effective performance evaluation include commitment by senior management, well-educated and experienced staff, and an appropriate budget for necessary information technology projects. It is also very important that the performance evaluation process itself be well defined and structured.

2.3 Performance Evaluation: Component Activities

Feedback provided by performance evaluation relates to major questions important for the asset owner and other stakeholders. Associated with each question is a major component activity. Narrowly speaking, performance evaluation consists of performance measurement, attribution, appraisal, and presentation. Although manager selection considers many aspects of a manager in addition to evidence of skill in past performance—such as investment philosophy and risk control processes—manager selection is traditionally presented alongside performance appraisal. In the Certificate in Investment Performance Measurement (CIPM®) curriculum, manager selection is a component activity of performance evaluation. Exhibit 3 illustrates these activities.

Exhibit 3 Performance Evaluation: Major Component Activities

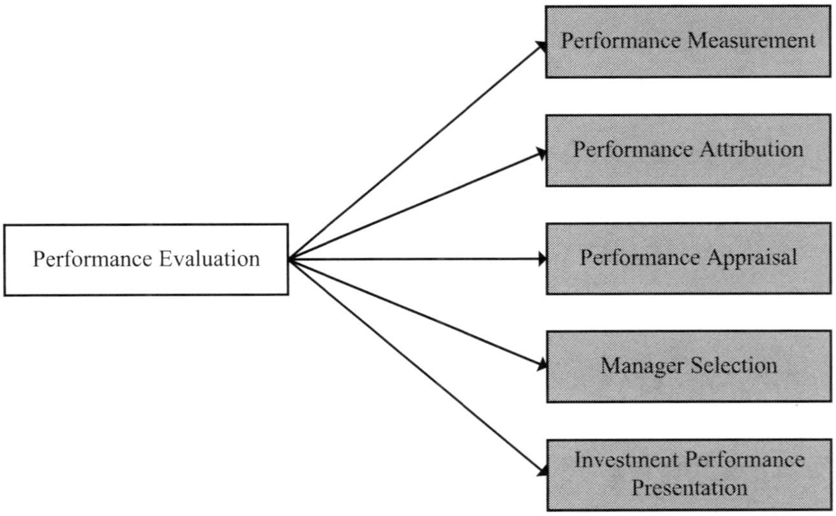

Performance evaluation answers a number of key questions within asset management:

- What was the portfolio's past performance, and what may be expected in the future?
- How did the portfolio produce its observed performance, and what are the expected sources of expected future performance?
- Was the observed portfolio's performance the result of investment skill or luck?
- Which portfolio managers should be hired, retained, or dismissed?
- What performance information should be presented, and in what way?

2.3.1 *What may be expected in the future?*

Performance measurement answers the first question, the calculation of risk and return of the portfolio. Performance may either address a past time period (*ex post* performance) or look forward to a future time period (*ex ante* performance). "*Ex post*" and "*ex ante*" are Latin words that mean, respectively, "after the fact" and "before the fact."

"Return" may be defined as the percentage gain or loss in wealth resulting from holding an investment over a specified period.[4] Risk means different things to different stakeholders at different times. The Oxford English Dictionary provides a good

4 As defined in Bacon, Cariño, and Stancil (2011) in the CIPM curriculum.

definition of risk: "the potential impact of an event determined by combining the likelihood of the event occurring with the impact should it occur." Risk is the combination of exposure and uncertainty.[5] Risk within asset management may be broadly categorized into

- compliance risk,
- operational risk,
- liquidity risk,
- counterparty risk, and
- portfolio risk.

Performance measurement is concerned with portfolio risk. Are the risks of the portfolio of assets—for example, market risk, interest rate risk, credit risk, and currency risks—managed to the client's expectations?

Both return and risk can be viewed from *ex post* or *ex ante* perspectives. *Ex post*, or historical, risk is the analysis of risk after the event; it answers the question, How risky was the portfolio in the past? *Ex ante*, or prospective, risk is forward looking, based on a snapshot of the current securities and instruments in the portfolio and their historical relationship with each other. It is an estimate or forecast of the future risk of the portfolio.

In its coverage of performance evaluation, the CIPM curriculum begins with rate of return measurement because "calculation of rates of return is the crucial first step in performance evaluation: Without accurate rates of return, we can make no further progress in analyzing performance."[6] The motto "garbage in, garbage out" supports the importance of this component—the first step, in fact, of the performance evaluation process. Logically, the reading on return measurement is followed by coverage of risk measurement in the CIPM curriculum.

2.3.2 *How did the investment portfolio produce its observed performance, and what are the expected sources of expected future performance?*

Performance attribution is concerned with identifying and quantifying the sources of risk and return of a portfolio, and it answers the second question. Performance attribution is the key tool for performance analysts. It allows them to participate in the investment decision process and demonstrably add value. Attribution analysis allows the analyst to understand the sources of risk and return in a portfolio and communicate that understanding to portfolio managers, senior management, asset owners, and other stakeholders.

Effective attribution requires the analyst to thoroughly understand the decision process and quantify the decisions actually made. The attribution analysis must fit the investment decision process. There is less value in analyzing factors that are not part of the decision process other than to identify weaknesses and gaps in the current process. Bond managers, more concerned with the changing shape of the yield curve and credit risk, will manage portfolios in a different way from equity managers and will likely require a different attribution approach. Multi-currency strategies, portfolios with derivative instruments, overlay portfolios, illiquid assets, and bottom-up security-level strategies may each require a different approach aligned with the manager's decision process.

Following the two dimensions of performance—return and risk—attribution questions can be analyzed from two perspectives.

5 Grégoire (2007, p. 309).
6 Bacon et al. (2011).

Focusing on return, analysts apply the tools of return attribution. Because most portfolios are assigned a benchmark or reference point for assessing the portfolio manager's management of a portfolio, relative return attribution is usually defined as a set of techniques used to identify the sources of a portfolio's excess return—against the assigned benchmark.

Focusing on risk, analysts apply the tools of risk attribution. Risk attribution is a set of techniques used to identify and quantify the sources of risk in a portfolio as well as the impact of investment decisions contributing to the portfolio's total risk. In contrast to return attribution, which typically is performed only *ex post* (i.e., looking at the portfolio's historical returns), risk attribution can be performed on both an *ex post* basis (i.e., considering the risk of the portfolio in past periods) and an *ex ante* basis (i.e., considering the risk associated with the current portfolio holdings).

Thus, performance attribution properly consists of return attribution and risk attribution, although many practitioners informally use the term "performance attribution" to refer only to return attribution. The asset management industry, however, appears to be moving to integrate risk into performance analytics. Consequently, the performance analytics function is being integrated with risk management or risk control.

2.3.3 *Was the observed investment portfolio's performance the result of investment skill or luck?*

Performance appraisal is concerned with identifying and measuring investment skill, and it answers the third question. Performance appraisal distinctively treats returns in conjunction with risk. Were the returns (or rewards) earned sufficient compensation for the risks taken? Thus, part of the study of performance appraisal concerns making full adjustment to returns for the risks incurred (risk-adjusted returns). The complexity of the issues addressed suggests that, as in the CIPM curriculum, the topic of performance appraisal should be covered after performance measurement and attribution.

It should be obvious that performance appraisal can provide helpful information in the selection of active investment managers. Of course, many considerations besides questions of active investment skill may be important to an investment client—for example, financial stability and reputation of the investment management company, its operational risk management, and the quality of investment reporting. In that sense, investment manager selection is a broader topic than performance appraisal. Because of the connections between them, however, manager selection is often grouped with and studied along with or after performance appraisal, as in the CIPM curriculum.

2.3.4 *Which portfolio managers should be hired, retained, or dismissed?*

Manager selection is broadly understood as the analysis of whether to hire, retain, or dismiss a portfolio manager, and it answers the fourth question. Manager selection is used as shorthand to include all three aspects of hiring, retaining, and dismissing managers, and thus, it includes not only selection but also monitoring of manager performance.

In general, manager selection considers both quantitative and qualitative information and addresses not only observed portfolio performance but also operational and organizational factors that affect the repeatability of performance; the financial stability, creditworthiness, and integrity of the investment manager; operational risk management; and any other factors that are important to the client. Portfolio manager turnover, analyst capabilities, and the quality of the investment decision-making process are examples of organizational factors that can affect performance repeatability.

The three activities of hiring, retaining, and dismissing managers each have some unique considerations. For example, the decision to hire involves becoming acquainted in detail with an organization and its operational setup, reputation, risk management, internal control system, and regulatory supervision. When a client is deciding whether to retain a manager, she may have gained considerable further experience with the manager. Such experience includes not only the experience with the manager's investment performance but also further operational experience, such as the quality of client relationship management and investment reporting. Considerations not present when the manager was hired may be important—for example, whether an investment strategy or style should be retained or changed to better reflect changed circumstances or investment objectives. In replacing a manager, a client also needs to consider the costs and risks in transitioning assets from the old to the new portfolio manager.

2.3.5 *What investment performance information should be presented, and in what way?*

Investment performance presentation is concerned with providing information about the performance of investment portfolios, and it answers the final key question.

Among stakeholders external to the investment manager, it is useful to distinguish between two kinds of consumers of performance information: prospective clients and existing clients. Reporting to prospective clients is very much sales driven—prepared from the perspective of the investment manager to reflect the manager's track record and skills. Therefore, this type of reporting often needs to adhere to specific regulations or industry best practices that aim to protect less informed, non-professional investors. The Global Investment Performance Standards (GIPS®) address this need. Reporting to existing clients has other focuses, including explaining the investment manager's recent investment decisions and information relevant to evaluating progress in achieving client objectives. Among the other stakeholders external to the investment manager that can shape performance presentation are regulators. Internal performance reporting to management is also a related topic.

2.4 Factors Defining the Output of Performance Evaluation Activities

In general, performance evaluation handles performance information or data in any format provided by the preparer for the intended user. Four factors characterize the output of a performance evaluation activity:

- the performance information to be analyzed,
- the intended user of the performance evaluation,
- the intended use of the performance evaluation, and
- the preparer of the performance evaluation.

- *Performance information:* profit and loss figures; performance figures (return and risk), both *ex ante* (forward looking) and *ex post* (historical); contributions to absolute or relative return and risk; performance appraisal measures; individual investment, portfolio, benchmark, composite,[7] and peer group performance figures; or performance analytics, including performance attribution or investment style analysis
- *Intended user:* prospective or existing clients; marketing officers; client relationship managers; compliance officers; performance analysts; portfolio managers; investment committee members; senior management; investment consultants; journalists; or regulators

7 A "composite" in this context is an aggregation of one or more portfolios managed according to a similar investment mandate, objective, or strategy.

- *Intended use:* determination of the sources of the absolute or relative return and risk; monitoring the implementation of the investment strategy; monitoring agreed risk limits, investment restrictions, or portfolio characteristics; product review; performance assessment; analysis of investment skills; or peer group comparisons
- *Preparer:* custodian; fund administrator; research department; investment management company; broker; financial analyst; investment adviser; investment consultant; independent performance measurer; investment controller; risk manager; performance analyst; reporting specialist; compliance officer; or the asset owner

Various performance evaluation activities can be characterized along these dimensions. For example, consider the production of a return attribution. Exhibit 4 illustrates a sample return attribution report for a multi-asset-class portfolio. This report consists of information analyzing the sources of investment returns in terms of investment management decisions—in particular, asset allocation and security selection.[8] In assigning responsibility for those results, it would be important to know whether the asset class weighting decisions were the responsibility of the client or were delegated to an external party, in particular an external investment manager. If the client made tactical asset allocation decisions but delegated security selection to external managers, the asset class results would be attributed to the client and the security selection results to the delegated portfolio managers. The return attribution report may be used by the performance analyst and/or head of portfolio management (for monitoring the implementation of the promised investment strategy) or by the client (for monitoring the quality of the individual investment management decisions).

Exhibit 4 Sample Return Attribution Report

	Portfolio			Benchmark			Management Effects			
	Return	Weight	Contribution	Return	Weight	Contribution	Asset Allocation	Security Selection	Interaction	Total
Cash	0.50%	15.00%	0.08%	0.05%	10.00%	0.01%	0.00%	0.05%	0.02%	0.04%
Domestic bonds	-1.50%	20.00%	-0.30%	-0.80%	25.00%	-0.20%	0.04%	-0.18%	0.04%	-0.10%
Foreign bonds	1.25%	5.00%	0.06%	1.20%	8.00%	0.10%	-0.04%	0.00%	0.00%	-0.03%
Domestic equities	5.00%	20.00%	1.00%	3.50%	15.00%	0.53%	0.18%	0.23%	0.08%	0.48%
Foreign equities	2.50%	15.00%	0.38%	4.50%	10.00%	0.45%	0.23%	-0.20%	-0.10%	-0.08%
Mortgages	0.35%	1.00%	0.00%	0.25%	2.00%	0.01%	0.00%	0.00%	0.00%	0.00%
Real estate	-4.50%	5.00%	-0.23%	-3.50%	10.00%	-0.35%	0.18%	-0.10%	0.05%	0.13%
Commodities	0.50%	8.00%	0.04%	-1.50%	5.00%	-0.08%	-0.05%	0.10%	0.06%	0.12%
Private equity	2.00%	8.00%	0.16%	0.50%	5.00%	0.03%	0.02%	0.08%	0.05%	0.14%
Hedge funds	-0.50%	3.00%	-0.02%	1.00%	10.00%	0.10%	-0.07%	-0.15%	0.11%	-0.12%
Total	**1.18%**	**100.00%**	**1.18%**	**0.58%**	**100.00%**	**0.58%**	**0.48%**	**-0.17%**	**0.29%**	**0.60%**

8 The asset allocation effect measures the contribution to excess return (relative to the benchmark return) resulting from over- or underweighting asset classes. The security selection effect measures the contribution to excess return resulting from over- or underweighting individual securities within the respective asset classes. The interaction effect is a combined effect and measures the contribution to excess return resulting from the over- or underweighting of out- or underperforming asset classes.

In Exhibit 4, the decision to overweight domestic equities at 20% versus a benchmark weight of 15% contributed +0.18% in added return—the asset allocation effect. In addition, the selection of individual stocks in the domestic equities segment contributed a further +0.23%—the security selection effect—for a total added return (management effect) of +0.48% for the investment in domestic equities; (tactical) asset allocation was most successful within the foreign equities asset class—with a contribution of +0.23%. In contrast, all active security selection decisions combined removed 17 bps of excess returns. If the entity responsible for security selection claimed capability in that area, further analysis would be appropriate, potentially leading to continuing with security selection, possibly with improvements in process, or abandoning it.

Another example of a performance evaluation activity is a risk contribution analysis. Exhibit 5 illustrates a sample risk contribution report for an equity portfolio. This report consists of information analyzing the sources of absolute investment (total) risk—here measured by standard deviation (volatility) of returns—in terms of Global Industry Classification Standard (GICS) sectors (in particular, energy, materials, industrials, and so on). The report provides investment managers with feedback on an equity portfolio's current risk exposures to individual GICS sectors. These risk contributions may be used as a test of whether the portfolio manager constructed the equity portfolio risk exposures as he claimed to in the first place. The preparer of the risk contribution report may be a risk analyst performing a special analysis for the head of equity portfolio management or a consultant hired by an investor. The report may be used by the risk manager or the head of equity portfolio management (for monitoring either the risk exposures or the proposed investment strategy) or by the investor (for investment guideline monitoring or performance review).

In Exhibit 5, the total risk of the equity portfolio is expressed as the expected volatility, and it is 14.00%. Furthermore, the contribution of each sector to the total risk is presented: The largest contributor to volatility is the financial sector (with a contribution of 2.52%), followed by the telecommunication services sector (1.92%). An additional kind of investment risk analysis for the portfolio is a risk attribution, in which the contributions of individual investment decisions (e.g., to under- and overweight certain GICS sectors relative to a benchmark) to the total excess risk are analyzed.

Other sets of characteristics can define other kinds of performance evaluation activities, such as scenario analysis, composite performance analysis, performance watch lists, investment style analysis, peer group comparisons, or even a combination of these.

Exhibit 5 Sample Risk Contribution Report

GICS	Marginal Contribution*	Weight	Contribution
Energy	12.00%	6.00%	0.72%
Materials	10.00	8.00	0.80
Industrials	13.00	14.00	1.82
Consumer discretionary	15.00	12.00	1.80
Consumer staples	14.00	7.00	0.98
Health care	16.00	6.00	0.96
Financials	18.00	14.00	2.52
Information technology	18.00	8.00	1.44
Telecommunication services	16.00	12.00	1.92

(continued)

Exhibit 5 (Continued)

GICS	Marginal Contribution*	Weight	Contribution
Utilities	8.00	13.00	1.04
Total risk			**14.00%**

* "Marginal contribution" of a sector measures the sensitivity of the portfolio's total risk to a small change in the asset holdings. For example, if the portfolio manager increases the holding in the consumer discretionary sector by 1%, the total risk of the portfolio will increase by 15% (change in the asset holdings multiplied by the marginal contribution).
Source: Risk Measurement and Risk Attribution (CFA Institute, 2012)

3 THE SCOPE OF THE PERFORMANCE EVALUATION PROCESS

Section 2.3 described how a set of major questions of interest to investment managers, asset owners, prospective clients, and other stakeholders can be used to distinguish among the major activities or component processes of performance evaluation. Actually, performance evaluation can address many more questions. This section provides more detailed information on the scope of performance evaluation.

Exhibit 6 presents a fairly general representation of the performance evaluation process. It is a recurring production, analytical, and communication process that uses input from, but also generates feedback to, the various participants and stakeholders in the investment management process. In practice, this process is not standardized, because it depends on specific organizational characteristics and on the historical development of the performance-related department(s) and related sub-processes. For example, at one extreme, performance measurement, attribution, presentation, and appraisal may be centralized for all types of investment products or client segments and managed within one department. At the other extreme, all of these processes might be separately managed and uncoordinated. In some organizations, the performance measurement function and performance analysis function (attribution and appraisal) are separated, with performance measurement more aligned with the operations function in the back office and performance analysis closely supporting portfolio managers and risk management in the front office. Increasingly, performance evaluation and all its elements are joined with risk control in the middle office of asset managers.

Exhibit 6 Generic Performance Evaluation

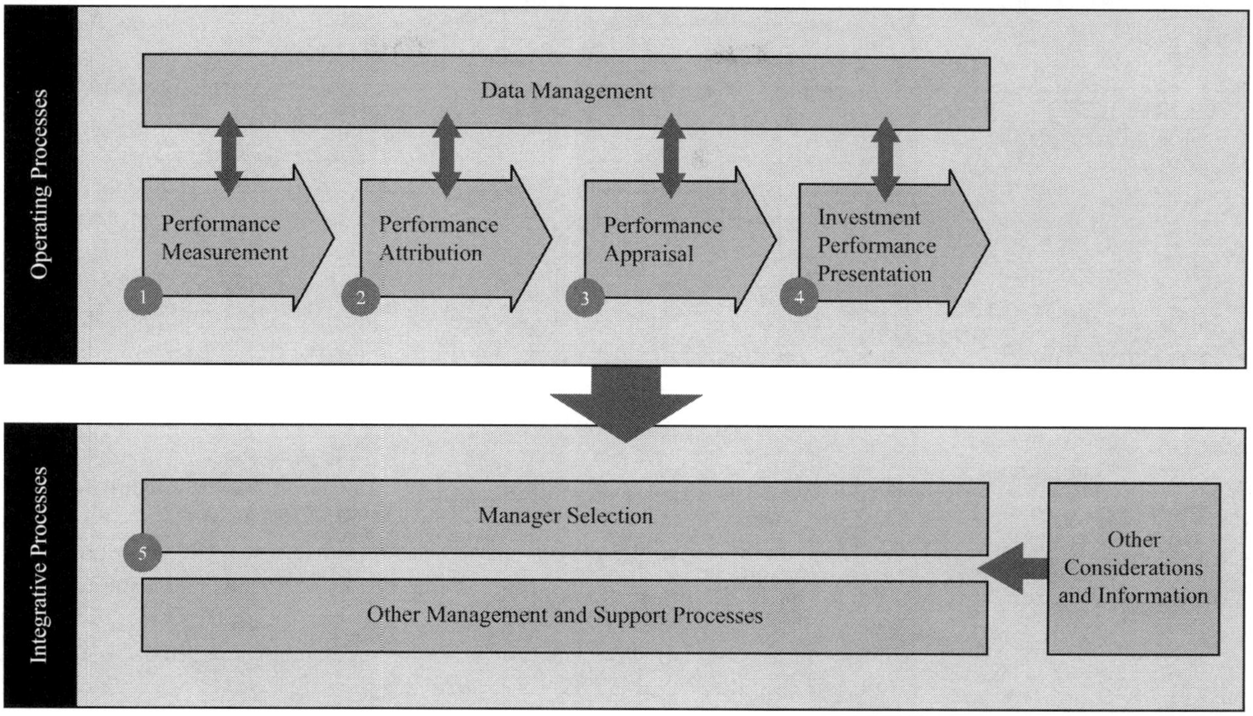

Exhibit 6 illustrates that the overall process is usually split into operating processes—covering performance measurement, attribution, appraisal, and presentation—and integrative processes, including manager selection and other management or support processes. Exhibit 6 also highlights that manager selection often uses a wide range of information, including qualitative information that may be only indirectly related to performance.

Operating processes are typically production oriented and data management driven and are used for calculating, managing, visualizing, and reporting performance figures. In contrast, integrative processes focus less on processing and more on detailed analysis, including qualitative analysis, of investment performance and on activities that depend on such analysis. Here, performance evaluation acts as a management information system, providing information to enable the senior management to make future-oriented management decisions—for example, on investment products to be introduced or withdrawn from the marketplace, on investment processes to be adjusted to better meet investors' expectations or to improve future performance, and on determining remuneration of portfolios managers.

3.1 Scope of Performance Measurement

The first step of the performance evaluation process, performance measurement, deals with all aspects of return and risk measurement for portfolios. Often, performance measurement is taken to be synonymous with return calculation, but it should be understood more broadly to cover the measurement of return as well as risk, whether on an absolute basis or compared with a selected benchmark.

Performance measurement poses various challenges. The complexity starts with ensuring the quality of the input data underlying performance, such as valuation of securities and investment instruments, in terms of both their accuracy and their comparability with the benchmark. Even for liquid marketable securities, such as "blue chip" equities, prices may be available from various sources (e.g., stock exchanges) and consistency must be monitored to ensure that the portfolio and its benchmark use the same pricing source. "Corporate action" events (e.g., share splits and dividend payments) must also be consistently accounted for, with respect to using the "ex-date" or "value date" convention. Valuation of fixed-income securities may be subject to different interest accrual assumptions. Over-the-counter derivatives, such as non-traded options or swaps, are usually estimated at fair value using a model, and it is important that such models be accurate. Private equity investments, such as private equity funds that hold portfolios of non-traded companies, pose big challenges in terms of determining their accurate values and, hence, meaningful returns. Different return methodologies and different assumptions may apply to different asset categories and different situations. Performance analysts will require detailed and well-documented policies and procedures to avoid self-selection of return methodologies and assumptions designed to improve the apparent performance of the portfolio manager.

Calculating rates of return appears simple when timely and accurate prices are available. More than one measurement methodology is often available, however, and in such cases, a return calculation's intended purpose can be an important consideration in choosing the appropriate calculation. Two major return measurement methodologies are the money-weighted rate of return (MWRR) and the time-weighted rate of return (TWRR). Broadly speaking, MWRR is the compound rate of growth that would produce the ending value of the portfolios given the timing and magnitude of all cash flows over the measurement period. In contrast, TWRR is the compound rate of growth of one unit of money invested in the portfolio at the start of the measurement period. TWRR neutralizes the impact of cash flow into and out of the portfolio—decisions that are typically beyond the manager's control—in order to isolate and better measure returns that derive from the manager's decision making. These concepts need to be presented in detail to be fully appreciated; the reading on rate of return measurement will do that.

Performance measurement also concerns measuring risk, both absolute and relative. Absolute risk relates to the risk of a portfolio, a benchmark, or a composite on a standalone basis—that is, not compared with anything else. In contrast, relative risk concerns risk relative to some reference point, such as a market index.

3.2 Scope of Performance Attribution

Performance attribution is the second major component of the performance evaluation process. It deals with all aspects of explaining what accounts for the return and risk of portfolios.

Performance attribution is often seen as synonymous with return attribution, but—as illustrated in Exhibit 7—this approach addresses only one aspect of performance. Performance attribution covers the decomposition of excess return as well as relative risk and brings both aspects of performance together by decomposing the risk-adjusted return.

Exhibit 7 Overview of Performance Attribution

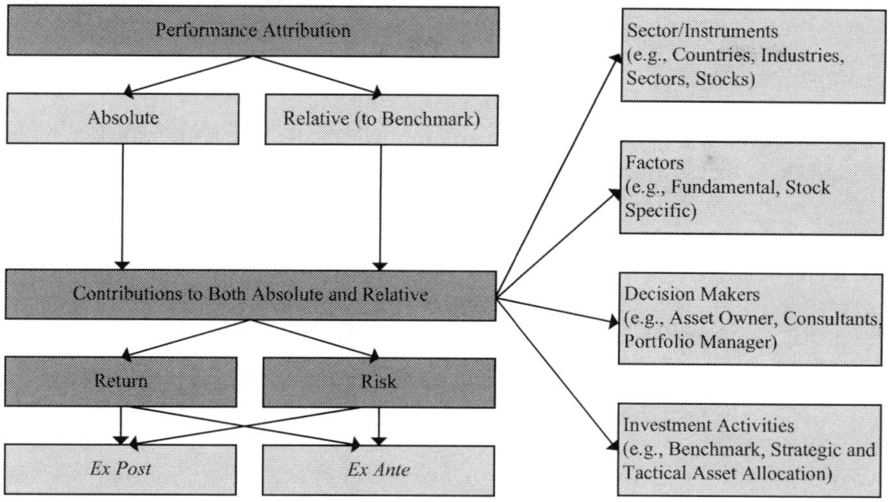

Exhibit 7 also shows that performance attribution may be conducted not only on an absolute but also on a relative basis. Absolute attribution—often also called "contribution analysis"—deals with the decomposition of standalone return and risk measures. For example, if a portfolio that is invested one-half in government bonds and one-half in corporate bonds returned 8% in a year and the returns on government bonds and corporate bonds were, respectively, 6% and 10%, a return contribution analysis (absolute return analysis) would be as follows: The contribution of the allocation to government bonds to the portfolio return was (1/2) × 6% = 3%, and the contribution of corporate bonds was (1/2) × 10% = 5%; 3% + 5% = 8%. This approach of explaining a whole (8%) by analysis of the parts (3% and 5%) is characteristic of attribution analysis in general. Further contribution analysis could also be performed within individual asset classes—for example, for the corporate bonds with respect to contribution from movements of the yield curve and credit spreads. A relative return attribution analysis would explain the portfolio's total excess return in relation to its benchmark and would attribute the sources of excess return to investment decisions. Exhibit 5 previously illustrated a risk contribution—also called "absolute risk attribution."

A key point is that performance attribution analysis needs to consider who was responsible for each investment decision—that is, it must be consistent with the specific investment decision-making process. Consider, for example, a charity with the following characteristics: (a) The board of directors meets annually to decide on the normal allocation of funds to asset classes—the "policy portfolio" or "strategic asset allocation"—and the benchmark for the overall portfolio (the "policy benchmark"); (b) the charity's treasurer decides on short-run deviations from the strategic asset allocation ("tactical asset allocation"); and (c) monies allocated to equities and bonds are turned over to hired external equity and fixed-income managers, respectively, who are responsible for selecting market sector allocations and individual securities within those sectors. An appropriate relative return attribution analysis would seek to quantify the impact of the treasurer's tactical asset allocation decisions and the equity and fixed-income managers' sector and security selection decisions. The comparison point for the treasurer would be the return to the policy portfolio, and those for the external managers would be the benchmarks they were assigned after considering their respective investment disciplines.

The feedback provided by performance attribution into the investment management process can be useful in many ways. The following are two examples of such feedback and how it is used by different decision makers.

- The sector allocation (i.e., industry groups) and security selection effects of an equity portfolio versus the relevant equity benchmark highlight the investment decisions that led to the excess return and where specifically—for instance, in what sector or by which investments—the portfolio manager added value. This information can lead to improved decision making. For example, if the sector allocation effect was consistently negative for a considerable period and the security selection effect was consistently positive during the same period, one might conclude that the investment manager is sector neutral to the benchmark and that she takes active bets against the benchmark only through security selection.
- The level of a portfolio's expected total excess risk in relation to a benchmark is a measure of the level of active risk of the portfolio management (the variability of a manager's deviations from the benchmark). It might serve as an investment restriction or risk budget—for example, expressed in terms of tracking risk—that a portfolio manager would need to observe. However, an investor might use tracking risk to check whether an active portfolio manager (a) has taken excessive risk in the portfolio in order to increase its performance or (b) has not managed the portfolio as actively as expected. If such an investor concludes that the manager is running an almost indexed investment, he might negotiate a reduction in management fees or even cancel the investment management contract.

A very simple scenario in Exhibit 8 illustrates well how performance attribution introduces feedback into the investment management process and how the respective performance information may be used in practice—using stylized data.

Exhibit 8

Feedback from Performance Evaluation: Attribution

Spring Investment Management (SIM) manages an equity portfolio for Mr. Cleaver. Cleaver chose SIM to manage the equity investments because the portfolio manager convinced him that the proposed active investment style should lead to substantial outperformance. Cleaver asked a performance analyst, Mr. Fairborn, to measure the investment performance (over a two-year period) of his equity portfolio managed by SIM. The portfolio delivered –5.5% return (annualized, on a TWRR basis), compared with its benchmark's –4.8% return. Cleaver specifically wished to have a closer look at the source of the equity portfolio's excess (in this case negative) return. Fairborn prepared the following on the basis of historical data.

Fairborn's Attribution Analysis

Panel A: Absolute and Excess Returns

	Weights		Returns		Excess
	Portfolio	Index	Portfolio	Index	Returns
Sector A	50.00%	60.00%	–8.00%	–7.00%	–1.00%
Sector B	50.00%	40.00%	–3.00%	–1.50%	–1.50%
Total	100.00%	100.00%	–5.50%	–4.80%	–0.70%

Exhibit 8 (Continued)

*Panel B: Management Effects**

	Sector Allocation Effect	Security Selection Effect	Total
Sector A	+0.70%	−0.50%	+0.20%
Sector B	−0.15%	−0.75%	−0.90%
Total	+0.55%	−1.25%	−0.70%

* For the record, the excess return is decomposed using the Brinson–Hood–Beebower model, assuming that the two sectors are independently managed by different portfolio managers. Here the interaction effect is assigned to the security selection effect, and for simplicity, the whole time period was treated as a single measurement period. Details are provided in the CIPM curriculum reading on return attribution.

Looking at this additional investment performance information, Cleaver came to the following conclusions:

a The management effects do not correspond with the expectations, because SIM claimed an active sector allocation investment approach that avoids taking big security bets. It turns out that security selection more than offset the positive effect of sector allocation.

b The equity portfolio and its portfolio manager need to be further investigated to enable Cleaver to better understand the sources of portfolio performance.

3.3 Scope of Performance Appraisal

As discussed, one of the major issues addressed by performance appraisal is identifying active investment skill. Such analysis may result in various conclusions.

- If the analysis concludes that superior results are based on investment skill, then normally no further action is needed except to check whether the manager's investment strategy or style is still appropriate in a forward-looking sense. In contrast, if the analysis concludes that the superior results are likely the result of luck or are not sustainable, then the rationale of the investment strategy or style for the coming investment period and/or the adequacy of the portfolio manager should be analyzed in detail.
- If the analysis concludes that inferior results are based on lack of active investment skill, then the rationale for the investment strategy or style for the coming investment period and the adequacy of the portfolio manager are in question. In contrast, if the analysis concludes that the inferior results were based on bad luck, then normally no further action is needed to improve future performance except to check whether the investment strategy or style still makes sense.

Often, performance appraisal is misunderstood as pertaining only to what happened in the past. As illustrated on the left-hand side of Exhibit 9, performance appraisal can deal with analyzing and interpreting historical investment performance. In contrast, as shown on the right-hand side of Exhibit 9, the second part of the performance appraisal cycle—maybe the more important one—takes the results of the historical performance interpretation as well as current information and draws conclusions used as feedback for selecting managers (for the asset owner) or for improving the investment management process (for the asset management company). Producing historical performance information by itself has little value if not used as input or feedback into the investment management process to define, confirm, or adjust future actions. For example, suppose the portfolio manager's investment philosophy favored securities that fell out of favor with most investors during the measurement period. The next activity would be to analyze whether the underlying investment idea and strategy are still rational for the coming period.

The outcome of this analysis will help an investor choose between the following alternatives: (a) Adhere to the investment idea and strategy in the hope public sentiment will change or (b) discontinue investing in the manager's strategy if it is believed either that the public sentiment will not change or that a structural change occurred in the financial markets such that the strategy no longer makes sense.

Exhibit 9 Performance Appraisal Cycle

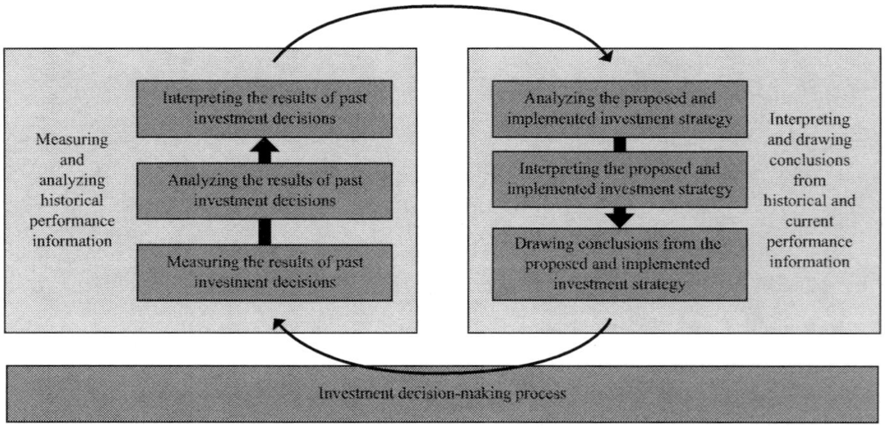

Despite the arsenal of available quantitative performance appraisal tools, qualitative criteria and subjective judgment are often important in a performance appraisal's final conclusions. That is why a performance appraisal should be conducted by very experienced performance analysts who have a broad knowledge of and long experience with investment management. The problems that may complicate a strictly quantitatively oriented performance appraisal include the following:

- asset owner investment restrictions that place constraints on the manager in implementing the investment strategy;
- opaque investment guidelines or decision making;
- changes to the investment management process, the investment strategy, the investment guidelines, or the manager team during the period being analyzed;
- lack of an appropriate investable benchmark for the investment strategy; and
- taxes and other costs that reduce the return of the portfolio but are not under control of the portfolio manager.

Performance appraisal is often part of performance review meetings. The purpose of these meetings is to discuss with all stakeholders whether the portfolio is still on track to meet the investment objectives and to discuss any corrective measures that might improve the future performance or whether the assets invested with the manager should be increased, decreased, or removed entirely.

Using simplified data, Exhibits 10 and 11 illustrate how performance appraisal produces feedback in the investment management process.

Exhibit 10

Feedback from Performance Evaluation: Appraisal

Following the analytics provided by the performance analyst, Mr. Fairborn (see Exhibit 8), Mr. Cleaver decided to have an even closer look at the equity portfolio managed by SIM. He called the portfolio manager, Mr. Sill, and mentioned his concerns about the performance of the equity portfolio. He also mentioned that the first analytic results did not support a conclusion that SIM was following the originally proposed and approved investment strategy. Sill was quite surprised about Cleaver's feedback and promised to send him a return attribution report examining SIM's investment professionalism.

After speaking with a SIM internal performance analyst, Sill sent the promised return attribution report—knowing that Cleaver already received a different analysis from Fairborn. The following is a summary of what Sill sent to Cleaver, all based on historical data.

Sill's Attribution Analysis

Panel A: Absolute and Excess Returns

	Weights		Returns		Excess Returns
	Portfolio	Index	Portfolio	Index	
Sector 1	64.20%	40.00%	−6.50%	−6.52%	+0.02%
Sector 2	35.80%	60.00%	−3.70%	−3.65%	−0.05%
Total	100.00%	100.00%	−5.50%	−4.80%	−0.70%

Panel B: Management Effects*

	Sector Allocation Effect	Security Selection Effect	Total
Sector 1	−1.58%	+0.01%	−1.57%
Sector 2	+0.88%	−0.02%	+0.87%
Total	−0.69%	−0.01%	−0.70%

* For the record, the excess return is decomposed using the Brinson–Hood–Beebower model, assuming that the two sectors are independently managed by different portfolio managers. Here the interaction effect is assigned to the security selection effect, and for simplicity, the whole time period was treated as a single measurement period. Details are provided in the CIPM curriculum reading on return attribution.

Looking at the return attribution report provided by SIM, Cleaver came to the following conclusions:

a The return attribution in Exhibit 8 did not reflect the relevant classification scheme of the investment strategy. The management effects do correspond with the expectations because SIM sold an active sector allocation investment approach without taking big security bets.

b The active asset allocation investment approach was not profitable over the measurement period, and a detailed discussion on the pursued investment strategy and the portfolio manager's investment skill is needed.

Exhibit 11

Feedback from Performance Evaluation: Appraisal (continued)

Following the detailed return attribution on the equity portfolio provided by SIM (see Exhibit 10), Mr. Cleaver asked for a performance review meeting with SIM to discuss whether corrective measures are necessary. To prepare for the meeting, Cleaver asked the performance analyst, Mr. Fairborn, to gather and summarize other important information relevant to assessing the performance of the equity portfolio. Furthermore, he asked Fairborn to provide some performance statistics on comparable investment products available in the market.

The performance review meeting went well and was very helpful for Cleaver to get the whole picture, to better understand what happened over the last two years, and to decide on subsequent actions.

Looking at the additional investment performance information and other relevant but non-performance-related information, Cleaver came to the following conclusions:

- **a** The performance comparison with other investment products was not of great help because not many alternatives were available for investment. Furthermore, despite the short history of 24 months of data, the performance appraisal measures used were quite comparable.
- **b** The portfolio manager could prove that he implemented the proposed investment strategy—by using a different sector classification than that used by Fairborn—but had to confirm that since inception, the active investment approach did not achieve positive results. Furthermore, the portfolio manager could not convince Cleaver that the past and current financial circumstances did not affect the rationale of the pursued investment approach.
- **c** It is necessary to investigate other investment strategies and approaches for managing his equity portfolio.

3.4 Scope of Manager Selection

Manager selection is closely related to performance appraisal but also often very much involves an evaluation of the investment philosophy and process, as well as the asset manager's human resources, ethical underpinning, and organizational strengths and weaknesses. Manager selection includes both (a) the initial selection of managers and (b) the continuous monitoring and reassessment of their performance, not only in relation to return and risk but also with respect to compliance with investment guidelines, quality of reporting, and "soft factors." Soft factors include reputation in the marketplace and client relationship management. Manager selection (including hiring, monitoring, and firing decisions) uses performance appraisal analysis along with information about investment managers gained from their written materials, their presentations, company visits, audit reports, and interviews, among other sources. Selection is also guided by the particular needs and requirements of the entity choosing the manager, and investment consultants often play a significant role by screening a vast number of investment managers for those most likely to satisfy an investor's needs. Investment consultants may use proprietary databases, know-how, and techniques, as well as personal relationships and experience with other clients.

Hiring investment managers initially involves searching using specific screening criteria, both quantitative and qualitative. This process also requires a great deal of data management—gathering and maintaining information on each investment manager. This information comes from detailed questionnaires completed by investment managers covering various aspects of the manager's products and processes, as well as from other sources external to the manager. Often, the relevant manager universe is screened to identify those managers deemed most capable of managing a portfolio according to the asset owner's expectations. After further analysis to narrow the list down to a shortlist, detailed discussions or presentations take place to give the various managers the opportunity to explain why they are able to meet the asset owner's expectations. Finally, a pricing discussion leads to a final proposal or decision.

The manager selection process requires asset owners to obtain full, transparent, and accurate information about the managers in question to enable asset owners to make well-founded decisions. An inherent conflict exists because managers are obviously interested in winning the investment mandate and are tempted to present themselves in the best possible light. Asset owners should, therefore, apply certain safeguards and techniques, ask relevant questions, and apply reasonability checks to the information provided by the managers. Among the first questions that the manager should be challenged with are inquiries about its compliance with relevant regulations, being subject to regulatory supervision, and compliance with industry ethical guidelines, such as the GIPS standards and the CFA Institute Asset Manager Code. Negative responses to these inquiries do not necessarily exclude the manager from the selection process but do represent a possible warning sign and should be challenged by asset owners.

The presentation of historical performance information introduces many ethical concerns. Asset owners should pay particular attention to matters that are prone to potential misrepresentation, such as the following:

- claiming GIPS compliance but showing performance figures that do not originate from a GIPS-compliant performance presentation;
- showing portfolios or strategies that do not represent the asset owner's objectives;
- "cherry picking" portfolios—that is, showing portfolios with good performance and hiding those with bad performance (e.g., portfolios managed in the past that have since been liquidated because of poor performance);
- showing model and backtested performance instead of the "real" track record when it is available and not disclosing it as such;
- using return calculation methodologies that are inappropriate or not transparent;
- selecting unsuitable benchmarks to give the false impression of outperformance;
- "hiding" the strategy's risk profile—for example, by not presenting appropriate risk statistics and risk-adjusted returns or ratios;
- cherry picking time periods—that is, showing periods of good performance and hiding periods of bad performance;
- presenting attribution analysis that does not fit the investment process; and
- hiding the impact of fees, taxes, and transaction costs.

Many asset owners lack the necessary personnel resources to perform onsite due diligence at the manager's place of business. In such cases, it is also advisable to obtain the most recent audited reports on internal controls at the investment management firm for useful insights into the manager's internal control system around the investment management process and operational risk management. In addition, it is advisable to require that the firm's claim of compliance with the GIPS standards be independently verified.

Effective ongoing monitoring of managers depends heavily on the quality of the reporting provided by the manager (or by the appointed third party, such as a custodian bank or investment consultant). The content, form, and frequency of the reporting ideally should be specified in cooperation between asset owner and asset manager, and the methodology, assumptions, appropriate risk measures, and conventions underlying the calculation of statistics used in the reporting should be clear to the asset owner. The manager must also be responsive to asset owner queries and be available for periodic presentations and explanations of investment results.

3.5 Scope of Performance Presentation

Performance presentation is the fourth major component of performance evaluation. It deals with all aspects of the illustration of performance information for portfolios or investment products. Performance presentation summarizes the information produced by performance measurement, performance attribution, and performance appraisal. It is sometimes supplemented by data and information produced or delivered by other processes, such as financial research, investment accounting, or compliance monitoring. Performance presentation is viewed as investment reporting, which focuses on the presentation of the returns achieved and the risks taken within an investment portfolio during some specified measurement period.

Different kinds of performance presentations can be defined considering four determining factors: (a) the performance information presented, (b) the intended user of the presentation, (c) the intended use of the presentation, and (d) the preparer of the presentation. In practice, performance presentations are often tailored to fit specific needs and circumstances. In general, these presentations are used in sales (including client relationship management), management, and monitoring processes. Along these lines, Exhibit 12 illustrates major areas of focus of performance presentation—especially from an investment manager's point of view.

Exhibit 12 Performance Presentations: Major Area of Focus

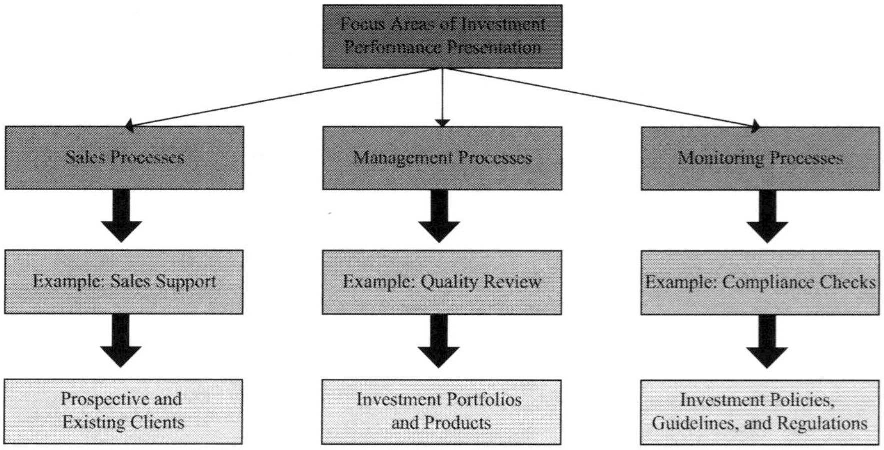

In sales, performance presentations are used to attract new clients by illustrating managers' performance capabilities. Furthermore, as part of the after-sales support, the presentations are also used to increase transparency on portfolio performance for existing clients and as a tool to increase client retention.

Because of their importance within the sales process, these kinds of external presentations bear a high risk for being in some way biased or misleading. For example, an investment manager might present the performance track record of a sample of its best-performing portfolios instead of a composite constructed in accordance with the GIPS standards that represents the complete performance track record.

As Exhibit 12 illustrates, performance presentations are used to provide feedback on the investment management process. An example would be a watch list used by the investment manager to highlight and to monitor portfolios with performance problems based on company-specific performance quality criteria.

The monitoring role of performance presentation focuses on compliance with all relevant investment restrictions and provisions. Client agreements increasingly contain specific portfolio characteristics expressed in terms of performance measures—especially risk measures, such as limits for an investment portfolio's expected tracking risk or target volatility. Other investment restrictions include—for example, for a fixed-income portfolio—the maximum average duration, the minimum credit rating of a single bond, or minimum hedged ratios for foreign currencies.

SUMMARY

This reading introduces performance evaluation and outlines the performance evaluation process and its major parts. Among the points made are the following.

- Performance evaluation refers to the measurement, analysis, presentation, interpretation, and assessment of performance.
- Performance evaluation is the quality control of the investment decision process, enabling asset managers to calculate risk and return, understand the behavior of a portfolio of assets, communicate with asset owners and other stakeholders, and determine how performance can be improved.
- Performance evaluation is an integral part of the investment management decision process because it provides feedback on the effects of investment activities and the decisions on the performance of portfolios. This information is useful to internal stakeholders, such as portfolio managers, senior management, risk managers, compliance professionals, and marketing and sales staff, as well as external stakeholders, such as asset owners, investment consultants, and regulators.
- The information provided by performance evaluation helps evaluate progress toward achieving asset owner goals and consistency with the investment mandate.
- The performance evaluation process is divided into five activities: performance measurement, performance attribution, performance appraisal, manager selection, and investment performance presentation. Manager selection uses a range of information beyond the quantitative information provided by performance evaluation.
- Performance measurement is two dimensional, relating to both risk and return.
- Performance attribution quantifies the sources of investment performance and provides feedback on how investment decisions affect both risk and return.
- Performance appraisal concerns the identification and measurement of investment skill, and it involves analyzing and interpreting return in relation to risk.
- Manager selection concerns the question of whether to hire, retain, or dismiss a manager and incorporates many sources of quantitative and qualitative information, including performance appraisal measures and soft factors on all aspects of the investment managers under consideration.
- Performance presentation relates to the presentation of investment performance and involves documenting the returns and risk of portfolios. In an extremely competitive industry, performance presentations offer significant

opportunities for asset managers to misrepresent performance, self-select methodologies, choose favorable time periods, data mine risk measures, and provide misleading presentations. Compliance with ethical self-regulation standards, such as the GIPS standards, helps reduce the risk of asset managers providing false and misleading performance information.

REFERENCES

Bacon, Carl, David Cariño, and Arin Stancil. 2011. Performance Evaluation: Rate-of-Return Measurement. Charlottesville, VA: CFA Institute.

Grégoire, Philippe. 2007. "Risk Attribution." In *Advanced Portfolio Attribution Analysis*, edited by Carl Bacon. London: Risk Books.

PRACTICE PROBLEMS

1 Which of the following *best* describes how performance evaluation fits into the asset management process? Performance evaluation:

A provides information that reduces most risk.

B serves in a feedback role that helps investment managers align portfolios with asset owner objectives.

C is part of the asset owner reporting function, which occurs only at the end of the management process.

2 From the perspective of the investment firm, an effective performance evaluation process addresses:

A appropriate budgeting for necessary information technology (IT) projects.

B potential performance problems and unintended business or investment risks.

C quantitative but not qualitative aspects of the investment decision-making process.

3 Performance appraisal is *best* described as addressing the:

A calculation of risk statistics.

B identification of investment skill.

C identification of the investment decisions that added value.

4 Performance attribution primarily concerns:

A the past performance of a portfolio.

B identifying and quantifying the sources of portfolio performance.

C quantifying the valued added to portfolio performance by active investment managers.

5 The decision to retain or dismiss an investment manager is *best* described as part of which component activity of performance evaluation?

A Manager selection

B Manager oversight

C Performance appraisal

6 What are the five major component activities of the performance evaluation process?

A Performance measurement, performance attribution, performance appraisal, manager selection, and GIPS compliance

B Performance measurement, return attribution, risk attribution, manager selection, and investment performance presentation

C Performance measurement, performance attribution, performance appraisal, manager selection, and investment performance presentation

7 The subject of performance measurement can *best* be described as:

A measuring a manager's investment skill.

B calculating a portfolio's risk and return metrics.

C identifying the sources of a portfolio's excess return relative to its benchmark.

8 Manager selection relates *most* to:

A the factors that affect the repeatability of performance.

B how performance information should be presented.

C how the investment portfolio produced its observed performance.

9 Which of the following is *most likely* to appear in a reporting presentation prepared for a prospective client?

A Return attribution report

B GIPS performance presentation

C Report on compliance with tracking risk limits

10 Which factors define the specific characteristics of the output of a performance evaluation activity?

A Intended user, intended use, and performance attribution measures

B Performance information, risk measures, and risk-adjusted returns

C Performance information, intended user, intended use, and preparer

11 A risk contribution report is *best* described as addressing the:

A sources of absolute investment risk.

B contributions of the individual investment decisions to total excess risk.

C sources of excess return earned expressed as the return contribution for each unit of excess risk taken.

12 An investor has a portfolio that contains equity investments in three sectors. Security selection is delegated to an external investment manager. As part of her evaluation of portfolio performance, the investor identifies the management effects as illustrated the following table:

	Sector Allocation Effect (%)	Security Selection Effect (%)	Total (%)
Sector A	−2.0	1.5	−0.5
Sector B	0.1	−0.2	−0.1
Sector C	−3.0	1.0	−2.0

The table presents an example of an analysis that is typically used in performance:

A appraisal.

B attribution.

C measurement.

13 An investor is evaluating the performance report of a manager's composite. The composite consists of US large-cap equity portfolios. Which of the following is *most likely* to indicate a potential misrepresentation?

A Using the S&P 500 Index as a benchmark to calculate excess returns

B Excluding the performance of terminated portfolios in the composite

C Using and disclosing backtested performance information to fill in a track record gap

14 A mutual fund firm has recently revised the performance presentation of a composite included in its marketing material. Which of the following is *most likely* to indicate a potential misrepresentation? The performance presentation:

A does not show the impact of fees.

B does not include a risk attribution analysis.

C has not been examined by an independent verifier.

SOLUTIONS

1 B is correct. Performance evaluation plays a feedback role in investment management. A is incorrect because although performance evaluation supports monitoring of risk, it does not address risk reduction per se. C is incorrect because performance evaluation is ongoing within the investment management process and is not just part of the client reporting function.

2 B is correct. The feedback provided by an effective performance evaluation process should identify potential performance problems and unintended business or investment risks. A is incorrect because determining appropriate budgeting for necessary IT projects is not an objective of an effective performance evaluation process per se. C is incorrect because qualitative information is important as well; for example, such information is important in performance appraisal and manager selection.

3 B is correct. Performance appraisal concerns the identification and measurement of investment skill. A is incorrect because such calculations are the output of performance measurement. C is incorrect because identifying the investment decisions that added value is the domain of performance attribution.

4 B is correct. Performance attribution relates to the sources of portfolio performance. A is incorrect because the past performance of a portfolio is the subject of performance measurement. C is incorrect because quantifying added value is the subject of performance appraisal.

5 A is correct. Manager selection is defined to include the initial selection of investment managers and subsequent retention and dismissal decisions. B is incorrect because "manager oversight" is not a description of a component activity of performance evaluation. C is incorrect because performance appraisal concerns the identification of investment skill.

6 C is correct. A is incorrect because although GIPS compliance can facilitate effective and ethical investment performance presentation, it is not a standalone performance evaluation activity but, rather, is part of investment performance presentation. B is incorrect because return attribution and risk attribution together constitute performance attribution and performance appraisal has been omitted.

7 B is correct. Performance measurement involves the measurement of the return and risk of a portfolio.

8 A is correct. In general, manager selection considers both quantitative and qualitative information and addresses not only observed portfolio performance but also operational and organizational factors that affect the repeatability of performance.

9 B is correct. Reporting to prospective clients is very much sales driven, and such presentations are prepared from the perspective of the investment manager to reflect the manager's track record and skills. The Global Investment Performance Standards (GIPS) address this need.

10 C is correct. Investment performance information, intended user, intended use, and preparer are the four factors that define performance evaluation output. A is incorrect because investment performance information and preparer are omitted and performance attribution measures are a specific type of performance evaluation output but are not a factor that defines the characteristics of the output. B is incorrect because intended user, intended use, and preparer are omitted; risk measures and risk-adjusted returns are examples of performance evaluation outputs, not factors that define the outputs.

11 A is correct. A risk contribution report consists of information analyzing the sources of absolute investment risk. B is incorrect because a risk attribution report, not a risk contribution report, analyzes the contribution of the individual investment decisions to total excess risk. C is incorrect because a risk contribution report does not analyze the sources of excess return.

12 B is correct. The table is an example of return attribution analysis, which is typically performed as part of the performance attribution process.

13 B is correct. The manager selection process requires investors to obtain full, transparent, and true information about the manager. The inclusion of only survivor portfolios is an example of cherry picking, which means including only portfolios with good performance to hide those with bad performance. Therefore, it should be challenged.

14 A is correct. The fact that the presentation does not include information on fees is a warning sign of a potential misrepresentation.

READING

4

Performance Evaluation: Rate-of-Return Measurement

by Carl R. Bacon, CIPM, David R. Cariño, PhD, and
Arin Stancil, CFA, CIPM

Carl R. Bacon, CIPM, is at StatPro and the University of Manchester (United Kingdom). David R. Cariño, PhD (USA). Arin Stancil, CFA, CIPM (United Kingdom).

LEARNING OUTCOMES

Mastery	*The candidate should be able to:*
□	**a.** explain the treatment of investment income (e.g., dividends and interest) in calculating holding period rates of return;
□	**b.** calculate and interpret the holding period rate of return on a stock or bond investment;
□	**c.** calculate and interpret a portfolio rate of return;
□	**d.** calculate the home currency equivalent of a non-domestic rate of return and explain a decomposition of the home currency equivalent return;
□	**e.** calculate and interpret rates of return that result from short positions and leveraged positions;
□	**f.** distinguish between book value and market value, realized and unrealized gains and losses, trade date accounting and settlement date accounting, and show how these elements are treated in determining the asset values to be used in calculating rates of return;
□	**g.** explain the major bases for calculating rates of return: nominal versus real, gross-of-fees versus net-of-fees, pre-tax versus post-tax, and leveraged versus cash basis;
□	**h.** explain and demonstrate discrete and continuous compounding;
□	**i.** convert rates of return to an annual basis and explain when annualization is or is not appropriate;
□	**j.** compare arithmetic and geometric mean rates of return;
□	**k.** explain arithmetic and geometric bases for calculating excess returns;
□	**l.** calculate and interpret money-weighted and time-weighted rates of return;
□	**m.** describe unit value pricing;

(continued)

LEARNING OUTCOMES

Mastery	The candidate should be able to:
☐	**n.** explain the issues raised by external cash flows for performance evaluation;
☐	**o.** explain major approximation methods to a true time-weighted rate of return;
☐	**p.** compare the methods used to calculate composite returns;
☐	**q.** explain the condition of consistency in calculating the time-weighted rates of return of portfolio segments and the overall portfolio.

1 INTRODUCTION

The **rate of return** on an investment over a specified time period is the percent gain or loss in wealth resulting from holding the investment over that period. The rate of return is an essential concept in investing. For example, in comparing investment managers, investors often evaluate the returns the managers have achieved over various time horizons and in various market conditions. When calculated properly, the rate of return enables valid comparisons to be made among managed portfolios, despite differences in the amounts invested and in other circumstances. Rates of return are measured and analyzed by performance analysts and investment consultants, who need to be proficient in calculating and interpreting them.

Rate of return is a *measurement*—a number calculated from more basic primitive data. The calculation of rates of return is the crucial first step in performance evaluation: Without accurate rates of return, we can make no further progress in analyzing performance. The purpose of this reading is to define the various forms of return useful for performance analysis, document methods of calculation, highlight calculation issues, provide guidance for appropriate use, and, hence, build the foundations for more detailed evaluation.

The reading is organized as follows: Section 2 presents the fundamentals of rate-of-return calculation over a single investment holding period without external cash flows (i.e., without client-initiated additions to or withdrawals from the portfolio). Section 3 covers the principles of compounding and averaging rates of return. Section 4 introduces rate-of-return measurement in the presence of external cash flows. Section 5 provides conclusions and a summary.

For those without an investment background or desiring a refresher, the Appendix to this reading provides a brief overview of the features of common shares and bonds and an explanation of the mathematical notations used in this reading.

2 SINGLE-PERIOD RATES OF RETURN

Performance analysts more commonly analyze portfolios than individual assets. An investment portfolio, or **portfolio** for short, is defined as a collection of one or more assets. Such assets may be common shares (common stock) and bonds, derivative instruments, other securities, or even other portfolios.[1] A portfolio may consist of a single security, or it may comprise all the assets of a large pension fund. The principles of performance measurement apply equally to portfolios with small and large numbers of holdings and of any asset size.

The primary inputs to performance measurement are records of portfolio values over time. The holdings of a portfolio are the quantities (for example, numbers of shares in the case of stocks) of each asset in the portfolio. The value of the portfolio is the sum of the values of the component holdings; that sum is calculated by multiplying the quantities of the component holdings by their respective per unit values. Consider a portfolio made up of common stock and bonds. Five hundred shares of common stock valued at €30 per share give a value of €15,000 (= 500 × €30) for the common stock component. Fifty €100 par value bonds with a market value of €98 each give a value of €4,900 (= 50 × €98) for the bond component. The value of the portfolio is thus €15,000 + €4,900 = €19,900.

Specific procedures to determine value vary by asset type. For some assets, such as the shares of the largest publicly traded corporations, up-to-date market prices are readily available and are used for value. Where such market prices are not available, values might need to be estimated (a process called valuation or **appraisal**). Data for performance measurement are critically dependent on the accounting and record-keeping systems that maintain values of assets over time. Pricing sources, timing of records (e.g., concerning cash flows or corporate actions), and other variables may introduce differences in calculated performance.

2.1 Holding Period Rates of Return

A **holding period** is an interval between two points in time over which an asset or portfolio is assumed to be held. A holding period may be of any specified length and is typically based on calendar units, such as years, quarters, months, or days. The term **holding period rate of return** is used to underscore the time period over which the rate of return was earned and is defined as the percentage gain or loss in wealth resulting from holding some asset or portfolio over the stated holding period; thus it is calculated as the change in wealth resulting from holding some investment for a stated time period divided by the initial amount invested.

In this Section 2, on single-period rates of return, and the following Section 3, on multi-period rates of return, we assume that there are no deposits to or withdrawals from the portfolio, which are types of cash flows known as external cash flows. (Section 4 addresses calculating rates of return when external cash flows have taken place.)

Consider a single portfolio or security held over a given holding period. Given the beginning market value V_0 and the ending market value V_1 of the portfolio or security—and it is important to be clear to which V refers—the **return relative** (also referred to as the **value relative** or **wealth ratio**) is the ratio of ending (denoted "1") to beginning (denoted "0") value:

$$\text{Return relative} = \frac{V_1}{V_0}$$

In calculating return relatives, we need to take account of investment income that the owner of a portfolio or asset has received or is entitled to receive from holding the investment over the stated holding period. Thus, if V_1 represents the ending portfolio value, it must include income that the portfolio has received or is entitled to. If we are concerned with an individual security, a term for investment income that the owner of the security has received or is entitled to may need to accompany V_1 in the

1 An example of a "portfolio of portfolios" is one that consists of shares of different US mutual funds or UK unit trusts (these are types of investments that pool the money of investors).

numerator. We will illustrate these points later. The holding period rate of return R is the return relative minus one, or, equivalently, the change in value over the holding period as a fraction of the beginning value:

$$R = \frac{V_1}{V_0} - 1 = \frac{V_1 - V_0}{V_0} \quad (1)$$

The result is usually expressed as a percentage (%). A few writers reserve "return" for a gain (loss) in units of money and "rate of return" for gains (losses) in relation to the amount invested, but most use the terms interchangeably in the sense of "rate of return." Returns that are less than 1 percent are often expressed in **basis points**, abbreviated as **bps**, or hundredths of 1 percent. For example, if the beginning value of a portfolio is €100 and seven days later its value is €100.7, the seven-day holding period return is (€100.7 – €100)/€100 = €0.7/€100 = 0.007 or 0.7%, which can also be expressed as 70 bps (70/100 of 1 percent). Example 1 illustrates such a calculation.

EXAMPLE 1

Holding Period Rate-of-Return Calculations

1 A six-month £10,000 certificate of deposit is redeemed at maturity for £10,200. The six-month holding period return is *closest* to:

A 1.02%.

B 1.96%.

C 2.00%.

2 A securities account had no deposit or withdrawal transactions during the month of April. Account values (in thousands) reported by the record keeper were as follows:

	31 March	30 April
Equity securities	€1,029,234.12	€1,108,314.67
Cash	€52,078.23	€41,596.05

The portfolio return of the account for April is *closest* to:

A 6.34%.

B 7.68%.

C 11.72%.

3 A portfolio held 1,500 shares of BP plc common stock over the month of April 2010. Closing (i.e., final) price quotes for a BP share on the London Stock Exchange for the beginning and ending dates of the holding period were

31 March 2010	£6.234
30 April 2010	£5.755

Based only on the information given, calculate the holding period rate of return on the position in BP shares for the month of April 2010.

A 0.92%

B –7.68%

C –8.32%

Solution to 1:

C is correct.

$$R = \frac{V_1 - V_0}{V_0} = \frac{£10{,}200 - £10{,}000}{£10{,}000} = \frac{£200}{£10{,}000} = 0.02 \text{ or } 2.00\%$$

Solution to 2:

A is correct. The portfolio makes up the entire account, for which there were no external cash flows. The portfolio return can be calculated from beginning and ending market values.

$$\text{Beginning value } V_0 = €1{,}029{,}234.12 + €52{,}078.23 = €1{,}081{,}312.35$$
$$\text{Ending value } V_1 = €1{,}108{,}314.67 + €41{,}596.05 = €1{,}149{,}910.72$$

$$\text{Holding period return } R = \frac{V_1 - V_0}{V_0} = \frac{€1{,}149{,}910.72 - €1{,}081{,}312.35}{€1{,}081{,}312.35}$$
$$= 0.0634 = 6.34\%$$

Solution to 3:

B is correct.

$$\text{Beginning value } V_0 = 1{,}500 \times £6.234 = £9{,}351.00$$
$$\text{Ending value } V_1 = 1{,}500 \times £5.755 = £8{,}632.50$$

$$\text{Holding period return } R = \frac{V_1 - V_0}{V_0} = \frac{£8{,}632.50 - £9{,}351.00}{£9{,}351.00}$$
$$= -0.0768 = -7.68\%$$

Because the portfolio consists of only one security, an alternate approach would be to calculate the rate of return as a per-share value of the single security:

$$\text{Holding period return } R = \frac{V_1}{V_0} - 1 = \frac{£5.755}{£6.234} - 1$$
$$= -0.0768 = -7.68\%$$

In all the examples that follow, an equals sign ("=") will be used at the final return calculation even though the returns have usually been rounded to the nearest basis point. It should be understood that intermediate results are calculated to full precision.

The calculation of holding period returns for a portfolio presents several practical problems:

- The choice of holding period is constrained by the availability of portfolio valuations for the beginning and the end of the holding period. It is common, for example, to calculate a monthly return based on valuations as of the last trading days of consecutive months, which might not coincide with the last calendar days of the months (as can happen when the last calendar day of a month falls on a Saturday or Sunday). The holding period is defined by the valuation dates in such cases.
- Some circumstances may lead to various assets in a portfolio reflecting differently dated values. For example, if different assets in a portfolio trade on different exchanges, the trading days might not coincide for all exchanges (because of holidays or local customs) and trading hours might differ for the various exchanges. Time zone differences in markets can also be an obstacle. Even within a given marketplace, some securities trade more frequently than others.

For the sake of accuracy, all the assets in a portfolio should be valued as close to the same time as is practicable. Differences in the timing of the prices used for valuation can be a source of uncertainty in rate-of-return calculation.

In the examples presented so far, nothing has been said about the calculation of holding period return when income from securities is received during the holding period. **Income** in this context (sometimes called **investment income**) refers to cash payments made to owners of an asset and is a source of return called the **income return**. The income return is distinct from the **price return** (or **capital gains return**), which is the return from changes in asset price. The holding period return combines both the income return and the price return. The term **total return** is often used as a synonym of holding period return to emphasize that both components of return are included in the return being reported.

For common shares, representing ownership in a corporation, income is in the form of discretionary payments known as **dividends**. For bonds, income payments are contractual obligations, the timing and amount of which are specified in the bond's contract (known as the bond's indenture); the income on bonds is known as **interest** (or **coupon interest** or coupon). (If these facts are new to you, reviewing the Appendix should be useful.)

How do we calculate a holding period rate of return when we need to account for investment income?

The simplest case arises when any income payment D occurs at the end of the holding period so that there is no question of reinvesting income. Equation 2 is appropriate in that case.

$$R = \frac{V_1 - V_0 + D}{V_0} = \frac{V_1 - V_0}{V_0} + \frac{D}{V_0} \tag{2}$$

The expression says that holding period return (or total return) is the sum of price return $[(V_1 - V_0)/V_0]$ and income return (D/V_0). No assumptions have to be made, and there is no alternative correct expression.

To illustrate this, consider a single asset held for a single-month holding period. The beginning-of-month price was \$100, and the end-of-month price was \$106. In addition, income of \$2 was received at the end of the month. The price return is calculated as

$$\text{Price return} = \frac{V_1 - V_0}{V_0} = \frac{\$106 - \$100}{\$100} = 0.06 = 6.00\%$$

The income return is

$$\text{Income return} = \frac{D}{V_0} = \frac{\$2}{\$100} = 0.02 = 2.00\%$$

The total return is then the sum of the price and income returns:

$$\text{Total return} = \text{Price return} + \text{Income return} = 6.00\% + 2.00\% = 8.00\%$$

The total return can also be calculated independently from the price and income returns, using Equation 2:

$$\text{Total return} = \frac{V_1 - V_0 + D}{V_0} = \frac{\$106 - \$100 + \$2}{\$100} = \frac{\$8}{\$100} = 0.08 = 8.00\%$$

EXAMPLE 2

Holding Period Return When Income Is Received at End of Holding Period

1 An asset was held for the month of April 2011. The end of March 2011 price was \$228.78, and the end of April 2011 price was \$226.35. In addition, income of \$10 was received at the end of April. What was the asset's total return for the month of April?

A −1.06%

B 3.31%

C 4.37%

2 An institution lent \$1,000.00 to an individual on 1 February 2011. On 30 September 2011, the institution received \$1,080.00, including \$80.00 interest and \$1,000 capital repayment. What price return did the institution realize on the loan for the holding period 1 February–30 September 2011?

A 0%

B 8%

C 12%

Solution to 1:

B is correct.

$$\text{Total return} = \frac{V_1 - V_0 + D}{V_0} = \frac{\$226.35 - \$228.78 + \$10}{\$228.78} = \frac{\$7.57}{\$228.78} = 0.0331 = 3.31\%$$

The price and income returns can also be calculated separately as follows:

$$\text{Price return} = \frac{V_1 - V_0}{V_0} = \frac{\$226.35 - \$228.78}{\$228.78} = \frac{-\$2.43}{\$228.78} = -0.0106 = -1.06\%$$

$$\text{Income return} = \frac{D}{V_0} = \frac{\$10}{\$228.78} = 0.0437 = 4.37\%$$

$$\text{Total return} = \text{Price return} + \text{Income return} = -1.06\% + 4.37\% = 3.31\%$$

Solution to 2:

A is correct.

$$\text{Price return} = \frac{\$1,000 - \$1,000}{\$1,000} = 0.0 = 0.0\%$$

The income and total returns are thus

$$\text{Income return} = \frac{\$80}{\$1,000} = 0.08 = 8.0\%$$

$$\text{Total return} = \frac{\$1,000 - \$1,000 + \$80}{\$1,000} = 0.08 = 8.0\%$$

or Total return = Price return + Income return = 0.0% + 8.0% = 8.0%

If income is received during a holding period and reinvested into a portfolio (**reinvested income**), then the portfolio value at the end of the period reflects the return from the price appreciation of the beginning-of-period investment and the value of the additional assets purchased with the reinvested income. To calculate the income return component of holding period returns, assumptions must be made regarding gains from the income component subsequent to when the income was reinvested. Usually, one of two assumptions is made. In the first case, any gains from reinvested income are included in the income return. In the second, such gains are included in the price return.

Case 1. One common assumption is that income is immediately reinvested proportionately in all the assets of a portfolio according to the percentage of the total market value of the portfolio that each asset represents. That means that nothing is assumed to change in how money is allocated among the portfolio's holdings. This assumption is typically used in constructing stock market indexes, which are notional portfolios of stocks (i.e., managed virtually on paper by the index creator). An index portfolio value is typically calculated in two ways: first, with the income reinvested in all assets of the portfolio (a **total return index**), and second, on a capital only basis (a **price index**). The portfolio values with income reinvested are used to calculate the total return of the portfolio with Equation 1:

$$R = \frac{V_1 - V_0}{V_0}$$

where V_1 includes reinvested income. The price return is

$$R = \frac{V_1^x - V_0^x}{V_0^x}$$

where the superscript x (for "ex" or "without") indicates values without reinvested income (based on the price index). The total return minus the price return can be interpreted as the income return:

$$\frac{V_1 - V_0}{V_0} - \frac{V_1^x - V_0^x}{V_0^x} \tag{3}$$

The *income return* in this case includes the gains from reinvesting the income into the entire portfolio.

For example, consider a total return index portfolio that increases in value from 1,327.44 to 1,360.14 and an associated price return index that increases in value from 980.21 to 1,002.07 over the same period. Because the ending value of the total return index is inclusive of reinvested income, the total return for the portfolio can be calculated using Equation 1:

$$R = \frac{V_1 - V_0}{V_0} = \frac{1{,}360.14 - 1{,}327.44}{1{,}327.44} = 0.0246 = 2.46\%$$

The price return can be derived using values without reinvested income—in this case, a beginning price of 980.21 and an ending price of 1,002.07:

$$R = \frac{V_1^x - V_0^x}{V_0^x} = \frac{1{,}002.07 - 980.21}{980.21} = 0.0223 = 2.23\%$$

The total return minus the price return can be interpreted as the income return:

$$\frac{V_1 - V_0}{V_0} - \frac{V_1^x - V_0^x}{V_0^x}$$

The *income return* in this case includes the gains from reinvesting the income into the entire portfolio:

$$R = \frac{V_1 - V_0}{V_0} - \frac{V_1^x - V_0^x}{V_0^x} = 2.46\% - 2.23\% = 0.23\%$$

Case 2. The second assumption that may be made, often simpler to execute, is to include gains from reinvested income in the price return. In most portfolios, it is complicated to account for investment gains that are attributable to reinvested income apart from those of other assets in the portfolio. It is usually straightforward, however, to calculate the amount of income reinvested over a holding period. In this case, the total return R of a portfolio still can be written as Equation 1, and the decomposition into price and income return is

$$R = \frac{(V_1 - D) - V_0}{V_0} + \frac{D}{V_0} \qquad (4)$$

where V_0 is the beginning market value, V_1 is the ending market value *including* the reinvested income, and D is the income received. Price return is found by deducting the income from the ending value:

Price return = $[(V_1 - D) - V_0]/V_0$

Income return = D/V_0

For example, let V_0 = €100, V_1 = €106, and D = €2. The price return, defined to include gains from reinvested income, is [(€106 – €2) – €100]/€100 = (€104 – €100)/€100 = 0.04 or 4 percent; the income return is €2/€100 = 0.02 or 2 percent; and the total return is 4% + 2% = 6%.

EXAMPLE 3

Holding Period Return Calculation When Income Is Received and Reinvested during the Holding Period

1 A portfolio held one asset for the month of January 2011. The beginning-of-month portfolio value was $100 million. During the month, income of $2 million was received and reinvested in portfolio securities. Investment gains of $0.05 million resulted from the reinvested income. At the end of the month, the total value of the portfolio was $108.05 million. Based only on the information given, calculate the price, income, and total returns for the month, where income return is defined to include gains from reinvested income.

2 A portfolio held one asset for the month of April 2011. The beginning-of-month portfolio value was $228.78 million. During the month, income of $10 million was received, and interest on that $10 million was earned for the rest of the month. At the end of the month, the total value of the portfolio was $236.85 million. Based only on the information given, calculate the price, income, and total returns for the month, where price return is defined to include gains from reinvested income.

Solution to 1:

The income received is already included in the portfolio's ending value and, therefore, does not need to be added back when calculating the total return.

$$\text{Total return} = \frac{V_1 - V_0}{V_0} = \frac{\$108.05 - \$100}{\$100} = \frac{\$8.05}{\$100} = 0.0805 = 8.05\%$$

The income return, defined to include gains from reinvested income, can be calculated directly as

$$\frac{\$2 + \$0.05}{\$100} = \frac{\$2.05}{\$100} = 0.0205 = 2.05\%$$

Therefore, the price return was 6 percent: Price return = Total return – Income return = 8.05% – 2.05% = 6.00%.

Solution to 2:

The income received is already included in the portfolio's ending value and, therefore, does not need to be added back when calculating the total return.

$$\text{Total return} = \frac{V_1 - V_0}{V_0} = \frac{\$236.85 - \$228.78}{\$228.78} = \frac{\$8.07}{\$228.78} = 0.0353 = 3.53\%$$

The price return, defined to include gains from reinvested income, is

$$\begin{aligned}\text{Price Return} &= \frac{V_1 - V_0 - D}{V_0} \\ &= \frac{\$236.85 - \$228.78 - \$10}{\$228.78} \\ &= \frac{-\$1.93}{\$228.78} = -0.0084 = -0.84\%\end{aligned}$$

The income return is

$$\text{Income return} = \frac{D}{V_0} = \frac{\$10}{\$228.78} = 0.0437 = 4.37\%$$

We can check that the sum of the price and income returns equals the total return previously calculated: Total return = Price return + Income return = –0.84% + 4.37% = 3.53%.

In this example, the income return reflects only the income received ($10 million) and not any subsequent gain from investing the income. Any gains from the reinvested income are *included in the price return.*

2.1.1 *Common Shares*

When a dividend is announced, a certain date is set—the **ex-dividend date**—from which point forward a purchaser of a share is not entitled to the dividend payment. The trading day before the ex-dividend day is the last one in which an investor can purchase a share so as to appear as the owner of record as of a date called the record date; only owners as of that date are entitled to receive the dividend.[2] The date at which the dividend amount is actually paid—the **pay date**—can be weeks later.

Consider a portfolio with beginning and ending values V_0 and V_1, respectively, consisting initially of a single share of common stock. If the portfolio holds the stock over a period starting prior to the ex-dividend date and ending after the ex-dividend date but before the pay date and if the portfolio is valued after the ex-dividend date, the value of the dividend should be included in the portfolio value as accrued income when calculating total return because ownership of the dividend remains with the owner at the time the stock went ex-dividend. The expressions given for price and income return are then applicable.

2 The **record date** may be defined as the date on which an investor needs to be on record as an owner of a share to receive a dividend that has been declared on it. Most commonly, payment for a share purchase (as for bond purchases) is made three business days after the transaction date ("$T + 3$ settlement"), and the stock's record date is thus commonly two business days after the ex-dividend date.

EXAMPLE 4

Calculation of Income Return, Price Return, and Total Return for a Stock

Exxon Mobil Corporation (XOM) announced a dividend of \$0.44 per share in February 2011. The ex-dividend date was 8 February 2011, and the pay date was 10 March 2011. Closing prices of XOM on the New York Stock Exchange were

Date	Closing Price
31 January 2011	\$80.680
7 February 2011	\$83.930
8 February 2011	\$82.980
28 February 2011	\$85.530

Calculate the income return, price return, and total return on holding XOM from the close of trading on the 7 February through 8 February 2011 (assuming purchase at the close of trading on 7 February 2011) and for the month of February.

Solution:

The closing price of XOM on 8 February is ex-dividend—that is, the value of owning a share without owning the dividend. The ending value of the portfolio should include the value of the dividend even though it had not yet been paid. Thus, we use portfolio value as given in the last column in calculating return. Because the pay date is after 28 February, the issue of reinvestment of the dividend does not arise.

	Closing Price	Dividend Recognized on Ex-Dividend Date Forward	Portfolio Value
31 January 2011	\$80.680		\$80.680
7 February 2011	\$83.930		\$83.930
8 February 2011	\$82.980	\$0.44	\$83.420
28 February 2011	\$85.530	\$0.44	\$85.970

For 8 February,

$$\text{Price return} = \frac{(V_1 - D) - V_0}{V_0} = \frac{(\$83.42 - \$0.44) - \$83.93}{\$83.93}$$

$$= -0.0113 = -1.13\%$$

$$\text{Income return} = \frac{D}{V_0} = \frac{\$0.44}{\$83.93} = 0.0052 = 0.52\%$$

$$\text{Total return} = \frac{(V_1 - D) - V_0}{V_0} + \frac{D}{V_0} = \frac{(\$83.42 - \$0.44) - \$83.93}{\$83.93} + \frac{\$0.44}{\$83.93}$$

$$= -0.0061 = -0.61\%$$

Written differently, Total return = Price return + Income return = −1.13% + 0.52% = −0.61%.

For the month of February,

$$\text{Price return} = \frac{(V_1 - D) - V_0}{V_0} = \frac{(\$85.97 - \$0.44) - \$80.68}{\$80.68} = 0.0601 = 6.01\%$$

$$\text{Income return} = \frac{D}{V_0} = \frac{\$0.44}{\$80.68} = 0.0055 = 0.55\%$$

$$\text{Total return} = \frac{(V_1 - D) - V_0}{V_0} + \frac{D}{V_0} = \frac{(\$85.97 - \$0.44) - \$80.68}{\$80.68} + \frac{\$0.44}{\$80.68}$$

$$= 0.0656 = 6.56\%$$

Written differently, Total return = Price return + Income return = 6.01% + 0.55% = 6.56%.

2.1.2 *Portfolio Return Calculated from Returns to Individual Holdings*

How do we calculate the holding period return on a portfolio consisting of many assets when the information given consists only of data for the individual assets? If we can calculate the returns on the individual assets, the return on a portfolio that buys and holds the assets can be calculated as a weighted average of the assets' returns, using the beginning-of-period portfolio weights for the assets. Let R_i be the return on asset i and w_i be the portfolio weight of asset i—that is, w_i = (beginning-of-period market value of asset i)/(beginning-of-period market value of portfolio containing asset i)—so that the sum of portfolio weights equals 1. Denoting by R_p the return on the portfolio,

$$R_p = \sum_{i=1}^{n} w_i R_i \tag{5}$$

Thus, if the portfolio consists of three assets with respective weights of 0.20, 0.50 and 0.30 and returns of 2%, 6%, and 12%, then the portfolio return is 7%, calculated as follows:

$$R_p = \sum_{i=1}^{3} w_i R_i = w_1 R_1 + w_2 R_2 + w_3 R_3 = (0.20)(2\%) + (0.50)(6\%) + (0.30)(12\%) = 7\%$$

EXAMPLE 5

Calculating Portfolio Return from the Returns of Component Assets

A portfolio consists of four assets with respective portfolio weights of 0.40, 0.25, 0.20, and 0.15. Over the year, the assets achieved returns of –10%, 4%, 20%, and 24%, respectively. The portfolio's rate of return was closest to:

A 4.6%.

B 9.5%.

C 9.8%.

Solution:

A is correct. 0.40(–10%) + 0.25(4%) + 0.20(20%) + 0.15(24%) = 4.6 percent.

2.1.3 *Bonds*

The return calculations given thus far have been illustrated using common shares. There are important distinctions between the income on common shares (dividends) and the income on bonds (interest). A common stock investor receives a declared dividend if he or she appears as the owner of record on a stated date (the so-called record date for receipt of the dividend); otherwise, whatever the length of time the investor held the shares, no part of the declared dividend is received. In contrast, when a bond is sold, the seller receives the price quoted in the transaction plus a share of the upcoming interest payment, known as **accrued interest** (AI), which is proportional to the fraction of days between interest payments that the bond has been held by the seller.[3] For example, if a $1,000 face value bond with $20 semi-annual interest payments is sold for $960 exactly halfway between interest payment dates, the seller would receive $960 + (1/2)$20 = $970. The $10 difference is accrued interest: interest that has been earned by the bond seller (but not yet paid by the bond issuer) since the last interest payment. Conventional price quotes exclude the value of coupon interest accrued to the date of the quote. The price without accrued interest is called the **clean price**; here, the clean price is $960. The price with accrued interest, here $970, is sometimes called the **dirty price**. The dirty price represents the value at which the asset can be exchanged for other assets in the market.

The price with accrued interest is the relevant one for calculating the rate of return on a bond using Equation 1. Adapted to bonds and, for simplicity, limiting ourselves to the case in which the bond is purchased and sold within a single period between interest payments, we obtain[4]

$$\text{Total return} = \frac{(\text{Ending dirty price} - \text{Beginning dirty price})}{\text{Beginning dirty price}}$$

$$= \frac{\begin{bmatrix}(\text{Ending clean price} - \text{Beginning clean price}) \\ + \text{ Change in accrued interest}\end{bmatrix}}{\text{Beginning dirty price}} \quad \text{(6a)}$$

where

Change in AI = Ending AI – Beginning AI[5]

$$\text{Price return} = \frac{(\text{Ending clean price} - \text{Beginning clean price})}{\text{Beginning dirty price}} \quad \text{(6b)}$$

$$\text{Income return} = \frac{\text{Change in accrued interest}}{\text{Beginning dirty price}} \quad \text{(6c)}$$

Assume the bond just described is purchased halfway between interest payments for $970 (including accrued interest). The bond is sold three-fourths of the way into the six-month period for $950 plus accrued interest of (3/4)($20) = $15. The amount realized on the sale is $950 + $15 = $965.

The holding period return for the period beginning with the date the bond was purchased at a cost of $970 and ending on the date it was sold for total proceeds of $965 is

($965 – $970)/$970 = –0.52%

The price return is ($950 – $960)/$970 = –1.03 percent. Based on a change of accrued interest of $15 – $10 = $5, the income return is $5/$970 = 0.52 percent. The two return components sum to –0.52 percent (apart from rounding error).

3 When a bond is purchased, one pays AI counting from the last coupon payment date through the settlement date of the trade. The details of accrued interest calculations are beyond the scope of this reading and, in fact, differ across markets. One complication is that different markets make different assumptions about the number of days in a month and/or a year when calculating accrued interest (e.g., the US bond market assumes 30 days in all months and 360 days in a year). Some bonds, such as those in default, trade without accrued interest (they are said to trade "flat").

4 For longer periods, one would need to account for the receipt and reinvestment of coupon payments. Note that the income return shown in Equation 6c does not have a coupon payment component.

5 That is, the accrued interest received if the bond is sold at the end of the holding period minus the accrued interest paid when the bond was purchased at the beginning of the holding period.

Bonds, like common shares, can be thought of as having an "ex-date," or **ex-coupon date**: The entire coupon will be paid to the investor owning the bond on the day before the ex-coupon date. However, whereas for common shares the record date and the ex-dividend date are typically somewhat arbitrary,[6] for specific types of bonds the ex-coupon date is often set predictably in relation to trade settlement periods. For example, US corporate bond trades typically settle in three business days (e.g., on Thursday if the trade is on Monday, assuming Monday through Thursday are all days that are open for trading). If that Thursday is the coupon payment date, the Monday is effectively the ex-coupon date because a buyer on Monday does not receive the upcoming interest payment and the transaction is without accrued interest.[7]

Exhibit 1 shows the relationship between clean and dirty prices and accrued interest over time assuming the clean price remains constant over the period.

Exhibit 1 Relationship between Price and Accrued Interest for a Bond

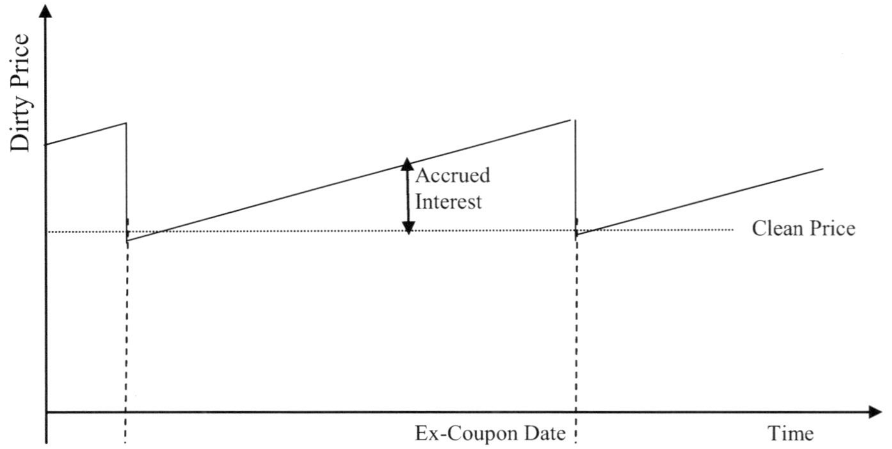

EXAMPLE 6

Calculation of Holding Period Return for a Bond

A $1,000 face value, 4 percent coupon, semi-annual pay bond is issued on 1 January and purchased at par. The first coupon will be paid on 1 July. The bond is quoted at a clean price of $1,020 on 31 January.

1 Calculate the rate of return on the bond for January.

2 Calculate the price return on the bond for January.

3 Calculate the income return on the bond for January.

Solution to 1:

Because the bond was held for one month, 1/6 of the semi-annual coupon payment needs to be accrued.

Semi-annual coupon = $1,000 × 4% × 0.5 = $20

6 For equities, the period between the ex-dividend date and the payment date is typically longer.

7 Trades carried out in a longer ex-coupon period (the ex-coupon date through the payment date) are often settled on the basis of *subtracting* interest from the clean price. Details vary by market; for example, gilts (UK government bonds) usually go ex-coupon seven days before the payment date.

$$\text{Accrued interest} = \$20 \times (1/6) = \$3.33$$

Using Equation 6a,

$$\text{Total return} = \frac{\$1{,}020 - \$1{,}000 + \$3.33}{\$1{,}000} = 0.0233 = 2.33\%$$

Solution to 2:

Using Equation 6b,

$$\text{Price return} = \frac{\$1{,}020 - \$1{,}000}{\$1{,}000} = 0.0200 = 2.00\%$$

Note that the dirty and clean prices are the same on 1 January because there is no accrued interest.

Solution to 3:

The income return accounts for the portion of the coupon payment that has been earned but not yet received. Using Equation 6c,

$$\text{Income return} = \frac{\$3.33}{\$1{,}000} = 0.0033 = 0.33\%$$

EXAMPLE 7

Calculation of Income Return, Price Return, and Total Return for a Bond

A \$1,000 face value, 4 percent coupon, semi-annual pay bond is issued on 1 January and purchased at par. The first coupon will be paid on 1 July. The bond is quoted on each of the following dates at the clean prices noted:

31 March at \$1,040

31 May at \$1,055

Calculate the holding period return for the bond including the price and income return components for the period 31 March to 31 May.

Solution:

$$\text{Accrued interest to 31 March} = \$20 \times (3/6) = \$10.00$$

$$\text{Accrued interest to 31 May} = \$20 \times (5/6) = \$16.67$$

Change in accrued interest: \$6.67

$$\text{Dirty price on 31 March} = \$1{,}040 + \$10 = \$1{,}050 = V_0$$

$$\text{Total return} = \frac{\$1{,}055 - \$1{,}040 + \$6.67}{\$1{,}050} = 0.0206 = 2.06\%$$

$$\text{Price return} = \frac{\$1{,}055 - \$1{,}040}{\$1{,}050} = 0.0143 = 1.43\%$$

$$\text{Income return} = \frac{\$6.67}{\$1{,}050} = 0.0064 = 0.64\%$$

2.1.4 *Cash in Portfolio Performance*

In a typical portfolio, such as a brokerage account, there is usually a provision for holding money that is not otherwise invested in securities in cash and cash equivalents. Such investments may be called the **liquidity reserve** asset, or simply cash. Income from dividends or coupon interest and sales of securities typically increase the value of the liquidity reserve, whereas purchases of securities typically decrease the liquidity reserve. When money is deposited to or withdrawn from the account, the money flows into or out of the liquidity reserve.

EXAMPLE 8

Value of a Liquidity Reserve

On 31 March, an investor has a portfolio consisting of 9,000 shares of stock and $10,000 cash. The stock has a dividend receivable of $0.10 per share; its pay date is 30 April. The stock's 31 March price is $10 per share, and the cash earns interest of 1.2 percent annually (10 bps per month). At the end of the month, the share price of the stock is $10.50. Consider the receivable dividend as part of the liquidity reserve. Calculate the ending values of the stock holdings, the liquidity reserve, and the total portfolio, along with the returns of the portfolio and its components for the month.

Solution:

The cash asset earns 10 bps on the $10,000 value, and the $900 receivable dividend earns no interest until it is paid. The beginning and ending values of the portfolio components are

	31 March	30 April	Return
Stock	9,000 × $10 = $90,000	9,000 × $10.50 = $94,500	5.00%
Liquidity reserve:			
Cash asset	$10,000	($10,000 × 1.001) + $900 = $10,910	
Receivable dividend	9,000 × $0.10 = $900	$0	
Liquidity reserve total	$10,900	$10,910	0.09%
Portfolio total	$100,900	$105,410	4.47%

Note that although the cash asset pays 1.2 percent annually, the return of the liquidity reserve was 9 bps for the month instead of 10 bps because cash from the dividend was not received until the end of the month.

The value of the liquidity reserve is an important component in calculating portfolio performance, and care should be taken in its accounting. (Note that the Global Investment Performance Standards [GIPS®] require returns from cash and cash equivalents held in portfolios to be included in all return calculations [CFA Institute 2010].)

2.1.5 *Returns on Foreign Assets*

A **domestic asset** is an asset that trades in the investor's home currency (the one he or she typically uses for spending). An example is a US government bond from the perspective of a US-domiciled investor. This same bond is a non-domestic asset from a eurozone investor's perspective: *Domestic* refers to a relation between the asset and the investor, not an inherent property of the asset. **Foreign assets** (or **non-domestic assets**) are assets denominated in currencies other than the investor's domestic (base) currency. The **domestic currency** (also called **base currency** or **home currency**) is the currency in which the portfolio is valued for return calculations because consumption takes place chiefly in that currency. Suppose an investor holds a foreign asset. In the (foreign) market in which the asset trades, the asset goes up in value by 10 percent (as measured in that market). From this investor's perspective, 10 percent is the asset's return in foreign currency terms—its **foreign-currency return**. This return is often called the **local currency return** (or local return) because it is the return of the asset expressed in local-currency terms, where "local" refers to that asset's market. The investor can restate the foreign-currency return in home-currency terms—that is, as a **domestic-currency return**. The domestic-currency return would reflect the foreign-currency return and any currency exchange rate gains or losses over the holding period.

To value a foreign-currency-denominated asset in an investor's base currency, the **spot exchange rate** is required, which is the rate at which foreign currency can be exchanged for immediate delivery of the base currency. If V^{FC} is the value of an asset in a foreign currency (FC) and $S^{d/f}$ is the spot exchange rate measured as the number of domestic-currency units required to buy a unit of foreign currency—indicated by the superscript d/f—then the value V of the asset in the domestic currency is $V^{FC}S^{d/f}$.[8] For example, if the value of an asset in a foreign currency (V^{FC}) is 2.5678 and the spot exchange rate ($S^{d/f}$) is 0.6982, then the value in the domestic currency is 2.5678 × 0.6982 = 1.7928.

Using subscripts 0 and 1 to denote the beginning and ending times of a holding period, respectively, the base-currency return of a foreign-currency asset can be written as

$$R = \frac{V_1}{V_0} - 1 = \frac{V_1^{FC} S_1^{d/f}}{V_0^{FC} S_0^{d/f}} - 1 \quad (7)$$

Building off the previous example, if the value of the asset in the foreign currency $\left(V_1^{FC}\right)$ changed to 2.7837 and the spot exchange rate $\left(S_1^{d/f}\right)$ moved to 0.6876, applying Equation 7, the holding period return would be

$$R = \frac{V_1^{FC} S_1^{d/f}}{V_0^{FC} S_0^{d/f}} - 1 = \frac{(2.7837)(0.6876)}{(2.5678)(0.6982)} - 1 = \frac{1.9141}{1.7928} - 1 = 0.0676 = 6.76\%$$

In the local currency, the return can be calculated as $R^{FC} = \left(V_1^{FC} / V_0^{FC}\right) - 1$; as mentioned earlier, this return can be referred to either as the foreign-currency or local-currency return or just the local return. The **currency return** is defined as $R^C = \left(S_1^{d/f} / S_0^{d/f}\right) - 1$; it represents the percentage change in the exchange rate over the period being considered (equivalently, the return from holding one unit of foreign currency). The return of an asset in base currency terms shown in Equation 7 can now be expressed as

$$R = (1 + R^{FC})(1 + R^C) - 1 \quad (8a)$$

or

$$R = R^{FC} + R^C + (R^{FC})(R^C) \quad (8b)$$

8 An exchange rate quotation of the form "domestic-currency units per foreign-currency unit" is known as a **direct quotation**; exchange rates can also be quoted in terms of "foreign-currency units per domestic-currency unit" which is an **indirect quotation**.

Equation 8a shows the base-currency return on an investment denominated in a foreign currency as the product of one plus the investment's local return and one plus the currency return. Equation 8b carries through the multiplication and shows the base-currency return as the sum of the local return, the currency return, and the cross-product between the local and currency returns.

To illustrate, suppose a eurozone investor makes a \$100 million investment that, in one year's time, is worth \$110 million. The US dollar is the foreign currency from this investor's perspective: V_0^{FC} = \$100 and V_1^{FC} = \$110. In foreign-currency (US dollar) terms, the return is 10 percent:

$$R^{FC} = \left(V_1^{FC}/V_0^{FC}\right) - 1 = \$110/\$100 - 1 = 0.10 = 10.00\%.$$

When the investment is made, €0.7 buys \$1 (one can write the exchange rate as €0.7/\$1). One year later, the dollar has appreciated against the euro; in other words, a given amount of dollars buys more euros or, equivalently, the euro cost of \$1 is greater. Suppose, in particular, that the exchange rate has increased to €0.735/\$1. Thus, $S_0^{d/f} = 0.70$ and $S_1^{d/f} = 0.735$ and the currency return can be computed as 5%:

$$R^{C} = \left(S_1^{d/f}/S_0^{d/f}\right) - 1 = (0.735/0.70) - 1 = 0.05 = 5\%$$

According to Equation 7,

$$R = \frac{V_1^{FC}S_1^{d/f}}{V_0^{FC}S_0^{d/f}} - 1 = \frac{\$110 \times €0.735/\$1}{\$100 \times €0.7/\$1} - 1 = \frac{€80.85}{€70} - 1 = 0.1550 = 15.5\%$$

Equivalently, using Equation 8a:

$$R = (1 + R^{FC})(1 + R^{C}) - 1 = (1.10)(1.05) - 1 = 0.1550 = 15.5\%$$

The return of 15.5 percent in the investor's home currency exceeds the investment's local return of 10 percent. What has happened? The investor has benefited by the appreciation of the US dollar against the euro because in converting dollars to euros at $t = 1$, a dollar buys more euros than before.

The impact of currency return can also be analyzed in monetary terms, as shown in Exhibit 2.

Exhibit 2 Impact of Currency on Returns

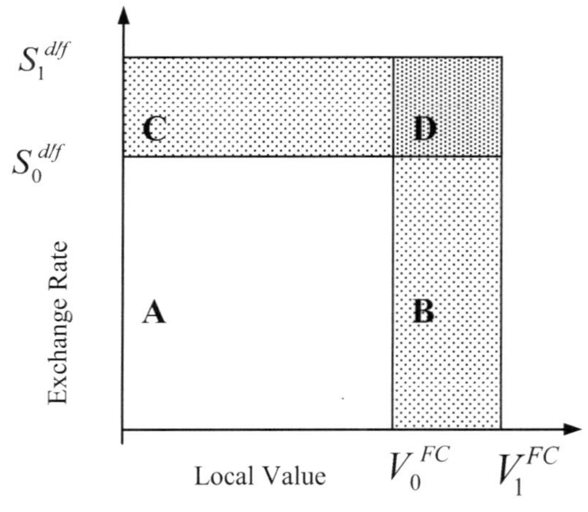

Area A is the initial value: $V_0^F S_0^{d/f}$.

Area B is the gain from the local return only: $\left(V_1^{FC} - V_0^{FC}\right)S_0^{d/f}$.

Area C is the gain from currency return only: $V_0^{FC}\left(S_1^{d/f} - S_0^{d/f}\right)$.

Area D is the gain from the interaction of both the local return and currency returns and is a consequence of both. Area D is found by subtracting areas A, C, and B from the total area $V_1^{FC}S_1^{d/f}$:

$$V_1^{FC}S_1^{d/f} - V_0^{FC}S_0^{d/f} - V_0^{FC}\left(S_1^{d/f} - S_0^{d/f}\right) - \left(V_1^{FC} - V_0^{FC}\right)S_0^{d/f}$$
$$= \left(V_1^{FC} - V_0^{FC}\right)\left(S_1^{d/f} - S_0^{d/f}\right)$$

Using information from the previous example,

Area A = (\$100 × €0.7/\$1) = €70

Area B = (\$110 – \$100)(€0.7/\$1) = €7

Area C = \$100(€0.735/\$1 – €0.7/\$1) = €3.5

Area D = €80.85 – €70 – €3.5 – €7 = €0.35

where, in the calculation of Area D, €80.85 = \$110(€0.735/\$1) is the ending value of the asset in euros.

Note that B + C + D, the total gain (€10.85), equals the first two terms in the expression for D, $V_1^{FC}S_1^{d/f} - V_0^{FC}S_0^{d/f}$. Therefore, the base-currency rate of return equals

$$\frac{V_1^{FC}S_1^{d/f} - V_0^{FC}S_0^{d/f}}{V_0^{FC}S_0^{d/f}} = \frac{V_1^{FC}S_1^{d/f}}{V_0^{FC}S_0^{d/f}} - 1 = \frac{€80.85}{€70} - 1 = 15.5\%$$

which is Equation 7 above.

The base-currency rate of return can also be derived by dividing the total gain (B + C + D) by the initial value (A).

$$R = \frac{€7 + €3.5 + €0.35}{€70} = \frac{€10.85}{€70} = 0.155 = 15.5\%$$

This expression shows that the interaction effect €0.35/€70 = 0.5% explains why the base-currency return is slightly higher than the sum of the local and currency returns (10% + 5%).

If a portfolio consists of a collection of assets in multiple currencies, all the assets must be converted to the base currency using the respective spot exchange rates in order to calculate a base currency return. Once a portfolio return has been calculated in a currency, by using Equation 7 one can convert the return to any other currency.

EXAMPLE 9

Holding Period Return for a Portfolio of Assets in Multiple Currencies

A portfolio holds assets in US dollars (\$), UK sterling (£), and Japanese yen (¥). Calculate performance in the base currency of euros (€), and then convert this return into \$, £, and ¥ returns.

	31 March	30 April
US equities	\$56.7 million	\$63.4 million
UK equities	£23.5 million	£26.7 million
Japanese equities	¥1,500 million	¥1,350 million

(continued)

	31 March	30 April
One US dollar buys this many euros:[a]	0.75	0.70
One UK pound sterling buys this many euros:	1.20	1.30
One Japanese yen buys this many euros:	0.009091	0.010000

[a] Another way to express the same thing is that this is the euro cost of one US dollar.

Solution:

Calculate total portfolio beginning and ending values in euros by multiplying each group of assets by the applicable exchange rate.

Beginning value: (\$56.7 × 0.75) + (£23.5 × 1.20) + (¥1,500 × 0.009091) = €84.36

Ending value: (\$63.4 × 0.7) + (£26.7 × 1.30) + (¥1,350 × 0.010000) = €92.59

$$\text{Portfolio return in €} = \frac{92.59}{84.36} - 1 = 9.76\%$$

The base-currency return in € can be converted into any other currency return by applying the appropriate currency return:

$$\text{Portfolio return in \$} = (1.0976)\left(\frac{0.75}{0.70}\right) - 1 = (1.0976)(1.0714) - 1 = 17.6\%$$

$$\text{Portfolio return in £} = (1.0976)\left(\frac{1.20}{1.30}\right) - 1 = (1.0976)(0.9231) - 1 = 1.32\%$$

$$\text{Portfolio return in ¥} = (1.0976)\left(\frac{0.009091}{0.010000}\right) - 1 = (1.0976)(0.909100) - 1$$
$$= -0.22\%$$

Alternatively, the return in each currency can be obtained by recalculating the beginning and ending values in each currency as follows:

$$\text{Beginning value in \$: \$56.7} + £23.5 \times \frac{1.2}{0.75} + ¥1{,}500 \times \frac{0.009091}{0.75} = \$112.48$$

$$\text{Ending value in \$: \$63.4} + £26.7 \times \frac{1.3}{0.7} + ¥1{,}350 \times \frac{0.01}{0.7} = \$132.27$$

$$\text{Portfolio return in \$: } \frac{\$132.27}{\$112.48} - 1 = 17.6\%$$

$$\text{Beginning value in £: \$56.7} \times \frac{0.75}{1.2} + £23.5 + ¥1{,}500 \times \frac{0.009091}{1.2} = £70.30$$

$$\text{Ending value in £: \$63.4} \times \frac{0.7}{1.3} + £26.7 + ¥1{,}350 \times \frac{0.01}{1.3} = £71.22$$

$$\text{Portfolio return in £: } \frac{£71.22}{£70.30} - 1 = 1.31\%$$

Beginning value in

$$¥\text{: \$56.7} \times \frac{0.75}{0.009091} + £23.5 \times \frac{1.2}{0.009091} + ¥1{,}500 = ¥9{,}279.67$$

$$\text{Ending Value in ¥: } \$63.4 \times \frac{0.7}{0.01} + £26.7 \times \frac{1.3}{0.01} + ¥1{,}350 = ¥9{,}259$$

$$\text{Portfolio return in ¥: } \frac{¥9{,}259}{¥9{,}279.67} - 1 = -0.22\%$$

The dollar return looks higher because the dollar fell against the euro, but both the pound and yen appreciated against the euro, generating lower returns in these base currencies.

2.1.6 *Short and Leveraged Positions*

Although we have defined a portfolio as a collection of assets, the concept of return can be extended to a collection of liabilities, which may be thought of as "negative assets." Liabilities can be modeled similarly to assets sold short, or "short holdings." The return of a portfolio consisting only of liabilities is sometimes called a **liability return**. The return of a portfolio of both assets and liabilities is sometimes called a **surplus return**. When a portfolio consists of both long and short positions, care must be taken to segment the assets into those held long and those held short. It is important to maintain the convention that if an asset falls in value, then the return on that individual asset is negative whether the holding is long or short. It is the combination of a negative holding with a negative return that results in a profit.

Consider the following data for the assets and liabilities of a pension fund:

Pension Assets	
Beginning value on 1 January 2010	€100
Change in value in 2010	7%

Pension Liabilities	
Beginning value on 1 January 2010	€60
Change in value in 2010	15%

Note: Euro values are in millions.

The fund's beginning surplus would be calculated by subtracting the value of liabilities from the value of assets: €100 – €60 = €40. The ending surplus is €100(1.07) – €60(1.15) = €107– €69 = €38. The surplus return is calculated as the percentage change in surplus: (€38 – €40)/€40 = –0.05 or –5 percent.

The following example illustrates the calculation of return for a portfolio with long and short positions.

EXAMPLE 10

Calculating Returns for Portfolios with Long and Short Positions

A portfolio holds two long shares of Stock A, valued at \$25 per share. In addition, the portfolio sells short one share of Stock B, valued at \$30 per share. One month later, both stocks A and B are valued at \$28 per share. Based only on the facts given, calculate the one-month returns on the long position, the short position, and the total portfolio.[9]

Solution:

The long-position, short-position, and total portfolio returns are 12 percent, –6.67 percent, and 40 percent, respectively. The total portfolio return can be arrived at in one of two ways: as a weighted average of long- and short-position returns or by netting long and short beginning and ending amounts.

1 ***Weighted average of long- and short-position returns:***

Long-position return

Beginning value = \$25 × 2 = \$50
Ending value = \$28 × 2 = \$56.

Thus, the return on the long position is

$$R = \frac{\$56 - \$50}{\$50} = \frac{\$6}{\$50} = 0.12 = 12.00\%$$

Short-position return
The return on the short position is

$$R = \frac{\$28 - \$30}{\$30} = \frac{-\$2}{\$30} = -0.0667 = -6.67\%$$

The initial equity is the amount invested in the long position minus the amount invested in the short position: \$50 – \$30 = \$20. The long position represents 250 percent of the beginning portfolio equity (\$50/\$20 = 2.5), and the short position represents –150 percent (–\$30/\$20 = –1.5). Multiplying the returns by the respective position weights yields the total portfolio return:

$$R = (12.00\% \times 2.5) + (-6.67\% \times -1.5) = 30\% + 10\% = 40\%$$

2 ***Netting long- and short-position amounts:***

The initial equity, as already noted, is \$50 – \$30 = \$20. This is the denominator. The long position gained \$56 – \$50 = \$6. From this we subtract the gain on the short position: \$28 – \$30 = –\$2 (i.e., a negative gain); thus the numerator reduces to \$6 – (–\$2) = \$6 + \$2 = \$8.

$$R = \frac{(\$56 - \$50) - (\$28 - \$30)}{(\$50 - \$30)} = \frac{\$8}{\$20} = 0.40 = 40\%$$

9 In practice, factors arise that complicate the rate of return calculation. For example, the short seller may have to deposit collateral over and above the short sale proceeds when selling short. Short sellers sometimes negotiate for short sale proceeds to earn interest. For the sake of simplicity, these and other complicating factors are ignored here.

Leverage is the use of borrowing[10] or various financial instruments to magnify potential gains and losses relative to the investor's equity position. The **leveraged return** (or **levered return**) represents the actual return achieved based on the capital invested—that is, on the leveraged (levered) equity. The **cash basis return** represents the unleveraged return on the underlying investment—that is, the return on total capital invested including the amount financed by borrowing.

The successful use of leverage involves earning a cash basis return that is in excess of the cost of borrowed funds. This result can most easily be shown by an example.

Suppose an investor has equity capital of \$400 million to invest. The investor borrows \$100 million at an interest rate (i) of 5 percent per year; thus, in one year, interest of 5% × \$100 million = \$5 million is payable. In total, after borrowing, the investor has \$500 million of total capital invested. The rate of return earned on this sum is the cash basis return, denoted R_{CB}.

Suppose \$40 million is earned on the \$500 million in one year. Then, R_{CB} = \$40/\$500 = 0.08 or 8%. If R_{LE} is the return on levered equity, R_{LE} = \$35/\$400 = 0.0875 or 8.75%. The numerator is \$40 million minus the \$5 million cost of borrowing, or \$35 million. The denominator in the expression is \$400 million, the equity in the investment.

A simple expression is available for the return on the equity in a portfolio that uses leverage. Defining the leverage ratio as L = Market value of margin debt/(Market value of margin debt + Market value of equity), the expression is

$$R_{LE} = \frac{R_{CB} - iL}{1 - L} \tag{9}$$

In the case presented, L = \$100/(\$100 + \$400) = 0.20. Thus,

$$R_{LE} = \frac{R_{CB} - iL}{1 - L} = \frac{0.08 - 0.05(0.2)}{1 - 0.20} = \frac{0.07}{0.80} = 0.0875 = 8.75\%$$

which confirms the result found. In Equation 9, note that as the use of debt relative to equity increases, the leverage ratio becomes larger and $1 - L$ becomes smaller, which tends to magnify returns.[11]

EXAMPLE 11

Leveraged and Cash Basis Returns

A portfolio purchased 100 shares of common stock valued at \$48 per share. Half the purchase price was paid with cash, while the remainder was paid for using borrowed money. One month later, the stock appreciated to \$50 per share. The annual interest rate on borrowing is 2 percent. Calculate the cash basis and leveraged returns for the investment over the one-month holding period.

Solution:

Initial equity exposure = 100 × \$48 = \$4,800

Final equity exposure = 100 × \$50 = \$5,000

Net profit = \$5,000 – \$4,800 = \$200

$$\text{Cash basis return } (R_{CB}) = \frac{\$200}{\$4{,}800} = 0.0417 = 4.17\%$$

Initial margin = \$4,800/2 = \$2,400

10 The use of borrowing in this context is sometimes called the use of **margin**.

11 The denominator effect tends to outweigh the effect of iL in the numerator of Equation 9.

Leverage ratio (L) = \$2,400/\$4,800 = 0.50

$$\text{Leveraged return } (R_{LE}) = \frac{\$200 - [\$2{,}400 \times (0.02/12)]}{\$2{,}400} = \frac{\$196}{\$2{,}400}$$
$$= 0.0817 = 8.17\%$$

Equivalently, using Equation 9,

$$R_{LE} = \frac{R_{BC} - iL}{1 - L} = \frac{0.0417 - [(0.5) \times (0.02/12)]}{0.5} = \frac{0.04087}{0.5}$$
$$= 0.0817 = 8.17\%$$

2.1.7 *Accounting and Trade Considerations*

We have defined rate of return as the change in value of a portfolio. **Market value** is the price at which investors can buy or sell an investment at a given time multiplied by the quantity held plus any accrued income. Market value provides the clearest indication of an investor's true economic wealth. Other accounting measures of value are useful for various purposes, but returns calculated for performance evaluation are almost always calculated from market values.

2.1.7.1 Book Value vs. Market Value In the context of a securities portfolio, the accounting concept of **book value** (sometimes also called **cost value** or **cost basis**) is the value of an asset recorded at the time it was purchased. Because market prices change over time, market values of assets diverge from book values over time. Moreover, accounting conventions (such as average cost basis accounting) can cause book values to change over time. For example, if 10 shares of stock were purchased at \$10 per share and later 10 more shares were purchased at \$14 per share, the cost value under average cost accounting would be \$240, or \$12 per share. Although a return can be calculated from book values—(12 – 10)/10 or 20% from the time of the first purchase to the time of the second purchase in this example—such a return may not accurately reflect the change in the owner's wealth. The return based on market values in the example is (14 – 10)/10, or 40%.

2.1.7.2 Fair Value vs. Market Value Fair value is the amount at which an investment could be exchanged in a current arm's-length transaction between willing parties in which the parties each act knowledgeably and prudently. In the case of liquid securities, fair value and market value will typically be the same. Where they will diverge is in the case of illiquid or infrequently traded investments where a market price is not readily available or is based on a transaction that occurred so long ago that its relevance is questionable (a stale price). In such a case, assumptions often must be made to arrive at the best estimate of fair value. It should be noted that beginning 1 January 2010, the GIPS standards require portfolio valuations to be based on fair value.

2.1.7.3 Realized and Unrealized Gains and Losses If an asset's market value has changed from its book value (which, in the simplest case, might be thought of as the market value at the time the asset was purchased), then the difference between the market value and the book value reflects an investment gain or loss. Such a gain (or loss) is called an **unrealized gain (loss)**. Regulation to which the portfolio is subject may require an asset's value to be restated at market value, or **marked to market**, at certain intervals or in certain events (such as the sale of the asset). At that point, the unrealized gains are said to be realized.[12] For illustration, assume an asset is purchased for $100 and then appreciates to $110. Prior to selling the asset, the $10 gain is unrealized. Upon the sale of the asset, the unrealized gain converts to a realized gain.

Many tax jurisdictions distinguish between realized and unrealized gains and treat such gains differently in assessing taxes. Consequently, in taxable accounts, record keepers may report realized and unrealized gains and losses on account statements. For performance measurement, tax payments may constitute cash flows out of a portfolio and must be accounted for. The treatment and management of taxable portfolios can be complex because of the obvious dependence on tax laws and the status of unrealized versus realized gains.

2.1.7.4 Trade Date Accounting vs. Settlement Date Accounting Trade date accounting recognizes the value of assets and liabilities on the date of purchase or sale. **Settlement date accounting**, on the other hand, recognizes the value of assets or liabilities on the date when the actual exchange of cash and investments is completed. Because trade date accounting accurately captures the timing of the investment decision and reflects the correct economic value of the portfolio assets as of the transaction date, valuations as of the trade date are more appropriate for use in performance measurement. Further, the GIPS standards require that, for periods beginning on or after 1 January 2005, firms use trade date accounting.

2.2 Factors Affecting Returns and Related Adjustments

A number of costs can affect the actual increments to wealth, so different types of return can be defined. The following section introduces inflation.

2.2.1 *Inflation: Nominal Returns vs. Real Returns*

Economists distinguish between **nominal prices** (actual transaction prices, with no adjustment for inflation) and **real prices** (nominal prices adjusted for changes in purchasing power of currency units over time). The change in purchasing power is a measure of monetary inflation. In many countries, the price levels of standard baskets of goods are calculated and maintained by government agencies. A price index is a number calculated from such standardized baskets, from which a change in the price index can be interpreted as inflation. Examples of such price indexes are the consumer price index (CPI) in many countries and the Retail Prices Index (RPI) in the United Kingdom. Other examples of price indexes used to measure inflation are the Producer Price Index and the GDP deflator.

Market values of assets can be converted to alternate base currencies by means of spot exchange rates, but the "real" value of financial assets can only be defined with respect to a chosen price index. If I is the value of the consumer price index, then an **inflation rate**, IR, over a given period can be calculated as the percentage change in the index over the period. Using subscripts 0 and 1 to denote the beginning and the end of the period,

$$IR = \frac{I_1}{I_0} - 1$$

12 An asset can also be marked to market for performance measurement purposes, which is a paper transaction that does not result in gains or losses being realized.

Given this measure of inflation, the "real value" of the currency alone has changed by IR. Therefore, the real value of a portfolio at the end of the period can be calculated by discounting the nominal value, V_1, by the rate of inflation, or $V_1/(1 + IR)$. A **real return**, R^{real}, can thus be defined as

$$R^{real} = \frac{V_1/V_0}{I_1/I_0} - 1 = \frac{1 + R}{1 + IR} - 1 = \frac{R - IR}{1 + IR} \quad (10)$$

where R is the **nominal return** of the portfolio. For example, if R is 0.10 and IR is 0.04, then R^{real} = (0.10 – 0.04)/1.04 = 0.0577 or 5.77 percent. For small values of IR, the denominator adjustment in Equation 10 is small and the approximation $R^{real} = R - IR$ = 0.10 – 0.04 = 0.06 or 6 percent is sometimes used. The corresponding expression for the nominal rate of return is

$$R = (1 + IR)(1 + R^{real}) - 1 \quad (11)$$

We emphasize here, however, that the real return in this equation is derived using the given price level index and cannot be measured independently.

Equation 11 can be interpreted further by multiplying out the right-hand side:

$$1 + R = 1 + IR + R^{real} + (IR \times R^{real})$$

The nominal return R is approximately the sum of the inflation rate IR and the real return R^{real}. The additional cross-product term $IR \times R^{real}$ represents the additional change from compounding. The formula for the real return R^{real} in Equation 10 as noted is called the **geometric difference** between the nominal return and the inflation rate. As seen, it is equal to the **arithmetic difference** $R - IR$ (sometimes used by itself as an approximation) divided by the inflation return relative (1 + IR). Arithmetic and geometric differences arise naturally when portfolio returns are compared with other reference rates of return such as the inflation rate above or benchmark returns.

EXAMPLE 12

Nominal Return, Inflation Rate, and Real Return

Calculate the real return of a portfolio given the following nominal return and inflation rate.

Portfolio return	8.7 percent
Inflation rate	3.2 percent

Solution:

1.087/1.032 – 1 = 5.33%.

2.2.2 *Fees: Gross-of-Fees Returns vs. Net-of-Fees Returns*

From the perspective of an investor, investment management fees are a cost of investing; therefore, a return that reflects the fees, or a **net-of-fee return**, is of value. From the perspective of a portfolio manager, however, some fees are not a direct consequence of portfolio decisions; portfolios managed identically might be offered at varying fee levels to different clients. Further, net-of-fee returns may not fairly reflect the skill of the manager when compared with a benchmark because benchmark returns typically are not calculated with a deduction for fees.

Consequently, portfolio managers and analysts tend to prefer **gross-of-fee returns** for analyzing the consequences of portfolio decisions. More specifically, gross-of-fee returns are the returns based on portfolio values reduced by any trading expenses incurred during the period but not reduced by investment management fees; net-of-fee returns are gross-of-fee returns reduced by investment management fees. Investment management fees are typically asset based (a percentage of assets under management)[13] or performance based (determined by the performance of the portfolio on an absolute basis or relative to a benchmark) but may take other forms as well.

Depending on the setting, fees may be incorporated into portfolio accounting in different ways. In regulated mutual funds, the **net asset value** (NAV) of the fund is based on valuing the portfolio net of any liabilities including fees and expenses which are payable. In such a setting, calculating performance from net asset values automatically gives a net-of-fee return. In institutional funds settings, it is common for the investor to agree that the fees will be accrued per the investment management contract terms and paid at discrete dates. If the investor requires the fee payment is treated as capital leaving the portfolio (i.e., as an external cash flow as discussed in Section 4), the calculated returns would be gross-of-fee returns. If, instead, the fee payment is treated as a simple reduction in the portfolio value, the calculated returns would be net-of-fee returns. Under the latter treatment, fees are typically accrued as a negative value between fee payment dates to ensure all intermediate period returns are calculated net-of-fees.[14] Performance fees are also similarly accrued, normally based on the theoretical payment given the excess return achieved to date. If negative excess performance is suffered in subsequent periods, this may lead to the strange result in which the net-of-fee return is greater than the gross-of-fee return as the performance fee accrual is unwound.

As mentioned, either net-of-fee or gross-of-fee returns might be more readily calculated depending on the setting and the available portfolio accounting data. Given a net-of-fee return, an analyst may want to calculate a gross-of-fee return, or vice versa. Typically, approximations are used to calculate one from the other. To derive net-of-fee returns from gross-of-fee returns, one must first determine the type of investment management fee being charged and the frequency at which the fees are incurred. As an example, assume an annual asset-based fee of 0.50 percent (50 bps) is charged on a monthly basis (equal to 0.0050/12 of the daily average of the value of assets under management during a month). To calculate an approximate net-of-fee return from a gross-of-fee return, the geometric difference[15] between the gross-of-fee return and the fee percentage per month can be calculated. Similarly, to calculate an approximate gross-of-fee return from a net-of-fee return, the assumed fee percentage can be compounded with the net-of-fee return.

EXAMPLE 13

Gross-of-Fee and Net-of-Fee Returns

1 Calculate the net-of-fee return for Portfolio A and the gross-of-fee return for Portfolio B. Assume, as a simplification, that fees are accrued throughout the year and paid annually.

Portfolio A's gross-of-fee return for 2010: 13.5%; annual fee: 1.5%

Portfolio B's net-of-fee return for 2010: 10.4%; annual fee: 1.2%

2 Calculate the 2010 quarterly net-of-fee returns for Portfolio C. Assume, as a simplification, that fees are accrued and paid quarterly.

Portfolio C's annual fee: 1.2%, paid quarterly

Portfolio C's quarterly gross-of-fee returns for 2010:

13 A fee calculated as a percentage of assets under management is called an *ad valorem* fee.

14 Another scenario is one where the fees are paid by the client from a separate account, not deducted from the portfolio. Under such a scenario the gross-of-fee return is calculated by ignoring the fee payment.

15 Calculating the geometric difference between two percentages involves adding 1 to each percentage, dividing the terms by each other, and then subtracting 1 from the result.

1Q: 2.41%, 2Q: –1.68%, 3Q: 3.72%, 4Q: 0.28%

Solution to 1:

Portfolio A's net-of-fee return is

$$R = \frac{(1 + 13.5\%)}{(1 + 1.5\%)} - 1 = \frac{1.135}{1.015} - 1 = 11.8\%$$

Portfolio B's gross-of-fee return is

$R = (1 + 10.4\%)(1 + 1.2\%) - 1 = 1.104 \times 1.012 - 1 = 11.7\%$

Solution to 2:

Given the stated annual fee rate of 1.2 percent, the quarterly fee rate is 0.012/4 = 0.0030. Portfolio C's net-of-fee returns are

$$1Q = \frac{1.0241}{1.0030} - 1 = 0.0210 = 2.10\%$$

$$2Q = \frac{0.9832}{1.0030} - 1 = -0.0197 = -1.97\%$$

$$3Q = \frac{1.0372}{1.0030} - 1 = 0.0341 = 3.41\%$$

$$4Q = \frac{1.0028}{1.0030} - 1 = -0.0002 = -0.02\%$$

2.2.3 *Taxes: Pre-Tax Returns vs. Post-Tax Returns*

Because of the nature of tax laws in many jurisdictions, calculating post-tax returns can be complicated. Because a tax liability is typically incurred when an asset is sold, assumptions about when assets are sold are critical. In a taxable portfolio, the decision to sell assets might be made either by the asset owner or by the portfolio manager. Therefore, a return that reflects the impact of taxes must be based on assumptions regarding the sale of assets and the tax rate at which the gains are taxed.

Mutual funds in the United States are required to report, or distribute, dividends and capital gains that are realized by the fund each year. Realized capital gains might have resulted from sell decisions made by the portfolio manager. Even if dividends and realized capital gains are reinvested in the portfolio, such distributions create a tax liability for the fund investors. Another type of tax liability occurs when an investor redeems shares of a mutual fund. In this event, unrealized capital gains are realized and become taxable. Obviously, post-tax returns must be accompanied with the assumptions by which they are calculated to enable correct interpretation of the returns.

EXAMPLE 14

Pre-Tax and Post-Tax Returns

1 An asset was purchased for $3,500,000 and then later sold for $3,750,000. The applicable capital gains tax rate is 35 percent. Calculate the pre-tax and post-tax holding period returns.

2 For an initial investment of \$1,000 at the beginning of the year, a mutual fund reported dividend amounts of \$20 and distributed capital gains of \$34 for the year. If the account was liquidated at the end of the year, an additional capital gain of \$132 would be realized. Assume the following tax rates:

Tax rate on dividend income: 35%

Tax rate on capital gains: 15%

Calculate the pre-tax return, the post-tax return assuming the account is not liquidated at the end of the year, and the post-tax post-redemption return assuming the account is liquidated.

Solution to 1:

$$\text{Pre-tax return} = \frac{\$3{,}750{,}000}{\$3{,}500{,}000} - 1 = 0.0714 = 7.14\%$$

Capital gain = \$3,750,000 – \$3,500,000 = \$250,000

Post-tax capital gain = \$250,000(1 – 35%) = \$162,500

$$\text{Post-tax return} = \frac{\$162{,}500}{\$3{,}500{,}000} = 0.0464 = 4.64\%$$

Solution to 2:

Gains after taxes can be calculated using the information in the table below:

	Pre-tax amount	Tax rate	Tax	Post-tax amount
Dividend income	\$20.00	35%	\$7.00	\$13.00
Capital gain distribution	\$34.00	15%	\$5.10	\$28.90
Post-redemption gain	\$132.00	15%	\$19.80	\$112.20

$$\text{Pre-tax return} = \frac{\$20 + \$34 + \$132}{\$1{,}000} = 0.1860 = 18.60\%$$

Post-tax pre-redemption return

$$= \frac{\$13.00 + \$28.90 + \$132.00}{\$1{,}000} = 0.1739 = 17.39\%$$

Post-tax post-redemption return

$$= \frac{\$13.00 + \$28.90 + \$112.20}{\$1{,}000} = 0.1541 = 15.41\%$$

MECHANICS OF MULTI-PERIOD RETURNS

3

In principle, a return over a long holding period (a year, for instance) can be calculated in the same manner as that for a shorter holding period (such as a month) using beginning and ending market values—if there are no external cash flows within the period. It is common, however, to calculate returns over short holding periods and then to combine or link returns over multiple periods. Such a procedure is necessary when external cash flows exist, as we explain in Section 4. Storing return (or return relative) data allows users the flexibility of calculating returns over arbitrary holding periods.

3.1 Compounding Rates of Return

If returns are generated at a constant rate over time, the portfolio's value will grow faster than it will if returns are generated in proportion to time. Such growth is called geometric growth, as opposed to linear growth. This fact is the result of **compounding**. A compounded return over two periods can be calculated as

$$(1 + R_1)(1 + R_2) - 1 = R_1 + R_2 + R_1R_2$$

where the subscripts indicate time periods. The term $R_1 + R_2$ reflects linear growth in value over time, while the interaction term R_1R_2 represents "interest on interest," the key to geometric growth, also known as compound growth.

3.1.1 *Chain Linking Returns*

Suppose a portfolio is valued at month ends over the course of a year. Let V_t be the portfolio value at the end of month t, and let V_0 be the portfolio value at the beginning of the year. If there were no external cash flows into or out of the portfolio during the year, then the return relative for the year can be written as the product of the monthly return relatives,

$$\frac{V_{12}}{V_0} = \frac{V_1}{V_0} \times \frac{V_2}{V_1} \times \cdots \times \frac{V_{12}}{V_{11}} \quad (12)$$

because the intermediate values V_1, V_2, ..., V_{11} cancel in the expression on the right-hand side. Substituting the monthly holding period returns $V_t/V_{t-1} = 1 + R_t$ into the preceding expression leaves

$$\frac{V_{12}}{V_0} = (1 + R_1)(1 + R_2)\cdots(1 + R_{12})$$

More generally, if $R = V_T/V_0 - 1$ is the return over T periods, then R can be calculated from the **linking formula**:

$$R = \prod_{t=1}^{T}(1 + R_t) - 1 \quad (13)$$

where the product operator $\Pi(\bullet)$ denotes the product of terms. The procedure described by this formula is also called **chain linking** returns or **geometric compounding** of returns. When there are no external cash flows, the cumulative return R can be interpreted as the change in value of the portfolio as a fraction of the beginning value.

EXAMPLE 15

Chain Linking Returns

Calculate the cumulative return for the following 5 years:

Year 1	10.5%
Year 2	–3.6%
Year 3	20.7%
Year 4	6.4%
Year 5	12.3%

Solution:

$1.105 \times 0.964 \times 1.207 \times 1.064 \times 1.123 - 1 = 53.63\%$.

Equation 13 applies to compounding **discrete returns** (returns measured over finite time intervals). The compounding of discrete returns is called **discrete compounding**. It is also possible to define a continuously compounded return: the return which results when a finite time interval is divided into infinitely many parts. The compounding of continuously compounded returns is called **continuous compounding**. The next section explains these concepts in detail.

3.1.2 *Discrete and Continuous Compounding*

Whenever an interest rate is quoted, the compounding frequency must be specified. By convention, the **stated annual rate** of interest is the periodic rate multiplied by the number n of compounding periods per year. Thus, the periodic rate associated with a stated annual rate i is i/n. The **effective annual rate** is defined as[16]

$$\text{EAR} = \left(1 + \frac{i}{n}\right)^n - 1 \quad (14)$$

Thus, if the stated annual rate is 12 percent and there are 12 compounding periods per year, the periodic rate is 12%/12 = 1% and the EAR = $(1.01)^{12} - 1 = 0.1268$ or 12.68 percent. In other words, a dollar invested at a 12 percent stated annual rate with monthly compounding produces the same amount in one year as one dollar invested at 12.68 percent without compounding.

In principle, the compounding frequency can be increased without bound, resulting in continuous compounding. For a given nominal rate, as the compounding frequency gets large, the annual return approaches a limit

$$\lim_{n \to \infty} \left(1 + \frac{i}{n}\right)^n = e^i$$

where e is the base of the natural logarithm, a constant approximately equal to 2.718. Also, one dollar invested at an annual rate R without compounding gives the same ending amount as $i_c = \ln(1 + R)$ compounded continuously. Consequently, i_c is called a continuously compounded return. For example, Exhibit 3 shows the nominal rates at different compounding frequencies that give the same effective annual rate. The EAR associated with i_c compounded continuously is $\exp(i_c) - 1$. Thus, 11.3329 percent continuously compounded is equal to $e^{0.113329} - 1 = .12$ or 12 percent.

Exhibit 3 Equivalent Effective Annual Rates of Return

Compounding Frequency	Stated Annual Rate (%)
Annual	12.0000
Semi-annual	11.6601
Quarterly	11.4949
Monthly	11.3866
Weekly	11.3452
Daily (365 days)	11.3346
Continuously compounded	11.3329

16 The terminology for the concepts introduced here follows CFA® curriculum usage; a wide variety of synonyms may be encountered in various world markets.

Although the interpretation of continuous compounding justifies the terminology, the use of logarithms can also be thought of as simply a transformation. A useful property of logarithms is the fact that the logarithm of a product is equal to the sum of the logarithms of individual terms. For example, the linking formula, Equation 13, can be written as

$$R = \exp\left(\sum_{t=1}^{T} \ln\left(1 + R_t\right)\right) - 1$$

where exp(•) is the exponential function. Computationally, it is sometimes convenient to calculate sums of terms instead of products.

EXAMPLE 16

Continuously Compounded Returns

1 What is the continuously compounded rate that produces the same cumulative return as in the solution to Example 15?

A 42.94%

B 47.28%

C 53.63%

2 Given a stated interest rate of 10.9 percent paid semi-annually, calculate the effective annual rate.

A 11.0%

B 11.1%

C 11.2%

Solution to 1:

A is correct. ln(1 + 53.63%) = 42.94%

Solution to 2:

C is correct.

$$R = \left(1 + \frac{i}{n}\right)^n - 1 = \left(1 + \frac{0.109}{2}\right)^2 - 1 = 1.1120 - 1 = 11.2\%$$

3.1.3 *Practical Issues*

Although some investments (such as term deposits) have well-defined compounding periods, in performance measurement the holding period of a return is generally dictated by the availability of valuation data. The periodicity of the return is not a characteristic of the investment; it is a parameter chosen by the performance measurer. In principle, market values may exist at any point in time regardless of whether they are measured and recorded. For analytical purposes, discrete compounding and continuous compounding constitute alternative models of growth. The models are equivalent if portfolio values match at the given valuation time points. The choice of holding period or the use of continuous compounding depends on the nature of the analyst's task at hand and the data with which the analyst is working.

EXAMPLE 17

Equivalent Returns with Different Compounding Intervals

Calculate the effective annual rate given the stated annual rate and number of compounding periods for the three cases given below.

Stated Annual Rate	Number of Compounding Periods per Year	Effective Annual Rate?
12%	4	A
10%	12	B
8%	continuous	C

Solution to A:

The periodic rate of return is 12%/4 = 3%. EAR = $(1.03)^4 - 1 = 0.1255$ or 12.55%.

Solution to B:

The periodic rate of return is 10%/12 = 0.8333%. EAR = $(1.008333)^{12} - 1 = 0.1047$ or 10.47%.

Solution to C:

$e^{0.08} - 1 = 0.0833$ or 8.33 percent.

3.2 Averaging Rates of Return

Returns calculated over multiple holding periods can be summarized by averaging over time. Two methods of averaging, arithmetic and geometric, give different results and are useful for different purposes.

3.2.1 *Arithmetic Mean Rate of Return*

Given a collection R_t $(t = 1, \ldots, T)$ of returns over time, the **arithmetic mean rate of return** is calculated as

$$\bar{R} = \frac{1}{T}\sum_{t=1}^{T} R_t \tag{15}$$

The arithmetic mean has well-known statistical properties, which make the calculation important for many analytical purposes. We address this point further in Section 3.2.3.

If the holding period of the return is $1/n$ years (where $n = 12$ corresponds to monthly, for example), then T periods span T/n years. The **annualized arithmetic mean rate of return** is the arithmetic mean multiplied by n:

$$\bar{R}^{ann} = n\bar{R} = \frac{n}{T}\sum_{t=1}^{T} R_t \tag{16}$$

3.2.2 *Geometric Mean Rate of Return*

The **geometric mean rate of return** is defined by the formula

$$\bar{R}_G = \left(\prod_{t=1}^{T}(1 + R_t)\right)^{1/T} - 1 \tag{17}$$

The geometric mean return can be interpreted as the constant periodic rate of return that results in the same ending value created by the given returns if there are no external cash flows. This fact is seen by linking the returns on both sides of the equation:

$$\left(1+\bar{R}_G\right)^T=\prod_{t=1}^{T}\left(1+R_t\right)=\frac{V_T}{V_0}$$

The **annualized geometric mean rate of return** is the constant rate, assuming annual compounding, that results in the same ending value. Assuming the periodic returns consist of n periods per year, T periods span T/n years. The annualized geometric mean return can be calculated as

$$\overline{RG}^{ann}=\left(1+\bar{R}_G\right)^n-1=\left(\prod_{t=1}^{T}\left(1+R_t\right)\right)^{n/T}-1 \quad (18)$$

The annualized geometric mean return is also called compound annual return or simply "annualized return."

EXAMPLE 18

Arithmetic and Geometric Mean Rates of Return, Annualized

Calculate arithmetic and geometric mean rates of return using the returns below (repeated from Example 15):

Year 1	10.5%
Year 2	–3.6%
Year 3	20.7%
Year 4	6.4%
Year 5	12.3%

Solution:

$$\text{Arithmetic mean}=\frac{10.5\%-3.6\%+20.7\%+6.4\%+12.3\%}{5}=9.26\%$$

$$\text{Geometric mean}=(1.105\times0.964\times1.207\times1.064\times1.123)^{1/5}-1=8.967\%$$

Given the different ways of averaging (arithmetic and geometric), users of return data should take note of what a data provider or performance reporter means by "mean return." When presenting historical portfolio returns, the geometric, rather than arithmetic, mean return must be used. The geometric mean is more accurate when measuring portfolio returns. It takes into account the compounding interaction between individual returns in addition to the returns themselves. When used in the context of investment returns, the arithmetic mean can be misleading concerning the effects of a series of returns on final wealth, as illustrated in Example 19.

EXAMPLE 19

Arithmetic and Geometric Mean Rates of Return, Annualized

Calculate arithmetic and geometric mean rates of return using the returns for the following five years, and then determine which measure is more appropriate:

Year 1	100%
Year 2	–25%
Year 3	0%
Year 4	50%
Year 5	–75%

Solution:

$$\text{Arithmetic mean} = \frac{100\% - 25\% + 0\% + 50\% - 75\%}{5} = 10.00\%$$

$$\text{Geometric mean} = (2.000 \times 0.750 \times 1.000 \times 1.500 \times 0.250)^{1/5} - 1 = -10.87\%$$

The geometric mean is more appropriate. The positive 10 percent arithmetic mean return implies that the portfolio has added value on an average annual basis. However, the compound growth rate for the five-year period is –43.75 percent, which indicates the opposite. The geometric mean more accurately reflects reality.

Although the formulas for mean returns can be annualized, caution should be used if the number T of returns is less than the number n of periods per year. In this case, the returns span a period less than a year and annualizing may be misleading. Annualizing for periods less than one year results in simulated or hypothetical performance and is thus considered a poor performance measurement practice.

EXAMPLE 20

Annualizing Partial-Year Returns

A portfolio achieved a return of 12 percent during first quarter 2011 and a return of 8 percent during second quarter 2011. Calculate the annualized rate of return for the full year 2011 and explain why the result is or is not appropriate.

Solution:

Annualized return would be $(1.12 \times 1.08)^{2/1} - 1 = 46.31\%$, but annualizing partial-year returns is not appropriate because doing so assumes that the performance results achieved during the partial year will continue at the same pace for the remainder of the year. The annualized results would be hypothetical and potentially misleading and, therefore, should not be included in performance presentation materials.

3.2.3 *Observations about the Arithmetic and Geometric Means*[17]

One property of arithmetic and geometric mean returns is notable: The geometric mean return is less than or equal to the arithmetic mean return:[18]

$$\bar{R}_G \leq \bar{R}$$

A good approximation of the difference can be calculated from

$$\bar{R}_G \cong \bar{R} - \frac{1}{2}s^2 \quad (19)$$

where s is the sample standard deviation of the returns R_t:

$$s^2 = \frac{1}{T-1}\sum_{t=1}^{T}\left(R_t - \bar{R}\right)^2$$

Thus, if the arithmetic mean return is 10 percent and the standard deviation of returns is 0.20, according to Equation 19 the geometric mean return is approximately $0.10 - ½(0.20)^2 = 0.08$ or 8 percent.

Arithmetic and geometric mean returns are useful for different purposes. If we need to estimate an expected or average return over a one-period horizon of stated length, a historical arithmetic mean return is an appropriate estimator. For statistical analysis, when a model is fitted with parameters estimated from data, the arithmetic mean normally is the appropriate estimator. The geometric mean is affected by volatility, whereas the arithmetic mean is not. In contrast, for summarizing the effect on wealth of observed investment returns, the geometric mean return is the only return to use: It represents the compound rate of growth of an investment—that is, the rate of return that if earned each period on the initial investment would match the actual cumulative return achieved.

EXAMPLE 21

Arithmetic and Geometric Mean Rates of Return, Volatility Dependence

Exhibit 4 gives quarterly returns for the Russell 3000 Index, a broad market index of US equities, and for three-month Libor, a rate commonly used as a proxy for the risk-free rate. Calculate arithmetic and geometric mean quarterly rates of return using the returns for the three-year period presented.

Exhibit 4 Quarterly Total Returns of Two Indexes (Percent)

Quarter Ending	3-Month Libor USD	Russell 3000 Index
31-Mar-2006	1.16	5.34
30-Jun-2006	1.27	−1.94
30-Sep-2006	1.33	4.61
31-Dec-2006	1.31	7.09

17 For further reading on this subject, consult Christopherson, Cariño, and Ferson (2009).

18 This fact can be shown by using logarithms:

$$\ln\left(1+\bar{R}_G\right) = \ln\left\{\left[\prod_{t=1}^{T}(1+R_t)\right]^{1/T}\right\} = \frac{1}{T}\sum_{t=1}^{T}\ln(1+R_t) \leq \ln\left(\frac{1}{T}\sum_{t=1}^{T}(1+R_t)\right) = \ln\left(1+\bar{R}\right)$$

where the inequality follows from concavity of the logarithm function. Strict inequality holds if not all the R_t are equal. The amount by which the geometric average is less depends on the volatility: The greater the volatility of the returns, the greater the difference between the two averages.

Exhibit 4 (Continued)

Quarter Ending	3-Month Libor USD	Russell 3000 Index
31-Mar-2007	1.31	1.24
30-Jun-2007	1.31	5.95
30-Sep-2007	1.33	1.53
31-Dec-2007	1.27	−3.35
31-Mar-2008	0.81	−9.50
30-Jun-2008	0.68	−1.62
30-Sep-2008	0.72	−8.58
31-Dec-2008	0.69	−22.74

Solution:

The quarterly arithmetic means are as follows:

Three-month Libor USD:

$$\frac{(1.16 + 1.27 + 1.33 + 1.31 + 1.31 + 1.31 + 1.33 + 1.27 + 0.81 + 0.68 + 0.72 + 0.69)}{12}$$

$$= 1.10\%$$

Russell 3000 Index:

$$\frac{(5.34 - 1.94 + 4.61 + 7.09 + 1.24 + 5.95 + 1.53 - 3.35 - 9.5 - 1.62 - 8.58 - 22.74)}{12}$$

$$= -1.83\%$$

The quarterly geometric means are:

Three-month Libor USD:

$$(1.0116 \times 1.0127 \times 1.0133 \times 1.0131 \times 1.0131 \times 1.0131 \times 1.0133 \times 1.0127 \times 1.0081 \times 1.0068 \times 1.0072 \times 1.0069)^{1/12} - 1 = 1.10\%$$

Russell 3000 Index:

$$(1.0534 \times 0.9806 \times 1.0461 \times 1.0709 \times 1.0124 \times 1.0595 \times 1.0153 \times 0.9665 \times 0.905 \times 0.9838 \times 0.9142 \times 0.7726)^{1/12} - 1 = -2.20\%$$

Equation 19 provides a good approximation to the quarterly geometric mean for the Russell 3000 Index. The sample standard deviation of returns or s is 8.52 percent.

$$\bar{R}_G \cong -1.83\% - \frac{8.52\%^2}{2} = -1.83\% - 0.36\% = -2.19\%$$

The quarterly returns for the three-month Libor USD are relatively consistent during the three-year period, and because of the low volatility, the arithmetic and geometric returns are identical when rounded to two decimal places. The same cannot be said for the Russell 3000. The quarterly returns for this index vary significantly throughout the period under review, leading to considerable disparity between the arithmetic and geometric means. When evaluating more volatile assets or time periods, the differences between the arithmetic and geometric means will be even more extreme.

Geometric mean returns are useful for accurately summarizing the ending wealth that has been produced by an investment. From the definition in Section 3.2.2, we see that the portfolio ending value can be calculated from the beginning value and the geometric mean return—there is a one-to-one relationship between the geometric mean return and the relative value. In contrast, ending wealth cannot be recovered from the arithmetic mean return. In general, therefore, if the intent is to accurately summarize and report *past* returns, as is the case in performance evaluation, the geometric mean return must be used. If the intent is to forecast *future* returns or infer parameters of statistical models, the arithmetic mean return is more useful.

3.2.4 *Arithmetic and Geometric Excess Returns*

The difference between a portfolio return R and a benchmark return B is called the **excess return**. Excess return can be defined arithmetically or geometrically:

$$\text{Arithmetic excess return} = R - B$$

$$\text{Geometric excess return } G = \frac{1+R}{1+B} - 1 = \frac{R-B}{1+B}$$

Note that the geometric excess return is simply the arithmetic excess return divided by the wealth ratio of the benchmark.

The arithmetic excess return can be thought of as the profit in excess of a notional or benchmark fund expressed as a percentage of the initial amount invested. The geometric excess return can be thought of as the exact same profit in excess of the notional or benchmark fund, but it is expressed as a percentage of the *ending* value of the notional or benchmark fund.

EXAMPLE 22

Arithmetic and Geometric Excess Returns

Calculate both the geometric and arithmetic excess returns of the following portfolio for the month of May:

Portfolio 30 April	\$1,000,000
Portfolio 31 May	\$1,120,000
Benchmark return for May	10%

Solution:

$$\text{Portfolio return} = \frac{\$1{,}120{,}000 - \$1{,}000{,}000}{\$1{,}000{,}000} = 12\%$$

$$\text{Arithmetic excess return} = 12\% - 10\% = 2\%$$

$$\text{Geometric excess return} = \frac{1.12}{1.10} - 1 = 1.82\%$$

Note that if the portfolio had been invested in the benchmark, the notional value on 31 May would have been \$1,100,000. Thus the value added relative to investing in the benchmark was \$1,120,000 – \$1,100,000 = \$20,000. This, in turn, equates to an

$$\text{Arithmetic excess return} = \frac{\$20{,}000}{\$1{,}000{,}000} = 2\%$$

$$\text{and a Geometric excess return} = \frac{\$20{,}000}{\$1{,}100{,}000} = 1.82\%$$

For many practitioners, the simple subtraction between portfolio return and benchmark return or arithmetic excess return is the natural and intuitive presentation of excess return and is by far the most common method used worldwide. For other practitioners, the less intuitive geometric excess return is preferred because the returns are compoundable over time, are convertible across currencies, and are proportionate.

Geometric excess returns are compoundable because both the cumulative portfolio and benchmark returns are the compound of each sub-period, as follows:

$$1 + R = (1 + R_1) \times (1 + R_2) \times \ldots \times (1 + R_T)$$

and

$$1 + B = (1 + B_1) \times (1 + B_2) \times \ldots \times (1 + B_T)$$

Therefore, the cumulative geometric excess return is simply the compound of each sub-period's geometric excess return:

$$1 + G = \frac{1 + R}{1 + B} = \frac{(1 + R_1)}{(1 + B_1)} \times \frac{(1 + R_2)}{(1 + B_2)} \times \ldots \times \frac{(1 + R_T)}{(1 + B_T)}$$

$$1 + G = \frac{1 + R}{1 + B} = (1 + G_1) \times (1 + G_2) \times \ldots \times (1 + G_T)$$

No such relationship exists for arithmetic excess returns. They neither sum nor compound to the cumulative period excess returns.

EXAMPLE 23

Cumulative Arithmetic and Geometric Excess Returns

Calculate annual arithmetic and geometric excess returns for the portfolio data shown in the following table:

	1st Quarter	2nd Quarter	3rd Quarter	4th Quarter
Portfolio return	7.1%	11.5%	–5.0%	8.5%
Benchmark return	5.3%	14.1%	–6.2%	4.7%
Arithmetic excess	1.8%	–2.6%	1.2%	3.8%
Geometric excess	1.71%	–2.28%	1.28%	3.63%

Solution:

The annual portfolio and benchmark returns are

Portfolio: (1 + 7.1%) × (1 + 11.5%) × (1 – 5.0%) × (1 + 8.5%) – 1 = 23.09%

Benchmark: (1 + 5.3%) × (1 + 14.1%) × (1 – 6.2%) × (1 + 3.8%) – 1 = 17.99%

The annual arithmetic and geometric excess returns are thus

Arithmetic: 23.09% – 17.99% = 5.09%

$$\text{Geometric: } \frac{(1 + 23.09\%)}{(1 + 17.99\%)} - 1 = 4.32\%$$

The quarterly geometric excess returns compound to the same annual geometric excess return, as follows:

(1 + 1.71%) × (1 – 2.28%) × (1 + 1.28%) × (1 + 3.63%) – 1 = 4.32%

The quarterly arithmetic excess returns do not link directly to the annual arithmetic excess return.

Because geometric excess returns are compoundable, the annualized geometric excess return can be calculated in the same way as the annualized return using Equation 18. The annualized arithmetic excess return cannot be derived directly from the arithmetic cumulative return but can be derived from the annualized portfolio and benchmark returns.

EXAMPLE 24

Annualized Arithmetic and Geometric Excess Returns

Calculate annualized arithmetic and geometric excess returns for the three-year portfolio data shown in the following table:

	Year 1	Year 2	Year 3	Three-Year Cumulative
Portfolio return	17.6%	–5.7%	12.4%	24.65%
Benchmark return	15.8%	–7.6%	14.9%	22.94%
Arithmetic excess	1.8%	1.9%	–2.5%	1.71%
Geometric excess	1.55%	2.06%	–2.18%	1.39%

Solution:

Annualized portfolio return: $(1 + 24.65\%)^{1/3} - 1 = 7.62\%$

Annualized benchmark return: $(1 + 22.94\%)^{1/3} - 1 = 7.13\%$

Annualized geometric excess return: $(1 + 1.39\%)^{1/3} - 1 = 0.46\%$

or Annualized geometric excess return: $\frac{(1 + 7.62\%)}{(1 + 7.13\%)} - 1 = 0.46\%$

The annualized arithmetic excess return is more problematic and, by convention, is normally calculated as the arithmetic difference of the annualized portfolio and annualized benchmark returns:

Annualized arithmetic excess return: $7.62\% - 7.13\% = 0.49\%$

This result cannot be derived directly from the arithmetic difference of the three-year cumulative return, 1.71 percent.

Geometric excess returns are convertible across currencies. Using Equation 8a applied to both portfolio and benchmark returns, we observe the following relationship:

$$\frac{1+R}{1+B} = \frac{\left(1+R^{FC}\right)\times\left(1+R^{C}\right)}{\left(1+B^{FC}\right)\times\left(1+R^{C}\right)} = \frac{1+R^{FC}}{1+B^{FC}}$$

Note that the currency return in the benchmark is the same as the currency in the portfolio. This relationship means the geometric excess return will be the same in whatever base currency the portfolio and benchmark returns are presented. The arithmetic excess return will differ for each currency (provided there is a least some element of currency return). Clearly you cannot add different value simply by expressing the same portfolio and benchmark returns in different base currencies.

Currency conversions are particularly relevant for portfolio managers wishing to present portfolio performance to a client with a different domestic currency. Both portfolio and benchmark returns will be converted to the desired base currency return using the same exchange rates.

EXAMPLE 25

Geometric Excess Returns and Currency Conversions

Convert the portfolio data shown in the table below from US dollars into euros assuming the US dollar appreciated against the euro by 8 percent during the period.

Portfolio return	15.0%
Benchmark return	10.0%
Arithmetic excess return	5.0%
Geometric excess return	4.55%

Solution:

Portfolio return in euros: $(1 + 15\%) \times (1 + 8\%) - 1 = 24.2\%$

Benchmark return in euros: $(1 + 10\%) \times (1 + 8\%) - 1 = 18.80\%$

Arithmetic excess return in US dollars: $15\% - 10\% = 5\%$

Geometric excess return in US dollars: $\frac{(1+15\%)}{(1+10\%)} - 1 = 4.55\%$

Arithmetic excess return in euros: $24.2\% - 18.8\% = 5.4\%$

Geometric excess return in euros: $\frac{(1+24.2\%)}{(1+18.8\%)} - 1 = 4.55\%$

Note that the geometric excess return is the same in both currencies, whereas the arithmetic excess return appears to change.

Geometric excess returns are proportionate because they represent the added value relative to the growth in the benchmark. To illustrate this, take the example of two portfolio managers, one delivering 51 percent performance against a benchmark return of 50 percent and the other delivering 11 percent performance against a benchmark of 10 percent. The arithmetic excess returns of both managers are equivalent at 1 percent, but intuitively, the manager that has grown the portfolio by 11 percent against an opportunity of 10 percent has done better than the manager that has grown the portfolio by 51 percent against the opportunity of 50 percent. Geometrically, we capture that outperformance in that 11 percent versus 10 percent represents a $(1.11/1.10) - 1 = 0.91\%$ excess return, whereas 51 percent versus 50 percent represents only a $(1.51/1.50) - 1 = 0.67\%$ excess return.

4 RATES OF RETURN WITH EXTERNAL CASH FLOWS

We describe measures of return with external cash flows in this section. **External cash flows** are generally defined as capital (cash or investments) that enters or exits a portfolio. External cash flows occur, for example, as contributions by the plan sponsor or payments out of the portfolio to pension plan beneficiaries or as deposits and withdrawals by investors, in the case of a mutual fund or a personal portfolio.

There is an exception to the definition of external cash flow as capital that enters or exits the portfolio. If the intent is to calculate a return that reflects the impact of fees and expenses, which might literally be paid by transferring capital out of the portfolio, then such payments can be treated as reductions in the portfolio value. In this case, such payments would not be considered external cash flows. The calculation of net asset values (NAVs) of mutual funds is an example of such a treatment. Returns calculated from portfolio values recorded this way are considered net-of-fee returns. If, instead, fee payments are regarded as external cash flows and treated using the methods in this section, the resulting returns are gross-of-fee returns.

These external cash flows complicate the calculation of returns. For example, consider a bank account that began the year with a balance of \$100. Suppose we deposited an additional \$100 into the account near the end of the year. If the account pays 2 percent interest per year, we might have about \$202 in the account at the end of the year. A calculation from beginning and ending values, (202 – 100)/100 = 102%, would not give a meaningful measure of the interest paid by the bank.

Key issues for performance measurement raised by external cash flows are as follows:

- The external cash flows might not be the result of investment decisions by the portfolio manager. A calculated return that is influenced by external cash flows might not fairly depict the value of the manager's decisions.
- Returns cannot be calculated only from beginning and ending values. Valuations at other times may also be required, as well as information on the magnitude and timing of external cash flows.
- Valuations at the required dates and accurate records of the amounts and timing of cash flows might be expensive to obtain or simply unavailable. In this case, an approximate method of calculating return must be used.

This section describes measures of return with external cash flows and standard approximations for cases where complete valuation data are lacking.

4.1 Money-Weighted Rate of Return

The first return concept that we discuss here is the **internal rate of return** (IRR) calculation. Loosely speaking, the IRR is the constant rate of return that would produce the total ending value of a portfolio given the magnitude and timing of the cash flows. It gives greater weight to time periods where the portfolio has greater value than to periods where the portfolio has less value. For this reason, the IRR is also known as a **money-weighted rate of return**.

The IRR is calculated from the beginning value V_0 and ending value V_1 of the portfolio and from the amount and timing of the external cash flows. By convention, a cash flow into the portfolio is a positive flow. If a cash flow C occurred midway through a holding period, then the beginning and ending values would be related by

$$V_1 = V_0(1 + R) + C(1 + R)^{1/2}$$

If there were multiple cash flows C_k (k = 1, 2, ..., K), this expression generalizes to

$$V_1 = V_0(1 + R) + \sum_{k=1}^{K} C_k(1 + R)^{W_k} \quad (20)$$

where W_k is the fraction of the period over which cash flow k applies, namely,

$$W_k = \frac{\text{TD} - D_k}{\text{TD}} \quad (21)$$

where TD is the total number of calendar days in the period and D_k is the number of days since the beginning of the period. This **day-weighting fraction** assumes end-of-day cash flows. For beginning-of-day cash flows or other timing assumptions, the fraction should be adjusted accordingly. For example, assuming beginning-of-day cash flows, we would use TD – D_k + 1 in the numerator.

The IRR is the rate R that satisfies Equation 20. Unfortunately, there is no closed-form formula for the IRR and it must be calculated by a numerical approximation algorithm. This fact is rarely a problem because many spreadsheet programs and financial calculators have IRR functions. A possible problem arises, however, because for some patterns of cash flows, there are multiple values of R that satisfy Equation 20. For cash flows that are small relative to the beginning and ending values, however, an IRR can usually be found.

Notice that the IRR does not require valuations at the times of cash flows, only at the beginning and the end of a period. Of course, if there are no cash flows over a period, then the IRR gives exactly the same result as the familiar holding period return.

EXAMPLE 26

Internal Rate of Return: Calculation

Calculate the internal rate of return of a portfolio with the following valuation points and external cash flow (where dollar amounts are in millions):

Market value	31 March	\$56.3
Market value (prior to cash flow)	11 April	\$58.2
Contribution (made at end of the day)	11 April	\$9.8
Market value	30 April	\$69.6

Solution:

$69.6 = 56.3 \times (1 + R) + 9.8 \times (1 + R)^{19/30}$. $R = 5.61\%$ satisfies the above equation: $56.3 \times 1.0561 + 9.8 \times (1.0561)^{19/30} = 69.6$.

Note: The mid-period valuation on 11 April is not necessary for completing the IRR calculation.

4.2 Time-Weighted Rate of Return

The decision to make an external cash flow is normally not under the control of the portfolio manager. As we have noted, those decisions may significantly influence the money-weighted rate of return. A general principle of evaluation, however, is that a person or entity should be judged only on the basis of their own actions or actions under their control. To isolate the effects of the portfolio manager's decisions, the measure of return should be insensitive to external cash flows. Such a return measure is the time-weighted rate of return (TWRR).

In the investment management industry, the time-weighted rate of return is the preferred performance measure. The TWRR measures the compound rate of growth of \$1 initially invested in the portfolio over a stated measurement period. In contrast to the money-weighted rate of return, the time-weighted rate of return is not affected by cash withdrawals or additions to the portfolio. As noted earlier, the money-weighted return gives greater weight to time periods where the portfolio has greater value than to periods where the portfolio has less value. For example, if a client gives an investment manager more funds to invest at an unfavorable time, the money-weighted rate of return will tend to be depressed. If a client adds funds at a favorable time, the money-weighted return will tend to be elevated. The time-weighted rate of return removes these effects. The term "time-weighted" refers to the fact that returns are averaged over time. The key idea is to distinguish the growth in value due to the investments held from the growth in value due to external cash flows. To do so, the portfolio values *at the times of the cash flows* are required, in addition to the beginning and ending values.

Consider a given holding period within which external cash flows have occurred. Divide the period into sub-periods corresponding to the times of the cash flows, and let C_t be the cash flow at time t, as illustrated in Exhibit 5.

Exhibit 5 Times of Cash Flows

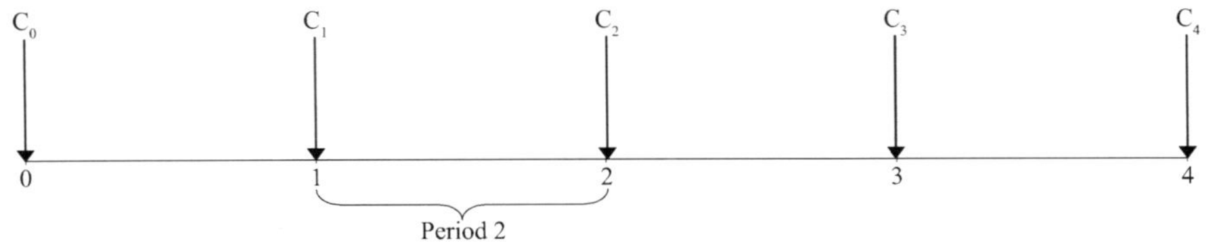

Let V_t be the market value of the portfolio *immediately before the cash flow* at time t, and let V_t' be the market value of the portfolio *immediately after the cash flow* at time t. These values are related by

$$V_t' = V_t + C_t$$

For completeness, let V_0 be the overall beginning value and let V_T be the overall ending value of the portfolio (before cash flow at time T). The time-weighted rate of return R for the full period is defined by

$$R = \left(\frac{V_1}{V_0} \times \frac{V_2}{V_1'} \times \frac{V_3}{V_2'} \times \frac{V_4}{V_3'} \times \cdots \times \frac{V_T}{V_{T-1}'}\right) - 1 \qquad (22)$$

Note that compared with Equation 12 in Section 3.1.1, the value V_t just before the cash flow at time t need not equal the value V_t' just after the cash flow at time t and, therefore, does not cancel in the preceding expression. This arises on the days when there is a cash flow, as we see in Example 27 below. It is natural, however, to define a holding period return as $R_t = V_{t+1}/V_t' - 1$ and to calculate the return over T periods by linking:

$$R = (1 + R_1)(1 + R_2) \ldots (1 + R_T) - 1 \qquad (23)$$

EXAMPLE 27

Time-Weighted Rate of Return: Calculation

1 Calculate the time-weighted rate of return of a portfolio with the following valuation points and external cash flow:

Market value	31 March	\$56.3 million
Market value (prior to cash flow)	11 April	\$58.2 million
Contribution (made at end of the day)	11 April	\$9.8 million
Market value	30 April	\$69.6 million

2 Calculate the time-weighted rate of return for the following portfolio:

Date (t)	Market Value (V_t) Prior to External Cash Flows	Transaction
30 April	\$73.7 million	
12 May	\$69.3 million	\$15.3 million contribution
17 May	\$87.3 million	\$2.7 million dividend reinvested

Date (t)	Market Value (V_t) Prior to External Cash Flows	Transaction
26 May	\$89.7 million	\$8.1 million withdrawal
31 May	\$84.7 million	

Solution to 1:

$$R = \frac{\$58.2}{\$56.3} \times \frac{\$69.6}{\$58.2 + \$9.8} - 1 = 1.03375 \times 1.02353 - 1 = 0.0581 = 5.81\%$$

Compare this result with the IRR calculated in Example 26.

Solution to 2:

$$R = \frac{\$69.3}{\$73.7} \times \frac{\$87.3}{\$69.3 + \$15.3} \times \frac{\$89.7}{\$87.3} \times \frac{\$84.7}{\$89.7 - \$8.1} - 1$$
$$= 0.9403 \times 1.0319 \times 1.0275 \times 1.038 - 1$$
$$= 0.0349 = 3.49\%$$

Note that it is not necessary for mathematical accuracy in calculating time-weighted rate of return to revalue the portfolio at the time a dividend is reinvested. In the solution above, the second and third factors can be combined as 89.7/(69.3 + 15.3), bypassing the valuation of the portfolio on May 17.

The time-weighted return has a natural interpretation in terms of the closely related concept of **unit value pricing** of mutual funds or other funds in which the assets of multiple investors are commingled (i.e., combined). In such a fund, investors may purchase or sell shares or units of the fund. The net asset value (NAV) of a unit of the fund is the total market value V of the portfolio (after netting liabilities) divided by the number of units U existing at the time of the valuation:

$$\text{NAV} = \frac{V}{U} \qquad (24)$$

When an investor deposits money to or withdraws money from the fund, the number of units changes. If V' is the market value of the portfolio immediately after the cash flow, then the new number of units U' is calculated from the NAV at that time:

$$U' = \frac{V'}{\text{NAV}}$$

The NAV of the unit does not change because of the cash flow—the number of units adjusts to maintain the identity NAV = V/U.

To illustrate this concept further, note that the change in the number of units resulting from a cash flow will be equal to the value of the cash flow divided by the NAV.

$$\Delta U = \frac{\text{CF}}{\text{NAV}}$$

Now consider two periods with an intervening cash flow. Returns calculated from the NAV can be linked over the two periods:

$$R = \frac{\text{NAV}_2}{\text{NAV}_0} - 1 = \left(\frac{\text{NAV}_1}{\text{NAV}_0} \times \frac{\text{NAV}_2}{\text{NAV}_1}\right) - 1 = \left(\frac{V_1/U_1}{V_0/U_0} \times \frac{V_2/U_2}{V_1'/U_1'}\right) - 1$$

In the expression on the right, we have substituted the identity NAV = V/U. Now, because the value V_1 is taken *immediately before the cash flow*, the number of units U_1 is equal to U_0 and cancels in the expression. Similarly, because the value V_1' is taken *immediately after the cash flow*, the number of units U_2 is equal to U_1'. Therefore, the return calculated from the NAV is equal to the time-weighted return defined above:

$$R = \frac{\text{NAV}_2}{\text{NAV}_0} - 1 = \left(\frac{V_1}{V_0} \times \frac{V_2}{V_1'}\right) - 1$$

If there are no cash flows, the formula for time-weighted return is equivalent to the linking formula (Equation 13). All the concepts of Section 3—compounding, arithmetic and geometric averaging, annualizing, and so on—are applicable. The interpretation of cumulative return, however, must be understood in terms of the growth of a unit value, instead of the growth of the total value of the fund, which is affected by cash flows.

EXAMPLE 28

Unit Value Pricing Method: Calculation

Using the data in Example 27, Question 2, assume that the number of units at the start is 10 million. Calculate the number of units added at each cash flow and the NAV at the start of the month, at each transaction, and at the end of the month.

Solution:

Date (*t*)	Market Value (millions)	Units before Flow (millions)	NAV	External Cash Flow (millions)	Added Units (millions)
30 Apr	\$73.7	10.0000	\$73.7/10.000 = 7.3700		0.0000
12 May	\$69.3	10.0000	\$69.3/10.000 = 6.9300	\$15.3	15.3/6.93 = 2.2078
17 May	\$87.3	12.2078	\$87.3/12.2078 = 7.1512		0.000
26 May	\$89.7	12.2078	\$89.7/12.2078 = 7.3478	–\$8.1	–8.1/7.3478 = –1.1024
31 May	\$84.7	11.1054	\$84.7/11.1054 = 7.6269		0.0000

The cumulative return calculated from NAV is (7.6269 – 7.3700)/7.3700 = 3.49%, which matches the conclusion that we derived in the solution to Question 2 of Example 27.

4.3 Practical Issues

The following sections address several key subtopics in time-weighted rate of return.

4.3.1 *When Is Time-Weighted Return Appropriate?*

A key difference between the time-weighted return and the internal rate of return is the treatment of external cash flows. Often, external cash flows result from decisions unrelated to the management of the portfolio; deposits and withdrawals by investors may be independent of decisions made by the portfolio manager. To usefully compare returns among alternate portfolios, either the pattern of cash flows must be the same for all the portfolios or the return measurement must be insensitive to cash flows. Consequently, time-weighted return is the preferred measure of return for comparing returns among alternative portfolios.

This point was emphasized in Cohen, Dean, Durand, Fama, Fisher, Shapiro, and Lorie (1968). This study, known as the BAI study, applied the term "time-weighted" to the method of measurement proposed by Dietz (1966). The BAI study described the internal rate of return (IRR) as a return that "measures the performance of the fund rather than the performance of the fund's manager."

Time-weighted methodologies are certainly preferred where there is a need to neutralize the impact of external cash flows. Money-weighted methodologies are typically used

- when accurate valuations and, therefore, time-weighted returns are not available (for example, for illiquid asset categories).
- when the manager is responsible for the timings of cash flows.
- when the time value of money is an important issue (for example, in a fund with a fixed termination date, an earlier distribution of capital is likely to improve the internal rate of return).

From the perspective of a client who directs the deposits to and withdrawals from a portfolio, the internal rate of return may be informative because it reflects the decisions made by the client. In some situations (in managing private equity, for example), the portfolio manager does direct the cash flows into the portfolio; in which case, the internal rate of return is an appropriate measure.

4.3.2 *Approximate Time-Weighted Return Methods*

A drawback of the time-weighted return is that an accurate valuation must be available at the time of all cash flows. Such valuations may be too expensive to obtain or simply unavailable. An approximation of the true time-weighted return must be used when the valuations are not available at the time of cash flows. The basic approximation procedure involves these steps:

1. Divide the overall time period into sub-periods corresponding to the availability of valuations. Typically, valuations are done at regular intervals, such as quarterly, monthly, or daily. (Note: For periods beginning on or after 1 January 2001, the GIPS standards require portfolios to be valued at least monthly.)
2. Calculate an approximate return for each sub-period.
3. Link the sub-period returns.

This procedure was first proposed by Dietz (1966). Variants of the method depend on the approximate return calculated in Step 2.[19]

4.3.2.1 Linked IRR Method (BAI Method) In step 2 of the basic approximation procedure, the sub-period return can be calculated using the IRR. In this case, the overall method is called the **linked IRR method**. This method is recommended in the Bank Administration Institute (BAI) study (Cohen et al. 1968) and is thus sometimes called the **BAI method**. Because the linked IRR method combines money-weighted sub-period returns by linking (which is the essence of time weighting), the method may be considered a hybrid method.

The linked IRR method effectively assumes that return is constant over a sub-period. As an approximation to a true time-weighted return, the result is reasonably insensitive to cash flows. The approximation degrades as the magnitudes of the cash flows increase. The BAI study recommended that if a cash flow exceeds 10 percent of the portfolio value, then the portfolio should be revalued to improve the accuracy of

19 Other approximation procedures that have been proposed are the index substitution method, the regression method, and the analyst's test method. See Bacon (2008). All three of these methods have largely fallen out of favor over the years.

the performance measurement. (Note: Effective 1 January 2010, the GIPS standards require managers to define what constitutes a large cash flow within the company and revalue the portfolio if the portfolio experiences a large cash flow.)

EXAMPLE 29

Linked IRR Method: Calculation

Calculate the quarterly linked IRR return of a portfolio with the following beginning and ending market values and external cash flows (dollar amounts are in millions):

Date (t)	Market Value (V_t)	External Cash Flow
31 March	\$100.3	
26 April		\$13.8
30 April	\$125.6	
03 May		\$17.8
22 May		–\$25.3
31 May	\$103.5	
18 June		\$15.6
30 June	\$142.7	

Solution:

Calculate IRR returns for each month.

April: $125.6 = 100.3 \times (1 + R) + 13.8 \times (1 + R)^{4/30}$

$R = 11.27\%$ satisfies the above equation: $100.3 \times 1.1127 + 13.8 \times (1.1127)^{4/30} = 125.6$

May: $103.5 = 125.6 \times (1 + R) + 17.8 \times (1 + R)^{28/31} - 25.3 \times (1 + R)^{9/31}$

$R = -10.89\%$ satisfies the above equation: $125.6 \times 0.8911 + 17.8 \times (0.8911)^{28/31} - 25.3 \times (0.8911)^{9/31} = 103.5$

June: $142.7 = 103.5 \times (1 + R) + 15.6 \times (1 + R)^{12/30}$

$R = 21.58\%$ satisfies the above equation: $103.5 \times 1.2158 + 15.6 \times (1.2158)^{12/30} = 142.7$

Linking monthly returns, we find that the linked IRR for the second quarter equals $1.1127 \times 0.8911 \times 1.2158 - 1 = 20.55\%$.

4.3.2.2 Linked Modified Dietz Method Dietz (1966) originally proposed a calculation for Step 2 of the basic approximation procedure that split the cash flows within a sub-period into two equal parts and assigned the pieces to the beginning and the end of the sub-period. Thus, half of the cash flow is added to the beginning value V_0 and half is subtracted from the ending value V_1. The simple or **original Dietz formula** is

$$R = \frac{V_1 - C/2}{V_0 + C/2} - 1$$

where C is the sum of all cash flows during the sub-period. Equivalently, this formula can be written as

$$R = \frac{V_1 - V_0 - C}{V_0 + C/2}$$

The obvious flaw in the simple Dietz formula is that it makes a general assumption that all cash flows occur at the midpoint of the time period being evaluated. If cash flows are actually concentrated closer to the beginning or end of the time period, the simple Dietz formula can produce distorted results. As a preferred alternative, if the timing of cash flows is available, then the simple Dietz formula can be modified to incorporate that level of detail. The **modified Dietz formula**[20] is

$$R = \frac{V_1 - V_0 - \sum_{k=1}^{K} C_k}{V_0 + \sum_{k=1}^{K} W_k C_k} \quad (25)$$

where W_k is the day-weighting fraction given by Equation 21. The modified Dietz formula is, in fact, a first-order approximation of the internal rate of return and is, therefore, a money-weighted return calculation for a single sub-period. (The same cannot be said for the simple Dietz formula because it does not accurately weight external cash flows over the performance period.) The fact that the modified Dietz formula is a first-order approximation of the internal rate of return can be seen by solving Equation 25 for V_1 and combining terms, leaving

$$V_1 = V_0 \times (1 + R) + \sum_{k=1}^{K} C_k \times (1 + W_k R)$$

which can then be compared with Equation 20.

In the modified Dietz formula, the weighted cash flows $\sum_{k=1}^{K} W_k C_k$ comprise a **beginning adjustment**, from which an **adjusted beginning value** can be calculated:

$$V_0^{adj} = V_0 + \sum_{k=1}^{K} W_k C_k \quad (26)$$

Similarly, by calculating a corresponding **adjusted ending value**,

$$V_1^{adj} = V_1 - \sum_{k=1}^{K} (1 - W_k) C_k \quad (27)$$

the modified Dietz formula can be written as

$$R = \frac{V_1^{adj}}{V_0^{adj}} - 1 = \frac{V_1^{adj} - V_0^{adj}}{V_0^{adj}}$$

completely analogous to the holding period return formula (Equation 1). If the modified Dietz formula is used to calculate the sub-period returns, which are then linked, the result is called the **linked modified Dietz method**. The linking process effectively creates a time-weighted return that approximates to a true time-weighted return.

EXAMPLE 30

Linked Modified Dietz Method: Calculation

Using the data from Example 29, calculate the quarterly linked modified Dietz return.

20 Dietz and Kirschman (1983) called this formula the **day-weighted Dietz formula**.

Solution:

Calculate modified Dietz returns for each month:

$$\text{April} \quad \frac{125.6 - 100.3 - 13.8}{100.3 + 13.8 \times \frac{4}{30}} = 11.26\%$$

$$\text{May} \quad \frac{103.5 - 125.6 - 17.8 + 25.3}{125.6 + 17.8 \times \frac{28}{31} - 25.3 \times \frac{9}{31}} = -10.87\%$$

$$\text{June} \quad \frac{142.7 - 103.5 - 15.6}{103.5 + 15.6 \times \frac{12}{30}} = 21.51\%$$

By linking monthly returns for the second quarter, we obtain 1.1126 × 0.8913 × 1.2151 – 1 = 20.50%. Over monthly periods with steady patterns of incremental cash flows, the IRR rarely differs very much from the modified Dietz return. Hence, the linked modified Dietz and linked IRR methods will tend to generate very similar results.

As mentioned previously, both approximate methods will tend to degrade as the magnitudes of the cash flows increase.

EXAMPLE 31

Approximate Methods Compared with True Time-Weighted Return

Suppose the data from Example 29 are supplemented with valuations at the times of the cash flows (dollar amounts are in millions):

Date (t)	Market Value before Cash Flow	Cash Flow	Market Value (V_t) after Cash Flow
31 March	\$100.30		\$100.30
26 April	\$114.10	\$13.80	\$127.90
30 April	\$125.60		\$125.60
3 May	\$190.50	\$17.80	\$208.30
22 May	\$260.20	–\$25.30	\$234.90
31 May	\$103.50		\$103.50
18 June	\$120.60	\$15.60	\$136.20
30 June	\$142.70		\$142.70

Calculate the true time-weighted returns for the months and for the full period. Compare the results with those from the linked IRR and linked modified Dietz methods.

Solution:

April: (114.10/100.30) × (125.60/127.90) – 1 = 11.71%

May: (190.50/125.60) × (260.20/208.30) × (103.50/234.90) – 1 = –16.52%

June: (120.60/103.50) × (142.70/136.20) – 1 = 22.08%

Second quarter: (1 + 0.1171) × (1 – 0.1652) × (1 + 0.2208) – 1= 13.85%

The true time-weighted return was 13.85 percent, compared with 20.50 percent using linked modified Dietz and 20.55 percent using linked IRR methods. The difference is due to the size of the cash flows, which are consistently large (nearly 10 percent of the portfolio value) and due to the high volatility of the returns.

4.3.3 *Consistency of Portfolio Segment Returns with the Overall Portfolio Return*

A portfolio can be divided into segments by asset class (stocks, bonds, cash, etc.), by sector, by country, by industry, or in other ways. Each segment can be regarded as a sub-portfolio for which returns can be calculated. The segment weights are the values of the segments as a fraction of the total portfolio value. For example, for a $200 million portfolio consisting of $100 million in stocks, $75 million in bonds, and $25 million in cash, the segment weights are 50 percent stocks, 37.5 percent bonds, and 12.5 percent cash. Portfolio return is found as the sum of the weighted returns of the segments. Weights and returns of segments may be calculated for a variety of analyses. It is important for weights and returns to be internally consistent: Weights must sum to one, and the weighted returns must sum to the total portfolio return.

With true time-weighted return, consistency is ensured if valuation of the segments coincides with valuation of the total portfolio. For example, suppose a portfolio is divided into two segments, stocks and bonds. Using superscripts to denote the two segments, the total beginning value V_0 is equal to the sum of the beginning value V_0^S of stocks and the beginning value V_0^B of bonds. Similarly, holding period ending values satisfy $V_1 = V_1^S + V_1^B$. The portfolio return can be written as

$$\frac{V_1}{V_0} - 1 = \frac{V_1^S + V_1^B}{V_0} - 1 = \left(\frac{V_0^S}{V_0} \times \frac{V_1^S}{V_0^S}\right) + \left(\frac{V_0^B}{V_0} \times \frac{V_1^B}{V_0^B}\right) - 1 \qquad (28)$$

Consequently, the beginning weights $w_S = V_0^S / V_0$ and $w_B = V_0^B / V_0$ are consistent with the segment returns $R_S = \left(V_1^S / V_0^S\right) - 1$ and $R_B = \left(V_1^B / V_0^B\right) - 1$. Equation 28 can be rewritten as $R = w_S R_S + w_B R_B$.

If there are cash flows without portfolio valuations, then a money-weighted method (modified Dietz or IRR) must be used for the portfolio return. If similar approximations are made for the segment returns, will the beginning weights still be consistent with the returns? Unfortunately, they will not be, in general, as shown by the following example.

EXAMPLE 32

Inconsistency of Beginning Weights with Money-Weighted Returns

Using the data from Example 29 for the month of June, suppose that the portfolio also held a second asset (Asset B) with a beginning value of $100 million that returned 10 percent for the month. Calculate the IRR and the modified Dietz return for the total portfolio. Further, calculate the weighted sum of the respective returns, using the beginning portfolio weights. (Dollar amounts are in millions.)

Date (t)	Asset A	Asset B	Market Value (V_t)	External Cash Flow
31 May	$103.5	$100.0	$203.5	
18 June				$15.6
30 June	$142.7	$110.0	$252.7	

Solution:

IRR = 16.04% because $203.5 \times 1.1604 + 15.6 \times (1.1604)^{12/30} = 252.7$.

$$\text{Modified Dietz return} = \frac{252.7 - 203.5 - 15.6}{203.5 + 15.6 \times \frac{12}{30}} = 16.02\%$$

$$\text{Beginning weights} = \frac{103.5}{203.5} = 50.86\% \text{ and } \frac{100.0}{203.5} = 49.14\%$$

Using the 21.58% IRR calculated in Example 29 for the month of June and the 21.51% modified Dietz return calculated in Example 30,

$$\text{Weighted IRR} = (0.5086 \times 0.2158) + (0.4914 \times 0.1000) = 15.89\% \neq 16.04\%$$

$$\begin{aligned}\text{Weighted modified Dietz return} &= (0.5086 \times 0.2151) + (0.4914 \times 0.1000)\\ &= 15.85\% \neq 16.02\%\end{aligned}$$

The weighted IRR calculation does not equal the portfolio IRR, nor does the weighted modified Dietz return equal the portfolio modified Dietz return, because the beginning weights are not consistent with the returns.

Using the modified Dietz formula, however, weights calculated from the adjusted beginning market values *are* consistent with the returns. To see this, we first note that the internal cash flow C of a segment is equal to

$$C = P - S - I$$

where

P = value of purchases
S = value of sales
I = value of income from assets in the segment

Income appears with a negative sign, as does sales, because both income and sales represent market values that can be used either for purchases within the segment or for transfers to other segments (or withdrawal from the total portfolio). For a given segment, the net value of purchases less sales less income equals the cash inflow to the segment.

Now, a cash flow between two assets creates flows at the segment level of equal value and opposite signs: A sale of one asset creates a purchase of another asset (into the liquidity reserve, perhaps). If all flows are correctly accounted for, then the sum of cash flows over all segments equals the cash flow at the total portfolio level. That is, for a portfolio segmented into stocks and bonds, if ΣC_S and ΣC_B are the sums of all cash flows at a given time into the stock and bond segments, respectively, then the cash flow into the overall portfolio is $C = \Sigma C_S + \Sigma C_B$. Consequently, the adjusted beginning value, Equation 26, and the adjusted ending value, Equation 27, can be segmented, respectively, as $V_0^{adj} = V_0^{adjS} + V_0^{adjB}$ and $V_1^{adj} = V_1^{adjS} + V_1^{adjB}$. The weights $w_S = V_0^{adjS} / V_0^{adj}$ and $w_B = V_0^{adjB} / V_0^{adj}$ are consistent with the returns $R_S = \left(V_1^{adjS} / V_0^{adjS}\right) - 1$ and $R_B = \left(V_1^{adjB} / V_0^{adjB}\right) - 1$. This consistency of weights and returns is a desirable feature of the modified Dietz formula.

Consistency should not be considered a trivial matter in practice. The data available for an analysis may consist of weights and returns that have been previously calculated for various uses. Sometimes weights and returns obtained from different data sources or systems might not be consistent with the return calculated at the total portfolio level. Simply defining the total portfolio return as the weighted sum of the segment returns may be a useful approach, but it is important to understand that weighted returns might not sum to the true total portfolio return.

EXAMPLE 33

Consistency of Weights and Returns: I

For the data in Example 32, calculate the adjusted beginning weights using the modified Dietz formula, and calculate the weighted sum of the modified Dietz returns. Confirm that the result is equal to the modified Dietz return of the portfolio.

Date (t)	Asset A	Asset B	Market Value (V_t)	External Cash Flow
31 May	\$103.5 million	\$100.0 million	\$203.5 million	
18 June				\$15.6 million
30 June	\$142.7 million	\$110.0 million	\$252.7 million	

Note that the cash flow of \$15.6 million was added entirely to Asset A.

Solution:

The adjusted beginning value of Asset A is 103.5 + 15.6 × 12/30 = 109.74. The adjusted beginning value of Asset B is 100.00 (there are no cash flows into Asset B). The adjusted beginning value of the portfolio is 203.5 + 15.6 × 12/30 = 209.74. The weighted modified Dietz return is

$$\left(\frac{109.74}{209.74} \times 0.2151\right) + \left(\frac{100.00}{209.74} \times 0.1000\right) = 16.02\%$$

Weights and returns calculated from adjusted beginning and ending values using the modified Dietz formula are consistent.

EXAMPLE 34

Consistency of Weights and Returns: II

Building on the data in Example 33, on 10 July the manager sells \$40 million out of Asset B, which was used to purchase an additional \$40 million of Asset A. On 31 July, the position in Asset A is valued at \$187.2 million and the position in Asset B is valued at \$72.4 million. For the month of July, calculate the adjusted beginning weights using the modified Dietz formula, and calculate the weighted sum of the modified Dietz returns. Confirm that the result is equal to the modified Dietz return of the portfolio.

Date (t)	Asset A	Asset B	Market Value (V_t)	Cash Flow from Asset B to Asset A
30 June	\$142.7 million	\$110.0 million	\$252.7 million	
10 July				\$40.0 million
31 July	\$187.2 million	\$72.4 million	\$259.6 million	

Solution:

- The adjusted beginning value of Asset A is 142.7 + 40.0(21/31) = 169.80. The modified Dietz return for Asset A is (187.2 – 142.7 – 40.0)/169.80 = 0.0265 = 2.65%.
- The adjusted beginning value of Asset B is 110.0 – 40.0(21/31) = 82.90. The modified Dietz return for Asset B is (72.4 – 110.0 + 40.0)/82.90 = 0.0289 = 2.89%.

The adjusted beginning value of the portfolio is 169.8 + 82.9 = 252.7. Note that this is the same as the beginning portfolio value without adjusting for cash flows (142.7 + 110.0 = 252.7). Because the cash flow between Assets A and B was internal, no adjustment at the portfolio level is necessary.

The weighted modified Dietz return is

$$\left(\frac{169.80}{252.70} \times 0.0265\right) + \left(\frac{82.90}{252.70} \times 0.0289\right) = 0.0273 = 2.73\%$$

Now, calculate the modified Dietz return of the total portfolio:

$$R = \frac{V_1 - V_0 - \sum_{k=1}^{K} C_k}{V_0 + \sum_{k=1}^{K} W_k C_k}$$

In this case, because there are no external cash flows (the cash flow was a transfer between sub-portfolios), the formula can be simplified as

$$R = \frac{V_1 - V_0}{V_0} = \frac{259.6 - 252.7}{252.7} = 0.0273 = 2.73\%$$

Again, weights and returns calculated from adjusted beginning and ending values using the modified Dietz formula are consistent, even after capital has been reallocated across segments.

4.4 Composite Returns

For both internal analysis and external presentation to prospective clients, managers typically group together portfolio returns to create a representative average (or **composite**) return. The GIPS standards define a composite as an aggregation of one or more portfolios managed according to a similar investment mandate, objective, or strategy and require that composite returns be calculated by asset weighting the individual portfolio returns using beginning-of-period market values or a method that reflects both beginning-of-period values and external cash flows.

As with portfolio returns, the more frequent the valuation points used in calculating composite returns, the more accurate the performance results will be. This is complicated by the fact that composites may include dozens (perhaps even hundreds or thousands) of accounts, all of which would need to be valued at the same point in time in order to calculate a true time-weighted rate of return. To reduce the complexity of composite performance calculations, various portfolio weighting methods have been developed. Acceptable methods include using weights calculated with beginning-of-period market values, using weights calculated from the denominator of the modified Dietz formula, or calculating the composite as a single portfolio consisting of all the assets of the constituent portfolios (i.e., the aggregate method).

The beginning market value weights approach is generally the simplest approach because it requires the fewest calculations. For example, consider a composite consisting of two portfolios: Portfolio A, with a beginning-of-month market value of

$25 million, and Portfolio B, with a beginning market value of $75 million. Portfolio A had a return for the month of 10 percent, and Portfolio B had a return for the month of 8 percent. Using the beginning-of-period market value approach, the composite return would be calculated as follows:

$$R = \frac{25}{100} \times 10.00\% + \frac{75}{100} \times 8.00\% = 8.50\%$$

The drawback, however, is that the weights of the individual portfolios do not take into account external cash flows throughout the period. When relying strictly on beginning-of-period market value weights, portfolios that experience positive cash flows during the period will be underweighted in the composite return calculation in relation to the assets that actually contributed to the portfolio return; at the same time, accounts that experience withdrawals will be overweighted. This issue is alleviated by applying weights calculated using the modified Dietz method because the weightings include both the beginning-of-period market values and weighted cash flows—although the calculations can get a bit more cumbersome.

Returning to our previous example, assume Portfolio A had experienced a $10 million contribution on the 12th day of a 31-day month. The composite return using modified Dietz weightings would be

$$\text{Weighted cash flow} = 10 \times \frac{19}{31} = 6.13$$

$$R = \frac{31.13}{106.13} \times 10.00\% + \frac{75}{106.13} \times 8.00\% = 8.59\%$$

The third approach, the aggregate method, compiles all the holdings of individual portfolios into one "super portfolio." Although mathematically accurate, this approach can be difficult to perform manually, particularly when working with a composite containing a large number of portfolios.

Continuing our example, assuming the end-of-period portfolio values are $38.12 million and $81 million, respectively, the composite would be calculated as

$$R = \frac{119.12 - 100 - 10}{100 + 10 \times \frac{19}{31}} = 8.59\%$$

Note that the aggregate method and the method using modified Dietz weightings produce the same result. This will not always be the case, as illustrated in the example below.

EXAMPLE 35

Calculating Composite Returns

Calculate the January composite return for the following constituent portfolios (in millions) using beginning market values, beginning market values plus external cash flows, and the aggregate method.

Portfolio	Market Value 31 Dec	Cash Flow 10 Jan	Cash Flow 18 Jan	Cash Flow 25 Jan	Market Value 31 Jan	Return
A	$10.2				$11.7	14.71%
B	$33.6				$39.5	17.56%
C	$16.7	$0.9			$20.1	14.44%
D	$25.1		–$1.2		$27.6	15.04%

(continued)

Portfolio	Market Value 31 Dec	Cash Flow 10 Jan	Cash Flow 18 Jan	Cash Flow 25 Jan	Market Value 31 Jan	Return
E	$151.3			$25.0*	$199.7	14.17%
Total	$236.9				$298.6	

* Note that the cash flow in Portfolio E on 25 January is defined as a large cash flow for both Portfolio E and in the context of the entire composite.
Value of Portfolio E on 25 Jan = $160.2 million
Value of entire composite on 25 Jan = $245.7 million

Solution:

For Portfolio E, the true time-weighted return for the month is calculated as follows:

$$R = \frac{160.2}{151.3} \times \frac{199.7}{160.2 + 25.0} - 1 = (1.0588)(1.0783) - 1 = 14.17\%$$

Beginning market value

$$\frac{10.2}{236.9} \times 14.71\% + \frac{33.6}{236.9} \times 17.56\% + \frac{16.70}{236.9} \times 14.44\%$$

$$+\frac{25.1}{236.9} \times 15.04\% + \frac{151.3}{236.9} \times 14.17\% = 14.79\%$$

Beginning market value plus external cash flow

Portfolio A	$10.2 + 0$	$= 10.2$	$\frac{10.2}{241.85}$	$= 4.22\%$
Portfolio B	$33.6 + 0$	$= 33.6$	$\frac{33.6}{241.85}$	$= 13.89\%$
Portfolio C	$16.7 + 0.9 \times \frac{21}{31}$	$= 17.31$	$\frac{17.31}{241.85}$	$= 7.16\%$
Portfolio D	$25.1 + -1.2 \times \frac{13}{31}$	$= 24.6$	$\frac{24.6}{241.85}$	$= 10.17\%$
Portfolio E	$151.3 + 25.0 \times \frac{6}{31}$	$= 156.14$	$\frac{156.14}{241.85}$	$= 64.56\%$
Total		$= 241.85$		$= 100\%$

$(4.22\% \times 14.71\%) + (13.89\% \times 17.56\%) + (7.16\% \times 14.44\%)$

$+ (10.17\% \times 15.04\%) + (64.56\% \times 14.17\%) = 14.77\%$

Aggregate method:
First sub-period return using modified Dietz

$$\frac{245.7 - 0.9 + 1.2 - 236.9}{236.9 + 0.9 \times \frac{15}{25} - 1.2 \times \frac{7}{25}} = 3.84\%$$

Second sub-period return

$$\frac{298.6}{245.7 + 25.0} - 1 = 10.31\%$$

Aggregate method total return: $(1 + 3.84\%) \times (1 + 10.31\%) - 1 = 14.55\%$

Note: The aggregate method produces a result different from the result of the beginning market value plus external cash flow method. This is because the market value plus external cash flow weighting does not take into account the revaluation of Portfolio E.

CONCLUSIONS AND SUMMARY

5

The calculation of the rate of return is complex, with many pitfalls for the unwary. There are many different acceptable calculation methodologies available to analysts resulting from the different treatment of external cash flows. Clearly there is an opportunity to manipulate returns by simply choosing the highest return or self-selecting methodologies in each period. This unethical approach must be avoided; managers should establish an internal policy for performance measurement and apply this policy consistently. Among the points made in this reading are the following:

- A holding period rate of return is the change in value created by holding the portfolio over a specified period of time. The portfolio values at the beginning and at the end of the period are essential data for calculating a holding period return.
- An internal cash flow is a transfer of value from one asset to another within a portfolio, whereas an external cash flow is a transfer of value into or out of a portfolio. Investment income (e.g., dividends or interest payments) may create an internal cash flow if the income is reinvested in the portfolio, or it may create an external cash flow if the income leaves the portfolio.
- Transactions such as purchases, sales, and income received typically create cash flows to or from a liquidity reserve, or cash asset. A portfolio rate of return can be calculated from the total value of the portfolio, which includes the liquidity reserve. The total value must also include accrued dividends and interest belonging to the portfolio.
- A portfolio of assets in multiple currencies must be converted to a base currency using currency exchange rates.
- Market values, rather than accounting concepts of book value, are preferred for calculating rates of return to accurately depict economic value.
- Various types of return can be calculated: nominal versus real, pre-tax versus post-tax, gross-of-fees versus net-of-fees, and leveraged versus cash basis returns.
- Returns over multiple holding periods can be chain linked, or compounded, to produce a cumulative return over a longer period.
- The periodicity of the return is not a characteristic of the investment; it is a parameter chosen by the performance measurer. For analytical purposes, discrete compounding or continuous compounding constitute alternative models of growth. The models are equivalent if portfolio values match at the given valuation time points.
- Two types of averages, arithmetic and geometric, are useful. Arithmetic averages can be used for statistical modeling and forecasting, having well-known properties. Geometric averages are used for accurately summarizing historical returns. Annualizing should be done only if the returns span a period longer than a year.

- An excess return is the difference between a portfolio return and a benchmark return. Excess returns can be calculated as either arithmetic differences or geometric differences.
- External cash flows complicate the calculation of returns because of their potential to distort performance results.
- Time-weighted rates of return are insensitive to external cash flows. The calculation requires valuations at the times of each cash flow. The time-weighted return can be interpreted as the growth of a unit value if the portfolio was treated as a mutual fund.
- Money-weighted rates of return are affected by external cash flows and may be appropriate if the cash flows are under the control of the portfolio manager.
- Because external cash flows are usually not under the control of the portfolio manager, time-weighted returns are preferred for comparing the performance of different funds.
- True time-weighted return can be approximated by valuing the portfolio periodically, calculating a money-weighted return for each period between valuations, and linking the results.
- If the sub-period returns are calculated using the internal rate of return (IRR), the method is called the linked IRR method. If the sub-period returns are calculated using the modified Dietz formula, the method is called the linked modified Dietz method.
- A portfolio can be divided into segments. If there are no cash flows during a period, returns calculated from the segments and weighted by the beginning weights will equal the return of the total portfolio. This condition is called consistency of weights and returns.
- If there are cash flows during a period, segment returns calculated with a money-weighted method will, in general, not be consistent with segment returns calculated with beginning weights. However, adjusted beginning weights and returns calculated with the modified Dietz formula are consistent and remain so as capital is allocated across portfolio segments.
- The GIPS standards prescribe methods of weighting multiple portfolios of a given portfolio management firm into a composite return.

APPENDIX

OPTIONAL SEGMENT

This appendix explains and concisely illustrates basic terminology and notation used in the "Rate-of-Return Measurement" reading. It should be helpful for candidates who do not have a background in investments.

1 Mathematical Notation

In this section, we discuss the use of summation and product operators. These operators are symbols used to represent mathematical operations—such as addition and multiplication—in a concise manner.

1.1 The Summation Operator

The summation operator, represented by the Greek letter sigma, Σ, can be used to represent an equation involving the adding (summation) of variables. Consider the following equation:

$$y = x_1 + x_2 + x_3 + x_4 + x_5$$

This equation can be represented using the summation operator as follows:

$$y = \sum_{t=1}^{5} x_t$$

The notation below and above sigma indicates how the addition can be performed as a set of steps. First, the index t is set equal to 1, resulting in $y = x_1$; t is then incremented to 2, resulting in $y = x_1 + x_2$; then t is incremented through 3, 4, and 5 (the limit indicated on top of sigma), resulting finally in $y = x_1 + x_2 + x_3 + x_4 + x_5$.

A memory aid is "the *s* in sigma stands for *sum*."

EXAMPLE A1

Calculating the Arithmetic Mean

The arithmetic mean of a set of items is equal to the sum of the items divided by the number of items summed. Given the following return data,

Year	Return
2006	10.6%
2007	2.5%
2008	0.5%
2009	24.5%
2010	14.2%

1 Give the expression for the arithmetic mean return using summation notation. Let R_t stand for the return in year t, and let T be the number of returns to be summed.

2 Calculate the arithmetic mean (or average) of the series.

Solution to 1:

Returns for five years are involved, so the formula to calculate the arithmetic mean return is

$$\text{Arithmetic mean return} = \frac{\sum_{t=1}^{5} R_t}{T}$$

Solution to 2:

$$\text{Arithmetic mean return} = \frac{10.6\% + 2.5\% + 0.5\% + 24.5\% + 14.2\%}{5} = 10.46\%$$

1.2 The Product Operator

The product operator, represented by the Greek letter pi, Π, is used to represent an equation involving the multiplication of a number of variables. For example, consider the following equation:

$$z = w_1 \times w_2 \times w_3 \times w_4 \times w_5$$

This equation can be represented in a concise manner using the product operator as follows:

$$z = \prod_{t=1}^{5} w_t$$

A memory aid is "the *p* in pi stands for *product*." (*Product* is the result of a multiplication.)

EXAMPLE A2

Calculating the Geometric Mean

The formula to calculate the geometric mean return is

$$\text{Geometric mean return} = \left[\prod_{t=1}^{5}(1 + R_t)\right]^{1/T} - 1$$

where R_t is the return for each year and T is the number of periods used in the calculation. Calculate the geometric mean return of the following series:

Year	Return
2006	20.6%
2007	22.5%
2008	7.5%
2009	4.5%
2010	10.2%

Solution:

Representing the annual returns in decimal form (e.g., 20.6% is written 0.206 in decimal form), the geometric mean return is

Geometric mean return

$= (1.206 \times 1.225 \times 1.075 \times 1.045 \times 1.102)^{1/5} - 1$
$= 0.1283 = 12.83\%$

2 Debt and Equity Securities: Overview

The debt market is a market for borrowing and consists of the bond market and the money market. Instruments that trade in the bond market have maturities that exceed one year, whereas money market instruments have maturities of one year or less. Governments and businesses are leading issuers of bonds. The issuer of a bond promises certain payments to bondholders specified in the bond's contract. Those promised payments are legal obligations of the bond issuer.

Equity securities can be categorized as common stock or preferred stock. Businesses are leading issuers of equity securities. In either case, any payments made to equity are not legal obligations of the equity issuer. Furthermore, payments to bond holders have priority over payments to equity holders. Common stock represents an ownership right in a company.

Preferred stock has characteristics of both debt and common stock. Like a debt instrument, preferred shareholders expect to receive a fixed payment and receive no voting rights. However, like common stock, the payment of dividends in a particular year is discretionary, although preferred dividends must be paid before any common share dividends are paid. If preferred dividend payments are skipped, they typically accumulate and must be paid before any common share dividends are paid out.

3 Debt Securities

In this section, we discuss basic concepts and calculations related to various types of debt securities.

3.1 Bonds and Notes

A bond represents an instrument that is issued as part of a borrowing agreement. The bond has a par value that represents the amount that must be repaid by the issuer to the lender when the bond matures. The par value is also referred to as the face value, principal value, redemption value, or maturity value. It is common practice to quote bond prices as a percentage of par value. Examples of bond quotes are provided in a separate section below.

Bonds generally trade in electronic (i.e., online) trading systems ("platforms") and in dealer markets (in which dealers stand ready to buy from investors who want to sell and then sell to investors who want to buy).

In most cases the issuer will pay the lender a periodic fixed interest payment known as the coupon. The coupon rate is quoted as an annual percentage of par value. The annual coupon payment is calculated as

$$\text{Annual coupon payment} = \text{Annual coupon rate} \times \text{Par value}$$

For example, if a bond has a par value of \$1,000 and pays an annual coupon rate of 4.75 percent, then the annual coupon is 0.0475 × \$1,000 = \$47.50.

If the bond pays interest every six months, as is the case in the United States, then the semi-annual coupon is calculated as follows:

$$\text{Semi-annual coupon} = \frac{\text{Annual coupon rate} \times \text{Par value}}{2}$$

The term to maturity of a bond is the number of years remaining until the principal value of the bond (or par value) is repaid to the lender. On that date, the debt ceases to exist. It is common practice to refer to the term to maturity of a bond as the maturity or term. Bonds with maturities of 1 to 5 years are sometimes referred to as short term, whereas bonds with maturities between 5 and 12 years are considered intermediate term. Bonds with maturities that exceed 12 years are considered long term. In the US Treasury market, securities with maturities of 1 to 10 years are called notes, whereas those with maturities of more than 10 years are called bonds.

Exhibit A1 below provides a summary of cash flows associated with a bond that pays an annual coupon of $\$c$, has a par value of $\$p$, and matures in four years.

Exhibit A1 Timeline of Cash Flows for a Bond

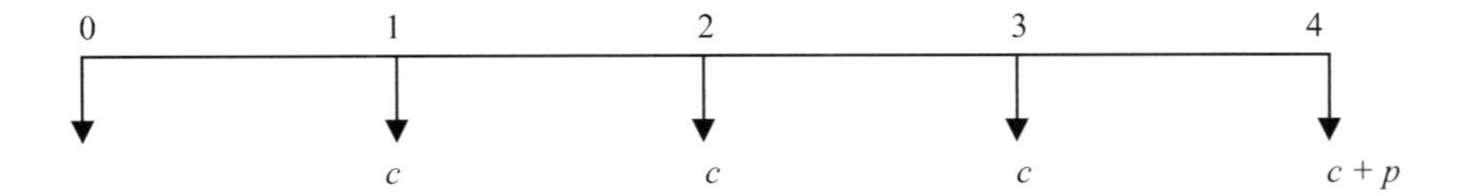

EXAMPLE A3

Treasury Bond Quotes

Exhibit A2 provides a quote for a US Treasury bond from the *Wall Street Journal* (1 June 2011).

Exhibit A2 Treasury Bond Quote

Maturity	Coupon	Bid	Asked	Chg	Asked yield
2041 May 15	4.375	102:22	102:23	+14	4.2152

This quote indicates that the bond matures 15 May 2041 and pays an annual coupon of 4.375 percent. In the United States, most bonds typically have a face value of \$1,000 and pay semi-annual interest. In this case the purchaser of the bond will receive \$21.875 every six months: (0.04375/2) × \$1,000 = \$21.875.

In the Treasury market, prices are quoted in 32nds.[21] The bid price of 102:22 is interpreted as $102\frac{22}{32}$ percent of \$1,000. This means that an investor wishing to sell this security would receive \$1,026.875. In a similar manner, an investor wishing to purchase this bond would have to pay \$1,027.1875; that is, the purchase price is $102\frac{23}{32}$ percent of \$1,000. The next column indicates that the price of the bond rose by \$4.375 or $\frac{14}{32}$ percent of \$1,000. The last column, titled *Asked yield,* indicates that an investor purchasing this bond can expect to earn an annualized yield (or yield to maturity) of 4.2152 percent. A later section provides more detail on the interpretation and calculation of the yield to maturity.

21 Quotation in 64ths and even 256ths is also possible.

EXAMPLE A4

Corporate Bond Quotes

Exhibit A3 provides a quote for a corporate bond obtained from the *Wall Street Journal* (1 June 2011).

Exhibit A3 Corporate Bond Quote

Issuer Name	Coupon	Maturity	Rating Moody's/ S&P/ Fitch	High	Low	Last	Change	Yield
WELLS FARGO & CO	5.625%	Dec 2017	A1/AA–/ AA–	113.094	111.500	112.793	0.293	3.421

Assuming a par value of $1,000, the bond pays interest of $28.125 every six months, calculated as (0.05625/2) × $1,000. The bond matures in December 2017. Corporate bonds receive a credit rating from three credit-rating agencies: Moody's, Standard & Poor's, and Fitch. These ratings are presented in the next column.

The next two columns indicate that the bond traded in a range of $1,130.94 to $1,115.00 during the day.[22] The bond closed at a price of $1,127.93. The change in price from open to the time of the quote is 0.293 as a percentage of par, or $2.93. The last column provides the yield to maturity of the bond. That is, the investor can expect to earn an annualized rate of approximately 3.421 percent if this bond is held to maturity.

3.1.1 *Calculating the Value of a Bond on a Coupon Date*

The value of a bond is the present value of future expected cash flows, to maturity, discounted by the bond's periodic yield to maturity *i*. Denoting the periodic coupon payment as *C*, the maturity as *N*, and the par value as *P*, the equation to calculate the value of a bond is

$$\text{Value} = \frac{C}{(1+i)^1} + \frac{C}{(1+i)^2} + \frac{C}{(1+i)^3} + \ldots + \frac{C}{(1+i)^N} + \frac{P}{(1+i)^N}$$

Or more compactly, using the summation notation Σ, the valuation equation is

$$\text{Value} = \sum_{n=1}^{N} \frac{C}{(1+i)^n} + \frac{P}{(1+i)^N}$$

A bond that sells at face value is referred to as a par value bond, and a bond that trades at a price above face value is referred to as a premium bond. A bond that trades at a price below face value is referred to as a discount bond.

22 Unlike the previous Treasury bond example, the quotes in this example are in cents (not in 32nds).

EXAMPLE A5

Bond Valuation on Coupon Date

By way of illustration, consider the following example. A bond has an annual coupon of 8 percent paid semi-annually. The bond matures in two years and has an annual yield to maturity of 10 percent. The par value is $1,000. The value of the bond is the present value of future expected payments:

$$\text{Value} = \frac{40}{(1+0.05)^1} + \frac{40}{(1+0.05)^2} + \frac{40}{(1+0.05)^3} + \frac{40}{(1+0.05)^4} + \frac{1{,}000}{(1+0.05)^4}$$
$$= \$964.54$$

The semi-annual coupon payment C is (0.08 × $1,000)/2 = $40. The periodic yield to maturity i is (0.10/2) = 0.05. The maturity N is four six-month periods.

3.1.2 *When a Bond Is Sold between Coupon Payment Dates*

When a bond is sold between coupon dates, the buyer of the bond will receive the full coupon on the next coupon payment. Because the buyer has not owned the bond through the full coupon period, the buyer must compensate the seller in an amount known as accrued interest. Accrued interest is proportional to the fraction of days between coupon payment dates that the bond was held by the seller. For example, if that fraction is ¼ and the coupon is $60, the amount of accrued interest is (1/4)($60) = $15. However, quoted bond prices do not generally include accrued interest. The quoted price is called the clean price. The clean price plus accrued interest is known as the full price or dirty price and is the amount of money actually received for the bond by the seller (apart from sales-related costs such as commissions). Thus, if the clean price was $920 and accrued interest was $15, the dirty price would be $935.

EXAMPLE A6

Bond Valuation between Coupon Dates

Suppose the quoted price of a bond is $900 and the bond pays an annual coupon of $50. The bond is sold halfway through coupon payment dates. Calculate the dirty price of the bond.

Solution:

The dirty price of the bond is $900 + (1/2)($50) = $925.

3.1.3 *Yield-to-Maturity Calculation*

The yield to maturity of a bond is the approximate average annual rate of return that an investor can expect to earn on a bond purchased today and held to maturity. It is also the discount rate that equates the present value of a bond's future cash flows to its price. Recall that we previously stated that the value of a bond is calculated as follows:

$$\text{Value} = \frac{C}{(1+i)^1} + \frac{C}{(1+i)^2} + \frac{C}{(1+i)^3} + \ldots + \frac{C}{(1+i)^N} + \frac{P}{(1+i)^N}$$

The yield to maturity in this equation is i. Given the price of the bond, the coupon payment, the face value, and the periods to maturity, the equation can be solved to obtain the yield to maturity. The yield to maturity consists of returns attributed to coupon payments as well as the capital gains or losses.

Yield to maturity = Current yield + Capital gains/losses yield

where Current yield = Coupon payment/Price of bond.

EXAMPLE A7

Yield to Maturity for a Discount Bond

A bond sells for \$975, carries an annual coupon rate of 5 percent paid semi-annually, matures in three years, and has a face value of \$1,000. The yield to maturity for this bond can be solved using the bond valuation equation provided above.

$$975 = \frac{25}{(1+i)^1} + \frac{25}{(1+i)^2} + \frac{25}{(1+i)^3} + \frac{25}{(1+i)^4} + \frac{25}{(1+i)^5} + \frac{1{,}025}{(1+i)^6}$$

Solving for i using a financial calculator or Microsoft Excel, we find that i = 2.96%. The bond's annualized yield to maturity is 2.96% × 2 = 5.92%.

The yield to maturity can be decomposed into the current yield and capital gains yield as follows:

5.92% = 5.13% + 0.79%

Current yield = Coupon payment/Price of bond = 50/975 = 5.13%. The capital gains yield is 0.79 percent and reflects the fact that the bond has been purchased at a discount to face value (\$975) and will pay \$1,000 at maturity.

3.2 Money Market Instruments

Money market instruments are highly marketable debt instruments with maturities not exceeding one year. Examples of money market instruments include US Treasury bills, commercial paper, bankers' acceptances, and repos or repurchase agreements. Most money market instruments carry a minimum face value of \$100,000. In the sections that follow, we provide a more detailed discussion of two well-known money market instruments: US Treasury bills and commercial paper.

3.2.1 *Treasury Bills*

The US government borrows money for short periods by issuing T-bills with initial maturities of 4, 13, 26, or 52 weeks. T-bills pay the full face value at maturity but do not make coupon payments. Investors purchase these instruments at a discount to face value, which is typically \$10,000. The difference between the purchase price and maturity value represents the investor's return from implicit interest.

Unlike Treasury bonds and corporate bonds, T-bills are quoted using a bank discount method. A T-bill quote from the *Wall Street Journal* (2 June 2011) is presented below.

Exhibit A4 Treasury Bill Quote

Maturity	Bid	Asked	Chg	Asked yield
2012 Mar 08	0.128	0.120	−0.003	0.121

The first column indicates that the T-bill matures 8 March 2012, which is 280 days from the date of the quote, 2 June 2011. The bid column indicates that the bid price or sale price is approximately 0.128 percent below the face value of $10,000, whereas the asked column indicates that the asked price or purchase price is approximately 0.12 percent below the face value of $10,000. The last column, the asked yield, is the annualized rate of return to the investor purchasing the bond today. It is also referred to as the bond equivalent yield. The asked price of the T-bill can be calculated using the following equation:

$$\text{Discount yield} = \frac{\text{Face value} - \text{Asked price}}{\text{Face value}} \times \frac{360}{\text{Days to maturity}}$$

We substitute the relevant terms into the equation:

$$0.0012 = \frac{\$10{,}000 - \text{Asked price}}{\$10{,}000} \times \frac{360}{280}$$

Solving for the asked price, we obtain

$$\text{Asked price} = \$10{,}000 - \left[\$10{,}000 \times 0.00120 \times \frac{280}{360}\right] = \$9{,}990.67$$

The asked yield or bond equivalent yield is then calculated using a 365-day year as[23]

$$\text{Asked yield} = \frac{\text{Face value} - \text{Asked price}}{\text{Asked price}} \times \frac{365}{\text{Days to maturity}}$$

$$= \frac{\$10{,}000 - \$9990.67}{\$9990.04} \times \frac{365}{280} = 0.00121 = 0.121\%$$

(or 0.122 percent based on using the rounded numbers given in the asked yield calculation).

3.2.2 *Commercial Paper*

Large, well-known companies issue short-term unsecured debt instruments called commercial paper. Maturities can be as long as 270 days, but they generally average about 30 days. These instruments typically have a face value of $100,000 and are a low-cost alternative to bank loans. Commercial paper issuance falls into one of four categories:

- AA non-financial
- A2/P2 non-financial
- AA financial
- AA asset-backed

The letters indicate perceived creditworthiness. These instruments trade in very liquid secondary markets and carry annualized yields in the range of 0.09 percent to 0.36 percent depending on maturity.

23 By money market convention, a 360-day year is frequently used to price contracts. However, the analyst can use the actual number of days in a year to most accurately determine the return or yield.

4 Equity Securities

In this section, we cover fundamental concepts regarding equity securities. We review a basic stock quote, the dividend payment chronology, valuation, and the basics of stock market index construction.

4.1 Common Shares

Common shares represent an ownership stake in a company. Common shareholders are entitled to vote at the company's annual meeting. At the discretion of the company, the shareholder may also receive a dividend payment. Common shareholders have a residual claim on the company's assets and income. That is, should the company be liquidated, common shareholders are the last in line to receive payments after all other claimants have been paid.

Common shareholders enjoy the benefit of limited liability. Should the company fail, the most that a common shareholder can lose is the original investment; that is, they are not liable for any liabilities of the company.

In the United States, stocks trade on exchanges, such as the NYSE and the NASDAQ, as well as on electronic communication networks (ECNs). We provide a quote below for IBM from the NYSE.

EXAMPLE A8

Stock Quote

Exhibit A5 below provides a stock quote from the *Wall Street Journal* (3 June 2011).

Exhibit A5 Stock Quote

	Open	High	Low	Close	Net Chg	% Chg
International Business Machines	166.44	167.10	165.71	166.09	−0.47	−0.28

	Vol	52 Week High	52 Week Low	Div	Yield	PE	YTD % Chg
International Business Machines	3,847,659	173.54	120.61	3.00	1.81	13.95	13.17

The stock opened trading at $166.44 and traded between $167.10 and $165.71 during the day, with the last trade taking place at $166.09. The stock pays an annual dividend of $3 per share. The dividend yield is 1.81 percent and is calculated by dividing the dividend per share by the price. The quote also indicates that the price-to-earnings (P/E) multiple is 13.95; that is, it trades at 13.95 times 12-month trailing earnings per share.

The main sources of return for a stock investment are price changes (capital gains/losses) and dividend income. The frequency of dividend payments during a year varies by country. Most companies in the United States and Canada pay dividends once every three months. European and Japanese companies typically pay dividends every six months. Annual dividend payments are common for Chinese companies.[24]

The chronology of dividend payments includes several notable dates: the declaration date, the ex-dividend date, the holder-of-record date, and the payment date. The declaration date is the day that the company announces a specific dividend payment. The ex-dividend date, or ex-date, is the first date that the share trades without the right to receive the next dividend. Investors who own the share before the ex-date receive the dividend; however, investors who purchase the share on or after the ex-dividend date will not receive the dividend. The holder-of-record date is two business days after the ex-dividend date and is the date that a shareholder is deemed by the company to have ownership of the stock. The payment date is the date the company makes the dividend payment. Exhibit A6 below provides a timeline of the dividend payment chronology.

Exhibit A6 Dividend Payment Timeline

A widely used equity valuation model is Gordon's constant growth model, sometimes referred to as the dividend discount model (DDM). It is a type of a discounted cash flow (DCF) model. Gordon's model maintains that the intrinsic value of a stock is the present value of all future dividend payments, assuming that they grow at a constant rate of g in perpetuity. Under these assumptions, the value, V_0, is calculated as

$$V_0 = \frac{D_1}{k - g}$$

where D_1 is the dividend payment expected next year and k is the required rate of return on the stock.

EXAMPLE A9

Calculating the Intrinsic Value of a Stock

A stock is expected to pay a dividend of \$1.50 per share next year. Dividends are expected to grow in perpetuity at a constant rate of 2.5 percent per year. The required rate of return on this stock is 7.25 percent. The intrinsic value according to Gordon's constant growth model is

$$V_0 = \frac{1.50}{0.0725 - 0.025} = \$31.5$$

24 George H. Troughton and Gregory Noronha, "Dividend and Share Repurchases: Basics" (Charlottesville, VA: CFA Institute, 2010).

4.1.1 *Stock Market Indexes*

A stock market index can be used to gauge the performance of overall equity markets or an equity market segment. In the United States, well-known stock market indicators include the Dow Jones Industrial Average (DJIA) and the S&P 500. The DJIA is a price weighted average of 30 large "blue chip" companies. This average is calculated by adding up the prices of the 30 shares and dividing by a divisor D that has been adjusted for stock splits and changes in the constituents of the 30 companies. The DJIA measures the return on a portfolio that holds one share of each of the 30 constituent stocks. The weight of each stock in the index is a function of the price of the stock.

The S&P 500 composite is a market value weighted index, where the market value of a stock is the stock price times the number of shares outstanding. This index measures the return of a portfolio of the 500 companies invested in proportion to each company's market value.

Stock indexes can provide a measure of price return or total return. A price return index reflects only changes in the prices of the stocks in the index, whereas a total return index measures changes in the prices of the stocks in the index as well as the reinvestment of dividend income.

Generally, the value of a price return index is calculated as follows:

$$\text{Price return index} = V^x = \frac{\sum_{i=1}^{N} n_i P_i}{D}$$

where the superscript x indicates that it is the value of the index without dividends reinvested.

The price return of the index, R, can be calculated by determining the percentage change in the index—for example, from Time 0 to Time 1:

$$R = \frac{V_1^x - V_0^x}{V_0^x}$$

where V_1^x is the value of the price return index at Time 1 and V_0^x is the value of the price return index at Time 0.

The return for a total return index is the price change for the index plus the return from dividend income generated by the component stocks. The return on a total return index is calculated as follows:

$$\text{Return on total return index} = \frac{V_1 - V_0}{V_0}$$

where V_1 and V_0 represent the values of the total return index (i.e., with dividends reinvested) at Time 1 and Time 0.

4.2 Preference Shares

Preference shares or preferred stock are equity instruments, but they share features of debt and common stock. Like debt instruments, preferred shareholders usually receive fixed payments. However, these dividends are paid at the discretion of the company, much like common shares. Dividends on preferred shares are generally cumulative; that is, if the company skips a dividend payment, it accumulates missed dividends and accumulated dividends must be paid to preference shareholders before the payment of any common share dividends.

5 Foreign Exchange Quotation

Domestic investors investing in foreign markets must account for the impact of currency exchange rates. An exchange rate is the number of units of one currency required to purchase one unit of another currency. An exchange rate can be quoted in two ways. For the US dollar and the euro, the two ways are

- €0.68493 per $1, which may be written €0.68493/$1 (or $:€ = 0.68493).[25] This means that €0.68493 buys $1 or, equivalently, $1 buys €0.68493.
- $1.46 per €1, which may be written $1.46/€1 (or €:$ = 1.46). This means that $1.46 buys €1 or, equivalently, €1 buys $1.46.

The two quotations are reciprocals of each other; that is, 1/0.68493 = 1.46.

EXAMPLE A10

Currency Appreciation and Depreciation

Suppose a US investor observes that the exchange rate between the US dollar and the UK pound is $1.64/£. If the exchange rate one week later is $1.75/£, it implies that the dollar has declined (or depreciated) against the pound because it takes more dollars to purchase one pound. Equivalently, the pound has strengthened (or appreciated) against the dollar because a pound now buys more dollars. The US investor in UK assets benefits from the depreciation of the dollar against the pound because on converting pounds back into dollars, he realizes a gain. By contrast, if the exchange rate one week later is $1.55/£, it indicates that the dollar has appreciated against the pound because it takes fewer dollars to purchase one pound.

END OPTIONAL SEGMENT

REFERENCES

Bacon, Carl R. 2008. *Practical Performance Measurement and Attribution*, 2nd ed. Chichester, U.K.: John Wiley & Sons Ltd.

CFA Institute. 2010. *Global Investment Performance Standards* (www.gipsstandards.org/standards/current/Pages/index.aspx).

Christopherson, Jon A., David R. Cariño, and Wayne E. Ferson. 2009. *Portfolio Performance Measurement and Benchmarking*. New York: McGraw-Hill.

Cohen, Kalman J., Joel Dean, David Durand, Eugene F. Fama, Lawrence Fisher, Eli Shapiro, and James H. Lorie. 1968. *Measuring the Investment Performance of Pension Funds: For the Purpose of Inter-Fund Comparison*. Park Ridge, IL: Bank Administration Institute.

Dietz, Peter O. 1966. *Pension Funds: Measuring Investment Performance*. New York: The Free Press, republished by TSG Publishing, Somerset, NJ, 2004.

Dietz, Peter O., and Jeannette R. Kirschman. 1983. "Evaluating Portfolio Performance." In *Managing Investment Portfolios: A Dynamic Process*. Edited by John L. Maginn and Donald L. Tuttle. Boston: Warren, Gorham & Lamont. Second edition published in 1990.

25 The different order of currency symbols in $:€ is not an error but a difference in quotation style; it can be read as "one dollar is priced at 0.68493 euros."

PRACTICE PROBLEMS

The following information relates to Questions 1 and 2

A 12 percent coupon bond was issued on 1 February 2011. The clean price for the bond was $930 on 31 March 2011 and $980 on 30 June 2011. The coupon is paid semi-annually.

1 Which of the following is *closest* to the price return from 31 March 2011 to 30 June 2011?

A 5.26%

B 5.38%

C 8.42%

2 Which of the following is *closest* to the total return from 31 March to 30 June 2011?

A 7.37%

B 8.42%

C 8.60%

---

3 A stock is held from 31 March 2011 to 30 June 2011. The 31 March 2011 stock price was $65 and the 30 June 2011 price was $83. The stock paid a $1.80 dividend on 1 February. On 15 June, the company announced that the same amount of dividend would be paid on 1 August. The ex-dividend dates are a week before pay date. Which of the following is *closest* to the total return for the equity investment from 31 March to 30 June?

A 27.69%

B 29.54%

C 30.46%

4 The value at the beginning of the year for a total return index was $1,213.47, and the end-of-year value was $1,336.42. During the year, dividend income of $7.92 was received and $5.24 of interest income was received. The value for the price index was $911.01 at the beginning of the year and $989.03 at the end of the year. If the gain from reinvested income is included in the income return, which of the following is *closest* to the income return for the index for the year?

A 1.08%

B 1.44%

C 1.57%

5 A 12% coupon bond was purchased on 1 June 2016. The clean price of the bond on the purchase date is 100. The bond pays annual coupons on 1 March. On 1 December 2016, the clean price of the bond is 102. The total return of the bond for the six-month period is *closest* to:

A 7.8%.

B 8.0%.

C 10.7%.

6 The total return for a bond is positive for a given period that lies between two interest payment dates. Given this information one:

A can conclude that the clean price has increased.

B can conclude that the clean price has decreased.

C cannot conclude whether the clean price has increased or decreased.

7 A 6 percent coupon bond was purchased for $1,000 at par when issued. The bond was sold four months later at a clean price of $1,050. Assuming that the coupon is paid semi-annually, which of the following is *closest* to the total return for the four-month holding period?

A 5.0%

B 7.0%

C 8.0%

8 A portfolio contains US dollars ($), UK pound sterling (£), and Japanese yen (¥) equities. The investor's base currency is the Japanese yen. The value of the equities in millions and the value of the currencies are shown in the following table for 31 January and 28 February of a given year.

	31 Jan	28 Feb
US equities	$110.20	$98.50
UK equities	£123.00	£135.00
Japanese equities	¥1,678.00	¥1,801.00
One US dollar buys this many euros:	0.8	0.9
One euro buys this many UK pounds sterling:	0.67	0.71
One Japanese yen buys this many euros:	0.008811	0.009126

Which of the following is *closest* to the portfolio's base-currency return for the month?

A −0.5%

B 3.0%

C 6.7%

The following information relates to Questions 9–11

An Italian investor owns 120,000 shares of a Swiss stock. The investor's base currency is the euro (€). The value of the stock in Swiss francs (CHF) and the currency values in the table below are for the beginning and end of a given year. The dividends were received at the end of the year.

	1 January	31 December
Share price	CHF 46.70	CHF 51.90
Dividend per share		CHF 2.30
€/CHF =	0.819672	0.862069

9 Which of the following is *closest* to the currency return that was made on the initial investment for this year?

A −4.9%

B 4.9%

C 5.2%

10 Which of the following is *closest* to the base-currency return for the year?

A 10.4%

B 21.2%

C 22.1%

11 Which of the following is *closest* to the return from the interaction of the local return and the currency return for the year?

A −0.8%

B 0.7%

C 0.8%

---

12 A UK investor held equity positions in US, Brazilian, and Japanese equities. The investor's base currency is the British pound (£). The equity returns for the holding period in the local currencies (LC) are shown below. The changes in the US dollar ($), the Brazilian real (R$), and the Japanese yen (¥), relative to the British pound, are also shown.

LC	Equity return in LC	Change in currency value relative to British pound
US	5%	−15%
Brazil	−4%	−6%
Japan	−12%	2%

The investor's base-currency return is greatest for the:

A US equity investment.

B Brazilian equity investment.

C Japanese equity investment.

13 An investor purchased 3,000 shares of stock at a price of $56. To purchase the stock, the investor financed 40 percent of the acquisition with borrowed funds. A month later, a dividend of $0.80 per share was received and the stock was sold at a price of $61. Trading expenses are $30 on the purchase and $30 on the sale. The interest on margin funds was 2 percent annually. Which of the following is *closest* to the monthly gross-of-fee return for the investment?

A 10.4%

B 17.1%

C 17.3%

14 An institutional investor has the long and short positions in the table below for one year.

Long Position	
Beginning Share Value	$410.00
Dividend	$3.20
Price Change	9.4%

Short Position	
Beginning Share Value	\$560.00
Dividend	\$1.20
Price Change	18.2%

The investor pays a fee of 0.75 percent times the beginning short position to borrow the shares. Assume this fee and the dividends occur at the end of the year and that the short position does not require margin. Which of the following is *closest* to the annual gross-of-fee return for this investment?

A −16.0%

B −15.4%

C −6.8%

15 The 2011 values for a pension fund are provided in the table below, in millions of dollars.

Pension Assets	
Beginning value on 1 January 2011	\$50.11
Change in value in 2011	6.3%

Pension Liabilities	
Beginning value on 1 January 2011	\$47.23
Change in value in 2011	8.4%

Which of the following is *closest* to the surplus return for this fund?

A −28.1%

B −2.1%

C 7.3%

16 A portfolio manager buys a stock and shortly thereafter sells it. The table below provides the sequence of events and stock prices associated with the transaction.

Date	Closing Stock Price	Event
2 May 2011	\$45.12	Purchase order is executed
3 May 2011	\$45.57	
4 May 2011	\$46.16	Sale order is executed
5 May 2011	\$46.91	Cash is exchanged for stock
6 May 2011	\$47.00	
9 May 2011	\$47.68	Stock is exchanged for cash

Which of the following is *closest* to the holding period return?

A 1.6%

B 2.3%

C 5.7%

17 A portfolio manager purchases 1,000 shares of stock in March 2011 and sells them later in the month. The purchase and the sale each incur a \$50 commission. The table below provides the sequence of events and stock prices associated with the transaction.

Date	Closing Stock Price	Event
7 March 2011	$21.39	Trade date of purchase
8 March 2011	$21.64	Ex-dividend date
9 March 2011	$22.02	
10 March 2011	$21.74	Settlement date of purchase
11 March 2011	$21.53	
14 March 2011	$21.36	Trade date of sale
15 March 2011	$21.40	
16 March 2011	$21.61	
17 March 2011	$21.41	Settlement date of sale
18 March 2011	$21.19	
5 April 2011	$20.70	$0.80 per share dividend paid

Which of the following is *closest* to the holding period return?

A −0.6%

B 1.7%

C 3.1%

18 An investor owns a stock during 2011. Inflation rose during 2011 as reflected in the Consumer Price Index (CPI). A dividend is received at the end of the year. The table below provides beginning- and end-of-year stock prices and CPI values.

	1 January 2011	31 December 2011
Stock price	$45.24	$38.56
Dividend paid		$2.55
CPI values	155.8	159.1

Which of the following is *closest* to the exact real return (the geometric difference between the nominal holding period return and the inflation rate) for the year?

A −11.25%

B −11.02%

C −7.20%

The following information relates to Questions 19 and 20

An initial investment of $2,500 in Fund A or Fund B generates a return of 9.5 percent per year. The tax rate applied to investment returns is 32 percent. An investment in Fund A would result in the realization of a tax on gains every year. An investment in Fund B defers the tax on gains until the investment is sold.

19 Over a one-year time horizon, which of the following is *closest* to the difference in post-tax percentage returns for an investment in Fund A versus that in Fund B?

A 3.04%

B 6.46%

C 32.00%

20 Assume both investments are liquidated in 10 years and that a tax is paid on Fund B's gain at that time. Which of the following is *closest* to the difference in post-tax annual percentage returns for an investment in Fund A versus that in Fund B?

A 0.75%

B 1.11%

C 3.04%

---

21 The portfolio manager for a pension fund incurs quarterly trading expenses of 0.20 percent. The annual investment management fee for the portfolio is 1.60 percent and is paid on a quarterly basis. The portfolio's quarterly gross-of-fees return is 5.0 percent. The pension fund sponsor (the employer) pays the fund's investment management fees. Which of the following is *closest* to the portfolio's quarterly net-of-fees return that should be used to evaluate the portfolio manager?

A 4.4%

B 4.6%

C 5.0%

22 An investor purchased a 7 percent coupon bond at par for $1,000.00 immediately after the payment of a coupon and held it 18 months. Coupons were received semi-annually and reinvested at the stated annual rate of 4 percent compounded semi-annually. The bond price when sold was $950.41. Which of the following is *closest* to the effective annual rate of return from the bond in the investor's portfolio?

A 3.7%

B 3.8%

C 5.8%

23 A fund has quarterly returns of –9.6%, 4.4%, and –4.7% for the first three quarters of the year. Which of the following is *closest* to the fourth quarter return that is required to restore the fund to its beginning-of-year value?

A 3.3%

B 9.9%

C 11.2%

24 A fund lost half its nominal value in the first year. Which of the following is *closest* to the annual nominal rate of return required over the next four years to restore the fund to its beginning real value? The inflation rate is 4 percent annually for all five years.

A 18.9%

B 20.1%

C 24.9%

25 An asset priced at $19 increases in price to $21 over one year. Which of the following is *closest* to the continuously compounded rate of return for the asset?

A 10.0%

B 10.5%

C 11.1%

26 An analyst observes the following year-end stock prices:

Year	Year-end stock price
1	\$9.14
2	\$9.23
3	\$8.88
4	\$8.93
5	\$9.22
6	\$9.99

Which of the following is *closest* to the compound annual rate of growth?

A 1.49%

B 1.79%

C 1.87%

The following information relates to Questions 27 and 28

Joan Bradham is a performance analyst for US-based Garnet Portfolio Management. While reviewing the historical performance of the firm's equity investments, she makes the following statements.

Statement #1 "If a series of equal contributions are made at the beginning of each year, the arithmetic mean is preferred over the geometric mean because arithmetic mean will provide the best representation of the investor's terminal wealth."

Statement #2 "Relative to the geometric mean, the arithmetic mean represents a more conservative estimate of an investment's average return because it is generally lower."

Turning her attention to the performance of the firm's money market fund, Bradham makes the following statements.

Statement #3 "The fund's most recent quarterly performance was quite impressive. The fund had a return of 3.2 percent, strongly outperforming its benchmark. I will report the annual performance of the money market fund to our investors as 13.4 percent, which I calculate as $1.032^4 - 1$."

Statement #4 "I have been examining the historical performance of the money market fund relative to global macroeconomic conditions. In the statistical analysis, I am predicting the arithmetic mean rather than the geometric mean because it is best suited for this usage."

27 Are Statement #1 and Statement #2 correct?

	Statement #1	Statement #2
A	No	No
B	No	Yes
C	Yes	Yes

28 Are Statement #3 and Statement # 4 correct?

	Statement #3	Statement #4
A	No	No
B	No	Yes
C	Yes	Yes

29 For a fund that uses unit value pricing and has intraperiod cash flows, the net asset value (NAV) of a unit is:

A calculated before deducting fund liabilities.

B used to calculate money-weighted rates of return.

C not affected by capital withdrawals from the fund.

The following information relates to Questions 30–32

John McMaan has just received from his portfolio manager a summary report on his investment returns for the 15-year period from 1 January 1996 to 31 December 2010. The benchmark given to the portfolio manager by McMaan has always been inflation.

Data on John McMaan's investment returns and inflation benchmark for the years 1996 through 2010

	Arithmetic averages		Geometric averages	
	Inflation	Portfolio return (nominal)	Inflation	Portfolio return (nominal)
1/1/1996 to 31/12/2010 (15 years)	4.4%	6.8%	4.0%	6.0%
1/1/2001 to 31/12/2010 (10 years)	3.8%	5.0%	3.0%	4.0%
1/1/2006 to 31/12/2010 (5 years)	2.0%	0.6%	1.5%	0.5%

30 The average annual real rate of return for the five-year period from 1 January 2001 to 31 December 2005, in analyzing historical portfolio returns, is *closest* to

A 2.6%.

B 3.0%.

C 3.8%.

31 Suppose that $1,000 was invested in McMaan's portfolio on 1 January 2006 when it could have bought 50 units of a given good. Suppose the price of that good increased with inflation from 1 January 2006 to 31 December 2010. The number of units of the same good that McMaan could have bought on 31 December 2010 with the accumulated value of the $1,000 is *closest* to (rounded down to a whole number of units)

A 46.

B 47.

C 52.

32 The highest variability of McMaan's portfolio returns, as measured by the variance, occurred in the period

A 1996–2000.

B 2001–2005.

C 2006–2010.

The following information relates to Questions 33–35

A 12 percent coupon bond is bought at par on 1 January 2011, the time of issuance. Semi-annual coupon payments are reinvested at market rates. The bond's quarterly value and the value of the portfolio (inclusive of reinvested coupons) are shown in the table below for an 18-month period.

	Bond Value	Coupons Paid	Total Value of Portfolio
1 January 2011	$1,000.00		$1,000.00
1 April 2011	$1,005.12		$1,005.12
1 July 2011	$1,022.11	$60.00	$1,082.11
1 October 2011	$992.29		$1,053.04
1 January 2012	$978.92	$60.00	$1,100.42
1 April 2012	$966.23		$1,089.24
1 July 2012	$933.90	$60.00	$1,118.44

33 Which of the following is *closest* to the portfolio's annualized time-weighted rate of return for the 18-month period?

A 7.7%

B 11.8%

C 18.3%

34 Assume that the coupons for the bond in the previous question are not reinvested but are withdrawn by the investor. Which of the following is *closest* to the portfolio's time-weighted rate of return?

A 1.9%

B 2.8%

C 7.6%

35 Using the same assumption—that the coupons for the bond are not reinvested but are withdrawn—which of the following is *closest* to the portfolio's money-weighted rate of return?

A −8.4%

B 3.8%

C 7.9%

---

36 Consider the use of the money-weighted return and time-weighted return for each of the following scenarios:

Scenario A	A portfolio manager manages a portfolio of illiquid microcap stocks and hedge fund investments for a trust. Although the trust requires annual, predetermined disbursements from the fund, the manager controls investment choices and the timing of the liquidation of investments to meet the disbursements. The manager prepares monthly valuations for the trustees.
Scenario B	A portfolio of publicly traded large-cap stocks and commodity futures for a client has performed quite well over time. The client's contributions, however, have been quite variable. In the fall of 2007, the client required a large disbursement for a divorce settlement. Contributions have been lumpy in nature because of the client's performance-based executive compensation.
Scenario C	A portfolio manager is preparing a presentation for a long-term client where the portfolio has underperformed its benchmarks, partly because the client had made a large, one-time contribution from an inheritance to the fund during a prolonged bear market. The client is considering a switch to another manager and wishes to know how much a dollar invested in the current fund at inception would be worth as of the most recent quarter.

In which of the scenarios would the money-weighted return be the *most* appropriate measure of the portfolio manager's performance?

A Scenario A

B Scenario B

C Scenario C

The following information relates to Questions 37 and 38

An investment account earns the following dividends and receives a contribution from the investor during 2010. Dividends are not reinvested in the account but, rather, are paid out to the investor. Account values reflect contributions and are after the payment of dividends.

	Dividends	Contributions	Account Value
1 January 2010			$237,000
1 July 2010	$8,000		$188,000
1 October 2010		$40,000	$220,000
31 December 2010	$8,000		$329,000

37 Which of the following is *closest* to the account's time-weighted rate of return for 2010?

A 13.6%

B 21.3%

C 48.2%

38 Which of the following is *closest* to the account's money-weighted rate of return using the IRR formula for 2010?

A 8.5%

B 21.1%

C 28.1%

The following information relates to Questions 39 and 40

A large manufacturer offers its employees a pension plan but has not paid retirement benefits yet. In April 2010, the company made a contribution to the plan. In October of that year, following a partial windup of the business, a large number of employees withdrew the value of their accumulated benefits. The pension fund earns quarterly dividends that are reinvested in the fund. The pension fund values shown in the table below reflect dividends, withdrawals by employees, and sponsor contributions (in thousands).

	Dividends	Withdrawals	Contributions	Fund Value
1 January 2010	$2,000			$93,200
1 April 2010	$2,000		$13,000	$111,300
1 July 2010	$2,000			$67,900
1 October 2010	$2,000	$21,000		$49,900
31 December 2010				$74,100

39 Which of the following is *closest* to the fund's time-weighted rate of return for 2010?

A −48.57%

B −29.78%

C −0.22%

40 Which of the following is *closest* to the fund's money-weighted return using the modified Dietz return formula for 2010?

A −31.2%

B −11.4%

C 2.2%

The following information relates to Questions 41 and 42

A mutual fund reports the following data:

- A fund's number of units at the end of August is 10 million.
- On 4 September a withdrawal is made of $8.3 million.
- On 22 September a contribution of $6.7 million is made.
- Market values in the table below are before portfolio transactions of the same date.

Additional data (all in millions except for NAV) are provided in the table. Data for the added units on 22 September and the units before flow on 30 September are purposely omitted.

Date	Market Value	Units before Flow	NAV	External Cash Flow	Added Units
31 August	$45.80	10.000	4.580		0.000
4 September	$42.30	10.000	4.230	($8.30)	−1.962
13 September	$37.70	8.038	4.690		0.000
22 September	$43.60	8.038	5.424	$6.70	?
30 September	$47.50	?	5.122		0.000

41 Which of the following is *closest* to the added units on 22 September?

A 0.810

B 0.834

C 1.235

42 Which of the following is *closest* to the time-weighted rate of return for September?

A 2.44%

B 3.71%

C 11.83%

The following information relates to Questions 43–45

The following table provides information for a portfolio composed of two assets, Asset A and Asset B, for the month of December. Contributions and withdrawals occur at the end of the day.

	Date (t)	Asset A	Asset B
Market Value	30 Nov	\$241.00	\$88.00
Contribution	3 Dec	\$34.00	\$12.00
Withdrawal	22 Dec	\$14.00	\$9.00
Market Value	31 Dec	\$289.00	\$86.00

43 Given the figures in the table, which of the following is *closest* to the IRR for December for Asset A?

A 3.5%

B 8.3%

C 10.5%

44 Given the figures in the table, which of the following is *closest* to the Modified Dietz return for December for Asset B?

A −5.49%

B −5.20%

C 1.25%

45 In this example, the modified Dietz return for the entire portfolio will be consistent with the modified Dietz return for the portfolio segments when the segment weightings are based on

A end-of-period values.

B beginning-of-period values.

C beginning-of-period values adjusted for external cash flows.

The following information relates to Questions 46–50

Stephan Ryan began investing money in a registered education saving plan (RESP) for two of his grandchildren, Laura and Noah, in 2009 and for his third grandchild, Sophia, in 2010. Ryan has decided that the investments would be initially in bonds in Laura's account, in stocks in Noah's account, and in real estate investment trusts in Sophia's account.

46 Financial data for the individual accounts for March and April 2009 are shown below. During that period, there was no purchase or sale of securities in any of the accounts and no contribution or withdrawal.

Data on the individual accounts of the RESP for March and April 2009 (in thousands of dollars except for returns)

	Laura	Noah
Market value on 1 March 2009	80.0	20.0
Coupons received on 15 March 2009 and reinvested in Laura's portfolio	3.2	—
Dividends received on 15 March 2009 and held in cash in Noah's portfolio	—	0.6

(continued)

(Continued)

	Laura	Noah
Total return from 1 March 2009 to 30 April 2009	5%	not available
Price return from 1 March 2009 to 30 April 2009	not available	−1%

The total return of the RESP for the period from 1 March 2009 to 30 April 2009 was equal to:

A 3.8%.

B 4.4%.

C 4.6%.

47 Data for the individual accounts for the year 2010 are shown below (amounts in thousands of dollars):

	Laura	Noah	Sophia	Total RESP Fund
Market value on 1 January	100.0	40.0	0	140.0
New contributions made on 31 January	10.0	20.0	30.0	60.0
Market value 31 December	105.0	65.0	31.0	201.0

If the method used is to weight the modified Dietz return of the individual accounts with the weights of those accounts at the beginning of the year, the RESP fund return in 2010 is *closest* to:

A −0.82%.

B −0.11%.

C 0.00%.

48 Based on the same data as in the previous question, if one weights the modified Dietz returns of the individual accounts with the adjusted beginning values (i.e., the weights of those accounts at the beginning of the year adjusted for the new contributions made during the year), the RESP fund return in 2010 is *closest* to:

A 0.51%.

B 0.69%.

C 1.18%.

49 Ryan is aware that there were large variations of returns in the RESP accounts during the year and decides to analyze the 2010 results using time-weighted rates of return. For that purpose he adds to his data the values of the accounts immediately before the new contributions were made. The complete financial data are presented below:

Data on Individual Accounts of the RESP for the year 2010 (amounts in thousands of dollars)

	Laura	Noah	Sophia	Total RESP Fund
Market value on 1 January	100.0	40.0	0	140.0
Market value on 31 January before new contributions	80.0	45.0	0	125.0

(Continued)

	Laura	Noah	Sophia	Total RESP Fund
New contributions made on 31 January	10.0	20.0	30.0	60.0
Market value 31 December	105.0	65.0	31.0	201.0

The contribution of Sophia's account return to the total RESP fund return for the period from 31 January to 31 December 2010 is *closest* to:

A 0.51%.

B 0.54%.

C 3.06%.

50 Based on the data in Question 50, Ryan intends to write the following in his summary report on the RESP fund:

"For the period from 1 January 2010 to 31 December 2010, the rate of return

- in Laura's account, that best reflects the influence of the timing of external cash flows, is below –4 percent." (**Statement 1**)
- "in Noah's account, that best reflects the investment management of the assets irrespective of the timing of external cash flows, is above 12 percent." (**Statement 2**)
- "in Sophia's account, that best reflects the investment management of the assets irrespective of the timing of external cash flows but still reflects the fact that money was deposited for the first time only on 31 January, is above 3.5 percent." (**Statement 3**)

Which of Ryan's statements is *incorrect*?

A Statement 1

B Statement 2

C Statement 3

SOLUTIONS

1 A is correct. The semi-annual coupon is 12%/2 X $1,000 = $60.00. There are two months between 1 February and 31 March, therefore the accrued interest from 1 February to 31 March is $60 X 2/6 = $20.If the bond was purchased on 31 March, the bond investor would pay $20 in accrued interest as well as the clean price of the bond, therefore the dirty price of the bond (total price) paid on 31 March would be $930.00 + $20 = $950.00. The clean price at the sale date is $980.00. The price return is the change in the clean prices of the bonds between 30 June and 31 March divided by the dirty price on 31 March:

$$\text{Price Return} = \frac{\$980 - \$930}{\$950} = 5.26\%$$

B is incorrect and is calculated by using the clean prices in both the denominator and the numerator. C is incorrect and is calculated using the dirty prices in both the numerator and denominator.

2 B is correct. From the previous question, the bond investor would pay $20 in accrued interest on 31 March. There are five months between 1 February and 30 June. The accrued interest from 1 February to 30 June is $60 × 5/6 = $50. If the bond is sold on 30 June, the bond investor receives $50 in accrued interest. So, the investor would pay $20 but would later receive $50; therefore, the investor would net $30 in interest. Thus, the change in accrued interest between 31 March and 30 June is $50 − $20 = $30. The income return is the change in accrued interest divided by the dirty price paid: $30/$950 = 3.16%.

Using the answer from the previous question, the total return is the sum of the income and price return: 3.16% + 5.26% = 8.42%. Or it can be shown as

$$\text{Total return} = \frac{\$980 - \$930 + \$30}{\$950} = 0.0842 = 8.42\%$$

Alternatively, we can calculate the total return as the percentage change in dirty prices. The dirty price on 30 June is $50 + $980 = $1,030.

$$\text{Total return} = \frac{\$1{,}030 - \$950}{\$950} = 0.0842 = 8.42\%$$

A is incorrect and is calculated by using two months of interest in the calculation of the income return. C is incorrect and is calculated by using the clean prices in the calculations of price and income return.

3 A is correct. There is no income return here because a dividend was not received. The investor purchased the stock after the January ex-dividend date and sold it before the July ex-dividend date. Note that there is no accrual of the dividend amount as there is for bond coupons. When investing in bonds, there is accrual of income between coupon payment dates and that accrual of income is paid to the seller from the buyer; the clean price, also called the quoted price, does not include that accrual of income. For stocks the present value of any expected dividend is included in the quoted stock price. So, the total return is equal to the price return because the income return is zero:

$$\text{Total return} = \frac{V_1 - V_0 + D}{V_0} = \frac{\$83 - \$65 + \$0}{\$65} = \frac{\$18.00}{\$65} = 0.2769 = 27.69\%$$

B is incorrect because four months of dividends are included in the income return component. C is incorrect because six months of dividends are included in the income return component.

4 C is correct. If the gain from reinvested income is included in the income return, we will calculate the total return for the index and subtract the price return to arrive at the income return. This question illustrates Case 1 in Section 2.1 of the text. The total return is calculated as

$$\text{Total return} = \frac{V_1 - V_0}{V_0} = \frac{\$1{,}336.42 - \$1{,}213.47}{\$1{,}213.47} = \frac{\$122.95}{\$1{,}213.47} = 0.1013 = 10.13\%$$

The price return is exclusive (x) of the gain from reinvested income and is

$$\text{Price return} = \frac{V_1^x - V_0^x}{V_0^x} = \frac{\$989.03 - \$911.01}{\$911.01} = \frac{\$78.02}{\$911.01} = 0.0856 = 8.56\%$$

The income return includes the gain from reinvested income and is the difference between the total return and the price return: 10.13% – 8.56% = 1.57%.

A is incorrect and is calculated as the sum of the dividend and interest income divided by the beginning-of-year total return index value:

$$\frac{D}{V_0} = \frac{\$7.92 + \$5.24}{\$1{,}213.47} = 0.0108 = 1.08\%$$

This response illustrates including gains from reinvested income in the price return, not the income return as specified. B is incorrect and is calculated as the sum of the dividend and interest income divided by the beginning-of-year price index value.

5 A is correct. The total return for a bond purchased and sold within a single period is calculated based on the change in the clean price plus any change in accrued interest. The change in the clean price was 2. On 1 June (purchase date), the bond had accrued interest of 3 = 100 × 12% × (3/12). As of 1 December (sell date), the bond had accrued interest of 9 = 100 × 12% × (9/12). The change in accrued interest is 9 – 3 = 6.

Total return is calculated as follows:

Total return = (Ending clean price – Beginning clean price + Change in accrued interest)/(Beginning dirty price),

Total return = (102 – 100 + 6)/(100 + 3),

Total return = 7.77%.

6 C is correct. From the information given, one cannot establish whether the clean price increased or decreased. The total return of a bond incorporates both the change in the clean price and the change in accrued interest. It is possible to have a positive total return along with a decrease in the clean price if the change in accrued interest is positive and larger than the decrease in the clean price.

7 B is correct. The semi-annual coupon is 6%/2 × \$1,000 = \$30. The accrued interest over four months is \$30 × 4/6 = \$20. When the bond is sold at the end of the four-month holding period, the investor receives \$20 in income. Because the bond was bought at par and is sold at the clean price of \$1,050, the holding period return is

$$\frac{\$1{,}050 - \$1{,}000 + \$20}{\$1{,}000} = 0.07 = 7.0\%$$

A is incorrect and omits the accrued interest. C is incorrect and is calculated by using six months of accrued interest.

8 A is correct. It will be easiest to convert all the portfolio values and corresponding returns to a common currency. We'll use the euro (the common currency in all the exchange rates is the euro) and then convert the euro values to yen values. First, let's restate the exchange rates in the table. For the beginning values, we have €0.80/\$, £0.67/€, and €0.008811/¥, respectively. For the ending values, we have €0.90/\$, €/£0.71, and €0.009126/¥, respectively. Then, converting the beginning and ending values to euros, we have

Beginning Value: (\$110.2 × €0.80/\$) + (£123.0 × €/£0.67) + (¥1,678.0 × €0.008811/¥) = €286.5269

Ending Value: (\$98.5 × €0.90/\$) + (£135.0 × €/£0.71) + (¥1,801.0 × €0.009126/¥) = €295.2268

Note that for each calculation, we simply set up the formula so the other currencies cancel and we are left a value in euros. Note also that the pound–euro calculation uses an exchange rate stated in terms of the euro. So, we must invert this rate in the calculation. The fund's return in euros is then €295.2268/€286.5269 – 1 = 3.0363%.

To convert this to a yen return, first calculate the euro appreciation/depreciation relative to the yen. Because we are interested in the euro change in value, we put that currency in the denominator of a percentage change calculation:

$$\frac{¥/€0.009126}{¥/€0.008811} - 1 = -3.4517\%$$

The return in yen is then the compounding of the equity return in euros and the euro change in value: (1.030363) × (1 – 0.034517) – 1 = –0.52%.

You can practice by calculating the returns in the dollar and pound. The change in the value of the euro relative to the dollar is

$$\frac{\$/€0.9}{\$/€0.8} - 1 = -11.11\%$$

The change in the value of dollar equity is (1.030363) × (1 – 0.1111) – 1 = –8.41%.

The change in the value of the euro relative to the pound is (again putting the euro in the denominator because it is its change we are interested in)

$$\frac{£0.71/€}{£0.67/€} - 1 = 5.9701\%$$

The change in the value of pound equity is (1.030363) × (1.059701) – 1 = 9.19%.

Another way of calculating the return in yen is to compare the beginning and ending values of the portfolio in yen. The beginning value in yen using the 31 January exchange rates is equal to

$$110.20 \text{ dollars} \times \frac{1}{0.008811}\left(\frac{\text{yen}}{\text{euro}}\right) \times 0.8\left(\frac{\text{euro}}{\text{dollar}}\right)$$

$$+\ 123.00 \text{ pounds} \times \frac{1}{0.008811}\left(\frac{\text{yen}}{\text{euro}}\right) \times \frac{1}{0.67}\left(\frac{\text{euro}}{\text{pound}}\right)$$

$$+\ 1{,}678 \text{ yen}$$

$$= 10{,}005.67 \text{ yen} + 20{,}835.56 \text{ yen} + 1{,}678 \text{ yen}$$

$$= 32{,}519.23 \text{ yen}$$

The ending value in yen, using the 28 February exchange rates, could be calculated in a similar manner and is equal to 32,350.07. So, the February return in yen is equal to

$$\frac{32{,}350.07 - 32{,}519.23}{32{,}519.23} = -0.52\%$$

B is incorrect because it is the return in euros. C is incorrect because it inverts the currency return.

9 C is correct. The currency return is defined as $R^C = \left(S_1^{d/f} / S_0^{d/f}\right) - 1.$

$$R^C = (0.862069/0.819672) - 1 = 5.17\%$$

CHF has strengthened against the euro because at year-end it takes fewer CHF to buy a euro.

A is incorrect because it inverts the currency return. B is incorrect because it uses the currency gain divided by the ending value (not the beginning value).

10 C is correct. The most direct method of calculating the return in the base currency (€) is to calculate the local return in Swiss francs and the currency change in value. The local return in Swiss francs factors in the capital gain and dividend:

$$\frac{\text{CHF}51.90 + 2.30}{\text{CHF}46.70} - 1 = 16.06\%$$

The base return (€) is then the compounded return of the holding period return in Swiss francs and the currency return (already calculated as 5.17%): (1.1606)(1.0517) – 1 = 22.06%.

A is incorrect because it inverts the currency return. B is incorrect because it does not use the entire currency return component (i.e., it does not include the interaction term).

11 C is correct.

The interaction return is the third term of Equation 8b in the reading:

$$R = R^{FC} + R^C + R^{FC}R^C$$

where

R = base-currency return

R^{FC} = local return

R^C = currency return

$R^{FC} \times R^C$ = return due to the interaction of the local return and the currency return

$$\text{Here, } R^{FC}R^C = \left[\frac{51.90 + 2.30}{46.70} - 1\right]\left[\frac{0.862069}{0.819672} - 1\right] = 0.83\%$$

A is incorrect because it inverts the currency return. B is incorrect because it divides the interaction gain by the ending value (not the beginning value).

12 B is correct. The investor's base-currency return will be a function of the change in the currency value (currency return), the equity return in local currency (local return), and the interaction between the two. This is shown in Equation 8:

$$R = (1 + R^C) \times (1 + R^{FC}) - 1$$
$$= R^C + R^{FC} + (R^C \times R^{FC})$$

In all three countries, the simple sum of the first two components is −10% (e.g., Japan: −12% + 2% = −10%). However, a simple sum of returns does not factor in the third term, the interaction between the equity local return and the currency return. Notice that the third term is positive for only the Brazilian market because it is the product of two negative values. Therefore, the Brazilian market will have a base-currency return slightly higher than −10%, whereas the US and Japanese markets will have returns slightly less than −10%. You can verify that the Brazilian market will provide the highest base-currency return:

United States: $R = (1 - 0.15)(1 + 0.05) - 1 = -10.75\%$

Brazil: $R = (1 - 0.06)(1 - 0.04) - 1 = -9.76\%$

Japan: $R = (1 + 0.02)(1 - 0.12) - 1 = -10.24\%$

The intuition as to why the Brazilian market's interaction term will be positive and slightly boost the return (even though both equity and currency returns are negative) can be understood from the text decomposition of returns into areas. In this example for Brazil, the calculation for Area C, the currency change in value, assumes that the beginning equity value is multiplied by a currency depreciation. However, the ending value for the Brazilian equity is actually what will be converted to British pounds. Because the ending equity value is smaller than the beginning value, the calculation for Area C overestimates the loss from the currency depreciation. The calculation for Area D, the interaction term, then corrects the overestimation.

13 B is correct. The total purchase price is 3,000 × \$56 = \$168,000. The investor must put up equity of 60% × \$168,000 = \$100,800. The remaining \$67,200 is borrowed. Including the trading expenses on the stock purchase, the total initial equity investment is \$100,830. In one month, the sales price is 3,000 × \$61 = \$183,000 and the capital gain is \$183,000 – \$168,000 = \$15,000. Dividends received are 3,000 × \$0.80 = \$2,400. Interest paid for the month is \$67,200 × 2%/12 = \$112.

Including the expenses on the sale, the gain on the transaction in one month is \$15,000 + \$2,400 – \$112 – \$30 = \$17,258. Subtracting the trading expenses on the purchase of \$30 results in a total gain of \$17,228. The return on the equity investment is \$17,228/\$100,830 = 17.1%.

Using the formula in the text, we would first estimate the cash basis return:

= (Capital gain + Dividends – Trading expenses)/Beginning investment

= (\$15,000 + \$2,400 – \$30 – \$30)/\$168,030 = 10.32%

The leverage ratio, L, equals 0.40 because the equity is 60%. Using the text formula,[1]

$$R_{LE} = \frac{R_{CB} - iL}{1 - L} = \frac{0.1032 - 0.02/12(0.4)}{1 - 0.40} = \frac{0.1025}{0.60} = 0.1709 = 17.1\%$$

A is incorrect because it assumes leverage is not used and omits trading costs. C is incorrect because it assumes leverage is used but at no interest cost. It also omits trading costs.

14 A is correct. The long-position price appreciation is $410 × 9.4% = $38.54. Adding the dividend provides a profit of $41.74. The stock short increases in price, so the investor suffers a loss of $560 × 18.2% = $101.92. The institutional investor owes a dividend of $1.20 to the stock owner. The borrowing cost is $560 × 0.75% = $4.20. The loss on the short position is then –$101.92 – $1.20 – $4.20 = –$107.32.

The initial investment is the cost of the long position because the short position does not require margin in this problem. The total return on both the long and short is ($41.74 – $107.32)/$410 = –16.0%. Note that the gain on the long position is outweighed by the loss on the short position. In a long position, the gains are unlimited because there is no limit on asset price appreciation. Losses are limited to the original investment amount. In a short position, however, gains are limited to 100 percent (the minimum stock price is zero) and losses are unlimited (the stock price upside is theoretically unlimited).

B is incorrect because it assumes that the dividend in the short position is received (rather than paid). C is incorrect because it assumes that an initial investment in the short position must be made.

15 A is correct. The fund's beginning surplus was $50.11 – $47.23 = $2.88. The pension assets have increased in value to $50.11 × 1.063 = $53.27. The pension liabilities have increased in value to $47.23 × 1.084 = $51.20. The new surplus is $53.27 – $51.20 = $2.07. The decline in the surplus on a percentage basis is $2.07/$2.88 – 1 = –28.1%.

B is incorrect because it is the return on the assets minus the return on the liabilities. C is incorrect because it is the return on a portfolio of assets and liabilities.

16 B is correct. 2 May is the trade date for the purchase, which is the appropriate date for accounting for the purchase. The stock price at which the order was executed on the trade date, $45.12, is also the appropriate price for accounting. The settlement date for the purchase is 5 May, which is when the portfolio manager pays the $45.12 cash for the stock.

The trade date for the sale is 4 May. The settlement date for the purchase is 9 May, which is when the portfolio manager receives $46.16 in cash for the stock. The goal of performance measurement is to determine whether the manager adds value. The trade date and the price on that date best reflect the timing and cash flow implication of the manager's decision. No dividends were paid, so the holding period return is

$$\frac{V_1 - V_0 + D}{V_0} = \frac{\$46.16 - \$45.12 + 0}{\$45.12} = \frac{\$1.04}{\$45.12} = 0.0230 = 2.30\%$$

1 If you carry this calculation out several decimal places, the 17.1% calculated using the text formula is not exactly the same as the 17.1% calculated previously. The latter return is 0.002% higher because the trading expenses increase the initial investment and are not margined.

A is incorrect because it uses settlement dates. C is incorrect because it uses the first trade date and last settlement date prices.

17 C is correct. We will use the 7 March and 14 March trade date prices ($21.39 and $21.36) to determine the capital gain from the purchase and sale. We use trade date prices, not settlement date prices, for manager evaluation because the order will be executed at trade date prices. Even though the pay date is in April, the investor will receive the dividend because the stock was purchased on the record date. The trading day before the ex-dividend day (8 March) is the record date (7 March). The record date is the last day an investor can own the share and be entitled to receive the dividend. The holding period return should recognize the value of the dividend even though it had not yet been paid.

The investor bought and sold 1,000 shares and received an $0.80 per share dividend. The commission was $50 on the purchase and $50 on the sale, so the holding period return is

$$= \frac{\$21{,}360 - \$21{,}390 + \$800 - \$50 - \$50}{\$21{,}390} = \frac{\$670}{\$21{,}390} = 0.0313 = 3.13\%$$

A is incorrect because it omits the dividends. B is incorrect because it uses settlement dates.

18 B is correct. The nominal holding period return is

$$\frac{V_1 - V_0 + D}{V_0} = \frac{\$38.56 - \$45.24 + \$2.55}{\$45.24} = \frac{-\$4.13}{\$45.24} = -0.0913 = -9.13\%$$

The inflation rate over the year is

$$IR = \frac{I_1}{I_0} - 1 = \frac{159.1}{155.8} - 1 = 2.12\%$$

To solve for the geometric difference (the real return calculated exactly) between the nominal holding period return and the inflation rate, we use

$$R^{real} = \frac{1 + R}{1 + IR} - 1 = \frac{1 - 0.0913}{1 + 0.0212} - 1 = -11.02\%$$

A is incorrect because −11.25% is the arithmetic difference (the approximate real return) between the nominal holding period return and the inflation rate. It is calculated as −9.13% − 2.12% = −11.25%. Although the approximate real return is acceptable in many cases, especially when the difference between the exact and approximate real returns is small, the question asks for the geometric difference (exact calculation of the real return). C is incorrect and compounds the nominal return with the inflation rate instead of discounting it.

19 A is correct. The pre-tax future value for an investment in Fund A or B is $2,500 × 1.095 = $2,737.50. Applying the tax to the $237.50 gain in the case of Fund A, the after-tax future value = $2,500 + $237.50 × (1 − 0.32) = $2,661.50.

Alternatively, we could have calculated the $2,661.50 by applying the tax to the return in the future value calculation: $\$2{,}500 \times [1 + 0.095(1 - 0.32)]^1 =$ $2,661.50. The term in brackets, [1 + 0.095(1 − 0.32)], is essentially an after-tax annual return.

The post-tax percentage return for an investment in Fund A is $\$2{,}661.50 = \$2{,}500 \times (1 + R)^1$ implies $R = 6.46\%$. This is a reduction of 9.5% − 6.46% = 3.04%. Note that it would have been simpler, but perhaps less instructive, to multiply the 9.5% return by the tax rate to obtain the performance difference: 9.5% × 0.32 = 3.04%.

The solution can also be obtained as follows:

Difference in post-tax return between Fund B and Fund A

= Rate of return with no tax – Rate of return after 32% tax

= 9.5% – 9.5% × (1 – 0.32)

= 3.04%

B is incorrect and is calculated as 9.5% × (1 – 0.32) = 6.46%. C is incorrect and is the reduction of future value from taxes of $76.00 ($2,737.50 – $2,661.50). On a percentage basis, this is the tax rate of 32.0% [$76.00/($2,737.50 – $2,500)].

20 A is correct. For Fund A, we can use the after-tax future value calculation from the previous question over 10 years: $2,500 × [1 + 0.095(1 – 0.32)]^{10} = $4,675.25. For Fund B, we apply the 32% tax rate against the cumulative gain over 10 years. The future value of Fund B is $2,500 × [1 + 0.095]^{10} = $6,195.57. The gain is $6,195.57 – $2,500 = $3,695.57. The tax on the gain is $3,695.57 × 0.32 = $1,182.58. The after-tax future value is $6,195.57 – $1,182.58 = $5,012.99.

The post-tax percentage return for an investment in Fund A is $4,675.25 = $2,500 × $(1 + R)^{10} \rightarrow R$ = 6.46%.

The post-tax percentage return for an investment in Fund B is $5,012.99 = $2,500 × $(1 + R)^{10} \rightarrow R$ = 7.21%.

Applying tax on an annual basis (Fund A) versus a tax applied on a deferred gain (Fund B) results in an annual return reduction of 7.21% – 6.46% = 0.75%.

The solution can also be obtained as follows:

Difference in post-tax return between Fund B and Fund A

= Rate of return when 32% tax is paid at end of 10 years only – Rate of return when 32% tax is paid annually

$$= \left\{\left[(1 + 0.095)^{10} - 1\right] \times (1 - 0.32) + 1\right\}^{1/10} - 1 \text{ minus } \left\{\left[1 + 0.095 \times (1 - 0.32)\right]^{10}\right\}^{1/10} - 1$$

= 7.21% – 6.46%

= 0.75%

B is incorrect and is calculated by taxing the entire future value for B (not just the gain). C is incorrect and is calculated as 9.5% – 6.46% = 3.04%.

21 B is correct. Trading expenses are already accounted for in the gross-of-fees return, so they are not netted from the fund's 5.0 percent return. Although the employer pays the fund's investment management fees, the net-of-fees return will still be net of the investment management fees.

To calculate the net-of-fees return, we calculate the quarterly investment management fee: 1.60%/4 = 0.40%. The net-of-fees return is then

$$\text{Net-of-fees return} = \frac{(1 + 5.0\%)}{(1 + 0.4\%)} - 1 = \frac{1.05}{1.004} - 1 = 4.6\%$$

A is incorrect and is calculated by including trading expenses in the calculation. C is incorrect and is calculated by omitting the investment management fees.

22 B is correct. To calculate the effective annual return for the bond over the 18-month holding period, the terminal value of the investment must be determined. The terminal value consists of the price of the bond at the end of the 18 months plus the sum of the coupons reinvested at the 4 percent interest rate compounded semi-annually or 2 percent per six-month period. The coupons are \$35 each (7%/2 × \$1,000). The first coupon (received 12 months ago) is reinvested for two 6-month periods, the second coupon is reinvested for one period, and the last coupon earns no interest. Their reinvested values at the end of the 18 months are

Terminal value of first coupon: $\$35 \times 1.02^2 = \$36.41$.

Terminal value of second coupon: $\$35 \times 1.02 = \$35.70$.

Terminal value of third coupon: \$35.00.

Sum of the value of the reinvested coupons is \$36.41 + \$35.70 + \$35.00 = \$107.11.

The bond price when sold was \$950.41, so the total terminal value is \$950.41 + \$107.11 = \$1,057.52. The purchase price for the bond was \$1,000. The return relative over 18 months is then \$1,057.52/\$1,000 = 1.0575.

To calculate an effective annual return from this 18-month return relative, we would take it to the 2/3 power (a year is two-thirds of an 18-month period) and subtract one: $1.0575^{2/3} - 1 = 3.80\%$.

A is incorrect because it omits the interest on the coupons. C is incorrect because it is the holding period return over 18 months.

23 C is correct. The compounded return relatives in the first three quarters are (1 − 0.096)(1.044)(1 − 0.047) = 0.8994. So, the account is at 89.94 percent of its original value at the start of the fourth quarter. To restore it to its full beginning value, we calculate the fourth-quarter return that will return the fund to a value of 1.0. Let the fourth-quarter return equal x:

$$0.8994(1 + x) = 1.00$$

$$x = 11.2\%$$

A is incorrect because it assumes the fourth-quarter return must offset the average of the first three quarters of returns. B is incorrect because it assumes the fourth-quarter return must offset the sum of the first three quarters of returns.

24 C is correct. In this problem, inflation is 4 percent a year for all five years, so a good that costs \$1.00 at Year 0 would cost $\$1.00 \times 1.04^5 = \$1.216653$ in Year 5. If the fund is worth \$0.50 at the end of the first year, the fund must provide the following return relative over the next four years to restore its beginning purchasing power:

$$\$1.216653/\$0.50 = 2.43331$$

Converting this to an annual return, we have $2.43331^{1/4} - 1 = 24.90\%$.

A is incorrect because it ignores inflation in all years. B is incorrect because it ignores inflation in the last four years.

25 A is correct. The holding period return is 21/19 − 1 = 10.53%. The continuously compounded rate of return is ln(1 + 0.1053) = 10.0%.

B is incorrect because it is the holding period return. C is incorrect because it is $e^{0.1053} - 1$.

26 B is correct. Because there are no external cash flows in this example, we can calculate the compound annual rate of growth (i.e., geometric mean of periodic returns) by using the beginning and ending prices to determine an annual rate of growth for the five years of growth: $(9.99/9.14)^{1/5} - 1 = 1.79\%$.

Alternatively, you can chain link the periodic return relatives and arrive at the same answer. The respective returns for the five years are 0.98%, –3.79%, 0.56%, 3.25%, and 8.35%. The product of (1.0098)(1 – 0.0379)(1.0056)(1.0325)(1.0835) is 1.0930. Taking the product to the one-fifth power and subtracting one, we arrive at the same answer as before: $1.0930^{1/5} - 1 = 1.79\%$.

A is incorrect because it uses six years in the exponentiation (not five). C is incorrect because it is an arithmetic mean of the periodic returns.

27 A is correct. Statement #1 is not correct. The geometric mean will provide the best representation of the investor's terminal wealth because the periodic returns are not independent events. The gain or loss from one period affects the return in future periods. The geometric mean reflects the compounding of returns, whereas the arithmetic mean does not. Statement #2 is also not correct. The geometric mean will be lower than the arithmetic mean as long as the returns are volatile. The geometric mean will only be equal to the arithmetic mean when the volatility of returns is zero.

28 B is correct. Statement #3 is not correct. A performance analyst should not annualize the performance for periods of less than a year and report it as the annual performance. By doing so, the presentation assumes that the quarter's performance would continue for the rest of year, which the fund may not be able to achieve.

Statement #4 is correct. When using statistical analysis where a model is fitted using historical data, the arithmetic mean is preferred over the geometric mean. The geometric mean is affected by return volatility, whereas the arithmetic mean is not.

29 C is correct. When capital withdrawals are made from a fund, the number of units adjusts to maintain the identity of the NAV per unit.

30 B is correct. In analyzing historical portfolio returns, one must use geometric (not arithmetic) averages; thus, the formula for the real rate of return is calculated as follows (using the 10-year average real rate of return in the numerator and the 5-year average real rate of return in the denominator):

$$\left[\frac{\left(\frac{1.04}{1.03}\right)^{10}}{\left(\frac{1.005}{1.015}\right)^{5}}\right]^{\frac{1}{5}} - 1 = 2.97\%$$

A is incorrect because it is simply the difference in the average arithmetic rates for the period 2001–2010 minus the difference in the average arithmetic rates for the period 2006–2010:

$$(5.0\% - 3.8\%) - (0.6\% - 2.0\%) = 2.6\%$$

C is incorrect because it calculates the average real rate of return for the period 2001–2005 using arithmetic rates (*not* geometric rates) as follows:

(2 × Average real rate from 2001–2010) – Average real rate from 2006–2010

$$= [2 \times (5.0\% - 3.8\%)] - (0.6\% - 2.0\%) = 3.8\%$$

31 B is correct. On 31 December 2010 the accumulated value of \$1,000 invested on 1 January 2006 is equal to $\$1,000 \times (1 + 0.005)^5 = \$1,025.25$; and the 50 units that had cost \$1,000 on 1 January 2006 cost $\$1,000 \times (1 + 0.015)^5 = \$1,077.28$. Thus, \$1,025.25 can buy \$1,025.25/\$1,077.28 × 50 = 47.6 or 47 (rounded down to the lower whole number of units).

A is incorrect because it uses five times the difference in the arithmetic averages of the portfolio return and inflation [5 × (0.006 – 0.02)] = –0.07 (i.e., a reduction factor of 7 percent to be applied to the 50 units or 3.5). The number of units purchased, rounded down, is 46 units. C is incorrect because it reverses the numerator and denominator values in the correct answer, B.

32 B is correct. We can calculate the approximate variance of portfolio returns as twice the difference between the arithmetic average and the geometric average of those returns.

- **For the period 2006–2010,**

  Variance = 2 × (0.6% – 0.5%) = 0.2%

- **For the period 2001–2005,** the averages must be calculated from the averages shown for the periods 2006–2010 and 2001–2010:

  a For arithmetic averages, let us denote the arithmetic average of return in period i by AAR_i; so we have

  $$\frac{5 \times AAR_{2001-2005} + 5 \times AAR_{2006-2010}}{10} = AAR_{2001-2010}$$

  or $AAR_{2001-2005} = 2 \times AAR_{2001-2010} - AAR_{2006-2010}$

  = (2 × 5.0%) – 0.6%

  = 9.4%

  b For geometric averages, let us denote the geometric average of return in period i by GAR_i; so we have

  $$(1 + GAR_{2001-2005})^5 \times (1 + GAR_{2006-2010})^5 = (1 + GAR_{2001-2010})^{10}$$

  or

  $$\left(GAR_{2001-2005}\right) = \left(\frac{\left(1 + GAR_{2001-2010}\right)^{10}}{\left(1 + GAR_{2006-2010}\right)^{5}}\right)^{\frac{1}{5}} - 1$$

  $$= \left[\frac{1.04^{10}}{1.005^{5}}\right]^{\frac{1}{5}} - 1 = 7.6\%$$

  c Geometric average of returns $= \left[\frac{1.04^{10}}{1.005^{5}}\right]^{\frac{1}{5}} - 1 = 7.6\%$

  Thus, variance = 2 × (9.4% – 7.6%) = 3.6%

- **For the period 1996–2000,** the averages must be calculated from the averages shown for the periods 1996–2010 and 2001–2010:

  Arithmetic average of returns = (3 × 6.8%) – (2 × 5.0%) = 10.4%

  Geometric average of returns $= \left[\frac{1.06^{15}}{1.04^{10}}\right]^{\frac{1}{5}} - 1 = 10.1\%$

  Thus, variance = 2 × (10.4% – 10.1%) = 0.6%

33 A is correct. Because there are no external cash flows, we do not need to examine the holding period returns for each quarter to calculate the time-weighted return. We can simply divide the terminal value by the beginning value to obtain the following return relative:

$1,118.44/$1,000.00 = 1.11844

We would take this value to the 2/3 power (one year represents two-thirds of an 18-month period) and subtract one:

$1.11844^{2/3} - 1 = 7.75\%$

Alternatively, the same annualized time-weighted return can be obtained using the quarterly holding period returns as follows: First, calculate each quarterly holding period return using the portfolio values. The first holding period return uses the April 2011 and January 2011 portfolio values:

$\$1{,}005.12/\$1{,}000 - 1 = 0.0051 = 0.51\%$

The second holding period return uses the July 2011 and April 2011 portfolio values:

$\$1{,}082.11/\$1{,}005.12 - 1 = 0.0766 = 7.66\%$

Note that we do not need to add the coupon in the return calculation because we are using portfolio values that are inclusive of coupons.

For the remaining holding period returns, you should calculate −2.69%, 4.50%, −1.02%, and 2.68%. Adding one to each holding period return and taking the product, we have $(1.0051)(1.0766)(1 - 0.0269)(1.0450)(1 - 0.0102)(1.0268) = 1.1183$.

If we take this to the 4/6 power (there are four quarters in a year and six quarters total) and subtract one, we have $(1.1183^{4/6}) - 1 = 7.74\%$. Your answer would be 7.75% if you carried intermediate calculations in your calculator's internal memory.

B is incorrect because it uses only the product of the periodic return relatives. C is incorrect because it inverts the exponent on the return calculation.

34 C is correct. If the coupons are not reinvested, there are withdrawals (i.e., external cash flows) from the portfolio, and a holding period return must be calculated whenever an external cash flow occurs. The first semi-annual holding period return relative uses the January 2011 and July 2011 bond prices and the $60 coupon:

$(\$1{,}022.11 + 60)/\$1{,}000 = 1.0821$

The second semi-annual holding period return relative uses the July 2011 and January 2012 bond prices and the $60 coupon:

$(\$978.92 + \$60)/\$1{,}022.11 = 1.0164$

Notice that in this second holding period return relative, the denominator is an amount ($1,022.11) that excludes the first coupon.

The third semi-annual holding period return relative uses the January 2012 and July 2012 bond prices and the $60 coupon:

$(\$933.90 + \$60)/\$978.92 = 1.0153$

Chain linking the return relatives, we have $(1.0821)(1.0164)(1.0153) = 1.1167$. If we take this to the 2/3 power (there are two semi-annual periods in a year and three total in this problem) and subtract one, we have $(1.1167^{2/3}) - 1 = 7.64\%$.

A is incorrect because it uses a one-sixth exponent in the return calculation. B is incorrect because it uses a one-fourth exponent in the return calculation.

35 C is correct. The money-weighted return is an IRR. The IRR satisfies the equation $933.90 + $60 = $1,000 × $(1 + R)^{3/2}$ – $60 × $(1 + R)^{2/2}$ – $60 × $(1 + R)^{1/2}$. The annual IRR is 7.91%. Note that the exponents in the equation are fractions of a year (e.g., the principal of $1,000 is invested 1.5 years before the terminal period).

The IRR calculation is most easily performed by entering the beginning bond price, the ending bond price, and external cash flows (i.e., the withdrawn coupons) as semi-annual inputs in a financial calculator's Cash Flow menu. Using the BA-II Plus,

CF0 = –1,000; CO1 = 60; FO1 = 1; CO2 = 60; FO2 = 1; CO3 = 933.90 + 60; CPT IRR = 3.879986744.

Notice that in contrast to the time-weighted return, we do not need the interim semi-annual bond valuations here. We only need the beginning bond price, the ending bond price, and external cash flows.

The calculator's answer is a semi-annual IRR in percent (because we had used semi-annual inputs). To convert it to an annual IRR, we convert it to a decimal, add one, raise it to the second power, and subtract one:

$(1.03879986744)^2 - 1 = 7.91\%$

We could also calculate the modified Dietz return as an approximation to the internal rate of return. The first coupon is withdrawn with two-thirds of the 18-month period remaining, and the second coupon is withdrawn with one-third of the 18-month period remaining. Using the formula from the text,

$$R = \frac{V_1 - V_0 - \sum_{k=1}^{K} C_k}{V_0 + \sum_{k=1}^{K} W_k C_k} = \frac{\$993.90 - \$1{,}000 + \$60 + \$60}{\$1{,}000 - \frac{2}{3}(\$60) - \frac{1}{3}(\$60)} = 12.1170\%$$

This is an 18-month return. To convert it to an annual return, we add one to its decimal form, raise it to the two-thirds power, and subtract one: $1.121170^{2/3} - 1 = 7.92\%$. This approximation is very close to the IRR we had calculated.

B is incorrect because it omits the last coupon. A is incorrect because it reverses the signs of the beginning and terminal cash flows.

36 A is correct. Scenario A presents the situation where the money-weighted return would be the most appropriate measure of the portfolio manager's performance. For the money-weighted return to be a proper measure of manager evaluation, the manager must control the timing of investment cash flows, which this manager does because he controls the timing of investment liquidation. The money-weighted return is also useful when the investments are illiquid because it does not require periodic valuations, as does the time-weighted return. The portfolio in this scenario is invested in microcap stocks and hedge funds, which have no ready secondary market to provide asset valuations.

In Scenario B, the assets of publicly traded large-cap stocks and commodity futures are liquid and can thus be readily valued. So the time-weighted return can be used here. Furthermore, the manager has no control over disbursements and contributions, so the money-weighted return would not be appropriate. In particular, the client's divorce in the 2007 is likely to result in the portfolio return being relatively high over time because the client required a large disbursement prior to the 2008 market decline.

In Scenario C, it does not appear that the manager has had complete control over the timing of the portfolio's investments because the client had a large, one-time contribution from an inheritance. Furthermore, the client wishes to know the terminal value of an initial investment, and the time-weighted return provides the most accurate measure of the compound rate of growth of $1 initially invested in a portfolio over a stated period.

37 B is correct. To calculate the time-weighted rate of return, first calculate the holding period returns using account values. The first holding period return is

[($188,000 + $8,000)/$237,000] – 1 = –0.1730 = –17.30%

Note that we add the dividend in the return calculation because the investor receives this value and because the account values shown exclude dividends.

The second holding period return is

[($220,000 – $40,000)/$188,000] – 1 = –0.0426 = –4.26%

The third holding period return including the dividend is

[$329,000 + $8,000)/$220,000] – 1 = 0.5318 = 53.18%

Adding one to each holding period return and taking the product, we have (1 – 0.1730)(1 – 0.0426)(1.5318) = 1.2129. Subtracting one, the time-weighted return is 21.29 percent. Note that the compounding is over a year and the time-weighted return desired is annual, so no exponentiation is needed.

A is incorrect because it omits the dividends in the holding period return calculations. C is incorrect because it omits the contribution in the holding period return.

38 C is correct. The first dividend is paid with 6/12 of the 12-month period remaining. The contribution is made with 3/12 of the 12-month period remaining. Calculating the money-weighted return as an IRR, the IRR will satisfy the equation $\$329{,}000 + \$8{,}000 = \$237{,}000 \times (1 + R)^{12/12} - \$8{,}000 \times (1 + R)^{6/12} + \$40{,}000 \times (1 + R)^{3/12}$. The annual IRR is 28.06 percent. Note that the equation above is in fractions of a year.

The IRR calculation is most easily performed by entering the beginning account value, the ending account value, and external cash flows (i.e., the dividends and contributions) as monthly inputs in a financial calculator's Cash Flow menu. We use months because they are the largest common denominator of time in the periodicity of the cash flows. We enter the dividends as positive values because they are paid out to the investor. Using the BA-II Plus,

CF0 = –237,000; CO1 = 0; F01 = 5; CO2 = 8,000; FO2 = 1; CO3 = 0; F03 = 2; CO4 = –40,000; FO4 = 1; CO5 = 0; F05 = 2; CO6 = 329,000 + 8,000; CPT IRR = 2.0824.

Note that the zeros for the COs tell the calculator that no cash flows occur during the periods between cash flows.

The calculator's answer is a monthly IRR in percent (because we had used monthly inputs). To convert it to an annual IRR, we convert it to a decimal, add one, raise it to the 12th power, and subtract one: $1.020824^{12} - 1 = 28.06\%$. Notice that in contrast to the time-weighted return, we do not need the periodic account valuations here. We need only the beginning account value, the ending account value, and external cash flows.

The time-weighted return of 21.28 percent is smaller than the money-weighted return of 28.06 percent because the contribution was made right before a period of favorable performance (the last period's holding period return was highest at 53.18 percent). If the portfolio manager does not control the timing of external cash flows, the money-weighted return is not as useful for manager evaluation because the client's contribution and withdrawal decisions can influence the account's performance.

We could also use the modified Dietz return as an approximation to the internal rate of return here. Using Equation 25 from the text,

$$R = \frac{V_1 - V_0 - \sum_{k=1}^{K} C_k}{V_0 + \sum_{k=1}^{K} W_k C_k} = \frac{\$329{,}000 + \$8{,}000 - \$237{,}000 + \$8{,}000 - \$40{,}000}{\$237{,}000 - \frac{6}{12}(\$8{,}000) + \frac{3}{12}(\$40{,}000)} = 27.98\%$$

This approximation is close to the IRR of 28.06 percent we had calculated but not exact. The difference between the IRR and the modified Dietz return will be larger when interim cash flows are relatively large (relative to the beginning and ending values) and when the interim cash flows occur earlier. This can be seen by comparing the last terms in the formulas for the IRR and the modified Dietz return in the text.

$$\text{IRR: } V_1 = V_0(1 + R) + \sum_{k=1}^{K} C_k (1 + R)^{W_k}$$

$$\text{Modified Dietz return: } V_1 = V_0 \times (1 + R) + \sum_{k=1}^{K} C_k \times (1 + W_k R)$$

The modified Dietz return formula shown here is a rewriting of Equation 25 previously shown.

A is incorrect because it fails to recognize the appropriate chronological spacing of the cash flows and assumes the periodic valuations are consecutive in the IRR calculation. B is incorrect because it omits the dividends in the IRR calculation.

39 C is correct. To calculate the time-weighted return, we calculate the holding period returns, which are defined by the occurrence of external cash flows. The first holding period return from January to April is

$$[(\$111{,}300 - \$13{,}000)/\$93{,}200] - 1 = 0.0547 = 5.47\%$$

Note that the contribution is subtracted from the ending value in the return calculation because the fund did not earn this amount. We do not need to add the dividend in the return calculation because we are using fund values that are inclusive of the reinvested dividends.

The second holding period return from April to October is

$$[(\$49{,}900 + \$21{,}000)/\$111{,}300] - 1 = -0.3630 = -36.30\%$$

Note that we add the \$21,000 in the numerator because the 1 October valuation will not reflect this cash flow received by the employees.

The third holding period return from October to December is

$$(\$74{,}100/\$49{,}900) - 1 = 0.4850 = 48.50\%$$

Adding one to each holding period return and taking the product, we have (1.0547)(1 – 0.3630)(1.4850) = 0.9977. Subtracting one, the time-weighted return is –0.23 percent. Note that the compounding is over a year and the time-weighted return desired is annual, so no exponentiation is needed.

A is incorrect because it reverses the signs of the contribution and the withdrawal. B is incorrect because it omits the withdrawal in the holding period return.

40 B is correct. The contribution is made with 9 of the 12 months remaining. The withdrawal is made with 3 of the 12 months remaining. Using Equation 25 from the text, the modified Dietz return is

$$\frac{74{,}100 - 93{,}200 - 13{,}000 + 21{,}000}{93{,}200 + 13{,}000 \times \dfrac{9}{12} - 21{,}000 \times \dfrac{3}{12}} = -11.36\%$$

We could also calculate the money-weighted return as an IRR. The IRR will satisfy the equation $74{,}100 = 93{,}200 \times (1 + R)^{12/12} + 13{,}000 \times (1 + R)^{9/12} - 21{,}000 \times (1 + R)^{3/12}$. The annual IRR is −11.37 percent. Calculating the money-weighted return as an IRR in a financial calculator's Cash Flow menu, we enter the beginning account value, the distribution, the contribution, and the ending account value as monthly inputs. Note that we do not need to enter the dividends because they are not outflows (they are reinvested in the account). Using the BA-II Plus,

CF0 = −93,200; CO1 = 0; F01 = 2; CO2 = −13,000; FO2 = 1; CO3 = 0; F03 = 5; CO4 = 21,000; FO4 = 1; CO5 = 0; F05 = 2; CO6 = 74,100; CPT IRR = −1.001

Note that the zeros for the COs tell the calculator that no cash flows occur during the periods between cash flows. The calculator's answer is a monthly IRR in percent (because we had used monthly inputs). To convert it to an annual IRR, we convert it to a decimal, add one, raise it to the 12th power, and subtract one: $0.9900^{12} - 1 = -11.37\%$. This is very close to the modified Dietz return of −11.36 percent we had calculated previously.

Notice that the money-weighted return of −11.4 percent is significantly lower than the time-weighted return, which is near zero at −0.22 percent. This is because the contribution was made right before a period of poor performance (the second period's holding period return was lowest at −36.30 percent) and also because a distribution was made right before a period of superior performance (the last period's holding period return was highest at 48.50 percent). Note that the timing of these external cash flows was beyond the control of the manager and was due to aspects of the pension fund's obligations to its employees. Because of this, the money-weighted return should not be used for manager evaluation here.

A is incorrect because it omits the withdrawal in the calculation. C is incorrect because it omits the contribution in the calculation.

41 C is correct. The number of units changes as withdrawals and contributions occur. The 22 September contribution of $6.70 increases the number of units as follows: $6.70/$5.424 = 1.235. The fund's number of units is increased from 8.038 to 9.273.

For practice, verify the decline in the number of units from the 4 September withdrawal. The 4 September withdrawal of $8.30 reduces the number of units by the NAV at that time: $8.30/$4.230 = 1.962. The fund's number of units is reduced from 10 to 8.038.

A is incorrect and is calculated by inverting the correct calculation. B is incorrect and is calculated by multiplying the ratio of the external cash flow to the market value by the NAV.

42 C is correct. The time-weighted return can be calculated using the beginning and ending NAV of the fund: \$5.122/\$4.580 – 1 = 11.83%. Note that you do not need to use daily fund values for every day in September (not shown in the table) to calculate the time-weighted rate of return. You also do not need to chain link the returns from the periodic NAVs shown in the table, although this will also provide the correct answer of 11.83 percent.

A is incorrect and is calculated by chain linking the returns from the periodic NAVs and reversing the signs of the external cash flows. B is incorrect and is calculated by chain linking the returns from the periodic market values and omitting the external cash flows.

The data below complete the table in the question:

	Market Value	Units before Flow	NAV	External Cash Flow	Added Units
31 Aug	\$45.80	10.000	4.580		0.00
4 Sep	\$42.30	10.000	4.230	(\$8.30)	–1.962
13 Sep	\$37.70	8.038	4.690		0.00
22 Sep	\$43.60	8.038	5.424	\$6.70	1.235
30 Sep	\$47.50	9.273	5.122		0.00

43 C is correct. The IRR satisfies the equation $289 = 241 \times (1 + R) + 34 \times (1 + R)^{28/31} - 14 \times (1 + R)^{9/31}$.

The IRR is 10.46 percent. The IRR calculation is most easily performed in a financial calculator's Cash Flow menu by using daily inputs. Using the BA-II Plus,

> CF0 = 241; CO1 = 0; F01 = 2; CO2 = 34; FO2 = 1; CO3 = 0; F03 = 18; CO4 = –14; FO4 = 1; CO5 = 0; F05 = 8; CO6 = –289; CPT IRR = 0.321485.

Note that the zeros for the COs tell the calculator that no cash flows occur during the periods between cash flows.

The calculator's answer is a daily IRR in percent (because we had used daily inputs). To convert it to a monthly IRR, we convert it to a decimal, add one, raise it to the 31st power, and subtract one: $1.00321485^{31} - 1 = 10.46\%$. You can practice the calculation of the IRR by determining it for Asset B. You should calculate –5.20 percent.

A is incorrect because it is the IRR if the time periods between external cash flows are ignored. B is incorrect and is calculated using a simple percentage return of the initial investment, the contribution, the withdrawal, and the terminal value.

44 B is correct. To calculate the modified Dietz return for December, first determine the portion of the month (W) between the contribution and month-end:

$$W = \frac{31 - 3}{31} = 0.9032$$

The portion of the month (W) between the withdrawal and month-end is

$$W = \frac{31 - 22}{31} = 0.2903$$

Next, adjust the beginning portfolio value in the numerator and ending portfolio value in the numerator by the contribution and the withdrawal as follows:

$$\text{Modified Dietz return} = \frac{\$86.00 - \$88.00 - \$12.00 + \$9.00}{\$88.00 + (\$12.00)(0.9032) - (\$9.00)(0.2903)} = -5.20\%$$

A is incorrect and is calculated by omitting the weights in the modified Dietz return calculation. C is incorrect and is calculated by reversing the signs of the contribution and the withdrawal in the modified Dietz return calculation.

You can practice the calculation of the modified Dietz return by determining it for Asset A. You should calculate 10.46 percent:

$$\text{Modified Dietz return} = \frac{\$289.00 - \$241.00 - \$34.00 + \$14.00}{\$241.00 + (\$34.00)(0.9032) - (\$14.00)(0.2903)} = 10.46\%$$

The modified Dietz return here is very close, but not equal, to the IRR calculated previously for Asset A. Using four decimal places for the percentage modified Dietz return, we would have 10.4616 percent. Using four decimal places for the IRR, we would have 10.4619 percent. The IRR and modified Dietz returns for Asset B are also very close but not exactly the same.

45 C is correct. The modified Dietz return for the entire portfolio will be consistent with the modified Dietz return calculated using portfolio segments when the beginning-of-period values are adjusted for external cash flows. The adjustment is implemented using values from the denominator of the modified Dietz formula.

You can confirm this consistency by calculating the modified Dietz return for the entire portfolio and comparing it with the portfolio return calculated using portfolio segments. Using the values for the entire portfolio below and the method shown in the previous answer, you should calculate a modified Dietz return for the portfolio of 6.32 percent.

	Date (t)	Asset A	Asset B	Market Value (V_t)
Market Value	30 Nov	241.00	88.00	329.00
Contribution Deposit	3 Dec	34.00	12.00	46.00
Withdrawal	22 Dec	14.00	9.00	23.00
Market Value	31 Dec	289.00	86.00	375.00

Using the segment returns where segment weights are adjusted for external cash flows, we can also calculate 6.32 percent. The beginning-of-period value adjusted using the modified Dietz formula denominator for Asset A is \$241 + (\$34 × 0.9032) – (\$14 × 0.2903) = \$267.645. For Asset B it is \$88 + (\$12 × 0.9032) – (\$9 × 0.2903) = \$96.226. The total adjusted weights are \$267.645 + \$96.226 = \$363.871.

Using the relative weighting of A and B with their respective modified Dietz returns of 10.46 percent and –5.20 percent from the previous answer results in the modified Dietz return for the portfolio of 6.32 percent: (267.645/363.871) × 10.46% + (96.226/363.871) × –5.20% = 6.32%.

46 B is correct. The return on a portfolio that buys and holds the assets can be calculated as a weighted average of the assets' returns using the beginning-of-period portfolio weights for the assets. Here we know the total return of

Laura's account (5%). The total return of Noah's account is equal to the given price return (–1%) plus the income return (= 0.6/20 or 3% since the dividends received were held in cash). Thus, we have

$$\text{Total return} = 5\% \times \frac{80}{80+20} + (-1\% + 3\%) \times \frac{20}{80+20} = 4.4\%$$

A is incorrect. It is obtained when one ignores the 3 percent income return in the above formula. C is incorrect. It is obtained when one ignores the –1 percent price return in the above formula.

47 A is correct. The RESP fund return using the beginning weights of the accounts is obtained as follows:

Laura's contribution to return + Noah's contribution to return + Sophia's contribution to return (where each contribution to return = Modified Dietz return × Beginning weight) =

$$\frac{105-100-10}{100+10\times\frac{11}{12}} \times \frac{100}{140} + \frac{65-40-20}{40+20\times\frac{11}{12}} \times \frac{40}{140} + \frac{31-0-30}{0+30\times\frac{11}{12}} \times \frac{0}{140}$$

$$= -3.27\% + 2.45\% + 0\% = -0.82\%$$

Note that the modified Dietz return for the total RESP fund is obtained as follows:

$$\frac{201-140-60}{140+60\times\frac{11}{12}} = 0.51\%$$

Thus, the weighted returns using beginning weights do not sum to the total portfolio return. This is not surprising given that in this particular instance, Sophia's contribution to return is zero in the RESP fund return using beginning weights simply because the beginning weight of Sophia's account is zero.

B is incorrect because in the denominator of each of the three terms in the formula above the proportion of the year applied to the new contribution is 1/12 rather than 11/12. C is incorrect because in the denominator of each of the three terms in the formula above, the new contribution is totally ignored.

48 A is correct. The RESP fund return using the beginning weights of the accounts adjusted for the new contributions is obtained as follows:

Laura's contribution to return + Noah's contribution to return + Sophia's contribution to return (where each contribution to return = Modified Dietz return × Beginning weight adjusted for the new contribution) =

$$\frac{105-100-10}{\mathbf{100+10\times\left(\frac{11}{12}\right)}} \times \frac{\mathbf{100+10\times\left(\frac{11}{12}\right)}}{100+10\times\left(\frac{11}{12}\right)+40+20\times\frac{11}{12}+0+30\times\frac{11}{12}}$$

$$+$$

$$\left[\frac{65-40-20}{\mathbf{40+20\times\left(\frac{11}{12}\right)}} \times \frac{\mathbf{40+20\times\left(\frac{11}{12}\right)}}{100+10\times\left(\frac{11}{12}\right)+40+20\times\frac{11}{12}+0+30\times\frac{11}{12}}\right]$$

$$+$$

$$\left[\frac{31-0-30}{\mathbf{0+30\times\left(\frac{11}{12}\right)}}\times\frac{\mathbf{0+30\times\left(\frac{11}{12}\right)}}{100+10\times\left(\frac{11}{12}\right)+40+20\times\frac{11}{12}+0+30\times\frac{11}{12}}\right]$$

The bold terms cancel, we use the common denominator, and then we are left with

$$=\frac{(105-100-10)+(65-40-20)+(31-0-30)}{100+10\times\left(\frac{11}{12}\right)+40+20\times\frac{11}{12}+0+30\times\frac{11}{12}}$$

$$=\frac{(105+65+31)-(100+40+0)-(10+20+30)}{100+40+0+(10+20+30)\times\left(\frac{11}{12}\right)}$$

$$=\frac{201-140-60}{140+60\times\frac{11}{12}}=0.51\%$$

Note that this is also the modified Dietz return for the total RESP fund. Thus, the weighted returns using beginning weights adjusted for contributions sum to the total portfolio return. The mathematical expression $\frac{201-140-60}{140+60\times\frac{11}{12}}$ above is the expression that we developed in the previous question for the modified Dietz return of the total RESP fund. Indeed, the modified Dietz return of a total portfolio is mathematically equivalent, as we have illustrated, to the sum of the weighted composite returns when the weights are the beginning weights adjusted for the contributions (and withdrawals) made.

Because the weights sum to 1 and the weighted returns sum to the total fund return, there is consistency between the segment returns (the three terms in the first mathematical expression above—that is, −2.56%, +2.56%, and +0.51%).

B is incorrect because in all of the expressions above, or equivalently in the simple mathematical expression $\frac{201-140-60}{140+60\times\frac{11}{12}}$, the weight used for the number of months is 1/12 rather than 11/12. C is incorrect because in all of the expressions above, or equivalently in the simple mathematical expression $\frac{201-140-60}{140+60\times\frac{11}{12}}$, the weight applied to the contribution is subtracted rather than added—that is, −60 × (11/12) rather than +60 × (11/12).

49 B is correct. The contribution to portfolio return of a segment return is the weighted return of the segment. Here, using time-weighted rate of return, there is no external cash flow involved and the weight used is the beginning weight of the segment. Hence, contribution to return is equal to

Segment return × Weight

$$=\frac{31-30}{30}\times\frac{30}{125+60}=0.54\%$$

Note that the contributions to return of the other two accounts for the same period would be as follows:

$$\text{Laura: } = \frac{105 - 90}{90} \times \frac{90}{185} = 8.11\%$$

$$\text{Noah: } = \frac{65 - 65}{65} \times \frac{65}{185} = 0.00\%$$

The sum of the three weights is equal to one and the sum of the contributions to returns (0.54% + 8.11% + 0.00%) is equal to the overall fund return:

$$(201 - 185)/185 = 8.65\%$$

Thus, account returns are consistent with the RESP fund return, which is always the case with true time-weighted rates of return when segments are valued at the same dates as the total portfolio.

A is incorrect. It is equal to Sophia's account return × (31/201), where (31/201) is the ending weight. C is incorrect. It is equal to Sophia's account return × (11/12).

50 C is correct (i.e., Statement 3 is incorrect). The money was invested for 11 months in 2010, and the rate of return for that 11-month period was 3.33 percent (= 31/30 – 1) and thus was below 3.5 percent. It would not be correct to annualize that rate to $1.03333^{12/11} - 1 = 3.64\%$ and make it represent the whole year 2010. Note that 3.64 percent is also the internal rate of return for the whole year 2010 [from $31 = 30 \times (1 + \text{IRR})^{11/12}$]. Also, it would not be correct to use the IRR because Ryan wants a return that is independent of the timing of the external cash flows.

A is incorrect (i.e., Statement 1 is correct). The money-weighted rate of return (IRR) of Laura's account is equal to –4.58 percent, obtained from

$$105 = 100 \times (1 + \text{IRR}) + 10 \times (1 + \text{IRR})^{11/12}$$

The modified Dietz method provides the same rate of return, –4.58 percent, calculated as follows:

$$\frac{105 - 100 - 10}{100 + 10 \times \frac{11}{12}}$$

B is incorrect (i.e., Statement 2 is correct). The time-weighted rate of return best reflects the manager's skill in investing the assets, irrespective of the timing of external cash flows. The time-weighted rate of return of Noah's account is equal to 12.5 percent, obtained as follows:

$$\frac{45}{40} \times \frac{65}{45 + 20} - 1$$

READING

5

Data Integrity

by Marcus Boudville and Adam Taylor

Marcus Boudville is at Aviva Investors (United Kingdom). Adam Taylor (United Kingdom).

LEARNING OUTCOMES

Mastery	*The candidate should be able to:*
☐	a. describe dimensions of data quality;
☐	b. describe elements of sound investment data governance;
☐	c. identify and describe common sources of data errors in the performance and risk measurement process;
☐	d. describe the errors that may arise in processing corporate actions and their effect on performance and risk measurement;
☐	e. explain return discrepancies in a portfolio or a composite that may arise from currency issues;
☐	f. determine whether a data revision necessitates a restatement of prior-period returns.

INTRODUCTION

1

Data that investment management firms use in performance measurement and reporting can take many different forms and can come from many different sources. The wide range of forms and sources can give rise to numerous data quality issues. These issues can be compounded by the data flowing between systems and departments. The calculation of performance relies on multiple "upstream" pieces of data—data sources. All such inputs affect the ultimate returns that are used by many stakeholders, including the firm's portfolio managers, existing and potential clients, and external consultants. Practitioners must always remember that returns are the product of multiple sets of data—with discrepancies—and be able to articulate the accuracy of those returns based on the known and potentially unknown issues. In this reading, we explain what is meant by data integrity, what the best data governance practices are, and what the common sources of data errors are. We also consider scenarios that require revision of prior-period returns.

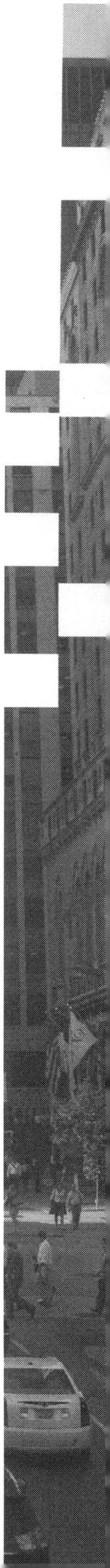

2 DIMENSIONS OF DATA QUALITY

The scope of what data is can be varied and wide ranging. Dictionary definitions vary too. One such definition describes data as "facts and statistics collected together for reference or analysis" (this definition comes from Oxford University Press). Ultimately, data is all information in all forms. In the context of investment performance measurement, it is easier to consider data as being in one of two distinct forms. The first form is structured in the sense that data sits within a system or application, such as an accounting or a portfolio performance system. It is extractable and organized in a way that makes it useful and suitable for the application's use. But data can also be less structured and can be found in Microsoft Excel spreadsheets, Microsoft Word documents, or paper documents. We will describe the dimensions of data quality, and by "dimensions," we mean the different ways in which we can think about data quality, as follows:

Accuracy: Data are valid and correct.

Completeness: Data are complete given the intended purpose.

Conformity: Data conform to standards and rules.

Consistency: There is a consistent application of rules across different systems.

Timeliness: Data must be available in time for use and regularly updated.

Lineage: There is a record and knowledge of where the data come from.

Such descriptions and examples are shown in Exhibit 1. These are characteristics or aspects of data that need to be considered when thinking about data quality. We consider both structured and unstructured data in the discussion of the dimensions. An overarching principle is that data should be "fit for purpose."

Exhibit 1 Dimensions of Data Quality

Dimension	Description	Examples and Scenarios
Accuracy	Data are valid and correct. There is an appropriate level of accuracy of the data for its intended purpose. This outcome can be achieved through validation to an authoritative source of data or by comparing multiple sources of the same data.	Example of arrangements where one could apply different accuracy rules: "Report any instances where the NAV has moved over 25 bps over a set period of time when being used for regulatory reports." "Report any instances where the NAV has moved over 40 bps over a set period of time when being used to prepare client reports."
Completeness	Achieved when the dataset is complete given the purpose for which it was intended. It is worth noting that some data are mandatory and some are optional; this will all be part of the expected data collection.	An operations analyst may have a list of all open positions in the Investment Book of Records (the internal firm register of open positions). The analyst expects this information to be held by various brokers and counterparties. As a result, he or she will compare the independent multiple broker and counterparty position records with the internal Investment Book of Records view.
Conformity	Ensuring that the data conforms to internally defined standards and rules. For example: • character length (maximum number of characters allowed) • character type (alphanumeric, integer, numeric, Boolean, float, string, array, etc.)	When transferring a file from System A into another system or application, a check is run to ensure that the character type of the attribute in the file being sent matches what is expected to be received from the data warehouse (the in-house data store). A breach is reported if a mismatch is found.

Exhibit 1 (Continued)

Dimension	Description	Examples and Scenarios
Consistency	Ensuring that data quality rules are applied consistently across one or many systems or applications for the same attribute or dataset.	Net asset value (NAV) information is held in systems A, B, and C. If there is a rule to "report any instance where the NAV has moved over 5 bps a day" in System A but in Systems B and C the number is set at 10 bps and 15 bps, respectively, then the data consumers will have differing levels of confidence within the NAV data attribute (within different systems).
Timeliness	With regard to data quality processes, timeliness would ensure that the data are being reviewed to ensure that they are not stale. The rule(s) will test whether the attribute has updated per the expected frequency. Actual frequency is compared with the expected frequency. Generally, timeliness refers to getting information at the right time and quickly enough to meet reporting and analytical requirements.	The NAV of a daily priced fund is expected to be updated on a daily basis. If the date of the NAV attribute value is not the expected most recent date, allowing for the time the attribute is expected to be updated and public holidays, then it is stale and not appropriate to use.
Lineage	Understanding where the data have come from (the origin), what happens to the data, and where the data move over time. It allows errors to be traced and helps ensure the data quality for all its intended purposes.	A particular data attribute is created and maintained in a particular system (say, ABC) and is distributed to a different system (DEF). For example, a performance system receives inputs from multiple source systems—where a particular source data item is missing or incorrect, it may be necessary to fix the problem at the source, and therefore, knowledge of the source of each data item is required.

Note: The above descriptions of different dimensions of data quality are broadly based on contributions by Brian Buzzelli (Acadian Asset Management).

EXAMPLE 1

Dimensions of Data Quality

The data governance officer, responsible for developing an environment that ensures transparency of all current data governance–related policies at a fund management firm, is meeting with an investment consultant to describe the firm's data governance arrangements. She describes how the firm ensures that when data move from one system to another, there are no issues or errors arising from a mismatch of data attributes.

What dimension of data quality is the data governance officer *most likely* describing?

A Accuracy

B Conformity

C Consistency

Solution

B is correct. The character type and attribute in the file being sent must match what is expected to be received from the data warehouse (the in-house data store). A breach is reported if a mismatch is found. A is incorrect because accuracy requires data to be valid and correct. C is incorrect because consistency is ensuring that data quality rules are applied consistently across one or many systems or applications for the same attribute or dataset.

3 DATA GOVERNANCE

In this section, we will explain what is meant by data governance and why it is important to the firm and its existing and potential clients. We will also describe desirable characteristics of sound data governance frameworks.

3.1 What Is Data Governance?

Data governance is the ownership and oversight of the firm's data over its life cycle. The **data life cycle**, as we will describe, is the sequence of stages that data will go through within a firm. Data governance provides overall management and integrity over data and drives good data management practices. Data governance will put in place the framework and oversight within the firm's departments to ensure the transparency, accuracy, and ownership of data across the organization. This outcome is achieved by implementing standards, policies, and procedures to support and guide the framework.

3.2 Why Data Governance Is Important

Failure to implement a robust data governance framework creates a number of risks to the firm's strategic and customer outcomes. It could also negatively affect the quality and accuracy of disclosures to regulators and asset owners. Not managing data appropriately erodes and may ultimately destroy the credibility of and reliance on the accuracy and completeness of the firm's data.

Sound data governance adds value to the organization in many different ways. The most substantial ones are as follows:

- It protects clients' interests and helps ensure accurate reporting to asset owners and regulators. Demonstrating strong data governance should also help win and retain business.
- It helps staff and management make more informed decisions and identify business opportunities (for example, reduction in duplication of data across the firm can result in reduced operational processes, leading to time and cost efficiencies).
- It provides senior management with a central view of how data are being managed across the organization. It also provides senior management with reassurance that data are being managed in a controlled, efficient, and consistent manner throughout the organization.

Exhibit 2 shows an example of an asset management firm's data governance framework. When such a framework exists, it typically features a committee that oversees the firm's data governance policy. In turn, it defines controls and processes that are implemented by **data owners**, individuals who are accountable for the data and its source. The exhibit also shows that data owners are responsible for defining the accuracy and completeness of all data within the data domains (of which the firm will typically have several, such as top-level "Performance") and data entities (a few dozen, such as "performance attribution" or "relative performance"). Data owners oversee and appoint data stewards who are responsible for monitoring the quality of data attributes (potentially thousands of actual data items—for example, ISIN [International Securities Identification Number], SEDOL [Stock Exchange Daily Official List], fund name, fund identifier, and security name). The framework exists to the benefit of both internal and external stakeholders.

Exhibit 2 Data Governance Framework

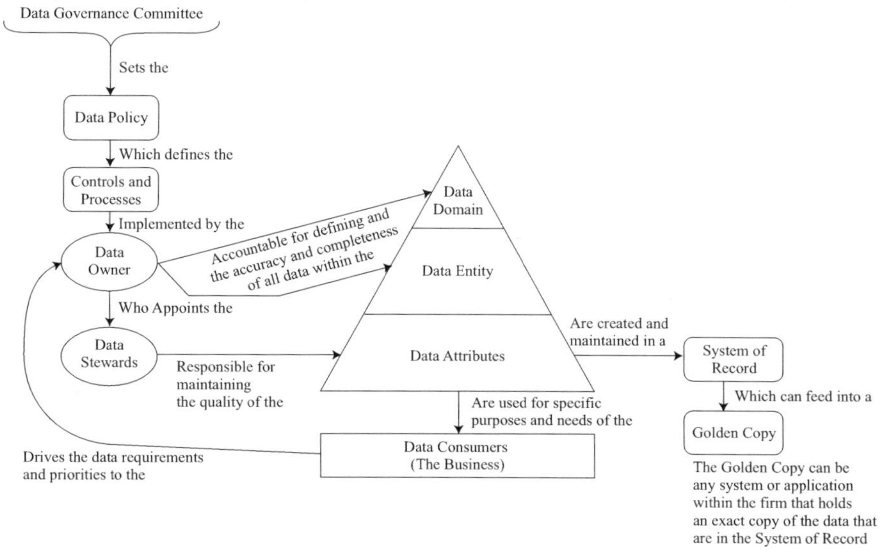

3.3 Features of Data Governance Framework

There are two main features of a data governance framework:

- The data life cycle and governance principles
- Key roles within the data governance framework

Next, we provide an overview of each.

3.3.1 *The Data Life Cycle and Governance Principles*

Exhibit 3 provides a high-level illustration of what a typical data life cycle would look like, reflecting the fact that data go through several stages. These span from creation, through secure storage, distribution, and use, all the way to retention and possible deletion, which we label as the "destruction" stage. The data owner is accountable for ensuring this life cycle is managed for the data that he or she is assigned ownership of. This life cycle should drive the principles that an organization adopts to ensure effective and good data governance principles, as shown in Exhibit 4.

Exhibit 3 Data Life Cycle

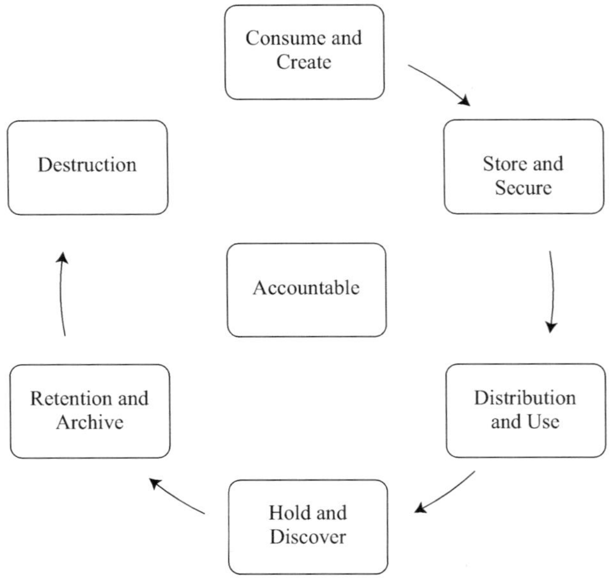

Exhibit 4 Data Governance Principles

Principle	Description
Accountable	Ensuring that the organization will implement a framework that will oversee and lead data governance and delegate roles and responsibilities to appropriate individuals. The organization will develop policies and controls to support individuals with their data governance–related roles and responsibilities.
Consume & Create	Ensuring that all data consumed or created by an organization have a purpose and reason and undergo review for quality to ensure accuracy and completeness is maintained in all circumstances.
Store & Secure	Ensuring that data are classified within the organization so that the appropriate level of security and encryption is applied at an attribute, file, and application level.
Distribution & Use	Ensuring the distribution and usage of the organization's data, both internally or externally, will be legal, with lineage documented. Business justification and purpose must be documented, making sure that the correct governance, assurance, and security arrangements are in place and sustained.
Hold & Discover	Ensuring that data will be held in a manner that allows for timely, efficient, and accurate discovery from any interested party, including regulatory bodies or clients that may legitimately request access to the data.

Exhibit 4 (Continued)

Principle	Description
Retention & Archive	Ensuring that data will be held for the appropriate amount of time, considering all legal, regulatory, business, and historical requirements.
Destruction	Ensuring that once data have passed the retention period or if there is a specific request from an authorized party that does not conflict with any legal or regulatory requirements, secure destruction arrangements are in place.

EXAMPLE 2

Data Governance Principles

An investment management firm has policies and arrangements to classify and handle data to ensure that the appropriate level of security and encryption is used for the data it holds. These policies will also ensure that data are held in a manner that allows timely, efficient, and accurate discovery from any legitimate party that requests to view it. Finally, the firm has secure data destruction arrangements in place. Data are subject to a destruction principle that requires that data be held for seven years or as long as there is secure storage capacity on the firm's systems. Once storage limits are reached, data can be destroyed until enough storage again exists in the system.

Which data governance principle is the firm *most likely* violating?

A Store and secure

B Hold and discover

C Destruction

Solution

C is correct. Data can be destroyed only once it has passed its retention period or if there is a specific request from an authorized party that does not conflict with any legal or regulatory requirements. A is incorrect because the store and secure principle is satisfied since the firm is ensuring an appropriate level of security and encryption. B is incorrect because the hold and discover principle is satisfied. The description states that policies must ensure that data are held in a manner that allows timely, efficient, and accurate discovery from any legitimate party.

3.3.2 *Key Roles within the Data Governance Framework*

The data governance framework features key roles that need to be assigned within an organization to support it, enable its functioning, and implement its principles. Exhibit 5 outlines some of the key roles that should be considered within a firm and a brief description of what the role holder's responsibilities should be. At the top level, the firm's executive committee includes a member responsible for the effective deployment of data governance capabilities. It also features a data governance officer who develops an environment that ensures transparency of all current data governance–related policies and objectives across the organization. The data governance officer is supported by the data governance leads, who are responsible for the day-to-day oversight of the principles and activities and for reporting any issues or violations to the data governance officer. Data owners and data stewards actually work with the data on day-to-day basis, as part of their performance measurement functions. It should be noted that each firm is different and that some roles may or may not exist. To maintain simplicity, we do not provide descriptions of some roles that exist in some firms (such as data protection officer or systems of record IT owner).

Exhibit 5 Key Roles in Data Governance Framework

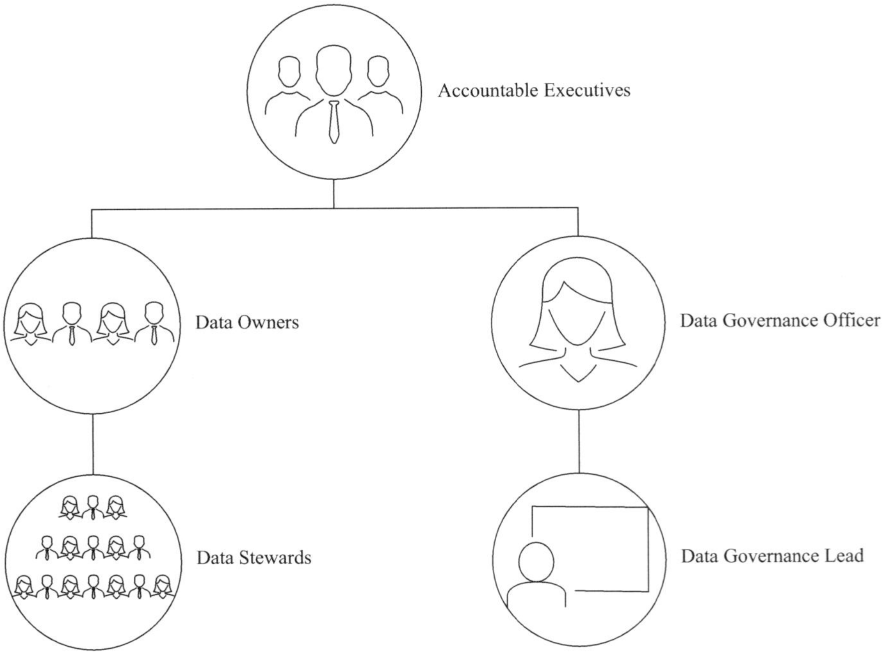

Role Name	Role Description
Accountable Executive	The accountable executive is a member of the executive committee and is responsible for the effective deployment of data governance capabilities to improve data within the organization and its use in achieving the organization's strategic goals and objectives.
Data Governance Officer	The individual who is responsible for developing an environment that ensures transparency of all current data governance–related policies and objectives for the organization.
Data Governance Lead	The person in this role provides day-to-day support for the data governance officer and is responsible for ensuring that all data governance–related principles and activities are operating as expected through the implementation (or "operationalization") of the data governance structure. He or she monitors for non-compliance, escalates any such occurrences to the data governance officer, and builds awareness within the organization. Typically, a firm would have one such person in place for each major business line.
Data Owner	The individual who is accountable for making sure data stewards are in place for the data that he or she has been assigned. They also act as the deciding vote on any changes to any of the data definitions, rules, systems of record, or usage for their dataset.
Data Steward	The individual responsible for ensuring data maintenance is upheld within a specific system of record.

DATA ERRORS IN THE PERFORMANCE AND RISK MEASUREMENT PROCESS

4

We begin our discussion of data errors with a high-level view of the typical data flows involved in the performance calculation and reporting process. Exhibit 6 illustrates the flows of data between departments. Data generated by portfolio management activity flow into the portfolio accounting system, where they are combined with external data sources. Operations teams validate and maintain data within the portfolio accounting system. The performance system receives data feeds from portfolio accounting and external sources for index data. Returns are then calculated, verified, and distributed to a variety of stakeholders (including portfolio managers, the compliance department, and the client servicing department). Note that portfolio accounting may be outsourced to an external provider, but the activities undertaken with regard to maintaining data will be the same whether performed in house or outsourced.

Exhibit 6 High-Level Performance Measurement Data Flows

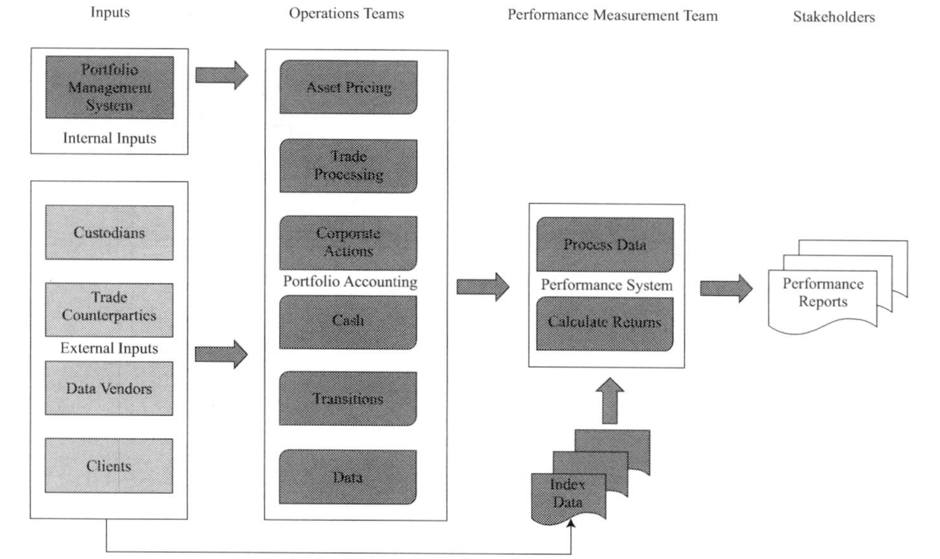

Any data errors feeding into the performance calculation may lead to inaccurate returns. As such, it is important for a performance analyst to understand all possible causes of error to enable efficient identification and resolution. It may be helpful to think of the impacts of data errors in terms of gain or loss on an individual asset or on the portfolio as a whole. We will often refer to such gains or losses as "false" gains or losses. Data errors will result in distortion of the return on the asset. In its most basic form,

$$\text{Return} = \frac{\text{Gain or loss}}{\text{Value invested}}.$$

Incorrect asset-level returns will "roll up" through any reporting hierarchy into the total portfolio level return. In turn, these will distort any *ex post* risk calculations.

There are numerous sources of potential data errors in performance measurement, and their impact can be characterized as one of two broad types:

- Incorrect or missing valuation of an asset or transaction
- Inconsistency between transactions and valuations, including associated cash impacts

Next, we will describe the main sources of data errors in performance. The concept of consistency can be understood by considering each investment transaction as affecting the four data elements shown in Exhibit 7. The timing of transaction bookings in the accounting system is a common cause of data inconsistency. Exhibit 7 shows how each asset purchase in a portfolio generates a change in asset position with an associated value increase. Each purchase also generates a payment obligation, which reduces the cash balance of the portfolio. One can view the top-left "Asset Purchase" as an investment decision where a transaction triggers a cash transaction obligation. Both elements then affect the value and balance.

Exhibit 7 Data Elements Created by an Asset Purchase

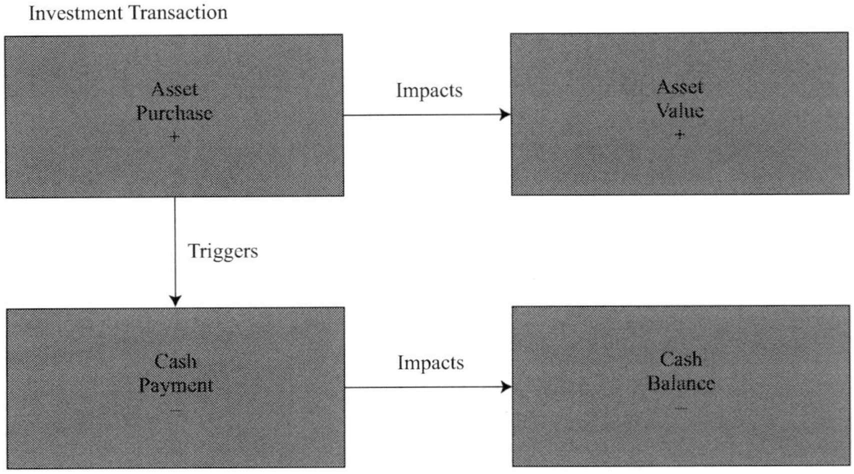

Inconsistency will also occur if backdated entries or corrections are made to accounting data that do not result in synchronized updating of each of these four data elements—asset purchase, asset value, cash payment, and cash balance. Where inconsistency occurs, false gains and losses will arise in individual time periods and on individual assets. Although these may net out over time at an aggregate level, they will be exposed where an error "crosses" a reporting period end. Their effects can crystalize in performance and risk attribution analysis, affecting the quality of output. Incorrectly calculated returns, if not spotted, may result in incorrect performance being reported to clients, causing reputational damage. Issues also may be caused by a firm's accounting policy leading to data being different from what is required for performance measurement. Accounting policies will not result in erroneous data per se, but their effects need to be understood to enable appropriate treatment in performance calculations. Doing so may require enrichment, as we will discuss, being applied to portfolio accounting data before they enter the performance system. Examples of areas where performance policies are required to determine calculation treatment include tax on income or security finance income, such as income from stock lending.

We will now look at common causes of data errors and policy-related issues in the performance measurement process.

4.1 Portfolio Accounting

The purpose of portfolio accounting systems is to maintain a book of records of investment activity. This book can be used for operational controls, such as reconciliations to third-party custody records, and for periodic client valuation reporting. The requirements that portfolio accounting fulfills may differ from the needs of performance measurement. For example, accounting data usually need to be accurate only at points in time, such as month end, whereas performance calculation requires full historical accuracy. The policies that an accounting system uses, such as which asset pricing sources are used, may not suit the purpose of measuring performance. These policies can, therefore, lead to errors in performance return. As illustrated in Exhibit 6, there are many different functions performed by operations teams who maintain the portfolio accounting records. Each of these areas represents a potential source of data errors.

4.2 Extraction, Enrichment, and Processing of Data

Unless returns are calculated directly within an accounting system, there is a risk that the process of extracting data from the accounting system and loading these data into the performance system will create data errors. So, although the data in the accounting system may be correct, the records of the data that flow into the performance system may not be. These can be inconsistencies between transactions and holdings and between asset and cash data. Further problems may occur where accounting data are being enriched in order to suit performance calculations. An example of enrichment would be applying rules to create a market value amount for an adjustment that is entered at book cost in the accounting system. Enrichment could also take the form of aggregation of data or mapping, such as converting accounting system codes into categories recognized by the performance system.

4.2.1 *Asset Pricing Policy and Valuations*

A firm's asset pricing policy will determine which pricing source, time, and basis is used for each asset class. A source could be a stock exchange or specialist data supplier, and examples of bases include bid price and last traded price. Price time refers to time of day that the price is struck. An example of price timing is "global close." For equity markets, global close prices reflect each local market's closing time. The firm pricing policy may use a basis different from that used by a fund's benchmark. Where this occurs, the price variance can generate noise when monitoring performance relative to a benchmark. This situation can be particularly challenging if a portfolio invests globally with a wide range of local market operating hours. In this case, the same asset's prices and, therefore, returns will differ in the portfolio versus the benchmark. With regard to valuation process, portfolio accounting may be concerned only with an accurate month-end record. Daily calculated performance will also need intramonth prices to be correct in order to avoid generation of false gain or loss. In these situations, any false gain or loss may net out over time but individual days' returns will be incorrect. This false gain or loss may affect the quality of performance and risk reports, as well as other performance analytics.

The illustration in Exhibit 8 shows how an incorrect asset price during a reporting period will affect the profile of daily returns. In the example, an asset price is incorrect at the end of Day 2, with the value being too low. The return for Day 2 with the incorrect price shows a sharp loss, followed by a steep gain on Day 3, when the asset price is corrected. The cumulative performance return profiles based on the correct time series of prices and the time series containing the error diverge on Day 2 and Day 3 but then realign. If uncorrected, this error would increase the calculated volatility of returns for the portfolio, which would lead to an overstatement of tracking error and other *ex post* risk measures.

Exhibit 8 Impact of Non-Month-End Asset Pricing Error

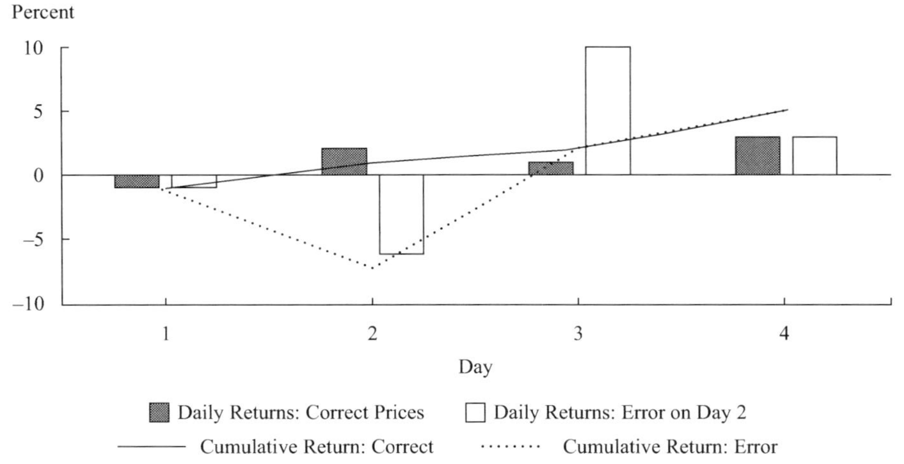

If a new asset is purchased—one not previously included on the portfolio accounting system—there may be a delay in the asset price flowing into the accounting system. This delay will have an impact similar to but potentially more extreme than an incorrect daily price. If there is no price, the asset may appear to be valued at zero, resulting in total loss.

Conventions regarding weekend pricing and accruals are also a potential area of inconsistency between portfolio and benchmark return calculation. In some cases, accruals will be updated on seven days each week, but in others, there are no weekend accrual increases. In some markets, static weekend accruals will result in Saturday and Sunday accrual increases all being captured in returns on the following Monday. In others, the markets are closed on Friday but are open on Sunday. Companies find it useful to have a policy on the treatment of weekends and holidays.

4.2.2 *Transaction Treatment*

For market trades involving a cash payment between counterparties, such as a purchase or sale of a bond, the accounting system transaction values will normally satisfy performance needs. However, for other transaction types, such as adjustments, transfers, and corporate actions, accounting may reflect book cost. In most instances, performance measurement needs to capture a market-valued transaction entry to ensure consistency with the valuation of assets, which is normally done on a mark-to-market basis. Exhibit 9 illustrates this transaction treatment for two portfolios between which the fund manager transfers an asset.

IMPACT OF TRANSACTIONS REFLECTED AT BOOK COST

In this example, an asset is transferred between two portfolios managed for the same client. This scenario could arise when a client wants the asset's cumulative gain or loss to be reflected on the receiving portfolio. Therefore, he or she asks for the transfer to be done at book cost. As a result, an asset valued at 150 is transferred between funds at a book cost of 120. This accounting treatment creates a false gain of 30 on the receiving fund, with a corresponding loss on the other fund. To be correct from a performance perspective, the transfer should be booked to reflect the prevailing market value of 150.

Exhibit 9 Impact of Transactions Reflected at Book Cost

	20 June	21 June	22 June
Fund A Value	150	0	0
Fund A Transfer Out		−120	
Daily Gain/Loss		−30	0
Fund B Value	0	150	150
Fund B Transfer In		120	
Daily Gain/Loss		30	0

4.3 Transaction Booking Errors

Within the operations department, a team will be monitoring and validating market trades to ensure that they can settle successfully. Should the team detect errors, corrections should flow back into performance calculations. If both the transaction record and the relevant valuation impact are not updated, consistently false gains or losses will arise. Exhibit 10 provides an illustration.

CORRECTION OF TRANSACTION ENTRY ERROR

In this example, a purchase was entered at half the correct size (100 instead of 200). In the middle table, the purchase is corrected but the valuation does not get aligned until two days later. This situation results in incorrect daily gains and losses, although the cumulative amount is accurate. With the fully corrected accounting data in the final table, gains and losses are accurate each day.

Exhibit 10 Asset Data without Cash Impacts

Original accounting entry	20 June	21 June	22 June
Asset purchase	100		
Asset value	100	101	102
Daily gain/loss	0	1	1

Only transaction corrected, not valuation	20 June	21 June	22 June
Asset purchase	200		
Asset value	100	101	204
Daily gain/loss	−100	1	103

(continued)

Exhibit 10 (Continued)

Fully corrected accounts	20 June	21 June	22 June
Asset purchase	200		
Asset value	200	202	204
Daily gain/loss	0	2	2

Building on the previous discussion and exhibit, cash effects must also be accounted for in synchronization with the asset side data. Exhibit 11 adds another layer of complexity with more data elements and with more potential for each data element to be inaccurate.

The first panel of Exhibit 11 shows the original entries. The adjustment in the middle table features updates to the asset side of the transaction and valuation and the cash impact of the transaction but not the cash balance. Daily gains and losses are incorrect in such a scenario, but the cumulative amount is accurate. With the fully corrected accounting data in the final table, gains and losses are accurate each day.

Exhibit 11 Correction of Transaction Entry Error: Asset and Cash Data Impacts

Original accounting entry	20 June	21 June	22 June
Asset purchase	100		
Cash payment	−100		
Asset value	100	101	102
Cash balance	−100	−100	−100
Daily gain/loss	0	1	1

Corrected except cash balance	20 June	21 June	22 June
Asset purchase	200		
Cash payment	−200		
Asset value	200	202	204
Cash balance	−100	−100	−200
Daily gain/loss	100	2	−98

Fully corrected accounts	20 June	21 June	22 June
Asset purchase	200		
Cash payment	−200		
Asset value	200	202	204
Cash balance	−200	−200	−200
Daily gain/loss	0	2	2

For non-market transactions, problems can also result from the incorrect or inconsistent use of transaction types. These problems may not be detected before they reach performance because the accounting impact could be correct. Once identified, the problem should be corrected at the source, in the portfolio accounting system. Return impacts will also occur if cash transaction entries are misclassified between cash flows and income or expenses, because of their different treatment in the performance calculation, where income and expenses will affect gain or loss but cash flows will not. If transactions are booked late in the accounting system, it may cause false gains and losses over individual time periods if holdings are not updated in synchronization. As with the examples in Exhibit 8 and Exhibit 9, cumulative gains and losses may still be accurate despite values on individual days being incorrect.

EXAMPLE 3

Backdated Correction to Portfolio Accounting Transaction Record

A colleague in the operations department informs the performance team that fund transactions have been corrected in the portfolio accounting system. In this case, a trade was originally booked to the wrong security. The operations department has performed its own checks and is satisfied that the result is correct. What is the best course of action for the performance team to take?

A Run periodic performance on the fund to ensure return and risk data are correct.

B Check and review the monthly security-level returns that have been calculated for the fund for the two relevant securities.

C Review the holdings and transactions relating to the securities in question in detail, for the purpose of consistency. Check that the cash impacts of the corrections are consistent with the security data changes.

Solution

C is correct. Inconsistencies between holdings and transactions will generate errors in the performance calculations at the security level. Inconsistencies between asset and cash data will also lead to inaccurate returns within the fund. A is incorrect because it does not include checking that the original booking to the wrong security has been fully cleaned up or that the overall cash impacts are corrected. Attribution may be incorrect at the security level. B is incorrect because although looking at the gain or loss on individual assets can be a good way to identify data errors, their impacts are often not visible when looking at longer time periods. Reviewing the daily returns would have been a better approach.

4.4 Security and Asset Setup

Certain errors within security setup in the accounting system will lead to incorrect transaction or valuation data being generated in the accounting data. An example of this problem is a security being set up with the wrong pricing currency, which would result in the security being incorrectly valued. This error would persist until the security record is corrected in the accounting system. If the security setup error is linked to an attribute that the accounting system uses to generate transaction records, this error will also persist until the security record is corrected. An example of this situation is the dividend payment date.

Security reference data, such as country and industry classifications or identifiers (for example, SEDOL or CUSIP), can cause issues if not processed correctly. There may also be inconsistencies between how the benchmark and how the portfolio classifies a security. For example, the benchmark provider may classify a security as a UK company if its shares are traded in London, but the company's business may be based in Asia and subject to factors unrelated to the UK economy. The portfolio may, therefore, classify it as a frontier or emerging market company. Depending on how it has been reflected in the accounting system, a reclassification could result in the original position disappearing and a new one appearing without a transaction to explain the movement in values. This situation will create distortions in performance attribution. This would also be true with any inconsistencies between the portfolio's and the benchmark's classification of assets.

4.5 Instrument-Specific Issues

There are a number of instruments that require performance teams to either make assumptions or address problems with a lack of timely data. Many fields, particularly in the case of derivatives and fixed-income instruments, may be inputted incorrectly—for example, in situations where derivatives reference other securities. We now turn our attention to some types of securities that, owing to their nature, are particularly prone to errors. Those instruments are fixed-income securities and illiquid assets, including OTC derivatives.

4.5.1 *Fixed-Income Securities*

Fixed-income securities are often subject to setup errors because many of their characteristics directly relate to the generation of valuation or coupon payments. Common problems include the following:

- Incorrect coupon rates or payment dates (a coupon is an income payment from a bond issuer to the holder; for conventional bonds, it would feature a fixed annual percentage value and specified dates on which payments are made).
- Accrued interest day-count conventions (coupon on a bond is accrued daily such that the bondholders earn a fraction of the coupon for each day they hold the bond; there are different methods, or "day count conventions," that may be applied to perform accrued interest calculations).

In periods when liquidity in bond markets dries up, price availability reduces, which can increase price volatility. If a firm's asset valuation policy does not align with the approach used by a fund's benchmark, it can lead to an increase in noise when looking at the relative performance of that fund. In the event of a default by a fixed-income security, there may be delays in decisions being made on appropriate accounting treatment. The decisions may trigger backdated write-downs or write-offs of coupons and principal.

Another issue may arise when a portfolio holds sinkable bonds that allow issuers to repay borrowings in installments. When this occurs, a transaction will be processed to reflect the repayment proceeds and a sinking factor is applied to a bond's price and accruals to reflect the reduced balance due on maturity. If these two accounting entries are not processed with the same effective date, false gain and loss impacts will be seen in the security-level return.

Mortgage-backed securities (MBSs) can have similar prepayment factors if principal is repaid periodically. The details of such payments are determined a month in arrears so that there is a time lag before the relevant information is available. This situation leads to backdated updates to valuations, accruals, and transactions in the portfolio accounting system.

EXAMPLE 4

Fixed-Income Performance Query

A portfolio manager's assistant is questioning the monthly total fund-level return on a bond fund that invests in a wide range of fixed-income instruments. Which of the following is the *least likely* contributor to an error?

A The fund has a substantial mortgage-backed security holding.

B A setup error on a newly purchased bond has resulted in the coupon rate being off by a factor of 10.

C An adjustment transaction moving a security between different identifiers has been entered at book cost instead of market value.

Solution

C is correct. An adjustment transaction entered at book cost instead of market value will net out at the total fund level, which is what is being challenged. Therefore, it is unlikely to be a contributor to a total fund-level error.

A is incorrect. Mortgage-backed securities are a likely cause of data problems because of the time lag in availability of information.

B is incorrect. An error in the coupon rate setup for a bond will affect the amount of income it accrues within its valuation and will affect the total fund-level return.

4.5.2 *Illiquid Assets*

The idiosyncratic nature of illiquid investments can be challenging for the operations teams that maintain their records on the accounting system. As Exhibit 12 shows, there is an inverse correlation between the liquidity of an asset and the likelihood of data issues arising. This issue can be thought of in terms of data availability, where at one end of the spectrum, an exchange-traded equity will have real-time data available through multiple sources. On the opposite end of the spectrum, a physical asset or bilateral private transaction is unique and will not have data readily available through third-party vendors. Instead, firms will need to design their own valuation models.

Exhibit 12 Data Challenges Increase as the Liquidity of an Asset Class Decreases

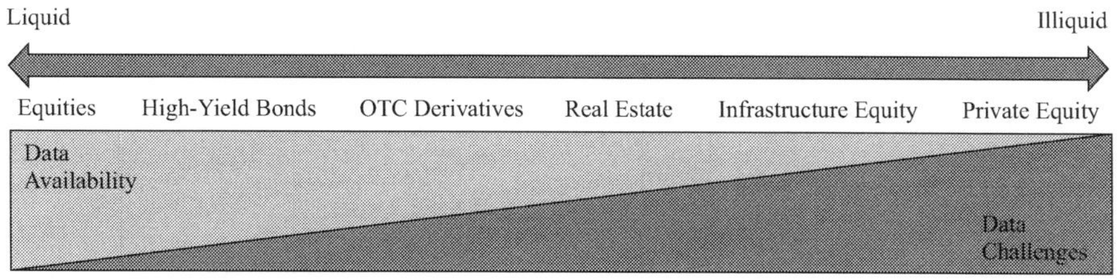

It is common for illiquid assets to be revalued only monthly or quarterly so that any price gain or loss will be posted on a single day. Prices may not be available until some time after the period end, which causes a valuation lag. Details of such transactions as drawdowns or distributions may not be available until after the pricing process has ended. This situation leads to backdating of entries, with the risk that valuation and transaction data reflect inconsistently. Exhibit 13 shows the possible treatment of a private equity investment.

VALUATION OF AN ILLIQUID ASSET

Exhibit 13 features a quarterly valued private equity investment of 100 units, worth 307, ahead of the March quarter end. For the first two days after quarter end, the valuation has not been updated and still shows the December values. On 3 April, the price applied to the investment is updated in the portfolio accounting system; on 7 April, details of a March distribution are available. This results in a return of capital of 20, which also reduces the holding from 100 to 95. The time lag of data availability leading to the need to backdate accounting entries heightens the probability that data are reflected inconsistently or incorrectly in the performance calculation.

Exhibit 13 Illustration of an Illiquid Asset Data Update Timeline

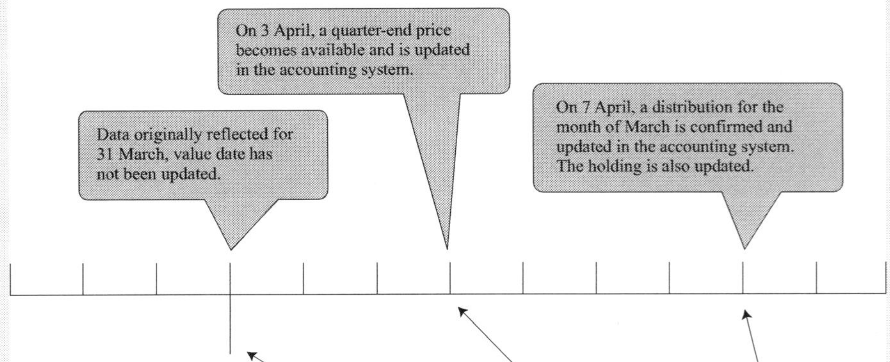

Accounting system entry dates:	31 March	3 April	7 April
Holding	100	100	95
Price	3.07	3.20	3.20
Valuation	307	320	304
Cash Distribution	0	0	20
Total value 31 March	307	320	304
March transactions	0	0	20

Although OTC derivative pricing models have become more standardized, the wide range of potential customized terms and conditions they have leads to a higher likelihood of setup errors. These can affect ongoing cash flows and valuation of the position, resulting in incorrect data. Model-based pricing causes further challenges for pricing teams because variations can occur against counterparty or administrator valuations. These variations can lead to price challenges and corrections, as well as potential time lags in price availability. Understanding the way complex derivatives are booked on accounting systems is also important for enabling the right data to be processed in the performance calculation. A common challenge involves the treatment of multiple legs within a swap transaction. Given these inherent complexities of data processing for illiquid assets, performance practitioners should consider adding controls to detect data issues.

EXAMPLE 5

Illiquid Asset Performance Error

A portfolio manager informs the operations and performance measurement team that the reported return that they have seen for an illiquid asset, a bilateral private transaction, in their fund is wrong. They know what the investment is yielding, and there have been no adverse events, so they know what the return should be. Which of the following is the *least likely* cause of error?

A The end-of-period price for an asset has not been updated.

B A cash distribution was recorded in the accounting system after performance had been calculated.

C An incorrect price for the illiquid asset was received from a third-party vendor.

Answer

C is correct. Pricing of illiquid assets will not normally be provided by an external market data vendor due to the customized nature of the instruments. A is incorrect because late availability of pricing is a common feature of illiquid assets. B is incorrect because time lags in the availability of information for cash flows relating to illiquid assets can lead to late capture in accounting data.

4.6 Index and Benchmark Data

Index data mostly come directly from an index provider or from other external firms that offer data services. In either scenario, the provider will probably run extensive quality controls before distributing the data, which means that revisions are relatively infrequent. Blended benchmarks involve the combining of two or more indexes to a specified set of weighting rules. An example of a weighting rule is floating weights. With floating weights, the starting allocation between indexes is specified, and then the ongoing weights move as a result of the individual index returns over time. Another example is fixed weights, where the same allocation between indexes is applied to a daily calculation. Rebalancing or re-fixing features starting weights that float for a specified duration, at the end of which they are reset to the same starting weights. Blended benchmark maintenance and calculation can lead to errors in benchmark returns.

DATA ERRORS ARISING FROM CORPORATE ACTIONS

5

A corporate action is an event that brings about a change in securities issued by a company. There are many different types of corporate actions, and each may feature any combination of the following:

- A cash payment or receipt
- A switch between or an issuance of existing securities
- The creation of and a switch to new securities
- Multiple currencies
- The reclassification of one or more securities

Exhibit 14 illustrates common features of corporate actions. The features influence the way that the corporate action is entered in the portfolio accounting.

Exhibit 14 Features of Common Types of Corporate Actions

Type	Optional	Cash Movement	Security Transaction	New Security	Description
New issue	Yes	Payment	Purchase	Yes	Capital raising via new security issuance
Rights issue	Yes	Payment	Multiple	Yes	Offer rights to existing shareholders to purchase new shares at discount. Rights are tradeable
Dividend	No	Receipt	Income	No	Distribution of profits in cash
Stock dividend	Yes	Receipt	Income/purchase	No	Dividend taken in the form of new shares instead of cash
Tender offer	Yes	Receipt	Sale	No	Company offers to buy back certain number of shares from shareholders
Bonus issue	No	No	Adjustment	No	New shares issued at no cost. Increases shares in issue and reduces price
Stock split	No	No	Adjustment	No	Increase in the number of shares in issue by a set ratio (e.g., 3:1). Will result in corresponding reduction in share price
Consolidation	No	No	Adjustment	No	Opposite of a stock split and will increase nominal price
Takeover/merger	No	Receipt	Yes	No	A company acquires another with payment in cash and/or shares
Spinoff	No	No	Adjustment	Yes	A company splits into two or more separately listed entities. Shareholders receive shares in new entities with decrease in value of existing holding

In order to check the data reflected for a corporate action, it is helpful to start with a clear understanding of what happened in the market:

- What assets does the portfolio hold that are affected by the corporate action—the starting position?
- What decisions were made (if the event is voluntary)?
- What transactions occurred as a result of the corporate action?
- What was the end result?

Similar to the case of non-market transactions, portfolio accounting records for corporate actions may be reflected in a way that does not suit the needs of performance calculation. Common problems with corporate actions data include the following:

- Transactional entries reflect book cost (not market value) equivalent.
- Holdings and transactions fall out of synchronization.

A lack of timeliness of information flow for corporate actions often leads to late portfolio accounting updates for both transactions and prices. As with all performance data, it is useful to think of corporate actions in terms of gain or loss on each individual line as well as in aggregate across relevant assets. If any data entries do not support accurate gain or loss calculated at these levels, return, risk, and attribution analysis may be inaccurate. Also in line with other performance data issues, the aggregate performance return from a corporate action over its full duration may be correct even where data errors affect individual lines or time period returns. This outcome can be caused by equal and opposite error impacts between security lines or from one day to the next.

Exhibit 15, Exhibit 16, and Exhibit 17 show how corporate actions can be structured and reflected in portfolio accounting systems. They illustrate a range of issues that can arise and lead to incorrect investment returns. For example, transactions that do not reflect market values cause performance data distortions, as do missing steps when creating temporary securities.

ILLUSTRATION OF A TAKEOVER

A UK company completes a takeover of a domestic rival in which shareholders of the target company receive 1 share in the acquirer for every 10 shares they hold. No cash payments are involved. The scenario illustrated relates to a fund that holds shares in both the acquirer and the target company, in the amounts shown. The original holdings are 100 shares and 200 shares, respectively, and in line with the terms of the takeover, the holder receives 1 share in the acquiring company, leading to a resulting position of 120 shares in the acquiring company.

Exhibit 15

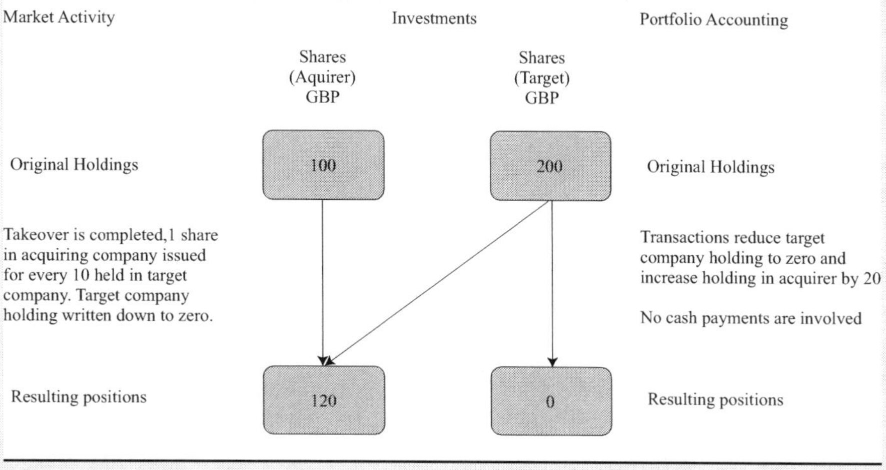

The accounting system entries for this corporate action are relatively straightforward because there are only two securities and two transactions involved. There is only one currency involved, which prevents the possibility of currency errors. These features should limit the likelihood of errors occurring.

As long as holdings and transaction movements are aligned for each security and between the two securities, there should be no data synchronization issues. At a total portfolio level, as long as the two transactional entries are of equal and opposite value, there should be no overall (incorrect) impact on returns. If the entries are not equal and opposite, then it will affect both the individual security returns and the total portfolio return. Under such circumstances, the security-level returns are potentially at risk of data error. If the transactional entries are recorded at book cost rather than market value, it would lead to incorrect returns on both of the security lines.

A simple check of the calculated returns can be performed where there are no cash movements involved. The return should simply reflect total ending value of assets divided by total starting value.

AN ILLUSTRATION OF A RIGHTS ISSUE

A company proposes a rights issue of 7 new shares at $1.78 for 15 existing shares (a rights issue allows a company to raise funds from existing shareholders by issuing new shares). The illustration assumes an initial holding of 150 shares in the company and that the rights issue is taken up. This situation results in a new total position of 220 shares.

Exhibit 16

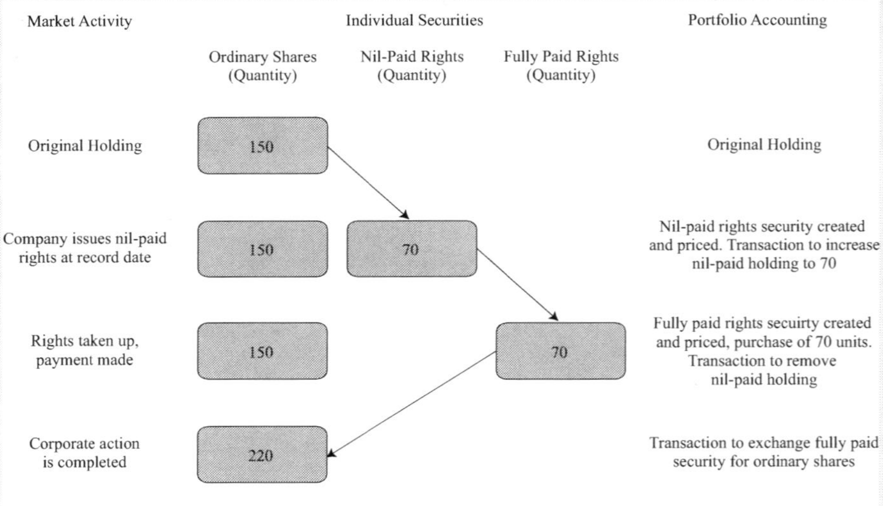

From an accounting perspective, the rights issue features the creation of two new temporary securities, transfers between the different securities, and a cash payment. If any of the transactions used to move between the lines of security do not reflect the prevailing market value of the respective line, it will lead to incorrect returns. Inconsistencies between holding and transaction data are also a potential source of error. This applies to each individual security and in aggregate for the three securities. Problems can occur if the newly created securities are not set up with classifications, such as industry or sector, aligned to the ordinary shares. This situation could lead to their return impacts appearing in different parts of attribution analysis.

AN ACQUISITION AND A MERGER

A US company whose shares are priced in dollars acquires a UK company priced in sterling. The transaction involves the creation of a new holding company that will wholly own all of both the acquiring company and the target once the transaction is completed. Shareholders in the target company are offered the chance to choose between cash and shares, but the acquirer has the right to determine the final split on the basis of rules that it has specified. Under the final terms of the deal, shareholders in the acquirer receive shares in the new company at a ratio of 1:1. Shareholders in the target company receive new company shares at a ratio of 1:4 (one new share for every four shares of the target company held) plus a payment of USD2 per share.

Exhibit 17 Example of an Acquisition and a Merger

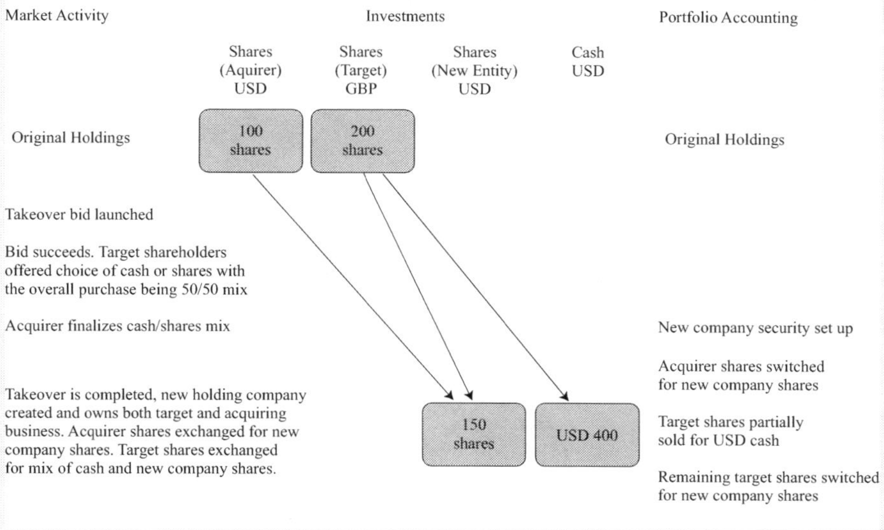

Reflecting this corporate action in the portfolio accounting system requires the creation of two new securities, transfers between securities, and a partial sale. As with the rights issue example, if the transfers reflect a book value, then performance will not be correct. The fact that the takeover is a cross-border action adds complexity because of the inclusion of securities in different currencies. This complexity adds another potential source of incorrect data for the performance calculation. Unlike the rights issue, the acquisition and merger happen in a single step, which makes it less likely to lead to synchronization issues between holdings and transactions. However, the optional element (the choice between cash or shares) means that the final payment details would likely have been calculated on the eve of the deal completing. This could lead to delays in the final transactions being booked in the accounting system, which does give rise to data synchronization issues.

EXAMPLE 6

Corporate Action Data Challenges

The manager of the corporate actions team in the operations department contacts the manager of the performance team to say she has heard that corporate actions are causing problems for performance reporting. She wants to know how her team can work with the performance team to minimize any future problems. Which of the following statements is *most* accurate?

A The calculation of performance needs adjustment transactions to be reflected at a market value because the use of book cost doesn't meet performance needs.

B Corporate actions can cause problems at the individual security level, but they do not affect total fund-level returns.

C New securities created as a result of cash dividends and tender offers need to be handled correctly; otherwise they may affect the accuracy of performance attribution.

Answer

A is correct. The statement is accurate because the use of book cost on transactions will affect calculated returns. B is incorrect because corporate actions can indeed cause problems at the individual security level, but they may also affect the overall fund-level return and risk. C is incorrect because cash dividends and tender offers do not result in new securities being created.

6 CURRENCY EXPOSURE AND RETURN DISCREPANCIES

For any portfolio that invests in assets outside of its own base currency, there will be performance impacts from currency exposure. These include both real investment impacts and, potentially, issues caused by accounting policies and calculation methodology.

6.1 Accounting Policy

The choice of exchange rates used for end-of-day asset valuation will influence the return on a portfolio. If the exchange rates used are not aligned with those in the relevant portfolio benchmark, it will make the assessment of relative performance difficult. For example, if a well-constructed index-tracking global equity portfolio were to use valuation exchange rates that are different from its benchmark, its performance would diverge from the benchmark return.

Although there are a multitude of daily exchange rates available, the London 4:00 p.m. rates are commonly used by major global index providers for end-of-day currency conversion. Aligning accounting valuation exchange rates to these rates will eliminate one source of return discrepancy from currency exposure.

Accounting policy will also determine which exchange rates are applied to transactions for conversion to base or reporting currency. Accounting policies tend to be simplistic, such as using end-of-day rates. More sophisticated approaches exist, such as linking trades to specific spot foreign exchange (FX) transactions.

For simplistic approaches, such as applying start-of-day or end-of-day exchange rates, there will be a policy calculation effect present on each asset for which a transaction occurs. Because the transaction creates a cash impact with opposite signage (i.e., buy asset = sell cash), there is an offsetting effect within the cash return. Consequently, at a total level, the portfolio return will not show any impact from the policy.

The impact of accounting policy exchange rates on transactions works differently for purchases and sales, as shown in Exhibit 18. This exhibit introduces the subject of the impact of exchange rate accounting policy, and Exhibit 19 builds on it. Candidates may find it useful to consider these exhibits together.

IMPACT OF FX RATE ACCOUNTING POLICY ON RETURNS

A euro-based portfolio starts with USD100 worth of assets, and the EUR/USD exchange rate is 1.1 (USD1.1 per EUR1). The assets are sold for proceeds of USD102, and at the end of the period, the EUR/USD rate is 1.05. The first sale proceeds row shows gain or loss on the asset using a start-of-period exchange rate for the trade. The bottom row shows the same calculation using the end-of-period exchange rate. A different base currency gain is calculated for the two rates.

Exhibit 18 Impact of FX Rate Accounting Policy on Returns, Excluding Cash

	Values		FX Rate	Gain/Loss	
	USD	EUR	EUR/USD	USD	EUR
Start-of-period value	100.00	90.91	1.10	—	—
Sale proceeds: Start FX	−102.00	−92.73	1.10	2	1.82
Sale proceeds: End FX	−102.00	−97.14	1.05	2	6.23

Exhibit 19 builds on Exhibit 18 and shows the same example with cash impacts included. It also shows sale and purchase scenarios. The transaction value in the sale and purchase scenarios has been set to create a gain of 2 on US dollar assets in both scenarios. In both tables, the same total fund gain in euros is observed, but the amounts attributed between assets and cash are different because of the exchange rate effect. Performance practitioners should be aware of the potential impact of FX accounting policy and use this potential impact as a channel of investigation when base currency returns on an asset are being questioned.

Exhibit 19 Impact of FX Rate Accounting Policy on Returns, Including Cash

Asset Sale

	USD			EUR			FX Rate
	Assets	Cash	Total	Assets	Cash	Total	EUR/USD
Start-of-period value	100.00		100.00	90.91		90.91	1.10
Transactions	−102.00	102.00		−92.73	92.73		1.10

(continued)

Exhibit 19 (Continued)

Asset Sale

	USD Assets	USD Cash	USD Total	EUR Assets	EUR Cash	EUR Total	FX Rate EUR/USD
End-of-period value		102.00	102.00		97.14	97.14	1.05
Gain/loss	2.00		2.00	1.82	4.41	6.23	

Asset Purchase

	USD Assets	USD Cash	USD Total	EUR Assets	EUR Cash	EUR Total	FX Rate EUR/USD
Start-of-period value		100.00	100.00		90.91	90.91	1.10
Transactions	100.00	−100.00		90.91	−90.91		1.10
End-of-period value	102.00		102.00	97.14		97.14	1.05
Gain/loss	2.00		2.00	6.23		6.23	

One scenario where transaction exchange rate policy will not "wash out" is when a portfolio experiences a cash flow (inflow or outflow) that is not in its own base currency. If this situation occurs, the choice of exchange rate to be applied will directly affect the starting valuation on which subsequent gains or losses are calculated. Such instances are likely to be rare because mutual funds have such mechanisms as currency share classes to deal with them and separate accounts will have a designated base currency.

6.2 Currency Hedging

Forward FX contracts, where rates at which currencies will be exchanged in a month are locked into today, can be used to reduce the currency exposure in particular assets or on a portfolio as a whole. Implementation of hedging is imperfect because the value of the assets being hedged will move with the market. This movement leaves the portfolio either over- or underhedged as the sold amount on the forward FX remains unchanged. This will generate a real return impact on the portfolio that can be quantified, and that the amount is not significant will be of interest to portfolio managers. Where a portfolio is managed against a currency-hedged benchmark, there may be relative performance impacts caused by the benchmark hedging methodology. A common approach in benchmark hedging methodology is for the index provider to take the currency composition of the index at the beginning of the month and use prevailing market rates to apply notional one-month forward FX positions back to 100% base currency. The forward contracts are revalued each day until month end, when they are replaced by new one-month forward hedges using the same process. This approach has the same imperfections as portfolio hedging, noted previously. It also means that where the portfolio hedging approach is different from the benchmark, there will be real relative return impacts. For example, the portfolio managers may use three-month forward FX contracts, or they may adjust hedging positions when asset trading occurs in the portfolio.

6.3 Dual Currencies

In some cases, an investment may be valued in one currency but pay dividends or coupons in another. Such instruments can be difficult for accounting systems to handle automatically because of this unusual feature since they may be able to use only a single currency. If this is the case, dividends and coupons may be accrued and recorded in one currency but settled in another. Such situations may require intervention, and the implied exchange rate (received amount/expected amount) can cause a performance impact if it varies from prevailing rates.

Similar situations occur with trades in securities within a restricted market. In a restricted market, the local government places controls that include limiting who is allowed to buy and sell the local currency. Here, securities traded in local currency may be settled by the custodian in a fund's base currency. The effective exchange rate applied to the trade will create a real performance impact if it diverges from prevailing rates used in portfolio accounting.

Exhibit 20 illustrates how performance can be affected when coupon proceeds in a restricted market currency are converted into another currency by an external custodian and then paid to the portfolio. Because the conversion is a real trade, its impact on performance is not an error. In this example, the fund receives USD392 less than it was expecting in dollar terms, which will result in the portfolio's cash return and total level return being lower by the basis point equivalent of USD392. The return on the bond will be unaffected because the accounting policy conversion amount of USD56,192 will be used for calculating its return.

Exhibit 20 Dual-Currency Coupon Payment

Coupon on Korean Won Bond		
Coupon proceeds	KRW	100,000,000
Accounting value of coupon converted	USD	56,192
Custodian executed FX sold	KRW	100,000,000
Custodian executed FX bought	USD	55,800
Performance impact from FX		−392

6.4 Global Investment Performance Standards (GIPS) Composites

Composites involve combining the performance track records of multiple funds using a weighted average approach. Combining portfolios with different base currencies is allowable if the investment strategies are similar and consistent with the composite definition, but the correct approach needs to be followed. If different currency track records are combined without first converting into a common currency, it will create meaningless results. This is due to both (1) combining different currency returns and (2) weighting using market values in different currencies.

In order to accurately construct composites containing funds with different base currencies, they must first be converted into a common currency. As long as the same exchange rates are applied to each portfolio and benchmark return, then the relative geometric return will remain consistent. Exhibit 21 illustrates the issue.

COMPOSITE CONSTITUENTS AND CURRENCIES

This example shows a composite made up of four constituent funds running similar investment strategies. The funds' base currencies are different. The total line in the first table shows the outcome if an incorrect approach is used—if local currency values are combined before converting to a common currency. The second table shows the correct results, where individual fund values and returns are first converted into the composite's base currency, the US dollar. The US dollar results are then combined to give the total composite return.

The individual funds' relative returns on a geometric basis are the same under both methodologies. The total composite relative return is distorted in the first table mainly by the overweighting due to Fund D being valued in Japanese yen. The individual funds' returns in the second table are also comparable because they are presented in a common currency, showing the correct calculation of the composite's relative return.

Exhibit 21 Converting Reporting Currencies for GIPS Composites

Global Treasury Composite: All Local Currency

Constituent	Base Currency	Value Base (m)	Fund Base CCY	Benchmark Base CCY	Relative Base CCY
Fund A	USD	350	6.6%	6.2%	0.4%
Fund B	EUR	1,000	8.3%	8.0%	0.3%
Fund C	EUR	275	8.4%	8.0%	0.4%
Fund D	JPY	50,000	3.6%	3.0%	0.6%
Total composite	Local	51,625	3.7%	3.1%	0.6%

Global Treasury Composite: Converted to USD

Constituent	Base Currency	Value Base (USD)	Fund USD	Benchmark USD	Relative USD
Fund A	USD	350	6.6%	6.2%	0.4%
Fund B	EUR	909	6.1%	5.8%	0.3%
Fund C	EUR	250	6.2%	5.8%	0.4%
Fund D	JPY	500	5.7%	5.1%	0.6%
Total composite	USD	2,009	6.1%	5.7%	0.4%

Calculations are based on currency moves over the period against the dollar of +2% for the euro and –2% for the Japanese yen and on market value conversion rates of 1.10 for EUR/USD and 100 for USD/JPY.

EXAMPLE 7

Accounting Policy on Exchange Rates

The client reporting team has challenged the returns on a global equity index tracking fund that aims to be fully currency hedged back to the US dollar. The total fund performance is out of line with the hedged benchmark. The unhedged portfolio return including cash is in line with the unhedged benchmark. The portfolio experienced a large cash inflow during the reporting period, which has seen high level of market volatility. Which of the following is the *most likely* cause of this outcome?

A It is due to the portfolio accounting policy choice of valuation FX rates being different from those used in the benchmark.

B The investment of the large inflow may not have been well executed.

C The hedging methodology is different for the fund and its benchmark.

Solution

C is correct. Hedging methodology may well be different for the portfolio and the benchmark. Any difference may be amplified because the portfolio has managed an inflow, which would likely result in an update to currency hedging positions. A is incorrect because it would result in a variance between fund and benchmark performance when looking at unhedged returns, excluding cash. B is incorrect because if it were the case, then it would affect the unhedged portfolio return.

DATA REVISIONS AND PRIOR-PERIOD RETURNS 7

Given the high volume of data that feeds into the performance calculation, it is almost inevitable that data errors that affect returns will occur. In some cases, errors may not be identified until after performance has been calculated and reports issued. If errors do occur, we have a range of considerations that need to be applied when deciding whether performance returns should be restated. Firms should develop and maintain a policy to ensure that the approach to restating returns is consistent and can be justified (firms that comply with GIPS must have an error correction policy in place). Next, we explain the main considerations for shaping a return restatement policy.

7.1 Status of Returns: Indicative, Preliminary, and Final Returns

Firms often produce a series of "indicative" returns. Portfolio management systems often calculate indicative performance using portfolio data that the firm holds or maintains. As the term "indicative" suggests, these are not formal or official returns and would not normally be subject to the need to restate. During the production of reports, a performance team will run validations on the returns and might issue a report to internal stakeholders to review and approve. Prior to receiving approvals, these numbers will be considered preliminary and would, therefore, not be subject to a restatement policy. The focus of our discussion of restatement policies is thus finalized returns. These can be thought of as those having passed validation checks and been issued to all stakeholders. Exhibit 22 provides and overview of the performance production process.

Exhibit 22 Performance: Returns Status

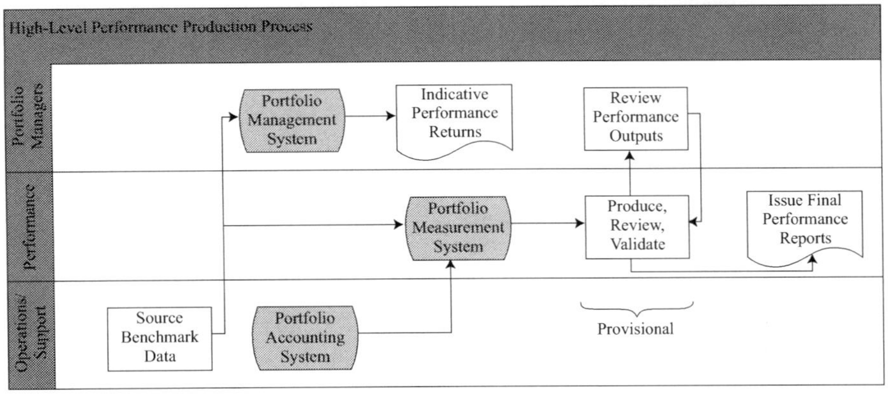

7.2 Stakeholders

The following are two key considerations in deciding whether to restate performance:

- Who are the stakeholders?
- What are the returns being used for?

Performance reports, and performance information in a wider sense, are made available to a wide range of stakeholder groups within the firm and to external parties. Each stakeholder will have his or her own interests in returns and may use them for different purposes. Understanding these purposes is important in order to determine whether a restatement of returns is necessary. Exhibit 23 shows the main stakeholder groups relevant for performance reporting.

Exhibit 23 Performance Measurement Stakeholders

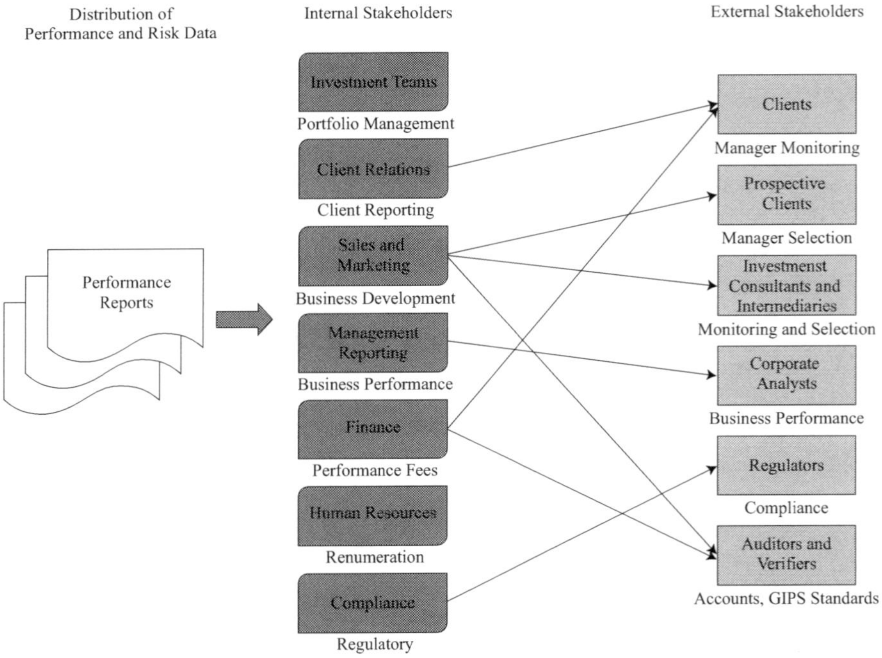

Stakeholders' use of fund returns can broadly be thought of as serving two purposes: information only or decision making. Many internal stakeholders receive performance reports for information purposes, meaning that decisions are not directly made on the basis of the performance numbers. In such cases, the impact of restatements is mainly one of reputational damage or of potentially undermining confidence in the performance team's outputs. Decision-making use includes stakeholders who use returns to calculate fees or payments. Examples include performance-related fees on a portfolio and portfolio manager bonus calculations. In both cases, there may be a financial impact as a result of restating performance. For performance-related fees, a restatement will also affect the client financially and will harm the investment manager's credibility. Whether to hire or retain an investment management firm is a key decision that will be based in part on investment performance. An extreme scenario is when a firm is hired on the basis of an overstated performance track record. In this situation, the firm may suffer reputational damage and could be exposed to mis-selling claims, in addition to being sanctioned by the regulator with potentially extreme consequences. Any form of decision-making use of fund returns is more likely to require a restatement in the event of a data error correction. This is why firms' controls need to be as good as possible to identify and resolve errors before publication, avoiding the need for restatements.

7.3 External Obligations

If an incorrect return has been issued to external stakeholders, specific rules apply. These rules include contractual stipulations in client agreements, local regulatory requirements, and Global Investment Performance Standards policies. Any obligations arising from these rules will need to be satisfied by the action taken in response to the data revision. Firms that are GIPS compliant will have a specific GIPS error correction policy, although this policy may focus on the impact at a composite level rather than the individual portfolio level (see the GIPS "Guidance Statement on Error Correction").

7.4 Materiality

Significance or materiality is an important factor to consider because the impact on returns of a data revision can range from zero to a large change. When determining materiality, an element of subjectivity may be required if there are no specified thresholds. Looking at the size of the return restatement in terms of proportions of risk budget or outperformance targets can provide a starting point, as Exhibit 24 illustrates.

Exhibit 24

Materiality of Performance Restatement

Consider two funds:

- A sovereign bond fund with an annual outperformance target of 0.5% over its benchmark
- An emerging market equity fund with an annual outperformance target of 2.5% over its benchmark.

Using 10% of the outperformance target as a restatement materiality rule would give materiality thresholds of 5 bps for the bond fund and 25 bps for the equity fund. In this case, a data revision that caused performance to change by 0.2% would require the bond fund's performance to be restated, but restatement would not be required for the equity fund's performance.

7.5 Implementing Revisions

Having determined the need to restate returns, there are options for executing the change:

- Full restatement—recalculate and reissue the performance report.
- Recalculate and include corrected history in the next reporting cycle accompanied by an explanation.

In each instance of restatement, a clear audit trail of any data or reporting changes should be kept, including reasons for any decisions that have been made. Clear communication to stakeholders is important to ensure full awareness and understanding of the impact, the cause of the error, and actions taken to prevent it from reoccurring.

EXAMPLE 8

Data Revisions

Staff in the pricing and valuation team in the operations department have alerted the performance team about a major pricing error on an illiquid asset in a fund that has been winning substantial amounts of new business. The error dates back over one year and has resulted in the asset being overvalued. The fund's fee structure includes a simple 0.5% per annum management fee. Which of the following stakeholders would be *most* affected from a decision-making perspective?

A Internal investment desk for monitoring and oversight of performance

B Recently won and prospective new clients because of inflated performance track record

C Fund managers responsible for the portfolio that holds the asset

Solution

B is correct. Existing and prospective clients may have made their decision to invest in the fund on the basis of incorrect performance. A and C are incorrect because this issue highlights failing controls, but the error discovery serves an information purpose for both the fund managers and the monitoring and oversight desk.

SUMMARY

- The scope of data can be varied and wide ranging. Ultimately, data is all information in all forms. It can be structured, sitting within a system or application and extractable and organized in a useful and suitable way, or it can be less structured and be found in spreadsheets or other documents.
- There are different ways in which dimensions of data quality can be described. They include accuracy (valid and correct), completeness (complete for its purpose), conformity (to standards and rules), consistency (of applications of rules across systems), timeliness (available in time for use), and lineage (knowledge of where it comes from).

- Data governance is the ownership and oversight of the firm's data over its life cycle. The data life cycle stages include creation, security and storage, distribution and use, holding and discovery, retention and archiving, and destruction.
- Governance provides overall management of the data over its life cycle and responsibility over the integrity of the data, leading to good data management practices.
- Data governance will put in place the framework and oversight within the firm's departments to ensure the transparency, accuracy, and ownership of data across the organization.
- Failure to implement a robust data governance framework creates a multitude of risks for the firm's strategic and customer outcomes.
- Data errors feeding into the performance calculation will lead to inaccurate returns. In turn, these will distort any *ex post* risk calculations.
- Data errors fall into two types: (1) incorrect valuation of an asset or transaction and (2) inconsistency between transactions and valuations, including associated cash impacts.
- Data errors include transaction booking errors, security and asset setup errors, and pricing and valuation issues.
- Fixed-income securities, with a wide variety of unique characteristics, are particularly prone to setup errors. Incorrect coupon rates or payment dates, accrued interest day-count conventions, or special features or structures, such as sinkable bonds or mortgage-backed securities, all pose challenges.
- Illiquid assets' unique characteristics and lack of data availability give rise to challenges in performance measurement. Time lags in data availability and customized terms and conditions of many derivatives are some of the issues that pose difficulties in valuations and return calculations.
- Corporate actions pose a range of data challenges. Common problems include transaction entries that reflect book cost equivalents rather than market values. Another common problem is synchronization issues between holdings and transactions.
- Return discrepancies may arise from currency exposures. Currency exposure itself does not cause return discrepancies, but treatment of currencies may. The key factors playing a role are the accounting policy chosen and the presence of currency hedging or dual currencies.
- Returns may require restatement if errors are identified after performance has been calculated and reports issued.
- Firms should develop and maintain policies to make sure the approach to restating returns is consistent and can be justified.
- Key considerations in restatements include stakeholders' roles and responsibilities and the ultimate purpose of the returns. Additional considerations include external obligations and materiality of errors.

PRACTICE PROBLEMS

1 A UK investment manager's new data warehouse uses the 12-character ISIN alphanumeric code to identify securities. In contrast, the firm's existing performance system (which receives feeds from the data warehouse) uses the seven-character SEDOL alphanumeric code for security identification. What dimension of data quality is of *most* concern in this situation?

A Lineage

B Conformity

C Consistency

2 The data in an accounting or performance system is said to be in structured form in the sense that:

A there are both a record and knowledge of where the data come from.

B the data are complete given the purpose for which they were intended.

C the data are extractable and organized in a manner suitable for the application's use.

3 In response to a verifier's question about data integrity measures, the firm's manager of performance reporting states that "her analysts review any instances where the NAV has moved more than 25 bps over a set period of time when being used for regulatory reports." The manager's response is an example of addressing which dimension of data quality?

A Accuracy

B Timeliness

C Consistency

4 Which data governance principle requires ensuring that all data generated by an organization undergo a quality review to guarantee accuracy and completeness?

A Hold & Discover

B Consume & Create

C Retention & Archive

5 The *second* stage of the investment data life cycle is referred to as:

A Store & Secure.

B Consume & Create.

C Distribution & Use.

6 In a data governance framework, the deciding vote on any changes to any of the data definitions, rules, systems of record, or usage for a dataset is cast by the data:

A owner.

B governance lead.

C governance officer.

7 In a data governance framework, ensuring that all governance-related principles are operating as expected and monitored for non-compliance is the responsibility of the data:

A steward.

B governance lead.

C governance officer.

8 Which of the following data are *most likely* to be enriched prior to being extracted from the accounting system?

A Returns that are calculated directly within an accounting system

B Adjustments that are entered at book cost in the accounting system

C Accounting system codes that are recognized by the performance system

9 Owing to their nature, which of the following asset classes is *most likely* to engender challenging data issues for operations teams that maintain their records on an accounting system?

A Real estate

B Private equity

C Infrastructure equity

10 Which of the following transactions recorded in the accounting system is *most likely* to satisfy the downstream performance system's requirements?

A An asset transfer between two portfolios at book cost

B A market trade involving cash payment between the counterparties

C The acquisition of a US company whose shares are priced in dollars by a Swiss company whose shares are priced in francs.

11 How many temporary securities must be created in the portfolio accounting system to reflect a rights issue that is taken up?

A One

B Two

C Three

12 An investment manager's global equity composite has four constituent funds, each with a different base currency. The firm claims compliance with the GIPS standards. Which of the following statements regarding the global equity composite is *most* accurate?

A The composite's benchmark-relative return is most meaningful when calculated in the constituent funds' base currencies.

B The individual funds' benchmark-relative returns in their base currencies are the same, on a geometric basis, as those calculated in a common currency.

C The individual funds' returns in their base currencies are comparable because each fund is managed according to similar investment strategies that are consistent with the composite definition.

13 Which of the following statements regarding a firm's exchange rate policy is *most* accurate?

A The choice of exchange rates used for end-of-day asset valuation will not influence the return on a portfolio.

B Applying start-of-day exchange rates to transactions will result in a policy calculation effect on each asset for which a transaction occurs.

C Applying end-of-day exchange rates to transactions will result in a policy calculation effect at the total portfolio level.

14 A domestic mid-cap growth fund with an annual outperformance target of 2.0% over its benchmark has generated a three-year annualized return of 19.33% for the period ending 31 December 2019. In addition to the management fee, the fund also charges a performance-based fee that is shared with the portfolio manager. An error from January 2016 that caused the year's annual return to be understated by 17 bps was discovered in April 2020. Which of the following stakeholders is *most likely* to be interested in a restatement of the fund's performance?

A An investment consultant

B The firm's human resources department

C A client whose account was opened on 31 March 2020

SOLUTIONS

1 B is correct. Conformity, as a data quality dimension, is described as ensuring that the data conform to internally defined standards and rules. For example, when transferring a file between two systems, a check is run to ensure that the character length of the attribute in the file being sent from the first system matches what is expected to be received by the second system. A is incorrect. Lineage, as a data quality dimension, can be defined as understanding where the data have come from (the origin), what happens to the data, and where the data move over time. It allows errors to be traced and helps ensure the data quality for all its intended purposes. C is incorrect. Consistency as a data quality dimension is described as the uniform application of data quality rules across one or more systems or applications for the same attribute or dataset. For example, if System A has a rule to "report any instance where the NAV has moved over 5 bps in a day," then other systems that hold NAV information also should apply this rule.

2 C is correct. In the context of investment performance measurement, it is helpful to consider data as being in one of two distinct forms. The first form is structured in the sense that data sitting within a system or application, such as an accounting system or portfolio performance system, are extractable and organized in a way that make them useful and suitable for the application's use. A is incorrect because the statement describes the "lineage" dimension of data quality, not the distinct form of data referred to as "structured." B is incorrect because the statement describes the "completeness" dimension of data quality, not the distinct form of data referred to as "structured."

3 A is correct. The accuracy dimension of data quality ensures that data are valid and correct. There is an appropriate level of accuracy of the data for its intended purpose. This outcome can be achieved through validation to an authoritative source of data or by comparing multiple sources of the same data. An example of an accuracy rule is, "Report any instances where the NAV has moved over 40 bps over a set period of time when being used for client reports." B is incorrect. The timeliness dimension of data quality ensures that the data are being reviewed in order to guarantee that they are not stale. The rules will test whether the attribute has been updated per the expected frequency. Actual frequency is compared with the expected frequency. Generally, timeliness refers to getting information at the right time and quickly enough to meet reporting and analytical requirements. C is incorrect. The consistency dimension of data quality ensures that data quality rules are applied consistently across one or more systems or applications for the same attribute or dataset.

4 B is correct. The Consume & Create data governance principle requires ensuring that all data consumed or created by an organization have a purpose and reason and undergo review for quality to guarantee that accuracy and completeness are maintained in all circumstances. A is incorrect. The Hold & Discover data governance principle requires ensuring that data will be held in a manner that allows for timely, efficient, and accurate discovery from any interested party, including regulatory bodies and clients that may legitimately request access to the data. C is incorrect. The Retention & Archive data governance principle requires ensuring that data will be held for the appropriate amount of time, considering all legal, regulatory, business, and historical requirements.

5 A is correct. Data go through several stages. These span from (1) Consume & Create, through (2) Store & Secure, (3) Distribution & Use, and (4) Hold & Discover, all the way to (5) Retention & Archive and possibly (6) Destruction.

B is incorrect. Consume & Create is the first stage of the investment data life cycle. C is incorrect. Distribution & Use is the third stage of the investment data life cycle.

6 A is correct. The data owner is accountable for making sure data stewards are in place for the data that he or she has been assigned. The data owner also acts as the deciding vote on any changes to any of the data definitions, rules, systems of record, or usage for his or her dataset. B is incorrect. The data governance lead provides day-to-day support for the data governance officer and is responsible for ensuring that all data governance–related principles and activities are operating as expected through the implementation (or “operationalization”) of the data governance structure. He or she monitors for non-compliance, escalates any such occurrences to the data governance officer, and builds awareness within the organization. C is incorrect. The data governance officer is responsible for developing an environment that ensures transparency of all current data governance–related policies and objectives for the organization.

7 B is correct. The data governance lead provides day-to-day support for the data governance officer and is responsible for ensuring that all data governance–related principles and activities are operating as expected through the implementation (or “operationalization”) of the data governance structure. He or she monitors for non-compliance, escalates any such occurrences to the data governance officer, and builds awareness within the organization. A is incorrect. The data steward is responsible for ensuring that data maintenance is upheld within a specific system of record. C is incorrect. The data governance officer is responsible for developing an environment that ensures transparency of all current data governance–related policies and objectives for the organization.

8 B is correct. Accounting data may need to be enriched in order to suit performance measurement calculations. An example of enrichment is the application of rules to create a market value amount for an adjustment that is entered into the accounting system at book cost. A is incorrect. There is a risk that the process of extracting data from the accounting system and loading these data into the performance system will create data errors, unless returns are calculated directly within an accounting system, mitigating the risk of incorrect performance numbers. C is incorrect. Enrichment can take the form of mapping, such as converting accounting system codes into categories recognized by the performance system. In this case, however, the accounting system codes do not require enrichment since they are already recognized by the performance system.

9 B is correct. There is an inverse correlation between the liquidity of an asset and the likelihood of data issues arising. Private equity is considered to be the least liquid investment class of the three choices. The issue can be thought of in terms of data availability, where at one end of the spectrum, an exchange-traded equity will have real-time data available through multiple sources. At the opposite end of the spectrum, a bilateral private transaction is unique and will not have data readily available through third-party vendors. Instead, firms will need to design their own valuation models. A is incorrect. Data challenges increase as the liquidity of asset classes decreases. Real estate as an investment class is considered more liquid than private equity and infrastructure equity. C is incorrect. As shown in Exhibit 12, although infrastructure equity as an asset class is less liquid than real estate, it is considered more liquid than private equity.

10 B is correct. For market trades involving a cash payment between counterparties, such as a purchase or sale of a bond, the accounting system transaction values will normally satisfy the performance system’s needs. A is incorrect. The accounting treatment of an asset transfer between two portfolios at book cost

can create a false gain on the receiving portfolio with a corresponding loss on the sending portfolio when the transferred asset's value is greater than its book cost. C is incorrect. The accounting for corporate actions may reflect book cost. In most instances, performance measurement needs to capture a market-valued transaction entry to ensure consistency with the valuation of assets, which is normally done on a mark-to-market basis.

11 B is correct. From an accounting perspective, the rights issue features the creation of two new temporary securities that must be created in the portfolio accounting system. A is incorrect. The rights issue features the creation of two (not one) new temporary securities. C is incorrect. The rights issue features the creation of two (not three) new temporary securities.

12 B is correct. The individual funds' benchmark-relative returns on a geometric basis are the same, whether the funds' and benchmark's local currency returns are used or the funds' and benchmark's returns are first converted into the composite's common currency. As long as the same exchange rates are applied to each fund and benchmark return, the relative geometric returns will remain consistent. A is incorrect. Combining portfolios with different base currencies is allowable if the investment strategies are similar and consistent with the composite definition and the constituent funds' values and returns are first converted into the composite's common currency. If different currency track records are combined without first converting into a common currency, it will create meaningless results. C is incorrect. The individual funds' returns are comparable when presented in a common currency.

13 B is correct. Applying start-of-day or end-of-day exchange rates will result in a policy calculation effect for each asset for which a transaction occurs. A is incorrect. The choice of exchange rates used for end-of-day asset valuation will influence the return on a portfolio. If the exchange rates used are not aligned with those in the relevant benchmark, it will make the assessment of relative performance difficult. C is incorrect. Applying start-of-day or end-of-day exchange rates will result in a policy calculation effect for each asset for which a transaction occurs. Because the transaction creates a cash impact with opposite signage (i.e., buy asset = sell cash), there is an offsetting effect within the cash return. Consequently, at a total level, the portfolio return will not show any impact from the policy.

14 B is correct. Internal stakeholders that use returns to calculate payments include the firm's human resources department. Remuneration to the portfolio manager of the mid-cap growth fund includes a bonus if performance targets are met. Consequently, there may be a direct financial impact for the portfolio manager as a result of any restated performance. The human resources department will use a restatement to determine whether the portfolio manager received the correct amount of compensation. A is incorrect. An investment consultant would likely consider a 17 bp annual return understatement that occurred more than four years earlier as serving an informational role, given that the mid-cap growth fund generated a three-year annualized return of 19.33% for the period ending 31 December 2019. C is incorrect. When determining materiality, there is an element of subjectivity required if there are no pre-specified thresholds. Looking at the size of the return restatement in terms of proportions of risk budget or outperformance targets can provide a starting point. Using 10% of the outperformance target as a restatement materiality rule (i.e., 20 bps), the error from January 2016 would be considered immaterial. In addition, although the error may undermine confidence in the performance team, the error understated, rather than overstated, the fund's performance.

PERFORMANCE EVALUATION:
STUDY SESSION

3

Return Attribution and Benchmark Analysis

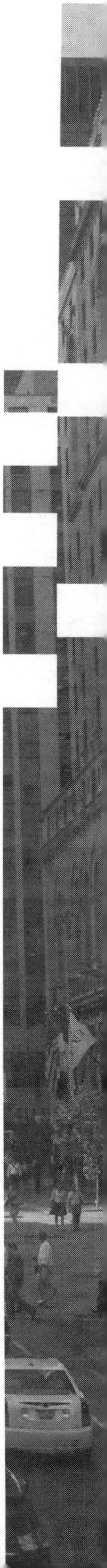

Return attribution is a set of techniques used to identify the sources of excess return of a portfolio against its benchmark in order to understand the consequences of active management decisions. "Return attribution" is often used interchangeably with "performance attribution" by practitioners. However, the first reading and the CIPM custom curriculum define performance attribution to include "return attribution" and "risk attribution." Risk attribution is introduced in the next study session.

Return attribution involves the selection of appropriate benchmarks. The second reading discusses the theory and practice of benchmark selection.

READING ASSIGNMENTS

6 Return Attribution
by Carl R. Bacon, CIPM, and Marc A. Wright, CFA

7 Introduction to Benchmarks
by C. Mitchell Conover, PhD, CFA, CIPM, Daniel Broby, FSIP, and David R. Cariño, PhD

READING

6

Return Attribution

by Carl R. Bacon, CIPM, and Marc A. Wright, CFA

Carl R. Bacon, CIPM, is at StatPro and the University of Manchester (United Kingdom). Marc A. Wright, CFA, is at Russell Investments (USA).

LEARNING OUTCOMES

Mastery	*The candidate should be able to:*
☐	**a.** explain purposes of return attribution and the role of return attribution in the investment decision-making process;
☐	**b.** distinguish between return attribution and return contribution analysis;
☐	**c.** distinguish between return attribution and risk attribution;
☐	**d.** describe the attributes of an effective attribution process;
☐	**e.** analyze the sources of performance of a portfolio using the Brinson–Hood–Beebower and Brinson–Fachler models;
☐	**f.** calculate and interpret arithmetic allocation, selection, and interaction attribution effects;
☐	**g.** explain the use of an interaction effect, including its advantages and disadvantages;
☐	**h.** calculate and interpret geometric allocation, selection, and interaction attribution effects;
☐	**i.** describe returns-based, holdings-based, and transactions-based attribution, including the advantages and disadvantages of each;
☐	**j.** distinguish between the effects of sponsors' and managers' investment decisions;
☐	**k.** calculate and interpret attribution analysis at different levels: plan sponsor, portfolio manager, country, industrial sector, and individual security;
☐	**l.** interpret the results of a factor model–based return attribution analysis;
☐	**m.** compare Brinson models (asset-grouping models) with factor models of attribution, including the advantages and disadvantages of each;
☐	**n.** explain why the standard Brinson approach may not be suitable for fixed-income strategies;
☐	**o.** describe the different types of fixed-income attribution models and interpret the results of a fixed-income attribution analysis;

(continued)

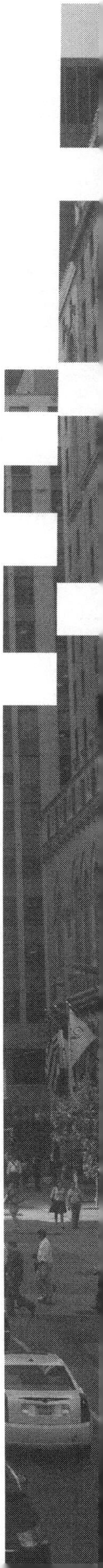

LEARNING OUTCOMES

Mastery	The candidate should be able to:
☐	**p.** explain the inputs necessary for a holdings-based and a transactions-based return attribution analysis and the problems associated with each;
☐	**q.** explain possible causes of residuals in attribution analysis;
☐	**r.** calculate and explain off-benchmark (zero-weight sector) attribution effects.

1 INTRODUCTION

A previous reading explained how rate of return is defined, measured, and interpreted. Investment performance measurement—establishing the returns earned by a portfolio—is essentially a descriptive process. Performance analysts also need to analyze performance records to evaluate how the portfolio was managed and which decisions were profitable or unprofitable. Questions they may want to answer about a portfolio include the following:

- Did the portfolio's return exceed, equal, or fall short of that of its assigned benchmark (reference point)?
- What active sector (e.g., industry) weighting decisions did the portfolio manager make? That, is, which sectors did he or she overweight (underweight) relative to the benchmark's weightings?
- Were active sector decisions profitable?
- Did the manager seek profits through individual security selection?
- Were individual security selection decisions profitable?
- Was the way the portfolio manager sought to add value consistent with the manager's self-description of his/her investment discipline?

The techniques of return attribution can provide answers to such questions and any question that addresses the consequences of investment decisions. Return attribution analysis is particularly important when performance is weak; portfolio managers must demonstrate an understanding of their performance, provide a rationale for their decisions, and generate confidence in their ability to add value in the future. Return attribution provides quality control for the investment process across asset management firms, illuminating key strengths and weaknesses essential to managing a complex business with multiple investment strategies. Return attribution also provides information that is helpful for investigating investment management skill—the subject of performance appraisal.

The balance of this reading is organized as follows. Section 2 provides an overview of the various types of return attribution analysis and their purposes. Section 3 presents arithmetic return attribution models, including the foundation Brinson models, and Section 4 presents geometric return attribution models. Section 5 contrasts holdings-based and transactions-based return attribution. Section 6 discusses the variations in the number of levels at which return attribution is performed. Section 7 introduces factor-based return attribution. The return attribution modeling presented up to Section 7 is developed with an equity focus; Section 8 offers a concise introduction to fixed-income return attribution, often considered to be a specialist area. Section 9 addresses several common problems in return attribution. Section 10 concludes and provides a summary.

RETURN ATTRIBUTION: AN OVERVIEW

2

To evaluate the performance of an actively managed portfolio, analysts often compare the portfolio's returns with those of its assigned benchmark. If we assume that the benchmark return represents the performance available from a passive investment in some appropriately selected segment of the market, then the difference between the performance return and the benchmark return represents the performance as a result of active investment decisions. The difference between the return on a portfolio and the return on its assigned benchmark is known in the investment performance field as the portfolio's **excess return**.[1] In this reading, outperformance (underperformance) is sometimes used to refer to positive (negative) excess return with respect to a benchmark. A dictionary definition of the verb "attribute" is "to explain something by indicating a cause." Return attribution can be defined as follows:

- **Return attribution** is a set of techniques used to identify the sources of the excess return of a portfolio against its benchmark in order to understand the consequences of active investment decisions.

2.1 Purposes of Return Attribution

Return attribution is part of the feedback loop of the portfolio management process, quantifying active decisions of portfolio managers, monitoring consistency, and informing senior management and clients. As a feedback mechanism, return attribution can be thought of as "backward looking" or *ex post*, meaning that it is used to evaluate the investment decisions for some historical time horizon. Return attribution allows us to look across a specific time horizon and identify which investment decisions have either added or detracted value from the portfolio, relative to its benchmark.

A Common Type of Return Attribution

Suppose a portfolio's return for the past year was 5.24% and the portfolio's benchmark return for that same time period was 3.24%. In this case, the portfolio achieved a positive arithmetic excess return of 2.00% (5.24% – 3.24% = 2.00%) over the past year.

Return attribution can then be applied to understand how the 2.00% was achieved. Was the return achieved by selecting securities that performed well relative to the benchmark or avoiding benchmark securities that performed relatively poorly (*security selection*)? Or was the return achieved by choosing to over-invest in (or overweight) a particular economic sector or asset category that outperformed the total benchmark for that period or to underinvest in or avoid (or underweight) an asset category that underperformed the total benchmark (*asset allocation*)?

1 The term *active return* is also frequently used to describe the excess return of a portfolio in relation to the benchmark return. We are consistent in using *excess return* only in the one sense given in the current reading; in other contexts, the reader should be aware that it can refer to a return in excess of the risk-free return.

Models of equity return attribution often attempt to separate the investment process into those two key decisions—selection and allocation—assigning both a magnitude and direction (plus or minus) for both decisions. For instance, using the above data, we might calculate the return attribution results shown in Exhibit 1:

Exhibit 1 Total Portfolio Return Attribution Analysis (Time Period: Past 12 Months)

Portfolio Return	Benchmark Return	Excess Return	Allocation Effect	Selection Effect
5.24%	3.24%	2.00%	–0.50%	2.50%

As we noted, the investment decisions generated a positive excess return of 200 basis points (bps) relative to the benchmark. We use the return attribution analysis to see how this 200 bps was generated. First, we should note that the *negative* allocation effect indicates that the asset allocation decisions over the past 12 months, whatever they were, had a negative impact on the total portfolio performance. They *subtracted* 50 bps from the excess return. In contrast, the *positive* selection effect indicates that the security selection decisions—decisions to overweight or underweight securities relative to their benchmark weights—*added* 250 bps to the excess return. Our return attribution analysis implies that the portfolio manager's security selection decision was far superior to his or her asset allocation decision for the time period examined.

When conducting a return attribution analysis, we need to also consider the different perspectives important to different roles within the investment process. The fund sponsor, for example, will be interested in different parts of the investment process than the portfolio manager because the fund sponsor will delegate some portion of the management to the portfolio manager. The fund sponsor will want to understand if any added value from the portfolio manager is consistent through time and consistent with the manager's stated investment discipline. Any added value derived from a source other than that explicitly described in the investment process may be random or not repeatable. Return attribution analysis can provide evidence in support of the claimed competencies of the portfolio manager. Prospective clients will want evidence of the investment process supported by return attribution analysis.

Return attribution may also identify other problems, such as holding too much cash in a rising market or unnecessarily high transaction costs when implementing part of the decision process.

2.2 Return Attribution vs. Return Contribution Analysis

Occasionally, performance analysts may conduct an *absolute* return attribution analysis, also known as return contribution analysis. We refer to it as absolute return attribution because, unlike return attribution as ordinarily understood, it is not calculated relative to a benchmark. Return contribution analysis uses only the weights and returns of the portfolio (without reference to the weights and returns of a benchmark).

- **Return contribution analysis** (**absolute return attribution**) identifies the contributions of portfolio components to the total return of a portfolio.

For return contribution analysis, we look at portfolio weights, component security or sector returns, and the weighted return or *contribution to return*. Contribution to return is calculated as the product of the security or sector weight multiplied by the security/sector return, as in:

$$R = \sum_{i=1}^{i=n} w_i R_i$$

where

n = the number of sectors or securities in the portfolio
w_i = the weight of the sector or security in the portfolio
R_i = the return of the sector or security in the portfolio
$w_i R_i$ = the contribution to portfolio return

The sum of the contributions to return is equal to the total portfolio return, R. Consider the example of a portfolio containing the three securities listed in Exhibit 2.

Exhibit 2 Return Contribution Analysis

	Weight (%)	Return (%)	Contribution(%)
Security A	25	4.80	1.20
Security B	50	2.50	1.25
Security C	25	−1.20	−0.30
Portfolio Total	100	2.15	Sum = 2.15

For each security, there is a weight, a return, and a contribution to return. The sum the contributions to return gives the total portfolio return: 1.20 + 1.25 + −0.30 = 2.15.

This return contribution analysis indicates that securities A and B made similar contributions to the total return (1.20 and 1.25 respectively). Although security B had a much larger weight in the portfolio (50%) than security A (25%), security B's significantly smaller return (2.5% versus 4.8%) produced a contribution almost equal to security A. Security C, with a negative return, had a negative contribution to the total portfolio return.

Return contribution analysis can tell us which securities have the greatest (and least) impact on the total portfolio return. But, as noted, the analysis does not include a comparison to a performance benchmark. So, although contribution analysis provides some insight into the *absolute* impact of individual securities (or groups of securities) on the portfolio, it is not informative about whether investment decisions added value *relative* to the benchmark.

EXAMPLE 1

Return Contribution Analysis

Return contribution analysis can be used to:

A measure the investment risk relative to the benchmark.

B compare the relative impact of securities within a portfolio.

C identify the investment value added from the asset weighting decisions relative to the benchmark.

Solution:

B is correct. Return contribution analysis is used to compare the weighted returns of separate investments within a portfolio, thus allowing the impact of those separate investments to be compared.

2.3 Return Attribution vs. Risk Attribution

Complementary to return attribution is risk attribution. Whereas return attribution analyzes the consequences of active investment decisions on returns, risk attribution analyzes the risk consequences of such decisions. Depending on the purpose of the analysis, risk may be viewed in absolute or benchmark-relative terms. For example, when risk relative to a benchmark is the focus, a risk attribution analysis might identify and evaluate a portfolio's deviations from a benchmark's exposures to risk factors. Risk attribution is presented in detail in a separate reading.

Performance attribution is defined to include return attribution and risk attribution (although in practice "performance attribution" is frequently used to just mean "return attribution").

EXAMPLE 2

Return and Risk Attribution

1 Return attribution can *best* be used to:

A measure volatility within a portfolio.

B adjust performance returns for external cash flows.

C analyze the value added by active investment decisions.

2 Return attribution attempts to identify investment management value added by:

A identifying which security selection decision was the best overall within the portfolio.

B focusing on the analysis of holdings that have made the greatest contribution to return.

C decomposing the excess return into the separate contributors to excess return from allocation and selection decisions relative to the benchmark.

3 Risk attribution is *best described* as concerned with identifying:

A the level of risk in a portfolio.

B contributions to a portfolio's alpha risk.

C the contributors to risk either in a benchmark-relative or absolute sense.

Solution to 1:

C is correct. Return attribution attempts to analyze whether value was added by active investment decisions.

Solution to 2:

C is correct. A typical return attribution analysis includes a decomposition of the excess return into the excess return generated by the asset allocation and security selection decisions separately.

Solution to 3:

C is correct. Risk attribution provides insight into the key contributors to risk.

2.4 Effective Return Attribution

Although first developed as an aid for portfolio management, return attribution analysis is equally useful for senior management, client relationship specialists, risk controllers, operations staff, and sales and marketing professionals on the one hand and clients and prospective clients on the other hand. In identifying the sources of excess return, it is the tool that allows performance analysts to add value and to participate in the investment decision process.

In effect, return attribution analysis is the tool that converts performance measurement information from the back office to information that is useful to the middle office control function. Effective return attribution analysis requires a deep understanding of the investment decision process; return attribution must reflect the active decisions of the portfolio manager. There is little value in analyzing factors that are not part of the investment decision process.

An effective return attribution process must:

- reconcile to the total portfolio return,
- reflect the investment decision process,
- quantify the active decisions of the portfolio manager, and
- provide a complete understanding of the excess return of the portfolio.

If the return generated by the return attribution analysis does not reconcile to the return presented to the client, then at best the return attribution is incomplete and at worst the quality of the return attribution analysis is brought into doubt. If the return attribution does not reflect the investment decision process, then the analysis will be of little value to either the portfolio manager or client. For example, if the portfolio manager is a genuine bottom up stock picker who ignores sector benchmark weights, then any value in measuring the impact of sector allocation against these weights relates not to measuring success in stock picking but to gauging the unintentional sector return effects of the manager's investment discipline.

Return attribution provides a good starting point for a dialogue with clients, explaining both positive and negative aspects of recent performance. In fact, return attribution analysis is particularly important when performance is weak; portfolios managers must demonstrate an understanding of their performance, provide a rationale for their decisions, and generate confidence in their ability to add value in the future. When it accurately reflects the investment decision-making process, return attribution provides quality control for the investment process; it provides senior management with the tool they need to manage a complex business with multiple investment strategies.

EXAMPLE 3

Effective Return Attribution

An effective return attribution process is best described as:

A adjusting fully for risk.

B identifying poor performance.

C quantifying the investment decision process.

Solution:

C is correct. Return attribution analysis does not focus on adjusting for risk, nor does it attempt to identify poor performance alone. Return attribution may be effective if it quantifies and thus reflects the investment decision process.

3 ARITHMETIC EQUITY RETURN ATTRIBUTION

The foundations of return attribution were established in two articles written by Brinson and Fachler (1985) and Brinson, Hood, and Beebower (1986); today these are collectively known as defining the **Brinson model**. The Brinson model could be called an **asset-grouping model** in the sense that it isolates attributions effects by comparing the returns of variously constructed portfolios or groups of assets.

These articles build on the assumption that the total portfolio and benchmark returns can be disaggregated as follows:

$$\text{Portfolio return } R = \sum_{i=1}^{i=n} w_i R_i \tag{1}$$

$$\text{Benchmark return } B = \sum_{i=1}^{i=n} W_i B_i \tag{2}$$

where

w_i = weight of the ith sector in the portfolio
R_i = return of the portfolio assets in the ith sector
W_i = weight of the benchmark in the ith sector
B_i = return of the benchmark in the ith sector
n = number of sectors or securities[2]

The sum of the weights in both the portfolio and benchmark is required to equal 100%. That is,

$$\sum_{i=1}^{i=n} w_i = 1 \text{ and } \sum_{i=1}^{i=n} W_i = 1$$

If the weights of the portfolio sum to less than 100%, it means some part of the portfolio is missing and the analysis will be incomplete. If the weights of the portfolio sum to greater than 100%, it means that either the total value of the portfolio is incorrect or the value of one or more sectors is incorrect. The total sum of the parts of the portfolio cannot be greater than the total portfolio size. The presence of leverage would require a negative weight (borrowings or short positions) to balance to 100%.

At this stage, we are concerned with only single period, single currency return attribution models. Multi-period, multi-currency models will be covered in other readings.

The challenge for attribution analysis is to quantify each of the portfolio manager's active decisions that explain the difference between the portfolio return R and the benchmark return B.

Exhibit 3 provides data for a three-sector domestic equity portfolio.

2 n is taken to refer to a number of sectors or securities depending on context. Null (zero weight) holdings are counted in n. For sectors, the number should be the same for portfolios and their benchmarks. The count of securities, however, will generally vary between a portfolio and its benchmark. In summations involving a portfolio and its benchmark, n can be understood to be the number of unique holdings that are in either the portfolio or the benchmark, counting cash as a holding.

Exhibit 3 Brinson Model Illustration

Sector	Portfolio Weight	Benchmark Weight	Portfolio Return	Benchmark Return
Energy	50%	50%	18%	10%
Health Care	30%	20%	–3%	–2%
Financials	20%	30%	10%	12%
Total	**100%**	**100%**	**10.1%**	**8.2%**

The total portfolio return $R = \sum_{i=1}^{i=n} w_i R_i$ is:

$$R = 50\% \times 18\% + 30\% \times -3\% + 20\% \times 10\% = 10.1\%$$

The total benchmark return $B = \sum_{i=1}^{i=n} W_i B_i$ is:

$$B = 50\% \times 10\% + 20\% \times -2\% + 30\% \times 12\% = 8.2\%$$

Thus, 10.1% – 8.2% = 1.9%. A return difference of 190 bps between the portfolio's and the benchmark's returns needs to be attributed to the portfolio manager's decision.

3.1 The Brinson–Hood–Beebower (BHB) Model

Brinson, Hood, and Beebower (1986) presented a breakdown of the arithmetic excess return assuming a simple two-step investment decision process in which the portfolio manager seeks to add value through both allocation and selection.

In return attribution, **allocation** refers to the value the portfolio manager adds by having different sector weights in the portfolio than the sector weights in the benchmark. A sector weight in the portfolio greater than the equivalent benchmark sector weight would be described as *overweight* and a lesser weight would be described as *underweight.*

Clearly, the portfolio manager will aim to overweight outperforming sectors and underweight underperforming sectors. In their original article, Brinson, Hood, and Beebower called this effect *timing. Allocation* is a more appropriate, and now more common, label.

Selection refers to the value the portfolio manager adds by holding individual securities or instruments within the sector in different-than-benchmark weights. The portfolio manager making selection decisions may or may not be the same portfolio manager making the allocation decisions. In fact, allocation decisions may often be made collectively by an asset allocation committee.

Again, the portfolio manager will aim to overweight outperforming securities relative to their respective benchmark and underweight underperforming securities relative to their respective benchmark.

3.1.1 *Allocation*

To identify the added value from allocation, we will calculate the return of an intermediate fund called the "allocation notional fund," which is one step away from the benchmark portfolio and one step toward the actual portfolio. The term notional is used in this context to describe the hypothetical return that results from the portfolio manager's allocation decisions but includes none of the selection decisions.

In the allocation notional fund, the sector weights of the actual fund are applied to the benchmark returns within each sector. By definition, the return on this notional fund includes all the portfolio manager's sector allocation decisions but excludes all individual security selection decisions (because benchmark returns are used within the sector).

Allocation notional fund return[3] is

$$B_S = \sum_{i=1}^{i=n} w_i B_i \tag{3}$$

The allocation notional return for the data from Exhibit 3 is:

$$B_S = 50\% \times 10\% + 30\% \times -2\% + 20\% \times 12\% = 6.8\%$$

The contribution from asset allocation is the difference between the allocation notional fund return and the benchmark return or:

$$B_S - B = \sum_{i=1}^{i=n} w_i B_i - \sum_{i=1}^{i=n} W_i B_i = \sum_{i=1}^{i=n} (w_i - W_i) B_i \tag{4}$$

The contribution to allocation in the ith sector is

$$A_i = (w_i - W_i) B_i \tag{5}$$

Note that the sum of sector contributions to allocation equals the arithmetic excess return from allocation:

$$\sum_{i=1}^{i=n} A_i = B_S - B \tag{6}$$

The contribution to arithmetic excess return from allocation for the portfolio data shown in Exhibit 3 is $B_S - B = 6.8\% - 8.2\% = -1.4\%$. Individual sector allocation effects $A_i = (w_i - W_i)B_i$ are as follows:

Energy	(50% – 50%) × 10% = 0.0%
Health care	(30% – 20%) × –2.0% = –0.2%
Financials	(20% – 30%) × 12% = –1.2%
Total	0.0% – 0.2% – 1.2% = –1.4%

The portfolio weight in the Energy sector is in line with the benchmark weight, therefore, there is no contribution to allocation in this sector.

There is, however, an overweight position of 10% in the Health Care sector, which when applied to the negative benchmark return of –2.0%, results in a contribution of –0.2%. The manager has overweighted a poorly performing sector.

It follows, if there is an overweight sector, there must be a least one other underweight sector. The 10% underweight position in Financials combined with a 12.0% benchmark return results in a contribution of –1.2%. The manager has underweighted a strongly performing sector. The total contribution to arithmetic excess return from sector allocation is –1.4%

3 The allocation notional fund will be renamed later to the semi-notional fund, which explains the subscript S in B_S.

EXAMPLE 4

Allocation Using the BHB Model

Exhibit 4 Three-Sector Portfolio Example

Sector	Portfolio Weight	Benchmark Weight	Portfolio Return	Benchmark Return
Technology	20%	30%	−11.0%	−10.0%
Telecommunications	30%	40%	−5.0%	−8.0%
Utilities	50%	30%	−8.0%	−5.0%
Total	**100%**	**100%**	**−7.7%**	**−7.7%**

Using the BHB model, the allocation effect of Utilities based on the portfolio data in Exhibit 4 is:

A −1.6%

B −1.5%

C −1.0%

Solution:

C is correct. $(w_i - W_i)B_i = (50\% - 30\%)(-5.0\%) = -1.0\%$. The portfolio was 20% overweight in a sector delivering −5% performance, thus contributing −1% to the overall allocation effect.

A is incorrect because $(w_i - W_i)R_i = (50\% - 30\%)(-8.0\%) = -1.6\%$. The portfolio return of −8% has been used rather than the benchmark return.

B is incorrect because $W_iB = 30\%(-5.0\%) = -1.5\%$ represents only the contribution to the benchmark return from Utilities.

3.1.2 *Selection*

To identify the added value from selection, we will calculate the return of a different intermediate fund called the "selection notional fund," which is also one step away from the benchmark return but isolates a different decision of the portfolio manager in the investment decision process. In the selection notional fund, the sector weights of the benchmark are maintained and applied to the sector returns achieved by the portfolio manager. By definition, the return on this notional fund includes the portfolio manager's individual selection decisions, but excludes any contribution from allocation effects.

Selection notional fund return is

$$R_S = \sum_{i=1}^{i=n} W_i R_i \tag{7}$$

Again using the data from Exhibit 3, the selection notional return is:

$$R_S = 50\% \times 18\% + 20\% \times -3\% + 30\% \times 10\% = 11.4\%$$

The contribution from selection is the difference between the selection notional fund return and the benchmark return:

$$R_S - B = \sum_{i=1}^{i=n} W_i R_i - \sum_{i=1}^{i=n} W_i B_i = \sum_{i=1}^{i=n} W_i \times (R_i - B_i) \tag{8}$$

The contribution to selection in sector i is:

$$S_i = W_i(R_i - B_i) \quad (9)$$

Note that:

$$\sum_{i=1}^{i=n} S_i = R_S - B \quad (10)$$

Exhibit 3 Brinson Model (BHB) Illustration (repeated)

Sector	Portfolio Weight	Benchmark Weight	Portfolio Return	Benchmark Return
Energy	50%	50%	18%	10%
Health Care	30%	20%	−3%	−2%
Financials	20%	30%	10%	12%
Total	**100%**	**100%**	**10.1%**	**8.2%**

For the portfolio data shown in Exhibit 3, the contribution to arithmetic excess return from selection is $R_S - B$ = 11.4% – 8.2% = 3.2%. Sector selection effects $S_i = W_i(R_i - B_i)$ are as follows:

Energy	50% × (18% – 10%) = 4.0%
Health Care	20% × (−3.0% + 2.0%) = −0.2%
Financials	30% × (10.0% – 12.0%) = −0.6%
Total	4.0% – 0.2% – 0.6% = 3.2%

Selection within the Energy sector added 800 bps to the benchmark sector return; applying the benchmark weight of 50% to this sector resulted in a 4.0% contribution to arithmetic excess return.

Selection in the Health Care sector subtracted 100 bps from the sector benchmark return sector; applying a 20% weighting thus resulted in a contribution of –0.2%.

Selection within Financials was also poor, subtracting 200 bps from the benchmark sector return; applying a 30% weighting thus generated a contribution of –0.6%.

Total contribution to arithmetic excess return from selection is 3.2 percentage points.

Combining allocation of −1.4% and selection of 3.2%, 1.8% of total added value of 1.9% is explained and 0.1% is so far unexplained. This 0.1% contribution to excess return is explained by the interaction of selection and allocation decisions.

EXAMPLE 5

Selection Using the BHB Model

Exhibit 5 The BHB Model and Selection

	Portfolio Weight	Benchmark Weight	Portfolio Return	Benchmark Return
Materials	30%	20%	12.0%	8.0%
Industrials	30%	20%	8.0%	10.0%

Exhibit 5 (Continued)

	Portfolio Weight	Benchmark Weight	Portfolio Return	Benchmark Return
Consumer Staples	40%	60%	5.0%	8.0%
Total	**100%**	**100%**	**8.0%**	**8.4%**

Using the BHB model, the selection effect of Industrials based on the portfolio data shown in Exhibit 5 is:

A –2.0%

B –0.6%

C –0.4%

Solution:

C is correct. $W_i(R_i - B_i) = (20\%)(8.0\% - 10.0\%) = -0.4\%$. In the industrials sector the portfolio manager underperformed by 2%. Applying the benchmark weight of 20%, the contribution to selection from Industrials is –0.4%.

A is incorrect because –2.0% is simply the arithmetic difference of return in the industrials sector: 8.0% – 10.0%= –2.0%.

B is incorrect because $w_i(R_i - B_i) = (30\%)(8.0\% - 10.0\%) = -0.6\%$. The portfolio weight has been used rather than the benchmark weight.

3.1.3 *Interaction*

In the BHB model, selection and allocation do not explain the arithmetic difference completely. For example, in the attribution analysis based on Exhibit 3, allocation (–1.4%) and selection (3.2%) together represent just 1.8 percentage points of the arithmetic difference between the portfolio return of 10.1% and the benchmark return of 8.2%; 0.1% (i.e., 10 bps) is missing. Thus, a third term, which will be called interaction, is required:

$$\text{Selection} + \text{Allocation} = (R_S - B) + (B_S - B)$$

or

$$= R_S + B_S - 2B \neq R - B$$

To achieve attribution factors that add up to the arithmetic difference between the portfolio and benchmark returns, we must introduce a third term called interaction:

$$\underbrace{R_S - B}_{\text{Selection}} + \underbrace{B_S - B}_{\text{Allocation}} + \underbrace{R - R_S - B_S + B}_{\text{Interaction}} = R - B \quad (11)$$

In their article, Brinson, Hood, and Beebower described this term as *Other;* interaction is perhaps a better description and is in common usage today. Interaction is not a residual, rather it is a directly calculable effect resulting from the combination of (or interaction between) allocation and selection effects, so that:

$$R - R_S - B_S + B = \sum_{i=1}^{i=n} w_i R_i - \sum_{i=1}^{i=n} W_i R_i - \sum_{i=1}^{i=n} w_i B_i + \sum_{i=1}^{i=n} W_i B_i$$

The right hand side simplifies to

$$\sum_{i=1}^{i=n} (w_i - W_i)(R_i - B_i) = \sum_{i=1}^{i=n} I_i \quad (12)$$

defining the contribution of sector i to interaction I_i as $I_i = (w_i - W_i)(R_i - B_i)$ or (Sector weighting difference)$_i$ × (Sector return difference)$_i$. Thus,

$$\sum_{i=1}^{i=n} I_i = R - R_S - B_S + B \quad (13)$$

Again using the portfolio data from Exhibit 3:

$$R - R_S - B_S + B = 10.1\% - 11.4\% - 6.8\% + 8.2\% = 0.1\%$$

Individual sector interaction effects, calculated as $I_i = (w_i - W_i)(R_i - B_i)$, are

Energy	(50% – 50) × (18% – 10%) = 0.0%
Health Care	(30% – 20%) × (–3.0% + 2.0%) = –0.1%
Financials	(20% – 30%) × (10.0% – 12.0%) = 0.2%
Total	0.0% – 0.1% + 0.2% = 0.1%

The overall contribution from interaction is small in this case. But the interaction effect need not be small; it is the combination of allocation and selection decisions and typically, although not necessarily, will be greater for larger asset allocation bets.

For the Energy sector, the portfolio weight is in line with the benchmark weight and thus there is no contribution to interaction.

For the Health Care sector, there is an allocation overweight decision of +10%. We have 10% more of portfolio value allocated to this underperforming sector than the benchmark has; because the manager had a negative selection in this sector, a negative contribution from interaction of –0.1% resulted.

In Financials, there is an underweight decision of 10% in this sector in which the manager also showed negative selection. We have less of this sector in which the manager underperforms the benchmark; therefore, the combined effect of being underweight in an underperforming sector is an added value of +0.2%. Total contribution from interaction is +0.1%.

The return attribution results are summarized in Exhibit 6.

Exhibit 6 BHB Return Attribution Results

	Portfolio Weight	Benchmark Weight	Portfolio Return	Benchmark Return	Allocation	Selection	Interaction
Energy	50%	50%	18%	10%	0.0%	4.0%	0.0%
Health Care	30%	20%	–3%	–2%	–0.2%	–0.2%	–0.1%
Financials	20%	30%	10%	12%	–1.2%	–0.6%	0.2%
Total	**100%**	**100%**	**10.1%**	**8.2%**	**–1.4%**	**3.2%**	**0.1%**

EXAMPLE 6

Interaction

Exhibit 7 Sample Portfolio Data

	Portfolio Weight	Benchmark Weight	Portfolio Return	Benchmark Return
Materials	30%	20%	12.0%	8.0%
Industrials	30%	20%	8.0%	10.0%
Consumer Staples	40%	60%	5.0%	8.0%
Total	**100%**	**100%**	**8.0%**	**8.4%**

Using the BHB model, the interaction effect of Industrials based on the portfolio data in Exhibit 7 is:

A −0.20%

B −0.04%

C 0.00%

Solution:

A is correct: $(w_i - W_i)(R_i - B_i)$ = (30% − 20%)(8.0% − 10.0%) = −0.2%. The portfolio is 10% overweight in a sector in which the manager underperformed by 200 bps; hence, there is an additional −0.2% contribution to performance.

B is incorrect: $(w_i - W_i)(R_i - B)$ = (30% − 20%)(8.0% − 8.4%) = −0.4%. Total benchmark return is used instead of benchmark sector return.

C is incorrect: $(w_i - W_i)(R_i - R)$ = (30% − 20%)(8.0% − 8.0%) = 0.00%. Total portfolio return is used instead of benchmark sector return

Exhibit 8 illustrates the Brinson framework for return attribution.

Exhibit 8 Brinson Framework for Return Attribution

		Selection: Actual	Selection: Passive
Allocation	Actual	**Quadrant I** Portfolio Return $R = \sum_{i=1}^{i=n} w_i R_i$	**Quadrant II** Allocation Notional $B_S = \sum_{i=1}^{i=n} w_i B_i$
Allocation	Passive	**Quadrant III** Selection Notional $R_S = \sum_{i=1}^{i=n} W_i R_i$	**Quadrant IV** Benchmark Return $B = \sum_{i=1}^{i=n} W_i B_i$

Excess returns are calculated as follows:

Asset allocation II − IV

Security selection III – IV

Interaction I – III – II + IV

Total I – IV

Graphically, Exhibit 9 illustrates the attribution factors for each sector i. The contribution to total portfolio return from sector i is the area w_iR_i; the contribution from the benchmark is area W_iB_i. Note that in this particular exhibit, $R_i > B_i$ and $w_i > W_i$.

The contribution to excess return in sector i is the sum of the areas representing Selection $W_i(R_i - B_i)$, Allocation $(w_i - W_i)B_i$, and Interaction $(w_i - W_i)(R_i - B_i)$.

Exhibit 9 Diagram of BHB Model

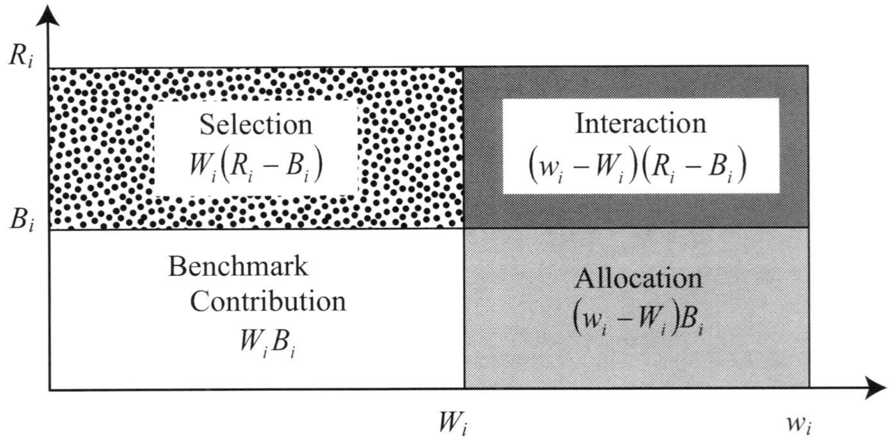

The BHB model successfully breaks down the sources of arithmetic excess return. But does it reflect the investment decision process of the portfolio manager?

For the most part, asset allocation decisions are made in the context of an overall benchmark return. The portfolio manager is not only seeking to be overweight in markets that make positive returns but also to be overweight in markets that outperform the overall benchmark. The portfolio manager will lose value by being overweight in a market with a positive return if that return is less than the overall benchmark. Therefore, in such a situation, a return attribution model is needed that better reflects the decision process by showing a negative allocation effect.

3.2 Brinson–Fachler Model

The Brinson–Fachler (BF) model differs from the BHB model only in how **individual sector allocation** effects are calculated.

In the BHB model, all overweight positions in sectors with positive returns will generate positive allocation effects irrespective of the overall benchmark return, whereas all overweight positions in negative markets will generate negative allocation effects.[4] Thus, overweighting a sector i that earns a positive return, $B_i > 0$, results in a positive allocation effect, $A_i = (w_i - W_i)\ B_i > 0$, even when the sector return is less than the overall benchmark return (i.e., $B_i < B$). When the sector return is negative, $0 > B_i$, overweighting produces a negative allocation effect, $A_i = (w_i - W_i)\ B_i < 0$.

4 In their original articles, Brinson, Hood, and Beebower and Brinson and Fachler did not emphasize this difference, but over the decades, performance measurement practitioners have attributed slightly different methodologies to each of these papers.

Clearly, if the portfolio manager is overweight in a negative market that has outperformed the overall benchmark, the effect should be positive.

The BF model solves this problem by modifying the asset allocation factor to compare returns with the overall benchmark as follows:

$$B_S - B = \sum_{i=1}^{i=n}(w_i - W_i)B_i = \sum_{i=1}^{i=n}(w_i - W_i)(B_i - B) \quad (14)$$

Because $\sum_{i=1}^{i=n} w_i = \sum_{i=1}^{i=n} W_i = 1$ the constant B can be introduced. The contribution to asset allocation in the ith sector is now:

$$A_i = (w_i - W_i)(B_i - B) \quad (15)$$

Note that in Equation 15 the allocation effect at the portfolio level, $B_S - B$, is unchanged from the BHB model.

Graphically extending Exhibit 9 to include the benchmark return, in Exhibit 10 we observe no change to the areas representing Selection and Interaction, but Allocation is now described by the area $(w_i - W_i)(B_i - B)$. Note that in this particular exhibit $R_i > B_i > B$ across all sectors because $\sum_{i=1}^{i=n} W_i B_i = B$

then $\sum_{i=1}^{i=n} W_i(B_i - B) = 0$,

and because $\sum_{i=1}^{i=n} w_i = \sum_{i=1}^{i=n} W_i = 1$

then $\sum_{i=1}^{i=n}(w_i - W_i)B = 0$.

Exhibit 10 Diagram of BF Model

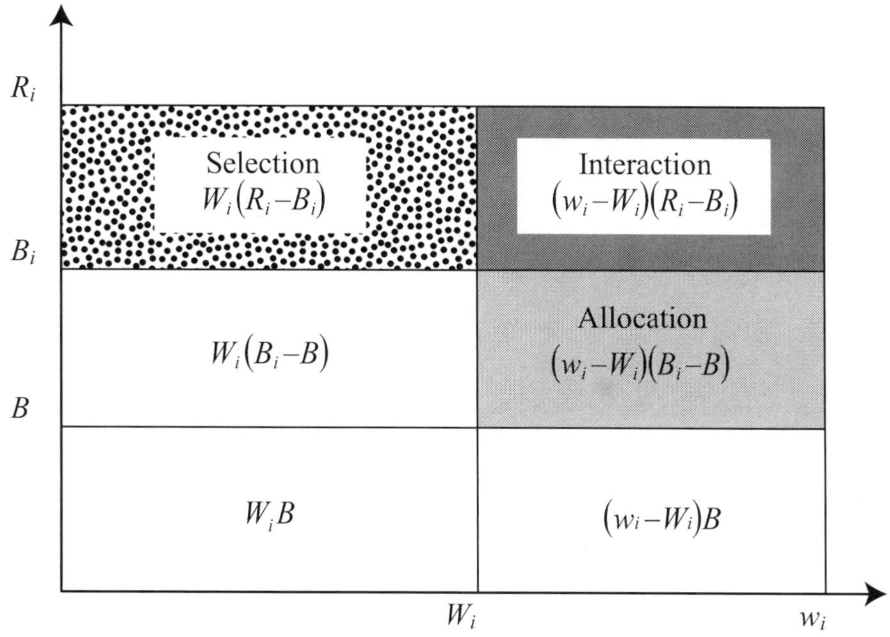

The only difference between the two versions of the Brinson model is the calculation of individual sector allocation effects. The BF model is more aligned with most portfolio manager's decision processes and thus far more popular.

The contribution to arithmetic excess return from sector allocation for the portfolio data shown in Exhibit 3 is $B_S - B$ = 6.8% − 8.2% = −1.4%. Revised BF sector allocation effects are calculated for the portfolio data in Exhibit 3 as follows, using $A_i = (w_i - W_i)(B_i - B)$:

Energy	(50% − 50%) × (10% − 8.2%) =0.0%
Health care	(30% − 20%) ×(−2.0% − 8.2%) = −1.02%
Financials	(20% − 30%) × (12% − 8.2%) = −0.38%
Total	0.0% − 1.02% − 0.38% = −1.4%

The impact in Healthcare is much greater. In addition to being overweight in a negative market, which cost −0.2%, the portfolio manager is correctly penalized the opportunity cost of not being invested in the overall market return of 8.2%, generating a further cost of 10% × −8.2% = −0.82% and resulting in a total impact of −1.02%. To describe it another way, the portfolio is 10% overweight in a market that is underperforming the overall market by −10.2% (−2.0% − 8.2%) and generating a loss of −1.02%

The impact in Financials is much smaller. Although being underweight in a positive market cost −1.2%, we must add back the opportunity cost of being invested in the overall market return of 8.2%, generating a contribution of −10% × −8.2% = 0.82% and resulting in a total impact of −0.38%. To describe it another way, the portfolio is 10% underweight in an industry that is outperforming the overall market by 3.8% (12.0% − 8.2%), generating a loss of −0.38%. As expected, at the portfolio level, the allocation effect of −1.4% remains the same as that calculated with the BHB model.

The revised attribution effects, which can be compared with the BHB results in Exhibit 6, are summarized in Exhibit 11. Readers will note that the exhibits differ only in the individual allocation effects.

Exhibit 11 BF Return Attribution Results

	Portfolio Weight	Benchmark Weight	Portfolio Return	Benchmark Return	Allocation	Selection	Interaction
Energy	50%	50%	18%	10%	0.0%	4.0%	0.0%
Health Care	30%	20%	−3%	−2%	−1.02%	−0.2%	−0.1%
Financials	20%	30%	10%	12%	−0.38%	−0.6%	0.2%
Total	**100%**	**100%**	**10.1%**	**8.2%**	**−1.4%**	**3.2%**	**0.1%**

EXAMPLE 7

Allocation Using the BF Model

Exhibit 12 Sample Portfolio Data

	Portfolio Weight	Benchmark Weight	Portfolio Return	Benchmark Return
Technology	20%	30%	−11.0%	−10.0%
Telecommunications	30%	40%	−5.0%	−8.0%

Exhibit 12 (Continued)

	Portfolio Weight	Benchmark Weight	Portfolio Return	Benchmark Return
Utilities	50%	30%	−8.0%	−5.0%
Total	**100%**	**100%**	**−7.7%**	**−7.7%**

Using the BF method, the allocation effect of Utilities based on the portfolio data in Exhibit 12 is:

A −1.50%

B 0.54%

C 1.35%

Solution:

B is correct: $(w_i - W_i)(B_i - B) = (50\% - 30\%)(-5.0\% + 7.7\%) = 0.54\%$. The portfolio was 20% overweight in a sector outperforming the overall benchmark by 2.7%, therefore contributing 0.54% to the overall allocation effect.

A is incorrect: $W_iB_i = 30\% \times -5.0\% = -1.5\%$ is the contribution to the benchmark return from Utilities.

C is incorrect: $w_i(B_i - B) = 50\% \times (-5.0\% + 7.7\%) = +1.35\%$. Only the portfolio weight of 50% has been used, not the overweight position of 20%.

3.3 Interaction Effect

A shortcoming of both Brinson models is the interaction or "other" term. Interaction is not part of the investment decision process because portfolio managers simply do not seek to add value through interaction decisions. It is a mathematical consequence of the other decisions; the interaction between allocation and selection effects.

For most investment decision processes, the allocation decision comes first and selection decisions follow after the cash has been allocated to the sector.

For genuine bottom-up stock pickers, sector allocation decisions are not made; therefore, the return attribution model should reflect this process and measure the contribution of each stock decision to the overall performance, ignoring allocation effects.

Interaction is not well understood because it is not intuitively part of the investment decision process and is thus often not attributed or interpreted correctly. In presentations of attribution data, it should not be ignored or not shown, randomly allocated to other factors, split proportionally, or simply split 50:50 between selection and allocation. These misuses of interaction would lead to potentially misleading presentations of return attribution effects.

Assuming allocation decisions are made first, the contribution from selection must be:

$$R - B_S = \sum_{i=1}^{i=n} w_i R_i - \sum_{i=1}^{i=n} w_i B_i = \sum_{i=1}^{i=n} w_i (R_i - B_i) \qquad (16)$$

This equation is equivalent to Quadrant I – Quadrant II in Exhibit 8. Using this definition for selection, the sum of selection and allocation conveniently adds up to the total excess return as follows:

$$\text{Selection} + \text{Allocation} = (R - B_S) + (B_S - B) = R - B$$

The contribution to selection in the ith sector is now:

$$S_i = w_i(R_i - B_i) \tag{17}$$

The revised impact on individual sectors is graphically demonstrated in Exhibit 13. Essentially, the interaction effect is included in the stock selection effect, which is consistent with most portfolio manager's decision processes.

Exhibit 13 Interaction Effect in BF Model

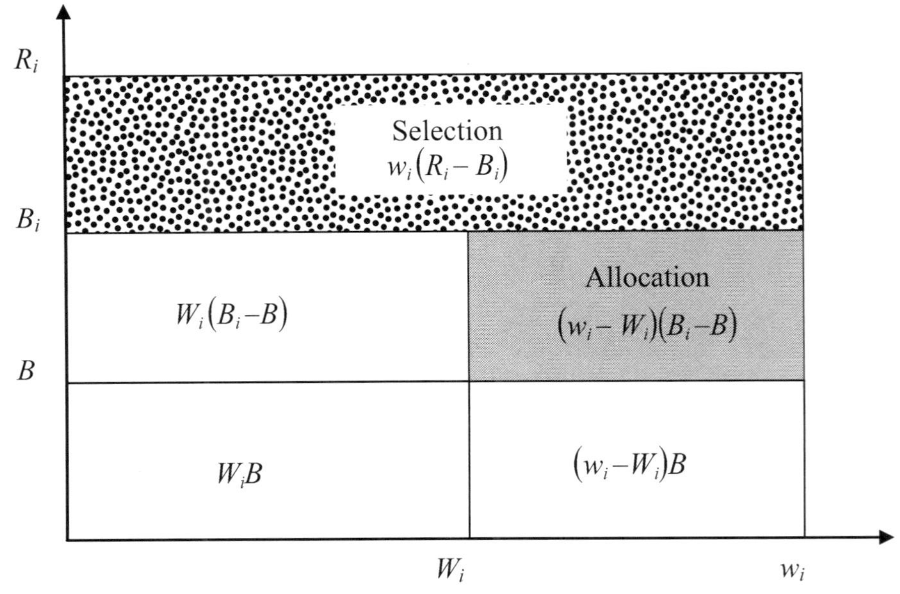

The revised total selection effect, including interaction using the portfolio data from Exhibit 3, is:

$$R - B_S = 10.1\% - 6.8\% = 3.3\%$$

The selection effects in each sector are:

Energy	50% × (18% – 10%) = 4.0%
Health Care	30% × (–3.0% + 2.0%) = –0.3%
Financials	20% × (10.0% – 12.0%) = –0.4%
Total	4.0% – 0.3% – 0.4% = 3.3%

Actual portfolio weights are now used to calculate selection effects rather than calculating what would have been the contribution to selection in that sector at the benchmark weight. There is no change in the selection effect for the Energy sector because the weight in the portfolio is the same as the weight in the benchmark. The selection effect in Health Care is now –0.3%, the sum of the previous –0.2% selection effect plus –0.1% interaction. The selection effect in Financials is now –0.4%, the sum of the previous –0.6% selection effect plus 0.2% interaction. The revised results are summarized in the Exhibit 14.

Exhibit 14 BF Results of Stock Selection and Interaction Combined

	Portfolio Weight	Benchmark Weight	Portfolio Return	Benchmark Return	Allocation	Selection
Energy	50%	50%	18%	10%	0.0%	4.0%
Health Care	30%	20%	−3%	−2%	−1.02%	−0.3%
Financials	20%	30%	10%	12%	−0.38%	−0.4%
Total	**100%**	**100%**	**10.1%**	**8.2%**	**−1.4%**	**3.3%**

In this example, in which allocation decisions are made first, interaction is appropriately included with selection. Combining selection with interaction allows the analyst to appropriately measure the impact of both the asset allocation and security selection decisions in the investment process.

Quadrant III (of Exhibit 8) of the Brinson model is now not required, which is an accurate reflection of most investment decision processes; cash is allocated to sectors and then this cash is used to purchase individual securities. Only the allocation notional fund is required to calculate return attribution, one step away from the benchmark portfolio, one step toward the final outcome of the portfolio return. Reflecting its intermediate position between the benchmark and portfolio return, the allocation notional fund is often renamed the "semi-notional fund." Rather than using the Brinson quadrants in Exhibit 8, it is preferable to think in terms of steps in the investment decision process as shown in Exhibit 15. Far more complex decision processes can be handled simply by identifying each individual step in the decision process and calculating a notional fund return corresponding to each step.

This analysis is a demonstration of an effective return attribution process. The analysis reflects the two-stage decision process of the portfolio manager: first sector allocation and then stock selection within sectors. We measure only the active decisions of the portfolio manager because they provide a complete understanding of the difference between the portfolio return and the benchmark return, and hence, provide a good explanation of the performance of the portfolio manager.

Exhibit 15 Steps in Investment Decision Process

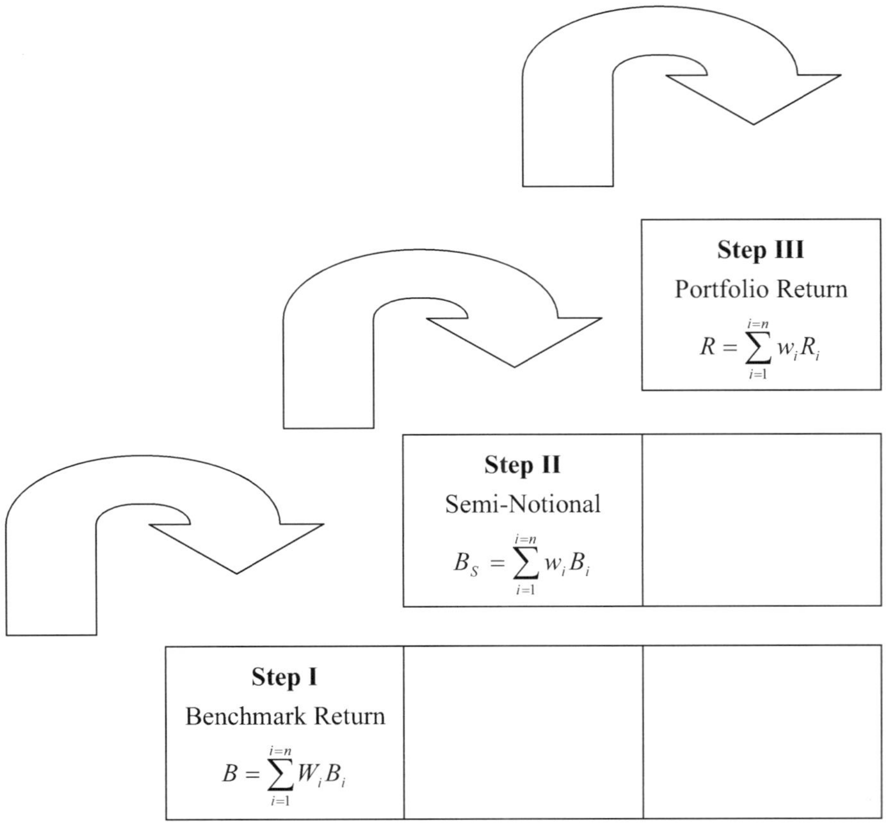

To summarize, the Brinson model attributes excess return to allocation and selection effects. There are two versions of the Brinson model: Brinson–Hood–Beebower and Brinson–Fachler. They differ only in the calculation of individual sector allocation effects. In both versions of the Brinson model, interaction may be calculated separately or included in the selection effect.

4 GEOMETRIC EQUITY RETURN ATTRIBUTION

The Brinson models described so far quantify arithmetic excess return only. A number of geometric excess return attribution models (*geometric methods*) have also been developed, such as Allen (1991), Bain (1996), Burnie, Knowles, and Teder (1998), and Bacon (2002, 2008). In effect, these models extend the Brinson model to attribute the geometric excess return defined as:

$$\frac{(1+R)}{(1+B)} - 1 \tag{18}$$

Using the portfolio data from Exhibit 3, the geometric excess return that we want to attribute is:

$$\frac{1.101}{1.082} - 1 = 1.76\%$$

The decision to use either the arithmetic model or geometric model is primarily driven by the preference of using arithmetic or geometric excess returns.

4.1 Allocation

To identify the contribution from allocation, we can use the same intermediate or semi-notional fund used in the Brinson method. But this time we use the geometric rather than the arithmetic difference, in effect the difference between Step 1 and Step 2 of the investment decision process. Step 1 is the benchmark.

$$\frac{(1+B_S)}{(1+B)}-1 \tag{19}$$

The contribution to geometric allocation in the ith sector is now

$$A_i^G=(w_i-W_i)\left(\frac{1+B_i}{1+B}-1\right) \tag{20}$$

Equation 20 is analogous to Equation 15; however, the geometric difference of the sector return against the overall benchmark is used rather than the arithmetic difference. Note the total geometric allocation A^G:

$$A^G=\sum_{i=1}^{i=n}A_i^G=\frac{(1+B_S)}{1+B}-1 \tag{21}$$

The geometric allocation effect for the portfolio data in Exhibit 3 is

$$\frac{(1+B_S)}{(1+B)}-1=\frac{1.068}{1.082}-1=-1.29\%$$

The individual sector allocation effects are

$$\text{Energy } (50\%-50\%)\times\left(\frac{1.10}{1.082}-1\right)=0.0\%$$

$$\text{Health Care } (30\%-20\%)\times\left(\frac{0.98}{1.082}-1\right)=-0.94\%$$

$$\text{Financials } (20\%-30\%)\times\left(\frac{1.12}{1.082}-1\right)=-0.35\%$$

Total: 0.0% – 0.94% – 0.35% = –1.29%

Given that the benchmark return is positive, the geometric excess return is a smaller negative number than the arithmetic excess return of –1.4%. The contributions to allocation are similar but slightly less than the arithmetic allocation. For comparison, the arithmetic effects are Energy 0.0%, Health Care –1.02%, and Financials –0.38%. With either method, the sign will always be the same.

EXAMPLE 8

Geometric Allocation: An Illustration

Exhibit 16 Sample Portfolio Data

	Portfolio Weight	Benchmark Weight	Portfolio Return	Benchmark Return
Technology	20%	30%	–11.0%	–10.0%
Telecommunications	30%	40%	–5.0%	–8.0%

(continued)

Exhibit 16 (Continued)

	Portfolio Weight	Benchmark Weight	Portfolio Return	Benchmark Return
Utilities	50%	30%	−8.0%	−5.0%
Total	**100%**	**100%**	**−7.7%**	**−7.7%**

Using the BF method, the geometric allocation effect of Utilities based on the portfolio data in Exhibit 16 is:

A 0.54%

B 0.59%

C 0.88%

Solution:

B is correct. $1 + B$ is calculated as $1 - 7.7\% = 1 - 0.077 = 0.923$ and $1 + B_i$ as $1 - 5.0\% = 1 - 0.05 = 0.95$. Thus,

$$(w_i - W_i)\left(\frac{1 + B_i}{1 + B} - 1\right) = (50\% - 30\%) \times \left(\frac{0.95}{0.923} - 1\right) = 0.59\%$$

The portfolio was 20% overweight in a sector geometrically outperforming the overall benchmark by 2.93%, therefore contributing 0.59% to the geometric excess return.

A is incorrect: $W_i\left(\frac{1 + B_i}{1 + B} - 1\right) = 30\% \times \left(\frac{0.95}{0.923} - 1\right) = 0.88\%$. The benchmark weight of 30% has been used incorrectly rather than the 20% overweight position.

C is incorrect: $(w_i - W_i)(B_i - B) = (50\% - 30\%) \times (-5.0\% + 7.7\%) = 0.54$. This is an arithmetic calculation.

4.2 Selection

To identify the contribution from selection, we can use the ratio of the portfolio return compared with the same intermediate or semi-notional return, effectively the difference between Step 2 and Step 3 of the decision process.

$$\frac{(1 + R)}{(1 + B_S)} - 1 \tag{22}$$

This approach implicitly includes interaction in the selection effect, which is in line with the decision process of most portfolio managers.[5]

The contribution of the ith sector to geometric selection is now

$$S_i^G = w_i\left(\frac{1 + R_i}{1 + B_i} - 1\right)\frac{(1 + B_i)}{(1 + B_S)} \tag{23}$$

Equation 23 can be compared with its arithmetic counterpart, Equation 9. In Equation 23, we use the geometric excess return between the portfolio sector return and the benchmark sector return rather than the arithmetic excess return. The

5 Although it is possible to calculate a geometric interaction effect this is rarely done in practice.

adjustment factor $\frac{1 + B_i}{1 + B_S}$ reflects the fact that equivalent geometric excess returns will add different value to the overall portfolio depending on the benchmark return in the sector. In short, outperformance in a rising market will contribute more excess return to the overall portfolio than equivalent outperformance in a falling market.

Note the total geometric selection S^G:

$$S^G = \sum_{i=1}^{i=n} S_i^G = \frac{(1 + R)}{(1 + B_S)} - 1 \tag{24}$$

The contribution to geometric excess return from selection is

$$\frac{(1 + R)}{(1 + B_S)} - 1 = \frac{1.101}{1.068} - 1 = 3.09\%$$

Individual sector selection effects are

$$\text{Energy } 50\% \times \left(\frac{1.18}{1.10} - 1\right) \times \frac{1.10}{1.068} = 3.75\%$$

$$\text{Health Care } 30\% \times \left(\frac{0.97}{0.98} - 1\right) \times \frac{0.98}{1.068} = -0.28\%$$

$$\text{Financials } 20\% \times \left(\frac{1.10}{1.12} - 1\right) \times \frac{1.12}{1.068} = -0.37\%$$

Total: 3.75% – 0.28% – 0.37% = 3.09%

Again, as expected, the geometric selection effects are similar to the arithmetic selection effects but slightly smaller in magnitude. The geometric return attribution effects are summarized in Exhibit 17:

Exhibit 17 Geometric Return Attribution with Stock Selection and Interaction Combined

	Portfolio Weight	Benchmark Weight	Portfolio Return	Benchmark Return	Allocation	Selection
Energy	50%	50%	18.0%	10%	0.0%	3.75%
Health Care	30%	20%	−3%	−2%	−0.94%	−0.28%
Financials	20%	30%	10%	12%	−0.35%	−0.37%
Total	**100%**	**100%**	**10.1%**	**8.2%**	**−1.29%**	**3.09%**

EXAMPLE 9

Geometric Selection

Exhibit 18 Sample Portfolio Data

	Portfolio Weight	Benchmark Weight	Portfolio Return	Benchmark Return
Materials	30%	20%	12.0%	8.0%
Industrials	30%	20%	8.0%	10.0%

(continued)

Exhibit 18 (Continued)

	Portfolio Weight	Benchmark Weight	Portfolio Return	Benchmark Return
Consumer Staples	40%	60%	6.0%	8.0%
Total	**100%**	**100%**	**8.4%**	**8.4%**

Using the BF method, the selection effect including interaction of Industrials based on the portfolio data in Exhibit 18 is:

A −0.60%

B −0.55%

C −0.40%

Solution:

B is correct: $w_i\left(\frac{1+R_i}{1+B_i}-1\right)\frac{(1+B_i)}{(1+B_S)} = 30\% \times \left(\frac{1.08}{1.1}-1\right)\times\frac{1.1}{1.086} = -0.55\%.$

Note that B_S = (30% × 8%) + (30% × 10%) + (40% × 8%) = 8.6%. In the industrials sector, the portfolio manager underperformed by 1.81% geometrically. The overall contribution from selection in this sector is thus −0.55%.

A is incorrect: $w_i(R_i - B_i)$ = 30% × (8.0% − 10.0%) = −0.6%. This is an arithmetic calculation.

C is incorrect: $W_i(R_i - B_i)$ = 20% × (8.0% − 10.0%) = −0.4%. This is an arithmetic calculation using the benchmark weight.

The total selection and allocation effects compound together to produce the geometric excess return:

$$\frac{(1+R)}{(1+B_S)}\frac{(1+B_S)}{(1+B)}-1=\frac{(1+R)}{(1+B)}-1$$

or

$$\left(1+S^G\right)\left(1+A^G\right)-1=\frac{(1+R)}{(1+B)}-1$$

For example, based on the data in Exhibit 3 from which we computed $R = 0.101$, $B_S = 0.068$, and $B = 0.082$:

$$\frac{1.101}{1.068}\times\frac{1.068}{1.082}-1=\frac{1.101}{1.082}-1=(1.0309)\times(1-0.0129)-1=1.76\%$$

5 HOLDINGS-BASED AND TRANSACTION-BASED RETURN ATTRIBUTION

We can distinguish between three types of attribution characterized by the information used to calculate attribution effects: returns -based, holdings-based, and transaction-based attribution. The types are listed in order of increasing information requirements. However, holdings-based and transaction-based attribution are the common types used in current practice.

5.1 Returns-Based Attribution

Returns-based (or factor) attribution uses only the total portfolio returns over a period of time to identify the factors that have generated the returns observed. Returns-based attribution is obviously most appropriate when the underlying portfolio holding information is unavailable, or not available with sufficient frequency, at the required level of detail. An example is hedge funds because these vehicles are not transparent in disclosure of holdings. This type of attribution is the quickest and easiest to implement, but because it does not access the underlying holdings, it is the least accurate.

5.2 Holdings-Based Attribution

Holdings-based attribution is calculated by reference to the underlying beginning-period holdings of the portfolio only. Typically, holdings-based attribution is calculated using monthly, weekly, or daily data, with shorter time periods leading to greater accuracy. For longer evaluation periods, the attribution results for the shorter measurement periods are linked together.

Holdings-based attribution fails to capture the impact of any transactions made between measurement periods and, therefore, will not reconcile to the actual portfolio return. The residual caused by ignoring transactions might be described as a timing or trading effect. Holdings-based analysis is appropriate for passive investment strategies with little turnover. Valuing the portfolio with the same prices used to calculate the underlying benchmark index will remove one potential difference between the portfolio and benchmark returns that is not a management effect.

5.3 Transaction-Based Attribution

Transaction-based attribution is calculated by using both the holdings of the portfolio and the transactions (purchases and sales) that occurred during the evaluation period. The difference between transaction-based and holdings-based attribution is the calculation of inputs to the attribution analysis. For holdings-based attribution, transactions are ignored and weights are calculated using the beginning period position exclusively. The returns are simply those returns that would have been achieved, including income and corporate actions (e.g., stock splits) but excluding any sales and purchases, if the beginning period holdings had been held to the end of the period.

For transaction-based attribution, both the weights and returns reflect all transactions during the period, including transaction costs. Transaction-based attribution is the most accurate type of attribution analysis. This type of attribution is also the most difficult and time consuming to implement. To obtain meaningful results, the underlying data must be complete, accurate, and reconciled from period to period. Because all the data is available, the entire excess return can be quantified and explained. The return used in the attribution analysis will reconcile with the return presented to the client, and attribution analysis can be used as a diagnostic tool to identify errors.

The choice of which type of attribution to use will very much depend on the availability and quality of the underlying data, reporting requirements for the client, and the complexity of the investment decision process. For example, in many cases, the lack of quality transaction data and/or the lack of turnover in the portfolio, may lead to daily holdings-based attribution that is just as informative as transaction-based attribution.

EXAMPLE 10

Types of Attribution

For an outside analyst, the most readily accomplished type of attribution to analyze the performance of a hedge fund is *most likely:*

A returns-based.

B holdings-based.

C transaction-based.

Solution:

A is correct. Because hedge funds generally do not disclose holdings to the public, returns -based analysis is much easier to accomplish than holdings-based or transaction-based analysis.

6 RETURN ATTRIBUTION ANALYSIS AT MULTIPLE LEVELS

The example used to demonstrate return attribution so far is a single country model in which the investment process allocates weight to industry sectors and then selects securities within each of those industry sectors. The same return attribution formulas for allocation and selection can be used at multiple levels in the entire decision process to evaluate different decisions. Consider an example in which the top level is the fund sponsor (e.g., a university endowment or a defined-benefit pension plan sponsor). At the fund sponsor level, the first decision might be to allocate a certain weight to asset classes—the strategic asset allocation. If the fund sponsor does not manage funds internally, they would delegate a second decision in the investment process to the investment managers who could decide on any tactical deviations from the strategic asset allocation. And the sponsor might choose a number of portfolio managers to manage against specific mandates within a given asset class. (Attribution at the sponsor level is sometimes called **macro attribution**; attribution at the portfolio manager level is sometimes called **micro attribution**.)

Using the investment decision process just described, the allocation formula can be used to measure the tactical asset allocation decision of the sponsor against its own strategic benchmark, which could be a weighted average of appropriate asset class indexes using the strategic asset allocation weights or a representation of the sponsor's liabilities, as in the case of many pension funds. The selection formula can be used to measure the added value of the performance of each of the portfolio managers relative to their assigned benchmarks. To the fund sponsor, the selection of portfolio managers is in effect a selection decision in the return attribution analysis performed at the highest level.

When we calculate return attribution, we have the opportunity to choose which level(s) to analyze. Consider the example of a fund sponsor who hires two investment managers for the equity portion of the fund. The overall fund has an equity allocation benchmark of:

50% Large-Cap Value Equities

25% Small-Cap Value Equities

25% Large-Cap Growth Equities

For this overall allocation, the fund sponsor hires Value Portfolio Manager to manage the large-cap and small-cap value allocations and Growth Portfolio Manager to manage the growth equity allocation. For a specific time period, this arrangement results in the performance shown in Exhibit 19.

Exhibit 19 Performance of Value and Growth Equity Managers

	Fund Weight	Fund Return	Benchmark Weight	Benchmark Return
Total	**100%**	**0.95**	**100%**	**−0.03**
Value Portfolio Manager	78%	0.99	75%	0.32
Small-cap value equities	20%	2.39	25%	1.52
Large-cap value equities	58%	0.51	50%	−0.28
Growth Portfolio Manager	22%	0.82	25%	−1.08
Large-cap growth equities	22%	0.82	25%	−1.08

You will note that this fund outperformed its total benchmark by 98 bps (95 bps compared with −3 bps). You will also note that the fund sponsor has allocated 78% of the total fund to the Value Portfolio Manager, exceeding the benchmark weight of 75%, with the remaining 22% allocated to the Growth Portfolio Manager, below the benchmark 25%. This overall weighting decision is that of the fund sponsor.

Within each of these total allocations, the portfolio manager has discretion about how to invest the assets. The managers have full discretion over the securities purchased, within the particular market segment benchmark. For this example, we assume that the Value Manager has full discretion to allocate between market cap segments—that is, how to divide the total 78% allocation to value equities between small cap and large cap.

Before we calculate our return attribution effects, we need to decide whom we want to evaluate. Do we want to evaluate the decisions of the portfolio manager, or those of the fund sponsor? In this first set of return attribution results, we will evaluate the portfolio manager's decisions. To do this, we will calculate the return attribution effects (using the BF approach) at the segment level (e.g., small-cap value, large-cap value, and large-cap growth). Using the earlier formulas, where:

$$\text{Allocation} = (w_i - W_i)(B_i - B)$$

$$\text{Selection + Interaction} = W_i(R_i - B_i) + (w_i - W_i)(R_i - B_i)$$

We can calculate the attribution effects for the small-cap value equities:

$$\text{Allocation} = (20\% - 25\%)[1.52 - (-0.03)] = -0.08$$

$$\text{Selection + Interaction} = [(25\%)(2.39 - 1.52)] + [(20\% - 25\%)(2.39 - 1.52)] = 0.17$$

Using the same approach for large-cap value equities and large-cap growth equities yields the results shown in Exhibit 20. (Note that numbers are shown to two decimal places and may not sum because of rounding.)

Exhibit 20 Segment Level Return Attribution

Return attribution (segment level)	Fund Weight	Selection + Interaction	Allocation	Total
Total	**100%**	**1.05**	**−0.07**	**0.98**
Value Portfolio Manager	78%	0.63	−0.10	0.53
Small-cap value equities	**20%**	**0.17**	**−0.08**	**0.10**
Large-cap value equities	**58%**	**0.46**	**−0.02**	**0.44**
Growth Portfolio Manager	22%	0.42	0.03	0.45
Large-cap growth equities	**22%**	**0.42**	**0.03**	**0.45**

In Exhibit 20, the attribution results in bold are calculated at the segment level. The attribution results at the next level above, the Value Portfolio Manager and Growth Portfolio Manager, are sums of the segment level results. For example, the allocation effect for the Value Portfolio Manager is equal to −0.08 + −0.02 = −0.10.

Because we are calculating the effects at the segment level and rolling up (summing) to a total for each manager, we are able to evaluate the specific decisions of the portfolio managers and their impact on the total fund. The total 98 bps of outperformance at the overall fund level is almost entirely the result of positive security selection decisions (105 bps in total). The decision of the Value Manager to underweight small cap in favor of large cap was a poor decision because the small-cap value benchmark outperformed the total benchmark (1.52% versus −0.03%) and the large-cap value benchmark underperformed the total benchmark (−0.28% versus −0.03%). Therefore, we calculate a negative allocation effect of −7 bps.

Separately, we can also evaluate the decisions of the fund sponsor. To do this, we perform a second return attribution analysis using the same set of weights and returns data in Exhibit 19, but we calculate the return attribution results at the portfolio manager level (rather than the segment level). For example, for the Value Portfolio Manager, we would calculate the effects as follows:

Allocation = (78% − 75%)[0.32 − (−0.03)] = 0.01

Selection + Interaction = [(75%)(0.99 − 0.32)] + [(78% − 75%)(0.99 − 0.32)] = 0.52

We calculate the effects in the same way for the Growth Portfolio Manager and obtain the results shown in Exhibit 21.

Exhibit 21 Return Attribution at the Portfolio Manager Level

Return Attribution (Portfolio Manager level)	Selection + Interaction	Allocation	Total
Total	0.94	0.04	0.98
Value Portfolio Manager	**0.52**	**0.01**	**0.53**
Small-cap value equities	–	–	–
Large-cap value equities	–	–	–
Growth Portfolio Manager	**0.42**	**0.03**	**0.45**
Large-cap growth equities	–	–	–

You will note that there are no return attribution effects at the segment level because we only calculated results at the manager level. Because we are measuring different decisions, the attribution results are different. There is still an overall positive security selection effect (94 bps), as we might expect. However, the total allocation effect is positive, not negative, because we are evaluating a *different* allocation decision. In this case, we are calculating the effect of the fund sponsor's decision to overweight value equities versus growth equities. We calculate a positive allocation of 4 bps, reflecting the overweighting of value equities (whose benchmark outperformed the total benchmark) and the underweighting of growth equities (whose benchmark underperformed the total benchmark).

Return attribution analysis is most often calculated with reference to the portfolio's agreed benchmark. But it is entirely possible to attribute one portfolio against another when using the same or similar investment strategy. The purpose of such analysis might be to explain an unexpected difference in return between two portfolios managed by the same portfolio manager using the same investment decision process.

Drilling down to the next level, the portfolio manager may well have a country allocation investment process.[6] At this level of analysis, the same allocation formula will calculate the impact of country allocation decisions within the manager's portfolio and the selection formula will calculate the impact of selection decisions within each country.

Drilling down another level, the portfolio manager may well have a sector allocation process, similar to that described earlier, within each country and thus the allocation formula can be used to calculate the impact of sector selection decisions within countries and the selection decisions within sectors.

Whatever the level of analysis, it is essential that the return attribution reflects the decision process of the portfolio manager. For example, a Eurozone investment strategy might use a country allocation process with security selection within each country or a sector allocation process with security selection within each industrial sector. Exhibits 22 and 23 illustrate the different analysis that might result from the same portfolio assuming a different investment process. In each case, an arithmetic Brinson and Fachler approach has been used.

Exhibit 22 Country Allocation

	Portfolio Weight	Benchmark Weight	Portfolio Return	Benchmark Return	Allocation	Selection
France	20%	30%	8.0%	6.0%	0.15%	0.40%
Germany	20	35	8.0	7.0	0.07	0.20
Holland	20	10	9.0	15.0	0.76	–1.20
Italy	30	15	10.0	9.0	0.23	0.30
Spain	10	10	3.0	3.5	0.00	–0.05
Total	**100%**	**100%**	**8.30**	**7.45%**	**1.20%**	**–0.35%**

6 For some portfolios, this next level may be asset classes.

Exhibit 23 Industry Sector Allocation

	Portfolio Weight	Benchmark Weight	Portfolio Return	Benchmark Return	Allocation	Selection
Energy	25%	30%	18.0%	12.0%	−0.23%	1.50%
Health Care	30	20	−3.0	−6.0	−1.35	0.90
Financial	20	30	10.0	12.0	−0.46	−0.40
Transportation	10	15	12.0	8.0	−0.03	0.40
Metals and Mining	15	5	10.0	5.0	−0.25	0.75
Total	**100%**	**100%**	**8.30%**	**7.45%**	**−2.30%**	**3.15%**

Exhibit 22 demonstrates good country allocation but negative security selection within countries, whereas Exhibit 23 demonstrates poor sector allocation but strongly positive security selection within industrial sectors. The message with regard to selection effects is completely different depending on the investment decision process used.

Drilling down to the lowest level, the same allocation and selection formulas can be used to calculate individual security decisions within sectors. For example, the allocation formula can determine the impact of over- or underweighting individual securities, whereas the selection formula will determine the contribution as a result of the returns of a security in the portfolio differing from the return of the same security in the benchmark. If the pricing sources used in the portfolio and the benchmark are identical, then any difference in return will be caused by transaction activity. Transaction activity as a result of trading expenses and bid–offer spreads will negatively affect returns, but very occasionally because of timing, the portfolio manager may be able to trade at advantageous prices during the day and recover all the transaction costs by the end of the day resulting in a positive effect.

Exhibit 24 shows the security level return attribution effects for a small portfolio of oil stocks against a customized benchmark consisting of the same oil stocks. This approach would be used by a pure stock picker, the only decisions in the portfolio being individual stock weighting and timing decisions.

Exhibit 24 Security Level Return Attribution Effects of Pure Stock Picker

	Portfolio Weight	Benchmark Weight	Portfolio Return	Benchmark Return	Allocation	Transaction Costs and Timing Effects
Chevron Corporation	24%	30%	10%	10%	−0.18%	0.0%
Conoco Phillips	21%	25%	8%	8%	−0.04%	0.0%
ExxonMobil	41%	35%	5%	6%	−0.06%	−0.41%
Marathon Oil	6%	5%	4%	4%	−0.03%	0.0%
Newfield Exploration	8%	5%	−5%	−5%	−0.36%	0.0%
Total	**100%**	**100%**	**5.97%**	**7.05%**	**−0.67%**	**−0.41%**

The arithmetic allocation effects of each security using the BF approach are as follows:

Chevron Corporation	(24% – 30%) × (10% – 7.05%) = –0.18%
Conoco Phillips	(21% – 25%) × (8.0% – 7.05%) = –0.04%
ExxonMobil	(41% – 35%) × (6.0% – 7.05%) = –0.06%
Marathon Oil	(6% – 5%) × (4.0% – 7.05%) = –0.03%
Newfield Exploration	(8% – 5%) × (–5.0% – 7.05%) = –0.36%

Allocation in this context measures the value added from individual security selection. There are transactions in only one security during the period—ExxonMobil—therefore, there are selection effects (transaction costs and timing) in only this security. The calculation is

ExxonMobil 41% × (5.0% – 6.0%) = –0.41%

EXAMPLE 11

Levels of Return Attribution

1 At the lowest level of return attribution analysis, the selection type formula is *most likely* used to analyze:

   A transactions costs.

   B security level decisions.

   C individual portfolio managers.

2 At the highest level of return attribution analysis, the selection type formula is *most likely* used to analyze:

   A allocation decisions

   B security level decisions.

   C individual portfolio managers.

Solution to 1:

A is correct. At the lowest level, return attribution analysis is used to investigate the differences in return of a security in the portfolio and the benchmark, which is most likely caused by transaction costs. At the lowest level the allocation formula will measure individual security decision and the contribution of portfolio managers are normally measured at the highest level.

Solution to 2:

C is correct. Selection type formulas are used to evaluate the selection ability of individual portfolio managers.

FACTOR MODELS IN RETURN ATTRIBUTION

7

Return attribution is used to identify the components of excess return relative to a benchmark. As we have seen, return attribution allows us to analyze that excess return by comparing the accounting information (weights and returns) in the portfolio with those in the benchmark. The models presented thus far focus on the security selection, asset allocation, and interaction of those factors. But what if we want to control for other decisions within the investment process? Another type of return attribution uses fundamental factor models to decompose the relative contributors to excess return of a number of different factors. Fundamental factor analysis allows us to quantify the impact of specific active investment decisions within the portfolio, showing how they add or remove value relative to the benchmark.

We want to remove the effects of the market in an effort to identify the excess return generated by the active investment decisions. To do that, we return to our definition of excess return: Excess return = $R - B$.

Practitioners use many different factor models to decompose excess returns. In constructing those models, they have the ability to choose which components to attribute (which factors to use). For example, they may choose to control for investment style, currency management, or fixed-income characteristics like duration to attribute those parts of the excess return that are the result of exposures to the specific factors. As we mentioned earlier, we want to focus our analysis only on those factors that contribute to the active investment management process.

Consistent in all of these models, no matter which factors are used, there will be a portion of the excess return that is not related to any factors. This term is known as **specific asset selection**. Taking from our equation for excess return, we separate the excess return into the portion due to factors and that portion due to specific asset selection.

As an example, we will focus on a model first introduced by Fama and French (1993) that expands on the traditional capital asset pricing model (CAPM) regression, adding two additional terms for size and value. In this model, we choose to restrict our analysis to a single currency equity market. This restriction allows us to exclude a multitude of other potential investment decisions, such as currency management or country selection. Within the single equity market, the three factors include:

1. RMRF standing for $(R_M - R_F)$ is the return on a market-value-weighted equity index minus the one-month T-bill rate (a proxy for the risk-free rate of return). The expected value is an equity risk premium, a factor shared with the CAPM.
2. SMB (small minus big) is the return on a portfolio of small-cap equities minus the return on a portfolio of large-cap equities. This factor captures a small-cap return premium.
3. HML (high minus low) is the return on a portfolio of high book-to-price equities minus the return on a portfolio of low book-to-price stocks. Recognizing that a high book-to-price ratio means a low price-to-book ratio (i.e., selling cheaply relative to book value), this factor represents a value return premium.[7]

The model itself is expressed as

$$R_P - R_F = \alpha + \beta_{mkt}\text{RMRF} + \beta_S\text{SMB} + \beta_V\text{HML} + \varepsilon_P$$

7 Using the book-to-price ratio avoids problems, such as division by zero, that are possible with the more familiar price-to-book ratio.

where

R_P = Portfolio Return
R_F = The return on a one-month T-bill, representing a default-risk-free return
R_M = Return on a market-value-weighted equity index
β_{mkt} = The sensitivity of the portfolio (minus risk free) returns to market (minus risk free) returns
β_S = The sensitivity of the portfolio (minus risk free) returns to SMB. A positive high number (greater than 1) suggests that the portfolio tends to hold/favor small-cap over large-cap equities.
β_V = The sensitivity of the portfolio (minus risk free) returns to HML. A positive high number (greater than 1) suggests that the portfolio tends to hold/favor value-oriented versus growth-oriented equities.
ε_P = Error term

By analyzing the results of a factor return attribution analysis, we can infer the relative strengths and/or weaknesses of the investment decisions. For example, using the Fama–French model provided earlier, we obtain the following results from the return attribution analysis.

Exhibit 25 Fama–French Factor Model

Factor	Portfolio Sensitivity	Benchmark Sensitivity	Difference	Factor Return	Absolute Contribution	Proportional Contribution
$R_M - R_F$	1.05	1.09	−0.04	6.88	−0.2752	29%
SMB	1.2	1.1	0.1	−3.82	−0.3820	40%
HML	0.3	0.25	0.05	−4.97	−0.2485	26%
		Return attributed to factors			−0.9057	96%
		Return attributed to specific asset selection			−0.0400	4%
				Excess return	−0.9457	100%

Source: Data are from http://mba.tuck.dartmouth.edu/pages/faculty/ken.french/data_library.html.

This analysis yields some interesting results, including information about this portfolio's investment approach, how the manager generated excess return, and his or her ability to consistently add value relative to the benchmark.

First, in terms of investment approach, note that both the portfolio and the benchmark have a much higher exposure to the SMB factor (1.2 and 1.1 respectively) relative to the other two factors in our analysis. This exposure suggests that both the portfolio and benchmark tend to hold smaller capitalization equities relative to large capitalization equities. Similarly, the HML factors for both portfolio and benchmark are relatively low (0.3 and 0.25 respectively), suggesting that both portfolio and benchmark have a relatively low exposure to the value equities. Given these findings, we might conclude that this particular manager has either a small-cap growth or small-cap neutral investment style.

Second, we know that the portfolio had a negative excess return for this particular time period (−0.9457). Not surprisingly, the largest contributor to this negative excess return was the impact of the largest factor, SMB. For this time period, SMB contributed a −0.382, or 40% of the negative excess return. The decision to invest in small-cap securities, above the benchmark, clearly hurt the overall performance because the small-cap tilted portfolio (SMB) under-performed during this period. Similarly, the excess exposure to HML relative to the benchmark also negatively affected the excess return (−0.2485 or 26%). Lastly, the under-exposure to the overall market relative to the benchmark, the positive $R_M - R_F$ factor, also had a negative impact (−0.2752 or 29%).

Using this analysis, can we draw any conclusions about the investment management skill of this particular manager? The analysis reveals that 96% of the excess return can be attributed to one of the three factors: market, size, and style. The remaining 4% of the excess return not explained by those factors has a negative contribution (−0.04).

Within the factors, a higher allocation to small cap (1.2 versus 1.1 in the benchmark) and away from a growth bias (0.3 to 0.25 in the benchmark) had a negative impact. Because both small cap (−3.82 to 6.88) and value style (−4.97 to 6.88) underperformed the broad market index, the portfolio was negatively affected by those particular investment styles. We cannot say with certainty that the manager intentionally made bets in favor of either small-cap or value stocks during the investment period, but those would be reasonable questions that an evaluator might pose to the portfolio manager.

EXAMPLE 12

Factor Models

Using the return attribution analysis in Exhibit 25, select the best answer to the following:

1 About how much of the excess return is explained by the HML factor?

- **A** 29%
- **B** 26%
- **C** 96%

2 By how much did the portfolio overweight HML, relative to the benchmark?

- **A** 0.10
- **B** 0.05
- **C** 0.09

3 The impact on the excess return of the decision to overweight HML was:

- **A** negative because the factor return attribution analysis results indicate an absolute impact from the HML factor of −0.2485.
- **B** negative because the factor return attribution analysis results indicate an HML factor return of −4.97.
- **C** positive because the factor return attribution analysis results indicate a difference of 0.05.

Solution to 1:

B is correct. The results indicate that the HML factor contributed 26% to the overall excess return.

Solution to 2:

B is correct. The results indicate that the portfolio was 0.30, the benchmark was 0.25, and thus the difference was 0.05, or 0.30 – 0.25.

Solution to 3:

A is correct. The absolute contribution column in Exhibit 25 indicates the overall contribution to excess return from each factor. B is not correct because although the HML factor return is negative, the impact on the excess return may be positive or negative, depending on whether the portfolio is overweight or underweight HML relative to the benchmark. C is not correct because the portfolio is overweight a negative factor, which has a negative impact on the excess return.

In Example 12, using factors for market, size, and style is one of many different approaches to factor-based return attribution. Many different approaches are currently available within the industry and, relative to the asset-grouping approach—which isolates attribution effects by comparing the returns of variously constructed portfolios or groups of assets—of the Brinson or geometric models, factor models offer the following advantages:

- They are much more flexible in that they can be tailored very closely to the investment process.
- Different factor models can be used with the same portfolios to elicit return attribution effects for varying investment decisions.
- Factor models can be very sophisticated and designed to measure many effects resulting from investment management decisions.

Some of the key disadvantages relative to asset-grouping approaches include:

- Factor models are generally applied to single asset class (equity or fixed-income) portfolios, whereas asset-grouping approaches can be used for total plans or balanced portfolios containing multiple asset classes.
- Factor models are dependent on the specific factors used in the analysis. There are clear limits to every factor model, which is why some practitioners will apply several different models.
- If the factor model is particularly complex, for instance some fixed-income factor models, the data and computer software costs can be significant.
- In general, fewer varieties of asset-grouping models are used in the industry, making asset-grouping analysis results much more recognizable. Practitioners may encounter a large variety of factor models in the industry.
- Asset-grouping models are often easier to understand in terms of investment decisions.

So, although factor models may be more complex and difficult to use, their return attribution results can be used together with some of the asset-grouping approaches to provide a more complete understanding of the merits of the investment process.

EXAMPLE 13

Advantages and Disadvantages of Factor Models

1 Which of the following is an advantage of factor models relative to an asset-grouping approach?

  A They can be tailored to very subtle investment decisions.

  B They are dependent on the specific factors used in the analysis.

  C A very limited variety of factor models exists in the industry.

2 Which models are more frequently used with balanced portfolios?

  A Factor models because they are easily configured to consider multiple asset classes within one model.

B Asset-grouping models because the data requirements are less.

C Asset-grouping models because they can be used with multiple asset classes.

Solution to 1:

A is correct. Factor models can be designed to take into account any number of factors, and can thus be constructed to analyze very small (subtle) investment decisions. B is not correct because dependency on the specific factors is a disadvantage relative to asset-grouping models. C is not correct because a very large variety of factor model approaches are common throughout the industry.

Solution to 2:

C is correct. Asset-grouping models are most commonly used with balanced or multi-asset-class portfolios. A is not correct because factor models are generally not used because the models are usually more difficult to apply to multiple asset classes. B is not correct because the data requirements do not make it easier to use asset-grouping models for multiple asset classes.

8 FIXED-INCOME RETURN ATTRIBUTION: AN OVERVIEW

Investing in fixed-income securities is different from investing in equities because different factors drive bond returns. Interest rate risk is the primary risk faced by fixed-income securities (bond prices generally move inversely to interest rate changes).[8] The risk of non-payment of promised interest and/or principal (default risk) is a secondary risk for fixed-income investors. For equity investors, company-specific differences are important because, for example, they can lead one company to overtake a competitor and lead to very different returns for investors in those issues. Fixed-income investors have a limited upside defined by promised interest and principal (at maturity) payments and are generally less concerned with individual issuer selection within a given credit rating band, especially for "high-grade" bonds. For example, investors in "speculative-grade" bonds pay more attention to individual issuer differences. The decisions in fixed-income investing generally revolve around the desired levels of interest rate risk (sensitivity, often summarized by a measure known as *duration*) and credit risk (which may depend on the extra expected return the marketplace is offering for bearing more risk than a government bond). As a consequence, fixed-income investment nearly always involves decisions relative to sensitivity to interest rate changes and credit quality. Exchange rate exposures (for multi-currency portfolios) are an example of other decisions that may be relevant.

The Brinson approach was designed chiefly with equity return attribution in mind and is suitable for only the simplest of fixed-income investment processes. Exhibit 26 shows hypothetical output from applying a Brinson approach to fixed-income attribution. Fixed-income indexes that can serve as benchmarks are readily available and the portfolio and benchmark can be segmented by various fixed-income categories. For instance, if we want to understand the impact of investment decisions across the yield curve, we could choose to segment the portfolio and benchmark by maturity bands of increasing length. This choice might provide a return attribution analysis as show in Exhibit 26.

8 If bond investors expect interest rates to increase, they will lower the interest rate exposure in their portfolios, such as by shortening maturities. Conversely, if they expect interest rates to fall, they will increase interest rate risk, such as by lengthening maturities.

Exhibit 26 Return Attribution Analysis by Maturity Band, USD Portfolio

Maturity	Portfolio Weight	Benchmark Weight	Portfolio Return	Benchmark Return	Selection and Interaction	Allocation
0–1 Year	20%	20%	0.15%	0.14%	0.00%	0.00%
1–3 Years	50%	30%	1.65%	1.55%	0.05%	−0.08%
4–9 Years	20%	30%	2.80%	2.75%	0.01%	−0.08%
10+ Years	10%	20%	3.35%	3.25%	0.01%	−0.13%
Total	**100%**	**100%**	**1.75%**	**1.97%**	**0.07%**	**−0.29%**

If we assume that the decision to invest in particular parts of the yield curve is a separate and distinct decision, then we could use the return attribution analysis to evaluate that yield curve weighting decision. With these results, we clearly see an overweighting along the shorter segments of the yield curve, with 1–3 years overweight (50% versus 30%), and both 4–9 and 10+ years underweight. The manager may have anticipated an increase in interest rates across maturities, when being underweight long maturities would tend to limit losses (because long bonds are typically more interest rate sensitive than short bonds); but the manager was incorrect. This analysis suggests that these maturity allocation decisions account for the under performance of the portfolio during this period. The allocation category essentially tries to capture interest rate exposure decisions (yield curve positioning), whereas selection and interaction cover all other decisions.

Although this Brinson methodology is somewhat useful, it only measures one allocation decision. In the Exhibit 26 example, we measured only allocation to different parts of the yield curve. However, most fixed-income decision processes include multiple decisions relative to the benchmark and in those cases a fixed-income attribution model designed to evaluate those multiple decisions is appropriate. For illustration, we will consider a hypothetical model based on two primary decisions: yield curve positioning and the credit spread (each of which is further analyzed into component decisions).

The most common measurement of a portfolio's interest rate risk is its duration. We define **duration** as the percentage change in bond price based on an unanticipated small change in interest rates (in particular, the market-required yield to maturity). In the absence of other factors, a higher duration means a higher sensitivity to changes in interest rates. **Convexity** is another interest rate risk measure that may be used in conjunction with duration. Broadly speaking, convexity captures the degree of nonlinearity (curvature) in the relationship between price change and yield change.

If the credit risk within a specific security is higher than that of a government bond, the debt issuer will need to pay a premium over the current government bond yield. That premium, known as the **credit spread**, will be higher for higher default-risk securities. The spread will change over time as the security's credit risk changes and as risk aversion in the marketplace increases and decreases.

The credit spread of any given security can be thought of as having two primary sources. The first source is related to industry **sector** (e.g., technology) because the market conditions in a sector affect all companies operating within it. The remaining portion of the credit risk that is not related to sector is defined as **security specific**.

In addition to the choice of interest rate sensitivity, fixed-income investment managers may also make investment decisions about the credit risk in their portfolios. They will look to add value to those portfolios, relative to their benchmarks, by anticipating the changes in those credit spreads. For example, if a manager expects the credit spreads for certain sectors to contract over time, that manager may choose to overweight those sectors in search of additional outperformance. When constructing our return attribution analysis, we want to be able to consider the relative impact of all these decisions. By considering more than one factor, multi-factor fixed-income return attribution models allow us to evaluate the merits of these multiple decisions on the portfolio.

Consider, for example, the decomposition of portfolio excess return shown in Exhibit 27.

Exhibit 27 An Example of a Fixed Income Return Attribution Model

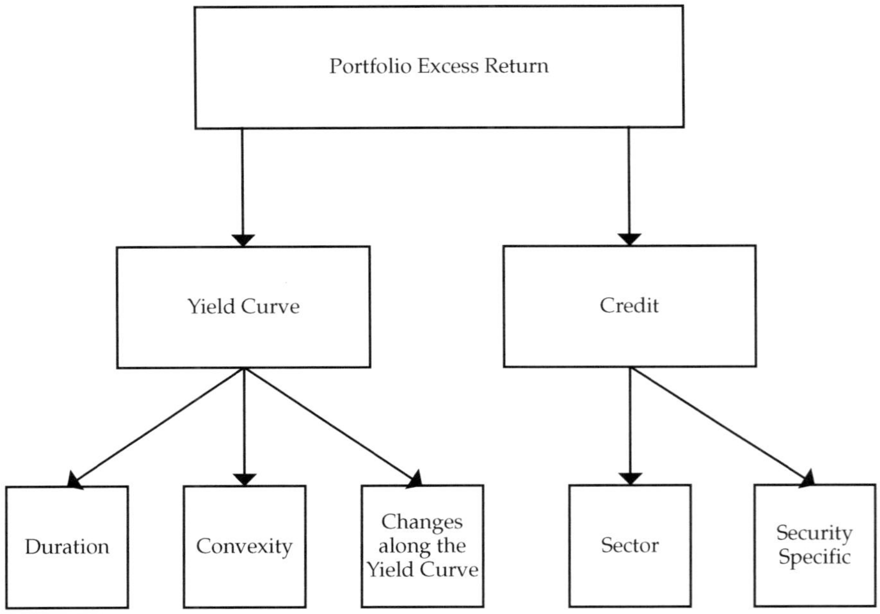

In this example, the excess portfolio return is divided into two primary decision areas: Yield curve positioning (or interest rate management) and credit positioning. The yield curve is then further broken down into the changes as a result of duration, convexity, and changes along the yield curve. With an upward sloping yield curve, there is generally a positive return to the passage of time, all else being equal. This element of return is sometimes called the roll-down. Credit is divided into the excess return generated by the sector bets and the security specific bets.

As a means of understanding fixed-income return attribution, we have included sample results for two different fixed-income portfolios, both managed relative to the same fixed-income benchmark. Fixed-income return attribution models tend to be data and computationally intensive and are typically calculated by one of many software products available in the marketplace. For our purposes, we will focus on understanding and interpreting the results.

In this example, we can compare the fixed-income return attribution results for two portfolio managers, Portfolio One and Portfolio Two. Portfolio One's manager claims an investment style that constructs portfolios to be very sensitive to interest rate changes. The manager invests heavily in specific economic models designed to identify the most under-valued economic sectors. The manager also acknowledges doing less research on specific fixed-income securities. Portfolio Two's manager focuses investment research primarily on predicting the relative changes in economic sectors and looks for specific bonds within those sectors. The manager does not look to add value through yield curve positioning relative to the benchmark.

Our analysis yields the results shown in Exhibit 28.

Exhibit 28 Fixed-Income Return Attribution Results

	Portfolio One	Portfolio Two
Total portfolio return	2.35	1.89
Total benchmark return	1.86	1.86
Total excess return	**0.49**	**0.03**
Yield curve total	**0.41**	**−0.17**
Duration	0.31	−0.25
Convexity	0.02	0.03
Changes along yield curve	0.08	0.05
Credit	**0.08**	**0.20**
Sector	0.29	0.11
Security specific	−0.21	0.09

In reviewing the results, we see that Portfolio One did manage to achieve a higher excess return than Portfolio Two over the same time period. That higher excess return appears to be the result primarily of the interest rate bets of Portfolio One over the investment period. Looking at a total of 49 bps of excess return, 41 bps were generated through those interest rate movement bets. Additionally, Portfolio One benefits from sector bets in relation to the benchmark, providing 29 bps of additional excess return. Portfolio Two also generated some positive excess return from both sector and security investment decisions, 20 bps, but it was mostly offset by losing 17 bps from yield curve positioning relative to the benchmark.

Considering our evaluation of each manager's investment strategies, we might infer the following. The claim that Portfolio One constructs portfolios that are positioned well to interest rate changes certainly appears true for this time period. For Portfolio Two, the decision to be consistent with the interest rate sensitivities of the benchmark may not be working as well as he or she hoped. Furthermore, the negative performance from interest rate sensitivity detracts from what might be an otherwise successful ability to identify well-performing securities within their benchmark sectors.

As with all return attribution analysis, we should remember that these fixed-income return attribution results help inform our understanding of the investment process for the particular measurement period. We need to combine these results with what we know to be true about the actual investment process through both qualitative analysis and additional quantitative data. And we may also want to extend our analysis to additional time periods or possibly even consider other factors.

When analyzing the fixed-income investment management process, practitioners may find that the standard Brinson return attribution models provide an adequate level of analysis. In most cases, however, they are likely to prefer the precision of a specialized, multi-factor approach that can be more closely tailored to the actual investment process. They will then have to decide whether those benefits from a specialized fixed-income return attribution approach will be worth the incremental costs, including specialized software models and much more in-depth data requirements.

EXAMPLE 14

Fixed-Income Attribution

1 Why might a specialized fixed-income return attribution analysis be preferable to a standard Brinson approach?

A Specialized fixed-income return attribution models are easier to implement than standard Brinson approach.

B Fixed-income return attribution models can be tailored to more closely match the fixed-income investment process.

C Fixed-income return attribution models have less specialized data and software requirements.

2 For Portfolio One in Exhibit 28, what is the most important contributor to excess return?

A The positioning of the portfolio's sensitivity to interest rates relative to the benchmark.

B The selection of securities within the portfolio versus the benchmark.

C The sector weighting of the portfolio relative to the benchmark.

3 For Portfolio Two in Exhibit 28, which factor most negatively affected the excess return?

A The positioning of the portfolio's sensitivity to interest rates relative to the benchmark.

B The selection of securities within the portfolio versus the benchmark.

C The sector weighting of the portfolio relative to the benchmark.

4 In Exhibit 28, what investment decision of Portfolio Two might be superior to that of Portfolio One?

A Sector bets

B Interest rate bets

C Security selection

Solution to 1:

B is correct. Fixed-income return attribution models can be closely tailored to match the investment process. A is not correct because fixed-income return attribution models are not typically easier to implement than the Brinson approach. C is not correct because fixed-income return attribution models typically require more data and sophisticated software.

Solution to 2:

A is correct. Portfolio One achieved 41 bps from the impact of yield curve positioning and 31 bps specifically from interest rate sensitivity (duration), both of which are higher than sector weighting (29 bps) and security selection (–21 bps).

Solution to 3:

A is correct. Portfolio Two lost 17 bps from the impact of yield curve positioning The –17 bps were offset by the positive sector weighting (11 bps) and security selection (9 bps).

Solution to 4:

C is correct. Portfolio Two gained 9 bps from security selection relative to −21 bps for Portfolio One. A is not correct because Portfolio Two gained only 11 bps relative to Portfolio One, which gained 29 bps from sector positioning. B is not correct because Portfolio One gained 41 bps relative to Portfolio Two, which lost 17 bps.

PROBLEMS IN RETURN ATTRIBUTION ANALYSIS

9

With such a key role in the analysis of the investment decision process, any anomalies revealed in the calculation of return attribution will inevitably attract a significant amount of attention. Considerable effort may be required to ensure the return attribution analysis genuinely reflects the decision process and that the data is of sufficient quality. Residuals of any size will naturally bring into question the accuracy of the return attribution analysis. A new step in the decision process, a new instrument, or a new strategy may require the redesign of the return attribution analysis to provide meaningful information.

9.1 Data Input

Clearly the quality of the return attribution analysis is only as good as the data input. The only inputs required for the Brinson model are portfolio weights and returns and benchmark weights and returns. If the difference between total portfolio return and total benchmark return is to be completely explained, then the sum of each sector weight and return for both the portfolio and benchmark, as described in Equations 1 and 2, must equal the total returns presented to the client.

For holdings-based return attribution the weight used is the beginning period weight for the sector expressed as a percentage of the total portfolio beginning period weight.

For example, the weights for the portfolio shown in Exhibit 3 were calculated for use in a holdings-based analysis as shown in Exhibit 29.

Exhibit 29 Holdings-Based Beginning Weights

	Beginning Market Value (millions)	Percentage Weight
Energy	$500	50%
Health Care	$300	30%
Financials	$200	20%
Total	**$1,000**	**100%**

The end market values for each sector and the returns used in the return attribution analysis are shown in Exhibit 30.

Exhibit 30 Holdings-Based Sector Returns

Sector	End Market Value (millions)	Return
Energy	\$590	$\frac{590}{500} - 1 = 18.0\%$
Healthcare	\$291	$\frac{291}{300} - 1 = -3.0\%$
Financials	\$220	$\frac{220}{200} - 1 = 10.0\%$
Total	\$1,101	$\frac{1101}{1000} - 1 = 10.1\%$

For transaction-based return attribution, the weight used must reflect the impact of transactions during the period and must be consistent with the underlying return calculation used. For example, if the calculation method used for the period is modified Dietz then the denominator in the modified Dietz calculation provides an appropriate weight for use in return attribution analysis.

The period of analysis for the portfolio data in Exhibit 30 is a 30-day month. Although ignored in the monthly holding analysis used previously, there are transactions at the end of the 10th day, namely a \$5 million outflow out of the health care sector into the financials sector. Using a transaction-based approach, the weights must now be adjusted using the denominator of the modified Dietz method of calculation as shown in Exhibit 31.

Exhibit 31 Transaction-Based Weights

Sector	Modified Dietz Denominator (\$ millions)	Percentage Weight
Energy	\$500	50%
Health Care	\$300 – (5 × 20/30) = \$296.67	29.67%
Financials	\$200 + (5 × 20/30) = \$203.33	20.33%
Total	**\$1,000**	**100%**

It is very important to use a consistent return methodology for each sector and the total portfolio return within the attribution analysis. For example, when a time-weighted return is used for one sector with a large cash flow and a modified Dietz return is used for all the other sectors, then the sum of sector weights and returns is unlikely to add up to the total return, which will lead to a residual in the attribution analysis.

9.2 Residuals

Residuals in return attribution can be caused by a number of reasons.

9.2.1 *Holdings-Based Return Attribution*

Because holdings-based return attribution naturally ignores transactions in the period, there will be a reconciliation difference or residual between the return implicitly used in the return attribution analysis and the return presented to the client.

9.2.2 *Errors in Portfolio and Benchmark Returns*

Any failure of the sum product of the weights and returns included in the return attribution of either the portfolio or benchmark to add up to the reported total portfolio or benchmark return will cause a residual.

Among the possible causes are (this list is not exhaustive):

- the failure to include all investment categories in the portfolio in the return attribution analysis;
- the failure to include all investment instruments, such as forward currency contracts or other derivative instruments; or
- mixing the return methodologies used to calculate sector returns and the total return.

In the benchmark, a residual might be caused by an error in the calculation of a customized benchmark, it might be an error caused by the index provider, or more likely it might be an unexpected transaction in a constituent security in the index, such as a corporate action.

9.2.3 *Incomplete Models*

The model itself may be incomplete and not identifying all the impacts within the investment decision process. One may need to add more factors to the model or try a different combination of factors that better explain the investment process.

9.2.4 *Multi-period Analysis*

Although multi-period analysis is beyond the scope of this reading, it should be noted that arithmetic excess returns naturally do not add up over multiple periods and, therefore, arithmetic return attribution analysis will also not normally add up. This characteristic will lead to a residual unless a geometric attribution methodology is used or more likely a smoothing algorithm is applied to the residual, redistributing the residual to other terms within the return attribution analysis.

EXAMPLE 15

Residuals

Residuals in return attribution analysis are *most likely* caused by:

A the interaction between investment decisions.

B portfolio transactions within the evaluation period.

C investing in securities not included in the benchmark.

Solution:

B is correct. The interaction between investment decisions is not a residual, but rather it is a directly calculable effect, so A is not correct. The return attribution of securities not included in the benchmark will depend on the investment process and should not lead to a residual.

9.3 Off-Benchmark Decisions

From time to time, if allowed by their investment mandate, portfolio managers may invest in securities not included in their benchmark (**off-benchmark decisions** or **zero-weight benchmark decisions**). The return attribution of these decisions depends on the rationale behind the decision in the first place.

For example, if an investment committee makes the decision to invest outside of the benchmark to specifically gain exposure to the transportation sector, a sector allocation decision has clearly been made and should be measured as such. If the benchmark does not include the transportation sector, its weight in the benchmark index will be zero and any allocation to transportation will thus be overweight. To measure the impact of this overweight decision, a suitable transportation sector index must be chosen.[9] This will not affect the overall benchmark return because the weight is zero. The portfolio manager will then invest in transportation securities to implement this sector decision; the selection impact of these securities is measured in the normal way.

But if the decision to invest in the transportation sector is solely the desire of the portfolio manager to purchase an individual security and allocation to the transportation sector did not feature in the investment process, then it would be inappropriate to measure the impact of being overweight the transportation sector. In this case, it would be more appropriate to measure the performance of the security against the overall benchmark thus ensuring its entire contribution to excess return, positive or negative, is always a selection effect.

A decision may be allocation driven but it may be impossible to identify an appropriate sector index. In such circumstances, the best proxy for the sector index return may well be the actual return achieved by the portfolio manager in that sector. This approach would result in the entire impact being allocated to allocation with no selection effect. In virtually all circumstances, it would be inappropriate to use a benchmark return of zero.

Three alternative presentations of a portfolio containing an off-benchmark decision are shown in Exhibit 32, Exhibit 33, and Exhibit 34.

Exhibit 32 Portfolio with an Off-Benchmark Decision (Scenario 1)

	Portfolio Weight	Benchmark Weight	Portfolio Return	Benchmark Return	Allocation	Selection
Energy	50%	50%	18%	10%	0.0%	4.0%
Health Care	30%	20%	−3%	−2%	−1.02%	−0.3%
Financials	15%	30%	10%	12%	−0.57%	−0.3%
Transportation	5%	0%	12%	4%	−0.21%	0.4%
Total	**100%**	**100%**	**10.2%**	**8.2%**	**−1.8%**	**+3.8%**

The arithmetic return attribution effects for transportation, assuming a sector allocation decision, are as follows:

Allocation: (5% − 0%) × (4% − 8.2%) = −0.21%

Selection (including interaction): 5% × (12% − 4%) = 0.4%

Alternatively, the arithmetic return attribution effects for transportation, assuming a selection only decision (note the change in benchmark for only the transportation sector) are:

9 Although the choice of sub-index will not impact the overall benchmark return because of the zero weight, this choice should be independent of the manager responsible for managing securities within the sector.

Exhibit 33 Portfolio with an Off-Benchmark Decision (Scenario 2)

	Portfolio Weight	Benchmark Weight	Portfolio Return	Benchmark Return	Allocation	Selection
Energy	50%	50%	18%	10%	0.0%	4.0%
Health Care	30%	20%	−3%	−2%	−1.02%	−0.3%
Financials	15%	30%	10%	12%	−0.57%	−0.3%
Transportation	5%	0%	12%	8.2%	0.0%	+0.19%
Total	**100%**	**100%**	**10.2%**	**8.2%**	**−1.59%**	**3.59%**

Allocation: (5% − 0%) × (8.2% − 8.2%) = 0.0%

Selection (including interaction): 5% × (12% − 8.2%) = 0.19%

Assuming an allocation-only decision (note the benchmark return is now identical to the portfolio return in the sector), the return attribution effects for transportation are:

Exhibit 34 Portfolio with an Off-Benchmark Decision (Scenario 3)

	Portfolio Weight	Benchmark Weight	Portfolio Return	Benchmark Return	Allocation	Selection
Energy	50%	50%	18%	10%	0.0%	4.0%
Health Care	30%	20%	−3%	−2%	−1.02%	−0.3%
Financials	15%	30%	10%	12%	−0.57%	−0.3%
Transportation	5%	0%	12%	12%	0.19%	0.0%
Total	**100%**	**100%**	**10.2%**	**8.2%**	**−1.4%**	**+3.4%**

Allocation: (5% − 0%) × (12.0% − 8.2%) = 0.19%

Selection (including interaction): 5% × (12% − 12%) = 0.0%

The overall effect for all three alternatives is the same—an impact of 0.19%. But in the first presentation, the fact that there has been an allocation to the transportation sector has been reflected in a cost of −0.21% offset by 0.4% contribution caused by outperformance against the transportation index. In the second presentation, the entire decision is selection driven. In the third presentation, the decision is allocation driven and the entire impact is reflected in asset allocation.

EXAMPLE 16

Off-Benchmark Decision

Off-benchmark investment decisions:

A exclusively cause allocation effects.

B may cause both allocation and selection effects.

C cannot be allocated because there is no benchmark.

Solution:

B is correct. The investment decision process will inform the method of return attribution and this may lead to both allocation and selection effects. Asset allocation effects may not result if the decision to invest outside the benchmark is an individual security driven decision.

10 CONCLUSION AND SUMMARY

Return attribution is an essential tool for all performance analysts. Return attribution is an invaluable aid to help ensure that portfolio returns are calculated correctly, facilitate a dialogue between portfolio managers and clients, generate a true understanding of the sources of added and subtracted value in the portfolio, and allow the performance analysts to participate in the investment decision process and thus add value. Among the points made in this reading are the following:

- Return attribution is an essential part of the investment decision process, identifying the sources of excess return.
- Return contribution identifies the sources of absolute return, whereas return attribution identifies the sources of relative return between the returns of the portfolio and the benchmark.
- Risk attribution complements return attribution by analyzing the risk consequences of active investment decisions, both absolute and relative to the benchmark.
- The foundation of return attribution analysis is the Brinson model formulated in the 1980s and presented in papers written by Brinson and Fachler and Brinson, Hood, and Beebower.
- The Brinson model quantifies excess return into allocation, selection and interaction effects.
- Interaction is a basic flaw of the Brinson model because it is not part of the investment decision process. The interaction effect can be removed by including it in the selection effect (in which allocation is the first decision).
- The Brinson model can be adapted for use with geometric excess returns.
- Return attribution can be calculated using returns -based, holdings-based, and transaction-based methodologies. Transaction-based attribution is the most complete and accurate method but also the most difficult to implement.
- Plan sponsors and portfolio managers make contributions to excess return at different levels in the investment decision process.
- The allocation and selection formulas can be applied at different levels in the investment decision process: sponsor level, manager level, country level, sector level, and security level.
- Another type of return attribution uses fundamental factor models to decompose relative contributors to excess return of any number of different factors.
- The Fama–French model uses factors for market, size, and style and is one of many different approaches to factor-based attribution.
- The Brinson model is adaptable for fixed income return attribution but may not be useful for that purpose if it does not correspond to the investment decision process being evaluated.

- Fixed-income managers are concerned with the sensitivity of their portfolios to the change in interest rates and spreads and they need to consider other characteristics specific to bonds, such as duration and credit risk.
- Holdings-based attribution only requires the holdings at the beginning of the period to calculate return attribution effects, assuming the portfolio manager does not undertake any transactions during the period.
- Residuals may be caused by using holdings-based analysis, errors in calculating both the portfolio or benchmark return, incomplete models, and multi-period analysis using arithmetic models.
- Any decision to invest outside the benchmark can be attributed, but only in the context of the investment decision process that led to that decision.

REFERENCES

Allen, Gregory C. 1991. "Performance Attribution of Global Equity Portfolios." *Journal of Portfolio Management*, vol. 18, no. 1 (Fall):59–65.

Bacon, Carl R. 2002. "Excess Returns—Arithmetic or Geometric." *Journal of Performance Measurement*, vol. 6, no. 3 (Spring):23–31.

Bacon, Carl R. 2008. *Practical Portfolio Performance Measurement and Attribution*. Hoboken, NJ: John Wiley & Sons.

Bain, William G. 1996. *Investment Performance Measurement*. Cambridge, England: Woodhead Publishing.

Brinson, Gary, and Nimrod Fachler. 1985. "Measuring Non-US Equity Portfolio Performance." *Journal of Portfolio Management*, vol. 11, no. 5 (Spring):73–76.

Brinson, Gary, Randolph Hood, and Gilbert Beebower. 1986. "Determinants of Portfolio Performance." *Financial Analysts Journal*, vol. 42, no. 4 (July–August):39–44.

Burnie, J.S., J.A. Knowles, and T.J. Teder. 1998. "Arithmetic and Geometric Attribution." *Journal of Performance Measurement*, vol. 3, no. 1 (Fall):59–68.

Fama, Eugene F., and Kenneth R. French. 1993. "Common Risk Factors in the Returns on Stocks and Bonds." *Journal of Financial Economics*, vol. 33, no. 1 (February):3–56.

PRACTICE PROBLEMS

1 Return attribution is *least* helpful for:

A identifying the sources of excess return over a benchmark.

B forecasting the excess return caused by overweighing an asset sector.

C determining whether a portfolio manager added value through security selection.

2 Return attribution is a set of techniques used to identify the sources of:

A absolute return of a portfolio.

B portfolio volatility for absolute return mandates.

C excess return of a portfolio over a benchmark return.

3 Return attribution is *best* described as a process that:

A helps a portfolio manager develop an investment strategy.

B measures the results of a portfolio manager's active decisions.

C determines the appropriateness of the portfolio manager's allocation or selection decisions.

4 Return contribution analyzes how:

A portfolio return differs from benchmark return.

B sector returns contribute to total portfolio return.

C active investment decisions contribute to total portfolio return.

5 Return contribution analysis differs from return attribution analysis in that return contribution:

A uses only the weights and returns of the portfolio, and not of the benchmark.

B explains the value added from investment decisions in comparison to the portfolio's benchmark.

C uses the Brinson model(s) to decompose returns based on allocation and security selection decisions.

6 Consider a portfolio and a benchmark containing the weights and returns given below:

	Portfolio Weight	Benchmark Weight	Sector Return	Benchmark Return
Industrial Sector	40%	50%	3.0%	2.0%
Consumer Goods Sector	60%	50%	5.0%	6.0%
Total	**100%**	**100%**	**4.2%**	**4.0%**

An analyst conducting a return contribution analysis would *most likely* conclude that:

A underweighting the industrial sector was a poor decision.

B overweighting the consumer goods sector was a good decision.

C overweighting the consumer goods sector reduced the portfolio value.

7 Risk attribution is *best* described as concerned with:

A analyzing the value added by active investment decisions.

B analyzing the volatility resulting from active investment decisions.

C decomposing the excess return into allocation and selection decisions.

8 Which of the following *best describes* an effective return attribution process? It:

A presents the historical risk of the portfolio.

B provides an understanding of portfolio excess returns.

C explains the return variability of the benchmark compared to that of the portfolio.

9 An effective attribution process *most likely*:

A ranks portfolio managers.

B reflects the investment decision process.

C attributes arithmetic excess returns but not geometric excess returns.

10 An effective return attribution process should:

A be used only internally within management.

B validate the selected benchmark as appropriate.

C reconcile to the total portfolio return presented to the client.

11 The Brinson–Fachler return attribution model improves upon the Brinson–Hood–Beebower model by:

A measuring the security selection effect relatively to the overall benchmark.

B producing a positive allocation effect for any manager who is overweight in a negative market that has outperformed the overall benchmark.

C producing a higher sum of sector contributions to allocation than the Brinson–Hood–Beebower model.

12 Consider a portfolio and a benchmark containing the weights and returns given below:

	Portfolio Weight	Benchmark Weight	Portfolio Return	Benchmark Return
Health Care	10%	20%	3%	–4%
Utilities	30%	30%	4%	–6%
Consumer Goods	60%	50%	–2%	–4%
Total	**100%**	**100%**	**0%**	**–5%**

The allocation effect in the consumer goods sector using the Brinson–Fachler model is:

A negative because the sector benchmark return is negative.

B negative because the sector portfolio return was negative.

C positive because the portfolio was overweight in a sector that outperformed the benchmark.

13 In the Brinson–Hood–Beebower (BHB) model, an underweight position in a sector with a negative benchmark return will generate a positive allocation effect in that sector:

A in all cases.

B only if the portfolio sector return is positive.

C only if the overall benchmark return is positive.

14 The Brinson–Hood–Beebower (BHB) model differs from the Brinson–Fachler (BF) model in how it calculates the:

A interaction effects.

B sector allocation effects.

C security selection effects.

15 Consider a portfolio and a benchmark containing the weights and returns given below:

	Portfolio Weight	Benchmark Weight	Portfolio Return	Benchmark Return
Energy	20%	25%	7.00%	5.00%
Health Care	25%	25%	10.00%	9.00%
Financial	30%	20%	−1.00%	2.00%
Information Technology	25%	30%	3.00%	2.00%
Total	**100%**	**100%**	**4.35%**	**4.50%**

Using the BHB model, which of the following effects is positive? The

A selection effect of Energy.

B allocation effect of Health Care.

C interaction effect of Information Technology.

16 The table below shows the excess returns for a three-sector portfolio and the returns and weights for its benchmark.

Sector	Benchmark Weight	Benchmark Return	Excess Return
Banking	30.0%	−2.0%	−2.0%
Transportation	45.0%	1.0%	3.0%
Communications	25.0%	−4.0%	−1.5%

Using the Brinson–Hood–Beebower (BHB) model, the total contribution to excess return from selection is *closest* to:

A −0.50%.

B 0.38%.

C 2.50%.

17 An equity portfolio is divided into three market capitalization segments and benchmarked against a broad market index. The segment weights and returns for a single period are as follows:

	Portfolio Weight	Benchmark Weight	Portfolio Return	Benchmark Return
Small Cap	40%	10%	8.5%	7.9%
Mid Cap	10%	20%	6.8%	7.3%
Large Cap	50%	70%	5.1%	5.1%
Total	**100%**	**100%**	**6.6%**	**5.8%**

Using the Brinson–Hood–Beebower (BHB) model, which of the following is *closest* to the allocation effect for the large cap segment?

A −1.0%

B 0.0%

C 0.1%

18 The exhibit below shows the weights and returns of a portfolio and its benchmark. It also shows the allocation, selection and interaction effect using the BHB model.

	Portfolio Weight	Benchmark Weight	Portfolio Return	Benchmark Return	Allocation	Selection	Interaction
Consumer Discretionary	25%	25%	8.00%	6.80%	0.00%	0.30%	0.00%
Consumer Staples	35%	25%	13.00%	14.00%	1.40%	−0.25%	−0.10%
Energy	10%	25%	−9.00%	−8.60%	1.29%	−0.10%	0.06%
Health Care	30%	25%	−3.00%	−1.00%	−0.05%	−0.50%	−0.10%
Total	**100%**	**100%**	**4.75%**	**2.80%**	**2.64%**	**−0.55%**	**−0.14%**

In terms of return attribution effects, which of the following contributed most to the total portfolio performance against the benchmark?

A Allocation plus selection decisions in energy

B Selection decision in consumer discretionary

C Allocation plus selection decisions in consumer staples

19 The exhibit below shows the weights and returns of a portfolio and its benchmark.

	Portfolio Weight	Benchmark Weight	Portfolio Return	Benchmark Return
Financials	15%	20%	−3.50%	−4.00%
Technology	30%	35%	22.00%	19.00%
Health Care	30%	17%	−3.00%	−2.00%
Consumer Staples	25%	28%	8.00%	10.00%
Total	**100%**	**100%**	**7.18%**	**8.31%**

The selection effect of the technology segment using the Brinson–Hood–Beebower model is *closest* to:

A −0.2%.

B 0.9%.

C 1.1%

20 The exhibit below shows the weights and returns of a portfolio and its benchmark.

	Portfolio Weight	Benchmark Weight	Portfolio Return	Benchmark Return
Health Care	10%	20%	3%	2%
Utilities	30%	30%	4%	4%
Consumer Goods	60%	50%	7%	8%
Total	**100%**	**100%**	**5.7%**	**5.6%**

According to the Brinson–Fachler attribution model, the allocation effect from the Consumer Goods sector is *closest* to:

A −0.50%.

B 0.24%.

C 0.80%.

21 In the context of Brinson attribution models, interaction is:

A small for larger allocation bets.

B a part of the investment decision making process.

C a mathematical consequence of the manager's allocation and selection decisions.

22 The exhibit below shows the weights and returns of a portfolio and its benchmarks, as well as the geometric allocation effect.

	Portfolio Weight	Benchmark Weight	Portfolio Return	Benchmark Return	Allocation Effect
Health Care	10%	20%	3%	4%	0.07%
Utilities	30%	30%	4%	3%	0.00%
Consumer Goods	60%	50%	7%	6%	0.12%
Total	**100%**	**100%**	**5.7%**	**4.7%**	**0.19%**

Assuming that security selection and interaction are combined, the geometric selection effect for the portfolio is *closest* to:

A 0.76%

B 0.81%

C 1.00%

23 The exhibit below shows the weights and returns of a portfolio and its benchmarks.

	Portfolio Weight	Benchmark Weight	Portfolio Return	Benchmark Return
Health Care	10%	20%	5%	7%
Utilities	30%	30%	4%	3%
Consumer Goods	60%	50%	7%	6%
Total	**100%**	**100%**	**5.9%**	**5.3%**

The geometric selection effect (including interaction) for the health care sector is *closest* to:

A −0.20%

B −0.19%

C −0.16%

24 The exhibit below shows the weights and returns of a portfolio and its benchmarks, as well as the geometric allocation and selection effects based on the Brinson–Fachler model.

	Portfolio Weight	Benchmark Weight	Portfolio Return	Benchmark Return	Allocation Effect	Selection Effect
Health Care	10%	20%	5%	2%	0.22%	0.29%
Utilities	30%	30%	4%	3%	0.00%	0.29%
Consumer Goods	60%	50%	8%	6%	0.16%	1.15%
Total	**100%**	**100%**	**6.5%**	**4.3%**	**0.38%**	**1.73%**

Which of the following effects from the changes to the asset allocation shown below is correct?

A Increasing the weight of utilities would have increased that sector's selection effect.

B Increasing the weight of health care would have increased the portfolio's allocation effect.

C Decreasing the weight of consumer goods would have increased that sector's allocation effect.

25 Which return attribution method would provide the *most* accurate analysis for an active portfolio manager?

A Returns-based

B Holdings-based

C Transactions-based

26 Which of the following is *most likely* a disadvantage of transactions-based return attribution compared to a holdings-based return attribution? Transaction-based:

A requires purchase and sale data inputs into the attribution analysis.

B increases the magnitude of residuals within the attribution analysis.

C necessitates reconciliation of attribution analysis to returns presented to a client.

27 Holdings-based attribution analysis:

A can be calculated over weekly or monthly holding periods.

B is the most time consuming attribution analysis to implement.

C is most appropriate when portfolio positions are not available.

28 The sponsor of an endowment fund does not manage assets internally but rather delegates most investment decisions to portfolio managers. Which of the following decisions is *most likely* to be retained by the sponsor?

A Security selection

B Tactical asset allocation

C Strategic asset allocation

The following information relates to Questions 29–31

The sponsor of a pension plan has hired two portfolio managers for the bond portion of his fund. The bond allocation benchmark of the fund is as follows:

50% long-term government bonds (Portfolio A)

30% long-term corporate bonds (Portfolio B)

20% short-term government bonds (Portfolio C)

The sponsor hires LT portfolio manager to manage Portfolio A and Portfolio B, and hires ST portfolio manager to manage Portfolio C. In the last fiscal year, the results were as follows:

	Fund Weight	Fund Return	Benchmark Weight	Benchmark Return
LT portfolio manager				
government	55%	3.50%	50%	4.00%
corporate	30%	2.50%	30%	2.00%
Total LT bonds	**85%**	**3.15%**	**80%**	**3.25%**

(continued)

	Fund Weight	Fund Return	Benchmark Weight	Benchmark Return
ST portfolio manager	15%	2.00%	20%	1.50%
Total all bonds	**100%**	**2.98%**	**100%**	**2.90%**

29 Evaluating the decisions of the sponsor for the last fiscal year, the allocation effect of the return attribution analysis for the LT portfolio manager, using the Brinson–Fachler approach, is *closest* to:

A −0.085%.

B 0.018%.

C 0.055%.

30 Evaluating the decisions of the LT portfolio manager for the last fiscal year, the allocation effect of the return attribution analysis, using the Brinson–Fachler approach, is *closest* to:

A −0.125%.

B 0.018%.

C 0.055%.

31 Assume that for the last fiscal year, with respect to LT bonds, it was observed that the allocation effect, when one evaluates the decisions of the sponsor, is less than the allocation effect, when one evaluates the decisions of the LT portfolio manager. The *most* appropriate conclusion to draw is that the:

A comparison is not valid.

B LT portfolio manager made better decisions than the sponsor.

C evaluation at the sponsor level should be completed by calculating the attribution at the segment level.

---

32 The results of a multiple factor return attribution analysis are presented below.

Factor	Portfolio Sensitivity	Benchmark Sensitivity	Difference	Factor Return	Contribution
Equity risk premium	0.02	0.05	−0.03	6.71%	−0.00201
Small cap return premium	0.35	0.50	−0.15	1.96%	−0.00294
Value return premium	1.30	1.11	0.19	−0.43%	−0.00082
				Return attributed to factors	−0.00577
				Return attributed to specific asset selection	−0.00009
				Excess return	−0.00586

Which of the following statements is a valid interpretation of the results?

A Excess exposure to value stocks negatively affected the excess return.

B Excess exposure to small cap stocks negatively affected the excess return.

C The largest contributor to negative excess return was the impact of the equity risk premium factor.

33 The results of a multiple factor return attribution analysis are presented below.

Factor	Portfolio Sensitivity	Benchmark Sensitivity	Difference	Factor Return	Contribution
Equity risk premium	0.05	0.05	0.00	4.99%	0.00000
Small cap return premium	0.56	0.50	0.06	2.31%	0.00139
Value return premium	0.31	1.21	−0.90	1.01%	−0.00909
				Return attributed to factors	−0.00770
				Return attributed to specific asset selection	−0.00009
				Excess return	−0.00779

The result that *best* shows that the impact on excess return of the decision to overweight the small-cap return premium factor was positive is the:

A small-cap factor return of 2.31%.

B contribution to excess return of 0.00139.

C difference in sensitivity of 0.06 for the small cap return premium.

34 The results of a multiple factor return attribution analysis are presented below.

Factor	Portfolio Sensitivity	Benchmark Sensitivity	Difference	Factor Return	Contribution
Equity risk premium	0.05	0.07	−0.02	3.04%	−0.00061
Small cap return premium	1.23	0.98	0.25	0.44%	0.00110
Value return premium	1.17	0.64	0.53	2.76%	0.01463
				Return attributed to factors	0.01512
				Return attributed to specific asset selection	−0.00009
				Excess return	0.01503

Based on the above results, which of the following conclusions is *most* appropriate? The portfolio manager employs a:

A passive investment approach.

B small-cap value investment style.

C large-cap growth investment style.

35 Compared to asset-grouping models of attribution, factor models:

A can be tailored more closely to the investment process.

B are easier to understand in terms of investment decisions.

C can be applied more directly to balanced portfolios containing multiple asset classes.

36 Comparing asset-grouping and factor models of attribution, factor models are:

A independent of the model specification.

B available in more varieties in the industry.

C relatively inexpensive to use due to computer advances.

37 Data and implementation costs aside, using a Brinson attribution approach for a fixed income portfolio would *most likely* be appropriate if:

A a customized multi-factor model supports the investment decision process.

B yield curve positioning is the only important factor in the investment decision process.

C yield curve positioning, credit spread positioning, and specific bond selection are the three most important factors in the investment decision process.

38 Which of the following *best* explains why the Brinson attribution approach may not be suitable for fixed income strategies?

A Appropriate fixed income benchmarks are not readily available.

B The approach cannot analyze the impact of decisions across the yield curve.

C The approach cannot match an investment decision process based on multi-factor risk models.

39 The results of a fixed income return attribution analysis are given below.

Description	Return
Portfolio	2.15%
Benchmark	1.24%
Changes along yield curve	0.08%
Convexity	0.02%
Duration	0.31%
Sector	0.29%
Security specific	0.21%

The excess return attributable to interest rate management is *closest* to:

A 0.08%

B 0.33%

C 0.41%

40 The results of a fixed income return attribution analysis are given below.

Description	Return
Portfolio	2.15%
Benchmark	2.19%
Changes along yield curve	−0.02%
Convexity	0.03%
Duration	0.14%
Sector	0.07%
Security Specific	−0.26%

Which of the following statements *best* interprets the analysis?

A The portfolio manager's contribution to excess return due to interest rate management was 0.17%.

B The portfolio manager's sector allocation ability exceeded his skill at interest rate management.

C The portfolio manager's selection skill was the major factor in the portfolio's underperformance relative to the benchmark.

41 In which of the following scenarios will holdings based attribution lead to the *best* results?

A The use of daily holdings for a portfolio with low turnover.

B The use of daily holdings for a portfolio with high turnover.

C The use of monthly holdings for a portfolio with high turnover.

42 Residuals in return attribution would *most* likely be increased by:

A switching from an arithmetic to a geometric attribution model.

B increasing the consistency of portfolio and benchmark weights and returns.

C switching from transaction-based attribution to holdings-based attribution analysis.

43 When performing a return attribution analysis for a large cap manager, a residual effect will *most likely* occur if:

A a small cap benchmark is used.

B the analysis covers a single period.

C the analysis uses beginning of period holdings.

44 Mary Alice invested in information technology stocks, although information technology is not included in her benchmark. Data on her portfolio and her benchmark are shown below.

	Portfolio Weight	Benchmark Weight	Portfolio Return	Benchmark Return
Energy	25%	35%	7.0%	5.0%
Health Care	30%	35%	10.0%	9.0%
Financial	35%	30%	−1.0%	2.0%
Information Technology	10%	0%	3.0%	2.0%
Total	**100%**	**100%**	**4.7%**	**5.5%**

Assuming the investment in information technology was a selection only decision, the selection (including interaction) effect is *closest* to:

A −0.35%.

B −0.25%.

C 0.10%.

45 The returns and weights of a portfolio and its benchmark for latest period are shown below. The investment committee made the decision to invest outside the benchmark specifically to gain exposure to the materials sector. To measure the impact of this decision, the committee chose a suitable materials sector index. For the period, the return on the materials sector index was 7.10%.

Sector	Portfolio Weight	Benchmark Weight	Portfolio Return	Benchmark Return
Consumer Discretionary	30%	35%	6.23%	7.00%
Consumer Staples	35%	40%	2.91%	2.55%
Industrials	30%	25%	3.00%	−5.67%
Materials	5%	0%	10.80%	7.10%
Total	100%	100%	4.33%	2.05%

The allocation effect for the materials sector is *closest* to:

A −0.10%

B 0.19%

C 0.25%

46 A portfolio manager believes that a company classified in the consumer staples sector will strongly outperform in the short term. The consumer staples sector is not part of his benchmark and he purchases the stock as an individual security. The result of the return attribution process should *most likely* indicate that the:

A selection effect only is zero.

B allocation effect only is zero.

C neither the allocation nor the selection effect are zero.

SOLUTIONS

1 B is correct. Return attribution is a "backward-looking" feedback mechanism. It cannot be used to forecast future investment returns.

A is incorrect because return attribution is defined as a set of techniques used to identify the sources of excess return. C is incorrect because return attribution shows the excess return resulting from the security selection decisions of a portfolio manager.

2 C is correct. Return attribution is a set of techniques used to identify the sources of the excess return of a portfolio against its benchmark.

A is incorrect. Return contribution (also called absolute return attribution), not return attribution, analyzes the contributions of portfolio components to the total return of a portfolio. C is incorrect. Risk attribution, not return attribution, is concerned with identifying the sources of portfolio volatility (or tracking risk) for absolute (or relative) return mandates.

3 B is correct. Because return attribution utilizes a benchmark to determine excess return, the results will reflect any value added from the portfolio manager's active decisions.

A is incorrect because the portfolio manager is expected to have formulated an investment strategy prior to any return attribution calculation. C is incorrect because return attribution is used to measure the results of active investment decisions. Considerations such as client suitability are not involved.

4 B is correct. Return contribution (also called *absolute* return attribution) analyzes the contributions of portfolio components to the total return of a portfolio, with no comparison to a benchmark.

A and C are incorrect because they refer to a comparative analysis to a benchmark.

5 A is correct. Return contribution is calculated as the sum of the product of the security/sector weight multiplied by the security/sector return, without the consideration of a benchmark. Only the weights and returns of the portfolio are utilized. Return attribution would include comparison with a benchmark.

Both B and C are incorrect because they claim that in return contribution, a calculated comparison is made to a benchmark.

6 B is correct. In this exhibit, because the portfolio return in the industrial sector was less than the return in the consumer goods sector, investing more in the consumer goods sector than in the industrial sector increased the portfolio's total return.

A is incorrect because the return in the industrial sector was less than in the consumer goods sector. Thus, investing less in the industrial sector than in the consumer goods sector was a good decision. The fact that the industrial sector investment outperformed its benchmark is not relevant to return contribution analysis. C is incorrect. Because the consumer goods sector return was positive, it contributed positively to total return and thus increased the portfolio value. The fact that the consumer goods sector investment underperformed against its benchmark is not relevant to contribution analysis.

7 B is correct. Risk attribution is concerned with analyzing the risk consequences of active investment decisions.

A is incorrect. Return attribution, not risk attribution, can best be used to analyze the value added by active investment decisions. C is incorrect. Return attribution, not risk attribution, attempts to identify investment management value added by decomposing the excess return into separate contributors to excess return from allocation and selection decisions relative to a benchmark.

8 B is correct. Return attribution should provide a complete understanding of a portfolio's excess returns.

A is incorrect because return attribution does not focus on measuring risk (risk attribution does). C is incorrect because return attribution compares the portfolio return to the benchmark return but does not compare the variability of those two returns.

9 B is correct. One of the attributes of an effective return attribution process is to reflect the investment decision process.

A is incorrect. Ranking portfolio managers is not part of an attribution process. C is incorrect because excess returns can be effectively calculated and attributed in either arithmetic or geometric terms.

10 C is correct. If the return generated by the return attribution does not reconcile to the return presented to the client the attribution will be considered incomplete and the quality of the analysis brought into question.

A is incorrect. Return attribution analysis can be used by portfolio managers to explain performance to clients. B is incorrect. Selection of an appropriate benchmark is made on an *ex ante* basis based upon the portfolio manager's intended investment strategy. It is not the role of return attribution to validate the benchmark.

11 B is correct. $(w_i - W_i)B_i$ represents the contribution to allocation for the ith sector in the Brinson–Hood–Beebower (BHB) model. In the Brinson–Fachler (BF) model, the contribution to allocation is $(w_i - W_i)(B_i - B)$. In the BHB model, B_i, or the return of the benchmark in the ith sector, could be negative and (given that $w_i > W_i$) would imply a negative allocation contribution. In the BF model, contribution to allocation would be negative only if the sector underperformed the overall benchmark, B.

A is incorrect because the formula for security selection are the same in the BF model and in the BHB model. C is incorrect because both models produce the same allocation effect at the portfolio level, $B_S - B$.

12 C is correct. The Brinson–Fachler (BF) model calculates the allocation effect as $(w_i - W_i)(B_i - B)$. In this case, the BF allocation effect in the consumer goods sector would be (0.6 – 0.5)(–0.04 – –0.05) = (0.10)(0.01) = 0.001 or 0.1%. The BF model takes in to account the fact that the manager was overweight a sector that outperformed the fund's benchmark, thus making a positive contribution to excess return.

A is incorrect as it is the Brinson–Hood–Beebower (BHB) allocation effect. The BHB allocation effect is given as $(w_i - W_i)B_i$. In this case, the BHB allocation effect in the consumer goods sector would be (0.6 – 0.5)(–0.04) = –0.004 or –0.4%. The BHB model does not take into account how the sector benchmark (B_i) performance relative to the overall benchmark return, B. B is incorrect because the use of the BF model implies a return attribution calculation, and thus a reference to a benchmark.

13 A is correct. An underweight position in sector i means that $(w_i - W_i)$ is negative. Given a negative sector benchmark return, B_i, the sector allocation effect $A_i = (w_i - W_i)B_i$ as the product of two negative numbers will always be positive.

14 B is correct. The only difference between the two models is the calculation of sector allocation effects, that is, $[(w_i - W_i) B_i]$ (BHB model) versus $[(w_i - W_i)(B_i - B)]$ (BF model).

A is incorrect. Both models use the same formula to calculate the interaction effects: $[(w_i - W_i)(R_i - B_i)]$. C is incorrect. Both models calculate selection effects as: $[W_i(R_i - B_i)]$.

15 A is correct. The selection effect of Energy is

$$W_i(R_i - B_i) = 25\% \times (7\% - 5\%) = 0.5\% > 0$$

B is incorrect because the allocation effect of Health Care is

$$(w_i - W_i)B_i = (25\% - 25\%) \times 9\% = 0$$

C is incorrect because the interaction effect of Information Technology is

$$(w_i - W_i)(R_i - B_i) = (25\% - 30\%) \times (3\% - 2\%) = -0.05\% < 0$$

16 B is correct. Using Equation 9, $S_i = W_i(R_i - B_i)$, we have:

Banking: 0.3(−0.02) = −0.006

Transportation: 0.45(0.03) = 0.0135

Communications: 0.25(−0.015) = −0.00375

Total: −0.006 + 0.0135 − 0.00375 = 0.0038, or 0.38%

A is incorrect. It is the sum of excess return but does not adjust for the benchmark weight in each sector. C is incorrect; it is the total benchmark return (−5.0%) multiplied by the total excess return (−0.5%).

17 A is correct. The formula to calculate the allocation effect for the *i*th segment is $A_i = (w_i - W_i)B_i = (0.5 - 0.7) \times 5.1\% = -1.02\%$ or −1.0%.

B is incorrect because 0.0 is the selection effect for the large cap segment. C is incorrect because 0.1% is the allocation effect using the Brinson–Fachler model: (0.5 − 0.7)(5.1% − 5.8%) = 0.14% or 0.1%

18 A is correct. The decision to underweight energy added 1.29% to the portfolio return but the security selection within energy was −0.10%. Ignoring interaction, energy was a positive contributor of 1.19% to overall performance.

B is incorrect. The attribution analysis shows a 0.30% in selection attribution; this indicates the manager outperformed the market and did add value in security selection but this was not the largest sector contributor to performance. C is incorrect. The contribution to overall performance from the allocation strategy of consumer staples was +1.40%; however the selection decisions cost the portfolio −0.25% resulting in a positive 1.15% in performance. This was not the largest sector contributor.

19 C is correct. Using Equation 9, $S_i = W_i(R_i - B_i)$, we have for the technology segment: 35%(22% − 19%) = 1.05% or 1.1%

B is incorrect. In this case the portfolio weight, rather than the benchmark weight, was used to calculate the selection attribution: 30%(22% − 19%) = 0.9%. A is incorrect. It is the interaction return: (30% − 35%) × (22% − 19%) = −0.15% or −0.2%.

20 B is correct. Using the Brinson–Fachler model, the allocation effect is measured by $(w_i - W_i)(B_i - B) = (0.60 - 0.50)(0.08 - 0.056) = 0.0024$ or 0.24%.

A is incorrect. It represents the contribution from selection: 0.50(0.07 − 0.08) = −0.005 or −0.50%. C is incorrect. It was found using the Brinson–Hood–Beebower model: (0.60 − 0.50)(0.08) = 0.008 or 0.80%.

21 C is correct. Interaction is a directly calculable effect resulting from the combination (or interaction) between allocation and selection effects.

A is incorrect because the interaction effect need not be small and typically will be greater for larger allocation bets. B is incorrect because interaction is not part of the investment decision making process, as portfolio managers do not seek to add value through interaction decisions.

22 A is correct. The formula for geometric excess return is $(1 + S^G)(1 + A^G) - 1 = (1 + R)/(1 + B) - 1$. The portfolio return ($R$), the benchmark return (B), and the geometric allocation effect for the portfolio (A^G) are all provided. Entering everything into the equation gives:

$$\left(1 + S^G\right)(1 + 0.0019) - 1 = \frac{(1 + 0.057)}{(1 + 0.047)} - 1$$

Solving for S^G gives $S^G = 0.0076$ or 0.76%. Alternatively, S^G can be calculated from Equation 24:

$$S^G = \frac{(1 + R)}{(1 + B_S)} - 1 = \frac{(1 + 0.057)}{(1 + 0.049)} - 1 = 0.0076$$

(Note that $B_S = 10\% \times 4\% + 30\% \times 3\% + 60\% \times 6\%$, using Equation 3).

B is incorrect because selection is calculated simply as a subtraction of the allocation effect from the excess return of the portfolio:

Selection = (Portfolio Return – Benchmark Return) – Allocation effect

Selection = (0.057 – 0.047) – 0.0019

Selection = 0.0081 or 0.81%

C is incorrect because it equals the total attribution effect or excess return.

23 B is correct. The contribution of the ith sector to geometric selection can be calculated using Equation 23:

$$S_i^G = \left(w_i\right)\left(\frac{(1 + R_i)}{(1 + B_i)} - 1\right)\frac{(1 + B_i)}{(1 + B_S)}, \text{ where } B_S = \sum_{i=1}^{n} w_i B_i$$

$$= (0.1)\left(\frac{(1 + 0.05)}{(1 + 0.07)} - 1\right)\frac{(1 + 0.07)}{(1 + 0.052)} \text{ for health care sector}$$

$= -0.0019$ or -0.19%.

A is incorrect because it is the arithmetic selection effect including interaction:

$= 10\% \times (5\% - 7\%)$

$= -0.0020$ or -0.20%

C is incorrect because it represents the geometric allocation effect:

$$= \left(w_i - W_i\right)\left(\frac{(1 + B_i)}{(1 + B)} - 1\right)$$

$$= (10\% - 20\%)\left(\frac{1 + 0.07}{1 + 0.053} - 1\right)$$

$= -0.0016$ or -0.16%.

24 A is correct. The contribution of the ith sector to geometric selection is

$$S_i^G = (w_i)\left(\frac{1+R_i}{1+B_i}-1\right)\left(\frac{1+B_i}{1+B_S}\right) = (w_i)\left(\frac{R_i - B_i}{1+B_S}\right)$$

The second term of the equation is positive since R_i (4%) is greater than B_i (3%). Therefore, increasing w_i (30%) would have increased S_i^G.

B is incorrect. The portfolio's allocation effect is given by

$$A^G = \frac{1+B_S}{1+B} - 1 = \frac{1+\sum_{i=1}^{i=n} w_i B_i}{1+B} - 1$$
$$= \frac{1+(0.10\times 0.02 + 0.30\times 0.03 + 0.60\times 0.06)}{1+0.043}$$

So increasing the weight of the health care sector (10%), and therefore decreasing the weight of either the utilities sector (30%) or of the consumer goods sector (60%), would have the effect of decreasing the numerator in this last equation since the benchmark return of health care (2%) is lower than the benchmark returns of the two other asset classes (3% and 6%).

C is incorrect. The contribution of the ith sector to geometric allocation is given by

$$A_i^G = (w_i - W_i)\left(\frac{1+B_i}{1+B} - 1\right)$$

Since for the consumer goods sector, B_i (6%), is greater than B (4.3%), the second factor in the above equation is positive, so that any decrease in w_i will bring a decrease in A_i^G.

25 C is correct. Transactions-based attribution uses both the holdings of the portfolio and the transactions (purchases and sales) that occurred during the evaluation period in the calculation. Because information on purchases and sales is included in the calculation, transactions-based attribution is considered to be the most accurate.

A and B are incorrect. Transactions are not included in holdings-based or returns-based attribution and these methods are therefore less accurate than transactions-based attribution.

26 A is correct. Transactions-based is the most difficult to type of attribution to implement. To obtain meaningful results, the underlying data inputs (purchases and sales) must be complete, accurate and reconciled from period to period and included in the calculation process.

B is incorrect. Using actual transaction data will not produce residuals like holdings-based transaction does. C is incorrect. With a transactions-based method, all the data is available so that the entire excess return can be quantified, explained, and reconciled with the actual return presented to the client.

27 A is correct. Holdings-based attribution analysis can be calculated over any time period.

B is incorrect because transaction-based attribution is the most difficult and time consuming to implement. C is incorrect. Holdings-based analysis requires information on portfolio positions. Returns-based attribution is most appropriate when the underlying portfolio holding information is unavailable.

28 C is correct. The strategic asset allocation of the fund is the responsibility of the fund sponsor. In fact this is the only decision the sponsor makes when he does not manage funds internally.

A is incorrect because security selection in each portfolio is the responsibility of the portfolio manager. B is incorrect because tactical deviations from the strategic asset allocation are the responsibility of the investment manager.

29 B is correct. The allocation effect at the sponsor level is equal to $(w_i - W_i)(B_i - B)$ where i refers to total LT bonds: (85% – 80%) × (3.25% –2.90%) = 0.018%.

A is incorrect because it is the selection plus interaction effect that was measured instead of the allocation effect: 80% (3.15% – 3.25%) + (85% – 80%) (3.15% – 3.25%) = –0.085%. C is incorrect because it evaluates the decision of the LT portfolio manager: (55% – 50%) × (4.00% – 2.90%) + (30% – 30%) × (2.00% – 2.90%) = 0.055%.

30 C is correct. The allocation effect at the LT portfolio manager is equal to $\Sigma(w_i - W_i)(B_i - B)$ where the summation is made over corporate bonds and government bonds: (55% – 50%) × (4.00% – 2.90%) + (30% – 30%) × (2.00% – 2.90%) = 0.055%

A is incorrect because it is the selection plus interaction effect that was measured instead of the allocation effect.

= 50% (3.50% – 4.00%) + (55% – 50%) (3.50% – 4.00%) + 30% (2.50% – 2.00%) + (30% – 30%) (2.50% – 2.00%)

= –0.125%

B is incorrect because it evaluates the decision at the sponsor level: (85% – 80%) × (3.25% – 2.90%) = 0.018%.

31 A is correct. A multi-level return attribution analysis depends on who is evaluated and one cannot directly compare the results of two analyses when these analyses are about different entities responsible for the investment decisions. For example, in this situation, if the sponsor is held responsible for the decision to invest 85%/15% in LT/ST, all allocation effects will be attributed to the sponsor.

B is incorrect because we cannot directly compare the allocation effect of a return attribution analysis at a sponsor level and the allocation effect of a return attribution analysis at a portfolio manager level. C is incorrect because when the allocation effect is analyzed at the sponsor level, there is no allocation analysis left at the segment level.

32 A is correct. Value factor return (–0.43%) times the portfolio's overweight position (0.19) equals a negative excess return impact of –0.00082.

B is incorrect. The portfolio was underweight in its exposure to small cap stocks. C is incorrect. The largest contributor to negative excess return was the impact of the small cap premium factor (–0.00294), not the impact of equity risk premium (–0.00201).

33 B is correct. The contribution column indicates the overall contribution to excess return of each factor. The contribution was 0.00139.

A is incorrect. Although the factor return is positive, the impact may be positive or negative, depending on whether the portfolio is under- or overweight the factor. C is incorrect. Although the portfolio is overweight the factor, the impact may be positive or negative, depending on whether the factor is positive or negative.

34 B is correct. The portfolio has high exposures to both the small-cap return premium factor (1.23) and the value return premium factor (1.17).

A is incorrect. The significant difference in sensitivities to both the small-cap return premium factor (0.25) and the value return premium factor (0.53) suggests the manager is not attempting to track the benchmark closely. C is incorrect. Positive high sensitivity numbers (greater than one) suggest that the portfolio tends to hold/favor small cap and value-oriented equities.

35 A is correct. Factor models are more flexible than asset-grouping models in that they can be tailored very closely to the investment process.

B is incorrect. Asset-grouping models are often easier to understand in terms of investment decisions. C is incorrect. Factor models are generally applied to single asset class portfolios.

36 B is correct. There is a large variety of factor models used in the industry.

A is incorrect. Factor models are dependent on the specific factors used in the analysis. C is incorrect. Factor models can be expensive to use. If the factor model is particularly complex, data and computer software costs can be significant.

37 B is correct. If only one factor (e.g., such as yield-curve positioning) is considered to be important in evaluating an investment manager, then a Brinson attribution approach would be an appropriate model to follow. The allocation effect would account for the manager's decisions regarding yield-curve positioning with any other decisions included in selection and interaction.

A is incorrect. The allocation effect measured by the Brinson approach would account only for one of the factors supporting the investment decision process with all other decisions included in selection and interaction. It would be more appropriate to develop a specialized, multi-factor approach that can be more closely tailored to the actual investment decision process. C is incorrect. The allocation effect measured by the Brinson approach would account only for one of the three factors supporting the investment decision process with the other two factors included globally in selection and interaction.

38 C is correct. The Brinson approach captures one factor in the allocation effect and combines all other factors in the selection and interaction effects. Thus, it is imprecise in dealing with multi-factor models.

A is incorrect. Fixed income indexes that can serve as benchmarks are readily available. As long as the investment decision process can be segmented in the fixed income categories of the benchmark, the Brinson approach can be appropriate. B is incorrect. Exhibit 26 is an example of the Brinson approach analyzing the impact of decisions across the yield curve.

39 C is correct. The impact of interest rate management is 0.41% (= 0.08% + 0.02% + 0.31%).

A is incorrect. This calculation considers changes along the yield curve (i.e., 0.08%) as the only component of interest rate management. B is incorrect. This calculation considers duration and convexity (i.e., 0.31% + 0.02%) as the only components of interest rate management.

40 C is correct. The manager's selection skill contributed the most (–0.26%) of any factor to the portfolio's underperformance.

A is incorrect. The manager's contribution to excess return due to interest rate management was 0.15% (= –0.02% + 0.03% + 0.14%). B is incorrect. The manager's skill at interest rate management exceeded his sector allocation ability (0.15% versus 0.07%).

41 A is correct. All else equal, (i) using shorter time periods in measuring holdings will yield more accurate results than longer time periods (this makes A better than C); and (ii) a portfolio with low turnover will likely have fewer transactions

(transactions cannot be not fully accounted for by holdings-based attribution and they lead to residuals) than a high turnover portfolio (this makes A better than B and A better than C).

B is incorrect because a portfolio with high turnover will lead to less accurate analysis in holdings-based attribution. C is incorrect because the use of longer time periods and a portfolio with high turnover will lead to less accurate analysis in holdings-based attribution.

42 C is correct. Holdings-based attribution suffers from greater residuals than transaction based attribution, due to the incomplete treatment of transactions.

A is incorrect because arithmetic excess returns do not add up over multiple periods and this will lead to a residual unless a geometric attribution methodology is used. Thus, switching to geometric attribution model will decrease residuals. B is incorrect because improving the quality of the data inputs so that the segment level and total level data are consistent, will increase the accuracy of the attribution results and decrease the residuals.

43 C is correct. By using beginning of period holdings and ignoring transactions (as in performing holdings-based attribution analysis), a residual effect called the timing or trading effect is produced.

A is incorrect because the choice of the benchmark itself, although it may affect the quality of the return attribution analysis, does not cause a residual effect. B is incorrect because a residual is more likely to occur in multi-period analysis than single period analysis, and more so with arithmetic return attribution.

44 B is correct. The selection (including interaction) effect of information technology is 10% × (3% – 5.5%) = –0.25%.

A is incorrect because it is the allocation effect assuming a sector allocation decision: (10% – 0%) × (2% – 5.5%) = –0.35%. C is incorrect because it is the selection effect assuming a sector allocation decision: 10% × (3% – 2%) = 0.1%.

45 C is correct. The return attribution of off-benchmark decisions depends on their rationale. This is clearly a sector allocation decision and should be measured as such. The calculation is (5% – 0%) × (7.10% – 2.05%) = 0.25%.

A is incorrect. This was calculated as (5% – 0%) × (0.00% – 2.05%) = –0.10%. B is incorrect. This was calculated as a selection effect: 5% × (10.80% – 7.10%) = 0.185% or 0.19%.

46 B is correct. The return attribution of off-benchmark decisions depends on their rationale. This is clearly a selection decision. The benchmark chosen for the consumer staples sector should be the overall benchmark return which will lead to a zero allocation effect.

A is incorrect. This is a selection decision, not a sector allocation decision. The selection effect would be zero only if it had been an allocation decision and if it had been impossible to identify an appropriate sector index. C is incorrect. Only the allocation effect is zero.

READING

7

Introduction to Benchmarks

by C. Mitchell Conover, PhD, CFA, CIPM, Daniel Broby, FSIP, and David R. Cariño, PhD

C. Mitchell Conover, PhD, CFA, CIPM, is at the University of Richmond (USA). Daniel Broby, FSIP, is at University of Strathclyde (United Kingdom). David R. Cariño, PhD (USA).

LEARNING OUTCOMES

Mastery	*The candidate should be able to:*
☐	**a.** define the term "benchmark" and distinguish between benchmarks and market indexes;
☐	**b.** describe how benchmarks are used in return attribution and performance appraisal;
☐	**c.** distinguish among types of benchmarks;
☐	**d.** explain desirable properties of benchmarks in the context of performance attribution;
☐	**e.** explain a portfolio's positions in terms of a market index's security positions, benchmark positions, style tilts, and active positions;
☐	**f.** identify and explain tests of benchmark quality;
☐	**g.** compare the theoretical advantages and disadvantages, data requirements, and costs of using each type of benchmark;
☐	**h.** interpret peer universe box charts;
☐	**i.** explain uses of asset class indexes;
☐	**j.** compare market-capitalization-weighting, equal-weighting, price-weighting, and fundamental-weighting index construction schemes, including their advantages and disadvantages;
☐	**k.** describe the purpose and effects of float adjustment of market capitalization indexes;
☐	**l.** explain the tradeoffs in constructing asset class indexes;
☐	**m.** describe classifications of equity investing styles and the construction of associated equity style indexes;
☐	**n.** explain bond market sectors and the construction of associated bond style indexes;
☐	**o.** describe the steps in constructing a custom benchmark;

(continued)

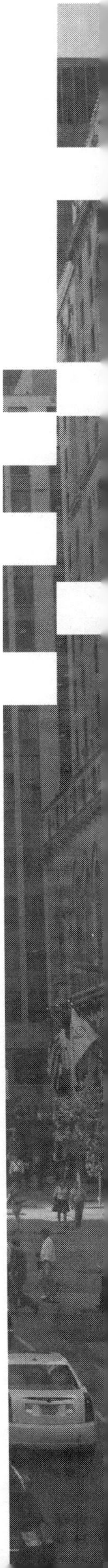

LEARNING OUTCOMES

Mastery	The candidate should be able to:
☐	p. describe considerations in using hedge fund benchmarks, liability-based benchmarks, and hedged benchmarks;
☐	q. describe the impact of benchmark misspecification on attribution and appraisal analysis;
☐	r. recommend and justify the choice of a benchmark for a portfolio given a description of portfolio objectives and management processes.

1 INTRODUCTION

The *Oxford English Dictionary* defines a **benchmark** as "a standard or point of reference against which things may be compared." In an investment context, a benchmark is a standard or point of reference for evaluating the performance of an investment portfolio. The selection of an appropriate benchmark depends on the objective and constraints that govern the portfolio's construction.

An investment benchmark is typically a collection of securities that characterizes a manager's preferred habitat of securities and risk. For example, an investor in German equities with characteristically small market capitalizations (and no other distinctive selection characteristics) might have a benchmark consisting of a broad portfolio of small-market-cap German equities. However, a benchmark can also be an absolute rate of return, or target return—for example, when the investment strategy targets achieving a specific rate of return and the strategy cannot be readily represented by a portfolio. Benchmarks can also take the form of peer group performance data against which an investment strategy is compared.

Benchmarks make it possible to determine how effectively active asset managers—managers who trade on perceived opportunities to earn superior risk-adjusted returns—have performed by measuring the effects of decisions to depart from benchmark weights. An ideal benchmark provides the manager and his investment clients with an objective means of evaluating how skillfully that manager implemented his investment strategy. Analysts can use it when attempting to identify active investment management skill. Well-chosen benchmarks allow returns to be accurately evaluated and decomposed. If the benchmark chosen is invalid, then all subsequent manager evaluation and analysis is incorrect. Throughout this reading, we refer to the ideal benchmark as one that is "valid," consistent with the literature in the field. Although a valid benchmark may be unattainable in certain circumstances, a performance analyst's goal should be to use a benchmark that allows the most accurate evaluation of manager performance.

Benchmarks are extremely important to owners of capital. Benchmarks communicate information about a manager's **investment universe** (the set of assets that may be considered for investment) and investment discipline. Managers often claim to beat "the market." The benchmark defines the relevant market and allows analysis of the manager's performance.

Benchmarks provide managers with a guidepost for acceptable levels of risk and return. They can be a powerful influence on investment decision making. As one investment authority has opined, "Benchmarks determine the performance of investment managers perhaps more than any other influence, including managers' determination to succeed and the resources and skills they bring to this task. We in the industry have largely overlooked this fact, perhaps at our peril."[1]

This reading will help the reader understand benchmarks. Among the questions it will answer are the following:

- How are benchmarks used?
- What are the properties of a valid benchmark, and how can they be tested for quality?
- What are the various types of benchmarks, and what are their advantages and disadvantages?
- How are indexes constructed?
- How are custom benchmarks constructed?
- What are some alternative benchmarks?
- What is the effect of poorly specified benchmarks on investment analysis?

The rest of the reading is organized as follows. Section 2 clarifies the distinction between two terms important in the discussion: benchmark and market index. Section 3 provides an overview of benchmarks and discusses how they are used, their types, their desirable properties, and how to ascertain their quality. Section 4 discusses the use of peer groups as benchmarks, Section 5 examines market indexes and style benchmarks, and Section 6 introduces custom benchmarks. Each of these sections assesses the various benchmarks' advantages and disadvantages. Section 7 examines hedge fund and liability-based benchmarks. Section 8 describes problems with benchmark misspecification, and the reading concludes with Section 9.

DISTINGUISHING BETWEEN A BENCHMARK AND A MARKET INDEX 2

Although the terms "benchmark" and "market index" (or simply "index") are often loosely used interchangeably, we must distinguish between them for an accurate discussion. A **market index** represents the performance of a specified security market, market segment, or asset class, usually computed from a collection of securities, that is aggregated to a single value and compared with the value of a base date. For example, the FTSE 100 Index is constructed to represent the broad performance of large-cap UK equities. The Bloomberg Barclays Sterling Aggregate Bond Index represents the performance of fixed-rate, investment-grade, sterling-denominated bonds; in contrast, the Bloomberg Barclays Sterling Gilts Index captures the performance of a narrower segment of the UK investment-grade debt market—UK government debt. The constituents of each of these indexes are selected for their appropriateness in representing the targeted market, market segment, or asset class.

A market index *may* be considered for use as a benchmark or comparison point for a manager; however, the most appropriate benchmark or reference point for a manager *need not* be an available market index. A good example in which a market index is an appropriate benchmark is the case of passive managers, who typically invest in a portfolio similar (or identical) to a chosen market index so as to closely track its performance. For example, the iShares Core (IVV) S&P 500 exchange-traded fund (ETF) seeks investment results, before fees and expenses, that correspond to the price and yield performance of US large-cap stocks as represented by the S&P 500 Index.

1 Siegel (2003, p. ix).

Because the fund's investment objective is to track the performance of the S&P 500, the S&P 500 is the appropriate benchmark for IVV, as it is for any other investment with an identical investment objective. An active US core equity manager whose investment universe is the S&P 500—that is, one that seeks to add value by under- or overweighting component securities of the S&P 500—and no other securities and that has no observable selection biases might also use the S&P 500 as its benchmark. Another active manager, however, might not follow an investment discipline for which an existing security market index is a valid reference point. Market indexes are typically meant to serve the general public's purposes and to have broad appeal as market barometers. Benchmarks must be appropriate for the specific investor (i.e., asset owner or sponsor) and any manager hired to manage money.[2] The fundamental requirements of indexes and valid benchmarks are formulated differently, as we will explain. Nevertheless, because market indexes can often serve as valid benchmarks (according to the facts of the case), performance analysts should become knowledgeable about market indexes.

The reader will find that writers and index providers vary in their preference for the plural of "index." For simplicity, throughout this reading we consistently use "indexes" rather than the Latin-inspired "indices" as the plural of "index."

EXAMPLE 1

Benchmark definition

A benchmark is *best* defined as:

A a point of reference against which things may be compared.

B a collection of securities.

C the average performance of competitor funds.

Solution:

A is correct. A benchmark is defined by the *Oxford English Dictionary* as "a standard or point of reference against which things may be compared." A collection of securities can be computed as a market index, which is one type of benchmark. The average performance of competitor funds in the form of a peer group is another type of benchmark.

3 BENCHMARKS IN PERFORMANCE ATTRIBUTION AND APPRAISAL: OVERVIEW

This section gives a general overview of benchmarks, including their uses, their types, their desirable properties, and tests of benchmark quality.

An asset owner is the owner of capital, perhaps a pension fund, endowment or sovereign wealth fund. The type of benchmark chosen will differ depending on the asset owner's characteristics. In a private wealth context, we would in general refer to the private investor as asset owner.

An asset manager is the professional manager of separate accounts or pooled assets structured in any of a variety of ways (e.g., a US mutual fund, a UK unit trust, a European Union Undertakings for Collective Investment in Transferable Securities

2 Amenc, Goltz, and Tang (2011, p. 68).

[UCITS] fund, an ETF, or a hedge fund). Although the asset owner could manage assets in house, in general, we will think of the asset manager as an external investment manager to whom management of a part of the asset owner's assets is delegated. The asset manager may have a mandate from the asset owner to follow either a passive or an active investment strategy.

- **Passive investment strategies** prominently include indexing.[3] Indexers seek to deliver returns comparable to those of a market index by investing in or replicating the index constituents.
- **Active investment strategies** seek to use a manager's insight to deliver returns in excess of those from a passive buy-and-hold strategy. These returns are referred to as the manager's active returns, and the variability of the active returns is referred to as active risk.

Benchmarks are vital for performance measurement when the assets are actively managed. Benchmarks are also relevant when passive strategies are used, however, as we discuss next.

3.1 Benchmarks: Investment Uses

There are several uses of benchmarks in investment practice, including the following:

- reference points for segments of the sponsor's (investor's or asset owner's) portfolio;
- communication of instructions to the manager;
- communication of instructions to a board of directors (or any oversight group) and consultants;
- identification and evaluation of current portfolio's risk exposures;
- interpretation of past performance and performance attribution;
- manager selection and appraisal;
- marketing of investment products; and
- demonstration of compliance with regulations, laws, or standards.

Asset owner benchmarks need to be distinguished from asset manager benchmarks. An asset owner's strategic asset allocation (policy portfolio) is the long-run allocation to asset classes consistent with the investor's objectives and constraints. From this allocation, a benchmark, often in the form of an investable market index, will be specified for each asset class in the strategic asset allocation. That practice implicitly and reasonably specifies a passive investment in the asset class as a neutral comparison point in measuring the owner's progress toward investment goals.

In general when we refer simply to benchmarks, the reference will be to benchmarks provided to managers that are appropriate references for their specific investment disciplines. Given the asset owner's understanding of the manager's investment discipline, the benchmark conveys to the manager the asset owner's expectations about how the assets will be invested and their expected risk and return. By conveying these expectations, benchmarks provide accountability, so that if a manager's security selection and subsequent performance frequently diverge far from the benchmark, it will be apparent that the manager's investment approach is inconsistent with the stated investment discipline. Benchmarks also ensure a degree of fairness in the sense that the manager will not be held to standards that the asset owner's board or consultants might arbitrarily impose.

---

3 "Buy and hold" is another example of a passive strategy. Indexing is by far the most important passive investment strategy in terms of assets committed to it, however, and the only one discussed in this reading.

Second, the benchmark communicates to the board and external consultants the manager's area of expertise and how a manager should subsequently invest and be evaluated. In a multiple-manager fund, benchmarks convey the managers' coverage areas, so that assets and securities that lack coverage or are overemphasized can be identified.

A third use of benchmarks is to identify and evaluate the manager's risk exposures. Managers often describe themselves as "value managers" or "growth managers." However, these terms are imprecise. An appropriate benchmark will have risk similar to the portfolio and be informative in revealing the manager's active risk exposures, which should help explain the manager's performance within his or her chosen investment style.

Another fundamental use of benchmarks is to attribute and appraise past performance and, in general, the consequences of the manager's investment decisions. The benchmark helps the asset owner determine and evaluate the manager's **excess return** (the difference between the portfolio return and the benchmark return, which may be either positive or negative). Return attribution identifies such things as whether the manager's security selection, industry bets (in equity analysis), or yield curve positioning (in fixed-income analysis) have added value. What caused the manager's performance to differ from the benchmark? If the benchmark is inappropriate, such differences may inaccurately reflect the manager's decision process. In the context of return attribution the benchmark must reflect the manager's decision process and ideally disaggregate into its constituent parts—that is to say, the sum of the parts should add up to the total benchmark return. Performance appraisal's chief focus is to distinguish active investment skill from luck.

Accounting or adjusting for risk may be accomplished in a variety of ways. One appraisal tool known as the information ratio (IR) attempts to measure the value added per unit of active risk. To calculate IR, the mean portfolio return in excess of the benchmark return is divided by the active risk.[4] If the benchmark is inappropriate, the calculated value of IR will not be informative. Thus, when benchmarks are used in performance appraisal, benchmark selection is obviously important.

Inappropriate benchmarks introduce noise into the investment manager assessment process and provide a misleading picture of manager performance. Good benchmarks enhance the effectiveness of manager assessment, whereas bad ones may lead to an inefficient or unintended allocation of assets and disguise managers' contributions.[5] As a result, benchmarks will also be instrumental in investment contracts that have an incentive compensation component that rewards outperformance (and potentially penalizes underperformance).

Furthermore, benchmarks play a role in the manager selection processes because they will influence the perception of a manager's skill. The analysis of past performance will involve a qualitative assessment of whether the manager's investment process is robust enough to produce repeatable outperformance in the future or, alternatively, whether a manager's past underperformance is likely to persist.

Benchmarks are also used to market investment products to potential investors. The Global Investment Performance Standards (GIPS®) require that if a benchmark exists, it must be included in a performance presentation with its description. If no benchmark is provided, a reason must be given. Marketing requires the communication and explanation of the investment process, of which the benchmark is an essential

4 This is the common definition used in industry. The numerator in the IR is most precisely defined as alpha, the excess return after completely adjusting for risk. If the risk of the portfolio and the benchmark are exactly the same (i.e., the beta of the portfolio with respect to the benchmark equals 1), the two are equivalent.

5 "Inefficient" is used in an investment context here, referring to an asset allocation that does not have an optimal risk–return trade-off.

descriptor of the investment strategy and a crucial determinant of excess returns. Excess returns have been found to be a significant determinant of investor inflows, so the choice of the benchmark will influence the fund's ability to attract new capital.

Lastly, benchmarks are used to demonstrate compliance with regulations, laws, and standards. Regulatory organizations use benchmarks as part of their oversight and surveillance, and as a result, benchmarks have become mandated in many jurisdictions. In 1998, the US SEC introduced a requirement that mutual funds self-designate a benchmark and present their historical returns alongside it in the prospectus. Many other jurisdictions now have similar rules. More generally, institutions are sometimes restricted from investing in specific instruments, such as below-investment-grade bonds. Benchmarks for such institutions have to be tailored accordingly.

EXAMPLE 2

Investment Uses of Benchmarks

1 Inappropriate benchmarks *most likely:*

  A encourage risk taking.

  B introduce noise into the performance appraisal process.

  C cannot be used for performance attribution.

2 In the context of return attribution, a good benchmark *most likely:*

  A can be disaggregated.

  B equals the total return of the portfolio.

  C represents the risk of the asset manager.

Solution to 1:

B is correct. Inappropriate benchmarks introduce noise into the investment appraisal process; they do not necessarily encourage risk taking. Inappropriate benchmarks can be used to calculate attribution, but the results may not be meaningful if not aligned with the manager's investment decision process.

Solution to 2:

A is correct. In a good benchmark, the sum of the parts should equal the total return. B is incorrect; the point of attribution is to identify the difference between the portfolio and benchmark return. C is incorrect; return attribution is not directly concerned with risk.

3.2 Types of Benchmarks

Given the uses described earlier, benchmarks are an important part of the investment process for both institutional and private wealth clients. In the following discussion, we introduce the types of benchmarks based on the discussion in Bailey, Richards, and Tierney (2007).[6] The five types of benchmarks introduced in this section are

- absolute (including target) return benchmarks;
- manager universes (peer groups);
- broad market indexes;
- style indexes; and
- custom benchmarks.

6 More detailed discussion for each benchmark is provided in the remainder of the reading.

An **absolute return benchmark** is simply a minimum target return that the manager is expected to beat. The return may be a stated minimum (e.g., 9%), stated as a spread above a market index (e.g., Euro Interbank Offered Rate + 4%), or determined from actuarial assumptions. An example of an absolute return benchmark is 30% per annum return for a private equity investment (e.g., a buyout fund—note that more-sophisticated benchmarks are available). Market-neutral long-short equity funds are another example of a type of fund sometimes given an absolute return benchmark. Such funds are run by managers who believe that they can identify over- and undervalued shares. Such a strategy consists of long and short positions in, respectively, perceived undervalued and overvalued equities, and it is constructed so that overall, the portfolio is expected to be insensitive to broad equity market movements—that is, market neutral with a market beta of zero. Because a market-neutral fund is in principle a zero–expected systematic risk investment, the benchmark may be specified as a three-month Treasury bill return; the investment objective may be to outperform the benchmark consistently by a given amount. Absolute benchmarks contain very little information other than the absolute target return.

A **manager universe**—or **manager peer group**—is a broad group of managers with similar investment disciplines. Manager universe benchmarks allow investors to make comparisons with the performance of other managers following similar investment disciplines. Managers are typically expected to beat the median manager return, which refers to the manager return that splits the sample of managers' returns in half. Manager universes are typically formed by asset class and the investment approach within that class. Hedge funds have often been evaluated relative to manager universe benchmarks provided by such vendors as Credit Suisse/Tremont, Hedge Fund Research, and Lipper TASS. Private equity funds are also commonly evaluated in this way; examples of data vendors are Burgiss, Cambridge Associates, Preqin, and Thomson Venture Economics. Investment magazines are prolific providers of peer group comparisons for investment funds (e.g., mutual funds in the United States and unit trusts in the United Kingdom); thus, a mutual fund investing in global equities might be ranked among all mutual funds with similar objectives over various time periods.

Broad market indexes are measures of broad asset class performance, such as the JP Morgan Emerging Markets Bond Index (EMBI) for emerging market bonds or the MSCI World Index for global developed market equities. Broad market indexes are well known, readily available, and easily understood. The number of market indexes has proliferated over time so as to serve a greater number and variety of both applications and end users. For example, in 1999, JP Morgan created the Emerging Markets Bond Index Global (EMBIG), which added less liquid issues and less creditworthy issues to the Emerging Markets Bond Index (EMBI). The performance of broad market indexes is widely reported in popular media, such as television.

Market indexes have also been more narrowly defined to represent investment styles within asset classes, resulting in style indexes. (An **investment style** can be defined as a natural grouping of investment disciplines that has some predictive power in explaining the future dispersion of returns across portfolios.)[7] In the late 1970s, researchers found that stock valuation (e.g., defined using the price-to-earnings ratio) and market capitalization explained much of stock return variation. In response, many index providers provided various style versions of their broad market indexes. For example, in 1999, Wilshire introduced value, growth, and size subsets of its US

7 See Brown and Goetzmann (1997).

Wilshire 5000 Total Market Index.[8] Style indexes are formed under the belief that a characteristic of an asset, such as a stock's dividend yield or a bond's credit rating, will be the primary determinant of its subsequent performance.

Lastly, custom benchmarks are custom built to accurately reflect the investment discipline of a particular manager or the strategic allocations of an asset owner. Such benchmarks are developed through discussions with the manager and often reflect the asset owner's specific investment restrictions. A cash weight may also be identified if appropriate. The benchmark is subsequently rebalanced on a periodic basis to ensure that it stays consistent with the manager's investment practice, asset owner's liabilities, or market movements. It is important that the asset owner and manager agree on and document the balancing frequency, because significant return differences can arise if fixed custom weights are rebalanced at different frequencies (e.g., daily, monthly, or quarterly). Custom benchmarks are also referred to as **strategy benchmarks** because they should reflect the manager's particular strategy. Custom benchmarks are particularly appropriate when the strategy cannot be closely matched to a broad market index or style index.

EXAMPLE 3

Types of Benchmarks

1 Which statement *best* describes a custom benchmark? It:

A replicates the manager's historical returns.

B reflects the manager's investment process.

C quantifies the return impact of systematic risk factors.

2 An investment fund taking long and short positions in equities is given as a benchmark the three-month Treasury bill return plus 150 bps. The fund's benchmark is *best* described as a(n):

A custom benchmark.

B peer group benchmark.

C absolute return benchmark.

Solution to 1:

B is correct. A custom benchmark reflects the manager's investment process. A is incorrect; a custom benchmark does not seek to replicate the manager's historical returns—that approach would eliminate any excess return. C is incorrect; on its own, a custom benchmark does not quantify the return impact of systematic risk factors.

Solution to 2:

C is correct. The benchmark of the Treasury bill return plus 150 bps is an absolute return benchmark. A custom benchmark would consist of securities that are consistent with the manager's investment process. A peer group benchmark would consist of the performance of managers similar to the fund.

8 Broadly speaking, a value investment style with respect to equity portfolio management is focused on paying a relatively low price with respect to earnings or assets per share. A growth investment style with respect to equity portfolio management is focused on investing in high-earnings-growth companies. Section 5.3 examines style in more detail.

In summary, the asset owner may select from a number of benchmarks. Given the variety of choices, we next examine a set of criteria that can be used to choose between the benchmarks.

3.3 Properties of a Valid Benchmark

Previously, we said that the choice the asset owner makes in regard to the portfolio and corresponding benchmark will have a strong effect on overall performance. Managers should be compared only with a benchmark that reflects the securities in which the manager has been charged to invest.

A valid benchmark is not simply a passive portfolio similar in composition to the manager's portfolio because it should satisfy certain validity criteria. We examine the characteristics of a valid benchmark by using the classic list from Bailey and Tierney (1998).[9]

- *Unambiguous.* The individual securities and their weights in a benchmark should be clearly identifiable. For example, we should be able to identify whether Nestlé is included in a global equity benchmark and its weight.
- *Investable.* It must be possible to replicate and hold the benchmark to earn its return (at least gross of expenses). The sponsor should have the option of moving assets from active management to a passive benchmark. If the benchmark is not investable, it is not a viable investment alternative.
- *Measurable.* It must be possible to measure the benchmark's return on a reasonably frequent and timely basis.
- *Appropriate.* The benchmark must be consistent with the manager's investment style or area of expertise.
- *Reflective of current investment opinions.* The manager should be familiar with the securities that constitute the benchmark and their factor exposures. The manager should be able to develop an opinion regarding their attractiveness as investments; she should not be given a mandate containing obscure securities about which she could not be expected to have knowledge.
- *Specified in advance.* The benchmark must be constructed prior to the evaluation period so that the manager is not judged against benchmarks created after the fact.
- *Accountable.* The manager should accept ownership of the benchmark and its securities and be willing to be held accountable to the benchmark.

The benchmark should be fully consistent with the manager's investment process, and the manager should be able to demonstrate the validity of his benchmark. By accepting the benchmark, the asset owner assumes responsibility for any discrepancies between the targeted portfolio and the benchmark.

The properties outlined by Bailey and Tierney (1998) help ensure that a benchmark will serve as a valid instrument for the purposes of evaluating the manager's performance. Although this list of qualities for a desirable benchmark may seem straightforward, we will show later that many commonly used benchmarks do not incorporate them.

9 This study was the first to include "accountable" in the list of characteristics.

3.4 Evaluating Benchmark Quality: Analysis Based on a Decomposition of Portfolio Holdings and Returns

Once a benchmark is constructed, we can evaluate its quality using tests. To understand these tests, it helps to first decompose the benchmark's returns. Using the decomposition from Bailey, Richards, and Tierney (2007), we can first state the identity where a portfolio's return (P) is equal to itself:

$$P = P$$

Then, add and subtract an appropriate benchmark (B) from the right-hand side of the equation:

$$P = B + (P - B)$$

Defining the manager's active management decisions (A) as the difference between the portfolio and benchmark returns ($P - B$), we have

$$P = B + A$$

Here, we see that the manager's return is a function of the benchmark return and the active management decisions.

Next, add and subtract the market index return (M) from the right-hand side of the equation:

$$P = M + (B - M) + A$$

Defining the manager's investment style (S) as the difference between the benchmark return and the market index ($B - M$) results in

$$P = M + S + A$$

The final equation states that a manager's portfolio return (P) is a result of the market index return (M), style (S), and active management return (A).

If the manager's portfolio is a broad market index, then S and $A = 0$ and, as expected, the portfolio earns the broad market return: $P = M$. If the benchmark used is a broad market index, then S is assumed to be zero, and the prediction is that the manager earns the market return and a return to active management: $P = M + A$. When a broad market index is used as a benchmark and the manager actually has style differences from it, however, the analysis and its return prediction are incorrect. In this case, the manager's style return (S) will be reflected in the measured active management component (A), such that an analysis of a manager's true value added will be obscured.

EXAMPLE 4

Decomposition of Portfolio Return

Note: In calculation questions, show final results to one decimal place.

1 Assume that the Courtland account has a return of –5.3% in a given month, during which the portfolio benchmark has a return of –5.5% and the market index has a return of –2.8%.

   A Calculate the Courtland account's return resulting from the manager's style.

   B Calculate the Courtland account's return resulting from active management.

2 Assume that Mr. Kuti's account has a return of 5.6% in a given month, during which the portfolio benchmark has a return of 5.1% and a market index has a return of 3.2%.

A Calculate the return resulting from the manager's style for Mr. Kuti's account.

B Calculate the return resulting from active management for Mr. Kuti's account.

3 An actively managed midcap value equity portfolio has a return of 9.24%. The portfolio is benchmarked to a mid-cap value index that has a return of 7.85%. A broad equity market index has a return of 8.92%. Calculate the return resulting from the portfolio manager's style.

4 A US large-cap value portfolio run by Anderson Investment Management returned 18.9% during the first three quarters of 2013. During the same period, a US large-cap value index had returns of 21.7% and a broad US equity index returned 25.2%.

A Calculate the return resulting from style.

B Calculate the return resulting from active management.

C Describe the implications of your answers to Parts A and B for assessing Anderson's performance relative to the benchmark and relative to the market.

Solution to 1:

A The return resulting from style is $S = B - M = -5.5\% - (-2.8\%) = \mathbf{-2.7\%}$.

B The return resulting from active management is $A = P - B = -5.3\% - (-5.5\%) = \mathbf{0.2\%}$.

Solution to 2:

A The return resulting from style is $S = B - M = 5.1\% - 3.2\% = \mathbf{1.9\%}$.

B The return resulting from active management is $A = P - B = 5.6\% - 5.1\% = \mathbf{0.5\%}$.

Solution to 3:

The return resulting from style is the style-specific benchmark return of 7.85% minus the broad market return of 8.92%—that is, −1.07%.

Solution to 4:

A The return resulting from style is the difference between the benchmark and the market index, or $S = (B - M) = (21.7\% - 25.2\%) = \mathbf{-3.5\%}$.

B The return resulting from active management is the difference between the portfolio and the benchmark, or $A = (P - B) = (18.9\% - 21.7\%) = \mathbf{-2.8\%}$.

C The implication of the style calculation is that large-cap value was out of favor in the period measured: That is, the US large-cap value index underperformed the US market index by 3.5%.

The implication of the active management calculation is that Anderson did not add value compared with the benchmark because its portfolio underperformed the portfolio benchmark. If Anderson is indeed a large-cap value manager and the US large-cap value index is an appropriate benchmark, then the client would have been better off investing in the passive alternative.

3.5 Tests of Benchmark Quality

The analysis facilitates a discussion of tests of benchmark quality from Bailey (1992b) and Bailey, Richards, and Tierney (2007). These tests are designed to reflect the previously discussed properties of a valid benchmark and the various uses to which benchmarks are applied.[10] Good benchmarks should possess the following characteristics:

1 The correlation between the manager's active return and style return should be statistically indistinguishable from zero.

Whether the manager's style is in or out of favor should have no effect on the manager's ability to generate excess returns. Intuitively, if a benchmark fully captures a manager's investment process, the residual variability in the manager's returns should not be explainable by the index.

2 Defining E as the difference between the manager's portfolio and a broad market index, the correlation between $E = (P - M)$ and the style return $S = (B - M)$ should be positive.

In other words, if the manager outperforms (underperforms) the broad market, the tendency should be for the manager's style to outperform (underperform) the market. Stated differently, the investment styles of the benchmark and portfolio should be similar if the benchmark is to explain a large proportion of the manager's returns.[11]

3 The standard deviation of $A = (P - B)$ should be less than the standard deviation of $E = (P - M)$:

$$\sigma_A < \sigma_E$$

In other words, the manager's portfolio should more closely track the benchmark than a market index. Stated differently, the tracking risk (i.e., the standard deviation) of ($A = P - B$) should be lower than the tracking risk of ($E = P - M$). This condition indicates that the benchmark is capturing important characteristics of the manager's investment process. If not, the evaluation of the manager's performance will be contaminated by noise introduced by a poor benchmark.[12]

4 Good benchmarks will have portfolio and benchmark sensitivities that are similar over time (i.e., of the same sign and comparable in magnitude). Although the risk sensitivities will not be the same in a given period when the manager takes active bets, over time, the benchmark should reflect the portfolio's risk. Otherwise, systematic bias exists between the benchmark and portfolio.

5 In the case of equities, the benchmark should exhibit low turnover, which is the proportion of benchmark market value used for purchasing new securities when it is rebalanced. Low turnover means that the benchmark can be held as a passive investment (so that it is investable). Bailey (1992b) estimated that turnover of 15%–20% per quarter is acceptably low benchmark turnover.[13] Fixed-income portfolios and benchmarks are inherently subject to turnover because of redemptions, calls, and other events, and the low turnover criterion is less clearly applicable to them.

10 Compared with Bailey (1992b), Criterion 7 has been modified to focus on equities.

11 These correlation requirements imply that the beta of the portfolio with respect to the benchmark is 1 and that, with respect to the market, the betas of the portfolio and benchmark will be similar. See Tierney and Bailey (1995, pp. 28–29).

12 For a given level of excess return, a good benchmark will also have a higher information ratio than a poor benchmark because of its lower tracking risk. See Bailey (1992a, p. 11).

13 His specification includes the reinvestment of income.

6 The benchmark should have investable position sizes, whereby the portfolio could replicate its positions without excessive trading costs. For example, the amount a benchmark holds in a small-capitalization stock should not exceed the tradeable value that a manager could attain.

7 If the benchmark contains many securities on which the manager has no opinion or that are inappropriate, then the manager will have a zero weight in those securities. Therefore, a high proportion of zero portfolio weights in the benchmark's securities may indicate a benchmark that is poorly representative of a manager's investment approach. Further investigation would be needed to determine whether the zero weights reflect an inappropriate benchmark or negative opinions of the manager.

EXAMPLE 5

Benchmark Attributes

1 A corporate pension fund sponsor announces that the fund's target for the coming year, based on historical capital market return data, is to earn 7.5%. The sponsor's target is *best* described as a:

- **A** return objective.
- **B** liability-based benchmark.
- **C** broad market index benchmark.

2 One way to identify systematic bias in a benchmark relative to an account is to examine the correlation between the return resulting from active management and the return resulting from the:

- **A** broad market.
- **B** manager's style.
- **C** benchmark's risk characteristics.

3 Which of the following characteristics suggests that a proposed benchmark is not satisfactory for an equity portfolio manager? The proposed benchmark:

- **A** is a style index.
- **B** is available as a passive investment option.
- **C** contains securities that the manager has not recently included in her portfolio.

Solution to 1:

A is correct. The fund's return target is an absolute return and is not a valid benchmark because it does not meet the benchmark validity criteria. There is no indication that the target is based on the pension fund's liabilities.

Solution to 2:

B is correct. The return resulting from active management is the difference between the portfolio return and the return of an appropriate benchmark ($A = P - B$). The return resulting from the manager's style is the difference between the benchmark return and the broad market return ($S = B - M$). A manager's ability to identify attractive and unattractive investment opportunities should be uncorrelated with whether the manager's style is in or out of favor relative to the overall market. Accordingly, a good benchmark—one that is free of systematic bias—will display a correlation between A and S that is not statistically different from zero. In other words, A and S should be uncorrelated.

Solution to 3:

C is correct. The proposed benchmark may not reflect the investment universe.

PEER GROUP BENCHMARKS

4

The following section focuses on peer group benchmarks. It describes them, explains why they are used, highlights some of their shortcomings, and sheds light on the interpretation of box charts.

4.1 Analysis of Peer Group Benchmarks

Peer group benchmarks consist of the performance data for similar managers (e.g., large cap) and are provided by such firms as Morningstar and Russell. Peer group comparisons answer the natural question of how a manager's performance compared with that of similar managers at similar institutions. Peer group benchmarks are widely cited in the financial press and advertisements, with funds in the United States frequently claiming that they beat the average of similar funds (i.e., their peers). For nontraditional investments, such as hedge funds and private equity, peer group benchmarks are often the only benchmark used.

Asset owners are interested in how the returns of managers they have hired, or are considering hiring, compare with the returns of other managers under consideration. For example, if the peer group consists of 100 managers and the portfolio manager's performance is ranked in the top 25, the manager is said to rank in the first quartile. Quartiles divide a sample into quarters. In performance rankings, investment industry use of the terms "quartiles" and "percentiles" (which divides a sample into hundredths) appear opposite of how these terms are defined in statistics because of the focus on ranking. (Statisticians refer to the top 25% as the fourth quartile and the worst 25% as the first quartile; for them, the top 25% in ranking are at the 75th percentile, which has 75% of observations below it.) Context and the use of words such as "top" and "bottom" usually make the intended meaning clear; this reading follows industry usage. The relevant comparison is how a manager's returns rank relative to others.

To facilitate such comparisons, service providers collect data and organize funds into peer groups. Typically, funds are classified by major asset classes, such as equities or bonds of a given country, or by common subcategories within asset classes. Categories may include common groupings, such as large- and small-cap equities or developed and emerging markets, and groupings based on investment approach or style, such as growth or value equity styles. The provider collects periodic returns from the funds and, in some cases, portfolio holdings. The summary statistics are provided to users who may then compare their own portfolios with that of a peer group.

Sometimes used as the benchmark in peer group comparisons, the median manager is the one whose performance falls in the middle of the manager universe distribution. If a fund manager achieves better returns than those of the median manager, the fund manager's performance will generally be viewed positively. In certain fields typically characterized by low transparency of investment processes and investment holdings, such as private equity and hedge funds, considerable reliance is often placed on peer group benchmarks; in such fields, top-quartile status in peer group rankings is often a highly sought after and highly marketable attribute.

From the returns of a peer group universe, various statistics can be calculated, such as the individual holding period returns (e.g., three-year returns).

Peer group comparisons and the use of the median manager are attractive because

- they are simple to understand and consistent with the belief that superior management should result in above-average returns;
- the data are readily available at low cost; and
- they are frequently used and are accepted as standards for performance evaluation.

As benchmarks, however, peer group comparisons and the use of the median manager have serious shortcomings. We compare them with the criteria for valid benchmarks presented previously.

- *Unambiguous.* Fails. The individual securities and their weights in a peer group universe are not clearly identifiable. The median manager is unlikely to disclose the composition and weightings of his portfolio.
- *Investable.* Fails. Neither the peer group nor its median manager are investable because without prior knowledge of the securities and their weightings, they cannot be replicated. Even if the holdings were known *ex ante*, the number of securities needed to replicate a peer group would be huge, resulting in high transaction costs for the passive portfolio.
- *Measurable.* Meets. One of the few advantages of peer group comparisons is that the returns are measurable.
- *Appropriate.* Fails. Peer groups are inappropriate benchmarks because the variety of investment approaches in most manager universes leads to a lack of comparability with the portfolio manager. The use of the median manager is also inappropriate because it describes the typical manager in the peer group, not the one to which the subject manager is most similar. Also, given that the median manager's portfolio holdings are usually unknown, it is impossible to determine how similar those holdings are to the manager's.
- *Reflective of current investment opinions.* Often fails. Among the portfolios in peer groups may be some that include securities not in a given manager's investment universe. Peer group portfolios are not always consistent with a manager's view of how individual securities should be classified (e.g., value or growth).
- *Specified in advance.* Fails. The portfolios in the first, second, third, and fourth quartiles change from one period to the next and are not known until the measurement period is over; they are thus not specified in advance. The median manager also cannot be specified in advance.
- *Accountable.* Sometimes fails. Although a manager may be willing to be held accountable to her peer group, many managers decline this comparison given the benchmark's shortcomings.

In addition to the problems in meeting the criteria for a valid (ideal) benchmark, peer groups have several other problems. First, the creation of a peer group is a subjective process. The asset owner must rely on the peer group creator to ensure that the data are accurate and that the group is suitable for evaluating the manager. Peer group selection depends to some degree on the creator's judgment and skill in investment analysis. A large-cap growth manager may appear superior in one large-cap growth peer group and inferior in a group from a different provider. There is no standardization or regulatory oversight in peer group construction. In a similar vein, Surz (2006) referred to classification bias, in which peer groups force managers into simplistic classifications that do not accurately or fully describe their investment approach. Also, for some investment styles, such as socially responsible investing, there may not be enough managers to form a robust peer group.

Second, the determination of which peer group managers are placed into is sometimes left to the manager's own discretion. Managers sometimes try to game the system and select a peer group in which they will look good.

Third, the data necessary to examine risk exposure, turnover, position sizes, active positions, and coverage for the median manager's portfolio are often unavailable. Fittingly, Bailey (1992a) referred to manager universes as investment "apparitions," where the only trace of their existence is the reported returns.

A fourth problem is that peer groups are often susceptible to survivorship bias. For example, suppose that in December 2013, a consultant constructs a manager universe for the period January 2004–December 2013. The consultant uses the returns for managers in existence in December 2013. There will be managers not reporting returns or not in existence in December 2013, however, who managed money during the historical period. These firms could have stopped reporting returns for several reasons. Publishing returns in a peer group acts as advertising, and if performance is poor, the management firm may have decided that it would rather keep its record private. Or the manager could have changed styles, shut the fund down altogether, or even merged it into another fund with a superior track record (thereby interring subpar performance). Whatever the reason, it is likely that these firms are poor performers. As a result, a peer group benchmark will have an upward bias. To mitigate survivorship bias, a benchmark should be constructed using all portfolio managers in existence over the course of the measurement period (in this case, January 2004–December 2013) instead of only those visible at the ending date of the measurement period. Furthermore, the returns for the non-survivors should be recorded until they exit the database, including their likely poor performance toward the end of their reporting period.

If survivorship bias exists in a peer group, the manager will be unfairly evaluated. Survivorship bias worsens as the measurement period increases because the non-survivors with the longest streaks of underperformance are most likely to exit. Furthermore, the rate of survivorship varies across equity styles and asset classes. For example, survivorship bias will likely be higher in a technology fund peer group benchmark than in an income fund peer group benchmark because technology funds generally have higher risk. Malkiel and Saha (2005) reported survivorship bias of 123 bps for equity mutual funds and 442 bps for hedge funds.

A fifth problem with peer groups is that the group is sometimes subject to herd behavior. For example, growth managers may shun tech stocks if the herd—that is, most growth managers—thinks that they are overvalued. Although we might expect a growth manager to hold tech stocks, the herd and hence the peer group do not, leading to an inappropriate benchmark. Consequently, information about how the peer group performs might not represent the true opportunity set for a given investor, and the universe will not represent an objective measurement of the investment opportunities.[14]

In sum, peer groups are not valid benchmarks, and when using them, analysts are not always able to discern the value added by the manager. Peer groups often obscure the manager's performance contribution, not define it. As a result, at least where better types of benchmarks are available, a portfolio manager's performance should not be evaluated relative to a peer group or the median manager. Much better benchmarks for evaluating performance exist. Nevertheless, given the natural desire to see how other portfolios are performing, peer group universes are commonly used tools in the investment industry.

14 Christopherson, Cariño, and Ferson (2009, ch. 20).

4.2 Interpreting Peer Universe Box Charts

Summary statistics of the peer group universe return distribution are typically reported in both tabular form and graphical display. A common graphical exhibit is a peer universe box chart, also known as a quartile chart, such as the one shown in Exhibit 1. The exhibit depicts the distribution of returns of US small-cap equity portfolios for the year 2011 and the three and five years ending 31 December 2011. This exhibit shows cumulative returns (annualized for periods longer than a year) to a particular ending date. An alternative exhibit might show individual year (or other holding period) returns sequentially across the page.

In Exhibit 1, the top and bottom of the boxes indicate the maximum and minimum return of the peer group. The solid line across the middle of each box shows the median return—that is, the return that lies in the middle of the distribution (half the distribution lies above the line and the other half lies below it). In industry performance rankings, a manager with a return in the top 19th percentile falls in the first quartile ranking of returns.

Exhibit 1 A Typical Peer Group Universe Box Chart

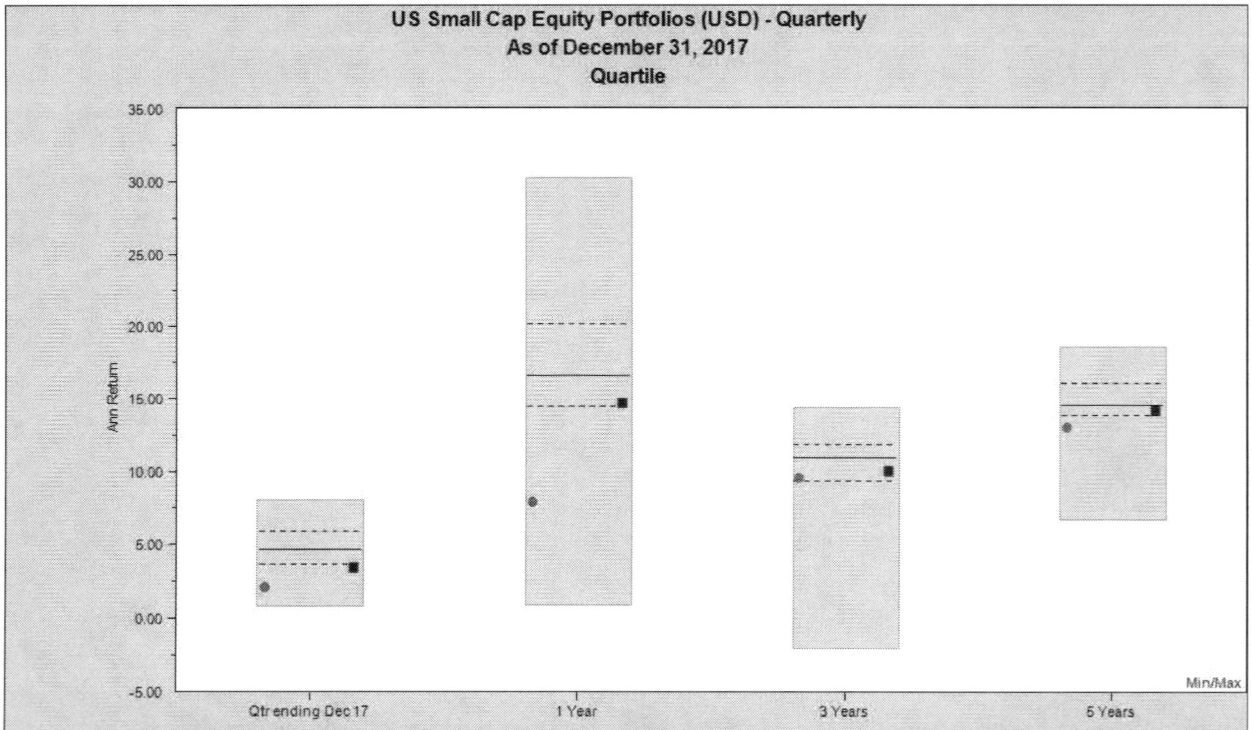

	Qtr ending Dec 17			1 Year			3 Years			5 Years		
	Value	%Tile	Rank	Value	%Tile	Rank	Value	%Tile	Rank	Value	%Tile	Rank
Maximum	8.02			30.26			14.45			18.58		
25th Percentile	5.84			20.20			11.86			16.10		
Median Percentile	4.65			16.61			10.94			14.56		
75th Percentile	3.61			14.48			9.36			13.87		
Minimum	0.77			0.86			-2.06			6.64		
# of Portfolios	82			76			68			64		
● Small Cap Fund	2.05	92	77	7.84	90	69	9.55	73	51	13.01	81	53
■ Small Cap Benchmark	3.34	82	68	14.65	75	58	9.96	62	43	14.12	71	46

Universe Source: The Bank of New York Mellon Corporation; Universe Status: Final

Source:

Such a manager's performance would be easily visualized in the box chart as lying above the top dashed line. The dashed lines show the 25th percentile (first quartile) and 75th percentile (third quartile) of the distribution. A portfolio manager plotted above the top dashed line has returns that lie in the top 25% of managers, whereas one plotted below the bottom dashed line has returns that lie in the bottom 25% of managers. The distance between the dashed lines is referred to as the interquartile range, which provides a measure of return variability surrounding the median. The interquartile range represents the middle 50% of data and provides a measure of variability not influenced by outlier returns (returns higher than the top 25% or below the bottom 25%). A larger interquartile range (i.e., a wider gap in the box chart) indicates that there is greater return variability.

Given an investor's typical preference for more return rather than less, an outcome in the upper quartile would be a welcome result. Normally, it is very difficult to achieve consistent upper-quartile performance, and most investment managers would be happy to achieve consistent results in the upper half of their peer group.

The box chart typically identifies the returns of relevant comparison indexes. Exhibit 1 identifies a small-cap fund account as a circle and the Small Cap Benchmark as a square. The performance for a universe of managers varies according to the measurement period. For the one-year period of 2017, universe returns were more variable, and the median was higher compared with the last quarter of 2017. In 2017, the small-cap fund had a return below the median and was in the fourth quartile. In the last quarter it also had return below the median and was also in the fourth quartile. Over the three-year period, the small-cap fund had third quartile return below the return of the Small Cap Benchmark.

Another common exhibit prepared from the same universe return data is a return/risk scatter chart, an example of which is shown in Exhibit 2. In this chart, the vertical axis depicts annualized return and the horizontal axis depicts annualized standard deviation of return, a measure of risk. Each point in the chart represents a portfolio in the universe. The crosshairs locate the median of each dimension. The small-cap fund is again plotted as a circle and the Small Cap Benchmark as a square. The scatter chart allows the viewer to quickly see where an identified account falls within the distribution of its peer group in two key dimensions of performance: return and risk. Over the five-year period, the small-cap fund had a lower return and more risk than the Small Cap Benchmark and the median universe.

Exhibit 2 A Typical Peer Group Universe Scatter Chart

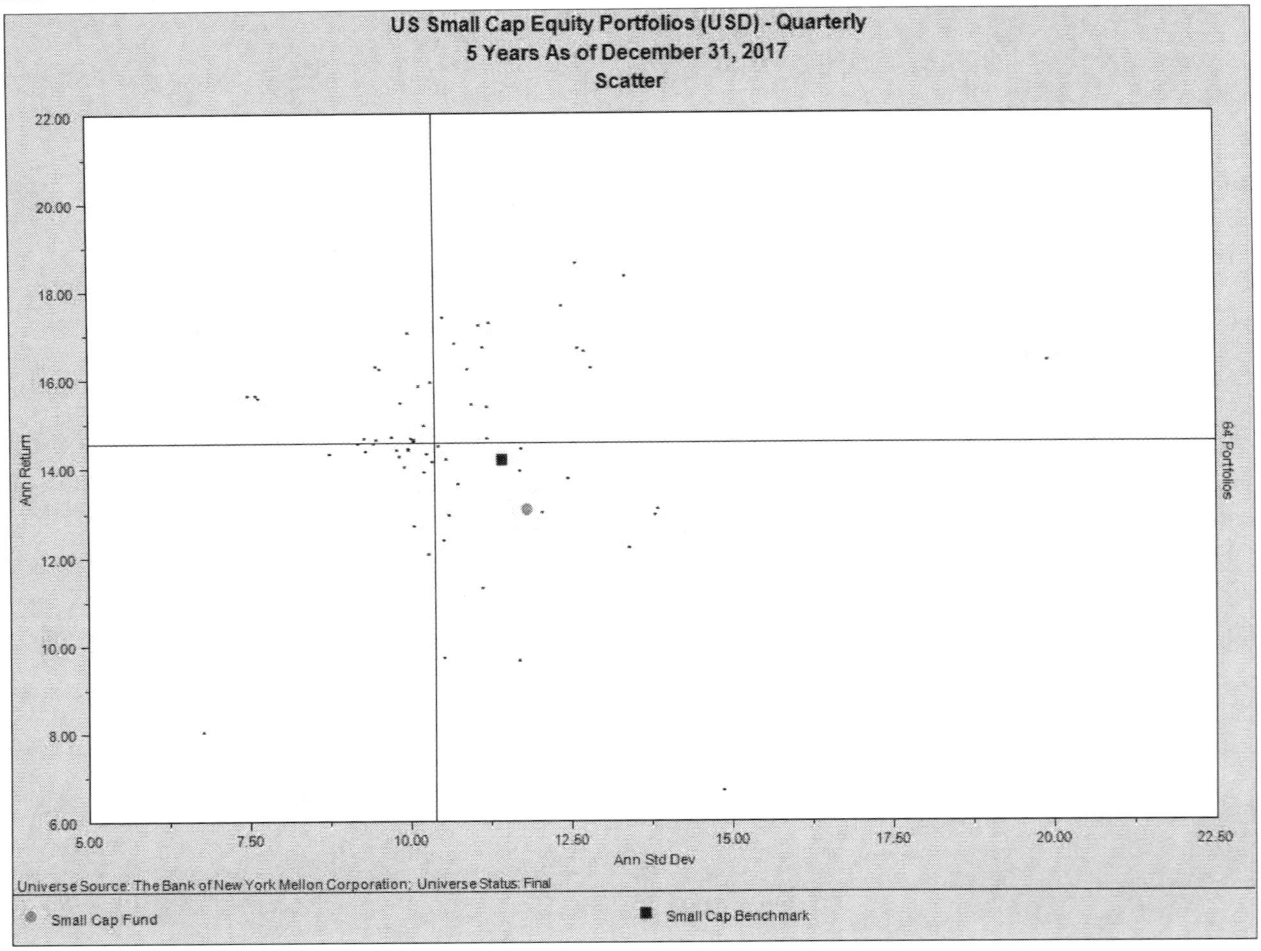

Source: © 2018 The Bank of New York Mellon Corporation. All rights reserved.

EXAMPLE 6

Peer Group Benchmarks

1 Which of the following is an advantage of peer group benchmarks?
   A They are inexpensive to construct.
   B The data on managers' holdings are readily available.
   C Managers have discretion over their classification category.

2 Which of the following validity criteria do peer group benchmarks typically satisfy? Peer group benchmarks are:
   A measurable.
   B specified in advance.
   C reflective of current investment opinions.

Solution to 1:

A is correct. Peer group benchmarks are inexpensive to construct. The data on managers' positions and their sizes, however, are not readily available. Managers often do have discretion regarding which peer group they are placed in, which is a disadvantage in that managers may try to game performance evaluation by trying to be placed in a peer group in which they will look good.

Solution to 2:

A is correct. Peer group benchmark returns are measurable. They are not specified in advance, however, and often do not reflect a manager's view of how individual securities should be classified.

MARKET INDEXES AND STYLE INDEXES

5

One of the most popular methods of assessing portfolio managers in the financial press is to compare their returns with those of a market index, such as the CAC 40, FTSE 100 Index, or Dow Jones Industrial Average (DJIA) for, respectively, French, UK, and US equities. The basic idea is that such indexes reasonably represent the performance of all securities in a market. Market indexes played a key role in modern portfolio theory, and the success of low-cost index funds furthered their popularity. They are more readily recognizable by the general public than most other benchmark types.

Currently, thousands of market indexes are available for more than 70 countries, spanning developed markets, such as the United States; emerging markets, such as Brazil; and smaller frontier markets, such as Kazakhstan. Indexes are created by traditional providers (e.g., MSCI), as well as exchanges (e.g., Euronext) and investment banks (e.g., Barclays). Equity indexes were the first to be developed but were soon followed by bond and alternative asset indexes.

In addition to the indexes mentioned, many other well-known broad market equity index series are provided by such vendors as FTSE, MSCI, Russell Investments, and S&P Dow Jones Indices. Major providers for broad market fixed-income indexes include Bloomberg Barclays, JP Morgan, IHS Markit, and S&P/Citigroup. Bond index examples include the S&P/Citigroup International Treasury Bond Index series, the Markit iBoxx USD Liquid Investment Grade Index, and the JP Morgan Emerging Markets Bond Index.

Given the abundance and the importance of security market indexes, it is constructive to understand their many uses. We discuss the uses of indexes in the approximate order that a sponsor would: as asset allocation proxies, investment management mandates, performance benchmarks, and portfolio analysis applications. Additionally, we discuss the use of indexes as a gauge of market sentiment and as the basis for investment vehicles.[15]

Asset allocation proxies Used for asset allocation, an index constructed consistently over time provides the investor a tool to measure asset class *ex ante* return, risk, and correlations. It allows investors to determine the incremental expected return and risk from adding a new asset to a portfolio. These measurements can be used to design an investment policy suitable for different risk aversion levels.

The assets of many large institutions are managed in a top-down manner, with decisions made at the highest level (e.g., the plan sponsor level) to allocate among broad asset classes. The expectations of asset class risk and return formed from indexes

15 Schoenfeld (2002), Schoenfeld (2003), and Siegel (2003) elaborated further on four uses of asset class indexes, to which we add two more.

can serve as proxies for the intended investments. The actual, specific investments within asset classes are usually chosen by managers separately from the asset allocation decision, with the assumption that the actual investments will be broadly in line with the characteristics of the index. Thus, the decision to implement a chosen security selection through the use of active management is made independently of the asset allocation decision.

Investment management mandates As a result of their effectiveness as asset allocation proxies, investment mandates can include a specified benchmark index. The benchmark index for a mandate communicates the asset owner's expectations to the asset manager: The manager is generally expected to select securities primarily from the constituents of the index. Exceeding an index return is frequently considered an objective of an actively managed portfolio (and matching the index return is the objective of a passively managed portfolio). Such an index will be valid as an evaluation tool, of course, only to the extent that it meets the criteria for a valid benchmark.

Performance benchmarks Indexes are often used as *ex post* performance benchmarks, where they answer the basic question, did the manager beat the market? With the development of the capital asset pricing model (CAPM) in the 1960s, the "market" index return representing the entirety of assets became important in investment theory. Investment practitioners subsequently looked to various indexes as proxies of this "market" return. The same benchmark validity criteria apply. Sometimes, a combination of more than one index is used to create a benchmark for the manager, under the assumption that the manager's portfolio cannot be captured by a single index.[16]

Portfolio analysis In addition to benchmarking the manager's performance, indexes can be used for more detailed portfolio analysis. In particular, return attribution of the manager's return against a benchmark will identify detailed sources of added and subtracted value and will be useful for investigating investment management skill.

Gauge of market sentiment Possibly the most common use of indexes is as a gauge of public or market sentiment. They answer the question, how did the market do today? Index values are cited incessantly in business media as an indicator of daily (and even intra-day) market movements. Such movements are influenced by a wide variety of factors, such as the prospects for economic expansion or recession, war and rumors of war, and general feelings of investor confidence. Market indexes provide a convenient summary statistic of expectations because they are succinctly summarized in a single number, the current return on the index. Market indexes convey the perceived importance of both past events and the probability of future events. As a specific example of the latter, the Chicago Board Options Exchange (CBOE) Market Volatility Index (VIX) is a frequently used measure of market uncertainty.

Basis for investment vehicles Indexes are also used as a basis for investments, such as index mutual funds, ETFs, and derivatives. Index funds, ETFs, and derivative instruments are created on the basis of indexes ranging in breadth from broad markets to narrow market segments and investment themes. The royalties from licensing indexes for such uses has been a major driver of the proliferation of market indexes. Derivative instruments, such as futures and options, are used in hedging, trading, and asset reallocation and have other uses as well. More recently, indexes have served as the basis for ETFs that straddle the line between passive and active investments, such as fundamentally weighted ETFs. These ETFs take active weights (non-market-value weights) in securities but do not actively trade portfolio securities. The ETFs seek to exploit market inefficiencies or target a particular style or risk factor.[17]

16 According to a survey of European portfolio managers, there is general agreement that a benchmark can be created from a combination of indexes (Amenc, Goltz, and Tang 2011, p. 67).
17 Christopherson (2012).

There is a great deal of research suggesting that it is difficult for active managers to earn their fees, so passive investments in low-cost index funds have become increasingly popular. There are also enhanced-index managers, who take active bets away from the index while simultaneously trying to limit their deviation from the index's risk. For an index to be useful as the basis for an investment vehicle, an investor must be able to replicate it at low cost without much difficulty.

In sum, indexes serve many vital purposes for asset owners and investors at large. There are aspects of index construction that can be more or less suited for a particular use. We next examine the construction of indexes.

5.1 Asset Class Index Construction

Indexes are created by defining a set of rules, which are then applied to a set of existing securities. Not all indexes are constructed in the same way, however. There are three primary choices in index construction: the inclusion criteria, security weighting, and index maintenance. In addition, index providers calculate index values from which returns can be calculated.

The first choice, the inclusion criteria, determines which specific population of securities the index represents. The greater the number of securities and the more diversified they are by industry and size, the better the index will measure broad market performance. A narrower universe will better measure performance of a specific group of securities. To serve as a benchmark, the inclusion criteria for an index should result in security composition similar to the manager's portfolio.

The second choice, the weighting of the securities, is usually a choice among price weighting, value weighting, or an alternative weighting. Some indexes weight some securities more than others, resulting in different return and risk. The sponsor should be aware of the differences before comparing the manager's portfolio with an index. Index maintenance and return calculation rules will also influence the applicability of the index as a benchmark.

Although the details vary by each index constructor, the general approach to constructing asset class indexes consists of creating rules for the following steps:

Define eligible securities The starting universe of securities, such as all common equity shares of companies within a given country, must first be identified. Typically, various eligibility rules are applied to improve the investability of the index. Some types of eligibility rules are as follows:

- Trading requirements: Eligible securities must be listed on a major exchange—for example, with over-the-counter traded securities ineligible for inclusion.
- Minimum trading price: Shares must trade at or above a minimum price.
- Minimum available shares (float): Companies with only a small portion of their shares available to the general public, for example, are ineligible.
- Minimum liquidity: Shares traded or value traded over a given period must be above a certain level.
- Company structure: Companies structured as limited partnerships, limited liability companies, and closed-end investment companies, for example, are ineligible.
- Share types: Preferred and convertible preferred stock, for example, are excluded from common share indexes.
- Country assignment: The country to which a security is assigned might depend on more criteria than the country of incorporation. Some companies choose to incorporate in a region for operations, tax, political, or other financial benefits.

For example, the country of the company's headquarters or the country where the company's shares are primarily traded might be taken into account in assigning a security to a country.

Inclusion criteria reduce the number of securities to a manageable number and are usually imposed in order to improve the investability of an index. The index provider also chooses whether to include all eligible securities or to further reduce the number. If a limit is imposed on the number of securities, then typically other rules are devised that are intended to keep the selected securities representative of the given market. For example, rules to ensure adequate representation of sectors or industries might be imposed.

The extent and detail of eligibility rules vary by index provider. Some providers choose to select eligible securities by a committee. In most cases, the index membership is best regarded as a sample of all securities that might be included. Ensuring that the sample is an adequate representation of the underlying market is ordinarily a goal of index providers.

Most index providers create a comprehensive family of indexes that cover nearly the entire range of market capitalizations (sizes) of companies. An index family may consist of indexes covering large-cap, mid-cap, and small-cap stocks as well as other variations. After defining eligible securities, rules assigning securities to the various capitalization tiers are applied.

Define index weighting Once the eligible securities are determined, rules for weighting the securities are applied. The security weighting is important because it directly affects index risk and return and also influences the index's validity as a manager's benchmark.

There are several weighting schemes commonly used:

- **Capitalization weighting**, also known as **market value weighting**, **market cap weighting**, or **cap weighting**. The most common weighting scheme used is capitalization weighting. In this scheme, constituents are held in proportion to their market capitalizations, calculated as price multiplied by available shares. *The performance of a value-weighted index represents the performance of a portfolio that holds all the outstanding value of each index security.* By far, market capitalization weighting has the greatest acceptance by investment professionals. This approach has several advantages, discussed later.

  Examples of US capitalization-weighted indexes include the S&P 500 and the Russell indexes. Global indexes that are capitalization weighted include the MSCI indexes. Non-US indexes include the Financial Times Actuaries Share Indexes (representing stocks on the London Stock Exchange), the Tokyo Stock Exchange Price Index (TOPIX), the CAC 40 in France, and the DAX 30 in Germany.

- **Price weighting**. In this scheme, constituents are weighted in proportion to their prices. The index value thereby can be interpreted simply as an average of the constituent prices. *The performance of a price-weighted index represents the performance of a portfolio that holds one unit of each index security.* Although the advantage of price weighting is its simplicity, the scheme offers little relevance to the way most investors weight their portfolios. The most notable price-weighted indexes are the Dow Jones Averages, which are widely quoted and have a long history. The Nikkei Stock Average is also a price-weighted index, representing stocks listed on the Tokyo Stock Exchange.

  Beyond cap weighting and price weighting, other forms of index weighting fall into a category called "alternative weighting." Some noteworthy approaches include the following:

- **Equal weighting**. In a pure equal-weighting scheme, all constituents are held at equal weights at specified rebalancing times. *The performance of an equal-weighted index represents the performance of a portfolio that invests the same amount of wealth in each index security.* Variations of this approach might weight groups of constituents (such as sectors or industries) equally. Equal-weighted indexes must be rebalanced periodically (e.g., quarterly) to reestablish the equal weighting because individual security returns will vary, causing security weights to drift from equal weights. The Value Line Composite Average is an equally weighted average of US stock returns.
- **Fundamental weighting**. This weighting scheme patented by Research Affiliates LLC uses company characteristics other than market values, such as sales, cash flow, book value, and dividends, to weight securities. By forming weights based on variables considered important for valuation, these indexes seek to weight securities using true *values,* rather than the market *prices* of capitalization and price weighting. Other organizations have created index funds based on similar weighting approaches, using other combinations of variables. *The performance of a fundamental-weighted index represents the performance of a portfolio that invests according to valuation metrics for a security.*
- **Optimization-based weighting** (minimum-variance and efficiency weighting schemes). Some evidence of abnormal risk-adjusted returns relative to low-volatility portfolios has been found. Minimum-variance portfolios are natural starting points for pursuing this apparent anomaly. Other indexes have been formed by maximizing the Sharpe ratio (excess return per unit of risk) and by seeking to equalize risk among all assets (an approach known as risk parity). These types of benchmarks blur the distinction between index design and investment strategy, with investment strategy now effectively embedded in the design of the index.

We discuss the relative advantages and disadvantages of these types of indexes in Section 5.3.

Nearly all capitalization-weighted indexes are adjusted for the free float. The *free float* is the amount of shares outstanding for a given company that is available to the public. This adjustment is intended to exclude the capitalization of a company that is not widely available for purchase and thus is not part of the investable opportunity set. The resulting index is called a free-float-adjusted market capitalization index, or float-weighted index for short. *A float-weighted index represents the performance of a portfolio that holds all the index securities available for trading.*

Some examples of share types removed are as follows:

- Cross ownership: shares held by another company that is also a member of the index.
- Large corporate or private holdings: for example, shares held by other companies or individuals that exceed 10% of shares outstanding.
- Employee-owned shares: for example, shares held by employee stock ownership plans.
- IPO lockups: shares locked up during an initial public offering are excluded.
- Government holdings: for example, holdings listed as "government of" are considered unavailable.

Adjustments for free float are particularly important in less developed markets, where governments, founding families, and other companies often hold a large portion of stock. Although, strictly speaking, such shares might be purchasable at some price, the premium that a buyer might need to pay for such shares would make them extremely unattractive to most buyers. Removing shares that are unavailable for purchase in this sense allows an index to be more easily replicated by an investor. If unavailable shares are included in an index and if many investors tried to replicate the index, there could be significant price distortions resulting from imbalances between supply and demand for the unavailable shares.[18] All the major global indexes are float adjusted, including those of S&P Dow Jones Global, FTSE, MSCI, Russell, and S&P/Citigroup.[19] Float adjustments result in the index being more investable. It should be noted that free float adjustments are subjective, and different index providers might reach different conclusions about the availability of shares in an index.

Index maintenance A variety of rules must be determined by an index constructor to provide for ongoing maintenance of an index. Some examples follow:

- Reconstitution and rebalancing intervals: Markets evolve, with companies appearing and disappearing through mergers, spinoffs, IPOs, bankruptcies, delistings, and so on. Further, small companies may grow to become large companies, and large companies may shrink. Inevitably, the constituents or the weights of an index might need to be reset to keep the index representative of its intended design. Some index providers choose to reconstitute their indexes based on a fixed time interval, such as annually or quarterly. For non-cap-weighted indexes, a rebalancing interval is necessary to maintain the weighting scheme. Index providers will take great care to ensure their rules do not result in securities regularly going in and out of the index, generating unnecessary turnover. Choosing when, or whether, to include a large IPO in an index will be a significant decision for the index provider.
- Corporate actions: Changes to shares outstanding may occur owing to buybacks, secondary offerings, spinoffs, stock distributions, and so on. Index providers typically handle these changes as they occur, by specified rules.
- Dividends: Dividends are typically accounted for through the calculation of index values, as described later. Indexes that incorporate dividends are called "total return indexes," whereas index values calculated without dividends are called "price return indexes."
- Suspensions: Index providers will need to determine rules for the pricing of suspended companies.

Free-Float Adjustment

In the discussion, we noted that a capitalization-weighted, float-adjusted index is the only index that all investors could realistically hold. Just prior to the widespread adoption of float adjustments, the most widely adopted global indexes were simply capitalization weighted.

Free-float adjustments can have dramatic effects on the weights of index constituents. On 30 November 2001, for example, the MSCI World Index began to change its market capitalization index rules to adjust for free float. The total turnover as a result of the subsequent inclusions and exclusions in the various index names was 25.8%. A total of 357 additions and 130 deletions were made to the MSCI World Index as it was then constituted. The greatest number of these

18 Schoenfeld (2003, pp. 77–78) provided an interesting anecdote regarding the potential problem with indexes that are not float adjusted. In 1999, the day before Yahoo! Inc. was to be added to the S&P 500, its price rose 24% over the course of the day. The reason is that on the next day, Yahoo! was added to the index at its full market capitalization weight, even though only about 10% of its shares were available to the public (most of its shares were held by employees, venture capitalists, and other investors). In 2004, a float adjustment was added to the S&P 500.

19 In 2012, the Dow Jones indexes were merged with those of Standard & Poor's.

additions and deletions was made to MSCI US and MSCI Japan sub-indexes. A total of 979 stocks, or 63% of stocks in the index, had free-float-adjustment factors applied to them. In Japan, the most tightly held market, every stock in its 325-member index had a free-float-adjustment factor of less than 100%.

EXAMPLE 7

Index Weighting Schemes

1 An index constituent is owned by the government, various mutual funds, and the general public in the following proportions: 40%, 20%, and 40%, respectively. Its total market capitalization is $120,000,000. How much of this constituent's capitalization should be reflected in a capitalization, free-float index?

   A $120,000,000

   B $72,000,000

   C $48,000,000

2 Which of the following construction methodologies will a large institutional fund manager *most likely* prefer for a broad market index?

   A Market capitalization

   B Market capitalization, weight capped

   C Market capitalization, free-float adjusted

3 Which of the following is an example of a broad market index?

   A A peer group index

   B A sector-specific index

   C A global equity index

Solution to 1:

B ($72,000,000) is correct. The government's stake is not traded and as such should be excluded from what is available to investors. A is incorrect because no adjustment is made. C is incorrect because mutual funds will trade in and out of a company, and their shares are therefore available for trading.

Solution to 2:

C is correct. A market capitalization, free-float-adjusted index will reflect the equity actually available for trading. A large institutional manager has to be concerned about whether she can realistically invest in all the index constituents. This might not be the case if A is selected. B is a special case in which the manager desires to cap her exposure to a particular segment of the market; no indication was given in the question that such is the case.

Solution to 3:

C is correct. A is incorrect because the peer group may well deviate from the broad market. B is too specific; it covers only a sub-segment of the market.

Index Returns and Time-Weighted Rates of Return

An index is a portfolio in the sense that it represents shares of securities held over time. An index value, however, is not simply the total market value of the shares held. Changes in holdings, such as those that occur when stocks are added to or deleted from the index, usually result in a change in the total market value represented by the index. The index value, however, must not change at such an occurrence; it is analogous to the concept of a unit value (or net asset value per unit) of a mutual fund or other fund in which the assets of multiple investors are commingled. The return that an index value is designed to measure is the time-weighted return of the index holdings.

Most modern indexes are valued at least daily and often more than once a day. To facilitate the calculation of index values, a method called the "divisor method" is commonly used. A quantity *U*, called the "divisor," is calculated, analogous to the total number of units in a unitized fund. Before the start of a trading day, the index provider disseminates the holdings of the index (numbers of shares and identifiers of constituents) and the divisor. During day *t*, the index value, IV, can be calculated by valuing the holdings and dividing by the divisor, U_t. If *V* is the value of the index holdings at any time during day *t*, then IV = V/U_t.

After the close of trading on a given day, the index provider makes several adjustments. The first adjustment is to account for dividends that may be associated with the holdings. In an ordinary portfolio, the dividend appears as a receivable on the ex-dividend date and normally is considered a cash flow into the liquidity reserve segment of the portfolio. In an index, there is no liquidity reserve; the dividend income is not represented in the market value and must be accounted for directly in the index value. At the end of day *t*, the index value is calculated as

$$\text{IV}_t = \frac{V_t + \text{DIV}_t}{U_t}$$

where DIV_t is the value of dividends of stocks that are assumed to be reinvested on day *t*. The dividend values are ordinarily based on holdings (the relevant number of shares multiplied by the dividend amount per share).[20] Conceptually, this calculation is equivalent to reinvesting the dividend amount proportionately among all holdings of the portfolio. The holdings (numbers of shares), however, are typically not adjusted for dividend income because an index that "holds" all the shares in a market cannot "buy" more shares with the dividend.

After adjusting the index value for dividends, the shares of the holdings are adjusted for corporate actions or any other additions to or deletions from the index per the construction rules. The shares added or removed are typically valued at closing prices, and the market value of the adjusted holdings, V_t', is calculated. The new divisor for the next day, *t* + 1, is then calculated:

$$U_{t+1} = \frac{V_t'}{\text{IV}_t}$$

Substituting the first equation given into the second gives a convenient formula for updating the divisor:

$$U_{t+1} = U_t \frac{V_t'}{V_t + \text{DIV}_t}$$

20 Typically, dividends are assumed to be reinvested on the ex-dividend date, with values based on holdings from the previous day. Assumptions may vary, depending on the provider or local conventions.

As mentioned, the calculated index values are intended to yield the time-weighted return of the index portfolio. To verify that the return calculated from index values is a time-weighted return, consider the return relative for day t calculated from index values, IV_t/IV_{t-1}. Substituting into this term using the first two equations given leaves

$$\frac{IV_t}{IV_{t-1}} = \frac{V_t + DIV_t}{V'_{t-1}}$$

This equation's numerator is effectively the portfolio value immediately before external cash flows at the end of day t, whereas the denominator is the portfolio value immediately after external cash flows at the end of day $t - 1$. Returns calculated from index values using the divisor method are thus time-weighted returns. The value after adjusting for share changes on day $t - 1$, V'_{t-1}—sometimes called the "beginning adjusted value for day t"—is disseminated with the holdings and the divisor; it should be interpreted as the opening holdings valued at the previous closing prices. At the inception date of an index, an index base value must be assigned to start the process.

When creating an index, index providers face several tradeoffs, which we examine next.

5.2 Index Construction Tradeoffs

Previously, we said that indexes are widely used to represent the performance of asset classes and the "market" in general. They are also increasingly used as a basis for investment vehicles. To satisfy these usages, index construction requires many choices, with accompanying tradeoffs.[21] We examine these tradeoffs following the discussion in Siegel (2003).

Completeness vs. investability In principle, striving for complete coverage of a market would suggest including every possible security in the investment universe available to investors. Doing so, however, would include many small-capitalization securities that are too illiquid and could not be purchased in amounts relevant to institutional investors. Eliminating hard-to-trade securities improves the investability of an index. Index designers must decide how broad their indexes can be while maintaining adequate investability.

As an example, the Wilshire 5000 is the broadest US equity index, representing more than 5,000 stocks. Many of its stocks are illiquid, however, and would be costly or very difficult to trade. As a result, no fund has ever tried to replicate the full sample of its securities. When index funds were created to track the Wilshire 5000, about 2,000 of its securities were untradeable. Indeed, one test of the investability of an index is to what extent there are investment funds that fully replicate it.

Investability is not, however, the same as liquidity, as emerging markets sometimes illustrate. A security may have excellent liquidity in its home country but may be uninvestable for non-domestic investors if the country's government imposes restrictions. An index representing investment opportunities to developed-world investors should exclude non-tradeable emerging securities, reflecting the free float of the market from a non-domestic investor's perspective.

Completeness and investability are important when indexes are used as a basis for investment vehicles. In choosing an index, the fund provider should consider how the index has balanced the tradeoff between completeness and investability. A

21 Schoenfeld (2003), Enderle, Pope, and Siegel (2003), and Christopherson, Cariño, and Ferson (2009) provided evaluations of existing indexes in terms of many of the criteria discussed here.

more complete index can provide broader, more diversified performance.[22] However, investability is an important concern for managers facing frequent and uncertain withdrawals. If investors suddenly withdraw funds, managers must quickly sell securities, possibly at low bid prices. Another consideration is that portfolios tracking more popular indexes tend to have lower trading costs, owing to their greater liquidity.

Reconstitution and rebalancing frequency vs. turnover The processes of reconstitution and rebalancing are designed to keep an index close to its intended membership and weighting criteria. Reconstitution refers to the process of adding and dropping securities from an index, whereas rebalancing refers to a readjustment in the weights of existing securities.

In principle, more frequent reconstitution and rebalancing would be desirable in order to improve representativeness, were it not for the fact that such activities create turnover in the index. Turnover is costly, in terms of transaction costs, bid–offer spread, and taxes for investors who wish to track an index because they must trade more often. Therefore, there is a conflict between representativeness and low turnover. Index designers must decide how often to reconstitute and rebalance their indexes while maintaining tolerable turnover.

Turnover is a potential concern for managers who track particular size and style indexes because they must trade as companies migrate from one classification to another. As a result, these indexes are less frequently reconstituted by providers. In contrast, the turnover in broad market indexes typically occurs among smaller issues, resulting in less trading when the index is reconstituted. Reconstitution is also less frequent for all-inclusive indexes than for those with a fixed number of securities (e.g., the S&P 500), where securities periodically enter and exit the index.

Rebalancing is of particular concern in international indexes, where float adjustments are more important. At one extreme, index creators could frequently adjust the float of index constituents to precise amounts. This adjustment would result in frequent rebalancing and high transaction costs for tracking portfolios. Instead, many index providers use bands to make float adjustments, where a range is used to capture the percentage of the issue's market cap that is free floating (e.g., 60%–70%). As long as the issue's estimated free float stays within the band, they do not adjust the issue's weight in the index. A narrower band would result in more frequent rebalancing. Determining a country's status—developed, emerging, or frontier, for example—is fraught with difficulties, because changing the status of a country from emerging to developed could significantly affect the country weights in both the developed and emerging markets indexes, with consequences for managers currently benchmarked against those indexes.

Objective and transparent rules vs. judgment Security prices rise when securities are added to an index and fall when they are deleted from an index. Index reconstitution results in decreased returns for managers tracking the index because they have to buy added securities at higher prices and sell deleted securities at lower prices. These price changes will be more acute for more popular indexes.

Transparency and objectivity are desirable characteristics of indexes because they allow investors to readily predict the changes in index constituents that might occur. This information enables investors to anticipate changes and trade accordingly, instead of reacting to them. Less transparency and the greater use of judgment by the index provider make it harder for investors to determine the constituents of an index and anticipate changes in it, making the index less investable and creating additional costs for tracking portfolios.

22 A more complete index, however, might also have a greater number of securities that have not traded recently, resulting in stale prices, with reported volatility and correlations that are understated. See Calverley, Meder, Singer, and Staub (2007, Section 2.2).

All index providers, however, exercise some degree of judgment in applying their methodologies. Doing so allows providers to adapt to changing circumstances or special situations that might not have been anticipated by explicit rules. Some providers intentionally use committees to choose index constituents, for example, in order to obtain certain characteristics that might be difficult to describe in rules. Index providers must decide when to use judgment in their methodologies and how much to use.

In sum, there are many choices and steps in index construction. An index provider must define the universe of eligible securities, determine the index weighting, and determine the rules for index maintenance and return calculation. From an index user's perspective, an index should be constructed using simple, transparent methods that are replicable. The index provider should publish clear, unambiguous construction rules, and the data should be available in a timely manner. Index users should have confidence in the index's construction and in the reliability and consistency of its return methodology.

EXAMPLE 8

Trade-offs in constructing asset class indexes

Larger, more comprehensive indexes tend to suffer from:

A investability issues.

B higher turnover.

C subjective choices of index providers.

Solution:

A is correct. Larger, more comprehensive or complete indexes are less investable because they include more hard-to-trade securities than smaller indexes. B is incorrect; larger indexes are less likely to suffer rebalancing leading to higher turnover than are smaller indexes. C is incorrect; larger indexes are more objective than smaller ones.

5.3 Weighting Schemes: Advantages and Disadvantages

In the following discussion, we compare the advantages and disadvantages of weighting schemes for indexes. We discuss their attributes in general and discuss the applicability of indexes as benchmarks.

5.3.1 *Capitalization-Weighted Indexes*

Capitalization weighting is used in most market indexes for good reasons. First, weighting companies by market value is an objective way of measuring the relative importance of constituents. Valuing securities at market prices clearly measures the market's assessment of their relative values. A security's price is a consensus estimate of its value formed by a multitude of investors, rather than a single index creator's estimate. Market prices and the number of tradeable securities are unambiguous measures of value at a point in time.

Second, a capitalization-weighted, float-adjusted index is the only index type that all investors could hold. If all investors held all the securities in cap-weighted indexes in proportion to their market value, then all shares would be held, with none left over. This property has been referred to as *macro consistency* (Siegel 2003). With other weighting methods, such as fundamental-weighted indexes, not all investors could hold the index. A cap-weighted index is thus the best representation of a typical investor's opportunity set. As a result, a capitalization-weighted index is superior at succinctly representing the effect of changes in a market's total value and investors' total wealth.

This property is closely related to one of the central results of the original CAPM: Under the assumptions of the CAPM, a cap-weighted portfolio of all assets is efficient, and all investors in a CAPM world would hold a proportional investment in the market portfolio. A cap-weighted index reflects this concept.

Third, a capitalization-weighted index requires less rebalancing than other indexes. In value weighting, changes in prices do not create a need to add or remove shares; the index remains cap weighted after a price change. A capitalization-weighted index also self-corrects for stock splits because they are reflected in the number of shares outstanding and price per share. If an investor tracks a capitalization-weighted index and there are no changes in the index constituents, then the portfolio will automatically track the index and no rebalancing is necessary. Other weighting schemes require periodic trades to bring the weights back to those required by the scheme.

Capitalization weighting has disadvantages, however. First, because they are market value weighted, these indexes could be overly influenced by overpriced securities. As a security's price increases through time, its representation in the index will grow. The capitalization-weighted index is thus potentially more susceptible to market bubbles and will not necessarily represent an efficient investment from a risk–return perspective. Second, the index may be overly concentrated because large issues will be weighted the most heavily. For example, in 2013, the 10 largest constituents of the S&P 500 represented approximately 19% of its value.[23] Some investors may prefer a more diversified portfolio. Similarly, active managers may desire weights that are different from those of the index, and institutional investors may be unable to track a capitalization-weighted index if they are subject to maximum holdings. Portfolio risk and return for these managers may, therefore, substantially deviate from the index, meaning that the index will not serve as a valid benchmark.

5.3.2 *Price-Weighted Indexes*

The main advantage of price-weighted indexes lies in the simplicity of their construction. Price-weighted indexes also have a long historical track record, which facilitates investment research. For example, the DJIA was first published in 1896.

Price-weighted indexes have several disadvantages. First, price-weighted indexes are overly influenced by the highest-priced securities, which have greater weights in the calculation of the indexes' returns.[24] Because price-weighted indexes weight by price instead of total market value, they do not necessarily reflect the issuing companies' economic importance. Second, stocks that appreciate will experience stock splits, and their weights in the index will decrease. Successful companies will become underrepresented, creating a downward bias in the index return. Lastly, price-weighted indexes assume an investor holds one unit of each security in the index, which does not describe how most investors form portfolios.

5.3.3 *Equal-Weighted Indexes*

The primary advantage of equal-weighted indexes is that they give smaller weights to large-cap securities (and larger weights to small-cap securities) than indexes formed by cap weighting. By reducing exposures to the largest-cap securities, the index is thereby less concentrated in those securities and more diversified. Proponents of this approach suggest that market prices do not always reflect true value and that equal

---

23 28 March 2013 S&P 500 Fact Sheet, available at http://www.spindices.com.

24 Some price-weighted indexes, such as the Nikkei 225 for Japanese equities, reduce the weighting of high-priced stocks to minimize this bias. See Gastineau, Olma, and Zielinski (2007) for an illustration and discussion.

weights reflect a more naive or informationless weighting of a portfolio, resulting in superior returns during particular historical periods. Second, these indexes may better represent "how the market did" because they provide the average of all index security returns.

Some argue, however, that this type of weighting results in a small-issuer bias, the primary disadvantage of equal-weighted indexes, because they include more small issuers than large ones. Second, to maintain equal weighting, strong-performing issues must be sold and weak performers must be bought, resulting in frequent rebalancing and high transaction costs for a portfolio tracking such an index. Third, the inclusion of small issuers means that investors tracking the index may be unable to find liquidity in some of these issues.

5.3.4 *Fundamental-Weighted Indexes*

The proponents of fundamental-weighted indexes argue that capitalization-weighted indexes overweight overvalued issues and underweight undervalued issues. Instead, weighting by valuation metrics, fundamental-weighted indexes attempt to avoid overweighting overvalued issues. Proponents also assert that these indexes will be more representative of an issuer's importance in an economy because they weight by fundamentals, rather than by market prices subject to bubbles.

A disadvantage of fundamental-weighted indexes is that they reflect the index provider's view of valuation, which may or may not be correct. The fact that there are different methods of constructing fundamental-weighted indexes in the industry demonstrates that they rely on subjective judgment. A second disadvantage is that they may be less diversified than capitalization-weighted indexes if the valuation screen is restrictive. Third, as mentioned previously, not all investors can hold a fundamental-weighted index because such indexes are weighted by valuation metrics, not by available liquidity (market capitalization). Fourth, the construction methodology used by these indexes is usually proprietary because they are created to market a fundamental-weighted fund. In this case, these indexes would not serve as valid benchmarks because their composition and weightings are not fully known.

Fifth, just because fundamental-weighted indexes have outperformed capitalization-weighted indexes during certain periods does not mean they will do so in the future and, more importantly, does not indicate that they are good indexes. As a reflection of "how the market did," an index should be judged on whether it is a representative sample, not on its performance. It is active management that is intended to deliver superior performance, not indexes. Index performance should be an outcome of index construction, not an objective. Furthermore, the reason why fundamental-weighted indexes have outperformed historically is that they are usually tilted toward small-cap value stocks, a well-documented effect in academic literature. For investors preferring a large-cap or growth emphasis, fundamental-weighted indexes would not serve as ideal benchmarks.

5.3.5 *Optimization-Based Weighted Indexes*

The advantage of these weighting schemes is that they attempt to find the combination of securities that provides the lowest risk or the highest Sharpe ratio. By using quantitative information on expected returns, standard deviations, and correlations, these indexes are intended to provide better risk–return tradeoffs than indexes formed using naive or passive approaches as in the case of equal or capitalization weighting. An optimization-based weighted index uses modern portfolio theory and attempts to provide a portfolio that plots on the efficient frontier.

The disadvantage of these indexes is that when minimizing risk, they may be over concentrated in low-risk sectors, such as utility stocks. As a result, the indexes may be less diversified and have future performance that is less stable. As a solution to this problem, constraints on the weights are sometimes used in the optimization, but these require subjective inputs to the process.[25] Second, the optimization requires historical data that are not necessarily indicative of future performance. Some optimizations use adjustments to historical data, but this process introduces subjectivity. Despite their conceptual appeal, the use of optimization-based weighted indexes as benchmarks is not widespread.

5.3.6 *Choosing an Equity Index Weighting Scheme When an Index Is Used as a Benchmark*

A natural categorization among indexes divides those that are cap weighted from those that are not. The objectivity, practicality, and theoretical underpinning of market capitalization weighting have made it the dominant scheme for constructing indexes. In most cases, benchmarks should be capitalization weighted and then float adjusted, reflecting the fact that most portfolio managers will take smaller positions in less available, less liquid securities. Of the index types examined, capitalization-weighted, float-adjusted indexes are considered the best for use as benchmarks because they are the most easily mimicked with the least amount of tracking risk and cost. The major equity index families published by FTSE, MSCI, Russell, and S&P as well as nearly all those published by S&P Dow Jones and Wilshire are cap weighted and float adjusted. In some cases, a non-float-adjusted version of an index may be published alongside a float-adjusted version for reasons of historical continuity.[26]

Non-cap-weighted indexes are often proposed to seek return (or risk-adjusted return) in excess of that provided by a cap-weighted index. The primacy of cap-weighted indexes as benchmarks is supported by the fact that a cap-weighted return must be calculated in order to determine by how much an alternate strategy might exceed it. As performance benchmarks, capitalization-weighted indexes are superior to the other index types because, simply put, they best tell us how a manager did relative to everyone else (i.e., the entire market). Price-weighted and equal-weighted indexes are best seen as particular market indicators that are generally not reasonable benchmarks. Fundamental-weighted indexes may or may not serve as viable investment strategies, but they do not serve the traditional representative role of an index, and their proprietary nature makes them difficult to use for manager evaluation.

In sum, capitalization-weighted indexes are the most likely type of index to serve as a valid benchmark for an investor. The next question is how they fare against the standards for benchmark validity discussed earlier. We next examine in more detail whether float-adjusted, capitalization-weighted indexes can serve as valid benchmarks.

5.3.7 *Market Indexes as Benchmarks*

From our previous discussion, we concluded that a capitalization-weighted, float-adjusted index would likely be the best index to use as a benchmark for most managers. Established indexes of that type are widely available, commonly accepted, and readily understood. In terms of the Bailey and Tierney (1998) tests of benchmark validity, these market indexes generally fulfill most criteria because they are easily measurable, unambiguous, specified in advance, and generally investable. Most managers would also be familiar with and have an opinion on index securities. Some sponsors may find market indexes acceptable as benchmarks if the manager selects from the same universe of securities as the benchmark and has no obvious style biases.

Capitalization-weighted, float-adjusted indexes may have several limitations for use as benchmarks, however. First, a value-weighted approach might be incompatible with a manager's investment approach. For example, as noted, value weighting may lead to concentration in large issues. Second, some construction rules might be less

25 Amenc, Goltz, and Tang (2011, pp. 35–44).

26 For example, the Dow Jones Wilshire 5000 (once known as the Wilshire 5000), representing US equities, is available in both float-adjusted and non-float-adjusted versions.

transparent than desired. As an example, consider float adjustment. Although float adjustment is desirable, some index providers do not fully disclose their adjustment process, and there is also no standardization of the process among providers. Moreover, as an index is reconstituted, its composition changes over time, sometimes in non-predictable ways. As a result, an index's style, sector, and risk exposures can change drastically over time. Even the performance of capitalization-weighted indexes typically is affected by index provider decisions over time.[27]

In terms of the Bailey and Tierney (1998) benchmark validity criteria, benchmarks may not be appropriate if the manager's style differs from the index's style. In this case, managers should not and likely would not be willing to be held accountable to the index. This shortcoming of market indexes as benchmarks reflects the fact that market indexes are designed to be representative of a market segment, not a particular manager's portfolio. The performance of a broad market index is usually influenced by many factors, few of which would be related to a manager's style or skill.

In summary, market indexes are similar to Swiss Army knives; they serve many useful purposes but are sometimes not the best tool for the job.[28] In light of the possibility that market indexes do not capture a manager's style, style indexes have been developed to evaluate managers, which we examine next.

5.4 Equity Style Indexes

In investing, the term "style" is used in at least four distinct yet related contexts.

Characteristics of individual stocks From at least the time of Graham and Dodd's influential book, *Security Analysis* (1934), investors have used the idea of analyzing company financial statements in order to identify stocks that are trading at less than their intrinsic values. Such stocks are known as "value stocks." A distinctly different approach to selecting stocks focuses on shares of companies with high rates of earnings growth. Such stocks are known as "growth stocks." The terms "value" and "growth" in this context are applied informally, characterizing the broad approaches toward selecting desirable companies to invest in.

Investment management style In the 1960s and 1970s in the United States, the investment management industry began a trend toward specialization. This trend was reinforced by the passage of the Employee Retirement Income Security Act of 1974 (ERISA), which raised the level of fiduciary responsibility to which pension funds needed to adhere. Consultants and plan sponsors began to research investment managers in order to find suitable managers for their funds. Groups of managers sharing similar investment approaches or philosophies tended to deliver similar returns. Examining the characteristics of their portfolios, such as price-to-earnings and price-to-book ratios, dividend yield, and beta, suggested that managers' portfolios tended to cluster on the basis of various characteristics. Managers also tended to focus on particular subsets of the broad market in selecting their portfolios. Broad categorizations of "investment style," based on portfolio holdings, emerged along the dimensions of size (capitalization) and value/growth.

Currently, investment managers are categorized along these and other dimensions in order to construct peer group universes. A common taxonomy is the "nine-box" categorization, depicted by large-, mid-, and small-cap segments along the size dimension and value, market oriented, and growth along the value/growth dimension. Any one of these categories may be called an "investment style": small-cap growth or mid-cap

27 See Amenc, Goltz, and Tang (2011, Section 2) for an excellent literature review and analysis of market index issues, upon which we base some of our discussion in this section.
28 This analogy is provided by Schoenfeld (2002).

value, for example. Finer groupings within the major categories are commonly proposed: for example, low-P/E (price-to-earnings ratio) managers, high-yield value managers, and growth at a reasonable price (GARP), which is a market-oriented substyle.

Style benchmarks With the growing importance of performance measurement and the evaluation of managers, in the 1980s, market indexes were created that were more appropriate for comparing the performance of managers of a given style than were available in the 1970s. The Russell family of US indexes, launched in 1984, introduced the first investable small-stock index, the Russell 2000, a subset of the Russell 3000. The first value/growth style indexes were launched by Russell in 1987. Style indexes were created by studying the holdings of managers that were categorized along the large/small and value/growth dimensions. Along the capitalization dimension, institutional portfolios were found to rarely hold stocks smaller than about the 3,000th largest stock; that observation established the lower cutoff of the Russell 2000 small-stock index. Other index providers followed with families of indexes spanning the space of large/small and value/growth styles.

In constructing value/growth indexes, profiles of value and growth manager portfolios suggest that value managers tend to hold portfolios with higher dividend yield and lower valuation ratios (lower P/Es), beta, return on equity, dividend growth, and forecasted growth than do growth managers. The index constructor must choose which variables to include as descriptors of the style. Russell indexes strive for simplicity by using a minimal set of variables. Other providers who offer style indexes—S&P Dow Jones Indices and MSCI—tend to use a larger set of descriptor variables, arguing that those variables contain additional information. As seen in the origins of value and growth investing, definitions of value and growth are traceable to manager behavior; there is much room for debate regarding the definition of value and growth stocks. Although particular investment approaches may involve elaborately detailed criteria for selecting stocks, an index provider's goal is to construct an index that broadly captures the essence of the investment style while maintaining the usual desirable properties of transparency, investability, objectivity, and so on.

Style factors While the money management industry was trending toward specialization of investment styles, academic research appeared that identified factors, or systematic influences on asset prices. Much of this research was a byproduct of attempts to empirically validate the CAPM, in which the broad market is theoretically a dominant factor. Around 1980, a small-cap effect (Banz 1981; Reinganum 1981) and a P/E effect (Basu 1977) were documented for US stocks. Bauman, Conover, and Miller (1998) documented these same effects in international markets. Fama and French (1992) combined these factors with broad market beta into a three-factor model. The three factors are beta (sensitivity to the broad market), the return on a small-cap portfolio minus the return on a large-cap portfolio (SMB), and the return on a high-B/M (book-to-market ratio) portfolio minus the return on a low-B/M portfolio (HML). This research stimulated much research into anomalies, or return patterns that could not be explained by the market factor alone. It also gave further support to the approach of practitioners in pursuing style investing and in creating style indexes by documenting evidence that such systematic influences on stock prices exist. Earlier work by Rosenberg, Reid, and Lanstein (1985) and others identified other factors affecting stock returns. Following this research, the term "style factors" was applied in the commercial world to any factor composed of fundamental stock characteristics other than industry membership factors. Thus, in formal factor models, there can simultaneously be a value factor and a growth factor (in addition to size, liquidity, etc.).

For use as the basis of investment products, recently style factor indexes, based on the style factors of a particular factor model, have appeared. These indexes are deliberately concentrated in their exposures to the targeted factor, and techniques are used to reduce or constrain exposures to non-targeted factors. Unlike style indexes, style factor indexes are not cap weighted, broadly diversified, or designed to represent a broad market index.

After a manager's style is characterized, he is often compared with a similar peer group. Previously, we discussed the shortcomings of peer groups as benchmarks. Using the criteria from Bailey and Tierney (1998), we determined that they fail all benchmark criteria except that they are measurable. Style indexes are also used as style benchmarks.

Style indexes are widely accepted and available. In terms of the validity criteria, they are measurable and specified in advance, and managers frequently take ownership of them. Style indexes are often investable, given that there are ETFs based on them. Importantly, however, a style index may not fully describe the manager's investment process, leading to an inappropriate benchmark. Previously, we used the decomposition of a manager's portfolio return (P) using the market index return (M), the style return (S), and the active management return (A):

$$P = M + S + A$$

From this decomposition, the evaluation of a manager's active management return depends on the specification of the manager's style. If the manager's style is misspecified, then the evaluation of the manager will be unsound. Specifically, because P and M are given for each measurement period, style returns and active management returns are inversely related. Algebraically,

$$\Delta A = -\Delta S$$

Understating the style return, $\Delta S < 0$, overstates the active management return; that is, $\Delta A > 0$. Similarly, overstating the style return, $\Delta S > 0$ understates the active management return, which means that $\Delta A < 0$.

EXAMPLE 9

Market and Style Indexes

1 A market index is *most likely* useful as a benchmark when the manager follows a:

A contrarian approach.

B market-oriented approach.

C aggressive growth approach.

2 Which of the following *best* describes the characteristics of style indexes? Style indexes typically:

A are not investable.

B cannot be measured after the fact.

C characterize some stocks as both value and growth.

Solution to 1:

B is correct. A market index is most likely useful as a benchmark when the manager follows a market-oriented approach. In this case, the manager's portfolio is most likely to resemble a broad market index and have the same style. As a result, a market-capitalization-weighted index would be most likely to serve as a valid benchmark for this manager.

Solution to 2:

C is correct. Most index providers use methodologies that allow for some stocks to be characterized as both partly value and partly growth. Style indexes are measurable and are often investable because there are many investment funds based on them.

5.5 Bond Indexes

The bond market may be separated into sectors, in which similar securities are grouped together. For example, the bond market can be divided by issuer: corporate bonds, government and government agency bonds, municipal bonds, and asset-backed securities (ABS) and mortgage-backed securities (MBS). Or bonds can be separated by credit risk sectors: investment-grade bonds (low credit risk) and high-yield bonds (higher credit risk). Within these classifications, even finer sectors could be defined. For example, corporate bonds could be separated into industrial, utility, and financial sectors. Investment-grade bonds could be separated by the specific investment rating (e.g., AAA, AA, A, BBB). Bonds can also be separated by other key features, such as fixed versus floating coupon rates, whether they are callable prior to maturity, and whether they are linked to inflation. In addition to returns, bond index providers will provide duration (a key systematic risk measure for bonds) at total and sector level.

The typical criteria used to construct a bond index concern country, credit risk, liquidity, maturity, currency, and sector classification. Typical inclusion criteria for US bond indexes are that a bond be publicly issued, be nonconvertible, be dollar denominated, have a fixed coupon or one that changes at specified intervals, have a maturity of one year or more, meet a minimum issue size, and fulfill the necessary credit rating.[29] Broad bond indexes are usually also available as sub-sectors, and indexes differentiated by maturity and credit risk are the most commonly available.

Compared with equities, there are more issuers of bonds. For example, governments and government entities issue bonds but not stocks. In addition, most issuers have only one type of common stock outstanding but several bond issues of different maturity, seniority, and other features. The total market capitalization of the global bond market was almost twice as large as that of the global equity market, estimated at $93 trillion compared with $54 trillion for global equities.[30]

Despite the larger number of corporate issues, most issues have less active secondary markets compared with equities. Even in developed markets, many bonds issues may not trade in the course of a typical day or their trades may not be reported because they may not trade through a centralized exchange. The most recent trade price in such cases is said to be "stale." The values of many issues constituting bond indexes do not represent recent trading but are estimated (appraised) based on the inferred current market value from their characteristics (an appraisal approach known as "matrix pricing"). Delays in data on spreads used in estimated prices can cause large errors in valuation. Several factors explain infrequent trading, including the long-term investment horizon of many bond investors, the limited number of distinct investors in many bond issues, and the limited size of many bond issues. Furthermore, corporate bond market trading data, although improving in many markets, have typically been less readily accessible than equity trading data. As a consequence of these facts, many bond indexes are not as investable as major equity indexes and may not represent bond markets as accurately as desired. Note that when appraised values are used, the potential exists for measured standard deviations and correlations to be biased downward because actual price fluctuations will be masked.

29 Mahseredjian and Friebel (2003).
30 Roxburgh, Lund, and Piotrowski (2011).

Because of the size and heterogeneity of bond issues and the issue of infrequent trading, one problem with using bond indexes as benchmarks is that a passive manager faces challenges in tracking a broad index. The full replication approach to tracking an index (buying all component securities according to their index weights) is much less common than for equity indexes. The effect on price from investing in less frequently traded bonds can be substantial because of their illiquidity. In practice, a passive bond fund manager usually buys a representative subset of the index (a sampling approach). To minimize problems with illiquidity, some providers create more-liquid subsets of their indexes. For example, JP Morgan has created a more liquid version of its emerging market government bond index, referred to as the EMBI Global Core Index. This index is more easily and cheaply replicable by investors and has lower tracking risk than the broader EMBI Global Index.

Second, owing to the heterogeneity of bonds, bond indexes that appear similar can often have very different composition and performance. For example, the Dow Jones Corporate Bond Index excludes bonds with sinking fund provisions, whereas the Bloomberg Barclays US Corporate Bond Index includes them. The FTSE Global Government Bond Index excludes callable and convertible bonds, whereas the Citigroup World Government Bond Index includes them in some countries.[31] Additionally, the assumptions concerning the reinvestment of coupon income are not consistent across indexes because some reinvest at a short-term rate and others do not. The investor and sponsor should understand the risk and return characteristics of the particular index they choose.

A third potential problem with using bond indexes as benchmarks is that index composition tends to change frequently. Although equity indexes are often reconstituted or rebalanced quarterly or annually, bond indexes are usually recreated monthly. The characteristics of outstanding bonds are continually changing as maturities change, issuers sell new bonds, and issuers call in others. For example, for the year ending July 2011, the Bloomberg Barclays US Aggregate Bond Index had more than a third of its value reconstituted in response to deletion and addition of issues. As the index composition changes, the index's risk can also change. For example, if the US government decreases its deficit spending, it would issue less debt, as it did in the 1990s. A shift in index weighting from government to corporate bonds would result in greater index risk. Fixed-income portfolio managers must track the effect of new issuance on sector weights and use cash flows to track such changes. Mitigating these changes is the fact that managed portfolios tend to be affected by maturities, issuer calls, changes in issuance among sectors, and so on, in the same direction and magnitude as indexes are. Nevertheless, investors and sponsors benchmarking to a bond index need to be aware of the possibility of changes in index composition. The calculation of a portfolio's excess returns relative to a bond index may not be reliable over time.

A fourth problem is what Siegel (2003) referred to as the "bums" problem. This problem arises because capitalization-weighted bond indexes give more weight to issuers that borrow the most (the "bums"). The bums in an index may be more likely to be downgraded in the future and experience lower returns. The bums problem is applicable to corporate as well as government issuers. With global bond indexes, the countries that go the most into debt have the most weight. For example, when launched in 1999, the EMBI Global had a 66% exposure to Latin American countries. Credit risk is increasingly a concern for developed country bonds as well, given the recent difficulties in the European Union.

An index heavily weighted by bums will likely have increased risk compared with an equally weighted index. Investors tracking such an index would be required to hold a riskier portfolio than they might otherwise desire, and the index and portfolio are

31 Amenc, Goltz, and Tang (2011, p. 46). Drenovak, Uroševic, and Jelic (2012) found that apparently similar European bond indexes have significantly different performance.

unlikely to be mean–variance efficient. A potential solution to this weighting problem is for the investor to track bond indexes that limit the weights of component securities from particular issuers. For example, JP Morgan provides diversified versions of its emerging market bond indexes, in which each country's representation is capped at 10%. However, such an index is more likely to contain smaller-value securities that are difficult to trade without incurring high transaction costs.

Another potential solution to the bums problem is to invest in bond indexes that limit the weights of component securities (e.g., diversified versions of JP Morgan emerging bond indexes), equal-weighted indexes (e.g., Dow Jones Equal Weight U.S. Issued Corporate Bond Index), GDP-weighted indexes (e.g., PIMCO Global Advantage Government Bond Index), fundamental-weighted indexes (e.g., the FTSE RAFI Sovereign Emerging Markets Local Currency Bond Index), or indexes with other weighting systems.[32] Such weighting schemes, however, may not solve the bums problem entirely, may contain bonds that are less liquid, or may be constructed using subjective inclusion criteria. Moreover, the arguments supporting the use of capitalization weighting for equity indexes also pertain here: They are objective, market-based measures of total security value. Market-value-weighted indexes are the only type of index that all investors could theoretically hold and the index type most commonly used as benchmarks. Indeed, it could be argued that if the "bums" really are bums, their prospects will be reflected in their market value and a capitalization-weighted index would not be overly influenced by them.

A fifth problem with using bond indexes as benchmarks is that asset owners and investors may be unable to find a bond index with risk characteristics that match their desired exposure. Because bonds differ in terms of credit rating, duration, prepayment risk, and other characteristics, a bond index will have a unique exposure that is unlikely to exactly match that desired for the portfolio. The risk characteristics of a bond index will reflect the bond issuers' preferences, which are not necessarily the same as those of investors. For example, if long-term interest rates are at historical lows, then many issuers will finance at the long end of the yield curve and the index will be dominated by these maturities.[33] For an investor desiring shorter durations, the bond index would not serve as a suitable benchmark. Asset owner requirements are most likely determined by the duration of their liabilities; the duration of public benchmarks are unlikely to match this duration. A portfolio's risk objectives depend on its risk tolerance and are not necessarily satisfied by an index.

Most investors using bond indexes as benchmarks will probably want to use composites of indexes and sub-indexes that best reflect their portfolios' targets for those sectors and exposures. In general, the bond indexes chosen to create a benchmark should align with the portfolio's sector and interest rate exposures, credit risk, currency risk, inflation risk, and other risk factors.[34] There are many specialized bond indexes that allow for a closer match to the portfolio. For example, a portfolio might have a target of 10% inflation-linked and 10% high-yield bonds, which would be measured against proportional positions in inflation-linked and high-yield indexes. Note that the 10% index proportions would typically be based on market values, not some alternative metric, such as company sales. The predominance of market value weighting here and elsewhere suggests that this objective measure is the most appropriate for use in benchmarks.

---

32 See Amenc, Goltz, and Tang (2011, pp. 51–52) for a discussion of various bond index weighting schemes.

33 Mizrach and Neely (2006) provided an example of index durations changing through time because of issuers' preferences. The US Treasury stopped issuing 30-year bonds in 2001 but started selling them again in 2006.

34 See Upbin (2012) for several examples of how bond sector indexes would be used to create a portfolio benchmark.

To evaluate bond indexes more generally as benchmarks, we again use the criteria from Bailey and Tierney (1998). Most bond indexes are unambiguous, measurable, and specified in advance. They are often not investable, however, given the large universe, heterogeneity, and illiquid nature of bonds. They may be inappropriate because a manager's style will often diverge from that of an index, whose composition can also change substantially over time. Lastly, they would likely not be reflective of current investment opinions or accountable if they contain unfamiliar securities. For example, many high-yield indexes contain emerging market securities, with which a US manager is unlikely to be familiar.[35]

In sum, although bond indexes fulfill traditional index roles, such as asset allocation proxies, gauges of market sentiment, and the basis for investment vehicles, the typical bond index is unlikely to be the optimal benchmark for an investor. We next examine the use of custom benchmarks, which are more likely to satisfy the requirements for a valid benchmark.

EXAMPLE 10

Bond Indexes

1 Which of the following statements is *most* accurate in the context of bond indexes?

  A Limiting the weight on "bums" may result in less liquid indexes.

  B Full replication is typically used by investors tracking bond indexes.

  C Indexes from different providers are similar because bonds are homogeneous.

2 Which of the following criteria for valid benchmarks is generally *not* met by most bond indexes?

  A Investable

  B Measurable

  C Unambiguous

Solution to 1:

A is correct. The bums problem refers to the fact that capitalization-weighted bond indexes can give more weight to issuers that borrow the most and thus may tend to have more default risk. A solution to this problem is to cap the weight in any one issue; however, doing so may result in more investment in smaller, less liquid issues. B is incorrect because full replication is not usually used for tracking bond indexes, because many issues are illiquid and it would be difficult to take a position in them. C is incorrect because indexes from different providers are often dissimilar, because bonds are heterogeneous.

Solution to 2:

A is correct. Bond indexes are often not investable because they typically consist of a large number of diverse, potentially illiquid bonds. Most bond indexes are unambiguous and measurable.

35 Levine, Drucker, and Rosenthal (2010).

6 CUSTOM BENCHMARKS

Previously, we noted that market indexes fulfilled several roles for investors: asset allocation proxies, investment management mandates, gauges of market sentiment, bases for investment vehicles, performance benchmarks, and use in portfolio analysis. In these last two roles, however, market indexes may not perform well if the portfolio has an investment process and holdings that differ from those of the index, so a custom benchmark may be considered.

6.1 Custom Benchmarks Explained in Terms of Portfolio Decomposition

The need for custom benchmarks can be explained through a decomposition of a manager's portfolio return (P) in terms of an appropriate benchmark (B) and the active management return (A):

$$P = B + A$$

Next, add and subtract the market index return (M) from the right-hand side of the equation:

$$P = M + (B - M) + A$$

The manager's investment style (S) is the difference between the benchmark return and the market index ($B - M$), which results in:

$$P = M + S + A$$

This final equation states that a manager's portfolio return (P) is a result of the market index return (M), style (S), and active management return (A).

Comparing the equations, we can see that a market index will serve as a valid benchmark if the benchmark is equal to the market index return ($B = M$)—that is, the manager's style return is equal to zero ($S = 0$). In this case, the portfolio return will equal the market index plus active return: $P = M + A$. This decomposition is valid when the manager pursues an enhanced indexing strategy or indexes. Kuenzi (2003) referred to this strategy as a published benchmark–centered discipline, which is often used by pension fund managers. The manager's primary goal in this case is to limit deviations from an index, with excess returns being a secondary goal.

Other managers have a primary goal of generating excess returns by exploiting market anomalies, taking risks outside an index, or using their competitive advantages. The market index will contain securities that the manager will not hold, and for those securities common to both, the manager's weights will not be neutral to (the same as) the benchmark's weights. Kuenzi (2003) referred to these strategies as manager strategy disciplines. In this case, the market index return will not equal the benchmark's return ($M \neq B$) and the manager's style return will be nonzero ($S \neq 0$). The portfolio return will equal the market index plus the style and active return: $P = M + S + A$.

In practice, most market indexes do not completely capture a manager's style. As a result, using a market index without the style return to describe a manager's return is poor practice because the measurement of the active return will be confounded by the inability of the market index to encompass the manager's style. In this case, the measured active return will reflect both the manager's style and the true active management return. A manager should not receive credit for investing in a particular style when that style is in favor, nor should she be penalized when that style is out of favor. If a sponsor hires a value manager to invest a portion of the fund according to that style, the manager should expect to be judged against that style. If a market index is used as a benchmark and does not capture the manager's style, then all subsequent portfolio manager evaluation and analysis will be invalid. For example, a manager investing in defensive stocks will underperform during bull markets and outperform during bear markets relative to a broad market index. The use of the market index will obscure the manager's skill during certain measurement periods.

Fundamentally, the design and purposes of market indexes and benchmarks are quite different. Whereas market indexes are useful for the purposes of market participants and the general public, they are usually less suitable for the internal purposes of measuring manager performance. A specific investment sponsor and manager will want a benchmark that accurately captures that manager's style and fulfills the criteria for a valid benchmark, which is best achieved by constructing a custom benchmark for the manager. A custom benchmark is also referred to as the normal or strategy portfolio because it represents the securities from which the manager normally chooses and reflects the sponsor's strategic (long-term) intention for the portfolio.

Most active managers have an investment philosophy that makes them focus on particular types of securities. The manager uses a research process to uncover the most attractive securities. A benchmark based on the pool of securities that the manager researches is referred to as a **custom security-based benchmark**. This custom benchmark selects securities from the manager's favorite "fishing holes."[36] The construction of a custom security-based benchmark requires a complete audit of the manager's investment processes and is based on a quantitative and qualitative assessment of the manager's investment style. The custom benchmark will reflect the securities and weighting that the manager normally chooses. An assessment of the manager's value added will be reflected in his performance relative to the custom benchmark. It will usually provide a more accurate and fair appraisal of the manager's performance than a market index.

6.2 Custom Benchmark Construction

In building a custom benchmark, three parties could be primarily responsible: the asset owner, a consultant or actuary hired by the asset owner, or the manager. Usually, a benchmark portfolio's design should largely be driven by the asset owner's liabilities.

By constructing the benchmark, the management firm gains insight into its investment process. In defining the investment objective more clearly, the manager can eliminate vague policies and inefficient procedures. With the manager as the primary driver of the benchmark, the manager is also more likely to agree to be held accountable to it. Lastly, with the manager creating the benchmark, there will be no need for multiple benchmarks created by multiple sponsors.

There is often a concern on the part of sponsors that the manager will build a "slow rabbit" benchmark that he can easily outperform. The manager should not typically have an incentive to build a benchmark of dissimilar securities, however, because his deviation from the benchmark would be expected to increase, resulting in increased tracking error (standard deviation of the active return). If a misfit benchmark is used, the possible increase in excess return would likely be offset by increased tracking error. If the information ratio (active return divided by tracking error) is used to evaluate the manager, it will be more difficult to find consistency in the manager's performance. The idea that using an inappropriate benchmark leads to unreliable information ratios is substantiated by the fact that information ratios differ by manager style.[37]

Although there is no single method that should be used to construct a custom benchmark, the following are the general steps, discussed in more detail later:[38]

- Identify the major features of the manager's investment process.

36 This analogy is from Bailey, Richards, and Tierney (1988, p. 26).
37 Bailey and Tierney (1993).
38 Bailey, Richards, and Tierney (1988).

- Select securities appropriate for the manager's investment process.
- Develop the security weighting for the benchmark and include a cash position.
- Review the preliminary benchmark portfolio and make modifications as appropriate.
- Rebalance the benchmark on a periodic basis.
- Prepare detailed documentation of all the foregoing steps prior to implementation.

6.2.1 *Identifying the Investment Process*

The process of identifying the manager's investment process and style relies on historical return data. Past data may be influenced, however, by active bets the manager has made outside her usual security universe. Although a long time span of data will reveal the manager's true investment process, the historical data may not be from a sufficiently long period. Therefore, qualitative factors, such as discussions with the manager and how the manager presents his style to potential clients in promotional literature, should also be used in identifying the investment process. The aim in benchmark construction is to make the benchmark forward looking and to base it on the investor's current investment process. It will be an *ex ante* assessment of the portfolio and not rely solely on past (*ex post*) holdings, as in other benchmark construction methods, such as returns-based analysis. This feature is particularly important for managers whose styles change over time.

6.2.2 *Security Selection*

Once the investment process is identified, the benchmark will be created with securities consistent with the manager's style using such criteria as market capitalization, P/E, and industry and market risk exposures. The values used in quantitative screens should be examined for relevancy by checking whether they provide benchmark securities consistent with the manager's investment process. A limitation of using quantitative screens is that they may not encompass such factors as a stock's management quality. Furthermore, some managers have security screens that are more conceptually than quantitatively based. Therefore, qualitative considerations, such as discussions with the manager's decision makers, should also be used in security selection.

The initial universe of securities chosen should be as inclusive as possible. However, securities for which there are insufficient data, that are not permissible (e.g., tobacco stocks excluded by a social screen), or of which the manager does not have an opinion should be deleted from the benchmark.

6.2.3 *Determining Security Weighting*

Instead of using the weighting from externally provided market indexes, a custom security-based benchmark weights securities and cash to reflect the manager's portfolio and is not necessarily capitalization weighted. The security weighting will be based on the manager's investment process and any client restrictions on holding particular securities. The manager may also have preferences for sector and country weighting that will be expressed in the custom benchmark.

It is important for the benchmark weights to reflect the manager's normal sector and country positions because, for example, a weight greater than the benchmark's could be interpreted as an overweight position during attribution analysis when in fact it reflects a misspecified benchmark that has incorrectly underweighted that sector or country. With the manager's normal positions correctly specified in the benchmark, her active bets can be clearly identified.

There is a temptation for sponsors to exclude cash from the benchmark, under the rationale that managers should not be compensated for cash allocations. Doing so, however, would misstate the manager's strategy and introduce noise into performance evaluation because a cash return has zero correlation with risky assets. Excluding cash would increase tracking error, making it more difficult to reliably evaluate the manager. For example, in a bear market, an equity manager would likely outperform a cashless benchmark even though he may deserve no credit for doing so.[39]

6.2.4 *Reviewing the Preliminary Benchmark*

After the preliminary benchmark is created, a manager will make final modifications to it. The manager is given time to review the benchmark before it is used to ensure that the benchmark is specified in advance. Often in this final review of the benchmark, much is learned about the manager's process. One of the benefits of creating a custom benchmark is that the types of securities and risks the manager takes will be described, which reminds both the sponsor and the manager of the strategy's exposures and the fact that the manager will be judged against the benchmark. If one party is comfortable with the strategy, changes to it should be considered. The importance of benchmark construction is highlighted by the fact that an inappropriate benchmark would provide the sponsor with a misleading view of the strategy's exposures.

6.2.5 *Rebalancing the Benchmark*

A custom benchmark evolves and is rebalanced over time because benchmark securities change and the manager's investment philosophy and universe of potential securities change. Benchmark composition changes through time in response to stock buybacks, mergers, liquidations, and other corporate events. Cash from dividends, coupon income, and other distributions have to be reinvested so that the benchmark stays true to the manager's asset allocation. Security characteristics also change; for example, a growth stock may become a value stock if the company falls on hard times. As a result, the security universe is rescreened to determine whether there are securities to add to or delete from the benchmark.

Many strategy custom benchmarks are combinations of published indexes. A global balanced strategy including both equites and bonds might well be represented by a mix of 50% MSCI World Index and 50% JP Morgan Global Government Bond Index. Although such a benchmark would be initially fixed at 50% global equities, 50% global bonds, by the end of any measurement period, market movements will have naturally changed these percentages. Asset owners will need to determine if these strategic allocations are to be reset (rebalanced) to 50%/50%—and if so, how often (daily, weekly, monthly, quarterly)—or allowed to float. The differences in resultant benchmark returns can be significant.

The return on the custom benchmark should be adjusted for the transaction costs incurred by rebalancing and reconstitution, although these costs are often ignored.

The rebalanced benchmark is submitted to the management firm for approval before its use so that the benchmark is properly specified in advance. The rebalancing of the benchmark ensures that it remains appropriate and reflective of the manager's investment opinions. The construction and maintenance of a benchmark will, however, require substantial resources, including data on fundamental security characteristics and computer resources, as well as a system for security weighting. The benchmark can be periodically tested for quality using analysis on return correlations, tracking error, risk factor sensitivities, turnover, weighting, and coverage, as discussed in Section 3.4.

6.2.6 *Advantages and Disadvantages of Custom Benchmarks*

The advantage of a properly constructed custom benchmark is that it fulfills all the benchmark validity criteria from Bailey and Tierney (1998). It is thus considered by many to be the most appropriate benchmark for evaluating a manager. Because

39 Bailey (1991) provided a comprehensive argument for including cash in a benchmark.

it changes as the manager's philosophy changes, it assists managers and sponsors in monitoring investment processes and risk. It allows the sponsor to determine a manager's current style without ambiguity so that the most efficient combination of managers that satisfies the fund's investment objectives can be chosen. The benchmark provides information as to which sectors and exposures a manager has so that gaps and overlaps in the fund's aggregate asset allocation relative to a targeted asset class allocation can be identified. A properly constructed benchmark also facilitates the determination of performance-based manager compensation.

The major disadvantage of custom benchmarks is that they are costly to construct and maintain because of the time and effort required to collect and analyze data. Furthermore, the manager must be a willing participant in the process because of the information required. Because they often are not based on published indexes, custom benchmarks may also lack transparency. Despite their cost, investors, especially large institutions, will typically find that custom benchmarks are worth the investment, given the amount of capital at stake.

6.2.7 *Tradeoffs in Custom Benchmark Inclusiveness*

Compared with peer universes, market indexes, and style indexes, a custom benchmark provides the highest hurdle for a manager wishing to demonstrate excess returns because it closely matches the manager's usual investment process. Strictly speaking, the custom benchmark is the ideal evaluation tool because it so closely mimics the manager's style.

Constructing a custom benchmark requires a delicate balance. The benchmark must reflect the securities from which the manager normally chooses, but it should not subsume the manager's active decisions. The manager's active return will result from bets on particular securities and their weighting. The manager may exclude some benchmark securities and may even temporarily include non-benchmark securities. Some benchmark securities may be overweighted and others underweighted. Active bets made by the manager often reflect proprietary trading strategies and result in the manager's added value. These bets should thus not be included in the benchmark.

During benchmark creation and rebalancing, the benchmark creator must make judgment calls regarding the benchmark's inclusiveness. At one extreme, the custom benchmark would always exactly match the portfolio. The closer the custom benchmark matches the manager's portfolio, however, the more incentive the manager has to take bets outside it to generate alpha, the return in excess of that expected given its risk. This incentive creates problems for a sponsor that wants to ensure that the fund satisfies its long-term strategic objectives and control its risk exposures. From the manager's perspective, a closer match creates a problem, making it more difficult to demonstrate skill and more likely that the sponsor would terminate their relationship.

Alternatively, instead of being a close match, the benchmark could be broader and more generic. A more generic benchmark would be more likely apply to several managers, thus allowing comparisons to the same benchmark. It would also allow for more investment flexibility for the manager. However, a more generic benchmark runs the risk of not adequately capturing a manager's style. It increases the "signal-to-noise" ratio and makes it harder to determine whether the manager added value on a statistically significant basis.

EXAMPLE 11

Custom Benchmarks

1 In which of the following scenarios is a custom benchmark for an equity manager *most* appropriate?

A The fund manager is an active stock picker.

B The stocks in the existing index do not appropriately cover the targeted asset class.

C The fund manager is unable to find a benchmark to explain his or her inferior performance.

2 The disadvantage of a custom benchmark is that it:

A is too complex to construct.

B cannot be used for return attribution.

C is expensive to construct and implement relative to the alternatives.

3 Which of the following statements on the characteristics of a properly constructed custom benchmark is *most* accurate? Such benchmarks are:

A measurable and appropriate.

B accountable but not unambiguous.

C specified in advance but not reflective of current investment opinions.

Solution to 1:

B is correct. The scenario in A does not exclude the selection of an existing index, and the scenario in C is an inappropriate (and potentially unethical) reason to choose a benchmark.

Solution to 2:

C is correct. A is incorrect; if they were too complex to construct, no such benchmarks would exist. B is incorrect because return attribution can be made relative to a custom universe of stocks.

Solution to 3:

A is correct. Custom benchmarks meet all validity criteria, so B and C are incorrect.

OTHER BENCHMARKS

7

The following sections introduce types of benchmarks besides custom benchmarks and those based on peer groups, market indexes, and style indexes.

7.1 Hedge Fund Benchmarks

Hedge funds are more complex than traditional funds in part because of their ability to pursue nonconventional strategies. They do not represent an asset class, such as equities or fixed income; rather, they reflect a manager's strategy for exploiting market inefficiencies. Hedge funds may have an unlimited investment universe, vary substantially from one to another, and can vary their strategies and asset allocations over time. These characteristics make it difficult to create a single standard against which hedge funds should be judged. Often, hedge funds have been promoted as absolute return vehicles, having an objective of providing a positive absolute return in all market environments. But this characterization is often misleading, as the record of hedge funds and a simple consideration of the objectives and risks in their investment disciplines show.[40]

40 The classic critique is a study by Waring and Siegel (2006).

Hedge fund benchmarks are also difficult to create because they can use higher leverage, sell assets short, take positions in derivatives, and be opportunistic in choice of strategy. Some hedge funds lever 20 times their capital base, which increases their expected return and risk. Short positions and derivatives used in long–short strategies can increase return or reduce risk. A manager's use of style, leverage, short positions, and derivatives may change over time, in which case the original benchmark will no longer be appropriate. As such, it will be more difficult to choose an appropriate benchmark that is consistent over time.

Hedge funds also typically lack transparency, are difficult to monitor, and are illiquid. Although a proprietary strategy and long-term focus can result in higher returns, evaluating performance also becomes more difficult. In contrast, benchmark determination for a traditional asset manager is relatively straightforward. From this discussion, it should be obvious that broad market indexes are inappropriate hedge fund benchmarks.

The risk-free rate (e.g., Libor) plus a spread (e.g., 3%–6%) is sometimes advocated as a hedge fund benchmark. The argument for using the risk-free rate is that investors desire a positive return and that arbitrage strategies are risk free, with the spread reflecting the active management return and management costs. Most funds, however—even those that target market-neutral strategies—are not completely free of systematic risk. Furthermore, many funds use leverage, which could magnify systematic risk. In this case, the spread should be adjusted upward.

Broad market indexes and the risk-free rate will be weakly correlated or uncorrelated with hedge fund returns, thus failing a benchmark quality test of Bailey (1992b) and Bailey, Richards, and Tierney (2007), whereby portfolio and benchmark factor sensitivities should be similar. Because of the shortcomings of broad market indexes and the risk-free rate, hedge fund manager universes from such providers as CSFB/Tremont are often used as hedge fund benchmarks. Comparing hedge fund managers with other managers is consistent with the fact that they pursue nonconventional strategies and are thus not comparable against a basket of traditional assets. Investors also use manager universes to screen the performance of prospective hedge fund manager hires.

As previously discussed, however, manager universes (peer groups) have serious shortcomings as benchmarks. In terms of the validity criteria, we determined that they fully satisfy only the measurability criteria.

Manager universes are also used to construct hedge fund indexes. These indexes report an average return for various categories of hedge funds. Hedge fund indexes are susceptible to survivorship bias, which results in misrepresentation of hedge fund performance.[41] When an index creator forms an index, sometimes the only companies included are those in existence (i.e., the survivors) when the index is created. Another form of survivorship bias is sometimes referred to as self-reporting bias or self-selection bias. Hedge funds voluntarily report to index providers. If managers decide to stop reporting their returns because of poor performance or because they exit the industry, their entire history of returns may be dropped from a database. In such cases, only successful funds will remain in the database, with the index return thus artificially overstated. Alternatively, however, large, successful funds may stop reporting because they cannot accept additional capital and are no longer motivated to make the effort to report results. In such cases, fund returns will be biased downward. As to which bias would prevail, there probably are more weak performers of all sizes than there are large, outstanding performers that are refusing additional capital. Therefore, it is likely that, in net terms, the self-reporting bias results in upwardly biased returns as well as downwardly biased risk.

41 Lhabitant (2004) Chapter 5 and Yau, Schneeweis, Robinson, and Weiss (2007) provide a discussion of hedge fund benchmark biases, upon which much of this discussion is based.

Another bias exists when additional managers' returns are added to an index. The index provider may add the entire return history of such managers to the index. The resulting bias is referred to as backfill bias, also called "inclusion bias" or "instant history bias." Consider a manager that launches several hedge funds. After an incubation period, some funds will be successful and others not. The manager could close the unsuccessful funds and advertise the success of the others by reporting only the successful funds' returns to an index. When the index provider adds the fund, the manager's historical record of attractive returns may be added to the index. The index provider may also have its own criteria for adding new funds (e.g., minimum assets under management) that are more likely to be met by successful funds. The combination of the manager's option to report and index provider criteria results in an upward bias in returns. Furthermore, some of the more successful hedge funds that report will be closed to new investors, thus potentially overstating the performance a sponsor could achieve in this asset class.

In addition to managers having discretion in reporting, self-reported hedge fund data are typically not confirmed by index providers and a fund's reported net asset value may be a managed value. Even if the manager has no intention to misreport the data, hedge funds hold illiquid assets that require some subjectivity in pricing. If the previous period's price is used as the current price or an appraisal is used, then the data will be smoothed. The presence of stale pricing will result in downward-biased standard deviations and temporal instability in correlations, with hedge funds potentially given larger portfolio allocations than are appropriate. The presence of stale pricing results in what is sometimes referred to as infrequent pricing or illiquidity bias.

Another potential problem with hedge fund indexes is their comparability. Some indexes contain a large number of funds and are more representative than others. Providers construct indexes using a variety of methodologies, so indexes differ from one provider to the next, even if they have the same style. For example, both interest rate arbitrage and forward yield curve arbitrage funds could be classified as fixed-income arbitrage funds, yet they have very different strategies and performance. Providers may also change the constituent funds, so the same index is not consistent from one period to the next. Survivorship and other biases will also vary by hedge fund style, creating problems in comparing the returns across various style indexes.

In addition to provider methods creating style comparability issues, the reporting of the funds creates additional difficulties because managers may intentionally misrepresent or vary their styles over time to boost relative or absolute performance. As an example of the latter, in periods when the merger market is dry, merger arbitrage managers may switch styles to obtain greater opportunities. Thus, investors may find that indexes do not serve as valid benchmarks because they do not match the manager's style. Indexes may have very different performance even if their stated styles are the same.

Another concern with hedge fund indexes is their weighting. Most traditional assets have indexes that are cap weighted, reflecting the economic importance of the underlying securities. In the case of hedge funds, however, the size of the underlying funds reflects the amount of money entrusted to the manager and nothing more. Consequently, the size of a hedge fund is not a capitalization in the traditional sense. Because of this fact, many hedge fund benchmarks are equally weighted, thereby reflecting the return of the average hedge fund. However, cap weighting reflects the investment availability of the underlying benchmark positions and the future value of a dollar invested. The fact that most investors' primary concern is how their average dollars would grow suggests that cap weighting is appropriate. In addition, most investments are compared against cap-weighted indexes and benchmarks, and consistency would require that hedge fund indexes be cap weighted too. Furthermore, equally weighted indexes are not easily investable because a tracking portfolio must be rebalanced often to maintain equal weighting. To maintain equal weighting, capital needs to be reallocated from winners (the best-performing hedge funds) to losers. Because hedge fund liquidity is limited, this process would be not only expensive but also difficult. On balance, capitalization weighting makes the most sense.

In sum, the record of hedge fund performance is distorted by the manager's option to report, and the data from index providers may present an overly rosy view of hedge fund risk and return. Used as traditional asset benchmarks, manager universes satisfy only the measurability criteria of Bailey and Tierney (1998). When applied to hedge funds, the use of manager universes becomes even more problematic because there are no regulatory requirements for hedge fund managers to report. Because of their private nature, hedge fund manager universes will not be unambiguous in composition, nor will they reflect the manager's knowledge. Thus, they cannot be specified in advance. They typically are neither investable nor appropriate, given the difficulties in classifying index style. Even the idea that hedge fund manager universe returns are measurable benchmarks is questionable, because manager fees are often privately negotiated and the investor's actual return may differ from that reflected in a hedge fund index's return series.

Because of their biases and issues in comparability and weighting, hedge fund indexes composed of manager universes will not serve as valid benchmarks. Manager universes are best used as a screen for hedge fund managers currently in existence. Factor-model-based, returns-based, and custom benchmarks are sometimes used to mimic a manager's risk exposures and construct useful benchmarks for individual funds. Bailey, Richards, and Tierney (2007) suggested creating separate benchmarks for a manager's long and short positions using a returns-based or custom benchmark process. The benchmarks for the long and short positions could then be combined in their respective proportions to create the manager's benchmark.

We next examine liability-based benchmarks, which shift the focus away from the manager's assets to create the benchmark.

7.2 Liability Benchmarks

So far, our focus has been asset-based benchmarks, in which the manager's performance is compared with the performance of a collection of assets. We now examine liability-based benchmarks, which focus on the asset's purpose—that is, the cash flows that the asset must generate obtain. Bernstein (2000, p. 5) made an argument for liability-based benchmarks in general. He stated that manager evaluation should be based on the question, "How much is this organization contributing to a return in excess of our required return, and at what level of volatility?" Bernstein believes these benchmarks are preferable to using cap-weighted security indexes, which are overweighted by the hot performers and for which the performance target is not defined quantitatively *a priori*. Liability-based benchmarks are superior because the manager knows the standard *ex ante* (e.g., a minimum return of 5%). For asset-based benchmarks, the manager is implicitly compared with a collection of the best-performing securities or managers. The users of asset-based benchmarks often assume that they can identify managers capable of consistently achieving an excess return, which is highly unlikely when a market is efficient.

In practice, liability-based benchmarks are used most frequently when the assets are required to pay a specific future liability (e.g., as in a defined benefit pension plan). Here, by necessity, the emphasis must be on the liabilities because a portfolio could outperform a market index but still fail to meet its liabilities. Furthermore, a market-value-weighted index would likely be an inappropriate benchmark because the liability often has a targeted asset allocation and risk exposures that are different from the index. For example, for the fixed-income portion of the benchmark, cap-weighted indexes are typically not suitable because their duration is usually shorter than that of most plans' liabilities. Also, if corporate bonds dominate the short end of the yield curve, the benchmark may contain more credit risk than the plan desires. Furthermore, as previously discussed, bond indexes are often not investable and are rebalanced frequently over time. As an alternative, a portfolio of individual bonds could be used as the benchmark, which should be well diversified to minimize idiosyncratic risk. Another alternative for the fixed-income portion of the liability-based benchmark has been developed recently: liability-driven investment (LDI) indexes. For example, in 2012, the Barclays–Russell LDI Index Series (now Bloomberg Barclays) was launched; these indexes were constructed to be investable. They may not describe a plan's particular liability structure as accurately as a portfolio constructed specifically for the plan, however.

To best determine how the entire plan asset allocation and liability-based benchmark should be constructed, the manager first needs to obtain the plan's projected future cash outflows from the plan trustee or actuary. Each plan will have its own unique characteristics, such as the availability of lump-sum payouts to retirees.

For example, in a pension, the manager should have knowledge of the following plan features:

- average number of years to retirement in the workforce;
- the percentage of the workforce that is retired;
- average participant life expectancy;
- whether the benefits are indexed to inflation;
- whether the plan offers an early retirement option;
- whether the sponsor has the ability to increase its plan contributions (e.g., whether the sponsor is profitable and diversified);
- the correlation between plan assets and the sponsoring company's operating assets (a lower correlation is desired so that the sponsor can make contributions when the plan requires funds); and
- whether the plan is a going concern (e.g., plans will eventually terminate if the sponsor has exited its business).

These characteristics influence the composition of the pension plan portfolio and hence its liability-based benchmark.

The primary goal of a pension plan is to generate a return that will satisfy the liabilities and minimize the risk of not meeting them. The two goals are distinct; for example, a plan's assets may generate a high return, but if the plan asset value is volatile and falls short of that required in a given year, the liabilities will not be met.

Historically, pension funds took very little gap risk, the risk that the assets move differently from the liabilities. The funds invested primarily in annuities and bonds successfully satisfied the liabilities. However, regulatory changes and benefits that were indexed with inflation caused the funds to change their asset allocations. More recently, Meder and Staub (2013) recognized that some plan liabilities grow as the economy grows and should be mimicked with equities. For example, if the economy and a company grow, the company's wage expenses will grow and so will the company's future liability. A failure to identify this liability risk could lead to a portfolio whose assets are insufficient to meet liabilities.

To minimize the risk that plan assets move differently from the liabilities, Meder and Staub (2013) proposed that the plan be constructed with liability-mimicking assets. Although traditionally, many plans focused only on interest rate risk, Meder and Staub proposed decomposing the risk of plan liabilities into interest rate risk, inflation risk, and risk from economic growth. In this liability-relative approach, plan assets are chosen for their ability to mimic the liability so that they are highly correlated. In contrast, when a portfolio is constructed using an asset-only approach, the emphasis is on portfolio efficiency and assets that have low correlations. The liability-relative approach takes a long-term view of the liabilities and does not focus solely on changes in fixed-income values arising from changes in interest rates. A decomposition of the liability risk exposure will help the portfolio manager better understand pension liabilities.

The pension obligation is first separated into that from inactive (no longer working) and active participants. The future benefits for inactive participants are fixed unless the benefits are indexed to inflation, so the relevant benchmark is a portfolio of bonds paying a nominal amount. If the benefits are indexed to inflation, the relevant benchmark is an inflation-indexed (real return) bond portfolio that satisfies the promised payments.

The obligations to active participants (current employees) can be separated into the amounts owed for past and future service. The obligations for past service are matched with nominal and inflation-indexed bonds, depending on whether they are fixed. Ongoing funds will have obligations from future benefits, which are from future wages to be earned, service to be rendered, and new plan entrants. The first component will grow with the economy and inflation prior to the retirement date. It is hedged with nominal bonds, inflation-indexed bonds, and equities. The second component reflects benefits that have not yet been earned but will be in the future. Because it is uncertain, however, this component is not usually modeled in the benchmark. The third component is also uncertain and not modeled. Additionally, there will be liability noise from non-market exposures, such as that owing to model uncertainty, which is unpredictable and cannot be hedged.

In sum, the best portfolio for a pension plan from an asset–liability management perspective is typically one consisting of nominal bonds, real return bonds, and common shares. The asset allocation is determined by the proportion of accrued versus future obligations, whether the benefits are inflation indexed, and whether the plan is growing. A younger workforce means that more is allocated to equities. Greater inflation indexing of the benefits would imply more inflation-indexed bonds. If the fund's managers outperform the benchmark constructed according to these principles, it will facilitate the pension obligations being met. Risk and noise that cannot be modeled in the benchmark may require future sponsor contributions. The goal for the pension plan is to outperform the benchmark while minimizing the risk of not meeting the obligations. A manager's skill will be required to avoid credit downgrades and defaults and select equity positions wisely. The manager will also have to honor any plan investment restrictions; for example, some plans have social investing concerns that will have to be reflected in the portfolio and benchmark. In a liability-relative benchmark, the benchmark and portfolio are structured to satisfy the return required to meet the future obligations as well as mimic the volatility of the liabilities.

EXAMPLE 12

Other Benchmarks

1 Which of the following *best* describes benchmarks for hedge funds?

- **A** The risk-free rate is widely used as a benchmark.
- **B** Manager universes are widely used as benchmarks.
- **C** Market indexes are widely used as benchmarks because indexes with returns that are highly correlated with hedge fund returns are generally available.

2 In which of the following cases is a liability-based benchmark *most* likely to be appropriate?

- **A** An income-oriented investor

B A defined benefit pension plan

C A hedge fund operating in fixed-income markets

Solution to 1:

B is correct. Choice A is incorrect because just earning the risk-free rate is not the investment objective of hedge funds. Choice C is incorrect because hedge fund returns are not in general highly correlated with market index returns.

Solution to 2:

B is correct. Such pension plans must meet the pension payments owed to retired plan participants.

7.3 Hedged Benchmarks

Many international index providers calculate and publish index returns in a specific base currency, in local currency terms, and hedged back to the base currency. In other words, they provide several different versions of returns of the same underlying index. Most international indexes use WM/Reuters London 4pm Closing spot rates (established in 1994) as standard exchange rates in the calculation of their international indexes, thus allowing fair comparison across a range of indexes and portfolios if managers choose to use the same exchange rates to value their portfolios.

Hedged benchmarks (often 100% hedged but also partially hedged, say 50%) reflect the asset owner's requirements. Asset owners may seek diversification through international assets while reducing the resulting currency risk by hedging using forward currency contracts or other currency derivative instruments. Hedged benchmarks also provide useful data that may be used in calculating detailed multi-currency attribution analysis.

Hedged calculation methods differ, one approach being to sell notional one-month forward contracts at the start of the month and then calculate a return based on the gain or loss of these contracts in conjunction with the gain or loss in the underlying securities. This method does not dynamically hedge currency positions caused by the market gains (or losses) of the underlying securities during the month and is therefore not fully hedged, leading to a residual currency element even in a supposedly 100% hedged benchmark. Some index providers offer both monthly and daily hedged variations. A daily hedged index will respond to the changing currency exposures caused by market movements of underlying assets. Typical international index data is shown in Exhibit 3.

Exhibit 3 Monthly Index Returns in Local Currency, in Base Currency, and Hedged in Base Currency

Country	Weight	Local Return	US Dollar Return	US Dollar Hedged Return
Australia	8.48%	0.81	6.28	0.56
France	23.31%	−3.03	0.53	−3.17
Japan	48.46%	2.68	6.23	2.84
Singapore	2.16%	−3.22	−1.88	−3.19
Switzerland	17.61%	0.47	3.89	0.57
Total	100%	0.67	4.32	0.72

It can also be observed from the data that interest rates in Japan must have been lower than in the United States at that time, because the hedged return is greater than the local return. In effect, within the forward currency contract, investors are borrowing yen at low interest rates and reinvesting at a higher interest rate in US dollars. Conversely, interest rates in Australia must have been higher than in the United States, because Australia's hedged return is lower than the local return. This is monthly data, and therefore interest rates must be 3% higher (0.81% – 0.56%) × 12 = 3% in Australia than in the United States. We next examine the consequences of poorly chosen benchmarks.

8 PROBLEMS IN BENCHMARK SELECTION

In this section, we address aspects of benchmark selection.

8.1 Benchmark Misspecification

As this reading has emphasized, great care has to be taken in benchmark selection to avoid misspecification. When benchmark specification errors occur, subsequent performance measurement will be incorrect. Misspecification affects both the attribution and the appraisal analyses, rendering them effectively useless.

Peer group benchmarking is particularly susceptible to selection problems. Selecting which peers to include is one problem, but also, such an approach risks sending the wrong signal to fund managers. Peer group benchmarks provide an incentive not to underperform the median fund manager and can result in herding around the median fund manager return. As a result, the fund manager's investment decisions can be biased by the structure of the benchmarks chosen.

Sometimes, benchmarks are chosen for the wrong reasons. Underperforming managers have been known to change benchmarks to improve their measured excess return, which is both inappropriate and unethical. The correct selection of a benchmark is as much a professional management issue as it is an ethical one. Research has shown that information ratios for managers of different style vary from those of the benchmark. As a result, one should be cautious in using a published information ratio and should discount any information ratio that uses an inappropriate benchmark.

The consequences of benchmark misspecification can be high for a plan sponsor because a manager's measured value-added can be undermined by benchmark error. Defining a "normal portfolio" (sometimes called "normal benchmark") to be the portfolio that most closely represents the manager's default or typical positions in her investment universe, a decomposition of the manager's return, when an inappropriate benchmark is used, is as follows (see, e.g., Gastineau, Olma, and Zielinski 2007):

Manager's "true" active return = Manager's return – Manager's normal portfolio return

Manager's "misfit" active return = Manager's normal portfolio return – Investor's benchmark return

In the decomposition, the term "investor's benchmark" refers to the benchmark the sponsor actually uses instead of the normal portfolio. The investor's benchmark is a broad market index and typically misses the manager's style. It is also referred to as the style bias.

This decomposition is useful for understanding the effect of a misspecified benchmark on performance appraisal. For example, consider a manager who invests in US value stocks. The sponsor uses the broad Russell 3000 equity index (the "investor's benchmark") to evaluate the manager. The manager's normal portfolio, however, is better represented by his universe of value stocks. The returns are as follows:

Manager return	15.0%
Russell 3000 return (investor's benchmark return)	10.0%
Normal portfolio return	18.0%

Although the manager has outperformed the investor's benchmark (15% for the manager versus 10% for the Russell 3000), the manager has not outperformed when correctly benchmarked against the normal portfolio:

- The manager's "true" active return is 15% − 18% = −3%.
- The manager's "misfit" active return is 18% − 10% = 8%.

Measuring the manager's results using the normal portfolio rather than the investor's benchmark more accurately evaluates performance. The manager's negative "true" active return indicates that the manager actually underperformed the normal portfolio. The positive "misfit" active return or style bias indicates that the manager is expected to outperform the broad market because her style (value stocks) outperformed the broad market; that is, the manager should outperform the broad market because her style has done so. When measured against the correct benchmark, we can ascertain that the manager does not demonstrate superior performance.

In addition, if an inappropriate benchmark is used, then the manager's tracking risk and resulting information ratio will also be measured incorrectly. It is difficult enough to determine whether a manager's performance resulted from luck or skill. Introducing an inappropriate benchmark makes the task that much harder. Unfortunately, in many instances, the effort that goes into benchmark selection is not always commensurate with its importance. Often, the benchmark used is a legacy of former managers, sponsors, or consultants and may no longer be appropriate.

If the manager is using a misspecified benchmark, then attribution models will misinterpret the weight difference between the portfolio and benchmark as an overweight or underweight. The excess return in each sector will also be incorrect, rendering the attribution analysis useless. The errors in the analysis are compounded over time when a multiperiod analysis is used.[42]

The benchmark choice can also influence the magnitude of the management fee. A manager's fee typically depends on the value of assets under management (AUM) and is often stated as a flat fee, such as 0.75% of the AUM. Sometimes, however, especially in the case of private equity and hedge funds, a performance fee is also paid. For example, the manager is paid 2.0% of the AUM plus 20% of any fund profits. In some cases, the performance fee is paid only for those returns in excess of some benchmark. In this case, benchmark considerations obviously arise because a lower benchmark hurdle results in more fees being paid.

Incentive performance fees are a problem for sponsors because they typically do not consider the risk the manager takes on. If a portfolio underperforms the benchmark, the manager is not penalized, but if the fund outperforms its benchmark, the fund manager collects a performance fee. The manager, therefore, has an incentive to take on greater risk relative to the benchmark. The result is that the portfolio may incur greater risk than the sponsor intended, thus creating a portfolio that is not aligned with its strategic purposes.

42 This consequence is important and goes strongly against the normal intuition or conventional wisdom that "things tend to balance out over time."

Mismatch can also occur by simply choosing an inappropriate construction methodology. For example, the shortcomings of capitalization-weighted equity indexes as benchmarks are amplified by the particular characteristics of many international and emerging markets. One concern is that these indexes are often highly concentrated, with a small number of companies that dominate the index. It thus often becomes difficult to construct a normal portfolio that represents a large universe of potential securities. Regional index weights can also be distorted by the pace of economic development, with larger weights assigned to fast-growing areas whose values can change rapidly, which would result in frequent rebalancing. An alternative is to use a GDP-weighted benchmark.

International benchmarks also require choices to be made on the currency exposure, because it introduces additional benchmark construction decisions and the potential for mismatches. Currencies affect risk and return and can be volatile over time. Currency analysis is very different from the skill set required for other asset classes. Fund managers address currency exposure by being either unhedged or hedged (partly or fully). An investor who allows currency exposure would use an unhedged benchmark. Investors seeking capital preservation may opt for currency-hedged benchmarks.

Other issues that can create a misspecified benchmark include the use of leverage and negative screening. Leverage refers to the use of borrowing and/or derivatives to increase a portfolio's risk exposure to a factor greater than its asset base. An approach to benchmarking a leveraged fund is to use a leveraged benchmark. Assuming the portfolio has leverage of 3 to 1, the benchmark needs to have 3 to 1 leverage as well. If not, the portfolio would have a tendency to outperform in bull markets and underperform in bear markets. Levered portfolios incur greater risk, so risk-adjusted returns should be measured when comparing the manager with a benchmark.

Negative screening excludes companies that are directly or partially involved in certain activities. An example of negative screens would be socially responsible screens wherein, for example, tobacco, alcohol, and gaming stocks are avoided. Any form of negative screening comes with benchmark effects and considerations. Although plan sponsor objectives are better met with negative screening, theory suggests that unscreened benchmarks have superior performance by virtue of having a wider universe. The best approach to handle negative screening is to define the benchmark constituents at the outset.

8.2 Benchmark Selection: An Example

In our discussion, we have emphasized that the benchmark should be constructed so as to be consistent with the portfolio's objectives and the manager's investment process. We now provide an example to illustrate the selection of a benchmark.

Consider a pension fund with the following sponsor characteristics, portfolio objectives, and manager investment process:

- The fund manager has full discretion to carry out the investment policy objectives, subject to federal and state laws, rules, and regulations. The fund is tax exempt.
- The sponsor is a US technology company with cyclical earnings and the majority of its sales in Japan.
- The sponsor is highly levered and has recently experienced financial difficulties.
- The sponsor has made large contributions to the fund owing to increased life expectancies and wishes to avoid future required contributions.
- Ten years ago, interest rates dropped to historic lows, and the sponsor's pension liability soared. As a result, the company switched from a defined benefit plan to a defined contribution plan for new employees to limit its future pension liabilities.

- The plan is fully funded.
- The percentage of plan participants who are now retired and receiving their pensions is 40%. The average duration of the liabilities is 12.5 years.
- The benefits are indexed to inflation. Future benefits will also increase as wages for current employees increase.
- The plan contains a lump sum provision whereby retirees can take a cash distribution at retirement in lieu of future payments. The plan will have to provide the required cash distributions at that time.
- The manager starts with the Bloomberg Barclays Global Treasury, Global Aggregate Corporate, and World Government Inflation-Linked Bond indexes as the target for bonds.
- Bonds will be used to provide liquidity and limit the risk exposure of the fund. Bonds also have a low correlation with the sponsor's cash flows.
- A total return approach will be used to meet required liquidity; however, the equity portion of the portfolio will be tilted toward dividend-paying stocks. Because the fund is tax exempt, capital gains are not favored over ordinary income.
- The preference for dividend-paying stocks is also consistent with the manager's belief that value stocks outperform growth stocks. The equity portfolio will be composed of value stocks, identified as low-price-to-book stocks.
- The manager starts with the MSCI World Index as the target for equities.
- The manager believes that the Japanese equity market is overvalued. The manager will also exclude Japanese stocks because of the sponsor's dependency on Japan.
- The manager will exclude technology stocks because of their high correlation with the sponsor's cash flows.
- The manager has full investment discretion and will be the primary benchmark creator.

One approach to benchmark construction would be to use a blend of the MSCI World Index and the Bloomberg Barclays bond indexes that reflects the intended portfolio asset allocation. Alternatively, a value style version of the MSCI World Index could be used for the equity portion. The portfolio's risk exposures could also be modeled with factor-model-based or returns-based benchmarks. These benchmark candidates, however, would contain many securities not consistent with the plan's strategic investment objectives. They may also misrepresent the manager's style.

The ideal benchmark will be a custom security-based benchmark whose assets, securities, and their weighting are chosen to mimic the liabilities. Construction of the benchmark will require a great deal of time and care. Data on securities in the indexes and the plan's characteristics and strategic investment objectives will be required.

A custom security-based benchmark would be constructed with the following attributes and features.

- The plan portfolio appears to have below-average ability to take risk because the manager prefers liquid, income-producing investments and the sponsor does not wish to make further contributions to the fund.
- The benchmark's asset allocation and security weighting should reflect the plan's liability duration of 12.5 years.
- Because pension benefits are indexed to inflation and future benefits will increase as the business grows in the future, the portfolio and benchmark will contain allocations to nominal bonds, inflation-indexed bonds, and equities.

- The Bloomberg Barclays Global Treasury, Global Aggregate Corporate, and World Government Inflation-Linked Bond indexes are the initial bond universe. From this universe, only investment-grade bonds and bonds with reasonable liquidity will be considered because of the plan's risk aversion, its need for liquidity, and the sponsor's wish to not make further contributions.
- The MSCI World Index is the initial equity universe. The equities selected for benchmark inclusion will be screened to ensure a composition of dividend-paying value stocks. Stocks with a large exposure to Japan and the technology industry will be excluded.
- The benchmark will have a cash allocation that, together with income from the investments, is sufficient to meet the liquidity required by retirement benefits due within the next year.
- The preliminary benchmark should be reviewed for consistency with the plan objectives and modified as appropriate.

Once constructed, the benchmark will be rebalanced through time to reflect changes in the investment process and ensure that it is still consistent with the fund's objectives. For example, the liability duration will decline through time, or the manager may change his views on the relative attractiveness of value and growth stocks.

SUMMARY

Although benchmark selection, construction, evaluation, and maintenance can be a demanding process, most managers are hired, retained, and often compensated based on their performance relative to a benchmark. Thus, benchmarks play key roles in the highly competitive investment management industry. This reading has provided a broad background for understanding their appropriate selection and uses. Among the points covered are the following:

- Benchmarks are a critical component of investment performance measurement and are distinct from market indexes.
- In addition to their use in performance measurement and attribution, benchmarks facilitate communication among asset owners, asset managers, and consultants; identify risk exposures; and assist with manager selection, marketing, and regulatory compliance.
- A valid benchmark will be unambiguous, investable, measurable, appropriate, reflective of current investment opinions, specified in advance, and accountable.
- A high-quality benchmark will exhibit the following: a correlation between the manager's active return and style return close to zero, a positive correlation between the style return and the difference in portfolio and market returns, a relatively low active return standard deviation, similar risk sensitivities for the benchmark and portfolio, low turnover, and investable position sizes.
- Although peer groups are simple to understand and intuitively attractive, they have serious methodological shortcomings and meet only the measurability criteria of a valid benchmark.
- Market indexes serve a variety of purposes and are valid benchmarks for many managed portfolios. They may not be valid benchmarks if they do not capture a particular manager's style.
- Style indexes may be a closer match for the manager's portfolio than market indexes and satisfy many of the benchmark validity criteria, but they may not fully describe the manager's investment process.

- Although bond indexes are usually not investable given the large universe, heterogeneity, and illiquid nature of bonds, bond portfolio managers inherently face similar challenges and often are suitably benchmarked to a bond index.
- Custom security-based benchmarks can fulfill all benchmark validity criteria but are costly to construct and maintain.
- Factor-model-based benchmarks are relatively easy to implement but are not widely used in the investment community and have other shortcomings.
- Using manager universes to form hedge fund benchmarks is problematic because managers are not required to report and, because of survivorship and other biases, the data may present an overly optimistic view of hedge fund performance.
- Liability-relative benchmarks are constructed to meet future obligations and to mimic the volatility of liabilities.
- A poorly specified benchmark will result in performance measurement, attribution, and appraisal analyses that are invalid.

REFERENCES

Amenc, Noel, Felix Goltz, and Lin Tang. 2011. *EDHEC-Risk European Index Survey 2011*. EDHEC Risk Institute (October): http://professoral.edhec.com/servlet/com.univ.collaboratif.utils.LectureFichiergw?ID_FICHIER=1328885973962.

Bailey, Jeffery V. 1991. "Why Include Cash in Your Benchmark?" *Investing* (Spring): 31–39.

Bailey, Jeffery V. 1992a. "Are Manager Universes Acceptable Benchmarks?" *Journal of Portfolio Management*, vol. 18, no. 3 (Spring):9–13.

Bailey, Jeffery V. 1992b. "Evaluating Benchmark Quality." *Financial Analysts Journal*, vol. 48, no. 3 (May/June):33–39.

Bailey, Jeffery V., and David E. Tierney. 1998. *Controlling Misfit Risk in Multiple-Manager Investment Programs*. Charlottesville, VA: Research Foundation of CFA Institute.

Bailey, Jeffery V., Thomas M. Richards, and David E. Tierney. 1988. "Benchmark Portfolios and the Manager/Plan Sponsor Relationship." *Journal of Corporate Finance*, Winter:25–32.

Bailey, Jeffery V., Thomas M. Richards, and David E. Tierney. 2007. "Evaluating Portfolio Performance." In *Managing Investment Portfolios: A Dynamic Process*, 3rd edition. Edited by John Maginn, Donald Tuttle, Dennis McLeavey, and Jerald Pinto. Hoboken, NJ: John Wiley & Sons.

Banz, Rolf W. 1981. "The Relationship between Return and Market Value of Common Stocks." *Journal of Financial Economics*, vol. 9, no. 1 (March):3–18.

Basu, S. 1977. "Investment Performance of Common Stocks in Relation to Their Price–Earnings Ratios: A Test of the Efficient Market Hypothesis." *Journal of Finance*, vol. 32, no. 3 (June):663–682.

Bauman, W. Scott, C. Mitchell Conover, and Robert E. Miller. 1998. "Growth versus Value and Large-Cap versus Small-Cap Stocks in International Markets." *Financial Analysts Journal*, vol. 54, no. 2 (March/April):75–89.

Bernstein, Peter L. 2000. "A Modest Proposal: Portfolio Management Practice for Modern Times." *Economics & Portfolio Strategy* (15 April).

Brown, Stephen, and William Goetzmann. 1997. "Mutual Fund Styles." *Journal of Financial Economics*, vol. 43, no. 3 (March):373–399.

Calverley, J.P., A.M. Meder, B.D. Singer, and R. Staub. 2007. "Capital Market Expectations." In *Managing Investment Portfolios: A Dynamic Process*, 3rd edition. Edited by John Maginn, Donald Tuttle, Dennis McLeavey, and Jerald Pinto. Hoboken, NJ: John Wiley & Sons.

Christopherson, Jon A. 2012. "The Making of a Better Benchmark." *Russell Research* (March).

Christopherson, Jon A., David R. Cariño, and Wayne E. Ferson. 2009. *Portfolio Performance Measurement and Benchmarking*. New York: McGraw–Hill.

Drenovak, M., B. Uroševic, and R. Jelic. 2012. "European Bond ETFs: Tracking Errors and the Sovereign Debt Crisis." *European Financial Management*,

Enderle, Francis J., Brad Pope, and Laurence B. Siegel. 2003. "Broad-Capitalization Indexes of the U.S. Equity Market." *Journal of Investing*, vol. 12, no. 1 (Spring):11–22.

Fama, Eugene F., and Kenneth R. French. 1992. "The Cross-Section of Expected Stock Returns." *Journal of Finance*, vol. 47, no. 2 (June):427–465.

Gastineau, Gary L., Andrew L. Olma, and Robert G. Zielinski. 2007. "Equity Portfolio Management." In *Managing Investment Portfolios: A Dynamic Process*, 3rd edition. Edited by John Maginn, Donald Tuttle, Dennis McLeavey, and Jerald Pinto. Hoboken, NJ: John Wiley & Sons.

Graham, B., and D. Dodd. 1934. *Security Analysis*. New York: McGraw–Hill.

Ibbotson, Roger G., Zhiwu Chen, Daniel Y.J. Kim, and Wendy Y. Hu. 2013. "Liquidity as an Investment Style." *Financial Analysts Journal*, vol. 69, no. 3 (May/June):30–44.

Kuenzi, David E. 2003. "Strategy Benchmarks." *Journal of Portfolio Management*, vol. 29, no. 2 (Winter):46–56.

Levine, Robert, Eve Drucker, and Steven Rosenthal. 2010. "The Problems and Challenges of High-Yield Bond Benchmarking." *Journal of Portfolio Management*, vol. 36, no. 4 (Summer):93–98.

Lhabitant, Francois-Serge. 2004. *Hedge Funds*. Hoboken NJ: John Wiley & Sons.

Mahseredjian, Vache, and Mark Friebel. 2003. "Fixed-Income Benchmarks." In *Active Index Investing: Maximizing Portfolio Performance and Minimizing Risk through Global Index Strategies*. Edited by Steven A. Schoenfeld. Hoboken, NJ: John Wiley & Sons.

Malkiel, Burton G., and Atanu Saha. 2005. "Hedge Funds: Risk and Return." *Financial Analysts Journal*, vol. 61, no. 6 (November/December):80–88.

Meder, Aaron, and Renato Staub. 2013. "Linking Pension Liabilities to Assets." *CFA Institute Level III Curriculum*. Charlottesville, VA: CFA Institute.

Mizrach, Bruce, and Christopher J. Neely. 2006. "The Transition to Electronic Communication Networks in the Secondary Treasury Market." *Federal Reserve Bank of St. Louis Review*, vol. 88, no. 6 (November/December):527–542.

Reinganum, Marc R. 1981. "Misspecification of Capital Asset Pricing: Empirical Anomalies Based on Earnings Yields and Market Values." *Journal of Financial Economics*, vol. 9, no. 1 (March):19–46.

Rosenberg, Barr, Kenneth Reid, and Ronald Lanstein. 1985. "Persuasive Evidence of Market Inefficiency." *Journal of Portfolio Management*, vol. 11, no. 3 (Spring):9–16.

Roxburgh, Charles, Susan Lund, and John Piotrowski. 2011. "Mapping Global Capital Markets." *McKinsey Global Institute* (August).

Schoenfeld, Steven A. 2002. "Perfection Impossible—Why Simply 'Good' Indexes Can Result in a More Perfect Solution." *Journal of Indexes* (2nd quarter).

Schoenfeld, Steven A. 2003. *Active Index Investing—Maximizing Portfolio Performance and Minimizing Risk through Global Index Strategies*. Hoboken, NJ: John Wiley & Sons.

Siegel, L. 2003. *Benchmarks and Investment Management*. Charlottesville, VA: Research Foundation of CFA Institute.

Surz, Ronald J. 2006. "A Fresh Look at Investment Performance Evaluation: Unifying Best Practices to Improve Timeliness and Accuracy." *Journal of Portfolio Management*, vol. 32, no. 4 (Summer):54–65.

Tierney, David E., and Jeffery V. Bailey. 1995. "Benchmark Orthogonality Properties." *Journal of Portfolio Management*, vol. 21, no. 3 (Spring):27–31.

Upbin, Brian. 2012. "Perspectives on Fixed-Income Index Design." *Journal of Indexes*, vol. 15, no. 1 (January/February):44–65.

Waring, M. Barton, and Laurence Siegel. 2006. "The Myth of the Absolute Return Investor." *Financial Analysts Journal*, vol. 62, no. 2 (March/April):14–21.

Yau, Jot, Thomas Schneeweis, Thomas Robinson, and Lisa Weiss. 2007. "Alternative Investments Portfolio Management." In *Managing Investment Portfolios: A Dynamic Process*, 3rd edition. Edited by John Maginn, Donald Tuttle, Dennis McLeavey, and Jerald Pinto. Hoboken, NJ: John Wiley & Sons.

PRACTICE PROBLEMS

1 In which scenario is the use of the S&P 500 Index as a benchmark *least appropriate*? A manager attempts to:

A exceed the performance of the S&P 500 by over- and underweighting stocks that are constituents of the index.

B match the performance of the S&P 500 with lower volatility by investing in value stocks that are constituents of the index.

C track the performance of the S&P 500 by investing in a representative sample of stocks that are constituents of the index.

2 For which of the following situations would the use of a market index be appropriate as a benchmark?

A An active manager has been given an absolute return mandate.

B An active small-cap manager seeks to replicate the performance of the S&P 500 Index.

C An active small-cap manager seeks to replicate the performance of the Russell 2000 Index.

3 The difference between the return of a portfolio and the appropriate benchmark is referred to as the manager's:

A excess return.

B return attribution.

C active return variance.

4 Which statement *best* describes features of custom security-based benchmarks?

A The factors included in the benchmark are the returns for various style indexes.

B The benchmark weights are essentially an average of the asset class indexes that best explains the portfolio's return.

C The benchmark is constructed by selecting securities and weightings consistent with the manager's investment process.

5 Absolute return benchmarks:

A are used only by market-neutral equity funds.

B may have target return based on actuarial assumptions.

C have a return that, once chosen, will not vary over the life of the portfolio.

6 Which of the following would **not** be considered a feature of a manager universe?

A Performance comparisons are made against the median manager return.

B It allows for a comparison of the risk of each manager within the universe.

C The manager universe is formed by including managers with similar investment approaches.

7 Which of the following benchmark types is *best* described as having a minimum target return?

A Returns-based benchmark

B Absolute return benchmark

C Manager universe

8 Which of the following is *least likely* to possess the desired properties of a benchmark for performance attribution?

A Manager universe (peer group)

B Absolute return benchmark

C Custom security-based benchmark

9 If a traditional small-cap investment manager uses the S&P 500 as a benchmark, which property of a valid benchmark is *most likely* to be violated?

A Measurable

B Appropriate

C Reflective of current investment opinions

10 In a month in which a manager has a particularly bad return compared to his benchmark, the manager states that the portfolio's benchmark should be replaced with another benchmark that tracks better. Replacing the benchmark would *most likely* violate which property of a valid benchmark?

A Investable

B Accountable

C Unambiguous

11 An appropriate benchmark is *most likely* to:

A reduce the usefulness of the information ratio.

B enhance the effectiveness of manager assessment.

C introduce a noise component into manager assessment.

12 The manager of a US mid-cap portfolio achieved an active return of −1.94% for the latest year. During the same period, the Russell Midcap Index returned 4.58% and the Russell 3000 Index returned 6.81%. If the manager is benchmarked to the Russell Midcap Index, the portfolio return is closest to:

A 2.64%.

B 4.87%.

C 9.45%.

13 A US large capitalization growth manager earned a total return of 6.7% (year-to-date). During the same period, the Russell 1000 Growth Index returned 8.2% and the Wilshire 5000 returned 5.3%. What are the most likely implications of the style and active management calculations?

A The US large-capitalization style was in favor, and the manager added value during the measurement period.

B The US large-capitalization style was out of favor, but the manager added value during the measurement period.

C The US large-capitalization style was in favor, but the manager did not add value during the measurement period.

14 During the month of December, a small-cap manager's portfolio return is 6.3%. During the same period, the MSCI USA Value Weighted Index return is 7.1% and the Russell 2000 small-cap index return is 5.9%. The return resulting from the portfolio manager's active management is *closest* to:

A −0.8%.

B 0.4%.

C 1.2%.

15 Which of the following characteristics is *most likely* observed in a good benchmark?

A The correlation between the manager's active return and style return should be statistically indistinguishable from zero.

B The correlation between (Portfolio return – Market index return) and the style return should be statistically indistinguishable from zero.

C The standard deviation of the manager's active return should be greater than the standard deviation of (Portfolio return – Market index return).

16 In which of the following scenarios would the use of an equity benchmark *most likely* be considered inappropriate?

A There is a low proportion of zero portfolio weights in benchmark securities.

B The intersection of portfolio and benchmark security market values is high.

C The proportion of benchmark market value used for purchasing new securities during rebalancing is 80% per quarter.

17 A portfolio manager uses a benchmark that contains a number of securities in which the manager has zero weights. The benchmark could still be considered valid if the:

A intersection of portfolio and benchmark security market value is low.

B portfolio's zero weights resulted from the manager having no opinion of the securities' value.

C portfolio and benchmark have high coverage and the zero-weight securities result from active management decisions.

18 A benchmark exhibiting low turnover:

A could be held as a passive investment.

B requires a high proportion of its market value to purchase new securities.

C is more likely composed of fixed-income rather than equity securities.

19 Of the following types of benchmarks, which would require the *least* amount of data to construct?

A Peer group

B Absolute return

C Custom security-based

20 Based on the manager universe table in Exhibit 1, which of the following statements is correct?

A The Small Cap Fund outperformed the market index.

B The median manager had a return that exceeded 16.25%.

C More than 50% of the managers in the peer group beat the market index.

Exhibit 1 Manager Universe

1 Year	Value	Percentile	Rank
Maximum	22.87		
25th Percentile	17.18		
Median Percentile	16.25		
75th Percentile	13.11		
Minimum	2.19		
No. of Portfolios	379		

(continued)

Exhibit 1 (Continued)

1 Year	Value	Percentile	Rank
Small Cap Fund	11.26	87	330
Russell 2000 Index	15.47	52	182

21 Given the statistics from the peer group analysis in Exhibit 2 and using the industry interpretation of quartile rankings, the manager of the Large Cap Fund was consistently ranked in the:

A first quartile.

B third quartile.

C interquartile range.

Exhibit 2 Peer Group Analysis

	Quarter Ending Mar 10			1 Year			3 Years			5 Years		
	Value	%Tile	Rank	Value	%Tile	Rank	Value	%Tile	Rank	Value	%Tile	Rank
Maximum	15.3			7.3			6.2			8.6		
25th Percentile	12.7			5.6			5.3			7.3		
Median Percentile	10.2			4.7			4.1			5.5		
75th Percentile	8.6			2.1			3.3			2.7		
Minimum	4.7			1.8			1.7			1.5		
No. of portfolios	234			229			215			199		
Large Cap Fund	14.5	3	7	5.9	19	44	5.7	2	5	7.4	4	7
Russell 1000 Index	10.3	49	115	4.7	50	115	4.2	51	110	5.7	53	105

22 Which of the following is a necessary condition for an index to be properly used as an *ex-post* performance benchmark?

A There is a high proportion of zero portfolio weights in the benchmark's securities.

B The correlation between the manager's active return and style return is statistically significant.

C The benchmark has investable position sizes that can be replicated by the portfolio without excessive trading costs.

23 Which of the following indexes would *best* serve as a benchmark for a large-cap growth investment management mandate?

A Equal-weighted

B Fundamental-weighted

C Float-adjusted cap-weighted

24 Which of the following uses of an asset class index *best* communicates the asset owner's expectations?

A Gauge of market sentiment

B Basis for investment vehicles

C Investment management mandates

25 Compared with market-capitalization-weighted indexes, which of the following is an advantage of price-weighted indexes?

A Simplicity of construction

B Less rebalancing required of tracking portfolios

C A more objective method of measuring the importance of index constituents

26 A disadvantage of a capitalization-weighted, float-adjusted index compared with a fundamental-weighted index is that:

A not all investors can hold a capitalization-weighted, float-adjusted, index-tracking portfolio.

B valuation screens may cause a capitalization-weighted index to be less diversified.

C a capitalization-weighted index may be overly influenced by overpriced securities.

27 During a period in which large-cap stocks outperform small-cap stocks:

A the need to rebalance an equal-weighted index should decline.

B an equal-weighted index should underperform a market-capitalization-weighted index.

C the weight to small company stocks should increase for a capitalization-weighted index.

28 Which of the following would represent an advantage of fundamental-weighted indexing over an index that is capitalization weighted?

A Fundamental-weighted indexes are proprietary.

B Overvalued issues will tend to be underweighted.

C Fundamental-weighted indexes reflect the index creator's view of valuation.

29 The free float adjustment to capitalization-weighted indexes:

A is less important in tracking emerging markets than developed economies.

B produces the only index to which all investors could realistically gain exposure.

C results in an index that holds all the constituent securities' shares outstanding.

30 Which of the following *best* characterizes a float-weighted index? A float-weighted index:

A is difficult to replicate.

B consists of securities not widely traded.

C contains only securities available to the public.

31 A difference between objective and transparent rules versus judgment in index construction is that:

A the use of judgment by the index provider prevents security prices from rising during index reconstitution.

B the use of judgment by the index provider makes it easier for investors to track an index.

C objective and transparent rules allow investors to predict the changes in index constituents that might occur.

32 Index investability may be improved by:

A increasing the amount of illiquid securities.

B decreasing the number of securities that are hard to trade.

C increasing exposure to securities whose ownership is restricted.

33 One characteristic of style factor indexes is that they:

A are market-capitalization weighted.

B are deliberately broad in their exposure to the targeted factor.

C can simultaneously include a value factor and a growth factor.

34 Which of the following is the *most accurate* description of a problem in assigning a manager to a single style?

A The techniques used to categorize a portfolio by size are diverse.

B Managers may move between categories as they perceive opportunities in changing markets.

C Fund managers report fund holdings only periodically; and if turnover is low, the reported holdings may not be representative of the manager's portfolio.

35 The *most likely* reason that an index provider would use a blended classification of stocks in the creation of an index is that a blended classification:

A decreases the turnover of the index.

B tends to increase the number of times the index needs to be reconstituted.

C allows for stocks in the index to be categorized as either 100 percent growth or 100 percent value.

36 Which statement *most accurately* explains why bond indexes are **not** as investable as equity indexes?

A There is infrequent trading as a result of the short-term investment horizon of many bond investors.

B Because of the heterogeneity of bond issues, bond indexes that appear similar can often have very different composition and performance.

C The total market capitalization of the global bond market is less than half as large as the global equity market.

37 Which statement is **not** related to the consequences of frequent changes in the composition of bond indexes?

A The calculation of a portfolio's excess return may not be reliable over time.

B As the composition of the index changes, the index's risk can also change.

C Capitalization-weighted bond indexes will give more weight to issuers that borrow the most.

38 The "bums" problem *most likely* arises from the use of a bond index that is:

A GDP weighted.

B equal weighted.

C capitalization weighted.

39 A published bond index would *most likely* fail to meet which of the following benchmark quality tests?

A Investable

B Measurable

C Unambiguous

40 When constructing a custom benchmark, excluding an allocation to cash:

A would decrease tracking error.

B is consistent with most manager allocations.

C would introduce noise into performance evaluation.

41 To determine security weightings for a custom benchmark, the benchmark should:

A be capitalization weighted.

B reflect the manager's normal positions.

C exclude cash from the custom benchmark.

42 Which of the following *best* represents an unintended consequence of using a custom benchmark to evaluate a manager's performance? A custom benchmark:

A makes the determination of manager style more difficult.

B decreases the likelihood that a sponsor would terminate the manager.

C encourages the manager to purchase securities outside the benchmark.

43 A manager invests in Russell 1000 Index stocks. A sponsor uses the S&P 500 Index to evaluate the manager. The manager's year-to-date performance is 12.3%. During the same period the Russell 1000 Index (the normal portfolio) returned 13.2% and the S&P 500 Index returned 10.0%. The manager's year-to-date "misfit" active return is:

A −0.9%.

B 2.3%.

C 3.2%.

44 Which of the following index types would be the *most* appropriate benchmark for a portfolio manager whose investment mandate is to minimize risk?

A Price weighted

B Capitalization weighted

C Optimization-based weighted

45 The manager's true active return is *best* measured by the manager's:

A return minus the investor's benchmark return.

B return minus the manager's normal portfolio return.

C normal portfolio return minus the investor's benchmark return.

SOLUTIONS

1 B is correct. A value manager should not be benchmarked to a broad market index (here the S&P 500) that is inappropriate to their style. A is incorrect because an active US core equity manager whose investment universe is the S&P 500 Index—that is, one that seeks to add value by under- or overweighting component securities of the S&P 500 Index—may be benchmarked on the S&P 500 Index. C is incorrect because if the investment objective is to track the performance of the S&P 500, the S&P 500 is the appropriate benchmark.

2 C is correct because the Russell 2000 is a small-cap index. A is incorrect because the manager's mandate does not involve a specific security market, market segment, or asset class. B is incorrect because a small-cap manager should not use the large-cap S&P 500 as a benchmark.

3 A is correct. The difference between the return of the portfolio and benchmark is referred to as the excess return. B is incorrect because return attribution identifies the sources of the manager's return (e.g., security selection and/or sector bets). C represents another way of describing the active risk of the manager.

4 C is correct. After the manager's investment process is identified, the custom security-based benchmark is constructed by selecting securities and weightings consistent with that process. A is incorrect. It is a returns-based benchmark where the factors are the returns for various style indexes. B is incorrect. A returns-based benchmark is a weighted average of the asset class indexes that best explains or tracks the portfolio's return.

5 B is correct. Absolute return benchmarks have target returns that may be determined from actuarial assumptions. A is incorrect. Market-neutral long/short equity funds are not the only users of absolute return benchmarks; for example, a buyout fund may have an absolute return benchmark. C is incorrect. The target return may be stated as a spread above a market index. Given that market indexes vary over time, any absolute benchmark tied to a market index will also vary over time.

6 B is correct because it is **not** a feature of a manager universe. A manager universe groups managers according to their investment discipline and then ranks each according to return. The created universe does not directly allow for a comparison of manager risk. Both A and C represent features of a manager universe.

7 B is correct. An absolute return benchmark is simply a minimum target return that the manager is expected to beat. A is incorrect. A returns-based benchmark is essentially a weighted average of the asset class indexes that best explains or tracks the portfolio's returns. C is incorrect. A manager universe benchmark compares a manager's performance with the performance of other managers following similar investment disciplines.

8 A is correct. The individual securities and their weights in a peer group universe are not clearly identifiable (they are not unambiguous). Without prior knowledge of the securities and their weightings, they cannot be replicated, so manager universes are not investable. The portfolios in the first, second, third, and fourth quartiles are not known until the measurement period is over, so manager universes are not specified in advance. B is incorrect. Absolute return benchmarks are specified in advance. C is incorrect. The advantage of a properly constructed custom security-based benchmark is that it fulfills all the benchmark validity criteria.

9 B is correct; it is the benchmark property most likely to be violated. To be considered appropriate, the benchmark must be consistent with the manager's investment style or area of expertise. Given that the manager is a traditional small-cap investor, the use of a large-cap index would not be appropriate. A is incorrect because the S&P 500 is a well-known large-cap index that is updated daily. C is incorrect because it is reasonable to assume that none of the issues contained in the S&P 500 would be considered "obscure." A small-cap equity manager should have some familiarity with the securities contained in the S&P 500 and could, if needed, develop an opinion regarding their attractiveness as an investment.

10 B is correct. The benchmark should not be considered valid if the manager is unwilling to be held accountable to the benchmark across time. A and C represent the least likely choices because having a high tracking error over a particular period would not necessarily result in the benchmark violating the investable or unambiguous properties.

11 B is correct. Good benchmarks enhance the effectiveness of manager assessment. A is incorrect. If the benchmark is *inappropriate*, the calculated value of IR will not be informative. C is incorrect. *Inappropriate* benchmarks introduce noise into the investment manager assessment process.

12 A is correct. A portfolio's return can be decomposed as: Portfolio return (P) = Market index (M) + (Benchmark (B) – Market index (M)) + Active return (A). Entering values from the problem yields $P = 6.81 + (4.58 - 6.81) + (-1.94) =$ 2.64%. B is incorrect: $P \neq M + A$; 6.81 + (–1.94) = 4.87%. C is incorrect: $P \neq M + B + A$; 6.81 + 4.58 + (–1.94) = 9.45%.

13 C is correct. The return from investment style is ($B - M$) = (8.2% – 5.3%) = 2.9%, so the large capitalization style was in favor. The return from active management is ($P - B$) = (6.7% – 8.2%) = –1.5%, so the manager did not add value. A is incorrect. The manager did not add value during the measurement period because the active management return is –1.5%. B is incorrect. The manager style was in favor (2.9%) and the manager did not add value during the measurement period (–1.5%)

14 B is correct. The active return is defined as $P - B$ and calculated as 6.3% – 5.9% = 0.4%. This is because the appropriate benchmark is the Russell 2000 small-cap index. A is incorrect because the manager should not be compared to a value index. This results in –0.8% (6.3% – 7.1%). C is incorrect because it calculates the active return as 7.1% – 5.9% = 1.2%.

15 A is correct. The correlation between the manager's active return and style return should be statistically indistinguishable from zero. B is incorrect. The correlation between $E = (P - M)$ and the style return $S = (B - M)$ should be positive. C is incorrect. The standard deviation of $A = (P - B)$ should be less than the standard deviation of $E = (P - M)$.

16 C is correct. The benchmark should exhibit low turnover, which is the proportion of benchmark market values used for purchasing new securities when it is rebalanced. Turnover of 15%–20% per quarter is acceptably low benchmark turnover. A is incorrect. A *high* proportion of zero portfolio weights in the benchmark's securities may indicate a benchmark that is poorly representative of a manager's investment approach. B is incorrect. There should be high coverage of the manager's portfolio in the benchmark.

17 C is correct. If there are many securities that have zero weights, then the benchmark could be considered inappropriate. If the benchmark has high coverage (of the portfolio) but the manager has made an active decision not to hold certain securities, however, then the benchmark could still be considered appropriate. A is incorrect because a low coverage likely implies that the benchmark

is a poor representation of the manager's investment approach. B is incorrect because if the manager has no opinion on the value of benchmark securities, the benchmark is inappropriate.

18 A is correct. One of the properties of a valid benchmark is that it is investable; a low turnover rate enhances the investability of a passive investment vehicle. B defines a benchmark with a high turnover and thus would be incorrect. C is incorrect because fixed-income securities have certain characteristics that can lead to a higher rate of turnover than equity securities.

19 B is correct. At a minimum, all that is needed to construct an absolute return benchmark is a stated minimum return. A is incorrect because it would be necessary to collect return data from the manager's portfolio as well as data from managers within the peer group. C is incorrect because a custom security-based benchmark would require data covering a history of a portfolio's sectors and exposures.

20 C is correct. The Russell 2000 was in the 52nd percentile, so 52% of the managers outperformed it. A is incorrect. The Small Cap Fund (11.26%) underperformed the Russell 2000 (15.47%). B is incorrect. The median manager earned exactly 16.25% because with 379 portfolios in the sample the median manager was at the center of the distribution (i.e., there were 189 managers both above and below the median manager).

21 A is correct. For each of the periods listed, the manager does not drop out of the top 25 percent of funds. Both B and C are incorrect because none of the manager's percentile ranks are below 25 percent.

22 C is correct. The benchmark should have investable position sizes, whereby its positions could be replicated by the portfolio without excessive trading costs. A is incorrect. A high proportion of zero portfolio weights in the benchmark's securities may indicate a benchmark that is poorly representative of a manager's investment approach. B is incorrect. The correlation between the manager's active return and style return should be statistically indistinguishable from zero.

23 C is correct. A float-adjusted, cap-weighted index would be the best choice because it can be replicated with the least amount of tracking risk and at a low cost. A is not the best choice because the "small-issuer bias" of an equal-weighted index implies that the index contains a larger weight to smaller-cap securities. Because portfolio managers tend to take smaller positions in securities that are less liquid and have less availability, an equal-weighted index would be expected to have higher tracking risk to a large-cap portfolio than a cap-weighted index. B would not be the best choice because proprietary construction of a fundamental-weighted index can limit the availability of its composition and weightings. Without such information, fundamental-weighted indexes could not serve as valid benchmarks.

24 C is correct. The benchmark index for a mandate communicates the asset owner's expectations. A is incorrect. When an asset class index is used as a gauge of market sentiment, it answers the question, "How did the market do today?" This answer does not convey the asset owner's expectations. B is incorrect. When an asset class index is used as the basis for an investment vehicle like an exchange traded fund, it does not communicate the asset owner's expectations.

25 A is correct. The advantage of price weighting is its simplicity. B is incorrect. A capitalization-weighted index requires less rebalancing than other methods. C is incorrect. The weighting of firms by market value is an objective way of measuring the relative importance of constituents.

26 C is correct. Capitalization-weighted indexes can be overly influenced by overpriced securities. A is incorrect. A capitalization-weighted, float-adjusted index is the only index type that all investors could hold. B is incorrect. Valuation screens are not used in a capitalization-weighted index.

27 B is correct. An equal-weighted index gives a higher weight to small stocks. During periods in which large companies outperform small, an equal-weighted index should underperform an index that favors large companies, such as the capitalization-weighted index. A is incorrect because in an equal-weighted index, strong performers must be sold and replaced with weaker performers, implying a constant or increasing need to rebalance. C is incorrect because in a capitalization-weighted index, the weight to larger company stocks would increase as their price increases.

28 B is correct. Because fundamental-weighted indexes use valuation metrics as weights, proponents argue that fundamental-weighted indexes, unlike cap-weighted indexes, will not over-weight overvalued issues. A is incorrect because this is a disadvantage of fundamental-weighted indexes. Their proprietary nature means that fundamental-weighted indexes would not serve as valid benchmarks because their composition and weightings are not fully known. C is incorrect because using the creator's view of valuation adds a subjective element to index creation and is seen as a disadvantage of fundamental-weight indexing.

29 B is correct. A capitalization weighted, float adjusted index is the only index that all investors could realistically gain exposure to. A is incorrect. Adjustments for free float are particularly important in less developed markets where governments, founding families, and other firms often hold a large portion of stock. C is incorrect. The free float is the amount of shares outstanding for a given firm that is available to the public. A free float adjustment to a capitalization-weighted index does not include all outstanding shares.

30 C is correct. A float-weighted index includes only securities outstanding that are available for purchase. A is incorrect because float adjusting removes securities that are unavailable for purchase, making the index easier to replicate. B is incorrect because the purpose of a float-weighted index is to remove securities that are not widely available for purchase to improve the investability of the index.

31 C is correct. Transparency and objectivity are desirable characteristics of indexes because they allow investors to readily predict changes that might occur in index constituents. A and B are both incorrect. The greater use of judgment by the index provider makes it harder for investors to anticipate changes in it, making the index less investable and creating additional costs for tracking portfolios. B is incorrect. The greater use of judgment by the index provider also makes it harder for investors to determine the constituents of an index and track it.

32 B is correct. Securities that are illiquid, costly, or difficult to trade should not be included in the index if investment managers cannot purchase them in sufficient size to be relevant. A is incorrect. Increasing the amount of illiquid securities, although improving the index's completeness, would decrease its investability because more securities would be added that investors may be unable to purchase in sufficient quantity. C is incorrect because ownership restrictions reduce the ability of all investors to take positions in the restricted securities. In this case, the index should exclude non-tradable securities to improve index investability.

33 C is correct. In formal factor models, there can simultaneously be a value factor and a growth factor (in addition to size, liquidity, etc.). A is incorrect. Style factor indexes are not cap weighted. B is incorrect. These indexes are deliberately concentrated in their exposures to the targeted factor.

34 B is correct. Managers will move between categories as they perceive opportunities in changing markets. A is incorrect. The techniques used to categorize a portfolio by size are relatively standard. C is incorrect. Fund managers report fund holdings only periodically and if turnover is *high*, the reported holdings may fail to represent the manager's portfolio.

35 A is correct. Allowing issues to be defined using a combination or blend of styles (e.g., value, growth) reduces index turnover because there is less movement across style boundaries. B is incorrect because a blended classification would be expected to reduce the number of issues that move across style boundaries, thus reducing the amount of reconstitution. C represents a non-blended classification.

36 B is correct. Because of the heterogeneity of bonds, bond indexes that appear similar can often have very different composition and performance. A is incorrect. There is infrequent trading in bonds because of the long-term investment horizon of many bond investors. C is incorrect. The total market capitalization of the global bond market is significantly larger than the global equity market.

37 C is correct. The "bums" problem arises because capitalization-weighted bond indexes will give more weight to issuers that borrow the most (the bums). Although this dynamic may present a problem with a bond index, it is unrelated to changes in index composition. A is incorrect. Investors and sponsors benchmarking to a bond index need to be aware of the possibility of changes in index composition. The calculation of a portfolio's excess returns relative to a bond index may not be reliable over time. B is incorrect. For example, a shift in index weighting from government to corporate bonds would result in greater index risk.

38 C is correct. In a cap-weighted index, those that borrow the most (the bums) have the highest weights. These issuers may be more likely to be downgraded in the future and/or have lower returns. A is incorrect because the use of a GDP-weighted index may be considered a possible solution to the bums problem. B is incorrect because an equal-weighted index would be expected to have a higher exposure to smaller issuers that would be expected to be less risky, everything else constant.

39 A is correct. Given such characteristics as a large universe, bond heterogeneity and illiquidity, a bond index would most likely fail to meet the investable test. Both B and C are considered to be properties of most bond indexes.

40 C is correct. Excluding cash from the benchmark would introduce noise into performance evaluation. A is incorrect. Excluding cash would *increase* tracking error, making it more difficult to reliably evaluate the manager. B is incorrect. Most managers will have an allocation to cash for fund redemptions, tactical reasons, or other purposes.

41 B is correct. With the manager's normal positions specified correctly, any active bets can be easily identified. A is incorrect because there is no requirement that a custom benchmark be capitalization weighted. C is incorrect because excluding cash would misrepresent the manager's strategy.

42 C is correct. The closer a benchmark represents a manager's portfolio, the greater the manager's incentive to purchase securities not included in the benchmark in order to generate excess returns. A is incorrect because if the benchmark exactly matched the manager's portfolio, style could be easily determined. B is incorrect because a more inclusive custom benchmark would make it more difficult for the manager to demonstrate skill, thus increasing the likelihood that the sponsor would terminate the manager.

43 C is correct. A manager's "misfit" active return = (Normal portfolio – Investor's benchmark), 13.2% – 10.0% = 3.2%. A is incorrect because the misfit active return ≠ (Portfolio – Normal portfolio); 12.3 – 13.2 = –0.9%. B is incorrect because the misfit active return ≠ (Portfolio – Investor's benchmark); 12.3 – 10.0 = 2.3%.

44 C is correct. An optimization-based weighted benchmark would be the most appropriate because quantitative variables, such as standard deviation, could be optimized to minimize risk in the portfolio. A is incorrect because a price-weighted index uses the prices of securities, not risk, in its formation. B is incorrect because a capitalization-weighted index is constructed by cap weighting securities; a measure of security risk is not considered.

45 B is correct. The manager's "true" active return equals the manager's return minus the manager's normal portfolio return. A is incorrect. The manager's return minus the investor's benchmark return is not the manager's true active return. C is incorrect. The manager's normal portfolio return minus the investor's benchmark return equals the manager's "misfit" active return.

Glossary

Abnormal return The return on an asset that is in excess of its required rate of return. Often synonymous with *alpha*.
Absolute return attribution See *return contribution*.
Absolute return benchmark A minimum target return that an investment manager is expected to beat.
Absolute risk Risk without comparison with a benchmark.
Accounting risks Risks arising from uncertainty about how a transaction should be recorded and the potential for accounting rules to change.
Accrual accounting the recording of transactions as income is earned or expenses are incurred, rather than when income is received, or expenses are paid.
Accrued interest The interest that has accumulated on a bond or other debt instrument since the most recent interest payment was made.
Active investment strategies An approach to investing in which the portfolio manager seeks to outperform a given benchmark portfolio.
Active return Portfolio return in excess of the benchmark return.
Active risk The variability of a manager's deviations from the benchmark.
Adjusted beginning value Beginning value plus any beginning adjustment.
Adjusted ending value Ending value plus any ending adjustment.
Adjusted R^2 A measure of goodness-of-fit of a regression that is adjusted for degrees of freedom. Hence, it does not automatically increase when another independent variable is added to a regression.
Advisory-only assets assets for which the firm provides investment recommendations but has no control over the implementation of the investment decisions and no trading authority.
Aggregate Return Method a composite return calculation method that combines all the assets and external cash flows for the portfolios included in the composite to calculate the composite return in the same manner as an individual portfolio.
Allocation In performance analytics, the decision to take sector weights in the portfolio different from the sector benchmark weights, and the value-added by such decisions.
Alpha The return on an asset in excess of the asset's required rate of return. Sometimes referred to as an *abnormal return*.
Annualized arithmetic mean rate of return The arithmetic mean rate of return stated on an annualized basis.
Annualized geometric mean rate of return The geometric mean rate of return stated on an annualized basis.
Appraisal The process of estimating the value of something; an estimate of value. *Note*: Often has the connotation of being done by an expert.
Appraisal ratio A measurement of the reward of active management relative to the risk of active management, calculated as the annualized alpha divided by the annualized residual risk. Both the alpha and the residual risk are computed from a factor regression. As first introduced by Treynor and Black, the measure used Jensen's alpha and the standard deviation of the portfolio's residual or non-systematic risk. Also referred to as the *Treynor–Black ratio* and the *Treynor–Black appraisal ratio*.
Arithmetic difference A difference between two numbers a and b that is found as $a - b$.
Arithmetic mean rate of return The arithmetic mean of a set of holding period rates of returns.
Arithmetic mean return The sum of a set of returns divided by the number of returns summed.
Asset-grouping model An attribution model that isolates attribution effects by comparing the returns of variously constructed portfolios or groups of assets (example: the Brinson model).
Asset owner an entity that manages investments, directly and/or through the use of external managers, on behalf of participants, beneficiaries, or the organization itself.
Asymmetric risk Risk focusing on the part of variability that reflects losses rather than total variability.
Average drawdown The average of a specified number of the largest drawdowns over a given period.
BAI method See *linked IRR method*.
Base currency See *domestic currency*.
Basis points Hundredths of 1 percent.
Beginning adjustment An adjustment to beginning portfolio value in order to better reflect the amount invested during a sub-period.
Beginning Assets Plus Weighted Cash Flows Method a composite return calculation method that weights the underlying portfolio returns using beginning-of-period values plus weighted cash flows. Each external cash flow is applied its proportionate weight during the period based on the day on which the cash flow occurred.
Beginning Assets Weighting Method a composite return calculation method that weights the underlying portfolio returns using beginning-of-period values.
Benchmark In an investments context, a standard or point of reference for evaluating the performance of an investment portfolio.
Beta A measure of systematic risk that is based on the covariance of an asset's or portfolio's return with the return of the overall market; a measure of the sensitivity of a given investment or portfolio to movements in the overall market.
Book value The value of an asset recorded at the time it was purchased. Also known as *cost value* or *cost basis*.
bps See *basis points*.
Brinson model The approach to return attribution established in various papers co-authored by Gary Brinson; the Brinson–Hood–Beebower and Brinson–Fachler models viewed as a group.
Broad distribution pooled fund a pooled fund that is regulated under a framework that permits the general public to purchase or hold the pooled fund's shares and that is not exclusively offered in one-on-one presentations.
Bundled fee a fee that can combine multiple fees into one total or "bundled" fee. Bundled fees can include any combination of investment management fees, transaction costs, custody fees, and/or administrative fees.
Cap weighting See *capitalization weighting*.

Capital gains return See *price return*.

Capitalization weighting The most common security weighting scheme in which constituents are held in proportion to their market capitalizations, calculated as price times available shares. Also known as *market value weighting*, *market cap weighting*, or *cap weighting*.

Carried interest the portion of profits on investments paid or allocated to the general partner of an investment vehicle.

Cash basis return The unleveraged return on an investment; the return on total capital invested including the amount financed by borrowing.

Chain linking With respect to returns, combining them using the linking formula. Also called *geometric compounding*.

Clean price Price quote on a bond that excludes the value of coupon interest accrued to the date of the quote; the price without accrued interest.

Coefficient of determination A measure of how well data points fit a linear statistical model, indicated in percentage terms from 0 to 100%. Also known as *R-squared* (R^2).

Composite An aggregation of one or more portfolios that are managed according to a similar investment mandate, objective, or strategy.

Composite definition detailed criteria that determine the assignment of portfolios to composites.

Composite description general information regarding the investment mandate, objective, or strategy of the composite.

Compounding The calculation of interest on principal and accrued interest.

Confidence interval A range that has a given probability that it will contain the parameter it is intended to estimate.

Continuous compounding The compounding of continuously compounded returns (returns measured over infinitely small time intervals).

Contribution to VaR A measure of the relative volatility of the different segments compared to the volatility of the total fund.

Convexity An interest rate risk measure used in conjunction with duration; captures the degree of nonlinearity (curvature) in the relation between price change and yield change.

Correlation A measure of linear relationship calculated as covariance divided by the product of the individual asset standard deviations.

Cost basis See *book value*.

Cost value See *book value*.

Costly information efficient market hypothesis See *rational efficient markets hypothesis*.

Counterparty risk The risk of loss caused by a counterparty's failure to make a payment.

Coupon interest See *interest*.

Covariance A measure of how any two assets move together over time.

Credit risk The risk of loss caused by a counterparty or debtor's failure to make a promised payment.

Credit spread A premium over and above the current government bond yield.

Cross-sectional analysis Analysis over a group as of a given time.

Currency return The percentage change in the exchange rate over the period being considered (equivalently, the return from holding one unit of foreign currency).

Custom security-based benchmark Benchmark that is custom built to accurately reflect the investment discipline of a particular investment manager. Also called a *strategy benchmark* because it reflects a manager's particular strategy.

Data governance The ownership and oversight of the firm's data over its life cycle.

Data life cycle The sequence of stages that data will go through within a firm.

Data owners Individuals who are accountable for the data and the data source.

Day-weighted Dietz formula See *modified Dietz formula*.

Day-weighting fraction With reference to the calculation of a money-weighted rate of return, the fraction of a period over which a particular cash flow applies.

Deciles Values that divide a distribution ranked smallest to largest into 10 equal parts.

Direct quotation Exchange rate quotation of the form of the number of domestic-currency units per unit of foreign-currency. Also called *direct quote*.

Dirty price Price quote on a bond that includes the value of coupon interest; the value at which the asset can be exchanged for other assets in the market.

Discrete compounding The compounding of discrete returns.

Discrete returns A return measured over a finite time interval.

Discretion the ability of the firm or asset owner to implement its intended strategy.

Distinct business entity a business unit that is organizationally and functionally segregated from other units, divisions, departments, or offices; retains discretion over the assets it manages; and has autonomy over the investment decision-making process.

Dividends The investment income that may be received from ownership of common or preference shares.

Domestic asset An asset that trades in the investor's home (base) currency (e.g., in Swiss francs for a Swiss investor).

Domestic currency The currency an investor uses for consumption purposes (e.g., Canadian dollars for a Canadian investor is his domestic currency). Also called *base currency* or *home currency*.

Domestic-currency return The rate of return expressed in the investor's home currency.

Downside risk The potential for loss.

Drawdown A decline in value (represented by a series of negative returns only) following a peak fund valuation. See *individual drawdown*.

Drawdown duration The time it takes to experience and then recover from the maximum drawdown; time from peak to trough to peak.

Drawdown measures Measures that capture various aspects of peak-to-trough declines.

Duration The percentage change in bond price given an unanticipated small change in interest rates.

Effective annual rate The amount by which a unit of currency will grow in a year, with interest on interest included.

Equal weighting A security weighting scheme in which all constituents are held at equal weights at specified rebalancing times.

***Ex ante* alpha** Alpha in a forward-looking sense. See *expected alpha*.

***Ex ante* risk** Risk looking to the future.

Ex-coupon date The first date that a bond trades without the coupon; date from which point forward a purchaser of a bond is not entitled to the coupon payment.

Ex-dividend date The first date that a share trades without the dividend; date from which point forward a purchaser of a share is not entitled to the dividend payment.

***Ex post* alpha** Historical alpha. See *realized alpha*.

***Ex post* risk** Risk in reference to a past record.

Excess return Used in various senses appropriate to context: 1) The difference between the portfolio return and the benchmark return, which may be either positive or negative; 2) The return in excess of the risk-free rate, thus representing the return for bearing risk.

Expected alpha The difference between the expected return and the required rate of return on an asset. Also called *ex ante alpha*.

External cash flow capital (cash or investments) that enters or exits a portfolio, excluding income (dividends or interest payments).

External cash flows Deposits to or withdrawals from a portfolio.

F-test With reference to an estimated regression, tests the null hypothesis that all of the coefficient estimates are zero versus the alternative hypothesis that one or more of the coefficient estimates is not equal to zero.

Factor-model-based benchmarks Benchmarks constructed by examining a portfolio's sensitivity to a set of factors, such as the return for a broad market index, company earnings growth, industry, or financial leverage.

Fair value the amount at which an investment could be sold in an arm's-length transaction between willing parties in an orderly transaction.

Fee-paying portfolios portfolios that are charged a fee for investment management services.

Financial risks Risks related to events in external financial markets.

Firm an entity that has been defined for compliance with the GIPS standards. The most common example of such an entity is an investment manager.

Foreign assets An asset denominated in currencies other than the investor's home (base) currency. Also called *non-domestic asset*.

Foreign-currency return The return on an asset held in a foreign market; also called the *local currency return* or *local return* because it is the return of the asset expressed in local-currency terms.

Frequency distribution A tabular display of data summarized into a relatively small number of intervals.

Fund manager The professional manager of separate accounts or pooled assets structured in a variety of ways.

Fundamental law of active management The relation that the information ratio of a portfolio manager is approximately equal to the information coefficient multiplied by the square root of the investment discipline's breadth (the number of independent, active investment decisions made each year). The expression was later expanded to include a multiplicative term that reflects how effectively investment insights are transferred to the information ratio.

Fundamental weighting Patented by Research Affiliates LLC, this scheme uses company characteristics such as sales, cash flow, book value, and dividends to weight securities.

Funding risk The risk that funding cannot readily be obtained.

Geometric compounding See *chain linking*.

Geometric difference A difference between two numbers a and b that is found as $[(1 + a)/(1 + b)] - 1$.

Geometric mean rate of return The compound growth rate associated with a set of holding period rates of returns.

GIPS Asset Owner Report an asset owner's presentation for a total fund or composite that contains all the information required by the GIPS standards and may also include recommended information or supplemental information.

GIPS Composite Report a presentation for a composite that contains all the information required by the GIPS standards and may also include recommended information or supplemental information.

GIPS Pooled Fund Report a presentation for a pooled fund that contains all the information required by the GIPS standards and may also include recommended information or supplemental information.

GIPS Report primary instrument through which GIPS-compliant information is communicated; may be a GIPS Composite Report, a GIPS Pooled Fund Report, or a GIPS Asset Owner Report.

Gross-of-fee returns The returns based on portfolio values reduced by any trading expenses incurred during the period, but not reduced by investment management fees.

Gross-of-fees return the return on investments reduced by any transaction costs (i.e., before the deduction of investment management fees).

Histogram A bar chart of data that have been grouped into a frequency distribution.

Holding period An interval between two points in time over which an asset or portfolio is assumed to be held.

Holding period rate of return The percentage gain or loss in wealth resulting from holding some asset or portfolio over the stated holding period. Also known as *rate or return* or *return*.

Home currency See *domestic currency*.

Idiosyncratic risk Risk that is firm or security specific.

Income Sometimes called *investment income*, refers to cash payments made to owners of an asset.

Income return The component of rate of return that derives from investment income.

Indirect quotation Exchange rate quoted in terms of the number of foreign-currency units per unit of domestic currency.

Individual drawdown A decline in value (represented by a series of negative returns only) following a peak fund valuation.

Individual sector allocation Allocation referring to a single sector (e.g., energy).

Inflation rate The rate of change in the purchasing power of a currency unit over time.

Information ratio A measure of return scaled by risk, calculated as the portfolio's mean excess return relative to its benchmark divided by the variability of that excess return.

Interest The investment income that may be received from ownership of debt instruments; payment for lending funds. The interest income on bonds is also known as *coupon interest* or *coupon*.

Internal dispersion a measure of the spread of the annual returns of individual portfolios within a composite. Measures may include, but are not limited to, high/low, range, and standard deviation (either using an asset-weighted or equal-weighted methodology).

Internal rate of return The constant rate of return that would produce the total ending value of a portfolio given the magnitude and timing of the cash flows. Also known as *money-weighted rate of return*.

Internal rate of return (IRR) the implied discount rate or effective compounded rate of return that equates the present value of cash outflows with the present value of cash inflows. A common method for calculating a money-weighted return.

Investment income See *income*.

Investment management fees the fees payable to the firm for managing a portfolio. Investment management fees are typically asset based, performance based, or a combination of the two but may take different forms as well. Investment management fees also include carried interest.

Investment manager an organization that manages assets on behalf of clients.

Investment performance appraisal The systematic evaluation of the investment performance of a fund or strategy in order to understand and assess the past decisions and abilities of a portfolio manager. Concerned with distinguishing skill from luck.

Investment style A natural grouping of investment disciplines that has some predictive power in explaining the future dispersion of returns across portfolios.

Investment universe The set of assets that may be considered for investment.

Jensen measure See *Jensen's alpha*.

Jensen's alpha Measures the return of a portfolio in excess of the theoretical required return given the equilibrium model for asset returns known as the CAPM. Also called *Jensen measure*.

Large cash flow the level at which the firm determines that an external cash flow may distort performance if the portfolio is not valued and a sub-period return is not calculated. Must be defined based on the value of cash flow or a percentage of the portfolio or composite assets.

Legal/contract risk Risk that arises from contract terms that are not clearly specified.

Leverage The use of borrowing or use of various financial instruments to magnify potential gains and losses relative to the investor's equity position.

Leveraged return With respect to a leveraged portfolio, the return achieved based on the capital invested. Also called *levered return*.

Levered return See *leveraged return*.

Liability return The return of a portfolio consisting only of liabilities.

Limited distribution pooled fund any pooled fund that is not a broad distribution pooled fund.

Linked IRR method A method for calculating an approximate time-weighted rate of return that involves linking together internal rate-of-return estimates for sub-periods. Also known as *BAI method*.

Linked modified Dietz method The linked IRR method based on using the modified Dietz method for calculating sub-period returns.

Linking the method by which sub-period returns are geometrically combined to calculate the period return, or by which periodic returns are geometrically combined to calculate longer-period returns.

Linking formula An expression for combining returns on a portfolio or asset over multiple periods so as to account for the cumulative effect on wealth.

Liquidity reserve Money held in cash and cash equivalents as a reserve.

Liquidity risk The risk that results from the inability to trade an asset quickly without a significant concession in price.

Local currency return See *foreign-currency return*.

M^2 An appraisal measure that indicates what a portfolio would have returned, assuming the same total risk as the market index.

M^2 alpha Difference between the risk-adjusted performance of the portfolio and the performance of the benchmark.

Macro attribution Attribution at the sponsor level.

Manager peer group See *manager universe*.

Manager universe A broad group of managers with similar investment disciplines. Also called *manager peer group*.

Margin With respect to trading, the use of borrowed money in making purchases; the collateral on deposit to meet potential performance obligations.

Marked to market A procedure used to revalue a financial asset or liability to its current market value.

Market cap weighting See *capitalization weighting*.

Market index Represents the performance of a specified security market, market segment, or asset class.

Market model A regression equation that specifies a linear relationship between the return on a security (or portfolio) and the return on a broad market index.

Market risk Risk related to market movements, e.g., unexpected changes in share prices, interest rates, currency exchange rates, and commodity prices.

Market value The price at which investors can buy or sell an investment at a given time multiplied by the quantity held, plus any accrued income.

Market value weighting See *capitalization weighting*.

Maximum drawdown The largest peak to trough loss within a period.

Mean absolute deviation A measure of dispersion calculated as the mean of the absolute values of deviations from the mean.

Median The "middlemost" observation; i.e., in a set of observations that has been ranked from highest to lowest, the median will lie in the middle.

Micro attribution Attribution at the portfolio manager level.

Model risk The risk that a model is incorrect or misapplied.

Modified Dietz formula With respect to the linked IRR method, a method for calculating sub-period returns that uses the actual dating of within-sub-period cash flows.

Modified Dietz Method a method for calculating portfolio returns that adjusts for daily-weighted external cash flows.

Money-weighted rate of return See *internal rate of return*.

Money-weighted return (MWR) a method of calculating returns that reflects the change in value and the timing and size of external cash flows.

Negative skewness The condition of being skewed towards smaller values; skewed to the left.

Net asset value The market value of assets minus the market value of liabilities, stated on a per-share or per-unit basis.

Net-of-fee return Investment return based on portfolio values, reduced by trading expenses and by the investment management fees; gross-of-fee returns reduced by investment management fees.

Net-of-Fees Return the return on investments reduced by both transaction costs and investment management fees.

Nominal prices Actual transaction prices with no adjustment for inflation.

Nominal return The rate of return based on actual transaction prices.

Non-diversifiable risk See *systematic risk*.

Non-domestic assets See *foreign asset*.

Non-fee-paying portfolios portfolios that are not charged a fee for investment management services.

Non-financial risks Includes operational risks, model risks, and settlement risks.

Off-benchmark decisions Decisions to invest in securities that are not included in the portfolio manager's benchmark.

Operational risk The risk of loss from failure in a company's systems or procedures or from external events such as acts of God, terrorist action, etc.

Optimization-based weighting Security weighting schemes using minimum-variance and efficiency.

Original Dietz formula With respect to the linked IRR method, a method for calculating sub-period returns that assumes that half of any within-sub-period cash flow is received at the beginning of the sub-period and half is received at the end.

P-value The smallest level of significance at which the null hypothesis can be rejected.

Passive investment strategies A buy-and-hold approach to investing in which an investor does not make portfolio changes based on short-term expectations of changing market or security performance.

Pay date The date at which a declared dividend is acutally paid.

Percentiles Values that divide a distribution into 100 equal parts.

Performance attribution Attribution, including return attribution and risk attribution; often used as a synonym for return attribution.

Performance examination a process by which an independent verifier conducts testing of a specific composite or pooled fund in accordance with the required performance examination procedures of the GIPS standards.

Plan sponsor The trustee, company, or employer responsible for a public or private institutional investment plan.

Pooled fund a portfolio whose ownership interests may be held by more than one investor.

Pooled fund description general information regarding the investment mandate, objective, or strategy of the pooled fund.

Portability a firm's ability to use performance from a past firm or affiliation and represent it as its own historical performance, if specific conditions have been met.

Portfolio An individually managed group of investments. A portfolio may be a segregated account or a pooled fund.

Portfolio risk The risk of a collection of assets.

Positive skewness The condition of being skewed towards larger values; skewed to the right.

Price index A securities index that reflects price changes but not investment income.

Price return The return earned from changes in asset price; also called *capital gain return*.

Price weighting Security weighting scheme in which constituents are weighted in proportion to their prices.

Priced risks Risks for which investors demand compensation for bearing (e.g., equity risk, company-specific factors, macroeconomic factors).

Private market investments investments that are illiquid, not publicly traded, and not traded on an exchange, including real assets (e.g., real estate and infrastructure), private equity, and similar investments.

Prospective client any person or entity that has expressed interest in one of the firm's composite strategies and qualifies to invest in the composite.

Prospective investor any person or entity that has expressed interest in one of the firm's pooled funds and qualifies to invest in the pooled fund.

Provisions individually itemized points that the principles of the GIPS standards are separated into. Each provision addresses a task or action as a requirement or a recommendation.

Quartiles Values that divide a distribution into four equal parts.

Quintiles Values that divide a distribution into five equal parts.

R^2 See *coefficient of determination*.

Rate of return The percent gain or loss in wealth resulting from holding an investment over a specific period of time.

Rational efficient markets hypothesis The hypothesis that, on average, active investors earn just enough incremental returns to cover costs of information acquisition.

Real prices Nominal prices adjusted for inflation.

Real return The nominal rate of return adjusted for inflation.

Realized alpha The difference between the actual holding-period return and the contemporaneous required return. Also called *ex post alpha*.

Recommendation a suggested task or action that should be followed or performed; identified in the GIPS standards by the word "should." A recommendation is considered to be best practice but is not a requirement.

Record date The date established by an issuer of a security for the purpose of determining the holders who are entitled to receive a dividend that has been declared; only owners as of the record date are entitled to receive the dividend.

Regulatory risk Risk of changes in regulations that adversely affect valuation.

Reinvested income Income that is received during a holding period and reinvested into a portfolio.

Relative risk Risk relative to some reference point.

Requirement a task or action that must be followed or performed; identified in the GIPS standards by the word "must."

Return attribution A set of techniques used to identify the sources of the excess return of a portfolio against its benchmark.

Return contribution analysis Analysis of the contributions of portfolio components to the total return of a portfolio.

Return relative The ratio of ending value to beginning value of a portfolio or security. Also called *value relative* or *wealth ratio*.

Returns-based benchmarks Benchmarks constructed by examining a portfolio's sensitivity to a set of factors, such as the returns for various style indexes (e.g., small-cap value, small-cap growth, large-cap value, and large-cap growth).

Reward-to-variability ratio See *Sharpe ratio*.

Risk Exposure to uncertainty.

Risk attribution The analysis of the sources of risk.

Sector A grouping of assets that share some common characteristics.

Security market line The graphical representation of the CAPM formula, showing the relationship between expected return and beta.

Security specific Belonging to the security rather than to the market or to the sector.

Segregated account a portfolio owned by a single client.

Selection The value the portfolio manager adds by holding individual securities or instruments within the sector in different-from-benchmark weights.

Semi-standard deviation The square root of the semi-variance.

Semi-variance An asymmetric risk mean that is similar to the variance except that only deviations below the mean are measured.

Settlement date accounting Recognition of the value of assets and/or liabilities on the date when the actual exchange of cash and investments is completed.

Settlement risk Risk of a breakdown in the settlement of a trade.

Sharpe ratio The average return in excess of the risk-free rate divided by the standard deviation of return; a measure of the average excess return earned per unit of standard deviation of return. Also known as the *reward-to-variability ratio*.
Significant cash flow the level at which the firm determines that one or more client-directed external cash flows may temporarily prevent the firm from implementing the composite strategy.
Sovereign/political risk Risk related to potential government actions.
Specific asset selection The portion of excess return that is due to individual asset selection.
Spot exchange rate The rate at which one currency can be exchanged for immediate delivery of another currency.
Stand-alone risk Risk independent of the performance of other assets.
Standard deviation The positive square root of variance.
Stated annual rate The stated interest rate for a year ignoring the effect of any compounding; the periodic rate multiplied by the number of compounding periods per year.
Strategy benchmarks *See custom security-based benchmark.*
Sub-advisor a third-party investment manager hired by the firm to manage some or all of the assets for which a firm has investment management responsibility.
Surplus return The return on a portfolio of both assets and liabilities (i.e., the return on the portfolio's equity).
Surplus risk Risk related to the value of surplus (vales of assets minus the value of liabilities).
Symmetric risk Risk related to both upside and downside.
Systematic risk Risk originating from broad financial market conditions and the macroeconomy; also called *non-diversifiable risk*.
***t*-statistic** The ratio of the departure of the estimate of a parameter from its hypothesized value divided by the estimate's standard error.
Tail risk The possibility of extreme losses.
Tail value at risk Equal to VaR plus the expected loss in excess of VaR, given that such excess loss occurs.
Target semi-standard deviation A measure of downside risk that focuses on deviations below a target value. Also called *target semideviation*.
Target semi-variance The same as the semi-variance, except that a specified target return is used instead of the mean return.
Target semideviation See *target semi-standard deviation*.
Tax risk Risk of unexpected changes in tax rates or rulings.
Temporary new account an account for temporarily holding client-directed external cash flows until they are either invested according to the composite strategy or disbursed.
Theoretical performance performance that is not derived from the investment of actual assets. Theoretical performance includes model, backtested, hypothetical simulated, indicative, *ex ante*, and forward-looking performance.
Time-series analysis Analysis of where the returns for an asset were examined over time.
Time-weighted return (TWR) a method of calculating returns that reflects the change in value and attempts to negate or neutralize the impact of external cash flows.
Total firm assets all discretionary and non-discretionary assets for which a firm has investment management responsibility.
Total fund a pool of assets managed by an asset owner according to a specific investment mandate, which is typically composed of multiple asset classes. The total fund usually consists of underlying portfolios, each representing of the strategies used to achieve the asset owner's investment mandate.
Total pooled fund fees all fees and expenses charged to the pooled fund, including but not limited to investment management fees and administrative fees.
Total return The rate of return that includes realized and unrealized gains and losses plus income for the measurement period.
Total return index A securities index that reflects both reinvested income and price changes.
Total risk The sum of systematic risk and non-systematic risk; also called *stand-alone risk*.
Tracking risk The standard deviation of the differences between a portfolio's returns and its benchmark's returns. Also called *tracking error* and *active risk*.
Trade date accounting recognizes the asset or liability on the date of the purchase or sale and not on the settlement date.
Transaction costs the costs of buying and selling investments. These costs typically take the form of brokerage commissions, exchange fees, and/or bid–offer spreads from brokers.
Treynor–Black appraisal ratio See *appraisal ratio*.
Treynor–Black ratio See *appraisal ratio*.
Treynor ratio A measure of risk-adjusted performance that relates a portfolio's returns in excess of the risk-free rate to a portfolio's beta.
Uncalled committed capital assets that have been pledged to the firm by clients or investors, but the firm has yet to call (or "draw down") the capital.
Unit value pricing A method for accounting for ownership interests in pooled investments that lends itself to calculating time-weighted rates of returns.
Unrealized gain (loss) The difference between the market value and the cost basis of an asset.
Value at risk An estimate of the loss that we expect to be exceeded with a given level of probability over a specified time period.
Value relative See *return relative*.
Variance The expected value or the mean of squared deviations from the mean.
Verification the process by which an independent verifier conducts testing of a firm or asset owner that claims compliance with the GIPS standards, in accordance with the required verification procedures of the GIPS standards.
Verifier a third party, independent from the firm or asset owner that claims compliance with the GIPS standards, that is hired to conduct a verification.
Wealth ratio *See return relative.*
Zero-weight benchmark decisions See *off-benchmark decisions*.

Made in the USA
Monee, IL
05 November 2026

67806907R00291